HOW TO PREPARE FOR THE

FUNDAMENTALS OF ENGINEERING

FE/EIT EXAM

Masoud Olia, Ph.D., P.E.
Wentworth Institute of Technology
Boston, Massachusetts

Contributors

Professor Armen S. Casparian
Wentworth Institute of Technology
Boston, Massachusetts

Professor Frederick Driscoll
Wentworth Institute of Technology
Boston, Massachusetts

Professor Mark Frisina, PE
Wentworth Institute of Technology
Boston, Massachusetts

Professor Thomas Hulbert, PE
Northeastern University
Boston, Massachusetts

Mohamad Metghalchi, Sc.D.
Northeastern University
Boston, Massachusetts

Richard Murphy, Ph.D.
Northeastern University
Boston, Massachusetts

Robert M. Scott
Exergy, Inc.
Hanson, Massachusetts

Professor David E. Stevens
Wentworth Institute of Technology
Boston, Massachusetts

BARRON'S

All inquiries should be addressed to:
Barron's Educational Series, Inc.
250 Wireless Boulevard
Hauppauge, New York 11788
http://www.barronseduc.com

Library of Congress Catalog Card No.: 99-45283

International Standard Book No.: 0-7641-0651-1

Library of Congress Cataloging-in-Publication Data

Olia, Masoud.
How to prepare for the fundamentals of engineering (FE/EIT) exam / Masoud Olia ; contributors, Armen Casparian ... [et al.]
p. cm
ISBN 0-7641-0651-1
1. Engineering—United States—Examinations—Study guides. 2. Engineering—Problems, exercises, etc. 3. Engineers—Certification—United States. I. Title. II. Casparian, Armen.

TA159.O45 1999
620′.0076 21—dc21 99-45283

PRINTED IN THE UNITED STATES OF AMERICA
987654321

CONTENTS

PREFACE

Whether you are a working, experienced engineer or a soon-to-be engineering graduate, *How to Prepare for the FE/EIT Exam* was written to help you pass the Fundamentals of Engineering Exam. Use this book in conjunction with the National Council of Engineering Examiners and Surveyors (NCEES)-supplied handbook of equations and formulas, and you will be well prepared to pass the FE exam.

Until now, preparing for the FE/EIT exam has been a time-consuming and sometimes costly proposition. *How to Prepare for the FE/EIT Exam* is the most efficient and effective way to study for the morning exam that is required of all examinees. This book also includes a review of the multiconcept, multipart questions found in the afternoon General Exam Option. While examinees can elect to take a discipline-specific exam (in either chemical, civil, electrical, industrial, or mechanical engineering), the majority choose the General Exam Option.

We have included a subject review and sample problems for each of the twelve subject areas covered by the FE exam. Each chapter includes exam-like problems as well as theoretical questions. Not only are the answers to the questions given but solutions to the problems are provided as well. Finally, a practice exam is included with answers and a scoring analysis.

This book is a collaborative work. How to best review each of the twelve exam subjects covered by the FE exam requires specialized knowledge. Experts weren't just "consulted" for certain chapters. A team of teaching professors, each an expert in his field and an experienced FE review course instructor, worked together to produce this book.

I am extremely thankful for the contributions made by the coauthors of this book, who are listed below. Their hard work and dedication made this project possible.

Professor Armen S. Casparian	*Wentworth Institute of Technology*
Professor Frederick F. Driscoll	*Wentworth Institute of Technology*
Professor Mark Frisina, PE	*Wentworth Institute of Technology*
Professor Thomas E. Hulbert, PE	*Northeastern University*
Mohamad Metghalchi, Sc.D.	*Northeastern University*
Richard J. Murphy, Ph.D.	*Northeastern University*
Robert M. Scott	*Exergy Incorporated*
Professor David E. Stevens	*Wentworth Institute of Technology*

Finally, I would like to thank my wife, Maria, for her support during the period I worked on this project. Without her encouragement and helpful input, completion of this book would not have been possible.

Passing the FE exam is your first step toward becoming a registered engineer. *How to Prepare for the FE/EIT Exam* will provide the information review and the practice problems needed to give you the confidence to pass the FE exam. We wish you continued success in your engineering career.

Masoud Olia, Ph.D., PE
Wentworth Institute of Technology
Boston, Massachusetts

INTRODUCTION

What is the FE Exam?

Passing the FE exam is the first step toward becoming a Registered, or Professional, Engineer (PE). Becoming a registered engineer is necessary to work as a consulting engineer and, in many industries, to advance to an engineering management position.

Registration requirements vary by state, but, in general, a registered engineering candidate must have graduated from an ABET-accredited engineering program, pass the FE exam, and, after several years as a practicing engineer, pass the PE exam in his or her specialty.

How to Apply

The FE exam is given twice a year, in April and in October. Contact your state Board of Registration well in advance to obtain an application and registration materials. State Board of Registration numbers are available from the NCEES website at www.ncees.org.

The FE Exam Format

The FE exam is an 8-hour "supplied reference" exam. "Supplied reference" means that a clean, unmarked copy of the NCEES *Fundamentals of Engineering (FE) Discipline-Specific Reference Handbook* will be supplied to each examinee upon entering the exam site. This is the only reference book that may be used for the exam.

The FE exam is divided into two 4-hour sessions. The morning session covers 120 multiple-choice questions, each worth one point. After a 1-hour break, the examinee may take either a more in-depth General Exam Option or a Discipline-Specific Option in either chemical, civil, electrical, industrial, or mechanical engineering. The afternoon-session exam contains 60 multiple-choice questions, each worth two points. *How to Prepare for the FE/EIT Exam* is designed to serve as a review for the morning exam required of all examinees as well as for the afternoon General Exam Option.

The approximate breakdown of questions by subject in each session is shown in the chart below.

The highest possible score for the morning session and for the afternoon session is the same: 120 points for each. You are not penalized for incorrect answers or for guessing. The scores from both sessions are added together to determine your total score. In recent years the passing score has been approximately 50 percent.

FE Exam Test-Taking Strategies

Because the FE Exam is a comprehensive exam, the best test-preparation strategy is to study all the exam subjects. To get the most benefit from your study time, however, concentrate your review on the subjects that

	Approx. Number of Questions	**Approx. Number of Questions**
Subject	***Morning Session All Examinees***	***Afternoon Session General Exam Option***
Mathematics	24	12
Electric Circuits	12	6
Statics	12	6
Chemistry	11	4
Thermodynamics	11	6
Dynamics	10	5
Fluid Mechanics	8	5
Materials Science	8	3
Mechanics of Materials	8	4
Computers	6	3
Engineering Economics	5	3
Ethics	5	3
Total Questions	**120**	**60**

have the most questions, as indicated in the breakdown of questions by subject presented above.

A major goal of the review process is to improve "recall," the ability to answer questions quickly. During the 4-hour morning session 120 questions must be answered. Generally, the questions are unrelated to each other, and each question must be answered, on average, in less than 2 minutes. During the 4-hour afternoon session 60 questions must be answered. The afternoon-session questions are often multipart; and each question must be answered, on average, in less than 4 minutes. It is essential, therefore, that you do not spend too much time on any one question.

If you are unsure of an answer, mark the question in your test booklet and circle your best guess. Reserve the last 10 minutes of test-taking time to reconsider your "guesses" and to transfer your final choices to the answer key.

Guessing is a valid test-taking strategy. You are not penalized for answering incorrectly. Answer each question; do not leave any answers blank.

Your recall speed will be greatly improved as you practice the problems in *How to Prepare for the FE/EIT Exam.* Remember that you will receive a clean copy of the NCEES FE Reference Handbook at the exam site. During your review, mark the equations and formulas that you use most frequently in your own copy of this handbook so that you will be familiar with their locations during the actual test. Similarly, become well acquainted with your calculator and its functions before exam day.

How to Use This Book

How to Prepare for the FE/EIT Exam is designed to give an overview of the concepts and equations used in the FE exam and to provide you with practice using FE exam-like problems.

This book is organized in the same order as the NCEES FE Reference Handbook to help you become acquainted with the formulas and equations that you will need for the test. Also, this book reflects the relative emphasis given to the various FE exam subjects; thus, Chapter 9 on mathematics has substantially more problems than Chapter 8 on materials science. Do not skip any chapters, however. Read each chapter review, and work all the sample problems in this book. It is only through actual practice on the problems that you will become familiar with the FE exam format.

Give yourself sufficient time to prepare. It is recommended that you allow 8 to 10 weeks of study time. If you have been out of school for several years, you may need more time to prepare for the FE exam.

One week before the FE exam, take the practice exam included in this book, using the NCEES Handbook as your only reference. If the results indicate a need for additional review, identify the areas on which you did poorly and concentrate your study on them. Leave yourself a couple of days for a brief overview of all the subject areas.

Do not study the night before the exam; instead, get a good night's sleep. By now you have done all you can academically to prepare for the FE exam. Through your understanding of the basic engineering principles, and by demonstrating the ability to apply these principles, you will pass the FE exam.

Mini-Diagnostic Exam

The purpose of this mini-diagnostic exam is to give direction to your study. The questions on this diagnostic exam are similar to those found on the FE morning exam, which is required of all examinees.

Taking this practice exam before you begin your FE/EIT study program will help you assess which areas you need to study and how to best allocate your time. This mini-diagnostic exam includes 38 questions—five questions from the area of mathematics and three questions from each of the other subject areas. Be sure to read the section on "FE Exam Test-Taking Strategies" before taking the diagnostic exam. Allow yourself 75 minutes to take this practice exam. Simulate exam-like conditions: Work in a quiet place, take the diagnostic exam in one sitting, and use your calculator and your copy of the NCEES FE Reference Handbook of equations and formulas.

Correct your exam and evaluate your results. If you scored more than one answer wrong in any one subject area, you may need to increase your study time in that area. If you were unable to complete the 38 questions in the time allotted, you may need to work on your problem-solving speed and/or recall. After taking the diagnostic exam and evaluating your results, begin your subject review with Chapter 1, Chemistry.

ANSWER SHEET: Mini-Diagnostic Exam

1. Ⓐ Ⓑ Ⓒ Ⓓ	9. Ⓐ Ⓑ Ⓒ Ⓓ	17. Ⓐ Ⓑ Ⓒ Ⓓ	25. Ⓐ Ⓑ Ⓒ Ⓓ	33. Ⓐ Ⓑ Ⓒ Ⓓ
2. Ⓐ Ⓑ Ⓒ Ⓓ	10. Ⓐ Ⓑ Ⓒ Ⓓ	18. Ⓐ Ⓑ Ⓒ Ⓓ	26. Ⓐ Ⓑ Ⓒ Ⓓ	34. Ⓐ Ⓑ Ⓒ Ⓓ
3. Ⓐ Ⓑ Ⓒ Ⓓ	11. Ⓐ Ⓑ Ⓒ Ⓓ	19. Ⓐ Ⓑ Ⓒ Ⓓ	27. Ⓐ Ⓑ Ⓒ Ⓓ	35. Ⓐ Ⓑ Ⓒ Ⓓ
4. Ⓐ Ⓑ Ⓒ Ⓓ	12. Ⓐ Ⓑ Ⓒ Ⓓ	20. Ⓐ Ⓑ Ⓒ Ⓓ	28. Ⓐ Ⓑ Ⓒ Ⓓ	36. Ⓐ Ⓑ Ⓒ Ⓓ
5. Ⓐ Ⓑ Ⓒ Ⓓ	13. Ⓐ Ⓑ Ⓒ Ⓓ	21. Ⓐ Ⓑ Ⓒ Ⓓ	29. Ⓐ Ⓑ Ⓒ Ⓓ	37. Ⓐ Ⓑ Ⓒ Ⓓ
6. Ⓐ Ⓑ Ⓒ Ⓓ	14. Ⓐ Ⓑ Ⓒ Ⓓ	22. Ⓐ Ⓑ Ⓒ Ⓓ	30. Ⓐ Ⓑ Ⓒ Ⓓ	38. Ⓐ Ⓑ Ⓒ Ⓓ
7. Ⓐ Ⓑ Ⓒ Ⓓ	15. Ⓐ Ⓑ Ⓒ Ⓓ	23. Ⓐ Ⓑ Ⓒ Ⓓ	31. Ⓐ Ⓑ Ⓒ Ⓓ	
8. Ⓐ Ⓑ Ⓒ Ⓓ	16. Ⓐ Ⓑ Ⓒ Ⓓ	24. Ⓐ Ⓑ Ⓒ Ⓓ	32. Ⓐ Ⓑ Ⓒ Ⓓ	

Mini-Diagnostic Exam

38 Questions

Directions: For each incomplete statement or question, select the answer that best completes the statement or answers the question. Then fill in the corresponding space on the answer sheet.

1. The distance between points (2,3) and (5,7) is
a. $\sqrt{149}$
b. 7
c. $\sqrt{7}$
d. 5

2. If $0 \leq x \leq \pi/2$, then $\tan x \cos x =$
a. $\sec x$
b. $\csc x$
c. $\cot x$
d. $\sin x$

3. The value of $\lim_{x \to 0} \left(\frac{8x^2}{\cos x - 1} \right)$ is
a. 0
b. 8
c. -16
d. $-\infty$

4. The value of $\int_a^b \frac{1}{x}\, dx$ is
a. $b^2 - a^2$
b. $\ln (b - a)$
c. $\frac{\ln b}{\ln a}$
d. $\ln \frac{b}{a}$

5. The solution of the differential equation $\frac{dy}{dx} = ky$, with initial condition $y = 1$ when $t = 0$, is
a. $y = \ln kt$
b. $y = e^{kt}$
c. $y = \sin kt$
d. $y^2 = 2t + k$

6.

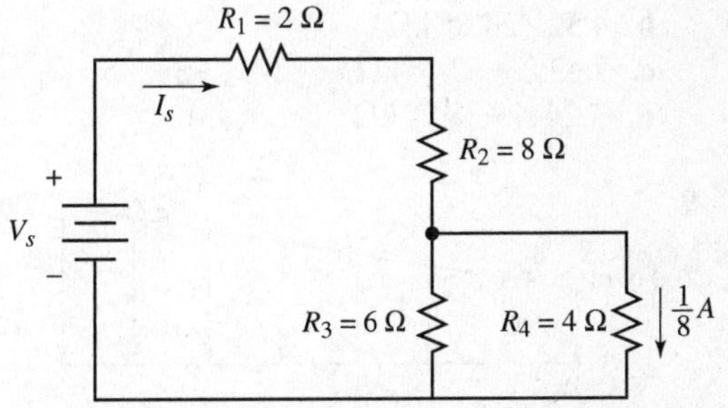

What is the total power delivered to the circuit shown above?
a. 1.52 W
b. 0.54 W
c. 2.14 W
d. 0.86 W

7.

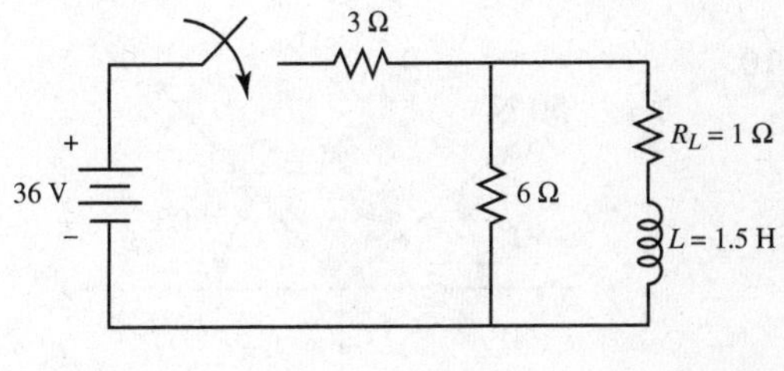

If the initial current in the inductor shown above is 0 ampere, what is the current through the inductor 0.25 second after the switch is closed?
a. 2.67 A
b. 1.95 A
c. 5.24 A
d. 3.15 A

8.

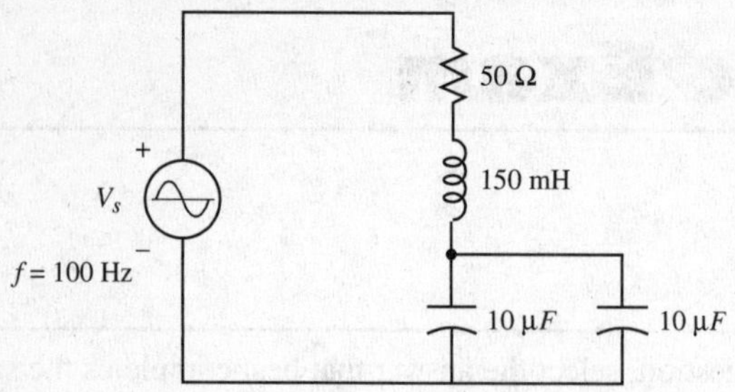

What is the input impedance for the circuit shown above?

a. 52.1∠16.3° kΩ
b. 4.52∠24.8° kΩ
c. 7.62∠−62.1° kΩ
d. 3.24∠−38.7° kΩ

9.

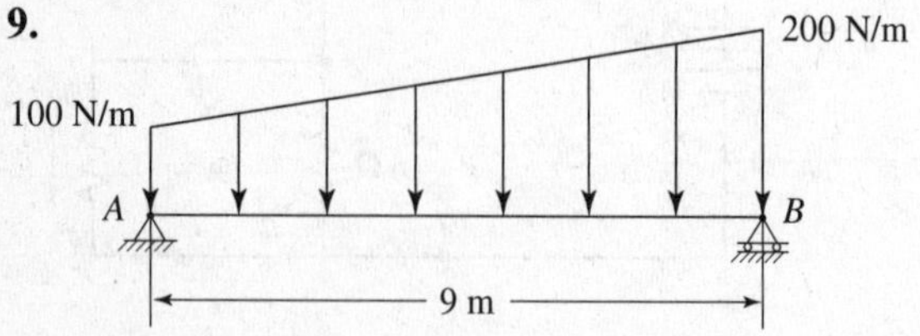

What is the reaction at the roller support (point *B*) in the above diagram?

a. 750 N
b. 600 N
c. 500 N
d. 525 N

10.

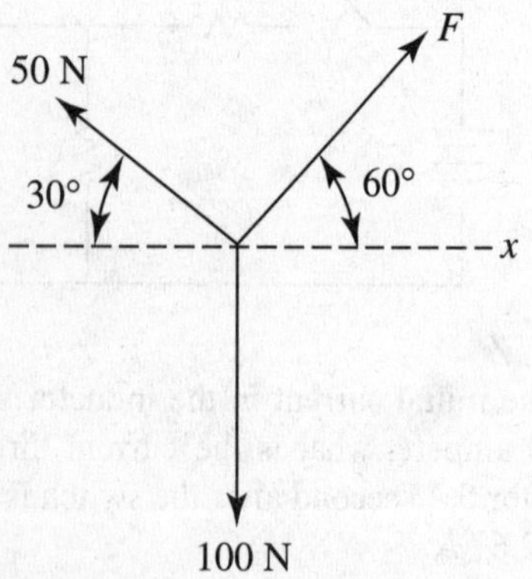

If the resultant of the forces shown in the above diagram is vertical, what is force **F**?

a. 50 N
b. 100 N
c. 86.6 N
d. 60 N

11. What is the angle between force **F** and the *x*-axis, where **F** = 30**i** + 50**j** − 20**k** newtons?
a. 30°
b. 65.8°
c. 60.9°
d. 12.8°

Questions 12–14

Air is compressed from an initial state of 100-kilopascal pressure and 25°C temperature to a final pressure of 500 kilopascals in a polytropic process ($n = 1.5$) in a piston and cylinder device.

12. What is the final temperature of the air?
a. 35°C
b. 43°C
c. 199°C
d. 237°C

13. What is the value of the work interaction in this process?
a. −122 kJ/kg
b. −10 kJ/kg
c. 10 kJ/kg
d. 120 kJ/kg

14. What is the amount of energy transfer via heat interaction?
a. −272 kJ/kg
b. −32 kJ/kg
c. 31 kJ/kg
d. 272 kJ/kg

---

15. The mass, in grams, of 2.5 moles of $Ca(NO_3)_2$ is
a. 255 g
b. 410 g
c. 164 g
d. 500 g

16. In the reaction below, how many grams of water are produced from the combustion of 300 grams of ethane, C_2H_6?

$$2C_2H_6 + 7O_2 \rightarrow 4CO_2 + 6H_2O$$

a. 540 g
b. 180 g
c. 1,080 g
d. 740 g

17. What happens to the volume of an ideal gas when the pressure is halved and the absolute temperature is doubled?
a. The volume is doubled.
b. The volume is halved.
c. The volume is quadrupled.
d. The volume is unchanged.

18. A long-range artillery rifle located at point *A* fires a shell at an angle of 45° with respect to the horizontal as illustrated below.

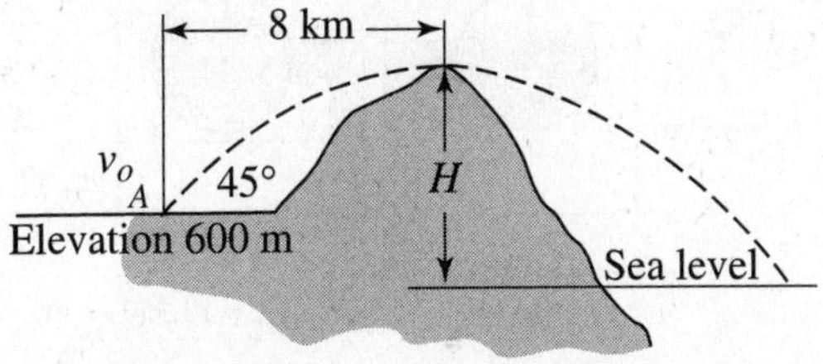

If the shell just barely clears the mountain peak at the top of its trajectory, the height *H* of the mountain peak above sea level is necessarily
a. 7,998.0 m
b. 4,600.0 m
c. 4,000.0 m
d. 12,600.0 m

19. A 60.0-kilogram crate at rest on a horizontal surface is suddenly subjected to a constant towing force as illustrated below.

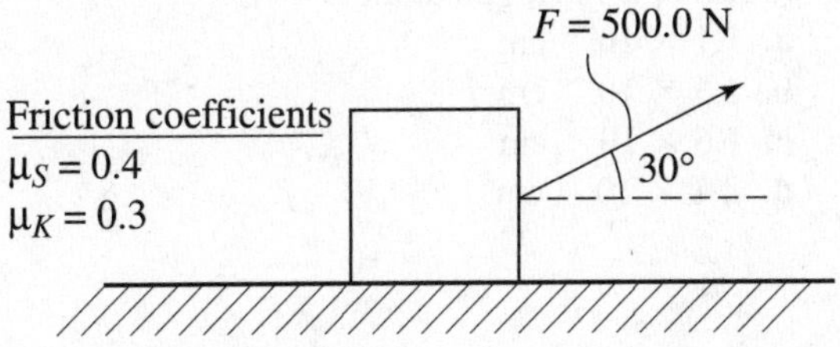

On the basis of the given values of the friction coefficients at the interface between the horizontal surface and the lower surface of the crate, the velocity of the crate at the instant when the towing force has been applied for 12.0 seconds will be
a. 66.2 m/s
b. 108.3 m/s
c. 497.4 m/s
d. 82.9 m/s

20. A racehorse gallops along a curved section of a track that has a radius of curvature of 400.0 feet. During its motion on the track, the horse's speed increases at a constant rate from 30 mph to 40 mph through a 6.0-second time interval. Within this period of motion, the magnitude of the horse's total acceleration when its speed is 35 mph should be
a. 2.4 ft/sec^2
b. 7.0 ft/sec^2
c. 8.9 ft/sec^2
d. 6.4 ft/sec^2

21. What is the average shear stress in the pin at *A* (double shear) in the diagram below? The diameter of the pin at *A* is 2 centimeters.

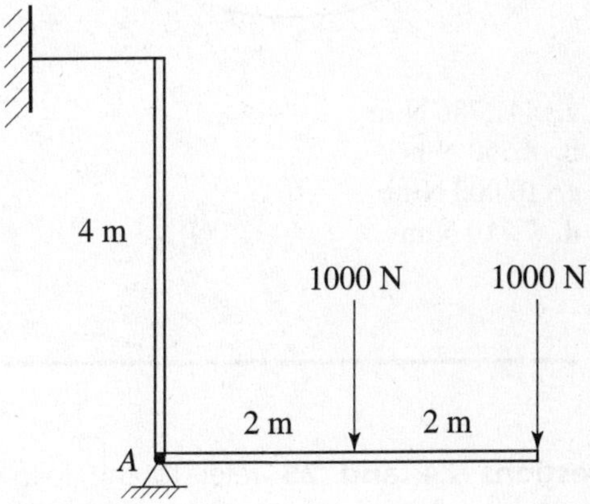

a. 7.96 MPa
b. 3.98 MPa
c. 6.36 MPa
d. 12.72 MPa

22. The maximum bending stress in the 6-centimeter-diameter shaft beam shown below is

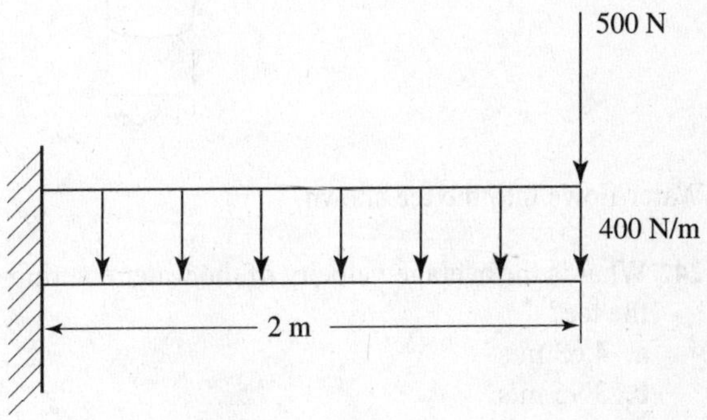

a. 84.88 MPa
b. 66.02 MPa
c. 112.6 MPa
d. 32.44 MPa

23. What is the torque T causing an angle of twist of 3 degrees in the solid shaft shown below? (G = 30 GPa)

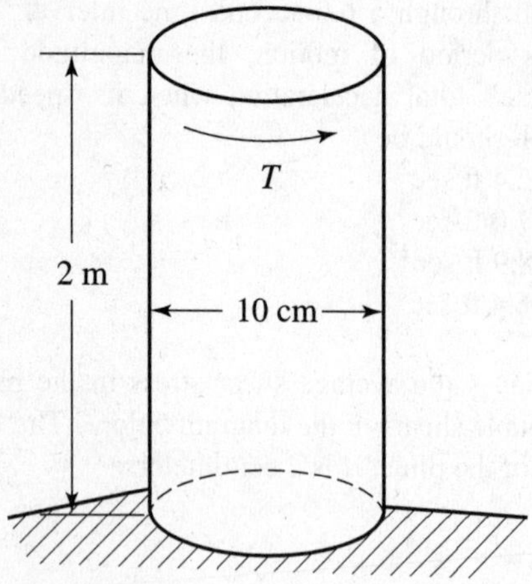

a. 441,786 N·m
b. 8,550 N·m
c. 10,000 N·m
d. 7,710 N·m

Questions 24 and 25 refer to the following diagram:

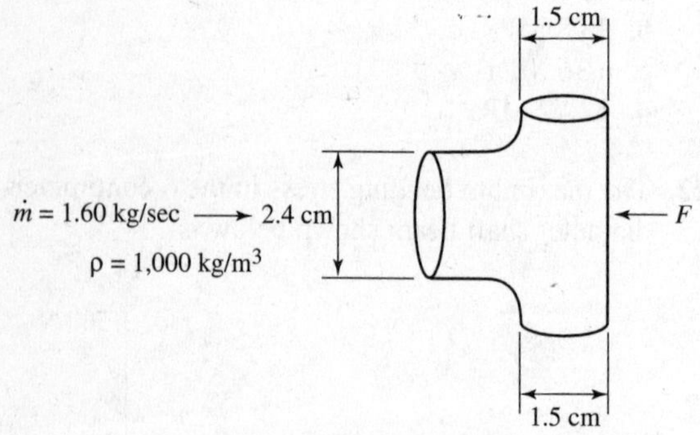

Water flows into the tee shown.

24. What is the average velocity of the water entering the tee?
a. 4.63 m/s
b. 3.95 m/s
c. 3.54 m/s
d. 0.35 m/s

25. What is the magnitude of the force (F) required to keep the tee stationary?
a. 5.66 N
b. 2.21 N
c. 6.32 N
d. 7.41 N

26.

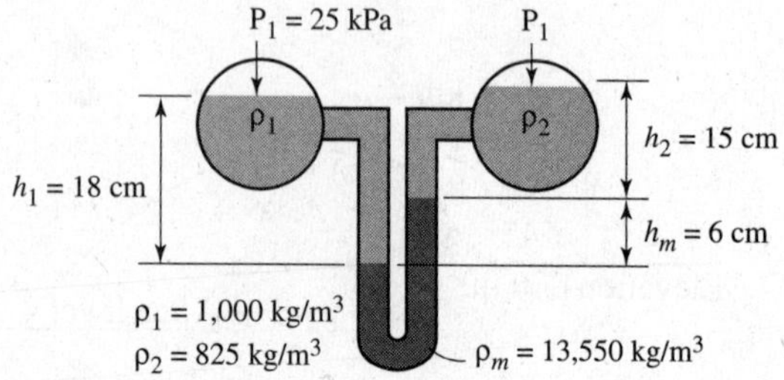

For the U-tube manometer shown above, what is the pressure in vessel 2 (p_2)?
a. 32.4 kPa
b. 33.5 kPa
c. 18.2 kPa
d. 17.6 kPa

27. The density of vanadium is 5.89 grams per centimeter $\frac{g}{cm^3}$, its atomic number is 23, its atomic weight is 50.94 atomic mass units (amu), and its structure is BCC. On the basis of these data, the radius of a vanadium atom is
a. 1.1×10^{-8} cm
b. 1.3×10^{-8} cm
c. 1.6×10^{-8} cm
d. 2.1×10^{-8} cm

28. Consider an alloy containing 49 weight percent copper and 51 weight percent nickel, and use the copper-nickel equilibrium phase diagram shown below.

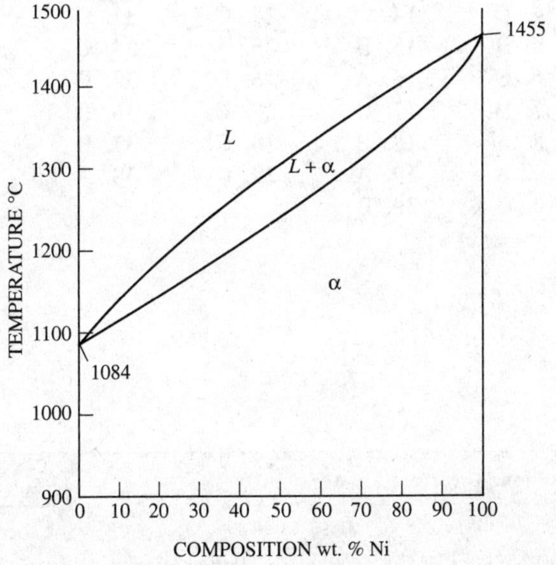

What is the percentage of liquid present in the alloy at 1,300°C?

a. 11%
b. 22%
c. 54%
d. 46%

29. The strong magnetic behavior exhibited by permanent magnets is called

a. paramagnetism
b. diamagnetism
c. ferromagnetism
d. superconductivity

30. In the following pseudo-code program segment, the second line is described as a (an)

```
REAL A, B
A=2
B=COS(A)
PRINT Y
```

a. statement
b. assignment
c. command
d. function

31. How many individual cells are in a spreadsheet in the range B3:I12?

a. 8
b. 10
c. 78
d. 80

32. Most memory in a computer remains on when the power is shut off. Which memory is *lost*?

a. A:
b. ROM
c. RAM
d. PROM

33. The Registered Professional Engineer's primary obligation is to

a. his/her client
b. his/her employer
c. the public welfare
d. the government

34. In engineering, legal and ethical requirements often overlap. Which of the following best describes the relationships between the two?

a. When legal and ethical requirements conflict, both can be ignored.
b. Legal actions are ethical actions.
c. Ethical requirements place more restrictions on behavior than legal requirements.
d. Legal and ethical actions have no relationship to each other.

35. Information, data, and analysis that you develop exclusively for a client

a. may be shared with your fellow employees
b. should remain confidential between you and the client
c. may be used on a subsequent project
d. should be shared with your superiors at a staff meeting

36. What amount of money would have to be deposited in a bank at the end of each year to accumulate a college fund of $50,000 at the end of 18 years? Interest on the account is 6%.

a. $1,520
b. $1,560
c. $1,580
d. $1,620

37. A company can manufacture a product with two different machines. Machine A has a $4.00 manufacturing cost per unit and a fixed cost of $3,000 for tools. Machine B costs $45,000 to purchase and has a $0.50 manufacturing cost per unit. With an annual anticipated volume of 7,000 units, the break-even point, in years, is most nearly

a. 1.5 yr
b. 1.7 yr
c. 1.9 yr
d. 2.1 yr

38. An automated measurement system has an initial cost of $36,000, and annual maintenance is $2,700. After 3 years the salvage value is $9,000. If the interest rate is 10%, the equivalent uniform annual cost is most nearly
   a. $14,457
   b. $14,658
   c. $14,860
   d. $15,020

Answer Key

1. D	11. C	21. B	30. B
2. D	12. D	22. A	31. D
3. C	13. A	23. D	32. C
4. D	14. C	24. C	33. C
5. B	15. B	25. A	34. C
6. B	16. A	26. D	35. B
7. D	17. C	27. B	36. D
8. A	18. B	28. C	37. B
9. A	19. A	29. C	38. A
10. C	20. B		

Diagnostic Chart

				Reason for Incorrect Answer			
Subject Area	*Total Number of Questions*	*Number Correct*	*Number Incorrect*	*Lack of Knowledge*	*Misread Problem*	*Careless or Mathematical Error*	*Wrong Guess*
Mathematics (1–5)	5						
Electric Circuits (6–8)	3						
Statics (9–11)	3						
Thermodynamics (12–14)	3						
Chemistry (15–17)	3						
Dynamics (18–20)	3						
Mechanics of Materials (21–23)	3						
Fluid Mechanics (24–26)	3						
Materials Science (27–29)	3						
Computers (30–32)	3						
Ethics (33–35)	3						
Economics (36–38)	3						
Total	38						

Answers Explained

1. **D** Distance $= \sqrt{(7-3)^2 + (5-2)^2}$
$= \sqrt{16+9} = 5$

2. **D** $\tan x \cos x = \dfrac{\sin x}{\cos x} \cdot \cos x = \sin x$, provided that $\cos x \neq 0$.

3. **C** By L'Hôpital's rule

$$\lim_{x\to 0}\left(\frac{8x^2}{\cos x - 1}\right) = \lim_{x\to 0}\left(\frac{16x}{-\sin x}\right)$$
$$= \lim_{x\to 0}\left(\frac{16}{-\cos x}\right) = -16$$

4. **D** $\int_a^b \frac{1}{x}\,dx = \ln x\,|_a^b = \ln b - \ln a = \ln\frac{b}{a}$, provided that $b > a > 0$.

5. **B** The differential equation $\frac{dy}{dt} - ky = 0$ is linear in y with integrating factor $e^{\int -k\,dt} = e^{-kt}$, where k is a constant. Hence, the general solution is

$$ye^{-kt} = c \quad \text{or} \quad y = ce^{kt}$$

If $y = 1$ when $t = 0$, then $c = 1$. Therefore, $y = e^{kt}$.

6. **B** Voltage across R_4: $V_4 = 4\ \Omega \times \frac{1}{8}\text{A} = \frac{1}{2}\text{V}$

Voltage across R_3: $1/2$ V because R_3 and R_4 are in parallel

Current through R_3: $I_3 = \dfrac{\frac{1}{2}\text{V}}{6\ \Omega} = \dfrac{1}{12}\text{A}$

Source current: $I_s = \frac{1}{12}\text{A} + \frac{1}{8}\text{A} = \frac{5}{24}\text{A}$

Voltage across R_2: $V_2 = \frac{5}{24}\text{A} \times 8\ \Omega = \frac{5}{3}\text{V}$

Voltage across R_1: $V_1 = \frac{5}{24}\text{A} \times 2\ \Omega = \frac{5}{12}\text{V}$

Apply Kirchhoff's voltage law to obtain

$$V_s = V_1 + V_2 + V_3$$
$$= \frac{5}{12}\text{V} + \frac{5}{3}\text{V} + \frac{1}{2}\text{V} = \frac{31}{12}\text{V}$$

Total power delivered to the system is

$$P_T = V_s I_s = \frac{31}{12}\text{V} \times \frac{5}{24}\text{A} \cong 0.54\text{ W}$$

7. **D** Consider R_L and L as a load and obtain a Thevenin equivalent circuit of R_1, R_2, and the source voltage.

$$E_{TH} = \frac{6\ \Omega}{3\ \Omega + 6\ \Omega} \times 36\text{ V} = 24\text{ V}$$

and

$$R_{TH} = \frac{3\ \Omega \times 6\ \Omega}{3\ \Omega + 6\ \Omega} = 2\ \Omega$$

The time constant of the circuit depends on L and $R_L + R_{TH}$ or

$$\tau = \frac{L}{R} = \frac{1.5\text{ H}}{3\ \Omega} = 0.5\text{ s}$$

The maximum current that can flow depends on E_{TH} and $R_L + R_{TH}$:

$$I_{max} = \frac{24\text{ V}}{1\ \Omega + 2\ \Omega} = 8\text{ A}$$

The inductor current is

$$I_L = 8\text{ A} \times \left(1 - e^{-\frac{0.25\text{ s}}{0.5\text{ s}}}\right) = 3.15\text{ A}$$

8. **A** Combine the capacitors into a single equivalent capacitor:

$$C_{eq} = 10\ \mu F + 10\ \mu F = 20\ \mu F$$

The capacitive reactance is

$$X_C = \frac{1}{2 \times \pi \times 100\text{ Hz} \times 20 \times 10^{-6}\text{ F}}$$
$$= 79.5\ \Omega$$

The inductive reactance is

$$X_L = 2 \times \pi \times 100\text{ Hz} \times 150\text{ mH} = 94.2\ \Omega$$

The input impedance is

$$Z_T = (50 + j94.2 - j79.6)\Omega$$
$$= (50 + j14.6)\Omega = 52.1\angle 16.3°\text{ k}\Omega$$

9. A $\sum M_A = 0$

$$B(9) - 900(4.5) - 450(6) = 0$$
$$B = 750 \text{ N}$$

10. C Since the resultant is vertical, $\Sigma F_x = 0$. Then

$$F \cos 60 - 50 \cos 30 = 0$$
$$F = 86.6 \text{ N}$$

11. C $\mathbf{F} = 30\mathbf{i} + 50\mathbf{j} - 20\mathbf{k}$

$$\cos \theta_x = \frac{F_x}{\sqrt{F_x^2 + F_y^2 + F_z^2}}$$
$$= \frac{30}{\sqrt{30^2 + 50^2 + (-20)^2}}$$
$$\theta = 60.9°$$

12. D $\dfrac{T_2}{T_1} = \left(\dfrac{p_2}{p_1}\right)^{\frac{n-1}{n}}$

$$T_2 = T_1\left(\frac{p_2}{p_1}\right)^{\frac{n-1}{n}}$$
$$= (298 \text{ K})\left(\frac{500 \text{ kPa}}{100 \text{ kPa}}\right)^{\left(\frac{1.5-1}{1.5}\right)}$$
$$= 510 \text{ K}$$
$$= 237°\text{C}$$

13. A $w = \int p\, dv$

$$= \frac{p_2v_2 - p_1v_1}{1 - n}$$
$$= \frac{R(T_2 - T_1)}{1 - n}$$
$$= \frac{\overline{R}(T_2 - T_1)}{M(1 - n)}$$
$$= \frac{\left(8.314 \frac{\text{kJ}}{\text{kmol K}}\right)(510 \text{ K} - 298 \text{ K})}{\left(29 \frac{\text{kg}}{\text{kmol}}\right)(1 - 1.5)}$$
$$= -122 \text{ kJ/kg}$$

14. C Energy balance:

$$\frac{dU}{dt} = \dot{Q} - \dot{W} + \sum \dot{m}_i h_i - \sum \dot{m}_e h_e$$
$$= \dot{Q} - \dot{W}$$

For a finite period of time:

$$\Delta U = Q - W$$
$$\Delta u = q - w$$
$$q = \Delta u + w$$
$$= c_v(T_2 - T_1) + w$$
$$= \left(0.718 \frac{\text{kJ}}{\text{kg K}}\right)(510 \text{ K} - 298 \text{ K}) - 122 \frac{\text{kJ}}{\text{kg}}$$
$$= 31 \text{ kJ/kg}$$

15. B First, determine the molar mass, MM.

$$\text{MM} = 40.01(1) + 14.01(2) + 16.00(6)$$
$$= 164.0 \text{ g/mol}$$

Then multiply the molar mass by 2.5 mol to get 410 g.

16. A The reaction is already balanced. Assume O_2 is in excess, and use the factor-label method.

$$300 \text{ g } C_2H_6 \frac{(1.0 \text{ mol } C_2H_6)}{(30.0 \text{ g } C_2H_6)}$$
$$\times \frac{(6.0 \text{ mol } H_2O)}{(2.0 \text{ mol } C_2H_6)} \frac{(18.0 \text{ g } H_2O)}{(1.0 \text{ mol } H_2O)} = 540 \text{ g}$$

17. C Check the general gas law, equation 1.1 in Chapter 1, and follow through with numbers.

18. B Projectile motion without air friction:

Elevation equation: $y(t) = y_o + v_{yo}t + \frac{1}{2}gt^2$

At position A, $y_o = 600$ m
At top of trajectory, $y = y_{max} = H$ at time t_M

$$x(t_M) = 8{,}000.0 \text{ m given}$$

Note, at y_{max}, $v_y = 0$ (velocity is entirely horizontal, v_x).

$$v_x = v_o \cos \alpha = v_o \cos 45° = 0.707v_o = \text{constant}$$

$$x(t) = v_x t = 0.707 v_o t \rightarrow$$
$$8{,}000.0 \text{ m} = 0.707 v_o t_M$$

$$t_M = \frac{11{,}315.4}{v_o}$$

$$y(t_M) = H = 600.0 \text{ m} + v_o \sin 45° \, t_M + \frac{1}{2}(-9.81)t_M^2 = 600.0 + 0.707 v_o t_M - 4.9 t_M^2$$

Since the vertical velocity component is $v_y(t) = v_{yo} - 9.81t$, at t_M write

$$0 = 0.707v_o - 9.81t_M \rightarrow t_M = 0.072v_o$$

Equate the previous expression for t_M to obtain

$$\frac{11{,}315.4}{v_o} = 0.072v_o \rightarrow v_o^2 = 157{,}158.0 \quad \text{and}$$

$$v_o = 396.4 \text{ m/s}$$
$$t_M = 0.072(396.4) = 28.5 \text{ s}$$

Substitute into the elevation equation above to obtain

$$H = 600.0 + 0.707(396.4)(28.5) - 4.9(28.5)^2 = 4{,}607.1 \text{ m} \approx 4{,}600 \text{ m}$$

19. A Use the impulse/momentum principle (IMP):

$$mv_1 + \text{IMP}_{1\rightarrow 2} = mv_2$$

Given $v_1 = 0$, obtain v_2 as follows:

Draw an FBD of the crate, and identify external forces: kinetic friction F_{FK}, normal reaction N_R, weight W, and towing F_T.

$$\text{IMP}_{1\rightarrow 2} = \sum F_x(\Delta t) \quad \text{and} \quad \Delta t = 12.0 \text{ s (given)}$$

$$\sum F_x = F_T \cos 30° - F_{FK} = (500.0 \text{ N})(0.866) - (0.3)N_R$$

From $\Sigma F_y = 0 \rightarrow F_T \sin 30° - W + N_R = 0$:

$$(500.0 \text{ N})(0.5) - (60)(9.81) + N_R = 0 \rightarrow$$
$$N_R = 588.6 - 250.0 = 338.6 \text{ N}$$

Substitute to obtain $\Sigma F_x = 433.0 \text{ N} - 0.3(338.6 \text{ N}) = 331.4 \text{ N}$

From the IMP equation:

$$0 + (331.4 \text{ N})(12.0 \text{ s}) = (60 \text{ kg})v_2$$

$$v_2 = \frac{3{,}977.0 \text{ N·s}}{60 \text{ kg}} = 66.2 \text{ m/s}$$

20. B Use tangential and normal coordinates:

$$R = 400.0 \text{ ft} = \text{constant}$$

Tangential acceleration:

$$a_T = \frac{\Delta V}{\Delta t} = \frac{(40 - 30)\text{mph}}{6.0 \text{ sec}} = 1.67 \text{ mph/sec} = 1.67\left(\frac{1.466 \text{ ft/sec}}{\text{mph}}\right) = 2.45 \text{ ft/sec}^2$$

Normal acceleration:

$$a_N = \frac{V^2}{R} = \frac{(35 \text{ mph})^2}{400.0 \text{ ft}} = \frac{[(35)(1.466)\text{ft/sec}]^2}{400 \text{ ft}} = 6.58 \text{ ft/sec}^2$$

Total acceleration magnitude:

$$a_{tot} = \sqrt{a_T^2 + a_N^2} = \sqrt{(2.45)^2 + (6.58)^2} = \sqrt{49.3} = 7.02 \text{ ft/sec}^2$$

21. B $\sum M_A = 0 \quad T(4) - 1{,}000(2) - 1{,}000(4) = 0$

$$T = 1{,}500 \text{ N}$$

$$\sum F_x = 0 \quad A_x = 1{,}500 \text{ N}$$
$$\sum F_y = 0 \quad A_y = 2{,}000 \text{ N}$$

Resultant pin reaction at A:

$$A = \sqrt{1{,}500^2 + 2{,}000^2} = 2{,}500 \text{ N}$$

Since the pin at A is in double shear, $V = A/2 = 1{,}250$ N. Then

$$\tau = \frac{V}{A_s} = \frac{1{,}250}{\frac{\pi}{4}(0.02)^2} = 3.98 \text{ MPa}$$

22. A The maximum moment occurs at the fixed support and is equal to

$$M_{max} = 800(1) + (500)(2) = 1{,}800 \text{ N·m}$$

Then

$$\sigma_{max} = \frac{M_{max}c}{I} = \frac{1{,}800(0.03)}{\frac{\pi}{64}(0.06)^4} = 84.88 \text{ MPa}$$

23. D $\phi = \dfrac{Tl}{GJ}$

Solve for torque, T:

$$T = \frac{\phi G J}{l} = \frac{\left(3\frac{\pi}{180}\right)(30 \times 10^9)\left(\frac{\pi}{32}(0.1)^4\right)}{2}$$

$$= 7{,}710 \text{ N·m}$$

Note that the unit for the angle of twist must be radians.

24. C $\bar{V} = \dfrac{Q}{A}$

$$Q = \frac{\dot{m}}{\rho} \qquad A = \frac{\pi D^2}{4}$$

$$= \frac{1.60\ \frac{\text{kg}}{\text{s}}}{1{,}000\ \frac{\text{kg}}{\text{m}^3}} \qquad = \frac{\pi(0.024 \text{ m})^2}{4}$$

$$= 1.60 \times 10^{-3}\ \frac{\text{m}^3}{\text{s}} \qquad = 4.52 \times 10^{-4} \text{ m}^2$$

$$\bar{V} = \frac{1.60 \times 10^{-3}\ \frac{\text{m}^3}{\text{s}}}{4.52 \times 10^{-4} \text{ m}^2}$$

$$= 3.54\ \frac{\text{m}}{\text{s}}$$

25. A $\sum \mathbf{F} = (\dot{m}\mathbf{V})_{\text{in}} - (\dot{m}\mathbf{V})_{\text{out}}$

This equation can be separated into its horizontal and vertical components:

$\sum \mathbf{F}_x = (\dot{m}\mathbf{V}_x)_{\text{in}} - (\dot{m}\mathbf{V}_x)_{\text{out}}$ and

$\sum \mathbf{F}_y = (\dot{m}\mathbf{V}_y)_{\text{in}} - (\dot{m}\mathbf{V}_y)_{\text{out}}$

The horizontal component of the outlet velocity, $(\mathbf{V}_x)_{\text{out}}$, and the vertical component of the inlet velocity, $(\mathbf{V}_y)_{\text{in}}$, are both zero. Also, because the tee is symmetric and both outlet ports have the same diameter, the momentum leaving each port will be of equal magnitude and opposite direction. Therefore:

$$\sum \mathbf{F}_y = 0$$

and

$$\sum \mathbf{F}_x = (\dot{m}\mathbf{V}_x)_{\text{in}} = \mathbf{F}$$

$$\mathbf{F} = \left(1.60\ \frac{\text{kg}}{\text{s}}\right)\left(3.54\ \frac{\text{m}}{\text{s}}\right)\left(\frac{\text{N}}{\frac{\text{kg m}}{\text{s}^2}}\right)$$

$$= 5.66 \text{ N}$$

26. D

$$p_2 = p_1 + \rho_1 g h_1 - \rho_m g h_m - \rho_2 g h_2$$

$$= 25 \text{ kPa} + \left(1{,}000\frac{\text{kg}}{\text{m}^3}\right)\left(9.81\frac{\text{m}}{\text{s}^2}\right)(0.18 \text{ m})\left(\frac{\text{N}}{\frac{\text{kg·m}}{\text{s}^2}}\right)$$

$$\times \left(\frac{\text{kPa}}{1{,}000\frac{\text{N}}{\text{m}^2}}\right) - \left(13{,}550\frac{\text{kg}}{\text{m}^3}\right)\left(9.81\frac{\text{m}}{\text{s}^2}\right)(0.06 \text{ m})$$

$$\times \left(\frac{\text{N}}{\frac{\text{kg·m}}{\text{s}^2}}\right)\left(\frac{\text{kPa}}{1{,}000\frac{\text{N}}{\text{m}^2}}\right) - \left(825\frac{\text{kg}}{\text{m}^3}\right)\left(9.81\frac{\text{m}}{\text{s}^2}\right)$$

$$\times (0.15 \text{ m})\left(\frac{\text{N}}{\frac{\text{kg·m}}{\text{s}^2}}\right)\left(\frac{\text{kPa}}{1{,}000\frac{\text{N}}{\text{m}^2}}\right)$$

$$= 25 \text{ kPa} + 1.76 \text{ kPa} - 7.98 \text{ kPa} - 1.21 \text{ kPa}$$

$$= 17.57 \text{ kPa}$$

27. B The structure is BCC, so there are 2 atoms in a unit cell. Obtain the radius by finding the lattice parameter from the volume. The radius is, for BCC, $4r = a\sqrt{3}$.

$$\text{Volume} = \frac{\text{mass}}{\rho} = \frac{2 \cdot 50.94}{6.023 \times 10^{23} \cdot 5.89}$$

$$= 2.87 \times 10^{-23} \text{ cm}^3$$

Then

$$r = \frac{\sqrt{3}}{4}(\text{volume})^{\frac{1}{3}} = \frac{\sqrt{3} \cdot (2.87 \times 10^{-23})^{\frac{1}{3}}}{4}$$

$$= 1.32 \times 10^{-8} \text{ cm}$$

28. C $f_L = \dfrac{C_S - C_o}{C_S - C_L} = \dfrac{58 - 51}{58 - 45} = .54$

29. C

30. B Line 2 *assigns* the value used later in the program. *Statement* is an instruction; *command* directs the computer to take action; *function* performs a specific action, as in COS.

31. D B to I is 8 columns; 3 to 12 is 10 rows. Therefore, there are 80 cells.

32. C A: is usually the slot for a 3 1/2-in. diskette. ROM is read-only memory, and PROM is programmable read-only memory.

33. C

34. C

35. B

36. D

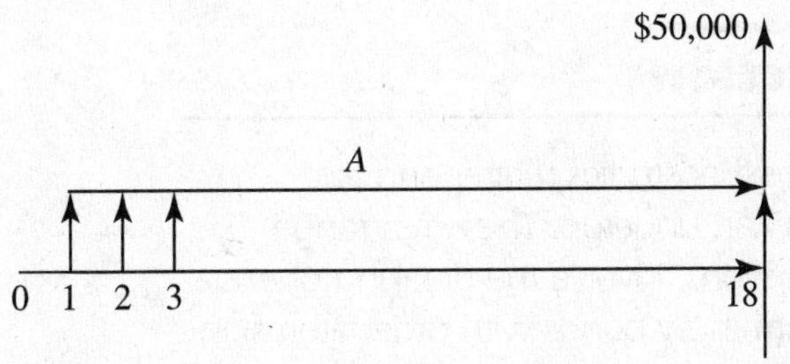

$A = \$50,000(A/F,6,18)$
$= \$50,000(0.0324) = \$1,620$

37. B Break-even analysis:

Set costs of Machine A = costs of Machine B

Let x = break-even quantity. Then

$$4.00x + \$3,000 = 0.50x + \$45,000$$
$$3.5x = \$42,000$$
$$x = 12,000 \text{ units}$$

At 12,000 units B/E and usage of 7,000 units per year:

$$\frac{12,000}{7,000} = 1.7 \text{ yr}$$

38. A

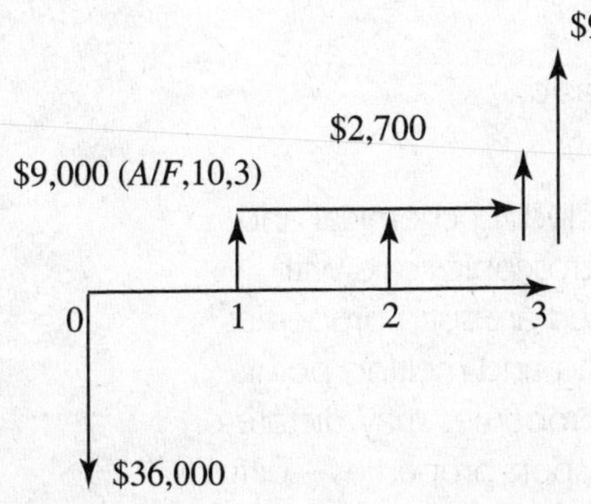

Annual cost $= \$36,000(A/P,10,3) + \$2,700 - \$9,000(A/F,10,3)$
$= \$36,000(0.4021) + \$2,700 - \$9,000(0.3021)$
$= \$14,476 + \$2,700 - \$2,719$
$= \$14,457$

C H A P T E R

1

Chemistry

Armen S. Casparian

Introduction

Chemistry is the branch of physical science that studies matter and the changes or "molecular rearrangements" it can undergo. These rearrangements, commonly known as chemical reactions, involve the breaking of existing chemical bonds between atoms to form new bonds with other atoms. In the process, different molecules with different properties are formed. Electrons may be gained or lost, and energy changes generally accompany the reaction. Chemical reactions, as distinguished from nuclear reactions, involve the exchange of only electrons—never protons or neutrons. In a sense, chemistry is the recycling of atoms.

Visible evidence of chemical reactions includes:

- Bubbling or fizzing, indicating the release of a gas.
- Color change.
- Temperature change.
- Formation of a precipitate.
- Dissolving of a solid.

Examples of common chemical reactions include:

- Rusting of iron or corrosion of any metal.
- Generation of current by a battery.
- Combustion of fuel to produce energy.
- Neutralization of excess stomach acid by an antacid.
- Hardening of concrete.

Chemistry also studies the structure of matter, including chemical and physical properties, correlating properties on the microscopic scale with behavior observed on the macroscopic scale. Included are such properties as vapor pressure, osmotic presssure, solubility, boiling and melting points, and energy and its transformations. Many of these properties may dictate or influence the outcome of a reaction. [The three transport properties—diffusion, viscosity, and thermal conductivity—are not discussed in this chapter.]

This chapter consists of 12 sections with individual topics discussed under each section. Solved examples reflecting fundamental principles and applications are included in most sections. Additional practice problems with answers are provided at the end of the chapter.

1.1 Basic Concepts, Definitions, Notation, and Units

Symbols and Notation

A. Chemistry is based on the premise that all matter is composed of some combination of the 92 naturally occurring elements. These elements are arranged in a particular order known as **the Periodic Chart** or **Periodic Table:** in horizontal rows called **periods,** by increasing atomic number, and in vertical columns called **groups or families,** by similar electron configurations, which in turn give rise to similar chemical properties. **Electron configurations** are ordered arrangements of electrons based on specific housing rules. Energy levels range from 1 to 7, and within each energy level or shell are sublevels or orbitals *s*, *p*, *d*, and *f*. Each of the four orbitals has a distinct shape and population limit: 1 *s* orbital with a maximum of 2 electrons; 3 *p* orbitals for a maximum of 6 electrons; 5 *d* orbitals for a maximum of 10 electrons; 7 *f* orbitals for a maximum of 14 electrons.

B. Members of the same family are called **congeners.** [Elements after uranium (atomic number 92), that is, elements 93 through 109, are manmade, radioactive, and increasingly unstable, and are not addressed in this chapter.] Some rows of the Periodic Table have names, such as the actinide (row 6) or lanthanide (row 7) series, while columns have such names as alkali metals (column 1A), alkaline-earth metals (column 2A), transition metals, halogens (column 7A), and noble (inert) gases (column 8A).

C. Each element is symbolized by either a single capital letter or a capital letter followed by a single lowercase letter. Thus, the number of elements from which a compound is made up can easily be determined by counting the number of capital letters.

D. The **atomic number,** ***Z,*** of an element is the number of protons in the nucleus of its atom. The atomic number, which is always an integer and uniquely identifies the element, is written as a *left-hand subscript* to the element's symbol, for example, ${}_6C$.

E. The **mass number,** ***A,*** of an element is the sum of the number of protons and number of neutrons in the nucleus. Protons and neutrons are arbitrarily assigned a mass number of one atomic mass unit (amu) each. Although an element can have only one atomic number, it may have more than one mass number. This fact gives rise to the phenomenon of isotopes. **Isotopes** are atoms with the same atomic number (hence represent the same element) but with different neutron numbers. An element may have several isotopes, one or more of which may be radioactive and hence unstable. For example, oxygen has three naturally occurring isotopes, all of which are stable, while carbon also has three, one of which is radioactive. The mathematical average of all of an element's isotopic mass numbers, weighted by the percent abundances in nature of these isotopes, constitutes the element's average **atomic mass.** It is impossible to theoretically predict how many isotopes an element may have, or how many may be radioactive. The isotopes of a given element have identical chemical properties (reactivities) but different physical properties. The mass number is expressed as a *left-hand superscript* to the element's symbol, for example, ${}^{12}C$.

F. The electronic charge of an element is zero; that is, the number of electrons equals the number of protons in the neutral or uncharged atom in its elemental state. If an atom gains or loses electrons, it becomes charged. A charged atom is called an **ion.** A positively charged ion has lost one or more electrons and is called a **cation,** while a negatively charged ion has gained one or more electrons and is called an **anion.** The charge or oxidation state on the ion is expressed as a *right-hand superscript* to the element's symbol.

Example 1.1

Uranium, the element with atomic number $Z =$ 92, has three naturally occurring isotopes: U-234, U-235, and U-238. Only U-235 is fissionable. When it combines with a halogen to form a compound, it commonly forms a cation with a +6 charge.

A. Using proper notation, write the symbol of the U-235 isotope, indicating its electronic charge (also known as the **valence** or **oxidation state**).

B. Determine the number of protons, neutrons, and electrons in one atom of this isotope.

Solution:

A. The symbol, written with proper notation, is:

$${}^{235}_{92}U^{+6}$$

B. This atom has 92 protons (note left-hand subscript).

It must also have 92 electrons, understood, in its neutral (uncharged) atom. However, since this atom has a charge of +6 (note right-hand superscript), it has *lost* six electrons to become positively charged. Hence, it now has only 86 electrons.

To compute the number of neutrons in this atom, simply subtract the atomic number (left-hand subscript) from the mass number (left-hand superscript): $235 - 92 = 143$ neutrons.

This is the isotope of uranium that is fissionable and produces nuclear energy.

Common Units of Measurement

Important, measurable quantities or variables, along with their symbols and common units of measurement, are as follows:

- Temperature, T, in degrees centigrade (Celsius) or Fahrenheit or in kelvin units (K).
- Mass, m, in grams (g).
- Number of moles, n, 6.022×10^{23} atoms, molecules, or formula units; see Section 1.2, page 18.
- **Molar mass,** *MM,* the mass in grams of 6.022×10^{23} atoms of an element or molecules of a compound; see Section 1.2, page 18. The terms **molecular weight** and **formula weight** are often used interchangeably with molar mass.
- **Avogadro's number** or **constant:** 6.022×10^{23} particles or items per mole.
- Volume, V, in cubic centimeters (cm^3) or liters (L).
- Pressure, P, in atmospheres (atm) or other suitable units.
- Density, d, in grams per cubic centimeter (g/cm^3) or grams per milliliter (g/mL).
- Concentration may be expressed in any one of several units, depending on the application; see Section 1.2, page 20.

Very often, amounts of substances either are given or must be calculated. They may be expressed in *grams* (unit of mass), *moles,* or *liters* (unit of volume).

1.2 Basic Calculations

Inorganic Nomenclature and Formula Writing

There are two methods to name inorganic compounds and write their chemical formulas:

1. The criss-cross method for ionic compounds.
2. The Greek prefix method for covalent compounds.

In order to decide which method is suitable, you must first decide what class of compound you are dealing with: **ionic** or **covalent.** Recall that ionic compounds are made up of a metal and a nonmetal; salts, such as sodium chloride or potassium nitrate, are ionic compounds. Covalent compounds are made up of two nonmetals; examples are carbon dioxide and phosphorous pentachloride. Ionic compounds are characterized by ionic bonds, in which one or more electrons have been transferred from the metal to the nonmetal atom, while covalent compounds are characterized by covalent bonds, in which electrons are shared between two atoms. If the sharing is unequal, the bond is said to be **polar-covalent,** and one end of the molecule has a partial positive charge while the other has a partial negative charge. Such molecules are referred to as **dipoles** and have dipole moments, which are quantitative measures of their polarity. If the sharing is equal, the bond is said to be nonpolar covalent; the molecule has no charge separation and hence no positive or negative end. In reality, most compounds are *not entirely* ionic or entirely covalent, but are a percentage of each.

If the compound in question is ionic, use the criss-cross method of nomenclature. Write the symbols of the metal and nonmetal elements side by side (recall that the nonmetal may be a single anion or a polyatomic oxoanion, such as sulfate or nitrate), along with their respective valences or oxidation states as right-hand superscripts. Then criss-cross the superscripts, that is, interchange them for the two elements, and write them as subscripts, omitting the plus or negative signs. If the two subscripts are the same, drop them both. In nomenclature, the name of the metal element is given first and that of the nonmetal element second, changing it to an "-ide" ending, such as chlor<u>ide</u> or sulf<u>ide</u>, or using the name of the oxoanion, like sulfate or nitrate.

If a compound is covalent, the Greek prefix method is used. Here, knowledge of valences is unnecessary, but you will need to know the first twelve numbers in Greek: mono, di, tri, tetra, penta, hexa, hepta, octa, nona, deca, unideca, and dodeca. The proper Greek prefix simply precedes each element in the formula. As above, the name of the second element takes on the suffix -ide.

You should remember that many compounds have chemical names as well as common names. A compound generally has only one correct chemical name but may have one or more common names. For example, the compound $Ca(OH)_2$ has the chemical name calcium hydroxide; it is also referred to commonly as slaked lime or hydrated lime.

Example 1.2

Write the correct chemical formula for each of the following compounds:

A. Calcium chloride　　**B.** Aluminum sulfate
C. Iron(III) phosphate　　**D.** Sulfur trioxide
E. Diphosphorus pentoxide

Solution:

Compounds **A–C** are ionic, so the criss-cross method applies.

Compounds **D** and **E** are covalent, so the Greek prefix method applies.

A. Calcium chloride: Ca^{2+} and Cl^{1-} are the two ions.

Criss-crossing gives: $CaCl_2$.

Note that the subscript 1 next to Ca has been omitted because 1's are understood and are not written when specifying numbers of atoms.

B. Aluminum sulfate: Al^{3+} and $(SO_4)^{2-}$ are the two ions.

Criss-crossing gives: $Al_2(SO_4)_3$.

Note that parentheses are necessary to express the fact that the subscript 3 refers to and thus multiplies both the sulfur and the oxygen atoms (subscripts) inside the parentheses.

C. Iron(III) phosphate: Fe^{3+} and $(PO_4)^{3-}$ are the two ions.

Note that the iron(III) notation refers to the Fe^{3+} species, to be distinguished from the Fe^{2+} species, written as iron(II). This is the modern way of distinguishing the ferric ion from the ferrous ion. This same system of notation, using Roman numerals in parentheses, is used for all transition metals with multiple oxidation states.

Criss-crossing gives: $Fe_3(PO_4)_3$.

Note that fine tuning is necessary. Since both subscripts are 3, they are omitted. Furthermore, the parentheses then become unnecessary and are dropped as well.

The fine-tuned answer is $FePO_4$.

D. Sulfur trioxide: S and O are the elements.

Sulfur is "mono" or 1 (understood and not written), and oxygen is "tri" or 3. Hence, the chemical formula is SO_3.

E. Diposphorus pentoxide: P and O are the elements.

Phosphorus is "di" or 2, and oxygen is "pent" or 5. Hence, the chemical formula is P_2O_5.

Example 1.3

Find the total number of atoms in one formula unit (molecule) of compounds **A, B,** and **C** in Example 1.2.

Solution:

In each case, simply add the subscripts next to all the atoms in the formula unit. Where parentheses are used, be sure to multiply subscripts inside parentheses by subscripts outside parentheses.

For $CaCl_2$: 1 Ca atom + 2 Cl atoms = 3 atoms total

For $Al_2(SO_4)_3$: 2 Al atoms + 3 S atoms + 12 O atoms = 17 atoms total

For $FePO_4$: 1 Fe atom + 1 P atom + 4 O atoms = 6 atoms total

Note: The percent oxygen (O) *by number* in $Al_2(SO_4)_3$ is $12/17 \times 100$ or 70.6%, while in $FePO_4$ it is $4/6 \times 100$ or 66.7%. Compare this calculation to the calculation for percent *by mass* in Example 1.5.

Calculating Oxidation States from Formulas

Occasionally, it may be necessary to determine the oxidation state or valence of an ion in a compound from its formula. This situation is often encountered with compounds or polyatomic complexes containing transition metal ions, which may have multiple oxidation states. A simple algebraic equation solves the problem, as illustrated in Example 1.4.

Example 1.4

Find the oxidation state or valence of each underlined atom.

A. $K\underline{Mn}O_4$ **B.** $(\underline{Cr_2}O_7)^{2-}$

Solution:

Here, it is necessary to know the oxidation states assigned to common "fixed" elements. Some guidelines include:

- Alkali metals are +1.
- Alkaline earth metals are +2.
- Oxygen is generally −2.
- Halides are generally −1.

Set up a simple algebraic equation based on the principle that the sum of the known charges of individual atoms in the formula, multiplied by their respective subscripts, must total the net charge on the formula unit of the compound or polyatomic ion.

A. For $KMnO_4$:

$$(+1)(1) + (x)(1) + (-2)(4) = 0$$

Note that x represents the oxidation state of the "unknown" Mn atom. The total is set to zero because the formula unit is electronically neutral or uncharged.

Solve for x: $x = +7$.

Thus, the oxidation state of Mn in $KmnO_4$ is +7. [The Mn ion itself can be expressed as either Mn^{7+} or Mn(VII).]

B. For $(Cr_2O_7)^{2-}$:

$$(x)(2) + (-2)(7) = -2$$

Note that x represents the oxidation state of the unknown Cr atom. The total is set to −2 because the net charge on the complex is −2.

Solve for x: $x = +6$.

Thus, the oxidation state of Cr in $(Cr_2O_7)^{2-}$ is +6. [The Cr ion itself can be expressed as either Cr^{6+} or Cr(VI).]

Determining the Percent Composition of a Compound

It is often important to be able to compute the percent composition of a compound. This ability is valuable, for example, when comparing compounds such as fertilizers or mineral supplements to determine which fertilizer contains the most nitrogen per unit mass of fertilizer, or which mineral supplement contains the most calcium per unit mass of tablet. This determination requires that you first calculate the molar mass of each of the compounds in question. It is assumed that you are familiar with calculating the molar mass of a compound from the atomic masses of the individual elements in the compound. Example 1.5 illustrates the method.

Example 1.5

Determine the percent composition, by mass, of each of the following compounds:

A. Calcium oxide, CaO (commonly known as lime or quicklime)

B. Calcium carbonate, $CaCO_3$ (commonly known as limestone)

Solution:

A. For CaO, the percent composition must be a two-part answer, because two elements make up CaO. Its molar mass is 56.1 g/mol. Thus:

$$\%\,Ca = \frac{(\text{atomic mass of Ca})(\#\text{ Ca atoms in 1 formula unit})}{\text{molar mass of CaO}} \times 100$$

$$= \frac{(40.1\text{ g Ca})(1)}{56.1\text{ g CaO}} \times 100$$

$$= 71.5\%$$

$$\%\,O = \frac{(\text{atomic mass of O})(\#\text{ O atoms in 1 formula unit})}{56.1\text{ g CaO}} \times 100$$

$$= \frac{(16.0\text{ g O})(1)}{56.1\text{ g CaO}} \times 100$$

$$= 28.5\%$$

B. For $CaCO_3$, the percent composition must be a three-part answer, because three elements make up $CaCO_3$. Its molar mass is 100.1 g/mol. In a similar fashion, then:

$$\% \text{ Ca} = \frac{(40.1 \text{ g Ca})(1)}{100.1 \text{ g CaCO}_3} \times 100$$
$$= 40.0\% \text{ Ca}$$

$$\% \text{ C} = \frac{(12.0 \text{ g C})(1)}{100.1 \text{ g CaCO}_3} \times 100$$
$$= 12.0\%$$

$$\% \text{ O} = \frac{(16.0 \text{ g O})(3)}{100.1 \text{ g CaCO}_3} \times 100$$
$$= 48.0\%$$

Note that CaO has a higher percent Ca content by mass than $CaCO_3$.

Determining Empirical and Molecular Formulas from Percent Composition

It is frequently useful to determine the chemical formula of an unknown compound. One method is **combustion analysis.** If the unknown compound is known to contain at least carbon and hydrogen, heating a measured amount in the presence of excess oxygen, a process known as combustion, produces carbon dioxide and water, which can be collected and weighed individually. All of the carbon atoms are contained in the carbon dioxide, and all of the hydrogen atoms are contained in the water. Since 1 mole of carbon dioxide is equivalent to 1 mole of carbon atoms, and 1 mole of water is equivalent to 2 moles of hydrogen atoms, the number of moles of carbon and hydrogen in the unknown compound can be determined. If oxygen is also present in the unknown, it is distributed over the carbon dioxide and water products; its mass can be found by difference and then converted to moles of oxygen in the original or unknown compound. The mass or moles of other elements, such as nitrogen and sulfur, which form known compounds with oxygen, can be determined in the same fashion. **Pyrolysis** is the intense heating of a compound or mixture in the absence of oxygen.

Alternatively, another method is known as **elemental analysis.** A measured amount of the unknown substance is heated until it decomposes into its constituent elements, which are collected and analyzed individually. The percent composition by mass of the compound is obtained.

Example 1.6 illustrates how percent composition data can be used to deduce the chemical formula and ultimately the identity of an unknown substance.

Example 1.6

The percent composition by mass of an unknown compound is 40.9% carbon, 4.57% hydrogen, and 54.5% oxygen. By a separate analysis, its molecular weight or molar mass is found to be 176 g/mol. Find for the unknown compound:

A. the empirical formula
B. the molecular formula

Solution:

A. Recall that the empirical formula represents the smallest group or combination of atoms, in the proper ratio, of which the molecule is composed. Assume a 100-g sample to work with. Then the given percentages can be translated directly into grams as follows:

$$40.9 \text{ g C}, 4.57 \text{ g H}, 54.5 \text{ g O}$$

Next, convert these masses to moles by dividing each one by its respective atomic mass:

$$40.9 \text{ g C}\left(\frac{1.00 \text{ mol C}}{12.01 \text{ g C}}\right) = 3.41 \text{ mol C}$$

$$4.57 \text{ g H}\left(\frac{1.00 \text{ mol H}}{1.008 \text{ g H}}\right) = 4.53 \text{ mol H}$$

$$54.5 \text{ g O}\left(\frac{1.00 \text{ mol O}}{16.0 \text{ g O}}\right) = 3.41 \text{ mol O}$$

At this point, the chemistry is done, and you could write the empirical formula in principle, using the calculated numbers as the subscripts: $C_{3.41}\,H_{4.53}\,O_{3.41}$.

Chemical formula rules stipulate, however, that these subscripts must not only be in the proper ratio but also must be whole numbers or integers. The problem now is to find a mathematical technique to maintain the ratio but change the subscripts into integers. One way is to divide through by the smallest number:

$$C_{3.41/3.41}\,H_{4.53/3.41}\,O_{3.41/3.41} = C_{1.00}\,H_{1.33}\,O_{1.00}$$

Only the 1.33 subscript is not an integer. This can be corrected by multiplying through by the factor 3:

$$C_{3.00}\,H_{4.00}\,O_{3.00}$$

This, then, is the empirical formula.

B. To find the molecular formula, simply divide the molar mass by the empirical mass, which should always be a whole number. Then multiply each of the subscripts in the empirical formula by this factor to obtain the molecular formula.

The empirical mass of the above chemical formula ($C_3H_4O_3$) is calculated in the same way as a molar mass would be and equals 88.0 g/mol. Thus, the factor is:

$$\frac{\text{Molar mass}}{\text{Empirical mass}} = \frac{176 \text{ g/mol}}{88 \text{ g/mol}} = 2.0$$

Therefore, the correct molecular formula is $C_6H_8O_6$.

This is the formula for ascorbic acid, commonly known as vitamin C.

Concentration Units for Aqueous Solutions

Several concentration units exist in chemistry to quantify the strengths of aqueous solutions. The reason for this great variety is that different applications and chemical formulas require different units. The term "concentration" always implies the existence of a **solute,** present as a gas, liquid, or solid, dissolved in a suitable **solvent** to form a **solution.** Unless otherwise specified, the solvent for liquid solutions is understood to be water—hence the designation "aqueous solution," abbreviated as (aq). The common definitions and units are as follows:

- Molarity, M = moles of solute/liter of solution.
- Molality, m = moles of solute/kilogram of solvent.
- Mole fraction, X = number of moles of component i/total number of moles.
- Percent by mass/mass = mass of solute in grams/mass of solution in grams.
- Percent by volume/volume = volume of solute in milliliters/total volume of solution in milliliters.

See pages 26 and 27 for specific applications and examples.

1.3 Gas Laws

The General Gas Law

Boyle's law (the pressure of a gas is inversely proportional to its volume) and **Charles's law** (the volume of a gas is directly proportional to its temperature) are generally combined into a more useful form known as the **general gas law,** expressed as

$$\frac{P_1V_1}{T_1} = \frac{P_2V_2}{T_2} \qquad [1.1]$$

It is understood that this law is valid only for a closed system in which the total number of gas molecules and hence the mass are constant. The general gas law can be applied to an individual gas (e.g., nitrogen or carbon dioxide) or a mixture of gases (e.g., air). It is assumed that the gas is ideal, that is, follows the ideal gas law (see next section) as its equation of state.

Pressures P and volumes V may be in any units as long as they are consistent. Temperature must be absolute and thus in kelvins. The subscripts 1 and 2 represent the initial and final states or conditions, respectively, for each quantity.

Example 1.7

A fixed quantity of gas occupies a volume of 2.0 L at a temperature of 20°C and a pressure of 1.0 atm. Find the volume that this gas would occupy at 40°C and 1.75 atm pressure.

Solution:

The general gas law (equation 1.1) applies. This is a problem in which the volume of a gas must be calculated at a new or different temperature and pressure. The data given are:

$$P_1 = 1.0 \text{ atm} \quad P_2 = 1.75 \text{ atm}$$

$$T_1 = 20°\text{C} + 273 \text{ K} = 293 \text{ K}$$
$$T_2 = 40°\text{C} + 273 \text{ K} = 313 \text{ K}$$

$$V_1 = 2.0 \text{ L} \quad V_2 = ?$$

Substitute these values into the general gas law and solve for V_2.

$$V_2 = \frac{P_1V_1T_2}{P_2T_1} = \frac{(1.0 \text{ atm})(2.0 \text{ L})(313 \text{ K})}{(1.75 \text{ atm})(293 \text{ K})}$$

$$= 1.22 \text{ L}$$

The Ideal Gas Law

The **ideal gas law,** known also as the **equation of state** for ideal gases, is a very useful and powerful problem-solving tool. It relates the pressure, volume, and temperature of a quantity of a gas. An **ideal gas** is a gas in which every molecule behaves independently of every other molecule (there is an absence of any intermolecular forces) and has no excluded volume. It is represented by the ideal gas law:

$$PV = nRT \quad [1.2]$$

where P = the pressure in atmospheres, torr, millimeters of mercury, pounds per square inch, pascals, etc.

V = the volume in liters, cubic centimeters, etc.

n = the number of moles of gas

= mass of gas in grams/molar mass in grams per mole

$= \dfrac{m}{MM}$

T = the absolute temperature in kelvin units

R = the universal gas constant in units consistent with the above values, that is, R = 0.0821 L · atm/K · mol; 8.31 J/K · mol, etc.

The ideal gas law contains four variables and the constant R. Given any three, the fourth can be found. In addition, this law can be used to find the molar mass or molecular weight if the mass of a gas is given.

Note that the ideal gas law is valid for a single, individual gas. If a mixture of gases is present, the ideal gas law is valid for each individual gas. In other words, a separate calculation using this law should be made for each gas present. The pressure of each gas thus calculated represents a partial pressure in the mixture. The total pressure can then be calculated according to Dalton's law (see the next section).

Example 1.8

Exactly 5.75 g of an unknown gas occupies 3.40 L at a temperature of 50°C and a pressure of 0.94 atm. Find the molar mass or molecular weight of the gas.

Solution:

The ideal gas law (equation 1.2) has many applications. One of them is to determine the molar mass of a gas.

$$PV = nRT = \left(\frac{m}{MM}\right) RT$$

In this case, you wish to solve for MM.

The data given in the problem are:

P = 0.94 atm R = 0.0821 L · atm/K · mol

V = 3.40 L T = 273 + 50°C = 323 K

m = 5.75 g

Substitute this information into the above equation, and solve for MM:

$$MM = \frac{mRT}{PV}$$

$$= \frac{(5.75 \text{ g})(0.0821 \text{ L} \cdot \text{atm/K} \cdot \text{mole})(323 \text{ K})}{(0.94 \text{ atm})(3.40 \text{ L})}$$

$$= 47.6 \text{ g/mol}$$

Dalton's Law of Partial Pressures

Dalton's law states: The total pressure exerted by a mixture of gases is equal to the sum of the partial pressures of all the gases in the mixture. Each partial pressure is the pressure that the gas would exert if the others gases were not present.

$$P_{total} = \Sigma P_i = P_1 + P_2 + P_3 + \ldots + P_n \quad [1.3]$$

This law is particularly useful when gases are collected in vessels above the surface of an aqueous or nonaqueous solution. In an aqueous solution, the partial pressure of water vapor may be subtracted from the total pressure to help determine the partial pressures of the other gases or vapors present. The percent composition of a gaseous mixture may then be calculated, based on Dalton's law. To calculate the composition of the *solution phase* (e.g., in mole percent) **Raoult's law** (see page 26) must be used.

Graham's Law of Effusion

Recall that kinetic molecular theory states that the average speed of molecules in motion is given by the **root mean square speed, U_{rms}:**

$$U_{rms} = \sqrt{\frac{3RT}{MM}}$$

Diffusion is the migration or mixing of molecules of different substances as a result of concentration gradients and random molecular motion. **Effusion** is the escape of gas molecules of a single substance through a tiny orifice (pinhole) of a vessel holding the gas. **Graham's law of effusion** states: The rates of effusion of two different gases escaping, A and B, are inversely proportional to the square roots of their molar masses:

$$\frac{\text{Effusion Rate}_A}{\text{Effusion Rate}_B} = \sqrt{\frac{MM_B}{MM_A}} \qquad [1.4]$$

Note that, at a fixed temperature, the *effusion time* is inversely proportional to the effusion rate, while the *mean distance traveled,* as well as the *amount of gas* effused, is directly proportional to the effusion rate.

Intermolecular Forces

Chemical bonds between atoms are generally referred to as **intramolecular forces.** They are categorized as ionic, covalent, or metallic. These are the bonds that are broken during a chemical reaction.

Significantly less in strength are **intermolecular forces.** These are the forces responsible for determining the boiling points, freezing points, and densities, for example, of substances. They also help determine whether two substances are soluble or miscible in one another, that is in part explained by the "like dissolves like" principle. There are four categories of intermolecular forces, listed below in order of decreasing strength:

- Dipole-dipole interactions (important in polar covalent interactions).
- Ion-dipole interactions.
- Hydrogen bonding (important in H—F, H—O, and H—N interactions).
- London dispersion or van der Waals forces (important in nonpolar interactions).

1.4 Chemical Reactions

Five Categories of Chemical Reactions

The purpose of categorizing a chemical reaction is to help predict the product or products of the reaction. In general, a chemical reaction is a process of molecular rearrangements, in which atoms change partners. Atoms are not destroyed or created. Total mass is conserved; that is, the mass of all of the reactants before the reaction must equal the mass of all of the products after the reaction, although the physical or chemical states of individual substances may change. This mass-conservation requirement explains why all chemical reactions must be properly balanced to be quantitatively valid and useful. Energy changes also accompany reactions—energy is either liberated or absorbed—since existing chemical bonds are broken and new bonds are formed.

With the letters A, B, C, and D used to represent simple elements or polyatomic ions, the five categories of reactions are as follows:

- Combination or synthesis

  $$A + B \rightarrow AB$$

- Decompostion

  $$AB \rightarrow A + B$$

- Single replacement/displacement

  $$A + BC \rightarrow AC + B$$

- Double replacement/displacement

  $$AB + CD \rightarrow AD + CB$$

- Combustion (complete or efficient)

  $$(CH)_x + O_2 \rightarrow H_2O + CO_2$$

The notation (g), (ℓ), (s), or (aq) immediately following a reactant or product is often employed to designate the chemical state of the substance.

Another class of reactions that cuts across all other reaction categories consists of **oxidation-reduction reactions.** Oxidation-reduction ("redox") reactions are reactions in which one substance is oxidized while another is simultaneously reduced. The processes of oxidation and reduction can be defined as follows. A substance is oxidized or reduced, respectively, if any *one* of the following conditions is met:

Oxidation	Reduction
■ The substance loses electrons.	■ The substance gains electrons.
■ The substance gains oxygen atoms.	■ The substance loses oxygen atoms.
■ The substance loses hydrogen atoms.	■ The substance gains hydrogen atoms.

Red-ox reactions are actually formed by the addition of two half-reactions—an oxidation reaction and a reduction reaction.

For example, each of the following shows an *oxidation reaction:*

$$Zn \rightarrow Zn^{2+} + 2e^-$$
[Zn has lost 2 electrons.] [1.5]

$$C + O_2 \rightarrow CO_2$$
[C has gained 2 O atoms.] [1.6]

And each of the following shows a *reduction reaction:*

$$Cu^{2+} + 2e^- \rightarrow Cu$$
[Cu^{2+} has gained 2 electrons.] [1.7]

$$C + 2H_2 \rightarrow CH_4$$
[C has gained 4 H atoms.] [1.8]

Each reaction also has an associated electromotive potential, measured in electron volts (eV) and found in electromotive potential tables. This topic is discussed more fully in Section 1.11.

Writing and Balancing Chemical Reactions

A chemical reaction consists of a reactant side (the left) and a product side (the right) separated by an arrow, which indicates *yields* or *produces.* Reactants and products are present as elements and/or compounds and are represented by appropriate symbols, as discussed in Section 1.1. Reactions must be balanced before they can be used in calculations to provide quantitative information. Again, a symbol placed immediately after the element or compound designates its chemical state: (g) for gas or vapor; (l) for liquid; (s) for solid, powder, precipitate, or crystal; (aq) for solution, where water is understood to be the solvent for the indicated solute.

The simplest balancing method is called *balancing by inspection.* Although this method is often interpreted to mean balancing by trial and error, three simple rules regarding the order of balancing must be followed:

1. Balance metal atoms or atoms present in the greatest number first.
2. Balance nonmetal atoms second.
3. Balance hydrogen and oxygen atoms last.

Balancing means inserting integers, known as **stoichiometric coefficients,** in front of elements or compounds to ensure the same number of like atoms on both sides of the reaction. Balancing requires that you keep track of every kind of atom that appears in the reaction. Subscripts of atoms in compounds are fixed by nature and cannot be altered to achieve balancing.

The following are examples of **balanced reactions:**

(A) $2Al(s) + 6HCl(aq) \rightarrow 2AlCl_3(aq) + 3H_2(g)$
(B) $3CaCl_2(aq) + 2Na_3PO4(aq) \rightarrow Ca_3(PO4)_2(s) + 6NaCl(aq)$
(C) $2C_4H_{10}(g) + 13O_2(g) \rightarrow 8CO_2(g) + 10H_2O(g)$
(D) $CaCO_3(s) \rightarrow CaO(s) + CO_2(g)$

The following points regarding these four reactions are noteworthy:

1. (A) is an example of a single-replacement reaction. (B) is an example of a double-replacement reaction. (C) is an example of a combustion reaction. (D) is an example of a decomposition reaction.
2. Only (C) is an example of a **homogeneous reaction,** since all of the reactants and products are present in the same physical state—gaseous. The other three are **heterogeneous reactions,** since the reactants and products are present in more than one state.
3. (A) and (C) are also examples of oxidation-reduction reactions. In (A), Al is oxidized while HCl is reduced; HCl is the **oxidizing agent** while Al is the reducing agent. In (C), C_4H_{10} is oxidized while O_2 is reduced; O_2 is the oxidizing agent, while C_4H_{10} is the **reducing agent.**
4. There are two, and only two, levels of interpretation of the stoichiometric coefficients that balance these reactions. Consider (C). On the microscopic or invisible level, the reaction states that 2 molecules of C_4H_{10} react with 13 molecules of O_2 to produce 8 molecules of CO_2 and 10 molecules of H_2O. On the macroscopic or visible level, the reaction states that 2 moles of C_4H_{10} [2 times the molar mass of C_4H_{10} = (2 mol)(58 g/mol) = **116 g**] react with 13 moles of O_2 [13 times the molar mass of oxygen = (13 mol)(32 g/mol) = **416 g**] to produce 8 moles of CO_2 [8 times the molar mass of CO_2 = (8 mol)(44 g/mol) = **352 g**] and 10 moles of H_2O [10 times the molar mass of H_2O = (10 mol)(18 g/mol) = **180 g**]. In other words, the only two correct units of stoichiometric coefficients are molecules and moles. The unit grams can be obtained by the use of molar masses, as shown, but is not directly readable.
5. Note, from point 4 above, that in (C) mass is automatically conserved. The total mass of reactants is 116 grams + 416 grams = 532 grams. The total mass of products is 352 grams + 180 grams = 532 grams. The **conservation of mass principle** requires that this equality always occur.

Simple Stoichiometry

The term "stoichiometry" refers to the mass relationships between two reactants, two products, or, more commonly, a reactant and a product. **Stoichiometry** depends on a balanced reaction, which is essential in predicting the amount of product generated by a given amount of reactant or, conversely, the amount of reactant required to generate a given amount of product. The method recommended in Example 1.9 is the **Factor-Label Method;** alternatively, the method of proportions is also used.

Example 1.9

Consider reaction (C), the complete combustion of butane with oxygen to produce carbon dioxide and water, presented in the previous section. Calculate the mass of carbon dioxide that can be produced from 816 g of butane, assuming oxygen is in abundant or unlimited supply.

Solution:

Since the reaction is balanced, you may proceed by setting up three conversion factors, written in parentheses and arranged from left to right, multiplying the given mass of carbon dioxide. Next, draw a connecting "tie" line between the 2 in front of the butane and the 8 in front of the carbon dioxide, since these are the only two substances of interest. This will form the basis of the middle conversion factor below. The first and third conversion factors are simply the molar masses of butane and carbon dioxide, respectively. Thus:

$$816 \text{ g } C_4H_{10} \times \frac{1.0 \text{ mol } C_4H_{10}}{58 \text{ g } C_4H_{10}} \times \frac{8 \text{ mol } CO_2}{2 \text{ mol } C_4H_{10}} \times \frac{44.0 \text{ g } CO_2}{1.0 \text{ mol } CO_2}$$

$$= 2{,}476 \text{ g } CO_2$$

Limiting Reagents

In many reactions, the reactants are not present in stoichiometric ratios. One of the reactants, called the **limiting reagent,** is present in short supply. This reactant determines the outcome of the reaction, that is, the maximum amount of any product of interest that can be generated. The other reactant or reactants are thus present **in excess.** In any reaction where two or more reactants are present and their respective amounts are given, the limiting reagent must be identified before the maximum amount of any product can be calculated.

Example 1.10

In an experiment, 50 g of hydrogen gas and 50 g of oxygen gas are ignited to form water. Calculate:

A. The mass of water formed.

B. The mass of any hydrogen or oxygen that is left over or unreacted.

Solution:

First, write the balanced chemical reaction as follows:

$$2H_2 + O_2 \rightarrow 2H_2O$$

Since the amounts of both reactants are given, one of the reactants may be the limiting reagent. To find which reactant is the limiting reagent, convert each mass given in grams into moles, and compare. Thus:

$$50 \text{ g } H_2 \times \frac{1.0 \text{ mol } H_2}{2.016 \text{ g } H_2} = 24.8 \text{ mol } H_2$$

$$50 \text{ g } O_2 \times \frac{1.0 \text{ mol } O_2}{32 \text{ g } O_2} = 1.56 \text{ mol } O_2$$

From the balanced reaction, it is clear that 2 mol of H_2 require 1 mol of O_2. Thus, 24.8 mol of H_2 would require 12.4 mol of O_2. However, only 1.56 mol of O_2 are actuallly present or available for reaction. Thus, O_2 is in short supply and is the limiting reagent. Also, H_2 is present in excess and will be left over after the reaction.

A. To find the mass of water produced, again apply the factor-label method, using the molar amount of O_2 present as the starting point.

$$1.56 \text{ mol } O_2 \times \frac{2 \text{ mol } H_2O}{1 \text{ mol } O_2} \times \frac{18.0 \text{ g } H_2O}{1.0 \text{ mol } H_2O}$$

$$= 56.2 \text{ g } H_2O$$

B. To find the mass of H_2 left over, subtract the amount of H_2 reacted with O_2 from the total mass of H_2 initially present and available in moles, since O_2 is the limiting reagent.

24.80 mol H_2 initally present
– 3.12 mol H_2 reacted (equivalent to 2 × 1.56 mol O_2)

$$21.68 \text{ mol } H_2 \text{ left over or unreacted} \times \frac{2.016 \text{ g } H_2}{1.0 \text{ mol } H_2}$$

$$= 43.7 \text{ g } H_2$$

Percent Yield

The result obtained in Example 1.10a is the theoretically predicted maximum amount of water. In reality, the amount of water actually collected may, for at least two reasons, be somewhat less. First, some reactions may not go to completion but instead may reach an equilibrium condition. Second, other reactions may have more than one pathway and may produce secondary or tertiary products that compete with the main route. In a sense, the percent yield of a reaction is a measure of its efficiency.

In either case, a **percent yield** may be computed as follows:

$$\% \text{ Yield} = \frac{\text{actual yield (g)}}{\text{theoretical yield (g)}} \times 100 \qquad [1.9]$$

Example 1.11

Suppose that, in Example 1.10, the actual mass of water collected or measured is 48.0 g. Compute the percent yield of the reaction.

Solution:

$$\% \text{ Yield} = \frac{48.0 \text{ g}}{56.2 \text{ g}} \times 100 = 90.2\%$$

Consecutive and Simultaneous Reactions

Reactions that are carried out one after another in sequence to yield a final product are called **consecutive reactions.** In **simultaneous reactions,** two or more products react independently of each other in separate reactions at the same time.

An example of a consecutive reaction involves the purification of titanium dioxide, TiO_2, the most widely used white pigment for paints. To free TiO_2 of unwanted colored impurities, it must first be converted into $TiCl_4$, and then reconverted into TiO_2.

$$2\,TiO_2(s)\ (\text{impure}) + 3C(s) + 4Cl_2(g) \rightarrow 2TiCl_4(g) + CO_2(g) + 2CO(g)$$

$$TiCl_4(g) + O_2(g) \rightarrow TiO_2(s)\ (\text{pure}) + 2\,Cl_2(g)$$

Note that the $TiCl_4$ product in the first reaction becomes a reactant in the second. This is the connecting link. For example, one could ask how many grams of carbon are required to produce 1.0 kilogram of pure TiO_2. First, it must be realized that 1 mole of TiO_2 (pure) requires 1 mole of $TiCl_4$. Then 2 moles of $TiCl_4$ requires 3 moles of carbon. In this way, using the factor-label method, a calculation with conversion factors can be set up, connecting $TiO_2(s)$ with C(s).

1.5 Colligative Properties of Solutions

Basic Concept

There are four colligative properties of solutions:

- Boiling-point elevation.
- Freezing-point depression.
- Vapor-pressure lowering.
- Osmotic pressure.

The term "colligative" means having to do with the *collection* or *number* of particles and/or ions dissolved in solution. It is an oversimplification, since size and polarity also play a role, albeit a less important one, in the chemistry of solutions.

Before describing each of the four colligative properties or effects in detail, it is useful to review the concept of a solution. A **solution** is a physical state wherein a solute has been dissolved completely and uniformly in a solvent, forming a solution of uniform composition. Unless specified otherwise, the solvent is assumed to be water, whose normal boiling point, freezing point, and density are well known. In the equations for each of the four properties, the concentration of the solution appears, although concentration units vary. It is critically important, when doing calculations with solutions, to distinguish among units of mass, volume, and density for solute, solvent, and solution, respectively.

For solutions, there are three types of solutes:

- Strong electrolytes.
- Nonelectrolytes.
- Weak electrolytes.

Strong electrolytes are generally ionic compounds, such as salts and strong acids and bases, that dissociate and ionize *completely,* that is, 100%, in water. The solutions they form with water become strong conductors of electric currents. Examples include NaCl, KNO_3, $CaCl_2$, HCl, and NaOH. Thus, 1 mole of NaCl produces 2 moles of ions or particles; 1 mole of $CaCl_2$ produces 3 moles of ions or particles (1 mole of Ca^{2+} ions and 2 moles of Cl^- ions). The **van't Hoff factor** is the total number of ions or particles per formula unit or mole: 2.0 for NaCl, 3.0 for $CaCl_2$, and so on. Experimentally measured van't Hoff factors are generally less than theoretically predicted ones for a given solute.

Nonelectrolytes are generally alcohols and sugars, such as ethanol (C_2H_5OH) and glucose ($C_6H_{12}O_6$), or other organic substances that dissolve in water but do not ionize. One mole of a nonelectrolyte always produces 1 mole of particles. Thus the van't Hoff factor is 1.0.

A **weak electrolyte,** such as acetic acid, is a substance that is only partially dissociated and ionized, typically 10% or less, leaving 90% or more undissociated and thereby behaving much like a nonelectrolyte. Its van't Hoff factor is greater than 1 but less than the total number of ions available for dissociation.

Boiling-Point Elevation

When a nonvolatile solute is dissolved in water or another suitable solvent, the normal boiling point of the solvent is always raised. The amount of elevation in temperature, ΔT, is given by the equation

$$\Delta T = iK_b\text{m} \qquad [1.10]$$

where i = the van't Hoff factor, discussed above,

m = the molality of the solution, that is, the number of moles of solute per kilogram of water or other solvent,

K_b = the ebullioscopic or boiling-point-elevation constant, characteristic of water (or other solvent) in °C · kg/mol.

Example 1.12

What is the boiling point of a solution made by dissolving 70 g of NaCl in 300 g of water? The K_b for water is 0.512°C · kg/mol.

Solution:

Use equation 1.10: $\Delta T = iK_b\text{m}$, and note that i = 2 for NaCl. Then:

$$\text{molality, m} = \frac{\text{mol NaCl}}{\text{kg H}_2\text{O}}$$

$$= \frac{70 \text{ g NaCl}/58.5 \text{ g/mol}}{0.300 \text{ kg H}_2\text{O}} = 3.99$$

$$\Delta T = (2)(0.512)(3.99 \text{ mol/kg}) = 4.08°\text{C}$$

$$T_{\text{new}} = T_{\text{norm}} + \Delta T = 100°\text{C} + 4.08°\text{C} = 104.1°\text{C}$$

Freezing-Point Depression

When a nonvolatile solute is dissolved in water or another suitable solvent, the normal freezing point of the solvent is always lowered. The amount of depression, ΔT, is given by the equation

$$\Delta T = iK_f\text{m} \qquad [1.11]$$

where I and m have the same definitions as for equation 1.10, and K_f = the cryoscopic or freezing-point depression constant in °C · kg/mol.

Example 1.13

The freezing-point depression equation is often used to find the molar mass of an unknown solute. Find the molar mass (also known as the molecular weight) of a substance when 1.14 g of it are dissolved in 100.0 g of liquid camphor, whose freezing point is lowered by 2.48°C. K_f for camphor is 37.9°C · kg/mol.

Solution:

Use equation 1.11: $\Delta T = iK_f\text{m}$. Assume that the unknown substance is an organic nonelectrolyte, so i = 1. Then:

$$\Delta T = 2.48°\text{C} \quad \text{and} \quad K_f = 37.9°\text{C} \cdot \text{kg/mol}$$

First, solve for the molality, m:

$$\text{m} = \frac{\Delta T}{i\,K_f} = \frac{2.48°\text{C}}{(1)(37.9)} = 0.0654 \text{ mol/kg}$$

But

$$\text{m} = \frac{\text{mol solute}}{\text{kg solvent}} = \frac{\text{g solute/molar mass solute}}{\text{kg solvent}}$$

Solve for molar mass, MM, of solute:

$$MM = \frac{\text{g solute}}{(\text{kg solvent})(\text{m})} = \frac{1.14 \text{ g}}{(0.100 \text{ kg})(0.0654)} = 174.3 \text{ g/mol}$$

Henry's Law

Henry's law concerns the solubility of a gas in a liquid, most often water. The law states that the solubility, S, of a gas in a liquid is directly proportional to the partial pressure, P, of the gas above the liquid; it can be written as follows:

$$S = k_\text{H}P \qquad [1.12]$$

where k_H, called Henry's constant, depends on the gas, the solvent, and the temperature. The law implies that, at constant temperature, doubling the partial pressure of a gas doubles its solubility.

Henry's law helps explain such phenomena as the bends experienced by deep-sea divers who surface too quickly and the carbonation of beverages in tightly capped bottles.

Raoult's Law for Vapor-Pressure Lowering

Raoult's law states that, when a nonvolatile solute is added to water or another solvent, the vapor pressure of the solvent is depressed. In other words, the vapor pressure of the solution is lower than the vapor pressure of the pure solvent. The vapor pressure of the solution is directly proportional to the mole fraction of the solvent multiplied by the vapor pressure of the pure solvent:

$$P_{\text{soln}} = X_{\text{solvent}}\, P°_{\text{solvent}} \qquad [1.13]$$

Where P_{soln} = the vapor pressure of the solution,

X_{solvent} = the mole fraction of the solvent

$$= \frac{\text{mol solvent}}{\text{mol solvent} + \text{mol solute}}$$

$P°_{\text{solvent}}$ = the vapor pressure of the pure solvent.

Vapor pressures are a measure of volatility. They may be expressed in any suitable units, such as atmospheres, millimeters of mercury, torr, and pounds per square inch. Note that Raoult's law applies to all ideal solutions (where solute and solvent molecules experience similar intermolecular forces, as in a benzene-toluene solution) and to all real but dilute solutions (where $X_{solvent} > 0.85$). For a binary system with only one solute and one solvent, Raoult's law may alternatively be expressed as follows:

$$P_{soln} - P_{solvent} = \Delta P = X_{solute} P_{solvent}^{\circ} \quad [1.14]$$

since

$$X_{solvent} + X_{solute} = 1 \quad [1.15]$$

Example 1.14

Calculate the vapor pressure at 100°C of a solution prepared by dissolving 10 g of sucrose, $C_{12}H_{22}O_{11}$, in 100 g of water.

Solution:

This is a real solution that is dilute, so Raoult's law should apply.

$$P_{soln} = X_{solvent} P_{solvent}^{\circ} = X_{H_2O} P_{H_2O}^{\circ}$$

where $P_{H_2O}^{\circ} = 760$ torr since the normal boiling point of water is 100°C, and its vapor pressure at that temperature must be equal to atmospheric pressure. On the other hand, the vapor pressures of pure solvents can always be looked up in tables.

To find X_{H_2O}, compute the number of moles of sucrose *and* the number of moles of water.

$$\text{moles of sucrose} = 10 \text{ g } C_{12}H_{22}O_{11} \times \frac{1.0 \text{ mol } C_{12}H_{22}O_{11}}{342.3 \text{ g } C_{12}H_{22}O_{11}} = 0.0292 \text{ mol}$$

$$\text{moles of water} = 100 \text{ g } H_2O \times \frac{1.0 \text{ mol } H_2O}{18.0 \text{ g } H_2O} = 5.55 \text{ mol}$$

Thus:

$$X_{H_2O} = \frac{5.55 \text{ mol}}{5.55 \text{ mol} + 0.0292 \text{ mol}} = 0.9948$$

Finally:

$$P_{soln} = (0.9948)(760 \text{ torr}) = 756 \text{ torr}$$

Additionally:

$$\Delta P = 760 \text{ torr} - 756 \text{ torr} = 4.0 \text{ torr}$$

Vapor pressure is a function of temperature. The dependence of the vapor pressure of a pure solvent on temperature is given by the **Clausius-Clapeyron equation:**

$$\ln\frac{P_2}{P_1} = \frac{\Delta H_{vap}^{\circ}}{R}\left(\frac{1}{T_1} - \frac{1}{T_2}\right) \quad [1.16]$$

where P_1 and P_2 are the vapor pressures at *absolute* temperatures T_1 and T_2, respectively, and must be in kelvins, and ΔH_{vap}° is the molar heat of vaporization of the pure solvent at its *normal* or *standard* boiling point.

A frequently useful, empirical approximation for many liquids, when *hydrogen bonding is unimportant*, is **Trouton's rule:**

$$\frac{\Delta H_{vap}^{\circ}}{T_b} = 85 \quad [1.17]$$

This ratio, expressed in joules per kelvin, allows the calculation of either the standard molar heat of vaporization, ΔH_{vap}°, or the boiling point, T_b, when one of the other is known.

Osmotic Pressure

Consider a U-tube in which a pure solvent such as water in the left arm is brought into contact with an aqueous solution made with a nonvolatile solute such as a sugar or protein in the right arm, and the two arms are separated by a semipermeable membrane (e.g., cellophane), permeable only to solvent molecules. The two sides or arms of the U-tube are initially at the same height. It is observed that a pressure develops across the membrane that drives solvent molecules from the left arm into the right arm in an apparent attempt to dilute the solution. This pressure is called the **osmotic pressure,** Π, and the process is known as osmosis. It is given by the equation:

$$\Pi = iMRT \quad [1.18]$$

where i = the van't Hoff factor,

M = the molarity of the solution,

R = the universal gas constant, 0.0821 L · atm/K · mol,

T = the absolute temperature in kelvins.

Some time later, the system in the U-tube reaches equilibrium, and a height differential, Δh, between the solution levels of the two arms is observed. Because of this height differential, a hydrostatic pressure, ΔP, exists and is given by the equation

$$\Delta P = \rho g \, \Delta h \qquad [1.19]$$

where ρ = the density of the solution, and g = the acceleration constant due to gravity.

The final hydrostatic pressure is equal to the initial osmotic pressure.

Osmometry can also be used to find the molar mass of an unknown substance dissolved in solution through its molarity, M, when the other quantities are measured experimentally.

1.6 Acids, Bases, and Salts

Basic Concept

Substances known as acids and bases are commonly encountered and have important chemical properties. Therefore, this group of substances deserves separate treatment.

An **acid** is any substance that, when dissolved in water, produces or causes to be produced hydrogen ions, H^+. A **base** is any substance that, when dissolved in water, produces or causes to be produced hydroxide ions, OH^-. The **Brönsted-Lowry model** stresses the fact that acids are *proton donors* and bases are *proton acceptors,* as well as the notion of *conjugate* (meaning "related") acids and bases. The **Lewis model** states that acids are substances that are electron-pair acceptors and bases are substances that are electron-pair donors. This concept broadens the meaning of acids and bases considerably to include many salts that would otherwise be excluded. Realistically, since a hydrogen ion is a bare proton, it is too reactive to exist as a stable species by itself. Hence, the real acid species is the hydronium ion, H_3O^+, a protonated water molecule, that is, $[H^+(H_2O)]$. Acids are powerful dehyrating agents.

When an acid and a base are added together, a neutralization (a double-replacement reaction) ensues, with water and a salt as the neutralization products. Quantitatively, 1 mole of acid exactly neutralizes 1 mole of base.

Acids and bases may be strong or weak. This property is determined by molecular structure and is different from concentration. A strong acid is one that dissociates and ionzies completely—100%—into its hydrogen/hydronium ions and anions, known as its conjugate base. Similarly, a strong base is one that dissociates and ionizes completely into hydroxide ions and its cations, known as its conjugate acid. Weak acids and bases, in contrast, dissociate and ionize less than 100%, typically less than 10%, into their respective ions. Recall that these substances are weak electrolytes, while strong acids and bases are strong electrolytes.

There are four common strong acids. All others can be assumed, by exclusion, to be weak.

- Hydrochloric acid, HCl [HBr and HI are also strong but uncommon; HF is weak.]
- Nitric acid, HNO_3 [This is a *monoporotic acid* since it has only one hydrogen ion.]
- Sulfuric acid, H_2SO_4 [This is a *diprotic acid* since it has two hydrogen ions.]
- Perchloric acid, $HclO_4$

Examples of weak acids include acetic acid, boric acid, hydrofluoric acid, ascorbic acid, carbonic acid, and phosphoric acid.

Examples of strong bases are sodium hydroxide (NaOH) are potassium hydroxide (KOH). Examples of weak bases are ammonia (NH_3), which, when dissolved in water, becomes ammonium hydroxide (NH_4OH) and organic amines.

When dissolved in water, **oxides of metals** (e.g., CaO, K_2O, MgO) are generally basic, while **oxides of nonmetals** (e.g., CO_2, SO_2, SO_3) are generally acidic.

Concentration Units and the pH Scale

Two units are routinely used to express concentrations of acids and bases:

- Molarity, M
- pH scale

Molarity is defined as the number of moles of H^+ ion for acids or of OH^- ion for bases per liter of solution. Concentration is symbolized by the use of brackets; that is, [ ] means moles per liter of the bracketed quantity.

The **pH,** representing the power of hydrogen ions, can be calculated from molarity. This value is useful for solutions whose acidic concentrations are less than 1.0 M, for example, 3.5×10^{-3} M.

$$pH = -\log[H^+] \qquad [1.20]$$

Equation 1.20 may also be written as follows:

$$[H^+] = 10^{-pH} \qquad [1.21]$$

The pH scale runs from 0 to 14, because of the autoionization of water. Recall that K_w for water is 1.0×10^{-14} at 25°C, since $K_w = [H^+][OH^-] = 1.0 \times 10^{-14}$.

The pOH may be analogously computed for basic solutions:

$$pOH = -\log[OH^-] \qquad [1.22]$$

In addition, since

$$pH + pOH = 14 \qquad [1.23]$$

you can always find pOH from pH, or vice-versa.

For the more commonly used pH, the **acid range** of solutions is **0 to 7,** while the **basic** (or **alkaline**) **range** is **7 to 14.** A pH of 7.0 represents a neutral solution such as distilled water. The pH values of common substances are shown in Figure 1.1.

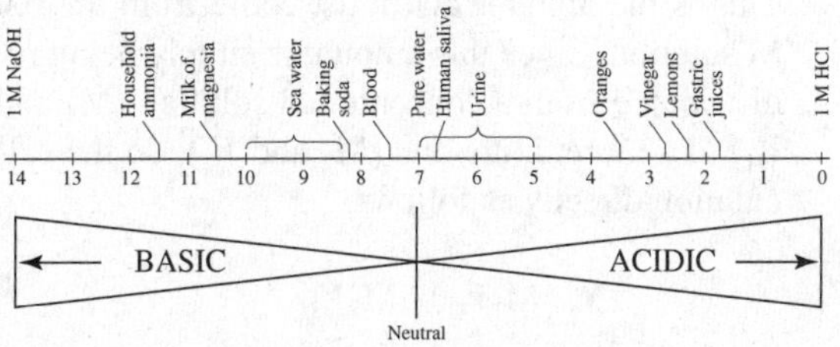

Figure 1.1 The pH values of common substances

Properties of acids include:

- They taste sour.
- They neutalize bases to produce water and a salt.
- They feel slippery.
- They react with metals to yield H_2 gas.

Calculations for Strong Acids and Bases

Examples 1.15 to 1.22 represent routinely encountered problems and calculations for strong acids and bases. In general, 1 mole of acid (H^+ ion) neutralizes 1 mole of base (OH^- ion) to produce 1 mole of water (H_2O).

Example 1.15

An aqueous solution of hydrochloric acid is 0.034 M. Find:

A. $[H^+]$
B. $[Cl^-]$

Solution:

Since HCl is a strong acid, it dissociates and ionizes completely (100%) into its component ions. Thus:

A. $[H^+] = 0.034$ M
B. $[Cl^-] = 0.034$ M

It is safe to assume that [HCl] in terms of molecules is 0.

Example 1.16

For a 0.035 M HNO_3 solution find:

A. $[H^+]$
B. pH

Solution:

A. HNO_3 is a strong acid. Thus, a 0.035 M solution of HNO_3 yields 0.035 M H^+ ions (and 0.035 M NO_3^- ions), since there is complete dissociation and ionization.

$[H^+] = 0.035$ M

B. $pH = -\log[H^+] = -\log(0.035\text{ M}) = 1.46$

Example 1.17

Find $[OH^-]$ for the solution in Example 1.16.

Solution:

Since this is an aqueous solution,

$$[H^+][OH^-] = K_w = 1.0 \times 10^{-14}$$

Thus:

$$[OH^-] = \frac{K_w}{[H^+]} = \frac{1.0 \times 10^{-14}}{0.035\text{ M}} = 2.86 \times 10^{-13}\text{ M}$$

This shows a very small OH^- ion concentration, but not zero, and illustrates the constant and reciprocal nature of H^+ ions and OH^- ions.

Example 1.18

A sample of lemon juice has a pH of 2.4. Find its $[H^+]$.

Solution:

Recall that $[H^+] = 10^{-pH}$. Thus:

$$[H^+] = 10^{-2.4} = 4.0 \times 10^{-3}\text{ M}$$

Example 1.19

Find, for a 0.014 M solution of slaked lime, $Ca(OH)_2$:

A. $[OH^-]$
B. pH

Solution:

A. The subscript 2 next to (OH^-) indicates that 1 mol of $Ca(OH)_2$ produces 2 mol of OH^- ions (along with 1 mol of Ca^{2+} ions).

It is assumed that $Ca(OH)_2$ is a strong base. Thus:

$$[OH^-] = 2(0.014\text{ M}) = 0.028\text{ M}$$

B. Furthermore, $pOH = -\log\ [OH^-] = -\log(0.028\text{ M}) = 1.55$. Then:

$$pH = 14.0 - pOH = 14.0 - 1.55 = 12.45$$

Example 1.20 Acid-Base Reaction

A laboratory technician mixes 400 mL of a 0.125 M NaOH solution with 600 mL of a 0.100 M HCl solution. Find the pH of the resulting solution.

Solution:

First compute the number of moles of acid and base to determine whether they are equal or, if not, which one is present in excess.

$$\text{moles of } H^+ = (\text{volume HCl})(\text{molarity HCl}) = 0.060 \text{ mol}$$

$$\text{moles of } OH^- = (\text{volume NaOH})(\text{molarity NaOH}) = 0.050 \text{ mol}$$

Since 0.06 mol of $H^+ > 0.05$ mol of OH^-, the final solution will be acidic.

Furthermore, since 1 mol of acid reacts exactly with 1 mol of base, subtract moles of base from moles of acid: 0.060 mol − 0.050 mol = **0.010 mol of H^+ left over or unreacted,** and present after mixing. This amount is in a total or combined volume of 1000 mL or 1.00 L. Thus:

$$[H^+] = \frac{0.01 \text{ mol } H^+}{1.0 \text{ L}} = 0.01 \text{ M}$$

$$\text{pH} = 2.0$$

Example 1.21 Acid-Base Titration/Neutralization

A laboratory technician wishes to find the concentration of an unknown base. He performs a titration in which 42.50 mL of 0.150 M HCl exactly neutralizes 25.00 mL of the base. Determine the concentration of the unknown base.

Solution:

Since moles of acid (A) equal moles of base (B) at the **endpoint** (point of neutralization), use the relationship

$$V_A M_A = V_B M_B$$

Solve for M_B:

$$M_B = \frac{V_A M_A}{V_B} = \frac{(42.50 \text{ mL})(0.150 \text{ M})}{25.00 \text{ mL}} = 0.255 \text{ M}$$

Example 1.22 Dilution of a Solution

A laboratory technician is asked to prepare 500 mL of a 0.750 M solution of HCl. The stock solution of HCl that she has is labeled 6.0 M. How much (what volume) should she take from the stock solution bottle?

Solution:

The total number of moles of HCl ultimately desired in solution is:

$$\text{moles of HCl} = V_{HCl} M_{HCl} = (0.500 \text{ L})(0.750 \text{ mol/L}) = 0.0375 \text{ mol}$$

This is the amount that must come from the 6.0 M solution. Since this amount is simply being redistributed from a concentrated solution (M_1 and V_1) to a more dilute one (M_2 and V_2), do the calculation directly as follows:

$$M_1 V_1 = M_2 V_2$$

Solve for V_1, substituting the values:

$$V_1 = \frac{(0.750 \text{ M})(0.500 \text{ L})}{6.0 \text{ M}} = 0.0625 \text{ L} = 62.5 \text{ mL of stock solution}$$

This same strategy can be applied to *any* dilution problem.

Calculations for Weak Acids and Bases

In contrast to strong acids and bases, weak acids and bases dissociate and ionize into H^+ ions and OH^- ions, respectively, but to a very limited extent—normally less than 10% and more commonly less than 5%. Thus, for every 100 molecules of acid initially present, typically fewer than 5 molecules dissociate and ionize into hydrogen ions. Weak acids produce few hydrogen ions, while weak bases produce few hydroxide ions. Their reactions are governed by an equilibrium acid (a) or base (b) constant: K_a or K_b.

For example, acetic acid (found in vinegar) is a weak acid. Its equilibrium is represented as follows:

$$CH_3COOH(aq) + H2O(l) \rightleftharpoons H_3O^+(aq) + CH_3COO^-(aq) \quad [1.24]$$

Here, H_3O^+ is the active acid species, and CH_3COO^- is called the **conjugate base** of acetic acid. Note that the double arrows indicate an equilibrium process, meaning that this reaction does not go to completion and that all four chemical species in the reaction are present at any given time in varying concentrations. The equilibrium concept is reviewed in Section 1.7.

The equilibrium acid constant expression, K_a, is as follows:

$$K_a = \frac{[H_3O^+][CH_3COO^-]}{[CH_3COOH]} \qquad [1.25]$$

The K_a value for acetic acid at room temperature is 1.75×10^{-5}.

The average percent dissociation and ionization, depending on initial concentration of the parent acid and temperature, is about 3 to 5%.

Table 1.1 gives K_a and K_b values for weak acids and bases, respectively, at 25°C.

There are two ways to compute $[H^+]$ or $[H_3O^+]$ for a solution of a weak acid. If the percent dissociation/ionization is given, simply multiply this by the initial concentration of the acid to obtain $[H^+]$. See Example 1.23. If the K_a value is given along with the initial concentration of the acid, equation 1.23 for K_a can be rearranged and solved for $[H_3O^+]$. See Example 1.24.

Example 1.23

A solution of 0.14 M nitrous acid, HNO_2, is 5.7% ionized. Calculate $[H^+]$.

Solution:

Nitrous acid is obviously a weak acid since its percent ionization is given as less than 10%, and certainly much less than 100%. Thus:

$$[H^+] = 5.7\% \times 0.14\ M = 7.98 \times 10^{-3}\ M$$

Table 1.1 Weak Acid and Base Constants at 25°C

Monoprotic Acids		K_a
$HC_2O_2Cl_3$	Trichloroacetic acid (Cl_3CCO_2H)	2.2×10^{-1}
HIO_3	Iodic acid	1.69×10^{-1}
$HC_2HO_2Cl_2$	Dichloracetic acid (Cl_2CHCO_2H)	5.0×10^{-2}
$HC_2H_2O_2Cl$	Chloroacetic acid (ClH_2CCO_2H)	1.36×10^{-3}
HNO_2	Nitrous acid	7.1×10^{-4}
HF	Hydrofluoric acid	6.8×10^{-4}
HOCN	Cyanic acid	3.5×10^{-4}
$HCHO_2$	Formic acid (HCO_2H)	1.8×10^{-4}
$HC_3H_5O_3$	Lactic acid ($CH_3CH(OH)CO_2H$)	1.38×10^{-4}
$HC_4H_3N_2O_3$	Barbituric acid	9.8×10^{-5}
$HC_7H_5O_2$	Benzoic acid ($C_6H_5CO_2H$)	6.28×10^{-5}
$HC_4H_7O_2$	Butanoic acid ($CH_3CH_2CH_2CO_2H$)	1.52×10^{-5}
HN_3	Hydrazoic acid	1.8×10^{-5}
$HC_2H_3O_2$	Acetic acid (CH_3CO_2H)	1.8×10^{-5}
$HC_3H_5O_2$	Propanoic acid ($CH_3CH_2CO_2H$)	1.34×10^{-5}
HOCl	Hypochlorous acid	3.0×10^{-8}
HOBr	Hypobromous acid	2.1×10^{-9}
HCN	Hydrocyanic acid	6.2×10^{-10}
HC_6H_5O	Phenol	1.3×10^{-10}
Hol	Hypoiodous acid	2.3×10^{-11}
H_2O_2	Hydrogen peroxide	1.8×10^{-12}

Polyprotic Acids		K_{a1}	K_{a2}	K_{a3}
H_2SO_4	Sulfuric acid	Large	1.0×10^{-2}	
H_2CrO_4	Chromic acid	5.0	1.5×10^{-6}	
$H_2C_2O_4$	Oxalic acid	5.6×10^{-2}	5.4×10^{-5}	
H_3PO_3	Phosphorous acid	3×10^{-2}	1.6×10^{-7}	
H_2SO_3	Sulfurous acid	1.2×10^{-2}	6.6×10^{-8}	
H_2SeO_3	Selenous acid	4.5×10^{-3}	1.1×10^{-8}	
H_2TeO_3	Tellurous acid	3.3×10^{-3}	2.0×10^{-8}	
$H_2C_3H_2O_4$	Malonic acid ($HO_2CCH_2CO_2H$)	1.4×10^{-3}	2.0×10^{-6}	
$H_2C_8H_4O_4$	Phthalic acid	1.1×10^{-3}	3.9×10^{-6}	
$H_2C_4H_4O_6$	Tartaric acid	9.2×10^{-4}	4.3×10^{-5}	
$H_2C_6H_6O_6$	Ascorbic acid	7.9×10^{-5}	1.6×10^{-12}	
H_2CO_3	Carbonic acid	4.5×10^{-7}	4.7×10^{-11}	
H_3PO_4	Phosphoric acid	7.1×10^{-3}	6.3×10^{-8}	4.5×10^{-13}
H_3AsO_4	Arsenic acid	5.6×10^{-3}	1.7×10^{-7}	4.0×10^{-12}
$H_3C_6H_5O_7$	Citric acid	7.1×10^{-4}	1.7×10^{-5}	6.3×10^{-6}

Weak Bases		K_b
$(CH_3)_2NH$	Dimethylamine	9.6×10^{-4}
CH_3NH_2	Methylamine	4.4×10^{-4}
$CH_3CH_2NH_2$	Ethylamine	4.3×10^{-4}
$(CH_3)_3N$	Trimethylamine	7.4×10^{-5}
NH_3	Ammonia	1.8×10^{-5}
N_2H_4	Hydrazine	9.6×10^{-7}
NH_2OH	Hydroxylamine	6.6×10^{-9}
C_5H_5N	Pyridine	1.5×10^{-9}
$C_6H_5NH_2$	Aniline	4.1×10^{-10}
PH_3	Phosphine	10^{-28}

Example 1.24

K_a for formic acid, HCOOH, contained in bee stings, is 1.8×10^{-4}. Find the pH of a solution that initally contains 0.20 mol of HCOOH in 500 mL of solution.

Solution:

Since formic acid has a K_a value, it must be a weak acid. Its equilibrium equation and K_a expression are as follows:

$$HCOOH(aq) + H_2O(l) \rightleftharpoons H_3O^+(aq) + HCOO^-(aq)$$

$$K_a = \frac{[H_3O^+][HCOO^-]}{[HCOOH]} = 1.8 \times 10^{-4}$$

The strategy used in solving this type of problem is one that is commonly used in other equilibrium problems discussed in Section 1.7. The above expression for K_a equated to its value is a useful equation; it can be solved for $[H_3O^+]$, which can then be converted into pH.

The *initial concentration* of HCOOH is given:

$$[HCOOH] = \frac{0.20 \text{ mol}}{0.500 \text{ L}} = 0.400 \text{ M}$$

However, all concentrations inserted into the K_a expression must be equilibrium or final values. Therefore, let x = the number of moles per liter of HCOOH that dissociate and ionize into products. Since 1 mol of HCOOH produces 1 mol of H_3O^+ *and* 1 mol of $HCOO^-$, and all products come from only one reactant, *at equilibrium,* then:

$$[H_3O^+] = x, \quad [HCOO^-] = x, \quad [HCOOH] = 0.40 - x$$

Substitute these values into the K_a expression and equation:

$$\frac{(x)(x)}{0.40 - x} = 1.8 \times 10^{-4}$$

This is a quadratic equation in x. A simplifying assumption may be made. Since $x << 0.40$, it may be neglected in the denominator, reducing this to an easier-to-solve abridged quadratic equation. Then:

$$x^2 = (1.8 \times 10^{-4})(0.40)$$

$$x = 8.49 \times 10^{-3}\ \text{M}$$

Thus:

$$[H_3O^+] = 8.49 \times 10^{-3}\ \text{M}$$

Also:

$$\text{pH} = -\log[H_3O^+] = -\log(8.49 \times 10^{-3}\ \text{M}) = 2.07$$

Note: A good rule of thumb to follow to determine whether the simplifying assumption is justified is as follows: Let M_a = initial molarity of acid; then

If $M_a/K_a > 100$, $M_a - x \cong M_a$ is a good approximation.

The error incurred is usually only 1 or 2%, which is generally acceptable. The M_a/K_a ratio in the example above produces a value of about 2,000.

Hydrolysis

Some compounds that appear neutral actually have acidic or alkaline properties. For example, when sodium acetate, $NaCH_3COO$, is dissolved in water, it reacts with water to form acetic acid (a weak acid) and hydroxide ion. This process is called **hydrolysis,** and the resulting solution is slightly alkaline. Remember that the acetate ion is the conjugate base of acetic acid. Other basic salts in this category include sodium cyanide, potassium nitrite, and lithium carbonate.

Similarly, ammonium chloride, NH_4Cl, produces a slightly acidic solution when dissolved in water, again because of hydrolysis. Ammonium ion is the **conjugate acid** of ammonium hydroxide, and/or ammonia, NH_3, is the conjugate base of NH_4^+. Another salt in this category is aluminum chloride, $AlCl_3$. Gases such as CO_2 and SO_2 also undergo hydrolysis and produce H^+ ions and HCO_3^- and HSO_3^- ions, respectively.

Example 1.25

Calculate the pH of a 0.20 M solution of ammonim chloride, NH_4Cl.

Solution:

NH_4Cl is the salt of a weak base, NH_3, and hence hydrolyzes when dissolved in water to form a slightly acidic solution.

$$NH_4^+(aq) + H_2O(l) \rightleftharpoons H_3O^+(aq) + NH_3(aq)$$

The hydrolysis constant expression, K_h, can be expressed as follows:

$$K_h = \frac{[H_3O^+][NH_3]}{[NH_4^+]}$$

The value for K_h is not given but can be found by applying the relationship

$$K_h = \frac{K_w}{K_b} = \frac{1.0 \times 10^{-14}}{1.8 \times 10^{-5}} = 5.56 \times 10^{-10}$$

where K_b is the value of the equilibrium base constant for NH_3 in H_2O. It is analogous to K_a:

$$NH_3 + H_2O \rightleftharpoons NH_4^+ + OH^-$$

The same strategy is now used as in Example 1.24. *At equilibrium,* then:

$$[H_3O^+] = x, \quad [NH_3] = x, \quad [NH_4^+] = 0.20 - x$$

Therefore:

$$5.56 \times 10^{-10} = \frac{(x)(x)}{0.20 - x}$$

Use the same simplifying assumption as above, assume $x << 0.20$ M, and solve for x:

$$x^2 = (0.20\ \text{M})(5.56 \times 10^{-10})$$

$$x = 1.1 \times 10^{-5}$$

Thus:

$$[H_3O^+] = 1.1 \times 10^{-5}$$

and

$$\text{pH} = -\log[H_3O^+] = -\log(1.1 \times 10^{-5}\ \text{M}) = 4.96$$

The pH is less than 7.0, reflecting an acidic solution, as expected.

Note: For the hydrolysis of an ion producing a *basic* solution, $K_h = K_w/K_a$.

Buffer Solutions and the Henderson-Hasselbalch Equation

Buffer solutions are solutions that protect against large shifts in pH in the event of a shock due to the sudden addition of a strong acid or base. The pH of a buffer solution does, however, change slightly. Such a solution can be made with a combination of either:

- A weak acid and its salt (conjugate base).
- A weak base and its salt (conjugate acid).

Thus, acetic acid plus sodium acetate constitutes a buffer system, as does ammonium hydroxide plus ammonium chloride.

To determine the pH of a buffer solution, the **Henderson-Hasselbalch equation** may be used. In the case of a weak acid (e.g., CH_3COOH) and its conjugate base salt (e.g., $NaCH_3COO$):

$$pH = pK_a + \log \frac{[\text{conjugate base}]}{[\text{weak acid}]} \qquad [1.26]$$

The buffering capacity of a system refers to the amount of acid or base it can absorb before its pH changes. Buffering capacity is generally at a maximum when [weak acid] = [conjugate base], so that $pH = pK_a$.

Amphoterism

Amphoterism refers to the property of certain compounds to act as both acids and bases. For example, the compound $Al(OH)_3$, which is categorically a base, may react with acid to form $[Al\,(H_2O)_6]^{3+}$ *and* with excess base to form $[Al(OH)_4]^{-1}$. Both of these species are termed **complex ions** and are water soluble. They are governed by complex-ion equilibrium constants, as explained in Section 1.7. Aluminum oxide, Al_2O_3, is also amphoteric. The hydroxides, as well as the oxides, of zinc(II) and chromium(III) are similarly amphoteric.

1.7 Chemical Equilibrium

Basic Concept

In reality, most reactions do not go to completion even if the reactants are present in stoichiometric amounts or ratios. Rather, they reach a condition of equilibrium, denoted by double arrows in the reaction equation. **Equilibrium** means that there is a balance between the reactant side and the product side, or simply between the reactants and the products. The equilibrium condition is dynamic, not static, allowing microscopic changes in reactant and product concentrations, such that no *net* change in reactant or product concentrations occurs, to take place, provided that no external stresses are applied. At any given time all species in the reaction equation—reactants and products—are present at equilibrium in varying amounts. These varying amounts, however, are related and connected to one another in a mathematical formula known as the **equilibrium constant expression, K_c.**

For an equilibrium reaction, which can be generally represented as

$$aA + bB \rightleftharpoons gG + hH \qquad [1.27]$$

the K_c expression is

$$K_c = \frac{[G]^g[H]^h}{[A]^a[B]^b} \qquad [1.28]$$

where a, b, g, and h represent the stoichiometric coefficients in the balanced reaction, and the brackets [] stipulate molar concentrations.

Four *points of caution* regarding this expression are noteworthy:

1. Only concentrations in units of molarity are permitted.
2. Only species that have concentrations can appear. Thus, species in the solution state (aq) or in the gaseous state (g) are included, but species that are pure solids (s) or pure liquids (l) are not.
3. K_c is a function of temperature (van't Hoff equation; see page 37).
4. The reaction must be at equilibrium.

A reaction in which all species are present in the same physical state (e.g., all gases or all solutions) is called a **homogeneous reaction,** while a reaction in which species are present in more than one physical state (i.e., mixed physical states) is called a **heterogeneous reaction.** If all species in a reaction are present in the gaseous state, an alternative form of the equilibrium constant expression can be written as K_p:

$$K_p = \frac{P_G{}^g P_H{}^h}{P_A{}^a P_B{}^b} \qquad [1.29]$$

Here, P represents the partial pressure of each gas present at equilibrium. Any pressure unit is acceptable as long as it is consistent with the others and with the units of K_P, but atmospheres and torr (1 torr = 1 mm Hg) are common.

A formula to convert K_c to K_p, and vice-versa, is as follows:

$$K_p = K_c\,(RT)^{\Delta n} \qquad [1.30]$$

where T = the absolute temperature in kelvins,

R = the gas constant in units consistent with partial pressures,

Δn = the total moles of product − the total moles of reactant (in the balanced reaction).

Example 1.26

Write the equilibrium constant expression K_c for the following reaction at 25°C:

$$2N_2O_5(g) \rightleftharpoons 4NO_2(g) + O_2(g)$$

Solution:

Note that this is a homogeneous, gas-phase reaction. All three substances can have concentrations in units of molarity and should appear in the K_c expression:

$$K_c = \frac{[NO_2]^4[O_2]}{[N_2O_5]^2}$$

If you were given a value for K_c and were asked to convert it to K_P, then, since all species are in the gaseous state, you could write:

$$K_p = K_c\,(RT)^{\Delta n}$$
$$= K_c\,(0.0821\text{ L} \cdot \text{atm/K} \cdot \text{mol} \times 298\text{ K})^3$$

since $\Delta n = (4 + 1) - 2 = 3$.

Example 1.27

For the reaction

$$2SO_2(g) + O_2(g) \rightleftharpoons 2SO_3(g)$$

at 827°C, the value for $K_c = 37.1$. What is the value for the reverse reaction?

Solution:

$$K_c(\text{reverse}) = \frac{1}{K_c(\text{forward})} = \frac{1}{37.1} = 0.0269$$

The Meaning of K_c

Reactions with K_c values significantly greater than 1 (e.g., on the order of 10^3 or larger) approach completion, and their equilibria lie far to the right or product side. In fact, reactions that go to completion have exceptionally large or even undefined K_c values. In contrast, reactions that have K_c values much less than 1 (e.g., on the order of 10^{-4} or smaller), as in the case of the K_a value for acetic acid in Section 1.6, do not undergo significant change, and their equilibria lie far to the left or reactant side—very little product forms. In the case of acids, the smaller the value of K_a, the weaker the acid.

Calculations for K_c

K_c values for a given reaction at a given temperature are always constant, regardless of which of the three approaches or pathways to equilibrium is followed:

- **Only** reactants present initially.
- **Only** products present initially.
- **Both** reactants **and** products present initially.

This concept, together with knowledge of the approach or pathway to equilibrium, can prove very valuable in developing a strategy to solve equilibrium problems, as shown in Example 1.28.

Example 1.28

The reaction below is carried out in a 5-L vessel at 600 K.

$$CO(g) + H_2O(g) \rightleftharpoons CO_2(g) + H_2(g)$$

At equilibrium, it is found that 0.020 mol of CO, 0.0215 mol of H_2O, 0.070 mol of CO_2, and 2.00 mol of H_2 are present. For this reaction, calculate:

A. K_c
B. K_p

Solution:

A. The reaction is balanced as it stands. All four substances are in the gaseous state and thus have concentrations that can be inserted into the K_c expression.

Since the *molar* amounts are given *at equilibrium,* all you need do is to divide each of them by the volume to convert it into molarity, and then substitute each into the K_c expression. Thus:

$$K_c = \frac{[CO_2][H_2]}{[CO][H_2O]}$$
$$= \frac{(0.070\text{ mol/5.0 L})(2.00\text{ mol/5.0 L})}{(0.020\text{ mol/5.0 L})(0.0215\text{ mol/5.0 L})}$$
$$= 326$$

B. To convert to K_p, simply use the conversion formula given in Equation 1.30:

$$K_p = K_c(RT)^{\Delta n}$$

Note that in this case, since

$$\Delta n = (1 + 1) - (1 + 1) = 0:$$
$$K_p = K_c$$

In fact, $K_p = K_c$ whenever the product side and the reactant side contain identical numbers of total moles.

Example 1.29

Ammonia gas, $NH_3(g)$, is introduced into a previously evacuated reaction vessel in such a way that its initial concentration is 0.500 M. The ammonia decomposes into nitrogen and hydrogen gases, according to the reaction given below, and eventually reaches equilibrium. The equilibrium concentration of nitrogen is found to be 0.116 M. Determine the value of K_c.

$$2NH_3(g) \rightleftharpoons N_2(g) + 3H_2(g)$$

Solution:

Knowing the approach or pathway to equilibrium is vital to solving this problem. It is clear in the statement that only reactant is present initially; therefore, all of the products are formed from the decomposition of NH_3. The equilibrium concentration of N2 is given as 0.116 M. Because of the 3 to 1 stoichiometric ratio between H_2 and N_2, 3(0.116 M) = 0.348 M of H_2 must have also formed and is present at equilibrium.

Also, because of the stoichiometric ratio between NH_3 and N_2, 2(0.116 M) = 0.232 M of NH_3 must have decomposed. Thus, the concentration of NH_3 remaining and present at equilibrium is 0.500 M − 0.232 M = 0.268 M. Therefore, the values for the three species *at equilibrium* are as follows:

$[NH_3] = 0.268$ M $[N_2] = 0.116$ M $[H_2] = 0.348$ M

Substitute these values into the K_c expression:

$$K_c = \frac{[N_2][H_2]^3}{[NH_3]^2}$$

$$= \frac{(0.116\ \text{M})(0.348\ \text{M})^3}{(0.268\ \text{M})^2}$$

$$= 0.0681\ \text{M}^2$$

Predicting Equilibrium Using a Test Quotient

It is often useful to know whether a reaction reached equilibrium and, if so, when. This information can be obtained by measuring the concentrations of all species in the reaction and then determining a test quotient, Q. Q is identical in form to K_c except that the values substituted into the expression may or may not be equilibrium concentrations. The criteria for equilibrium are as follows:

- If $Q = K_c$, the reaction is at equilibrium.
- If $Q < K_c$, the reaction is not at equilibrium and needs to proceed to the right.
- If $Q > K_c$, the reaction is not at equilibrium and needs to proceed to the left.

Example 1.30

Consider the reaction given in Example 1.27 along with the following concentrations:

$[SO_2] = 0.054$ M $[O_2] = 0.020$ M $[SO_3] = 0.012$ M

A. Is this reaction at equilibrium?
B. If not, in which direction will it proceed?

Solution:

A. $$Q = \frac{[SO_3]^2}{[SO_2]^2[O_2]} = \frac{(0.012\ \text{M})^2}{(0.054\ \text{M})^2(0.020\ \text{M})}$$

$$= 2.47$$

Since $K_c = 37.1$, Q does not equal K_c.

Thus, the reaction is not at equilibrium.

B. Since $Q < K_c$, the reaction must proceed to the right to reach equilibrium.

Stresses and Le Châtelier's Principle

Once a reaction has reached equilibrium, any external stress that is imposed results in a shift of the equilibrium and a subsequent change in the concentrations of the reactants and products involved. The direction of the shift—right (product side) or left (reactant side)—is in accordance with **Le Châtelier's principle,** which states: If a stress is imposed on a reaction at equilibrium, the reaction will shift either right or left in the way or direction that accommodates or relieves the stress.

There are five categories of stress:

- The reactant concentration or product concentration is increased or decreased.
- The temperature of the reaction is increased or decreased.
- The volume of the reaction vessel is increased or decreased.
- The pressure of the reaction is increased or decreased (in any one of three different ways).
- A catalyst is added to the reaction.

Example 1.31

Consider the following reaction already at equilibrium.

$$CS_2(g) + 3Cl_2(g) \rightleftharpoons S_2Cl_2(g) + CCl_4(g)$$

The enthalpy or heat of reaction is $\Delta H° = -84.3$ kJ.

Predict what will happen—increase, decrease, or no change—to the equilibrium concentration of CCl_4 when each of the following stresses is imposed:

A. Cl_2 is added.
B. S_2Cl_2 is removed.
C. The temperature is increased.
D. The volume of the reaction vessel is decreased.
E. The pressure is decreased by increasing the volume of the reaction vessel.
F. A catalyst is added.

Solution:

Use Le Châtelier's principle to answer each part.

A. Adding Cl_2 will cause the reaction to shift to the right, increasing $[CCl_4]$.
B. Removing S_2Cl_2 will cause the reaction to shift to the right, increasing $[CCl_4]$.
C. To answer this part, the meaning of $\Delta H°$ must be understood. This is the amount of heat energy either liberated or adsorbed in the reaction and may be expressed in either kilojoules (kJ) or kilocalories (kcal). If heat energy is liberated, the reaction is **exothermic,** and the sign of ΔH is by convention negative. If heat energy is absorbed, the reaction is **endothermic,** and the sign of ΔH is by convention positive. Here, the sign is negative, so heat is produced. Hence, since raising the temperature adds heat and heat behaves as a product, increasing the temperature will shift the reaction to the left, decreasing $[CCl_4]$.
D. In the balanced reaction, 4 molecules of reactant are reacting to form 2 molecules of product. Increasing the volume of the vessel favors the reactant or left side of the reaction, while decreasing the volume favors the product side. Hence, decreasing the volume will cause the reaction to shift to the right, increasing $[CCl_4]$. In the special case where the two sides of a reaction contain equal numbers of molecules, changing the volume has no effect.
E. If the pressure is decreased by increasing the volume, the effect can be evaluated as a volume stress. As discussed in part **d,** increasing the volume will cause the reaction to shift to the left and decrease $[CCl_4]$.

Note, however, that, if the pressure is increased or decreased by the addition of a reactant or product, the effect should be evaluated as a stress discussed in part **A** or **B.**

Also, note that, if the pressure is increased by the addition of an inert or unreactive gas, there is no effect on the equilibrium.

F. A catalyst speeds up the rate of reaction. Since the reaction has already reached equilibrium, adding a catalyst will have no effect.

Dependence of K_c on Temperature

The exact dependence of K_c (or K_p) on temperature is given by the **van't Hoff equation:**

$$\ln\frac{K_c(1)}{K_c(2)} = \frac{\Delta H_{RX}}{R}\left(\frac{1}{T_1} - \frac{1}{T_2}\right) \qquad [1.31]$$

where $K_c(1)$ is the equilibrium constant value at absolute temperature T_1 and $K_c(2)$ is the value at T_2, ΔH_{RX} is the enthalpy or heat of reaction, and R is the gas constant in units of either joules per mole or calories per mole, consistent with the units of ΔH_{RX}. The similarity of the van't Hoff equation to the Clausius-Clapeyron equation given in Section 1.5 is noteworthy.

1.8 Solubility Product Constants

Basic Concept

Like the acids and bases discussed in Section 1.6, another group of substances comprised generally of ionic compounds that have very limited solubility in water deserves separate treatment. Examples include magnesium hydroxide (commonly known as milk of magnesia, an antacid), barium sulfate (used in enemas to diagnose colonic tumors), and silver chloride (used in the photographic process). These substances, are generally referred to as "insoluble" or "slightly soluble," are governed by a solubility equilibrium expression and a solubility product constant known as K_{sp}, identical in concept to the principle of equilibrium discussed in Section 1.7.

The solubility of any salt depends on temperature. The solubility of most salts increases with increasing temperature. When a salt has dissolved to the maximum extent in a given volume of water at a given temperature, the solution is said to be **saturated.** Until that point is reached, the solution is **unsaturated.** If a saturated solution is heated above room temperature so that more salt can be dissolved and be held in solution, the solution is **supersaturated.** The solubility of a salt is commonly measured in units of moles per liter, grams per liter, or milligrams per liter (often referred to as parts per million or ppm).

If two liquids, such as ethanol and water, dissolve freely in each other, they are said to be **miscible** in all proportions. Oil and water are immiscible with each other.

Definition of Solubility Product Constant K_{sp}

Consider, for example, the slightly soluble salt $CaF_2(s)$ in equilibrium with water. Its limited dissociation and ionization in water can be expressed as follows:

$$CaF_2(s) \rightleftharpoons Ca^{2+}(aq) + 2\,F^-(aq) \quad [1.32]$$

and its **solubility product constant, K_{sp},** as

$$K_{sp} = [Ca^{2+}][F^-]^2 \quad [1.33]$$

Note that $[CaF_2(s)]$ does not appear in the K_{sp} expression since it represents the undissolved portion and is a pure solid.

Also note that $[Ca^{2+}]$ represents the concentration of Ca^{2+} ion actually dissolved in the water, while $[F^-]$ represents the F^- ion concentration actually dissolved in the water.

Note also that

$$[Ca^{2+}(aq)] = 2\,[F^-(aq)] = [CaF_2(aq)]$$

$CaF_2(aq)$ is dissolved.

The smaller the K_{sp} value, the lower the solubility of the salt.

Clearly, the K_{sp} value of a salt can be calculated by determining the solubility of each ion and then using equation 1.33. K_{sp} values, like other equilibrium constants, are functions of temperature.

Calculating Molar Solubility from K_{sp}

The molar solubility of any slightly soluble salt, along with the concentration of any of its ions, can be calculated from its K_{sp} value. The formula of the salt must be known, however, so that its dissociation and ionization can be written.

It is important to note that simply comparing the K_{sp} values of two salts to determine which has a higher or lower molar solubility can often be misleading. This comparison of numerical values is valid only when the two salts have the same stoichiometry, that is, the subscripts in the formulas are identical.

Table 1.2 lists K_{sp} values for many salts at 25°C.

Example 1.32

Calculate

A. the molar solubility of calcium flouride, CaF_2, and

B. the concentration of the flouride ion, in solution at 25°C. The K_{sp} of CaF_2 is 4.0×10^{-11} at 25°C.

Solution:

A. The equilibrium for this salt is as follows:

$$CaF_2(s) \rightleftharpoons Ca^{2+}(aq) + 2F^-(aq)$$

The K_{sp} expression is:

$$K_{sp} = [Ca^{2+}][F^-]^2 = 4.0 \times 10^{-11}$$

Let S = the solubility of the Ca^{2+} ion in moles per liter.

Then $2S$ = the solubility of the F^- ion.

Substitute S into the K_{sp} expression:

$$(S)(2S)^2 = 4.0 \times 10^{-11}$$

$$4S^3 = 4.0 \times 10^{-11}$$

$$S = 2.15 \times 10^{-4}\ M$$

Thus, the molar solubility of CaF_2 is 2.15×10^{-4} M. This is *also* $[Ca^{2+}]$.

B. $[F^-] = 2 \times 2.15 \times 10^{-4}\ M = 4.30 \times 10^{-4}\ M$

Example 1.33

The molar solubility of tin iodide, SnI_2, is 1.28×10^{-2} mol/L. What is K_{sp} for this compound?

Solution:

The solubility equilibrium for SnI_2 is:

$$SnI_2\ (s) \rightleftharpoons Sn^{2+}(aq) + 2I^-(aq)$$

The K_{sp} expression is:

$$K_{sp} = [Sn^{2+}][I^-]^2$$

Note that 1.0 mol of SnI_2 produces 1.0 mol of Sn^{2+}, but 2.0 mol of I^-.

$$[Sn^{2+}] = 1.28 \times 10^{-2}\ M$$

$$[I^-] = (2) \times 1.28 \times 10^{-2}\ M = 2.56 \times 10^{-2}\ M$$

Substitute these values into the K_{sp} expression:

$$K_{sp} = (1.28 \times 10^{-2}\ M)(2.56 \times 10^{-2}\ M)^2 = 8.4 \times 10^{-6}$$

Table 1.2 Solubility Product Constants at 25°C

Salt	*Solubility Equilibrium*	K_{sp}
Fluorides		
MgF_2	$MgF_2(s) \rightleftharpoons Mg^{2+}(aq) + 2F^-(aq)$	6.6×10^{-9}
CaF_2	$CaF_2(s) \rightleftharpoons Ca^{2+}(aq) + 2F^-(aq)$	3.9×10^{-11}
SrF_2	$SrF_2(s) \rightleftharpoons Sr^{2+}(aq) + 2F^-(aq)$	2.9×10^{-9}
BaF_2	$BaF_2(s) \rightleftharpoons Ba^{2+}(aq) + 2F^-(aq)$	1.7×10^{-6}
LiF	$LiF(s) \rightleftharpoons Li^+(aq) + F^-(aq)$	1.7×10^{-3}
PbF_2	$PbF_2(s) \rightleftharpoons Pb^{2+}(aq) + 2F^-(aq)$	3.6×10^{-8}
Chlorides		
CuCl	$CuCl(s) \rightleftharpoons Cu^+(aq) + Cl^-(aq)$	1.9×10^{-7}
AgCl	$AgCl(s) \rightleftharpoons Ag^+(aq) + Cl^-(aq)$	1.8×10^{-10}
Hg_2Cl_2	$Hg_2Cl_2(s) \rightleftharpoons Hg_2{}^{2+}(aq) + 2Cl^-(aq)$	1.2×10^{-18}
TlCl	$TlCl(s) \rightleftharpoons Tl^+(aq) + Cl^-(aq)$	1.8×10^{-4}
$PbCl_2$	$PbCl_2(s) \rightleftharpoons Pb^{2+}(aq) + 2Cl^-(aq)$	1.7×10^{-5}
$AuCl_3$	$AuCl_3(s) \rightleftharpoons Au^{3+}(aq) + 3Cl^-(aq)$	3.2×10^{-25}
Bromides		
CuBr	$CuBr(s) \rightleftharpoons Cu^+(aq) + Br^-(aq)$	5×10^{-9}
AgBr	$AgBr(s) \rightleftharpoons Ag^+(aq) + Br^-(aq)$	5.0×10^{-13}
Hg_2Br_2	$Hg_2{}^{2+}(s) \rightleftharpoons Hg_2{}^{2+}(aq) + 2Br^-(aq)$	5.6×10^{-23}
$HgBr_2$	$HgBr_2(s) \rightleftharpoons Hg^{2+}(aq) + 2Br^-(aq)$	1.3×10^{-19}
$PbBr_2$	$PbBr_2(s) \rightleftharpoons Pb^{2+}(aq) + 2Br^-(aq)$	2.1×10^{-6}
Iodides		
Cul	$Cul(s) \rightleftharpoons Cu^+(aq) + I^-(aq)$	1×10^{-12}
Agl	$Agl(s) \rightleftharpoons Ag^+(aq) + 1^-(aq)$	8.3×10^{-17}
Hg_2l_2	$Hg_2l_2(s) \rightleftharpoons Hg_2{}^{2+}(aq) + 21^-(aq)$	4.7×10^{-29}
Hgl_2	$Hgl_2(s) \rightleftharpoons Hg^{2+}(aq) + 21^-(aq)$	1.1×10^{-28}
Pbl_2	$Pbl_2(s) \rightleftharpoons Pb^{2+}(aq) + 21^-(aq)$	7.9×10^{-9}
Hydroxides		
$Mg(OH)_2$	$Mg(OH)_2(s) \rightleftharpoons Mg^{2+}(aq) + 2OH^-(aq)$	7.1×10^{-12}
$Ca(OH)_2$	$Ca(OH)_2(s) \rightleftharpoons Ca^{2+}(aq) + 2OH^-(aq)$	6.5×10^{-6}
$Mn(OH)_2$	$Mn(OH)_2(s) \rightleftharpoons Mn^{2+}(aq) + 2OH^-(aq)$	1.6×10^{-13}
$Fe(OH)_2$	$Fe(OH)_2(s) \rightleftharpoons Fe^{2+}(aq) + 2OH^-(aq)$	7.9×10^{-16}
$Fe(OH)_3$	$Fe(OH)_3(s) \rightleftharpoons Fe^{3+}(aq) + 3OH^-(aq)$	1.6×10^{-39}
$Co(OH)_2$	$Co(OH)_2(s) \rightleftharpoons Co^{2+}(aq) + 2OH^-(aq)$	1×10^{-15}
$Co(OH)_3$	$Co(OH)_3(s) \rightleftharpoons Co^{3+}(aq) + 3OH^-(aq)$	3×10^{-45}
$Ni(OH)_2$	$Ni(OH)_2(s) \rightleftharpoons Ni^{2+}(aq) + 2OH^-(aq)$	6×10^{-16}
$Cu(OH)_2$	$Cu(OH)_2(s) \rightleftharpoons Cu^{2+}(aq) + 2OH^-(aq)$	4.8×10^{-20}
$V(OH)_3$	$V(OH)_3(s) \rightleftharpoons V^{3+}(aq) + 3OH^-(aq)$	4×10^{-35}
$Cr(OH)_3$	$Cr(OH)_3(s) \rightleftharpoons Cr^{3+}(aq) + 3OH^-(aq)$	2×10^{-30}
Ag_2O	$Ag_2O(s) + H_2O \rightleftharpoons 2Ag^+(aq) + 2OH^-(aq)$	1.9×10^{-8}
$Zn(OH)_2$	$Zn(OH)_2(s) \rightleftharpoons Zn^{2+}(aq) + 2OH^-(aq)$	3.0×10^{-16}
$Cd(OH)_2$	$Cd(OH)_2(s) \rightleftharpoons Cd^{2+}(aq) + 2OH^-(aq)$	5.0×10^{-15}
$Al(OH)_3$ (alpha form)	$Al(OH)_3(s) \rightleftharpoons Al^{3+}(aq) + 3OH^-(aq)$	3×10^{-34}
Cyanides		
AgCN	$AgCN(s) \rightleftharpoons Ag^+(aq) + CN^-(aq)$	2.2×10^{-16}
$Zn(CN)_2$	$Zn(CN)_2(s) \rightleftharpoons Zn^{2+}(aq) + 2CN^-(aq)$	3×10^{-16}
Sulfites		
$CaSO_3$	$CaSO_3(s) \rightleftharpoons Ca^{2+}(aq) + SO_3{}^{2-}(aq)$	3×10^{-7}
Ag_2SO_3	$Ag_2SO_3(s) \rightleftharpoons 2Ag^+(aq) + SO_3{}^{2-}(aq)$	1.5×10^{-14}
$BaSO_3$	$BaSO_2(s) \rightleftharpoons Ba^{2+}(aq) + SO_3{}^{2-}(aq)$	8×10^{-7}

Solubility Product Constants (Continued)

Salt	*Solubility Equilibrium*	K_{sp}
Sulfates		
$CaSO_4$	$CaSO_4(s) \rightleftharpoons Ca^{2+}(aq) + SO_4^{2-}(aq)$	2.4×10^{-5}
$SrSO_4$	$SrSO_4(s) \rightleftharpoons Sr^{2+}(aq) + SO_4^{2-}(aq)$	3.2×10^{-7}
$BaSO_4$	$BaSO_4(s) \rightleftharpoons Ba^{2+}(aq) + SO_4^{2-}(aq)$	1.1×10^{-10}
$RaSO_4$	$RaSO_4(s) \rightleftharpoons Ra^{2+}(aq) + SO_4^{2-}(aq)$	4.3×10^{-11}
Ag_2SO_4	$Ag_2SO_4(s) \rightleftharpoons 2Ag^{+}(aq) + SO_4^{2-}(aq)$	1.5×10^{-5}
Hg_2SO_4	$Hg_2SO_4(s) \rightleftharpoons Hg_2^{2+}(aq) + SO_4^{2-}(aq)$	7.4×10^{-7}
$PbSO_4$	$PbSO_4(s) \rightleftharpoons Pb^{2+}(aq) + SO_4^{2-}(aq)$	1.6×10^{-8}
Chromates		
$BaCrO_4$	$BaCrO_4(s) \rightleftharpoons Ba^{2+}(aq) + CrO_4^{2-}(aq)$	2.1×10^{-10}
$CuCrO_4$	$CuCrO_4(s) \rightleftharpoons Ba^{2+}(aq) + CrO_4^{2-}(aq)$	3.6×10^{-6}
Ag_2CrO_4	$Ag_2CrO_4(s) \rightleftharpoons 2Ag^{+}(aq) + CrO_4^{2-}(aq)$	1.2×10^{-12}
Hg_2CrO_4	$Hg_2CrO_4(s) \rightleftharpoons Hg_2^{2+}(aq) + CrO_4^{2-}(aq)$	2.0×10^{-9}
$CaCrO_4$	$CaCrO_4(s) \rightleftharpoons Ca^{2+}(aq) + CrO_4^{2-}(aq)$	7.1×10^{-4}
$PbCrO_4$	$PbCrO_4(s) \rightleftharpoons Pb^{2+}(aq) + CrO_4^{2-}(aq)$	1.8×10^{-14}
Carbonates		
$MgCO_3$	$MgCO_3(s) \rightleftharpoons Mg^{2+}(aq) + CO_3^{2-}(aq)$	3.5×10^{-8}
$CaCO_3$	$CaCO_3(s) \rightleftharpoons Ca^{2+}(aq) + CO_3^{2-}(aq)$	4.5×10^{-9}
$SrCO_3$	$SrCO_3(s) \rightleftharpoons Sr^{2+}(aq) + CO_3^{2-}(aq)$	9.3×10^{-10}
$BaCO_3$	$BaCO_3(s) \rightleftharpoons Ba^{2+}(aq) + CO_3^{2-}(aq)$	5.0×10^{-9}
$MnCO_3$	$MnCO_3(s) \rightleftharpoons Mn^{2+}(aq) + CO_3^{2-}(aq)$	5.0×10^{-10}
$FeCO_3$	$FeCO_3(s) \rightleftharpoons Fe^{2+}(aq) + CO_3^{2-}(aq)$	2.1×10^{-11}
$CoCO_3$	$CoCO_3(s) \rightleftharpoons Co^{2+}(aq) + CO_3^{2-}(aq)$	1.0×10^{-10}
$NiCO_3$	$NiCO_3(s) \rightleftharpoons Ni^{2+}(aq) + CO_3^{2-}(aq)$	1.3×10^{-7}
$CuCO_3$	$CuCO_3(s) \rightleftharpoons Cu^{2+}(aq) + CO_3^{2-}(aq)$	2.3×10^{-10}
Ag_2CO_3	$Ag_2CO_3(s) \rightleftharpoons 2Ag^{+}(aq) + CO_3^{2-}(aq)$	8.1×10^{-12}
Hg_2CO_3	$Hg_2CO_3(s) \rightleftharpoons Hg_2^{2+}(aq) + CO_3^{2-}(aq)$	8.9×10^{-17}
$ZnCO_3$	$ZnCO_3(s) \rightleftharpoons Zn^{2+}(aq) + CO_3^{2-}(aq)$	1.0×10^{-10}
$CdCO_3$	$CdCO_3(s) \rightleftharpoons Cd^{2+}(aq) + CO_3^{2-}(aq)$	1.8×10^{-14}
$PbCO_3$	$PbCO_3(s) \rightleftharpoons Pb^{2+}(aq) + CO_3^{2-}(aq)$	7.4×10^{-14}
Phosphates		
$Mg_3(PO_4)_2$	$Mg_3(PO_4)_2(s) \rightleftharpoons 3Mg^{2+}(aq) + 2PO_4^{3-}(aq)$	6.3×10^{-26}
$SrHPO_4$	$SrHPO_4(s) \rightleftharpoons Sr^{2+}(aq) + HPO_4^{2-}(aq)$	1.2×10^{-7}
$BaHPO_4$	$BaHPO_4(s) \rightleftharpoons Ba^{2+}(aq) + HPO_4^{2-}(aq)$	4.0×10^{-8}
$LaPO_4$	$LaPO_4(s) \rightleftharpoons La^{3+}(aq) + PO_4^{3-}(aq)$	3.7×10^{-23}
$Fe_3(PO_4)_2$	$Fe_3(PO_4)_2(s) \rightleftharpoons 3Fe^{2+}(aq) + 2PO_4^{3-}(aq)$	1×10^{-36}
Ag_3PO_4	$Ag_3PO_4(s) \rightleftharpoons 3Ag^{+}(aq) + PO_4^{3-}(aq)$	2.8×10^{-18}
$FePO_4$	$FePO_4(s) \rightleftharpoons Fe^{3+}(aq) + PO_4^{3-}(aq)$	4.0×10^{-27}
$Zn_3(PO_4)_2$	$Zn_3(PO_4)_2(s) \rightleftharpoons 3Zn^{2+}(aq) + 2PO_4^{3-}(aq)$	5×10^{-36}
$Pb_3(PO_4)_2$	$Pb_3(PO_4)_2(s) \rightleftharpoons 3Pb^{2+}(aq) + 2PO_4^{3-}(aq)$	3.0×10^{-44}
$Ba_3(PO_4)_2$	$Ba_3(PO_4)_2(s) \rightleftharpoons 3Ba^{2+}(aq) + 2PO_4^{3-}(aq)$	5.8×10^{-38}
Ferrocyanides		
$Zn_2[Fe(CN)_6]$	$Zn_2[Fe(CN)_6](s) \rightleftharpoons 2Zn^{2+}(aq) + Fe(CN)_6^{4-}(aq)$	2.1×10^{-16}
$Cd_2[Fe(CN)_6]$	$Cd_2[Fe(CN)_6](s) \rightleftharpoons 2Cd^{2+}(aq) + Fe(CN)_6^{4-}(aq)$	4.2×10^{-18}
$Pb_2[Fe(CN)_6]$	$Pb_2[Fe(CN)_6](s) \rightleftharpoons 2Pb^{2+}(aq) + Fe(CN)_6^{4-}(aq)$	9.5×10^{-19}

Common and Uncommon Ion and pH Effects

Occasionally, the solvent in which a salt is to be dissolved is not pure water but rather contains an ion in common with the salt to be dissolved. The common ion may be a cation or an anion, such as Ca^{2+} or F^-. The common ion may also be the H^+ ion or OH^- ion, which manifests itself simply in a pH value less than or greater than 7, respectively. This is the **common ion effect,** and the net result is to significantly reduce the solubility of the salt in question.

The presence of a background salt with no ions in common with the salt to be dissolved is known as the **uncommon ion** or **salt effect.** In contrast, this effect slightly increases the solubility of the salt in question.

In general, most salts are more soluble in hot water than in cold; that is, the solubilities of most salts increase with increasing temperature. In the temperature range of 0 to 100°C, many common salts demonstrate a nearly linear relationship between solubility and temperature, with varying, positive slopes. Some notable exceptions include KNO_3, which shows an exponential relationship, and Li_2SO_4, which shows a linear but decreasing solubility with temperature.

Example 1.34

Magnesium hydroxide, $Mg(OH)_2$, is a common antacid and has a $K_{sp} = 1.8 \times 10^{-11}$. Find the molar solubility of $Mg(OH)_2$ in a solution whose pH is 13.12.

Solution:

To find the molar solubility of $Mg(OH)_2$ in distilled water, the method outlined in Example 1.32 would be followed. In this case, however, the solution is basic with an excess of OH^- ions. Since these OH^- ions are in common with the OH^- ions contained in $Mg(OH)_2$, the common ion effect must be taken into account because it will reduce the solubility of $Mg(OH)_2$.

First determine $[OH^-]$ as follows:

$$\text{pOH} = 14.00 - \text{pH} = 14.00 - 13.12 = 0.88$$

$$[OH^-] = 10^{-\text{pOH}} = 10^{-0.88} = 1.32 \times 10^{-1}\ \text{M}$$

The K_{sp} expression for $Mg(OH)_2$ is:

$$K_{sp} = [Mg^{2+}][OH^-]^2$$

Use the strategy outlined in Example 1.32.

Let $[Mg^{2+}] = S$

and $[OH^-] = 2S + 1.32 \times 10^{-1}$.

Substitute these values, along with the K_{sp} value, into the K_{sp} expression:

$$1.8 \times 10^{-11} = (S)(2S + 1.32 \times 10^{-1})^2$$

This is a cubic equation in S. To simplify the calculation, assume that $2S$ is negligible compared with 1.32×10^{-1} as an additive term. Then:

$$1.8 \times 10^{-11} = (S)(1.32 \times 10^{-1})^2$$

$$S = 1.0 \times 10^{-9}\ \text{M}$$

This result represents the solubility of $Mg(OH)_2$.

Predicting Precipitation

When two solutions are mixed, it is possible that an insoluble precipitate will form and settle to the bottom. Whether this happens depends on the identities of the ions present in the solutions and their respective concentrations. If the ions for a potentially insoluble precipitate are present, all that needs to be done to predict precipitation is to calculate a hypothetical solubility product constant, Q, in the same manner as K_{sp} is calculated. The Q value is then compared to the K_{sp} value, subject to the following criteria or conditions:

- If $Q \le K_{sp}$, no precipitate forms.
- If $Q > K_{sp}$, a precipitate forms.

In general, conditions that favor **completeness of precipitation** are:

- A very small value of K_{sp}.
- High initial ion concentrations.
- A concentration of common ion that considerably exceeds the concentration of the target ion to be precipitated.

Example 1.35

Will a precipitate form if 50.0 mL of 1.2×10^{-3} M $Pb(NO_3)_2$ are added to 50.0 mL of 2.0×10^{-4} M Na_2SO_4?

Solution:

The addition of the two solutions will result in a double-replacement reaction. Two products, $NaNO_3$ and $PbSO_4$, will form and are thus candidates as insoluble salts. A check of Table 1.2 reveals that only $PbSO_4$ has a K_{sp} value (1.6×10^{-8}) and is therefore a possible precipitate. To confirm whether a precipitate actually forms, evaluate Q as follows:

$$Q = [Pb^{2+}(aq)][SO_4^{2-}(aq)]$$

$$[Pb^{2+}(aq)] = \frac{(0.050\ L)(1.2 \times 10^{-3}\ M)}{0.100\ L} = 6.0 \times 10^{-4}\ M$$

$$[SO_4^{2-}(aq)] = \frac{(0.050\ L)(2.0 \times 10^{-4}\ M)}{0.100\ L} = 1.0 \times 10^{-4}\ M$$

Substitute these values for concentrations into the expression for Q:

$$Q = (6.0 \times 10^{-4}\ M)(1.0 \times 10^{-4}\ M) = 6.0 \times 10^{-8}$$

But $K_{sp} = 1.6 \times 10^{-8}$.

Since $Q > K_{sp}$, a precipitate forms!

1.9 Chemical Kinetics

Basic Concept

Chemical kinetics is the study of the rates and mechanisms of chemical reactions. The reaction rate is a kinetic property and depends on the mechanism. In contrast, thermodynamic properties (discussed in Section 1.10) are independent of mechanism. Thermodynamics can tell us whether or not a reaction is spontaneous, but kinetics tells us how fast the reaction occurs and if it happens fast enough to be of any interest or value.

The most common way to measure the rate of reaction is by the disappearance of a reactant, that is, the change in concentration of the reactant with time. Thus:

$$\text{Reaction rate} = \frac{-\Delta C}{\Delta t} = \frac{-(C_2 - C_1)}{t_2 - t_1} \quad [1.34]$$

where C = the change in the concentration of the reactant, and t = the elapsed time. Subscripts 1 and 2 refer to concentrations and corresponding times, respectively. The reactant concentration decreases with time, making $(C_2 - C_1)$ a negative quantity. The minus sign is used to make it a positive quantity.

The reaction rate can be calculated just as well from the change in concentration with time of a product, in which case $\Delta C/\Delta t$ is a positive quantity. It is important to remember that the reaction rate is constantly changing, so $\Delta C/\Delta t$ represents an average rate. The instantaneous rate is given by the first derivative, dC/dt.

Reaction Rate Laws, Orders, and Constants

For the general reaction:

$$aA + bB \rightarrow gG + hH \quad [1.35]$$

the **rate law or equation** is expressed as:

$$\text{Rate} = k[A]^x[B]^y \quad [1.36]$$

where k = the **rate constant** (in reciprocal time units), [A] and [B] represent the molar concentrations of reactants A and B, and x and y are exponents denoting the **order** of the reaction for the reactant species. The exponents x and y must be determined experimentally. The sum of the exponents $(x + y)$ is called the **overall order** of the reaction. In the present case, it is said that the reaction is x order in A, y order in B, and $(x + y)$ order overall.

Consider, for example, the following reaction:

$$NO_2(g) + CO(g) \rightleftharpoons NO(g) + CO_2(g) \quad [1.37]$$

Experimentally, it is determined that the rate law for this reaction is:

$$\text{Rate} = k[NO_2]^2 \quad [1.38]$$

This means that the rate is second order in NO_2, zeroth order in CO, and second order overall.

Consider, as another example, the decomposition of dinitrogen pentoxide, N_2O_5:

$$2N_2O_5(g) \rightleftharpoons 4NO_2(g) + O_2(g) \quad [1.39]$$

Here, it is experimentally determined that the rate law for this reaction is:

$$\text{Rate} = k[N_2O_5] \quad [1.40]$$

Thus, the rate of decomposition is first order in N_2O_5. The rate constant k is also experimentally measured:

$$k = 5.2 \times 10^{-3} \text{ at } 65°C.$$

First- and Second-Order Reactions

For any reaction that is known to be first order in a particular species, as in the N_2O_5 decomposition discussed above, the rate can be written as

$$\text{Rate} = \frac{-d[A]}{dt} = \frac{-\Delta[A]}{\Delta t} = k[A] \quad [1.41]$$

For a **first-order reaction,** this means that doubling the concentration of A doubles the reaction rate.

This equation may be integrated to give a more useful result:

$$\ln \frac{[A]_0}{[A]} = k\,\Delta t$$

This can also be written as

$$\ln[A] = \ln[A]_0 - k\,\Delta t \qquad [1.42]$$

In similar fashion, the integrated rate equation for a **second-order reaction** is:

$$\frac{1}{[A]} = \frac{1}{[A]_0} + k\,\Delta t \qquad [1.43]$$

Half-Life of a Reaction

A quantity defined as the half-life of the reaction can also be determined. The **half-life** is the time required for the concentration of the reactant to reach half of its initial value. For a *first-order reaction,* the half-life is independent of the initial concentration and is given as

$$t_{1/2} = \frac{0.693}{k} \qquad [1.44]$$

For a *second-order reaction,* the half-life depends on initial concentration and is given as

$$t_{1/2} = \frac{1}{k[A]_0} \qquad [1.45]$$

Example 1.36

Consider the reaction between peroxydisulfate ion, $S_2O_8^{2-}$, and iodide ion, I^-, shown below and the experimental data about the concentrations and reaction rates at 25°C given in the table that follows.

$$S_2O_8^{2-}(aq) + 3I^-(aq) \rightarrow 2SO_4^{2-}(aq) + I_3^-(aq)$$

Experiment	$[S_2O_8^{2-}]$	$[I^-]$	*Initial Rate*
1	0.080 M	0.034 M	2.2×10^{-4} M/sec
2	0.080 M	0.017 M	1.1×10^{-4} M/sec
3	0.016 M	0.017 M	2.2×10^{-4} M/sec

A. Write the rate law expression and determine the overall order, that is, $(x + y)$, for this reaction.

B. Determine the rate constant k for this reaction at 25°C.

Solution:

A. Examine the data in the preceding table. Comparing experiment 1 with 2, it is clear that doubling the iodide ion concentration, while holding the peroxydisulfate ion concentration constant, doubles the reaction rate. Similarly, comparing experiment 2 with 3 reveals that doubling the peroxydisulfate ion concentration, while holding the iodide ion concentration constant, also doubles the reaction rate.

Thus, this reaction is first order (linear) in iodide ion concentration, and first order (linear) in peroxydisulfate ion concentration. The rate law can be written as follows:

$$\text{Rate} = k[S_2O_8^{2-}]^x[I^-]^y$$

where $x = 1$ and $y = 1$.

Hence:

$$\text{Rate} = k[S_2O_8^{2-}]^1[I^-]^1$$

The overall order is $(x + y) = (1 + 1) = 2$, indicating second order overall.

B. The rate constant k can be determined using the data from any of the three experiments. Take the data from experiment 1, and use the rate law expression determined in part **a.** Thus:

$$2.2 \times 10^{-4}\ \text{M/sec} = k\,(0.034\ \text{M})^1(0.080\ \text{M})^1$$

$$k = 8.09 \times 10^{-2}\ (\text{M} \cdot \text{sec})^{-1}$$

Example 1.37

The thermal decomposition of phosphine, PH_3, is known to be a first-order reaction:

$$4PH_3(g) \rightarrow P_4(g) + 6H_2(g)$$

The half-life, $t_{1/2}$, is 35.0 sec at 680°C.

A. Compute the rate constant k for this reaction.

B. Find the time required for 75% of the initial concentration of PH_3 to decompose.

Solution:

A. For a first-order reaction, $t_{1/2} = 0.693/k$.

Hence:

$$k = \frac{0.693}{t_{1/2}} = \frac{0.693}{35.0\ \text{sec}}$$

$$= 0.0198\ \text{sec}^{-1}$$

B. To find the time, use the integrated, first-order rate law, equation 1.42, and solve for Δt.

If 75% of PH_3 is to decompose, 25% must remain! Thus:

$$[A]_0 = 100\% = 1.00$$
$$[A] = 25\% = 0.25$$

Substitute these values and solve for Δt:

$$\Delta t = 70.0 \text{ sec}$$

Dependence on Temperature: The Arrhenius Equation

The Arrhenius model for rates of reactions assumes that molecules must undergo collisions before they can react. The number of collisions per unit time is A, the **frequency factor.** This model also assumes that not all collisions will result in or lead to a reaction. Rather, only those with sufficient energy, called the **activation energy, E_a,** to allow molecules to reach an **activated complex** will achieve this result.

The rate constant k is a function of temperature and can be expressed theoretically as the **Arrhenius equation:**

$$k = Ae^{-Ea/RT} \qquad [1.46]$$

where A = the frequency factor, a measure of the number of collisions per second,

E_a = the activation energy in joules or calories per mole,

R = the universal gas constant in units consistent with those for E_a,

T = the absolute temperature in kelvins.

A more useful form of the equation can be written as

$$\ln k = \ln A - \frac{E_a}{RT} \qquad [1.47]$$

The rate constants k_1 and k_2 at two different temperatures, T_1 and T_2, are related as follows:

$$\ln\frac{k_1}{k_2} = \frac{E_a}{R}\left(\frac{1}{T_2} - \frac{1}{T_1}\right) \qquad [1.48]$$

Example 1.38

The reaction below is important in the chemistry of air pollution:

$$NO(g) + O_3(g) \rightarrow NO_2(g) + O_2(g)$$

The frequency factor $A = 8.7 \times 10^{12}$ sec^{-1} and the rate constant $k = 300$ sec^{-1} at 75°C.

A. Find the activation energy, E_a, in joules per mole for this reaction.

B. Find the rate constant k of this reaction at 0°C, assuming E_a to be constant.

Solution:

A. Use the Arrhenius equation and solve for E_a.

$$\ln k = \ln A - \frac{E_a}{RT}$$

Use $R = 8.31$ J/K · mole and $T = 273 + 75°C = 348$ K. Then:

$$\ln 300 = \ln 8.7 \times 10^{12} - \frac{E_a}{(8.31)(348)}$$

$$E_a = 69{,}700 \text{ J/mol or } 69.7 \text{ kJ/mol}$$

B. Denote the rate constant given at 75°C as k_1, and the rate constant at 0°C as k_2, and use

$$\ln\frac{k_1}{k_2} = \frac{E_a}{R}\left(\frac{1}{T_2} - \frac{1}{T_1}\right)$$

Substitute the above information, and solve for k_2.

$$\ln k_2 = \ln 300 - \frac{69{,}700}{8.31}\left(\frac{1}{273} - \frac{1}{348}\right)$$

$$= 5.7038 - 6.626 = -0.9222$$

$$k_2 = 0.3976 \text{ sec}^{-1}$$

Catalysis

Substances that increase the rate of reaction without themselves being consumed in the reaction are called **catalysts.** They work by lowering the activiation energy, E_a, or the barrier required for the reaction to proceed. A catalyst may be in the same physical state as the other species in the reaction (homogeneous catalysis) or in a different physical state (heterogeneous catalysis).

1.10 Chemical Thermodynamics and Thermochemistry

Basic Concept

Thermodynamics is the study of energy transformations. **Thermochemistry** is the study of the thermal energy changes that accompany chemical and physical changes. **Heat** is the energy transferred between objects or systems and is measured by temperature changes. Energy is a property of a substance or system; it cannot be measured directly.

Any process occurring within a system that produces or releases heat into the surroundings is called **exothermic,** and its value is given a negative sign by convention. Any process that absorbs heat from the surroundings into the system is called **endothermic,** and its value has a positive sign. Note that an exothermic reaction is not necessarily a spontaneous reaction, and its negative sign should *not* be interpreted as such. This type of interpretation and criterion is reserved for ΔG, the Gibbs free energy change, discussed on page 47.

Enthalpy and Hess's Law

Since chemical reactions involve the reforming of bonds, energy changes generally accompany reactions. To initiate a reaction, an activation energy, E_a, must first be supplied for the reactants to reach an activated complex, regardless of whether or not the reaction is spontaneous. When a reaction occurs, a change in **enthalpy,** that is, heat content, known as the **heat of reaction, ΔH_{RX},** is associated with the process. This is the amount of heat exchanged (liberated or absorbed) with the surroundings under constant external pressure and may be measured experimentally (directly) or calculated theoretically (indirectly) and expressed in either kilojoules (kJ) or kilocalories (kcal).

The enthalpy change known as the **standard heat of formation, $\Delta H_f°$,** is defined as the heat of reaction for a product derived only from its elements, the superscript ° meaning measured under normal conditions (usually NTP as opposed to STP).

Regardless of the reaction, **Hess's law** states: The enthalpy change of a chemical reaction is the same regardless of the number of steps or separate reactions. If the reaction of interest is the sum of several other reactions, the individual heats of reaction must be added algebraically. In other words:

$$\Delta H_{RX} = \Sigma \Delta H_{\text{products}} - \Sigma \Delta H_{\text{reactants}} \quad [1.49]$$

Example 1.39

The standard heats of formation, $\Delta H_f°$, for NO_2 and N_2O_4, are as follows: $\Delta H_f°[NO_2] = 33.9$ kJ/mole, $\Delta H_f°[N_2O_4] = -19.5$ kJ/mol. Predict or calculate the heat of reaction, ΔH_{RX}, for the following reaction at standard conditions.

$$2NO_2(g) \rightleftharpoons N_2O_4(g)$$

Solution:

Use Hess's law.

$$\Delta H_{RX}° = \Sigma \Delta H_{\text{products}} - \Sigma \Delta H_{\text{reactants}}$$
$$= \Delta H_f°[N_2O_4] - 2\Delta H_f°[NO_2]$$
$$= (1.00\ \text{mol})(-19.5\ \text{kJ/mol}) - (2\ \text{mol})(33.9\ \text{kJ/mol})$$
$$= -87.3\ \text{kJ}$$

Note that the negative sign means that the reaction is exothermic.

Example 1.40

Given the following reactions and data for $\Delta H°$:

$$N_2O_4(g) \rightarrow 2NO_2(g)\ \Delta H°(\text{I}) = 87.30\ \text{kJ}$$
$$2NO(g) + O_2(g) \rightarrow 2NO_2(g)\ \Delta H°(\text{II}) = -114.14\ \text{kJ}$$

Compute $\Delta H_{RX}°$ for the following reaction:

$$2NO(g) + O_2(g) \rightarrow N_2O_4(g)$$

Solution:

Recognize that, if the first given reaction is reversed and then added to the second reaction, the desired reaction is obtained, since the $2NO_2$ terms on opposite sides of the reaction cancel. Change the sign of $\Delta H°(\text{I})$, so that the value is -87.30 kJ, and then add the two $\Delta H°$ values. Thus:

$$\Delta H_{RX}° = \Delta H°(\text{I}) + \Delta H°(\text{II})$$
$$= -87.30\ \text{kJ} + (-114.14\ \text{kJ}) = -201.44\ \text{kJ}$$

Another way to solve this problem in principle is to use Hess's law and set the solution up as follows:

$$\Delta H_{RX}° = \Sigma \Delta H_{\text{products}} - \Sigma \Delta H_{\text{reactants}}$$
$$= \Delta H_f°[N_2O_4] - \{2\Delta H_f°[NO] + \Delta H_f°[O2]\}$$

The problem with this approach is that, while $\Delta H_f°[O_2] = 0$ and the value for $\Delta H_f°[N_2O_4]$ is given in Example 1.39, the value for $\Delta H_f°[NO]$ is unknown.

The First Law and the Conservation of Energy

In understanding the laws of thermodynamics, it is useful to define *system* and distinguish it from *surroundings* very carefully. In general, there are three types of systems:

1. **Closed system**—a system that no mass enters or leaves.
2. **Isolated system**—a system that no mass or heat enters or leaves.
3. **Open system**—a system that mass or heat can enter or leave.

Furthermore, there are two kinds of *boundaries/walls* or processes:

1. **Diathermal walls**—walls that permit the transfer of heat between system and surroundings.
2. **Adibatic walls**—walls that do not permit the transfer of heat between system and surroundings (e.g., good insulators).

The **first law of thermodynamics** can be stated in several ways. For example:

- The energy of the universe is constant. The total possible energy change is equal to the sum of the energy change of the system plus the energy change of the surroundings.
- During a chemical or physical change in any defined system, energy can neither be created nor destroyed, but only changes form.

Expressed in mathematical terms:

$$\Delta E = q - w \qquad [1.50]$$

where ΔE = the total internal energy change of the system,

q = the heat absorbed *by* the system *from* the surroundings,

w = the work done *by* the system *on* the surroundings.

For adiabatic processes, $q = 0$, so $\Delta E = -w$.

For isothermal changes in ideal gases, $\Delta E = 0$, since E is a function of temperature only.

For pressure-volume work of an ideal gas (i.e., expansion or contraction):

$$w = \int P\,dV = P\,\Delta V \text{ if } P \text{ is constant} \qquad [1.51]$$

$$= \int P\,dV = \int \frac{nRT}{V} dV$$

$$= nRT \ln \frac{V_2}{V_1} \quad \text{if } P \text{ is not constant} \qquad [1.52]$$

ΔE and ΔH are related by the equation $\Delta H = \Delta E + P\,\Delta V$ at constant P.

Other types of thermodynamic work may include electrical work and magnetic work.

Example 1.41

Ten moles of an ideal gas in a piston and cylinder assembly absorb 2,500 J of heat. The gas expands from 2.0 L to 8.5 L against a constant external pressure of 2.5 atms. What is the internal energy change of this system?

Solution:

$\Delta E = q - w = q - P\,\Delta V$

$= 2{,}500 \text{ J} - (2.5 \text{ atm})(8.5 \text{ L} - 2.0 \text{ L})$

$= 2{,}500 \text{ J} - 13.75 \text{ L} \cdot \text{atm} \times (101.3 \text{ J/L} \cdot \text{atm})$

$= 2{,}500 \text{ J} - 1{,}390 \text{ J} = 1{,}110 \text{ J}$

Since the answer is positive, this amount of energy is *gained* by the system.

The Second Law and Entropy

The **second law of thermodynamics** may be expressed in several ways. For example:

- The **entropy, *S*,** that is, the randomness or disorder, of the universe either stays the same or increases, but never decreases.
- During a physical change or chemical reaction, the *total* **entropy change, ΔS,** of the system plus the surroundings is either zero or positive, never negative. It may be calculated as the reversible heat q, either absorbed or liberated by a system, divided by the absolute temperature T:

$$\Delta S = \frac{q}{T} \qquad [1.53]$$

- The construction of a perpetual motion machine is impossible.
- It is impossible to build a heat engine with 100% efficiency.

A corollary of the second law, often referred to as the **zeroth law,** states: Heat always flows from regions of hot to regions of cold *spontaneously.*

Entropy is also a measure of the statistical disorder or randomness of a system. For all real or natural changes, which are spontaneous and irreversible, the entropy of a system increases, so the entropy *change,* ΔS, is positive. For idealized changes, which are reversible or infinitely slow, ΔS

is equal to zero. Mathematically, this may be expressed as follows:

$$\Delta S_{total} = \Delta S_{system} + \Delta S_{surroundings} = \Delta S_{universe} \geq 0 \quad [1.54]$$

For phase transitions, ΔS_{trans}

$$= \frac{q_{trans}}{T} = \frac{\Delta H_{trans}}{T} \quad [1.55]$$

where ΔH_{trans} may be ΔH_{vap} or ΔH_{fus}.

For the heating of any substance, without a phase transition, the heat gained or lost, q, may be expressed as

$$q = mC\,\Delta T \quad [1.56]$$

where m = the mass of the substance in grams or moles,

C = the specific heat or heat capacity in suitable units,

ΔT = the change in temperature in degrees Celsius or kelvins.

For other processes involving changes in temperature and/or volume:

$$\Delta S = C_v \ln\frac{T_2}{T_1} + nR \ln\frac{V_2}{V_1} \quad [1.57]$$

Example 1.42

One mole of an ideal gas expands reversibly and isothermally from an initial volume of 2 L to a final volume of 20 L. Calculate the entropy change, in calories/kelvin, of the system and the surroundings.

Solution:

Since this process is isothermal, $T_1 = T_2$, use $\Delta S = nR \ln V_2/V_1$. Then:

$$\Delta S_{sys} = (1.00 \text{ mol})(1.99 \text{ cal/K} \cdot \text{mol}) \ln \frac{20 \text{ L}}{2.0 \text{ L}}$$

= 4.57 cal/K or 4.57 eu ("eu" stands for entropy unit)

Since this is a reversible process:

$$\Delta S_{sys} = -\Delta S_{surr} = -4.57 \text{ cal/K}$$

Example 1.43

Calculate the entropy change when 100 g of water vaporizes at 100°C.

Solution:

This is a phase transition. Use $\Delta S = \Delta H_{vap}/T$ (equation 1.53), where ΔH_{vap} = 540 cal/g and T = 373 K. Then:

$$\Delta S = \frac{(540 \text{ cal/g})(100 \text{ g})}{373 \text{ K}} = 145 \text{ cal/K}$$

The Third Law and Absolute Zero

The **third law of thermodynamics** states that it is impossible to reach absolute zero in a finite number of steps. Another version states that the absolute entropy of a perfect crystal is zero at absolute zero, since every atom is perfectly in place and has no kinetic energy.

Gibbs Free Energy and the Spontaneity of a Reaction

The Gibbs free energy change, ΔG, is defined as:

$$\Delta G = \Delta H - T\,\Delta S \quad [1.58]$$

Its chief value is that it is an unequivocal measure and indication of a reaction's spontaneity. It includes both an enthalpy term, ΔH, and an entropy term, ΔS.

Every reaction wants to simultaneously reach a state of minimum energy and a state of maximum entropy. Thus, if the sign of ΔG is negative, the reaction proceeds spontaneously as written; if positive, the *reverse* reaction proceeds spontaneously.

For equilibrium reactions, ΔG can be expressed as:

$$\Delta G = -RT \ln K_c \quad \text{in general} \quad [1.59]$$

$$\Delta G = -RT \ln K_p \quad \text{for gas-phase reactions} \quad [1.60]$$

Example 1.44

For this reaction:

$$H_2(g) + S(s) \rightarrow H_2S(g)$$

$\Delta H_f° = -20.2$ kJ/mol and $\Delta S_f° = +43.1$ J/K · mol.

A. Compute $\Delta G°$ for the reaction.
B. Tell whether the reaction is spontaneous.

Solution:

A. Use $\Delta G = \Delta H - T\Delta S$. Note that the $\Delta G°$ that will be computed is really $\Delta G_f°$. At standard conditions, T = 298 K, and all quantities are 1.0 mol. Then:

$$\Delta G° = -20.2 \times 10^3 \text{ J} - (298 \text{ K})(+43.1 \text{ J/K})$$
$$= -33{,}908 \text{ J} = -33.9 \text{ kJ}$$

B. Since the sign of ΔG is negative, this reaction is spontaneous as written.

Example 1.45

At 1,500°C,

$$CO(g) + 2H_2(g) \rightleftharpoons CH_3OH(g)$$

and $K_p = 1.4 \times 10^{-7}$.

A. Compute ΔG for this reaction.

B. State whether the reaction is spontaneous.

Solution:

A. Use $\Delta G = -RT \ln K_p$. Then:

$$\Delta G = -(8.31 \text{ J/K} \cdot \text{mol})(1773 \text{ K}) \ln (1.4 \times 10^{-7})$$
$$= 233 \text{ kJ/mol}$$

B. Since the sign of ΔG is positive, this reaction is *not* spontaneous as written.

1.11 Electrochemistry

Basic Concept

One category of chemical reactions described briefly in Section 1.4 is oxidation-reduction reactions, or "red-ox" reactions for short. Recall the following criteria for each:

Oxidation	Reduction
▪ Loss of electrons	▪ Gain of electrons
▪ Gain of oxygen atoms	▪ Loss of oxygen atoms
▪ Loss of hydrogen atoms	▪ Gain of hydrogen atoms

If two different metals are placed in physical contact with their respective ionic solutions, and are then connected by a suitable conductor but separated by a salt bridge, forming a closed circuit, a potential difference or voltage and current flow are observed (see Figure 1.2 on page 51). This arrangement is known as an **electrochemical cell,** and the underlying electrochemical reaction involves simultaneous oxidation and reduction. Electrochemical cells are the basis of operation of all batteries. If the reaction and current flow are spontaneous, as in any battery, the cell is called a **voltaic** or **galvanic cell.** If, instead, electrical energy must be supplied, the cell is called an **electrolytic cell,** and the process is known as **electrolysis.**

An electrochemical cell is comprised of two **half-cells.** In one, called the **anode, oxidation** occurs; in the other, called the **cathode, reduction** occurs. Each reaction is called a **half-reaction.** The sum of the two half-reactions is the overall or net reaction. The rusting of iron or the corrosion of any metal involves an oxidation-reduction process, with a net electrolytic potential.

Units of measurement commonly used in electrochemistry include the volt (V), the electron volt (eV), the coulomb (C), and the ampere (A).

The Nernst Equation

The law describing the relationship between the concentrations of ionic solutions and the voltage produced in the net reaction is called the **Nernst equation** and is expressed as follows:

$$E_{\text{net}} = E_{\text{net}}° - \frac{RT}{nF} \ln Q \qquad [1.61]$$

where R = the gas constant = 8.31 J/K · mol,

T = the absolute temperature in kelvins,

F = the Faraday constant = 96,485 C/mol electrons,

n = the number of moles of electrons transferred per unit reaction,

Q = the ratio of molar concentrations of products to molar concentrations of reactants, for all (aq) or (g) species in solution [(s) or (l) species are excluded].

For the condition where T = 25°C = 298 K, and $\ln Q = 2.303 \log Q$, the Nernst equation can be simplified to:

$$E_{\text{net}} = E_{\text{net}}° - \frac{0.059}{n} \log Q \qquad [1.62]$$

Since 1 volt = 1 joule per coulomb and 1 ampere = 1 coulomb per second:

(current in amperes)(time in seconds)
= total charge transferred in coulombs

Also:

(potential in volts)(charge in coulombs)
= total energy produced or used in joules

Tables exist that present the reduction reactions of metals, along with selected nonmetals, and their corresponding potentials, relative to the standard hydrogen electrode, whose reduction potential is taken as zero. More extensive tables include reduction potentials organized separately, according to acidic and alkaline conditions. It is important to note that reduction reactions and potentials depend on the pH of solution, as well as the presence of any complexing agents. This listing is often referred to as the **electromotive series,** and the reduction potentials given are the $E°$ values in volts. If the E^0 value listed is positive, the reaction is spontaneous as written. If negative, the reverse reaction is spontaneous. The superscript zero refers to standard conditions, that is, a temperature of 25°C, a concentration of 1.00 M for any ionic solution, and a partial pressure of 1.00 atmosphere for any gas present.

The listing is also referred to as the **activity series** of metals, since they indicate which metal is more likely, relative to another, to release its electrons, oxidize, and react. For example, the metal lithium has the highest *negative* $E°$ value, −3.045 volt, while magnesium has an $E°$ value of −2.363 volt. Therefore, elemental lithium will oxidize and react more easily than elemental magnesium. The nonmetal fluorine has the highest *positive* $E°$ value, +2.87 volts, is easiest to reduce, and is the most electronegative element. In other words, a large negative $E°$ value means that the reactant is a good reducing agent, and a large positive $E°$ value indicates a good oxidizing agent.

Table 1.3 lists standard reduction potentials at 25°C for a number of half-cell reactions.

Table 1.3 Standard Reduction Potentials at 25°C

E° (volts)	*Half-Cell Reaction*
+2.87	$F_2(g) + 2e^- \rightleftharpoons 2F^-(aq)$
+2.08	$O_3(g) + 2H^+(aq) + 2e^- \rightleftharpoons O_2(g) + H_2O$
+2.05	$S_2O_8^{2-}(aq) + 2e^- \rightleftharpoons 2SO_4^{2-}(aq)$
+1.82	$Co^{3+}(aq) + e^- \rightleftharpoons Co^{2+}(aq)$
+1.77	$H_2O_2(aq) + 2H^+(aq) + 2e^- \rightleftharpoons 2H_2O$
+1.695	$MnO_4^-(aq) + 4H^+(aq) + 3e^- \rightleftharpoons MnO_2(s) + 2H_2O$
+1.69	$PbO_2(s) + SO_4^{2-}(aq) + 4H^+(aq) + 2e^- \rightleftharpoons PbSO_4(s) + 2H_2O$
+1.63	$2HOCl(aq) + 2H^+(aq) + 2e^- \rightleftharpoons Cl_2(g) + 2H_2O$
+1.51	$Mn^{3+}(aq) + e^- \rightleftharpoons Mn^{2+}(aq)$
+1.49	$MnO_4^-(aq) + 8H^+(aq) + 5e^- \rightleftharpoons Mn^{2+}(aq) + 4H_2O$
+1.46	$PbO_2(s) + 4H^+(aq) + 2e^- \rightleftharpoons Pb^{2+}(aq) + 2H_2O$
+1.44	$BrO_3^-(aq) + 6H^+(aq) + 6e^- \rightleftharpoons Br^-(aq) + 3H_2O$
+1.42	$Au^{3+}(aq) + 3e^- \rightleftharpoons Au(s)$
+1.36	$Cl_2(g) + 2e^- \rightleftharpoons 2Cl^-(aq)$
+1.33	$Cr_2O_7^{2-}(aq) + 14H^+(aq) + 6e^- \rightleftharpoons 2Cr^{3+}(aq) + 7H_2O$
+1.24	$O_3(g) + H_2O + 2e^- \rightleftharpoons O_2(g) + 2OH^-(aq)$
+1.23	$MnO_2(s) + 4H^+(aq) + 2e^- \rightleftharpoons Mn^{2+}(aq) + 2H_2O$
+1.23	$O_2(g) + 4H^+(aq) + 4e^- \rightleftharpoons 2H_2O$
+1.20	$Pt^{2+}(aq) + 2e^- \rightleftharpoons Pt(s)$
+1.07	$Br_2(aq) + 2e^- \rightleftharpoons 2Br^-(aq)$
+0.96	$NO_3^-(aq) + 4H^+(aq) + 3e^- \rightleftharpoons NO(g) + 2H_2O$
+0.94	$NO_3^-(aq) + 3H^+(aq) + 2e^- \rightleftharpoons HNO_2(aq) + H_2O$
+0.91	$2Hg^{2+}(aq) + 2e^- \rightleftharpoons Hg_2^{2+}(aq)$
+0.87	$HO_2^-(aq) + H_2O + 2e^- \rightleftharpoons 3OH^-(aq)$
+0.80	$NO_3^-(aq) + 4H^+(aq) + 2e^- \rightleftharpoons 2NO_2(g) + 2H_2O$
+0.80	$Ag^+(aq) + e^- \rightleftharpoons Ag(s)$
+0.77	$Fe^{3+}(aq) + e^- \rightleftharpoons Fe^{2+}(aq)$
+0.69	$O_2(g) + 2H^+(aq) + 2e^- \rightleftharpoons H_2O_2(aq)$
+0.54	$I_2(s) + 2e^- \rightleftharpoons 2I^-(aq)$
+0.49	$NiO_2(s) + 2H_2O + 2e^- \rightleftharpoons Ni(OH)_2(s) + 2OH^-(aq)$
+0.45	$SO_2(aq) + 4H^+(aq) + 4e^- \rightleftharpoons S(s) + 2H_2O$
+0.401	$O_2(g) + 2H_2O + 4e^- \rightleftharpoons 4OH^-(aq)$
+0.34	$Cu^{2+}(aq) + 2e^- \rightleftharpoons Cu(s)$

Table 1.3 Standard Reduction Potentials at 25°C (Continued)

E° (volts)	*Half-Cell Reaction*
+0.27	$Hg_2Cl_2(s) + 2e^- \rightleftharpoons 2Hg(l) + 2Cl^-(aq)$
+0.25	$PbO_2(s) + H_2O + 2e^- \rightleftharpoons PbO(s) + 2OH^-(aq)$
+0.2223	$AgCl(s) + e^- \rightleftharpoons Ag(s) + Cl^-(aq)$
+0.172	$SO_4^{2-}(aq) + 4H^+(aq) + 2e^- \rightleftharpoons H_2SO_3(aq) + H_2O$
+0.169	$S_4O_6^{2-}(aq) + 2e^- \rightleftharpoons 2S_2O_3^{2-}(aq)$
+0.16	$Cu^{2+}(aq) + e^- \rightleftharpoons Cu^+(aq)$
+0.15	$Sn^{4+}(aq) + 2e^- \rightleftharpoons Sn^{2+}(aq)$
+0.14	$S(s) + 2H^+(aq) + 2e^- \rightleftharpoons H_2S(g)$
+0.07	$AgBr(s) + e^- \rightleftharpoons Ag(s) + Br^-(aq)$
0.00	$2H^+(aq) + 2e^- \rightleftharpoons H_2(g)$
−0.13	$Pb^{2+}(aq) + 2e^- \rightleftharpoons Pb(s)$
−0.14	$Sn^{2+}(aq) + 2e^- \rightleftharpoons Sn(s)$
−0.15	$AgI(s) + e^- \rightleftharpoons Ag(s) + I^-(aq)$
−0.25	$Ni^{2+}(aq) + 2e^- \rightleftharpoons Ni(s)$
−0.28	$Co^{2+}(aq) + 2e^- \rightleftharpoons Co(s)$
−0.34	$In^{3+}(aq) + 3e^- \rightleftharpoons In(s)$
−0.34	$Tl^+(aq) + e^- \rightleftharpoons Tl(s)$
−0.36	$PbSO_4(s) + 2e^- \rightleftharpoons Pb(s) + SO_4^{2-}(aq)$
−0.40	$Cd^{2+}(aq) + 2e^- \rightleftharpoons Cd(s)$
−0.44	$Fe^{2+}(aq) + 2e^- \rightleftharpoons Fe(s)$
−0.56	$Ga^{3+}(aq) + 3e^- \rightleftharpoons Ga(s)$
−0.58	$PbO(s) + H_2O + 2e^- \rightleftharpoons Pb(s) + 2OH^-(aq)$
−0.74	$Cr^{3+}(aq) + 3e^- \rightleftharpoons Cr(s)$
−0.76	$Zn^{2+}(aq) + 2e^- \rightleftharpoons Zn(s)$
−0.81	$Cd(OH)_2(s) + 2e^- \rightleftharpoons Cd(s) + 2OH^-(aq)$
−0.83	$2H_2O + 2e^- \rightleftharpoons H_2(g) + 2OH^-(aq)$
−0.88	$Fe(OH)_2(s) + 2e^- \rightleftharpoons Fe(s) + 2OH^-(aq)$
−0.91	$Cr^{2+}(aq) + e^- \rightleftharpoons Cr(s)$
−1.16	$N_2(g) + 4H_2O + 4e^- \rightleftharpoons N_2O_4(aq) + 4OH^-(aq)$
−1.18	$V^{2+}(aq) + 2e^- \rightleftharpoons V(s)$
−1.216	$ZnO_2^-(aq) + 2H_2O + 2e^- \rightleftharpoons Zn(s) + 4OH^-(aq)$
−1.63	$Ti^{2+}(aq) + 2e^- \rightleftharpoons Ti(s)$
−1.66	$Al^{3+}(aq) + 3e^- \rightleftharpoons Al(s)$
−1.79	$U^{3+}(aq) + 3e^- \rightleftharpoons U(s)$
−2.02	$Sc^{3+}(aq) + 3e^- \rightleftharpoons Sc(s)$
−2.36	$La^{3+}(aq) + 3e^- \rightleftharpoons La(s)$
−2.37	$Y^{3+}(aq) + 3e^- \rightleftharpoons Y(s)$
−2.37	$Mg^{2+}(aq) + 2e^- \rightleftharpoons Mg(s)$
−2.71	$Na^+(aq) + e^- \rightleftharpoons Na(s)$
−2.76	$Ca^{2+}(aq) + 2e^- \rightleftharpoons Ca(s)$
−2.89	$Sr^{2+}(aq) + 2e^- \rightleftharpoons Sr(s)$
−2.90	$Ba^{2+}(aq) + 2e^- \rightleftharpoons Ba(s)$
−2.92	$Cs^+(aq) + e^- \rightleftharpoons Cs(s)$
−2.92	$K^+(aq) + e^- \rightleftharpoons K(s)$
−2.93	$Rb^+(aq) + e^- \rightleftharpoons Rb(s)$
−3.05	$Li^+(aq) + e^- \rightleftharpoons Li(s)$

A Simple Electrochemical Cell

Consider the copper/zinc electrochemical cell in Figure 1.2.

In the left half-cell, the **cathode,** Cu^{2+} ions in solution are being reduced to Cu^0, indicating copper metal or solid. In the right half-cell, the **anode,** Zn^0 is being oxidized to Zn^{2+} ions dissolved in solution. The anions—$SO_4^{2-}(aq)$—are spectator ions and do not participate in the reaction. The salt bridge is necessary to maintain electrical neutrality and retard polarization.

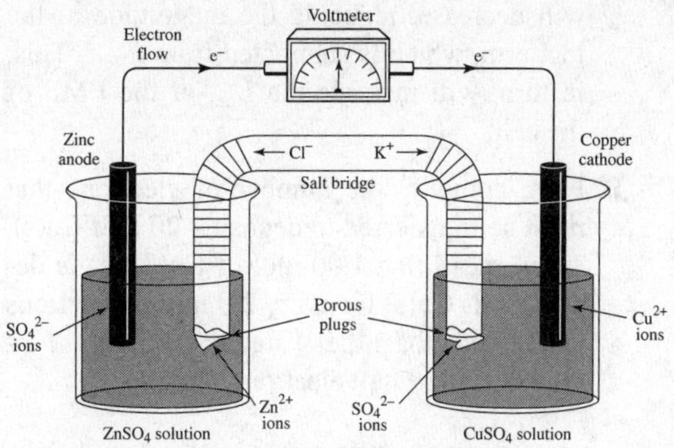

Figure 1.2. Electrochemical cell

The short-hand notation for this cell is as follows:

$$Zn(s)\,|\,ZnSO_4(aq)(1.00\text{ M})\,\|\,CuSO_4(aq)(1.00\text{ M})\,|\,Cu(s) \quad [1.63]$$

It is understood that the anode cell, where oxidation occurs, is written first and is separated by a double vertical line from the cathode cell, where reduction occurs. Single vertical lines separate the solid electrode from the aqueous solution into which it is placed. Concentrations of the solutions are expressed in parentheses.

The two half-reactions, followed by the net (algebraic sum) reaction, can be written as follows:

$$Cu^{2+}(aq) + 2e- \rightarrow Cu^0(s)\ E° = 0.337\text{ V} \quad [1.64]$$

$$Zn^0(s) \rightarrow Zn^{2+}(aq) + 2e-\ E° = 0.763\text{ V} \quad [1.65]$$

$$Cu^{2+}(aq) + Zn^0(s) \rightarrow Cu^0(s) + Zn^{2+}(aq)\ E_{net}° = 1.100\text{ V} \quad [1.66]$$

Note that the electrons exactly cancel each other in the two half-reactions, and do not appear in the net reaction. If this does not happen automatically, one or both of the half-reactions must be multiplied by a suitable coefficient (integer) or coefficients to obtain exact cancellation of electrons. Note also that the positive value (understood) for $E_{net}°$ indicates that this reaction proceeds spontaneously and produces 1.100 volts under standard conditions.

Useful Quantitative Relationships

1 mole of electrons (e^-) = 96,485 coulombs (C) [1.67]

charge (c) = current (C/sec) × time (sec) [1.68]

1 ampere (A) = 1 coulomb/1 second [1.69]

1 volt (V) = 1 joule (J)/1 coulomb [1.70]

Faraday constant F = 96,485 coulombs/mole e^- [1.71]

Gas constant R = 8.31 joules/kelvin · mole [1.72]

Number of moles of e^- = current × time/F [1.73]

Example 1.46

Consider the electrochemical cell with the following net reaction, which is observed to proceed spontaneously. All species are in their standard states, and T = 25°C.

$$Mg(s) + Sn^{2+}(aq) \rightarrow Mg^{2+}(aq) + Sn(s)$$

A. Write the two half-reactions with their respective $E°$ values.
B. Indicate which species is oxidized and which is reduced.
C. Identify the anode and cathode.
D. Compute $E_{net}°$.
E. Confirm that the reaction proceeds spontaneously.

Solution:

A. $Mg(s) \rightarrow Mg^{2+}(aq) + 2e^-$ $\quad E° = 2.370$ V

$Sn^{2+}(aq) + 2e^- \rightarrow Sn(s)$ $\quad E° = -0.140$ V

B. Mg(s) is oxidized to Mg^{2+}, while Sn^{2+} is reduced to Sn(s).
C. The anode is the electrode where oxidation takes place, while the cathode is the electrode where reduction takes place. Since Mg is oxidized, the half-cell containing the Mg electrode and $Mg^{2+}(aq)$ solution must be the anode (whatever the anion may be). Similarly, the cathode is the half-cell containing the Sn electrode dipping into $Sn^{2+}(aq)$ solution.
D. Adding the two half-cell potentials determined in part **a** gives $E_{net}°$ = 2.230 V.
E. Since $E_{net}°$ is a positive number, the net reaction must proceed spontaneously.

Example 1.47

Consider the reaction in Example 1.46. Instead of standard conditions of 1.00 M concentrations for each solution, assume now that the $Mg^{2+}(aq)$ solution is 0.85 M and that the $Sn^{2+}(aq)$ solution is 0.015 M. Find the $E_{net}°$ under these conditions, assuming T = 25°C.

Solution:

Since nonstandard conditions exist, the Nernst equation applies. However, use the simplified version of this equation, equation 1.60, since T = 25°C.

$$E_{net} = E_{net}° - \frac{0.059}{n} \log Q$$

In this case, $n = 2$, since 2 mol of electrons are exchanged in the *net* reaction.

Also:

$$Q = \frac{[Mg^{2+}(aq)]}{[Sn^{2+}(aq)]} = \frac{0.85 \text{ M}}{0.015 \text{ M}}$$

by checking the *net* reaction

$E_{net}°$ was calculated in part **d** of Example 1.46 as 2.230 V. Substituting gives:

$$E_{net} = 2.230 \text{ V} - \frac{0.059}{2} \log \frac{0.85 \text{ M}}{0.015 \text{ M}}$$

$$= 2.178 \text{ V}$$

Example 1.48

Compute the Gibbs free energy change, ΔG, for the cell in Example 1.47.

Solution:

$$\Delta G = -nFE_{net}$$

$$= -(2 \text{ mol e}^-)(96{,}485 \text{ C/mol e}^-)(2.178 \text{ V})$$

$$= -420,290 \text{ J or } -420.3 \text{ kJ}$$

Example 1.49

Consider the following cell reaction, in which all species are at standard-state conditions:

$$Cu^{2+}(aq) + H_2(g) \rightarrow Cu(s) + 2H^+(aq)$$

A. Predict the effect on the EMF (electromotive force) of this cell of adding NaOH solution to the hydrogen half-cell until the pH = 7.

B. Compute the number of coulombs required to deposit 4.20 g of Cu(s) in the copper half-cell.

C. How long in seconds will this deposition take if the measured current is 4.0 A?

Solution:

A. Refer to the simplified Nernst equation, (equation 1.60). The EMF is the E_{net}.

$$E_{net} = E_{net}° - \frac{0.059}{2} \log \frac{[H^+]^2}{[Cu^{2+}]}$$

If NaOH(aq) is added, H^+ ions (aq) will be neutralized, thereby raising the pH. $[H^+(aq)]$ will decrease, reducing the magnitude of the log term, which is subtracted from $E_{net}°$. This, in turn, will increase the E_{net} or the EMF of the cell.

B. First, compute the number of electrons that must be transferred to deposit 4.20 g of Cu(s). Then, recall that 1.00 mol of Cu^{2+}(aq) is deposited as Cu(s) for every 2.0 mol of electrons used, and that the Faraday constant F = 96,485 C/1.00 mol electrons. Thus:

$$4.20 \text{ g Cu(s)} \left(\frac{1.00 \text{ mol Cu}}{63.5 \text{ g Cu}}\right) = 0.06614 \text{ mol Cu(s) deposited}$$

$$0.06614 \text{ mol Cu(s)} \left(\frac{2 \text{ mol e}^-}{1.00 \text{ mol Cu(s)}}\right) = 0.1323 \text{ mol e}^-$$

$$0.1323 \text{ mol e}^- \left(\frac{96{,}485 \text{ C}}{1.00 \text{ mol e}^-}\right) = 1.28 \times 10^4 \text{ C}$$

C. $$\text{time, } t \text{ (sec)} = \frac{\text{charge (C)}}{\text{current (C/sec)}}$$

$$= \frac{1.28 \times 10^4 \text{ C}}{4.0 \text{ A}}$$

$$= 3.2 \times 10^3 \text{ sec}$$

This is about 10 hr.

1.12 Organic Chemistry

Basic Concept

Organic chemistry is the chemistry of carbon and its compounds. Carbon has the ability to bond to itself as well as to other elements including hydrogen, oxygen, nitrogen, sulfur, fluorine, chlorine, bromine, and iodine. The number of catalogued organic compounds (natural plus synthetic) is in the millions and rapidly expanding. In this section, the rules for the structures of simple organic compounds and the associated rules for nomenclature are outlined.

Hydrocarbons

Hydrocarbons are the simplest class of organic compounds and contain only carbon and hydrogen. Their classical names form the basis for naming more complex organic compounds. Carbon normally makes four covalent bonds. Compounds for which all possible carbon bonds contain hydrogen are called **alkanes** or **saturated hydrocarbons. Unsaturated hydrocarbons** contain one or more carbon-carbon double bonds or triple bonds, or **aromatic** (benzene-based) bonds. In general, unsaturated hydrocarbons are more reactive (by saturating or reducing agents) than their saturated counterparts.

The solubility of alkanes is related to the nonpolar nature of their molecules. Alkanes are water insoluble. Water molecules are polar and are bonded to one another by strong **hydrogen bonds.** Alkane molecules are nonpolar and are bonded by weak intermolecular **dispersion forces** (e.g., **London forces** and **van der Waals forces**). Therefore, alkane molecules are not readily attracted by water molecules and cannot become part of the water structure (an irregular but generally hexagonal network). This fact demonstrates the general solubility principle of **like dissolves like.** Because most alkanes have densities less than the density of water, these compounds usually float on top.

The structure of normal (*n*) or straight-chain alkanes is shown below. The chemical formula for alkanes is C_nH_{2n+2}.

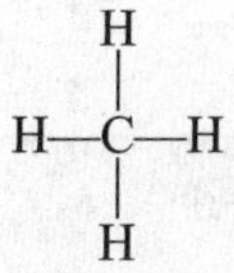

Methane, CH_4

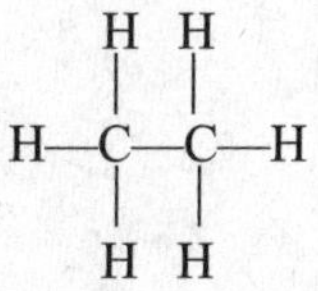

Ethane, C_2H_6

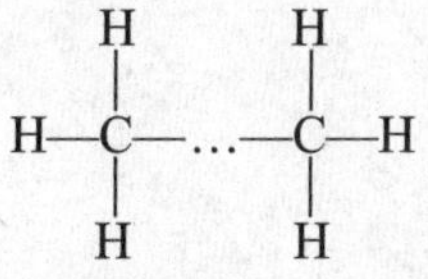

A general alkane structure

Table 1.4 lists formulas and properties for the first 10 hydrocarbons, known as the **homologous series,** along with the C_{20} and C_{30} hydrocarbons.

Alkanes can also be branched-chain hydrocarbons, which can form numerous isomers. **Isomers** are substances with the same chemical formula but different structural formulas, giving rise to different chemical and physical properties. To determine whether two compounds are isomers of each other, count the number of carbon atoms, hydrogen atoms, and any other type of atom present in each compound. If the numbers of each type of atom in the two compounds are equal, the compounds are isomers. The C_{20} hydrocarbon (eicosane), for example, has over 366,000 isomers.

The analogous series consists of hydrocarbons with one double bond; these are called **alkenes** and have the general formula C_nH_{2n}. Hydrocarbons with one triple bond are called **alkynes** and have the general formula C_nH_{2n-2}.

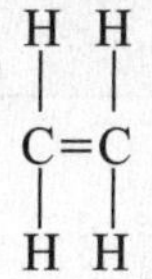

Ethylene or ethene, C_2H_4

$H{-}C{\equiv}C{-}H$ Acetylene or ethyne, C_2H_2

Many organic compounds have common names that were assigned before the formal system of nomenclature, called the **IUPAC system,** was developed in 1960. The following rules now apply to the naming of organic compounds:

1. Select the longest continuous chain of carbon atoms.
2. Number the carbon atoms in this chain, beginning with the end nearest a branch.
3. Assign the names and (position) numbers that indicate the branches of substituents (i.e., functional groups, including "-ene" for double bond and "-yne" for triple bond). If more than one of the same substituent appears, use Greek prefixes (di, tri, tetra, etc.). See Table 1.6, page 56, for the names of specific functional groups.
4. Number the longest continuous chain in such a way so that the substituents have the lowest possible numbers.

Example 1.50

Using the IUPAC system, name the three isomers of pentane and draw their structures.

Solution:

The three isomers of pentane are drawn below and labeled with both their common and IUPAC names.

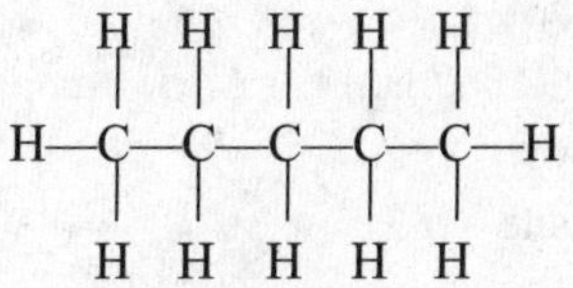

Normal pentane (C_5H_{12})

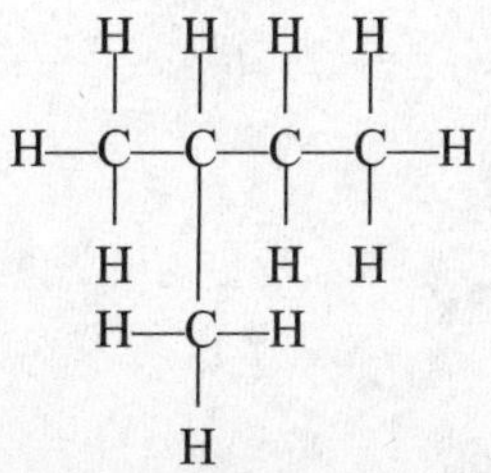

Isopentane 2-Methylbutane (C_5H_{12})

Table 1.4 The Homologous Series for Alkanes

Alkanes and Their Properties					
Name	*Molecular Formula*	*Condensed Formula*	*Melting Point (°C)*	*Boiling Point (°C)*	*State at 25°C*
Methane	CH_4	CH_4	−183	−162	Gas
Ethane	C_2H_6	CH_3CH_3	−172	−88	Gas
Propane	C_3H_8	$CH_3CH_2CH_3$	−188	−42	Gas
Butane	C_4H_{10}	$CH_3(CH_2)_2CH_3$*	−138	−0.5	Gas
Pentane	C_5H_{12}	$CH_3(CH_2)_3CH_3$	−130	36	Liquid
Hexane	C_6H_{14}	$CH_3(CH_2)_4CH_3$	−94	69	Liquid
Heptane	C_7H_{16}	$CH_3(CH_2)_5CH_3$	−91	98	Liquid
Octane	C_8H_{18}	$CH_3(CH_2)_6CH_3$	−57	126	Liquid
Nonane	C_9H_{20}	$CH_3(CH_2)_7CH_3$	−54	151	Liquid
Decane	$C_{10}H_{22}$	$CH_3(CH_2)_8CH_3$	−30	174	Liquid
Eicosane	$C_{20}H_{42}$	$CH_3(CH_2)_{18}CH_3$	36	343	Solid
Triacontane	$C_{30}H_{62}$	$CH_3(CH_2)_{28}CH_3$	66	446	Solid

*A condensed way to write the formulas of long alkane chains is to enclose CH_2 in parentheses and indicate the number of CH_2 units that occur in the chain as a subscript to the parentheses.

Table 1.5 Cyclic Hydrocarbons

Structural Formulas and Symbols for Common Cycloalkanes		
Name	*Structural Formula*	*Symbol*
Cyclopropane	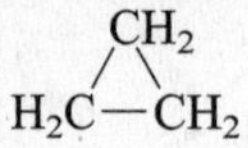	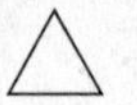
Cyclobutane	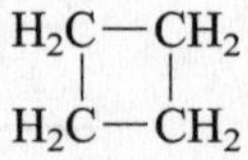	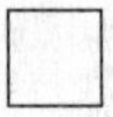
Cyclopentane	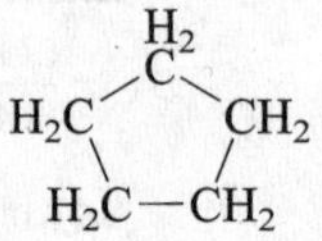	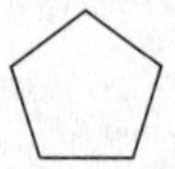
Cyclohexane	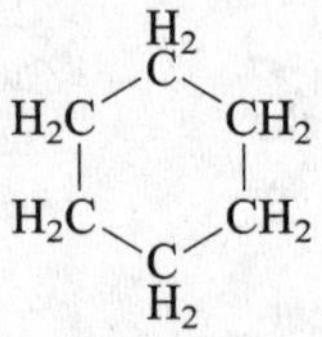	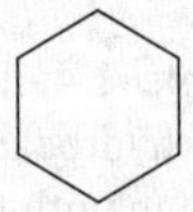
Cycloheptane	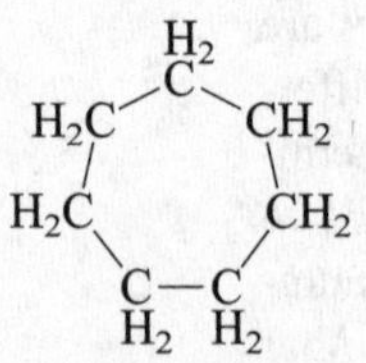	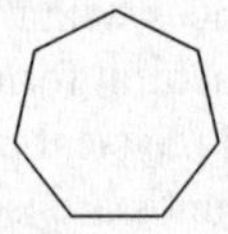
Cyclooctane	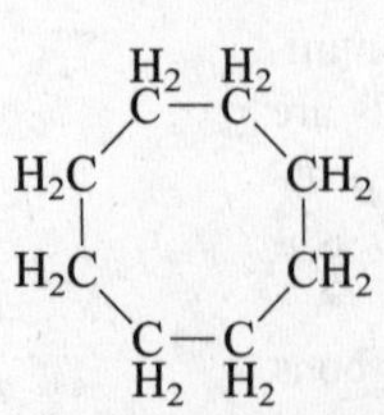	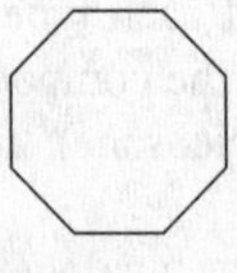

Benzene exhibits resonance.

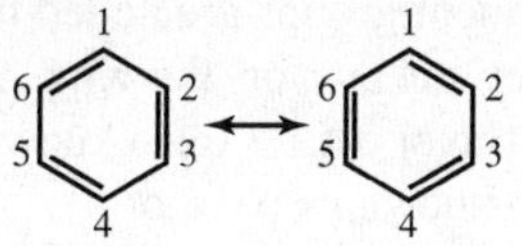

I II

In 1,2-dichlorobenzene, the two chlorine atoms are bonded to adjacent carbon atoms. In 1,3-dichlorobenzene, the two chlorine atoms are bonded to carbon atoms separated by one carbon atom, and in 1,4-dichlorobenzene the two chlorine atoms are separated by two carbon atoms.

Three prefixes, ortho, meta, and para, may be used to designate the position of groups. Ortho, or just *o,* means 1,2 disubstituted; meta, or *m,* means 1,3 disubstituted; and para, or *p,* means 1,4 disubstituted. Consider the following:

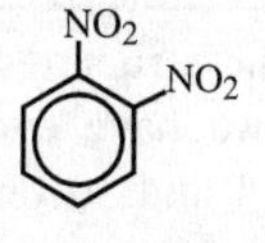

1,2-Dinitrobenzene
Orthodinitrobenzene
o-Dinitrobenzene

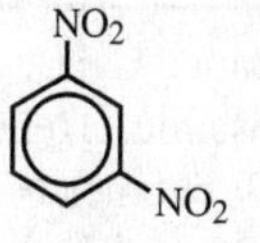

1,3-Dinitrobenzene
Metadinitrobenzene
m-Dinitrobenzene

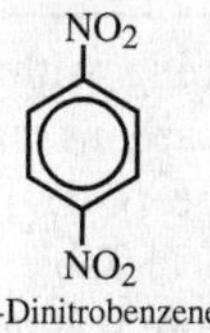

1,4-Dinitrobenzene
Paradinitrobenzene
p-Dinitrobenzene

In a toluene molecule, a methyl group replaces a hydrogen atom on the benzene ring. Any alkyl group can bond to the ring. If an ethyl group substitutes for a hydrogen atom in benzene, then ethylbenzene results.

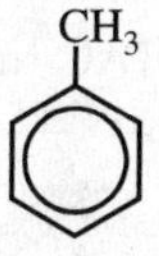

Toluene

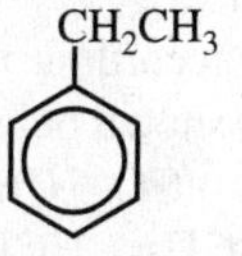

Ethylbenzene

Many aromatic compounds contain a functional group substituted for a hydrogen atom on the benzene ring. Consider each of the following:

Chlorobenzene

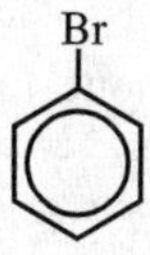

Bromobenzene

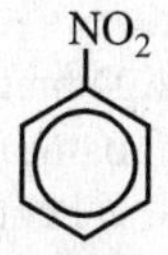

Nitrobenzene

Phenol

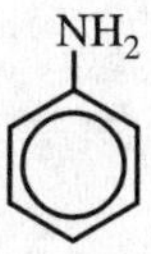

Aniline

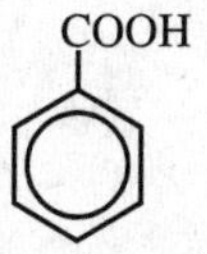

Benzoic acid

Benzaldehyde

On occasion, it is necessary to consider the benzene ring as a substituent group bonded to a chain or ring. If a hydrogen atom is removed from benzene, a phenyl group, C_6H_5—, results.

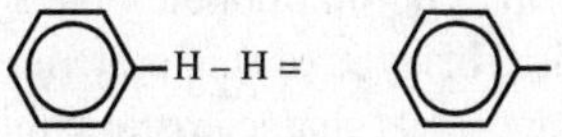

Benzene, C_6H_6 Phenyl group, C_6H_5—

Disubstituted benzenes can have three structural isomers. For example, the three isomers of dichlorobenzene are:

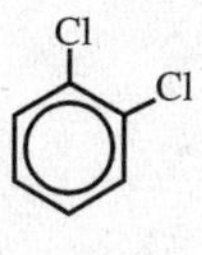

1,2-Dichlorobenzene

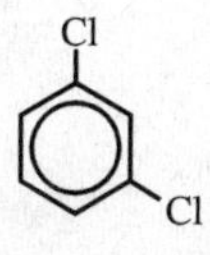

1,3-Dichlorobenzene

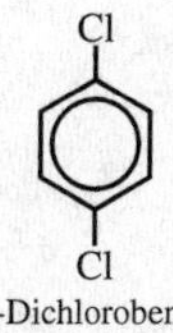

1,4-Dichlorobenzene

An example of a compound that contains a phenyl group is 3-phenylhexane.

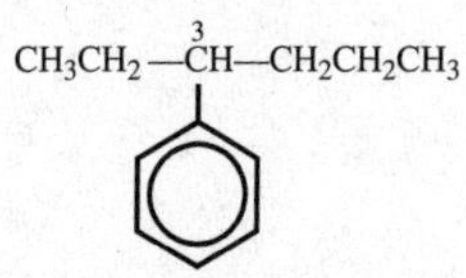

3-Phenylhexane

Figure 1.3 Aromatic hydrocarbons

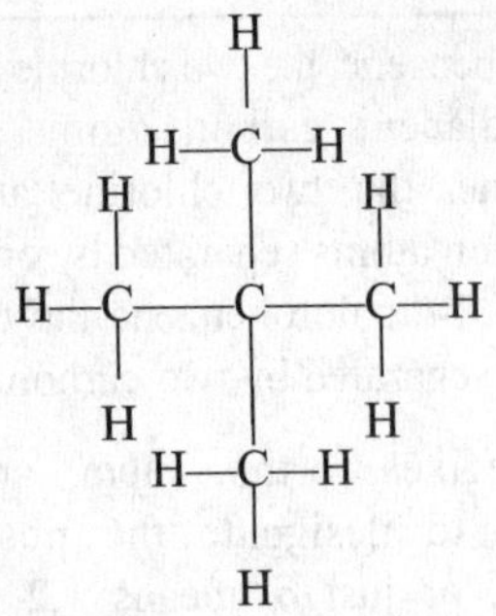

Neopentane 2,2-Dimethylpropane (C_5H_{12})

Cyclic Hydrocarbons

Beginning with propane, C_3H_8, cyclic structures of hydrocarbons are possible. Hence, we have cyclopropane (C_3H_6), cyclobutane, (C_4H_8), and so on as shown in Table 1.5. Ringed hydrocarbons are generally more reactive (because of ring tension) than their straight or branched-chain counterparts.

Aromatic Hydrocarbons

Compounds containing a benzene ring, C_6H_6, are classified as aromatic. The benzene ring, shown in Figure 1.3, has a system of alternating single and double bonds. Benzene has interesting properties. Even with three double bonds, benzene undergoes, not addition, but rather substitution, because it is relatively unreactive. It forms compounds such as toluene and monochloro-, dichloro-, and trichlorobenzene. The six carbon-carbon bonds are all equal and are hybrids of single and double bonds. They are longer than normal double bonds but shorter than single bonds. This type of ring system exhibits **resonance,** which gives it its characteristic stability.

For nomenclature purposes each of the six carbon atoms in the benzene ring is assigned a number, 1–6, in clockwise fashion. Common aromatic compounds—benzene derivatives—with their common names and IUPAC names are shown in Figure 1.3. When substituent groups are added two at a time, the positions they occupy on the ring may be 1,2 (also known as **ortho** or ***o***); 1,3 (also known as **meta** or ***m***); and 1,4 (also known as **para** or ***p***).

Functional Groups

When hydrogen atoms are replaced by certain other atoms, functional groups are formed. These functional groups give rise to discrete chemical and physical properties. The names of these functional groups, along with their structures, are listed in Table 1.6.

Example 1.51

Name, according to IUPAC rules, the four compounds shown below.

A. $CH_3—CO—CH_3$

B. $CH_3CH{=}CHCH_2CH_3$

C. $CH_3CH{=}C(Cl)CH(Cl)CH_3$

D. $CH_3CHOHCH_3$

Solution:

A. Dimethyl ketone (also acetone, the common name)

B. 2-Pentene

C. 3,4 Dichloro-2-pentene

D. 2-Propanol (also isopropanol, the common name)

Table 1.6 Functional Groups

Classes and Functional Groups of Organic Compounds				
Class	*Functional Group*	*Example of Expanded Structural Formula*	*Example of Condensed Structural Formula*	*Common Name*
Alkane	—	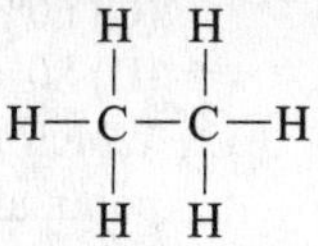	CH_3CH_3	Ethane
Alkene	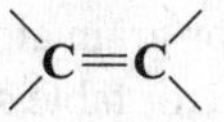	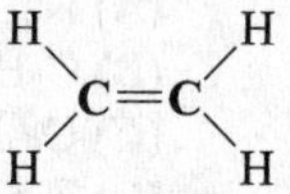	$H_2C{=}CH_2$	Ethylene
Alkyne	—C≡C—	H—C≡C—H	HC≡CH	Acetylene
Aromatic	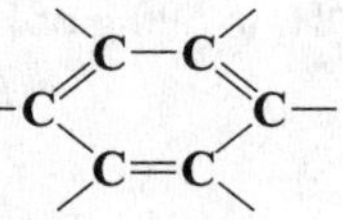	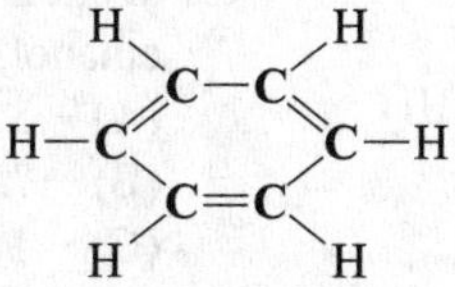		Benzene
Alcohol	**—O—H**	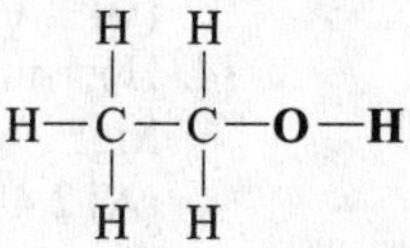	CH_3CH_2—OH	Ethyl alcohol
Ether	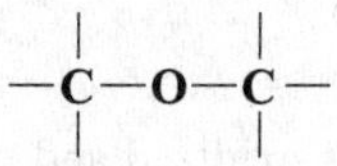	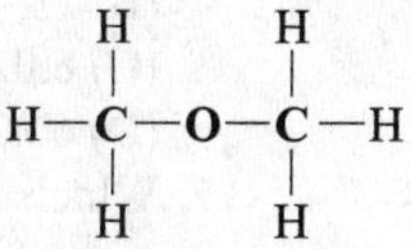	CH_3—O—CH_3	Dimethyl ether
Amine	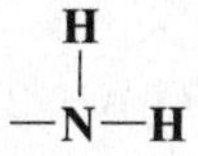	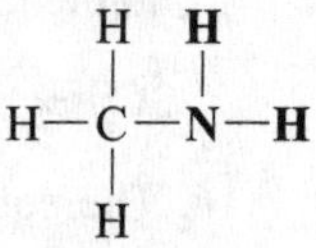	CH_3—NH_2	Methylamine
Aldehyde	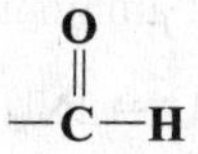	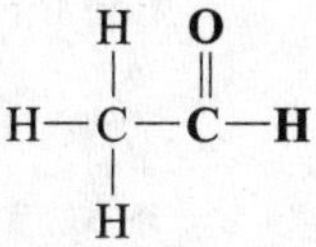	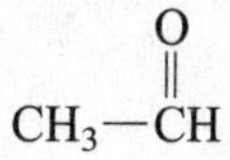	Acetaldehyde
Ketone	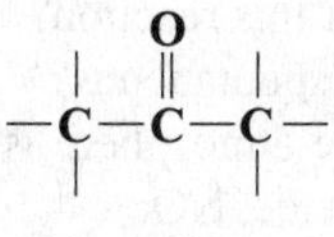	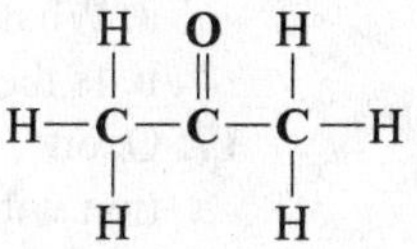	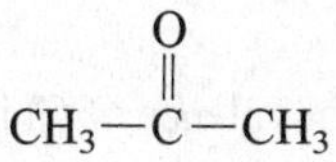	Acetone
Carboxylic acid	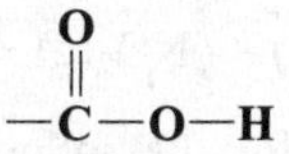	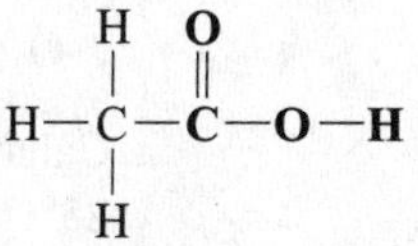	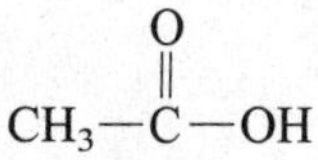	Acetic acid
Ester	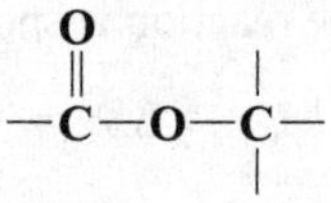	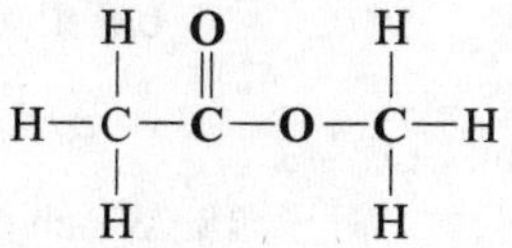	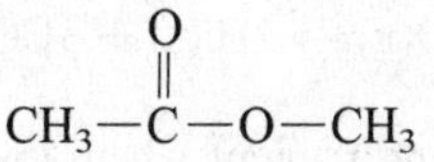	Methyl acetate
Amide	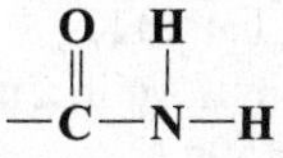	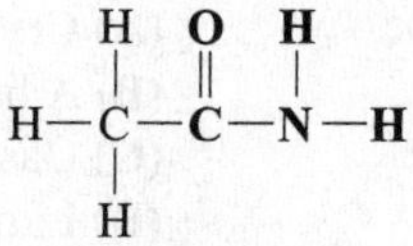	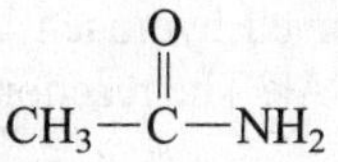	Acetamide
Halide	**—X** (X = F, Cl, Br, I)	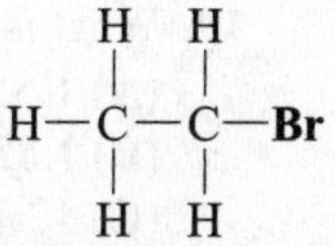	CH_3CH_2—Br	Ethyl bromide

PRACTICE PROBLEMS

1. An element has the electronic configuration $1s^2 2s^2 2p^4$.
   a. How many electrons and protons does one atom of this element have?
   b. Does this atom most likely form a stable cation or anion?
2. Each of the species Cl^-, Ar, K^+, and Ca^{2+} has the same number of
   (A) protons
   (B) electrons
   (C) neutrons
   (D) isotopes
3. The correct chemical formula for chromium(III) oxide is
   (A) CrO
   (B) Cr_3O_2
   (C) Cr_2O_3
   (D) Cr_3O_3
4. What is the correct chemical name for MnO_2?
5. Determine for urea, $CO(NH_2)_2$,
   a. the molar mass
   b. the percent nitrogen by mass
6. Determine the empirical formula of mustard gas, a chemical warfare agent, which has the following percent composition: 30.2% carbon, 5.07% hydrogen, 44.58% chlorine, and 20.16% sulfur.
7. How many atoms are represented in one formula unit of $Ca_3(PO_4)_2$, the main component of bone mass?
   (A) 16
   (B) 13
   (C) 9
   (D) 5
8. The oxidation number or valence of Cl in ClO_3^- is
   (A) +5
   (B) +3
   (C) +1
   (D) −1
9. In this reaction:

$$Fe_2O_3(s) + 3CO(g) \rightarrow 2Fe(s) + 3CO_2(g)$$

   what is the limiting reagent when 45.3 g of CO react with 79.8 g of Fe_2O_3?
10. In excess acid, how much hydrogen gas will be produced with 50 g of Al? The reaction is:

$$2\,Al(s) + 6\,HCl(aq) \rightarrow Al_2Cl_6(aq) + 3\,H_2(g)$$

   (A) 1.85 g
   (B) 3.7 g
   (C) 5.6 g
   (D) 11 g
11. In the reaction of problem 10, if only 4.5 g of H_2 (g) are actually produced, what is the percent yield of the reaction?
   (A) 20%
   (B) 40%
   (C) 60%
   (D) 80%
12. Which aqueous solution has the lowest freezing point, assuming that all are 1.0 molal?
   (A) NaCl (table salt)
   (B) C_2H_5OH (ethanol or grain alcohol)
   (C) $C_{12}H_{22}O_{11}$ (sucrose or table sugar)
   (D) $KAl(SO_4)_2$ (alum)
13. What is the freezing point of a solution of 92 g of ethanol, C_2H_5OH, in 500 g of H_2O?
   (A) −3.72°C
   (B) −7.44°C
   (C) −11.2°C
   (D) −15.0°C
14. How many atoms are represented by 1.0 ng of Mg?
   (A) 2.48×10^{13}
   (B) 1.24×10^{13}
   (C) 6.022×10^{13}
   (D) 6.022×10^{23}
15. Which element is oxidized and which is reduced in the following reaction?

$$3Cu + 8HNO_3 \rightarrow Cu(NO_3)_2 + 2NO + 4H_2O$$

16. The equilibrium constant at 427°C for the reaction for the formation of ammonia:

$$N_2(g) + 3H_2(g) \rightleftharpoons 2NH_3(g)$$

   is $K_p = 9.4 \times 10^{-5}$.
   a. What is ΔG for this reaction?
   b. Is the reaction spontaneous?
17. Ozone, O_3, in the atmosphere is subject to reaction with nitric oxide, NO:

$$O_3(g) + NO(g) \rightarrow NO_2(g) + O_2(g)$$

   a. Calculate $\Delta G°$ for the following reaction at 25°C from the given data.
   b. Tell whether the reaction is spontaneous.

$$\Delta H° = -199 \text{ kJ}, \qquad \Delta S° = -4.1 \text{ J/K}$$

18. Which of the following has the greatest entropy, *S*?
   (A) Crystalline NaCl at 10 K
   (B) A liquid solution of Ag in Cu at 500 K
   (C) Gaseous CH_4 at 500 K
   (D) Liquid He at 4 K
19. What is the pH of a 0.014 M $Ca(OH)_2$ solution?
   (A) 1.55
   (B) 1.85
   (C) 12.15
   (D) 12.45

20. A laboratory technician mixes 400 mL of 0.125 M HCl with 800 mL of 0.050 M HCl. What is the pH of the resulting solution?
(A) 1.12
(B) 2.50
(C) 10.5
(D) 12.2

21. Calculate the molar solubility of PbI_2 in a 0.15 M NaI solution.
(A) 1.3×10^{-3} M
(B) 6.2×10^{-7} M
(C) 3.5×10^{-7} M
(D) 7.9×10^{-9} M

22. Calculate $\Delta H_{RX}°$ for the reaction below from the standard heats of formation given in the table that follows:

$$Ca_3P_2(s) + 6HCl(g) \rightarrow 3CaCl_2(s) + 2PH_3(g)$$

Compound	ΔH^0_f (kJ/mol)
$Ca_3P_2(s)$	−504
$PH_3(g)$	+9
$HCl(g)$	−92
$CaCl_2(s)$	−794

23. a. Calculate $E_{net}°$ for a silver-aluminum cell in which the electrochemical reaction is as follows:

$$Al(s) + 3Ag^+(aq) \rightarrow Al^{3+}(aq) + Ag(s)$$

b. Would increasing $[Al^{3+}]$ increase or decrease the cell EMF?

24. At 160°C, $K_p = 0.750$ for the following decomposition:

$$PCl_5(g) \rightleftharpoons PCl_3(g) + Cl_2(g)$$

When a sample of PCl_5 (g) is introduced into a previously evacuated vessel at an initial partial pressure of 1.00 atm and allowed to reach equilibrium, what will be the partial pressure of PCl_3 (g)?
(A) 0.0569 atm
(B) 0.285 atm
(C) 0.569 atm
(D) 1.00 atm

25. The enzyme aspartase catalyzes the conversion of L-aspartate to fumarate plus ammonium ion. The equilibrium constant $K_c = 7.4 \times 10^{-3}$ at 29°C. ΔH_{RX} for the reaction is 14.40 kcal/mol.
a. Find K_c at the physiologically interesting temperature of 39°C (normal body temperature).
b. Determine ΔG for this reaction at 39°C.
c. Determine ΔS for this reaction at 39°C.

26. K_a for lactic acid, the acid responsible for dental caries, is 1.30×10^{-4}. Calculate, for a 0.200 M solution of lactic acid,
a. the pH
b. the percent ionization

27. Given that K_a for HCN is 4.0×10^{-10}, find the pH of a 0.50 M NaCN solution. [*Hint:* NaCN undergoes hydrolysis, since HCN is a weak acid, and the resulting solution is slightly basic.]
(A) 7.0
(B) 9.4
(C) 10.5
(D) 11.5

28. Will a precipitate form if 1.00 mg of Na_2CrO_4 is added to 225 mL of a 0.00015 M $AgNO_3$(aq) solution? K_{sp} for Ag_2CrO_4 is 1.2×10^{-12}.

29. a. Name the following four compounds using the IUPAC system:

C_6H_{14} $CH_3—O—CH_3$
C_2H_5OH $CH_2{=}CHCH_2CH_3$

b. Which are structural isomers?
c. Which is an unsaturated hydrocarbon?

30. Draw the structures for the following compounds:
a. paradichlorobenzene
b. 4,5-dibromo-2-octene
c. cyclohexanol

Answer Key

1. a. 8 electrons and 8 protons
b. anion
2. B
3. C
4. Manganese(IV) oxide
5. a. 60 g/mol
b. 46.6%
6. $C_4H_8C_{l2}S$
7. B
8. A
9. $Fe_2O_3(s)$
10. C
11. D
12. D
13. B
14. A
15. Cu is oxidized and N (in HNO_3) is reduced
16. a. +53.9 kJ/mol
b. No
17. a. −198 kJ
b. The reaction is spontaneous.
18. C
19. D
20. A
21. C

22. −1,308 kJ/mol

23. a. 2.46 V

b. Decrease

24. C

25. a. 1.60×10^{-2}

b. 2.56×10^3 cal/mol

c. 37.9 cal/K or 37.9 eu

26. a. 2.29

b. 2.54%

27. D

28. No, $Q < K_{sp}$

29. a. *n*-Hexane, dimethyl ether, ethanol or ethyl alcohol, 1-butene

b. Dimethyl ether and ethanol

c. 1-Butene

30. a.

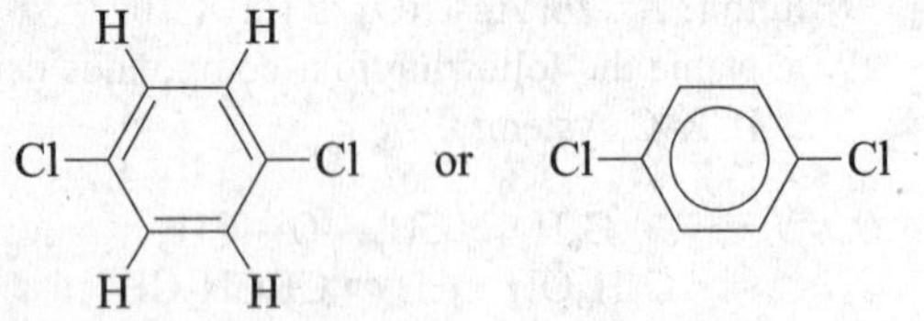

b.

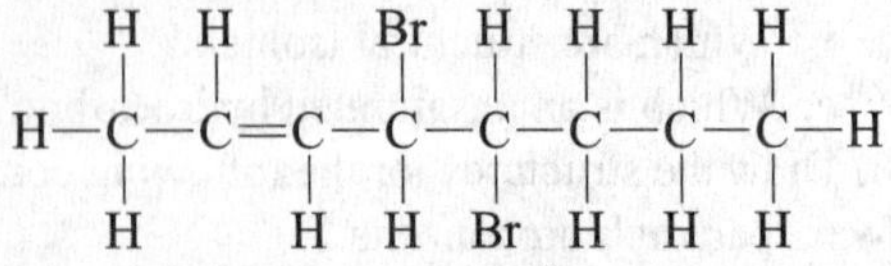

c.

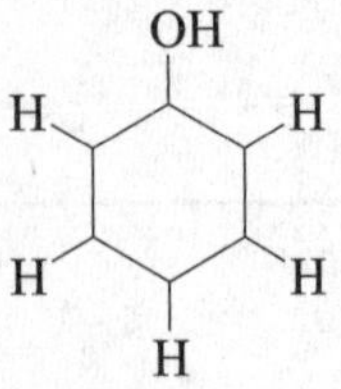

Answers Explained

1. a. Add the superscripts to get the total number of electrons: 8. Since the atom is neutral, 8 also represents the number of protons, and therefore the atomic number. Hence, the atom represented is oxygen.

b. Oxygen normally forms a stable anion, since it needs two more electrons to complete its second energy level and meet the octet rule.

2. **B** Cl^- has 17 protons and 18 electrons; Ar has 18 protons and 18 electrons; K^+ has 19 protons and 18 electrons; Ca^{2+} has 20 protons and 18 electrons. The number of neutrons or isotopes cannot be determined without the mass number. Thus, the only quantity in common is the number of electrons.

3. **C** Since chromium(III) oxide is ionic, use the criss-cross method with Cr^{3+} and O^{2-}. Thus, Cr_2O_3 is the correct chemical formula.

4. Since MnO_2 is an ionic compound, and manganese has multiple oxidation states, manganese(IV) oxide is the correct chemical name.

5. a. Molar mass is the sum of the atomic masses or weights, multiplied by the appropriate subscripts appearing in the formula, here $CO(NH_2)_2$. Thus:

$$\text{MM} = 12.01\text{ g}(1) + 16.00\text{ g}(1) + 14.01\text{ g}(2) + 1.008\text{ g}(4) = 60.0\text{ g/mol}$$

b. $$\text{Percent N (by mass)} = \frac{14.01\text{ g}(2)}{60.0\text{ g} \times 100} = 46.6\%$$

6. See Example 1.6. To convert percentages into grams, assume a 100.0-g sample. Then, convert grams of each element into moles using the atomic masses of carbon, hydrogen, chlorine, and sulfur. The result is: $C_{2.517}H_{5.030}Cl_{1.255}S_{0.630}$. Divide the number of moles of each element, that is, each subscript, by the smallest number, which is 0.630 mol, to obtain the empirical formula of mustard gas: $C_4H_8Cl_2S$.

7. **B** Add the subscripts in the chemical formula to obtain the total number of atoms: 13.

8. **A** See Example 1.4. Set up a simple algebraic equation as follows, letting x represent the unknown oxidation number of chlorine; −2 is the oxidation number of oxygen, and the sum is equal to the net charge on the oxoanion, −1:

$$x(1) + -2(3) = -1$$

Solve for x to obtain $x = +5$.

9. The limiting reagent is the reactant in short supply. To identify it, convert each reactant's mass, given in grams, into moles:

$$45.3\text{ g CO}\,\frac{(1.0\text{ mol CO})}{(28.0\text{ g CO})} = 1.62\text{ mol CO}$$

$$79.8\text{ g }Fe_2O_3\,\frac{(1.0\text{ mol }Fe_2O_3)}{(159.7\text{ g }Fe_2O_3)} = 0.500\text{ mol }Fe_2O_3$$

From the stoichiometry of the balanced reaction, it is clear that 1.0 mol Fe_2O_3 requires 3 mol CO, and 0.500 mol Fe_2O_3 would require 1.50 mol CO. Thus, CO is present in excess and Fe_2O_3 is the limiting reagent.

10. **C** In the given reaction, HCl is present in excess. Thus, Al is the limiting reagent, which determines the maximum yield of H_2 gas. Use the factor-label method:

$$50 \text{ g Al} \frac{(1.0 \text{ mol Al})}{(26.98 \text{ g Al})} \frac{(3 \text{ mol } H_2)}{(2 \text{ mol Al})} \frac{(2.016 \text{ g } H_2)}{(1.0 \text{ mol } H_2)} = 5.6 \text{ g } H_2$$

11. **D** See Example 1.12. Percent yield $= \frac{4.5 \text{ g}}{5.6 \text{ g}} \times 100 = 80\%$

12. **D** Refer to equation 1.11. Since all concentrations are the same, look for the solute that has the highest van't Hoff or i factor—the number of ions or particles per mole. For NaCl, $i = 2$; for C_2H_5OH, $i = 1$; for $C_{12}H_{22}O_{22}$, $i = 1$; for $KAl(SO_4)_2$, $i = 4$. Thus, alum produces the lowest freezing point.

13. **B** Use equation 1.11, and solve for ΔT. Molality m is given by the equation

$$m = \frac{\dfrac{92 \text{ g } C_2H_5OH}{46.0 \text{ g/mol} C_2H_5OH}}{0.500 \text{ kg } H_2O}$$

Also, $K_f(H_2O) = 1.86$, and $i = 1$ for C_2H_5OH.

Thus, $\Delta T = 7.44$ °C, and $T_f = -7.44$ °C.

14. **A** The given quantity, 1.0 ng, of magnesium $= 1.0 \times 10^{-9}$ g Mg. Use the factor-label method, the atomic mass of magnesium, and Avogadro's number:

$$1.0 \times 10^{-9} \text{ g Mg} \frac{(1.0 \text{ mol Mg})}{(24.31 \text{ g Mg})} \frac{(6.022 \times 10^{23} \text{ atoms Mg})}{(1.0 \text{ mol Mg})} = 2.48 \times 10^{13} \text{ atoms Mg}$$

15. In the given reaction, copper goes from an oxidation state of 0 to +2 in $Cu(NO_3)_2$, losing 2 electrons. Nitrogen goes from an oxidation state of +5 in HNO_3 to +2 in NO, gaining 3 electrons. Therefore, copper is oxidized, while nitrogen is reduced.

16. **a.** Use equation 1.60. The K_p value is given. Change 427°C to 700 K, and use $R = 8.31$ J/K·mol. Then, $\Delta G = +53{,}900$ J/mol $= +53.9$ kJ/mol.
    b. Since the sign for ΔG is positive, the reaction is *not* spontaneous.

17. **a.** Use equation 1.58, and substitute the values given. Convert 25°C to 298 K. Then, $\Delta G° = -198$ kJ.
    b. Since the sign of ΔG is negative, the reaction is spontaneous.

18. **C** Gas-phase systems have more kinetic energy and random motion and therefore greater entropy.

19. **D** Note that a 0.014 M $Ca(OH)_2$ solution is a strong base with 2 mol of OH^- per mole of $Ca(OH)_2$. First, find $[OH^-]$: $[OH^-] = 0.014$ M(2) $= 0.028$ M.

Then use equation 1.22, and substitute in 0.028 M to calculate pOH: pOH = 1.55. Finally, use equation 1.23 to calculate pH: pH = 12.45.

20. **A** This problem involves mixing two solutions of the same acid but with different concentrations. The strategy here is to find the number of moles of H^+ in the first solution and the number of moles of H^+ in the second solution, then add the numbers together, and divide the sum by the total volume (assume volumes are additive). The pH can then be found using equation 1.20.

$$\text{Moles } H_1^+ = V_1M_1 = (0.400 \text{ L})(0.125 \text{ M}) = 0.050$$
$$\text{Moles } H_2^+ = V_2M_2 = (0.800 \text{ L})(0.050 \text{ M}) = 0.040$$

Total moles $H^+ = 0.090$ Total volume $= 1200$ mL $= 1.2$ L

$$[H^+] = \frac{\text{total moles } H^+}{\text{total volume}} = \frac{0.090 \text{ mol}}{1.2 \text{ L}} = 0.075 \text{ M}$$

$$pH = -\log[H^+] = -\log(0.0750 \text{ M}) = 1.12$$

21. **C** This problem illustrates the common ion effect. The common ion is I^-, and the background concentration of I^- is given as 0.15 M, since NaI is a strong electrolyte. From Table 1.2, the K_{sp} of PbI_2 is 7.9×10^{-9}.

Let S represent the solubility of Pb^{2+}; then $2S$ represents the solubility of I^-. Set up the K_{sp} expression as follows:

$$K_{sp} = [Pb^{2+}][I^-]^2 = (S)(2S + 0.15 \text{ M})^2$$

Solve for S: $S = 3.5 \times 10^{-7}$ M.

This value also represents the molar solubility of PbI_2.

22. Use Hess's law, see Example 1.40, and use the heats of formation given in the table. Then:

$$\Delta H^\circ_{RX} = [2(9) + 3(-794)] - [1(-504) + 6(-92)] = -1{,}308 \text{ kJ/mol}$$

23. a. See Example 1.47. Assume all species are in their standard states. Find the E° values for aluminum and silver from Table 1.3, Standard Reduction Potentials, and add. Note that Al is oxidized while Ag^+ is reduced. Therefore:

$$E_{net}^\circ = 1.66 + 0.80 = 2.46 \text{ V}$$

b. See the Nernst equation, equation 1.61. Here, $Q = \frac{[Al^{3+}]}{[Ag^+]^3}$. Therefore, increasing $[Al^{3+}]$ would increase log Q but decrease the cell EMF.

24. C Use equation 1.29. Set up the K_p expression as follows:

$$K_p = \frac{[PCl_3][Cl_2]}{[PCl_5]} = \frac{(x)(x)}{1.00 \text{ atm} - x} = 0.750$$

Solve for x: $x = 0.569$ atm. This value represents the partial pressure of $PCl_3(g)$.

25. a. Use the van't Hoff equation, equation 1.31. $K_c = 1.60 \times 10^{-2}$.

b. Use equation 1.59. $\Delta G = 2.56 \times 10^3$ cal/mol.

c. Use equation 1.58 and solve for ΔS. $\Delta S = 37.9$ cal/K or 37.9 eu.

26. a. Follow the strategy outlined in Example 1.25. Lactic acid, $HC_3H_5O_3$, is a monoprotic acid like formic acid and acetic acid. The pH of lactic acid is 2.29.

b. The percent ionization, %I, is defined as $\frac{[H_3O^+]}{[HC_3H_5O_3]} \times 100$ and equals 2.54%.

27. D Follow the strategy outlined in Example 1.26, and use the hint given. The only difference is that NaCN produces a basic instead of an acidic solution. The pH of a 0.50 M NaCN solution is 11.5.

28. Assume that the total volume is 225 mL. This is also the volume for both Na_2CrO_4 and $AgNO_3$. Convert 1.0 mg of Na_2CrO_4 into moles, then into molarity. The molarity of $AgNO_3$ is given. Then follow the procedure of Example 1.36 to determine that a precipitate will *not* form.

29. a. See Example 1.51, Table 1.5 for homologous series for alkanes, and Table 1.8 for functional groups. The names of the four compounds are *n*-hexane, dimethyl ether, ethanol or ethyl alcohol, and l-butane, respectively.

b. Dimethyl ether and ethanol have the same chemical formula, although they have different structural formulas.

c. Only 1-butene has a double bond, which makes it unsaturated.

30. Follow the IUPAC rules for interpreting names and writing structures.

C H A P T E R

2

Computer Programming and Software Review

Thomas E. Hulbert, PE

Introduction

The FE/EIT exam requires a knowledge of no specific programming language to answer questions. However, the ability to analyze program segments from flow diagrams, pseudocode, and generic programming is required. Other questions are based on spreadsheets. This chapter reviews programming basics and provides an overview of Microsoft Excel. Sample problems are solved at the end of the chapter.

2.1 Flowcharting Symbols

A flowchart is a drawing that represents a specific procedure or algorithm. Since the flowchart is not a specific programming language but is a graphical technique, it is an effective way to structure a problem without using a specific language or coding. The most common flowcharting symbols that have developed over the years and have become pseudostandard are the following:

Terminal symbol begins and ends a flowchart.

Decision symbol indicates a point where a decision must be made or two items are compared.

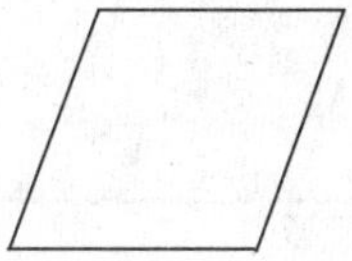

Input/output symbol defines flow to and from keyboard, memory, printer, and permanent data storage.

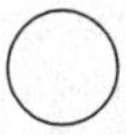

Connector symbol indicates that the flowchart continues elsewhere.

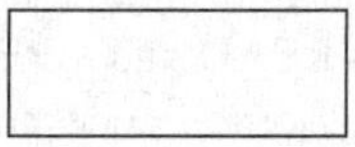

Processing symbol designates calculations or data manipulation.

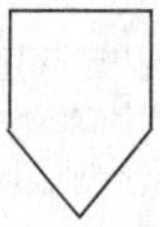

Off-page symbol indicates that the flowchart continues on the following page.

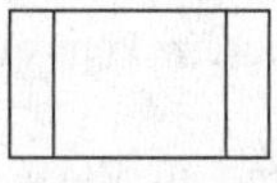

Predefined process symbol designates calculations or data manipulation.

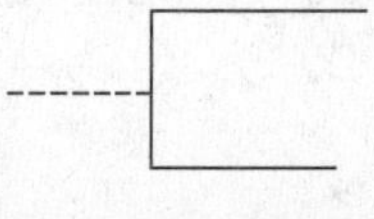

Annotation symbol indicates that comments are added.

2.2 Coding

Coding refers to the manner in which alphanumeric data and control characters are handled by series of bits. Characters that can be displayed or printed, including numerals and symbols (&, > , etc.), are alphanumeric data. Control characters (tab, carriage return, etc.) are keystrokes and are not recorded. Computers use binary numbers only; thus, all symbolic data must be expressed in binary codes.

The Extended Binary Coded Decimal Interchange Code (EBCDIC) is widely used on mainframe computers. It uses a byte (eight bits) for each character, allowing a maximum of 256 different characters. Since strings of bits are difficult to read, the hexadecimal or octal format is used to simplify working with EBCDIC data. Each byte is converted into two strings of four bits each. The two strings are then converted to hexadecimal (base −16) numbers. Since $(1111)_2 = (15)_{10} = (F)_{16}$, the largest possible EBCDIC character is coded FF in hexadecimal.

The American Standard Code for Information Interchange (ASCII) is a seven-bit code allowing 128 combinations. It is commonly used in microcomputers, although a higher order bit structure employing a 16-bit Unicode character format is being developed. ASCII-coded magnetic tape and disk files are used to transfer data and documents between computers that normally are unable to share data.

2.3 Program Design

A program is a sequence of instructions that performs a function in the computer. The program is designed to accomplish an algorithm. An **algorithm** is a problem-solving procedure that consists of a finite number of well-defined steps. Each step in the algorithm includes one or more instructions (such as READ and OPEN). These instructions are known as source code statements and are readable English phrases.

A computer will not normally understand source code statements. Source code is translated into machine-readable object code and absolute memory locations. Finally, an executable program is produced.

Software is an executable program kept on disk or tape.

Firmware is a program placed in ROM (read only memory) or EPROM (memory).

Hardware is the computer.

2.4 Low-Level Languages

Machine language instructions are understood by the computer's CPU (its native language). To make an instruction compatible, it consists of two parts:

The operation to be performed (op-code).
The operand expressed as a storage location.

Each instruction is expressed as a series of bits, a form known as intrinsic machine code. Octal and hexadecimal coding is a more convenient alternative. In either case, coding a machine language program is tedious and time consuming and is seldom done by hand.

Assembly language is more symbolic than machine language. Mnemonic codes are used to specify the operations, and the operands are referred to by variable names rather than by addresses. Blocks of code that are to be repeated at multiple locations in the program are known as macros. Macro instructions are written once and are referred to by symbolic names in the source code.

Assembly language code is translated into machine language by an assembler or macroassembler. After assembly, portions of other programs or function libraries are combined by a linker. In order to run, the program is placed in the computer's memory by a loader. Assembly language is preferred for highly efficient programs. However, the coding is difficult and cumbersome.

The following table compares several languages and the corresponding instructions.

Language	*Instruction*
FORTRAN	+
Assembly language	AR
Machine language	1A
Intrinsic machine code	1111 0001

2.5 High-Level Languages

Because the instructions for high-level languages resemble English, these languages are easier to use than low-level languages. An interpreter or a compiler, either of which is considered to be software, translates high-level statements into machine language. A compiler, when activated, performs the checking and conversion functions on all instructions, and a true stand-alone, executable program is created. An interpreter, however, checks the instructions and converts them line by line into machine code during execution, but produces no stand-alone program capable of use without the interpreter.

Interpreters can check syntax as each statement is entered by the programmer. For some languages and implementations of other languages there is little distinction between an interpreter and a compiler; in that case, the conversion software is known as a pseudo- or incremental compiler.

2.6 Microsoft Excel

To start Microsoft Excel for Windows, double-click the Microsoft Excel icon on the Microsoft Office Shortcut Bar or press Start and proceed through the program's pull-down menu to Excel and its icon. The Microsoft Excel window appears. If necessary, enlarge the window by clicking the Maximize button in the upper-right corner of the window.

To start Microsoft Excel for Macintosh, double-click the Microsoft Excel icon in the Finder. The Microsoft Excel window appears. If necessary, enlarge the window by clicking the zoom box in the upper-right corner of the window.

When Microsoft Excel starts, it creates a new, empty workbook. Workbooks can be reopened when Microsoft Excel is restarted by naming and saving them the first time in the startup directory or folder.

Opening a Workbook

The workbook is the normal document or file type in Microsoft Excel and is the electronic equivalent of a three-ring binder. Inside workbooks are sheets, such as worksheets and chart sheets. Each sheet's name appears on a tab at the bottom of the workbook. Sheets can be moved or copied between workbooks and can be rearranged within a workbook.

Open workbooks by double clicking them in the File Manager or Finder even if Excel has not been started. Also, open files in other formats such as Lotus 1-2-3; then create new workbooks in Microsoft Excel. Search your drive for a specific workbook, even if its name is not known, and create template workbooks that can be used a number of times.

Creating Worksheets

When a workbook is created or opened, Microsoft Excel displays it in a window. Several workbook windows can be open at the same time. In Microsoft Excel for Macintosh, the screen is slightly different.

Most of the work in Microsoft Excel will be on a worksheet, which is a grid of rows and columns. Each cell is the intersection of a row and a column and has a unique address, or reference. For example, the cell where column B and row 5 intersect is cell B5. It will be referenced in the white slot to the left and above the worksheet. Cell references are used when formulas are written or specific cells must be cited.

Generally, first select the cell or cells to work with, and then enter data or choose a command. Selected cells appear highlighted on the screen. The active cell is the cell in which data are entered when typing is started. Only one cell, indicated by a heavy border, is active at a time.

To change the active cell, move the mouse pointer into cell B4 and click. Notice that the cell's reference (B4) and its values (region) appear in the formula bar.

To scroll through the worksheet, proceed as follows:

1. Move the pointer to the down arrow in the vertical scroll bar on the right edge of the window, and then click. The worksheet scrolls down one row.
2. Click the scroll bar area below the scroll box. The worksheet scrolls down one screen.
3. Move the pointer into the scroll box. Hold the mouse button down, move the pointer back to the top of the vertical scroll bar, and then release the mouse button. This procedure is called dragging. The worksheet scrolls back up to the first row.
   To scroll any distance, drag the scroll box.
   To scroll down one page, click the scroll bar.
   To scroll down one row, click the down arrow.
   To enter the data, select the cell and fill in alpha or numeric information.

Microsoft Excel fills in the label based on the initial selection. This operation is called AutoFill, and it works with several types of data. For example, the days of the week and series of numbers can be filled by clicking and dragging on the appropriate cells.

Columns and rows can be totaled or averaged, and numerous formulas and functions are available. Data such as numbers, days, or other lists can also be entered with AutoFill. To move data around on the worksheet, drag it or use the Cut, Copy, and Paste commands on the Edit menu.

Building Formulas to Calculate Values

A formula can be used to do simple things, such as adding the values in two cells, or to perform much more complex operations. Here is how Microsoft Excel uses the SUM worksheet function to add two values together:

1. On a worksheet, write two numbers in A1 and A2, say 1 and 2.
2. Move the mouse to A3, and click.
3. Move the cursor to the tool bar and hit Σ. SUM(A1:A2) will appear in A3.
4. Hit ENTER, and the sum will appear in A3.

A formula in Microsoft Excel can always be recognized because it starts with an equal sign (=). You can see the formula itself only when editing the cell that contains the formula. Otherwise, the value produced by the formula is displayed.

A formula can be created that adds the amounts in a column, and that formula can be copied into the other columns. To total the column, select the cell where the total will be placed, and click the AutoSum button. Microsoft Excel looks at the data around the selected cell and guesses that you want to add the column of numbers above this cell. It writes the formula, suggesting the range of numbers to sum. Press ENTER to accept the proposed formula.

Formulas can be copied to different locations on the worksheet by dragging the fill handle or using COPY. The Function Wizard, located on the tool bar on the fx key, can simplify formula writing and also name cell references or ranges to create more understandable formulas.

When the Function Wizard opens, the function categories appear in the left box. Click on a category to bring up function names in the right box. The function name is explained in bold type below the category box. After highlighting category and function, click OK to finish and the formula will appear in the bold box on the worksheet and in the formula line above the cells. Editing can be done only in the formula line and acknowledged with the symbols to the left.

The basics for using Excel have been summarized above. If you are not familiar with a spreadsheet software package, open Excel and navigate through the basics. More advanced functions are explained through the highlighting on the various symbols or by referring to the Help functions.

2.7 Sample Problems

Examples 2.1 and 2.2 illustrate the appropriate approach to solving problems. Following these examples is a series of problems. An answer key and answer explanations are provided.

The first sample problem is a spreadsheet example.

Example 2.1

In a spreadsheet, the number in cell A3 is set to 5. Then A4 is set to A3 + \$A\$3, where \$ indicates absolute cell address. This formula is copied into cells A5 and A6. The number shown in cell A6 is most nearly

A. 10
B. 20
C. 25
D. 35

Solution:

First,

	A	
3	5	
4		Insert A3 + \$A\$3.
5		
6		

Then,

	A	
3	5	
4	10	
5		COPY A4 + \$3\$.
6		COPY A5 + \$3\$.

	A
3	5
4	10
5	15
6	20

The answer is choice (B).

The second sample problem involves a program segment from a BASIC program.

Example 2.2

The program segment

```
INPUT X, M
S = 1
T = 1
FOR K = 1 TO M
T = T*X/K
S = S + T
NEXT K
```

calculates the sum

A. $S = 1 + XT + 2XT + 3XT + \ldots + MXT$
B. $S = 1 + XT + (1/2)XT + (1/3)XT + \ldots + (1/M)XT$
C. $S = 1 + X/1 + X^2/2 + X^3/3 + \ldots + X^M/M$
D. $S = 1 + M/1! + M^2/2! + M^3/3! + \ldots + X^M/M!$

Solution:

As the program steps from one instruction to the next, the contents remain from the preceding iteration. Therefore, as T = T*X/K passes the first time, it is $X/1!$ S = S + T becomes $S = 1 + X/1!$.

At K = 2, $S = 1 + X/1 + X^2/1*2$.

At K = 3, $S = 1 + X/1! + X^2/2! + X^3/1*2*3$.

The answer is choice (D).

2.8 Summary

This chapter provides brief highlights of two rapidly changing areas: computer programming and spreadsheet software. It is strongly suggested that your preparations for the exam include referencing additional material on general programming and practice in using a spreadsheet package.

PRACTICE PROBLEMS

Number Systems (Refer to the NCEES *FE Reference Handbook,* "Electrical and Computer Engineering" section.)

1. Binary number 0101110 is what number in base 10?
(A) 32
(B) 46
(C) 48
(D) 56

2. Base-10 number 135 is equivalent to what binary number?
(A) 011000011
(B) 10000111
(C) 010001010
(D) 10000011

3. Base-5 number $(213144)_5$ converts to what binary number?
(A) 0 0111 0110 1101
(B) 1 0011 0111 1100
(C) 0 1101 1001 0101
(D) 1 1100 1000 0011

Computers

4. Which of the following best defines a compiler?
(A) hardware that is used to translate high-level language to assembly language
(B) hardware that collects and stores executable commands in a program
(C) software that processes and stores executable commands in a program
(D) software that is used to translate high-level language into machine code

5. Which of the following program flowchart symbols is used to compare two items?

(A) 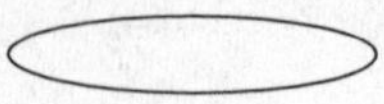

(B) 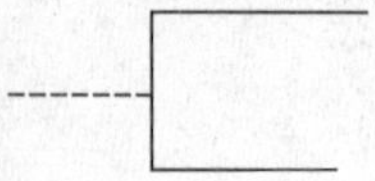

(C) 

(D) 

6. How many times will the line labeled "START" execute in the following program segment?

```
        I = 2
        J = 1
START   J = J + I
        I = J ^ 2
        IF J < 100 THEN GO TO START
        ELSE GO TO FINISH
FINISH  PRINT J
```

(A) 3
(B) 4
(C) 5
(D) 6

7. Based on the following program segment, what is the DECISION?

```
A = 1
B = 2
C = 3
D = 4
DECISION = I
IF (A > B) OR (C < D) THEN DECISION = G
IF (A < B) OR (C > D) THEN DECISION = H
IF (A > B) OR (C > D) THEN A = 5
IF (A < B) AND (C < D) THEN DECISION = J
```

(A) G
(B) H
(C) I
(D) J

Spreadsheets

8. In the following portion of a spreadsheet, the value of D1 is set to (A1 + B1 + C1)/3. This formula is copied into the range of cells D2:D3. The value of D4 is set to SUM(D1:D3)/4. What is the number in D4?

	A	B	C	D
1	1	2	3	
2	4	5	6	
3	7	8	9	
4				
5				

(A) 8
(B) 3.75
(C) 15
(D) 30

Questions 9–10

A segment of a spreadsheet is shown below. Use the numbers in the cells to answer Questions 9 and 10.

	A	B	C	D
1	20	21	22	23
2	5	A2^2	B2*A$1	
3	6	A3^2	B3*B$1	
4	7	A4^2	B4*C$1	
5	8	A5^2	B5*D$1	

9. What will be the top to bottom values in column B?
   (A) 25, 30, 35, 40
   (B) 25, 36, 49, 64
   (C) 40, 42, 44, 46
   (D) 5, 6, 7, 8
10. What will be the top to bottom values in column D?
   (A) 25, 36, 49, 64
   (B) 100, 126, 154, 184
   (C) 500, 756, 1078, 1472
   (D) 125, 196, 34

Answer Key

1. B	6. A
2. B	7. D
3. D	8. B
4. D	9. B
5. C	10. C

Answers Explained

1. **B** $2^6*0 = 0$
   $2^5*1 = 32$
   $2^4*0 = 0$
   $2^3*1 = 8$
   $2^2*1 = 4$
   $2^1*1 = 2$
   $2^0*0 = 0$
   46

2. **B** $2^7*1 = 128$
   $2^6*0 =$
   $2^5*0 =$
   $2^4*0 =$
   $2^3*0 =$
   $2^2*1 = 4$
   $2^1*1 = 2$
   $2^0*1 = 1$
   135
   Base-2 equivalent is 10000111.

3. **D** Convert base 5 to base 10.
   $(213144)_5$ $2*5^5 = 6250$
   $1*5^4 = 625$
   $3*5^3 = 375$
   $1*5^2 = 25$
   $4*5^1 = 20$
   $4*5^0 = 4$
   $(7299)_{10}$ $2^{12}*1 =$
   $2^{11}*1 =$
   $2^{10}*1 =$
   $2^9*0 =$
   $2^8*0 =$
   $2^7*1 =$
   $2^6*0 =$
   $2^5*0 =$
   $2^4*0 =$
   $2^3*0 =$
   $2^2*0 =$
   $2^1*1 =$
   $2^0*1 =$
   Base-2 equivalent is 1 1100 1000 0011.

4. **D** Compilers are software packages that convert programs. They take a high-level language and convert it into a machine code that the computer can understand (low-level language).

5. **C** The diamond represents a point where a decision must be made or where two items are compared. The other symbols are explained in Section 2.1.

6. **A** Set up a table of values for I and J during each loop. J is indexed before I, so the latest or new value of J is used to calculate I.

Loop	J	I
0(initial)	1	2
1	3	9
2	12	144
3	158	24964
4		

   After 3 loops, J > 100, so the program continues and prints.

7. **D** The program must be followed step by step from the first statement. The first and second IF statements are G and H. The third IF statement is not 5; however, the fourth IF statement is J. Therefore, DECISION is J.

8. B

	A	B	C	D	
1	1	2	3	**2**	
2	4	5	6	**5**	Copy formula from D1 to D2.
3	7	8	9	**8**	Copy from D2 to D3.
4				**3.75**	D4 is SUM(D1:D3)/4 or 15/4 = 3.75

9. B

	A	B	C	D	
1	20	21	22	23	
2	5	**25***			* A2^2=5*5=25
3	6	**36**			
4	7	**49**			
5	8	**64**			

10. C

	A	B	C	D	
1	20	21	22	23	
2	5	**25**	**500**		
3	6	**36**	**756****		**B3*B$1=756
4	7	**49**	**1078**		
5	8	**64**	**1472**		

CHAPTER

3

Dynamics

Mark Frisina, PE

Introduction

Dynamics is the study of motion and the forces that govern the motion. The Morning Session of the FE examination typically contains 9 to 15 examination problems related to various dynamics topics, and the Afternoon Sessions of the General Engineering and Mechanical Discipline exams have approximately 10% of the total questions in the area of dynamic systems. The following review modules are intended to assist the reader in reinforcing his or her knowledge of relevant dynamics principles and problem-solving techniques that are likely to appear on the FE exam.

3.1 Kinematics of Particles

Kinematics is the study of patterns of motion in space. This section focuses on describing two-dimensional plane motion and three-dimensional space motion by employing rectangular coordinates, tangential and normal coordinates, and radial and transverse components. The effect of forces on motion is outside the domain of kinematics. The most important parameters in particle kinematics are the vectors that represent position, velocity, and acceleration.

- $\mathbf{r}(t)$ is the *instantaneous* (time-dependent) *position vector* to a particle from a defined reference origin in space.
- *Instantaneous velocity* is defined as the time rate of change of the position vector and is represented by the relationship

$$\mathbf{v}(t) = \frac{d\mathbf{r}}{dt}, \qquad [3.1]$$

where v has typical units of m/s or ft/sec.

- *Instantaneous acceleration* is represented by the symbol $\mathbf{a}(t)$ and is defined as the rate of change of the velocity vector. The governing equation for acceleration is

$$\mathbf{a}(t) = \frac{d\mathbf{v}(t)}{dt} = \frac{d^2r}{dt^2} \qquad [3.2]$$

Generally, the units for acceleration are m/s^2 or ft/sec^2.

$$\mathbf{v}(t) = \frac{dx(t)}{dt\mathbf{i}} + \frac{dy(t)}{dt\mathbf{j}} + \frac{dz(t)}{dt\mathbf{k}} = \dot{x}\mathbf{i} + \dot{y}\mathbf{j} + \dot{z}\mathbf{k} \quad [3.3]$$

Acceleration vector:

$$\mathbf{a}(t) = \frac{d\mathbf{v}(t)}{dt} = \frac{d^2x(t)}{dt^2\mathbf{i}} + \frac{d^2y(t)}{dt^2\mathbf{j}} + \frac{d^2 z(t)}{dt^2\,\mathbf{k}}$$
$$= \ddot{x}\,\mathbf{i} + \ddot{y}\,\mathbf{j} + \ddot{z}\,\mathbf{k} \quad [3.4]$$

Rectilinear Motion

Rectilinear motion is straight-line motion in space or in a plane. In short, this motion is restricted to a single line of action in space or in a plane. If a particle's motion is confined to an x-axis (horizontal direction) as an example of rectilinear motion, then, if the initial position and velocity are denoted by x_0 and v_0, respectively, general equations for conditions of variable velocity $v(t)$ and acceleration $a(t)$ are given for motion from time t_0 to t:

- *Instantaneous position:*

  $$x(t) = x_0 + \int_{t_0}^{t} v(t)\, dt \quad [3.5]$$

- *Instantaneous velocity:*

  $$v(t) = v_0 + \int_{t_0}^{t} a(t)\, dt \quad [3.6]$$

- For *uniform-velocity* (v = constant), straight-line motion, which requires $a = 0$:

  $$x(t) = x_0 + v(t - t_0) \quad [3.7]$$

- The particle's *displacement* Δx is defined simply as the change of position:

  $$\Delta x = x(t) - x_0 = \int_{t_0}^{t} v(t)\, dt \quad [3.8]$$

In FE exam problems in which a velocity versus time graph is provided, displacement can be readily obtained by calculating the *net area* of the graph during a specified time interval. This capability is especially useful when the velocity graph contains several different $v(t)$ functions.

For *uniform acceleration* (a = constant) in rectilinear motion, the velocity is a linear function; and if the initial conditions x_0 and v_0 are given, the key equations are as follows:

$$x(t) = x_0 + v_0 t + \frac{at^2}{2} \quad \text{for } t_0 = 0 \quad [3.9]$$

$$v(t) = v_0 + at \quad [3.10]$$

$$v^2 = v_0{}^2 = 2a(x - x_0) \quad [3.11]$$

Example 3.1

The rectilinear motion of a particle is described by the equation

$$x(t) = 6t^2 - 24t + 7$$

where x is in meters.

Solve for the displacement at the instant when the velocity is zero.

Solution:

First determine the particle's velocity equation.

$$v(t) = \frac{dx(t)}{dt} = 12t - 24$$

Velocity $v = 0$ at $t = 2.0$ s.

$$\therefore \text{Displacement } \Delta x = \int v(t)dt$$
$$= \int_0^2 (12t - 4)dt$$
$$= (6t^2 - 24t)\Big|_0^2$$
$$= (24 - 48) - 0$$
$$= -24.0 \text{ m}$$

Plane Circular Motion

Plane circular motion requires that the particle traverse a path in a plane such that the *radius of curvature R is constant* with respect to a reference origin C, which is the center of curvature of the path. *Tangential* and *normal* coordinates are utilized to profile the circular-type motion; and with reference to Figure 3.1, it is important to recall that the tangential direction is along the line of action of the velocity and is typically positive when the motion results in an increase of angle ϕ in a counterclockwise direction. The normal direction is directed positively from the particle toward the center of curvature.

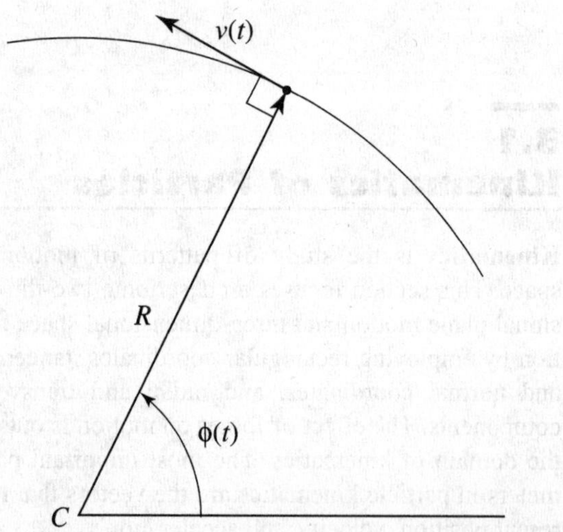

Figure 3.1

For circular motion, the governing equations are as follows:

- *Angular velocity:* $\omega = \frac{d\phi}{dt}$ (rad/s) [3.12]
- *Angular acceleration:*
  $\propto = \frac{d\omega}{dt}$ (rad/s^2) [3.13]
- *Tangential velocity:* $v(t) = R\omega$ [3.14]
- *Tangential acceleration:*
  $a_t = R\propto = \frac{R\,d\omega}{dt}$ [3.15]
- *Normal acceleration:*
  $a_n = \frac{v^2}{R} = R\omega^2$ [3.16]
- *Total acceleration* (scalar):
  $a(t) = \sqrt{a_t^{\,2} + a_n^{\,2}}$ [3.17]
- *Arc length* or distance along a curve:
  $s(t) = R\phi$ [3.18]

Example 3.2

A particle travels in a circular path along a plane surface in such a way that its radius of curvature is 60.0 m. If the angular measure is according to $\phi(t) = 4t^2 + 9$ rad, at what time will the particle's normal acceleration attain a value of 3,000 m/s^2?

Solution:

Since normal acceleration $a_n = v^2/R = 3{,}000$, the speed v of the particle is readily obtained with R specified.

$$v = \sqrt{3{,}000R} = \sqrt{180{,}000\ \text{m}^2/\text{s}^2} = 424.2\ \text{m/s}$$

$$= R\omega = (60.0\ \text{m})\left(\frac{d\phi}{dt}\right) = (60.0)(8.0t) = 424.2$$

$$\therefore t = \frac{424.2\ \text{m/s}}{480.0\ \text{m/s}^2} = 0.88\ \text{s}$$

Radial and Transverse Components of Plane Motion

Radial and transverse curvilinear motion occurs when the radius of curvature of a particle's path in a plane usually varies with time, except in the unique case of circular motion. In Figure 3.2 the *radial direction* is along the line of action from the reference origin to the particle, and the radial distance at any time t is denoted by $r(t)$. Note that the positive radial direction is directed away from the origin. The *transverse direction* is always perpendicular to the radial direction, and the positive transverse direction, denoted by the unit vector ε_θ, tends to cause an increase in the angle of the position vector in a counterclockwise sense as shown. Spiral motion and elliptical motion are classic examples of plane motion that are best profiled by radial and transverse components.

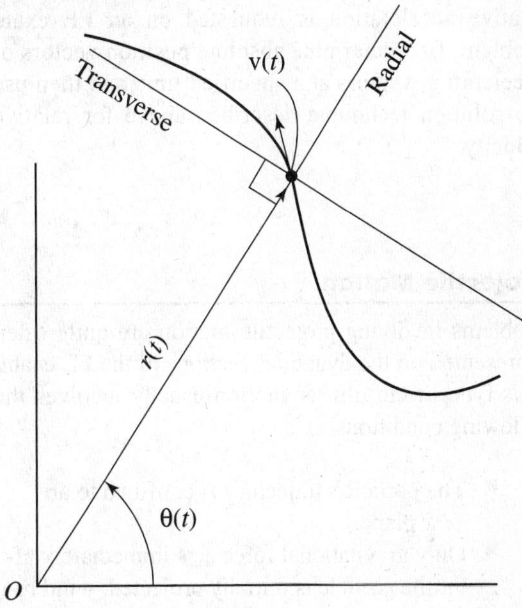

Figure 3.2

Radial and transverse components are effectively two-dimensional versions of cylindrical coordinates. FE exam problems related to radial and transverse components usually provide equations for radial distance $r(t)$ and angular measure $\theta(t)$, and typical problems often ask for computations of velocity and/or acceleration magnitudes using radial and transverse components. The governing equations of radial and transverse plane motion are as follows:

- *Radial velocity:* $v_r = \dot{r} = \frac{dr(t)}{dt}$ [3.19]
- *Tranverse velocity:* $v_\theta = r\dot{\theta}$ [3.20]
- *Total speed:* $v(t) = \sqrt{v_r^{\,2} + v_\theta^{\,2}}$ [3.21]
- *Radial acceleration:* $a_r = \ddot{r} - r\dot{\theta}^2$ [3.22]
- *Transverse acceleration:* $a_\theta = r + 2\dot{r}\dot{\theta}$ [3.23]
- *Total acceleration:* $a(t) = \sqrt{a_r^{\,2} + a_\theta^{\,2}}$ [3.24]

Relative Plane Motion

Relative motion of one object with respect to another in a plane is determined by taking the vector difference of the individual absolute quantities of the two objects measured with respect to a common reference datum. Specifically, if the relative velocity of object T is desired with respect to (as viewed from) object S, and if $\mathbf{v}_s$ and $\mathbf{v}_t$ are the instantaneous velocity vectors for S and T, respectively, then note the specific order of the vector subtraction in the following equation:

Relative velocity of T with respect to S: $\mathbf{v}_{T/S} = \mathbf{v}_T - \mathbf{v}_S$

Bear in mind that the solution to a vector subtraction is often found by setting up a *vector triangle* and calculating the magnitude and direction of the desired relative velocity through the use of the law of cosines and law of sines. If relative position and/or relative acceleration is requested on an FE exam problem, first determine absolute position vectors or acceleration vectors at a specified time and then use the solution technique described above for relative velocity.

Projectile Motion

Problems involving projectile motion are quite often represented on the dynamics sections of the FE exam. This type of curvilinear motion usually involves the following conditions:

- The particle's trajectory is confined to an x–y plane.
- Only gravitational force acts immediately after the particle is initially projected; wind resistance and aerodynamic forces are neglected.
- The initial elevation y_0 of the object is given relative to a datum.
- Other initial conditions, such as velocity v_0 and the projection angle θ that the velocity makes with the horizontal, may be provided or need to be determined.

Figure 3.3 illustrates the initial conditions listed above. Note that the object may have two different times at the same elevation because of the quadratic equation for $y(t)$ given below. Be prepared to solve for the maximum horizontal distance (range) R, which occurs at $y = 0$, as well as for the time required to reach maximum height y_m.

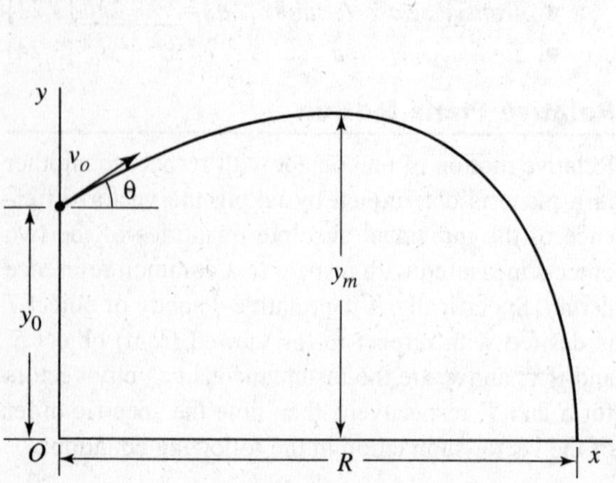

Figure 3.3

Projectile motion equations (assuming $t_0 = 0$):

$$x(t) = v_0 \cos \theta t$$

$$y(t) = y_0 + v_{y0}t - \frac{gt^2}{2} = y_0 + v_0 \sin \theta\, t - \frac{gt^2}{2}$$

$$v_x = v_0 \cos \theta = \text{constant}$$

$$v_y(t) = v_0 \sin \theta - gt$$

$$a_y = -g$$

Example 3.3

A football player claims that he can punt a ball over a 10.0-ft-high wall that is 35 yd away along a horizontal field. If the player kicks the ball from an elevation of 3.0 ft and the ball is projected at an initial speed of 60.0 ft/sec in a direction of 40° from the horizontal, will he successfully prove his claim?

Solution:

Assuming that wind resistance is negligible, first calculate the time when the ball reaches a horizontal position of 35 yd and then check the elevation at this position.

$$x(t) = v_x t = 35 \text{ yd} = 105.0 \text{ ft}$$

$$v_x = (60.0 \text{ ft/sec})\cos 40° = 45.96 \text{ ft/sec}$$

$$t = \frac{x(t)}{v_x} = \frac{105 \text{ ft}}{45.96 \text{ ft/sec}} = 2.28 \text{ sec}$$

Check whether elevation $y(t) \geq 10.0$ ft.

$$y(t) = y_0 + v_{y0}t - \frac{gt^2}{2}$$

$$= 3.0 + 60 \sin 40° t - \frac{(32.2)t^2}{2}$$

$$y(2.28) = 3.0 + 60(0.642)(2.28) - 16.1(2.28)^2$$

$$= 3.0 + 87.9 - 83.7$$

$$= 7.2 \text{ ft}$$

∴ The ball does not clear the wall.

3.2 Kinetics of Particles

Kinetics is the study of the effects of forces on motion. In particle dynamics, Newton's second law of motion is the governing principle.

Newton's Second Law of Motion

Newton's second law for a constant-mass object or particle: $\Sigma \mathbf{F} = m\mathbf{a}$

Here, $\Sigma \mathbf{F}$ is the *net external force* acting upon the object and typically has units of pounds force or kilonewtons, and a is the *acceleration vector,* which must have the same instantaneous direction as the net force.

Since numerous FE problems in kinetics are centered on the second law principle, the following general solution procedure is strongly recommended:

1. Construct an effective *free-body diagram* (FBD) of the object being analyzed. This requires identifying and drawing all external forces (known and/or unknown) acting upon the mass at their point of application.
2. Select an appropriate coordinate system and attach reference axes to the center of gravity (CG) of the body.
3. Resolve all known and/or unknown force components along each axis, paying strict attention to sign convention, and then write the second law equations along the established axial directions.
4. Solve the simultaneous component equations for the desired forces and/or accelerations, recognizing that only two unknowns can normally be solved in a two-dimensional problem.

Note also that conversion errors are often made in second law computations involving mass or weight, and observe the following cautions:

- When using $a = \Sigma F/m$, be aware that 50 lbf/50 lbm $\neq$ 1.0 ft/sec^2. The universal conversion 1.0 lbf = 32.2 lbm ft/sec^2 should be carefully employed.
- Avoid miscalculations of weight using the simple formula $W = mg$.

Proper use of the conversion given above (also known as g_c) will prevent errors.

Rectilinear Motion

Straight-line motion problems involving a fixed-mass object subjected to a system of external forces are typically solved utilizing scalar component versions of Newton's second law described above. For rectilinear motion in an x-y-z coordinate frame, where the object's instantaneous position is defined by the functions $x(t)$, $y(t)$, and $z(t)$, the governing component equations are as follows:

$$\Sigma F_x = ma_x = \frac{md^2\,x(t)}{dt^2} = m\ddot{x}$$

$$\Sigma F_y = ma_y = m\ddot{y} \quad \text{and} \quad \Sigma F_z = m\ddot{z} \qquad [3.25]$$

Note that the magnitude of the total (net) force acting upon the object is

$$\Sigma F = \sqrt{\Sigma F_x^{\,2} + \Sigma F_y^{\,2} + \Sigma F_z^{\,2}}$$

For motion along an *inclined plane*, a set of inclined and normal coordinates is employed, and the equations are

$$\Sigma F_I = ma_I \quad \text{and} \quad \Sigma F_n = ma_n \qquad [3.26]$$

Example 3.4

In Figure 3.4, a 150.0-kg crate is pulled up a frictionless inclined plane at 20° from the horizontal by a constant applied force F_A as shown. If the resulting acceleration is 7.0 m/s^2 along the incline, determine the magnitude of F_A.

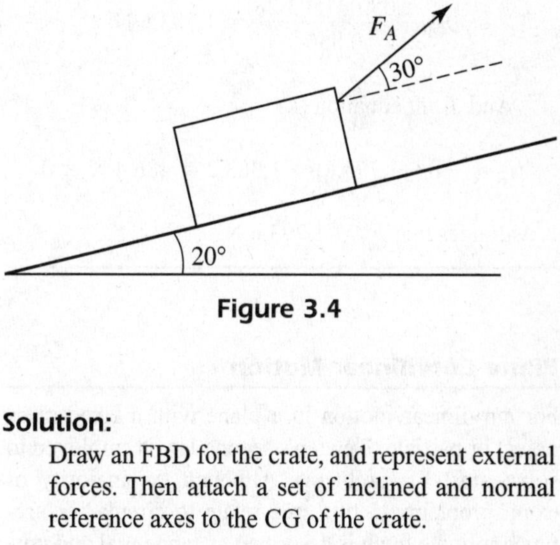

Figure 3.4

Solution:

Draw an FBD for the crate, and represent external forces. Then attach a set of inclined and normal reference axes to the CG of the crate.

Resolve the force components along the I and n directions as shown in Figure 3.5.

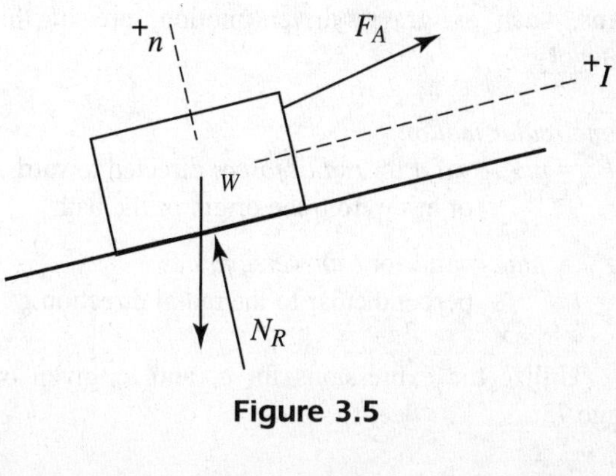

Figure 3.5

$F_{AI} = F_A \cos 30° = 0.866F_A$

$W_I = -W \sin 20° = -(150 \text{ kg})(9.81 \text{ m/s}^2)(0.342)$
$= -503.28 \text{ N}$

$F_{An} = F_A \sin 30° = 0.5F_A$

$W_n = -W \cos 20° = -(1{,}471.5 \text{ N})(0.940)$
$= -1{,}383.2 \text{ N}$

Write the second law equations:

$$\Sigma F_I = ma_I = (150 \text{ kg})(7.0 \text{ m/s}^2) = 1{,}050.0 \text{ N}$$

$$F_{AI} + W_I = 0.866\, F_A + (-503.28 \text{ N}) = 1{,}050.0 \text{ N} \quad (1)$$

$$\Sigma F_n = ma_n = 0 \text{ (assuming that crate remains in contact with incline)}$$

$$0.5F_A + (-1{,}383.2 \text{ N}) + N_R = 0 \quad (N_R \geq 0 \text{ required for contact}) \quad (2)$$

Then, from equation (1)

$$F_A \frac{1{,}050 + 503.28}{0.866} = 1{,}793.6 \text{ N}$$

And, from equation (2)

$$N_R = -0.5(1{,}793.6) + 1{,}383.2 = 486.4 \text{ N} \geq 0$$

$\therefore$ Validates that $F_A = 1{,}793.6$ N

Plane Curvilinear Motion

For curvilinear motion in a plane with a fixed-mass object or particle, Newton's second law is employed to solve most FE problems. Although the majority of exam problems in this area relate to circular or arc-type motion, which is described by tangential and normal components given in the following section, occasionally a few problems involve variable radii of curvature, and these are best solved by employing radial and transverse coordinates. Central-force problems, such as gravity-driven motion, are in this category.

Noncircular motion:

$\Sigma F_r = ma_r$, valid for *radial forces* directed toward or away from the origin of the path.

$\Sigma F_\theta = ma_\theta$, valid for *transverse forces* perpendicular to the radial direction.

Utilize the expressions for a_r and a_θ given on page 73.

Tangential and Normal Forces

For circular-type motion in a plane involving a fixed-mass object, *tangential and normal forces* are involved in the solution of a variety of FE problems. Specific problem categories that often appear include cable tension for an object traveling in a circular path, roller coasters requiring reaction forces, and centripetal forces/accelerations.

Tangential forces (circular or arc-type motion): $\Sigma F_t = ma_t = mR\alpha$ where radius R is a constant.

Normal force(s): $\Sigma F_n = ma_n = \dfrac{mv^2}{R} = mR^2\omega$

Note that *centripetal force* F_c is equivalent to the net normal force, and thus

$$F_c = \frac{mv^2}{R} \quad [3.27]$$

Example 3.5

A 1.8-kg ball attached to a 2.0-m inextensible cable swings in a vertical plane as illustrated in Figure 3.6. Determine the required speed of the ball (units of m/s) if the cable tension is 140.0 N when $\theta = 65°$.

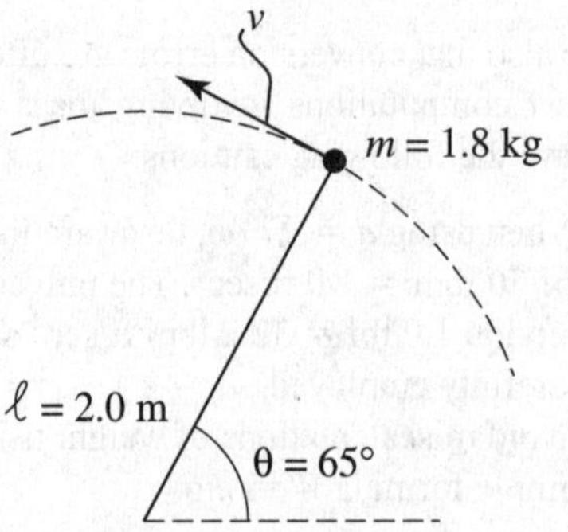

Figure 3.6

Solution:

Draw an FBD of the ball, as shown in Figure 3.7, and use the tangential and normal directions as references due to the circular motion. Since the cable tension is entirely along the normal direction, write the equation of motion in the n-direction, introducing the unknown speed v:

$$\Sigma F_n = \frac{mv^2}{R}$$

$$T + W_n = \frac{(1.8 \text{ kg})v^2}{2.0 \text{ m}}$$

$$140.0 \text{ N} + (1.8 \text{ kg})(9.81 \text{ m/s}^2) \cos 35° = (0.9 \text{ kg/m})v^2$$

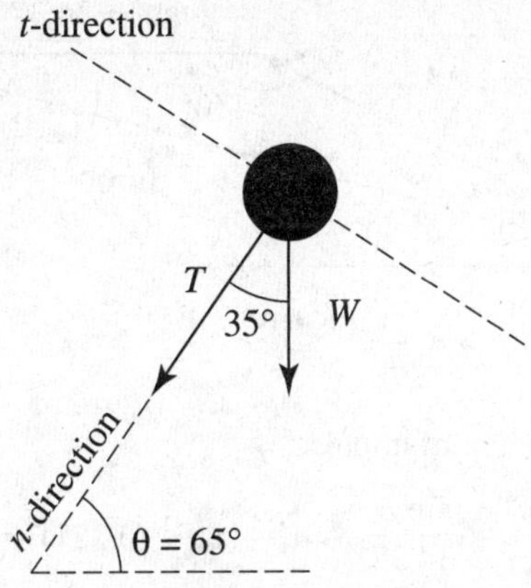

Figure 3.7

$$\frac{140.0 + 14.46}{0.9} \text{ N} \cdot \text{m/kg} = v^2$$

$$\therefore v = \sqrt{171.62 \text{ m}^2/\text{s}^2} = 13.1 \text{ m/s}$$

Note that in this case it was not necessary to involve tangential forces or accelerations to determine the speed.

Linear Momentum

The **linear momentum** of a constant-mass particle or object is a vector quantity **L**, which is simply defined as the product of the particle or object's mass and the instantaneous velocity vector:

$$\mathbf{L} = m\mathbf{v} \qquad [3.28]$$

Conventional units of **L** are lbf-sec or N · s.

Also, recall that for a fixed-mass object the net force acting equals the time rate of change of linear momentum. The equation

$$\Sigma\mathbf{F} = \frac{d\mathbf{L}}{dt} = \frac{md\mathbf{v}}{dt}$$

effectively restates Newton's second law.

An important ramification of the above equation is that, if the net force acting upon a fixed-mass object is zero, it is necessary that **L** = constant and the object's velocity remains constant. A clear example of this condition occurs when a puck travels across a horizontal "frictionless" air table at a constant speed.

For the dynamics section of the FE exam, an understanding of linear momentum concepts is essential in solving frequently represented *impact* and *impulse-momentum* problems (see pages 77–78).

Conservation of Linear Momentum

For a single particle having constant mass, it is required that the linear momentum remain constant (conserved) whenever the net force is zero over a specified period of time, as discussed above. Similarly, for a *system of constant-mass particles or rigid bodies,* if the net external force acting upon the system is zero, then the total sum of the individual linear momentum vectors for all members within the system must remain constant or *conserved:*

$$\Sigma\mathbf{F}_{sys} = 0 \rightarrow \mathbf{L}_{sys} = \text{constant} \qquad [3.29]$$

For a system of masses $m_1, m_2, \ldots, m_n$, *conservation of linear momentum* requires that

$$\begin{aligned} &m_1\mathbf{v}_1 + m_2\mathbf{v}_2 + \ldots + m_n\mathbf{v}_n \\ &= m_1\mathbf{v}_1' + m_2\mathbf{v}_2' + \ldots + m_n\mathbf{v}_n' \\ &= \text{constant} \end{aligned} \qquad [3.30]$$

The prime notation for velocities in the above equation signifies a later time condition. Note that, when $\Sigma\mathbf{F}_{sys} = 0$, linear momentum must be conserved in any or all directions.

Scalar equations may be written in a particular direction (such as the y- direction) as follows:

$$m_1v_{1y} + m_2v_{2y} + \ldots + m_nv_{ny} = m_1v_{1y}' + m_2v_{2y}' + \ldots + m_nv_{ny}' = \text{constant}$$

Equations similar to the one given above will be utilized later in solving impact (collision) problems, in which the elasticity of the colliding objects must also be given.

In solving problems involving the conservation of linear momentum principle, it is imperative to pay close attention to the sign conventions of all scalar velocities.

Impulse-Momentum Principle

Impulse is a vector represented by the symbol **Imp** and defined by the equation

$$\mathbf{Imp}_{1\rightarrow 2} = \int_1^2 \mathbf{F(t)}dt \qquad [3.31]$$

where **F(t)** is the impulsive force acting upon a rigid body or particle during a time period from $t_1 \le t \le t_2$. For a constant-mass object, the *impulse equals the change of linear momentum* according to the equation

$$\mathbf{Imp}_{1\rightarrow 2} = m(\mathbf{v}_2 - \mathbf{v}_1) \qquad [3.32]$$

If the impulsive force acting upon the object is constant during a specified time period, then

$$\mathbf{F}(t_2 - t_1) = m(\mathbf{v}_2 - \mathbf{v}_1)$$

Scalar impulse/momentum equations may be written in any direction, such as the x-direction below, for a constant-mass and a time-invariant impulsive force:

$$\text{Imp}_x = F_x(t_2 - t_1) = m(\mathbf{v}_{2x} - \mathbf{v}_{1x}) \quad [3.33]$$

Units of impulse are lbf-sec or N · s, and caution must be exercised in converting from interim units of lbm-ft/sec or kg · m/s. Also, recall that positive impulsive forces result in an increase of momentum, whereas negative impulsive forces are directed opposite the object's initial velocity and cause a reduction in momentum.

Impulse-momentum problems on the FE exam often test for the impulse time period required for a given force to produce a known velocity change. Vector-triangle solution methods are useful in avoiding a set of tedious scalar equations.

Example 3.6

A 5.0-oz baseball has an initial horizontal velocity of 110.0 ft/sec at the instant that it is struck by a bat. If the ball is in contact with the bat for 0.15 sec, and the ball leaves the bat with a velocity of 140.0 ft/sec at 30° with respect to the horizontal, solve for the magnitude and direction of the average force applied to the ball.

Solution:

First compute the initial and final momentum vectors; then construct a vector triangle to solve for impulse **Imp.** Assume that the bat force is constant (average value), and consider the ball's weight to be negligible in comparison.

Initial momentum: $m\mathbf{v}_1$

$$= \left(\frac{5}{16}\text{ lbm}\right)(110.0\text{ ft/sec}) = 34.37\text{ lbm-ft/sec}$$

Final momentum: $m\mathbf{v}_2$

$$= \left(\frac{5}{16}\text{ lbm}\right)(140.0\text{ ft/sec}) = 43.75\text{ lbm-ft/sec}$$

In the vector triangle shown in Figure 3.8, impulse **Imp** is the resultant of the difference of the momentum vectors, and its magnitude is calculated from the law of cosines:

$$\text{Imp} = \sqrt{(43.75)^2 + (34.37)^2 - 2(43.75)(34.37)\cos 150°}$$

$$= \sqrt{5{,}699.76} = 75.49\text{ lbm-ft/sec}$$

$$= \frac{75.49}{32.2} = 2.34\text{ lbf-sec}$$

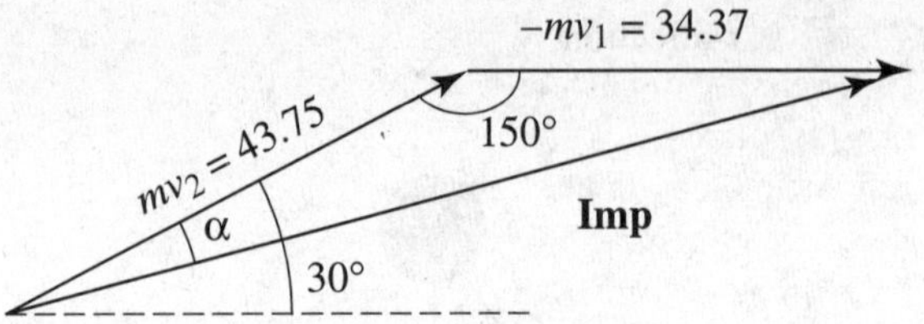

Figure 3.8

Direction of impulse:

$$\frac{\sin 150°}{75.49} = \frac{\sin\alpha}{34.37} \rightarrow \alpha = \sin^{-1}(0.227) = 13.16°$$

From the horizontal, the direction of **Imp** is $30.0 - 13.16 = 16.84°$, which must also be the direction of the bat (impulsive) force. Since

$$\mathbf{Imp} = \mathbf{F}(t_2 - t_1) = \mathbf{F}(0.15\text{ sec})$$

$$= 2.34\text{ lbf-sec} \rightarrow \mathbf{F} = \frac{2.34}{0.15} = 15.63\text{ lbf}$$

$\therefore$ **F** = 15.63 lbf at 16.84° with respect to the horizontal

Impact

An **impact** is a collision of two or more rigid bodies in which the forces of collision are equal and opposite (Newton's action/reaction principle) and the net external force acting upon the system is taken to be zero. As discussed in a preceding section, the *total linear momentum of the system of colliding bodies must be conserved* in all directions. The elasticity of the materials that constitute the colliding objects has a dramatic effect on the velocity of each object immediately after the impact. A coefficient of restitution ε is an important parameter in the solution of impact problems and is defined as

$$0 \le \varepsilon \le 1.0$$

where $\varepsilon = 0$ represents a *perfectly plastic impact* (objects join together after collision), and $\varepsilon = 1.0$ represents a *perfectly elastic impact* (objects experience no permanent deformation and energy is conserved).

Typical impact problems on the FE exam involve one of the following situations:

- Direct central impact (head-on collision) in which the lines of action of the initial velocities before collision are collinear with the line joining the centers of mass.
- Oblique collision (off-center) in which the initial velocities have components that are both parallel and perpendicular to the line joining the mass centers.

FE impact problems usually ask for the postcollision velocity of each object based upon a given value of ε. If velocities before and after impact are known for each object, then the value of ε may be called for. For a direct central impact involving two objects having masses m_1 and m_2, the following key equations are applicable (primes denote the condition immediately after impact):

$$m_1v_1 + m_2v_2 = m_1v_1' + m_2v_2' \qquad [3.34]$$
$$v_2' - v_1' = \varepsilon(v_1 - v_2)$$

Oblique collisions employ a set of equations similar to those above, except that all velocities must be components along the line of impact (n-direction), which is perpendicular to the tangential plane of impact.

Example 3.7

A 15.0-kg sphere having an initial velocity of 48.0 m/s along a frictionless horizontal surface collides with a 28.0-kg rectangular block at the instant when the block has a velocity of 9.0 m/s in the same direction. If the block's velocity becomes 30.0 m/s immediately after the impact, solve for the coefficient of restitution ε.

Solution:

Let the sphere and the block be denoted as objects 1 and 2, respectively. The conservation of linear momentum of a system for any impact requires that

$$(15.0\text{ kg})(48.0\text{ m/s}) + (28.0\text{ kg})(9.0\text{ m/s}) = (15.0\text{ kg})v_1' + (28.0\text{ kg})(30.0\text{ m/s})$$

$$(720 + 252)\text{kg}\cdot\text{m/s} = 15v_1' + 840\text{ kg}\cdot\text{m/s}$$

$$v_1' = \frac{972 - 840}{15} = 8.8\text{ m/s}$$

From the coefficient of restitution equation:

$$(30.0 - 8.8)\text{ m/s} = \varepsilon(48.0 - 9.0)\text{ m/s}$$

$$\therefore \varepsilon = \frac{21.2}{39.0} = 0.54$$

Angular Momentum

Angular momentum is a vector symbolized by **H** and defined as the "moment of momentum." For a constant-mass object that has position and velocity vectors **r** and **v**, respectively, from a reference origin O, as shown in Figure 3.9, the angular momentum is given by the cross product:

$$\mathbf{H} = \mathbf{r} \times m\mathbf{v} \qquad [3.35]$$

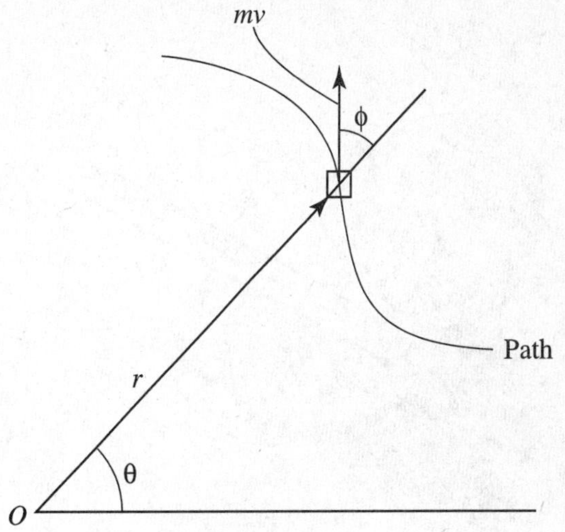

Figure 3.9

For most FE problems relating to angular momentum, both **r** and $m\mathbf{v}$ are in a two-dimensional plane and the direction of **H** is necessarily perpendicular to this plane according to the right-hand rule for cross products. The magnitude of angular momentum H is calculated using the angle ϕ between **r** and $m\mathbf{v}$ or using the object's angular velocity ω ($\omega = d\theta/dt$):

$$H = mrv\sin\phi = mr^2\omega \qquad [3.36]$$

The units for H are lbm-ft²/sec or kg · m²/s.

It is important to recall that the net moment (torque) acting upon a fixed-mass object is related to the rate of change of angular momentum:

$$\Sigma\mathbf{M} = \dot{\mathbf{H}} \qquad [3.37]$$

For circular or arc-type motion ($r = R$), the magnitude of the applied moment is related to the object's angular acceleration α according to the equation

$$\Sigma M = mR^2\alpha \qquad [3.38]$$

Example 3.8

The cam follower mechanism illustrated in Figure 3.10 contains arm AC, which rotates at a constant angular velocity ω = 300 rpm in a counterclockwise direction. If pin B is held against the cam lobes by a spring, and the distance of the pin from pivot point A is given by the equation

$$r = 100\cos 3\theta + 250$$

where r is measured in millimeters, determine the angular momentum of the pin about the pivot after 4.0 s of motion if the initial angle θ is assumed zero and the pin has a mass of 0.3 kg.

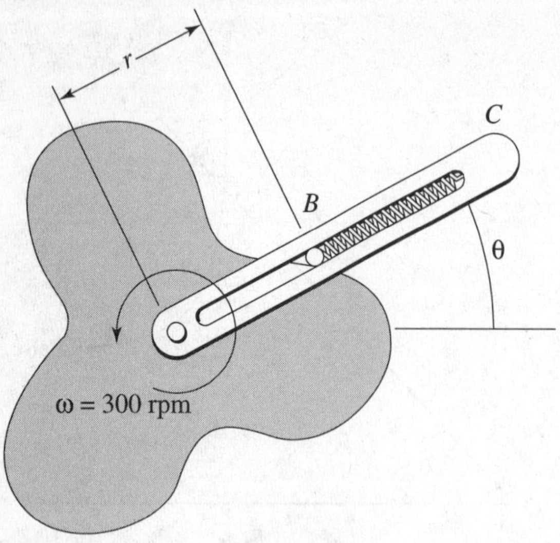

Figure 3.10

Solution:

Angular momentum for a fixed-mass object in plane motion is expressed as

$$H = mr^2\omega$$

In this case

$$\omega = (300 \text{ rev/min})(2\pi \text{ rad/rev})(\text{min}/60 \text{ s}) = 31.41 \text{ rad/s}$$

$$\text{since } \omega = \frac{d\theta}{dt} \rightarrow \theta = \int \omega\, dt = \omega t = 31.41t.$$

Substitute for θ into the expression for r to obtain

$$r = 100 \cos 3(31.41t) + 250$$

At $t = 4.0$ s,

$$r = 100 \cos[94.23(4.0)] + 250 = 349.7 \text{ mm} \approx 0.350 \text{ m}$$

$\therefore H = (0.3 \text{ kg})(0.350 \text{ m})^2(31.41 \text{ rad/s}) = 1.15 \text{ kg} \cdot \text{m}^2\text{/s}$

Central Force Motion; Conservation of Angular Momentum

For motion of a fixed-mass object or particle in a plane as presented in the preceding section, a *central force* is defined as an external force whose line of action is always collinear with that of the position vector. Essentially, a central force is one that is continually directed toward or away from the object's reference origin and that produces *no net moment or zero torque.* Examples of central forces are cable tensions, gravitational forces, and spring/elastic forces. Referring to equation 3.37 (moment = angular momentum change), central force motion requires that *angular momentum remain constant* (be conserved).

The following equations summarize the conditions for conservation of angular momentum:

$$\Sigma\mathbf{M} = 0 \rightarrow \dot{\mathbf{H}} = 0 \quad \text{and} \quad \mathbf{H} = \text{constant}$$

The magnitude of angular momentum is also constant.

$$H = mr\omega^2 = \text{constant}$$

$$mr_1^2\omega_1 = mr_2^2\omega_2 \rightarrow \text{For m = constant, then}$$

$$r_1^2\omega_1 = r_2^2\omega_2 = \text{constant}$$

Clearly, an object's angular velocity increases substantially when the distance of the object from a reference origin or spin axis is reduced.

3.3 Work and Energy

Work and energy problems often constitute a significant percentage of the total problems in the dynamics section of the FE exam. Therefore, a careful review of concepts such as the principle of work and kinetic energy, potential energy, kinetic friction, and conservation of energy is strongly recommended.

Work of a Force

For particle and rigid-body dynamics, *work W* is a scalar quantity that is the dot product of an external force or net force with the displacement vector of the object or particle.

The governing equation for this type of mechanical work is

$$W = \int \mathbf{F}\, dr \qquad [3.39]$$

The units of work are ft-lbf or N · m (equivalent to joules). For *rectilinear plane motion,* represented in the majority of FE exam problems related to work and energy, the equations listed below are useful when a *single force or net force component along the line of action of the displacement is constant:*

$W = F_x\,\Delta x$, where Δx is the displacement along the x-direction

$W = F_y\,\Delta y$

$W = F_I\,\Delta I$ (along an inclined direction) [3.40]

Positive work occurs when the applied force or net force component is in the same direction as the displacement, whereas *negative work* is the result of a (net) force that acts in a direction opposite to the displacement direction. Additionally, bear in mind that forces or components of forces that are perpendicular to the displacement direction produce zero work.

For curvilinear motion, the work due to a force or net force is given by equation 3.39; however, numerical calculations are somewhat tedious and are not often required on the FE exam. Usually, it is advisable to employ the principle of work and kinetic energy (discussed on page 83) to determine the work done along a curved path.

Example 3.9

A 600.0-kg milling machine that is being removed from a factory is lowered 14.0 m vertically by a rigging cable that has a constant tension of 5.0 kN. Determine the net work done on the machine during this process.

Solution:

An FBD of the machine is given in Figure 3.11, which shows the constant gravitational and cable tension forces **W** and $\mathbf{T}_c$, respectively, and the positive y-direction is assigned downward.

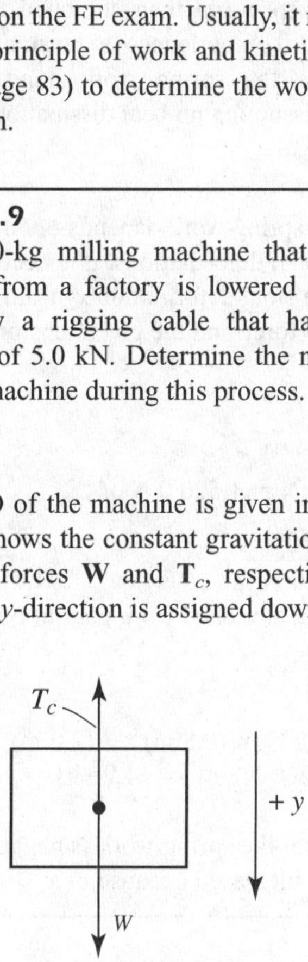

Figure 3.11

Since displacement Δy is given, the equation for net work is

$$W = F_y \, \Delta y$$

Here

$$F_y = W - T_c = (600.0 \text{ kg})(9.81 \text{ m/s}^2) - 5.0 \text{ kN}$$
$$= 5{,}886.0 - 5{,}000.0 = 886.0 \text{ N}$$

$$\Delta y = 14.0 \text{ m (positive displacement)}$$

$$\therefore W = (886.0 \text{ N})(14.0 \text{ m}) = 12{,}404 \text{ N} \cdot \text{m}$$
$$= 12{,}404 \text{ J or } 12.4 \text{ kJ}$$

Numerous other types of work-generating forces, such as kinetic friction and springs, are frequently incorporated into FE problems. These will be specifically reviewed in subsequent sections.

Kinetic Energy

Kinetic energy is the energy associated with an object's mass m and instantaneous speed v. (The standard abbreviation KE will be utilized for all references to kinetic energy in this section and beyond.) Like all other work/energy terms, kinetic energy is a scalar and is defined by the following equation for constant-mass objects and/or rigid bodies:

$$\text{KE} = \frac{1}{2}mv^2 \qquad [3.41]$$

Note that, in the IP system of units, inputting values of mass in pounds mass and of speed in ft/sec into the KE equation *will not directly yield ft-lbf results.* Your ability to employ the correct conversion(s) will influence your degree of success in identifying the correct answers to KE-related problems. In the SI system, utilizing kilograms and m/s for mass and speed terms in the KE equation will directly produce quantitative results in joules (or N · m).

The KE of a fixed-mass object can change only if a nonzero force or system of forces is applied that causes an acceleration or deceleration. This condition of zero net force also requires that the work done on an object having constant KE also be zero. In a later section, it will be shown that the amount of KE possessed by a rigid body is directly dependent upon the object's potential energy for a conservative process involving frictionless forces only.

Potential Energy

Potential energy is categorized into two major areas. *Gravitational* potential energy is the energy associated with an object's elevation with respect to a reference datum. *Elastic* potential energy is the energy stored in a compressed or stretched spring. This section focuses on gravitational potential energy; linear springs will be reviewed in the next section.

With the standard symbol PE utilized for potential energy, gravitational PE due to an object's elevation h with respect to a datum is defined as follows:

$$\text{PE} = \mathcal{W}h = mgh \qquad [3.42]$$

where $\mathcal{W}$ is the weight or gravitational force on the object, and g is the acceleration of gravity in the environment for which weight is being measured.

Gravity work (W_g) is the work due to a gravitational force for a given vertical displacement or elevation change Δh.

Later, it will be shown that for a frictionless process in which only gravitational force acts, the change in PE for a rigid body is equal and opposite to the change in KE.

Linear Springs

From the equation

$$W_g = W\,\Delta h = W(h_1 - h_2) \qquad [3.43]$$

gravity work is related to potential energy change as

$$W_g = \text{PE}_1 - \text{PE}_2 = -\Delta\text{PE}.$$

An object that experiences an increase in elevation, and therefore a positive PE change (increase), is subjected to negative gravity work because the force and the displacement are in opposite directions. Conversely, when elevation (and PE) is required, gravity work is positive, as shown previously in Example 3.9.

A **linear spring** is a spring that has a *constant stiffness k.* Recall that the force due to a spring is given by the simple equation

$$F_s = -kx \qquad [3.44]$$

where x represents the spring *deformation,* which is the amount by which the spring is stretched or compressed from natural (undeformed) position. The direction of a spring force on an attached object is opposite to the direction of the deformation, and stiffness constant k is measured typically in N/m or lbf/ft. A nonlinear spring exists when k varies with the spring length, as in an automobile coil spring.

The *potential energy* PE_s stored in a linear spring or an elastic material is due to the energy required to compress or stretch the spring and is computed from the equation

$$\text{PE}_s = \frac{1}{2}kx^2 \qquad [3.45]$$

Spring work W_s is related to the change in potential energy and is determined from the equation

$$W_s = \text{PE}_{s1} - \text{PE}_{s2} = \frac{1}{2}k(x_1{}^2 - x_2{}^2) \qquad [3.46]$$

where x_1 and x_2 signify the initial and final deformations, respectively.

Equation 3.46 is valid for both rectilinear and curvilinear motion and assumes no heat dissipation from the spring during compression or extension. Note that the work done by a spring is positive when the deformation decreases ($x_2 < x_1$) and the spring is unloading its potential energy.

Example 3.10

A linear spring having a stiffness of 750 N/m is initially compressed 0.8 m from its natural position. The spring is then stretched to a position such that it experiences a tension of 1.5 kN. Determine the spring work done during this process, assuming no heat dissipation.

Solution:

Since the spring work depends upon both the initial and final deformations, it is necessary first to obtain the final deformation x_2 from the equation for spring force and the given tension value.

$$x_2 = \frac{F_s}{k}$$

$$F_s = 1.5\text{ kN} = 1{,}500.0\text{ N}$$

$$x_2 = \frac{1{,}500.0\text{ N}}{750.0\text{ N/m}} = 2.0\text{ m stretched from natural position}$$

$$\therefore\ W_s = \frac{1}{2}k(x_1{}^2 - x_2{}^2)$$
$$= 375.0\text{ N/m}[(0.8\text{ m})^2 - (2.0\text{ m})^2]$$
$$= -1{,}260\text{ N}\cdot\text{m} = -1.26\text{ kJ}$$

Note that the spring work is negative since the PE has increased because of $x_2 > x_1$.

Kinetic Friction

Kinetic friction is the shearing force due to the sliding motion of a rigid body with respect to a surface of contact. The computation of kinetic friction simply involves determining the product of a *coefficient of kinetic friction* μ_k and the *normal reaction force* N_R acting upon the rigid body.

$$F_k = \mu_k N_R \qquad [3.47]$$

The value of μ_k is usually lower than the static friction coefficient μ_s for the same surfaces or objects in contact. It is also important to recognize that the direction of the kinetic friction force applied to a rigid body is opposite to the direction of the relative velocity of the body with respect to the contact surface or plane.

Most FE problems related to kinetic friction involve rectilinear motion, and a typical problem requires that the normal reaction be determined for an object on a horizontal or inclined surface in order to calculate F_k. Again, the use of effective free body diagrams is highly advantageous in solving problems incorporating kinetic friction.

The fact that kinetic friction forces oppose the velocity direction relative to the surface directly in contact with an object will cause a deceleration and consequently a decrease in the object's KE if the contacting surface is stationary. The *work done by a kinetic friction force is negative* relative to the surface of contact because this work opposes the displacement direction of an object, and kinetic friction work results in heat dissipation from a body. For this reason, kinetic friction forces are referred to as *nonconservative.*

Example 3.11

A mother pulls a sled containing her child across a horizontal snow-covered field as illustrated in Figure 3.12. The coefficient of kinetic friction μ_k between the base of the sled and the snow is estimated to be 0.15, and the pulling force is applied at a 30° angle with an assumed constant magnitude throughout the motion. The combined weight of child plus sled is known to be 65.0 lbf. If the sled travels 300.0 ft and the net work done on the child/sled system is 600.0 ft-lbf, determine:

A. the required pulling force
B. the friction force

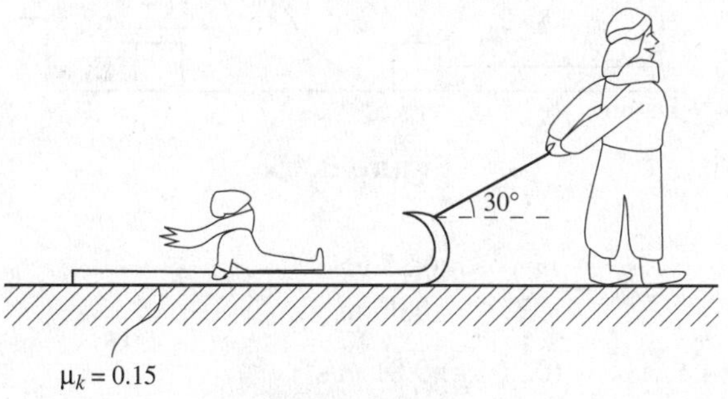

Figure 3.12

Solution:

Draw an FBD of the child/sled system, as shown in Figure 3.13, that displays all of the external forces acting on the system and the attached *x-y* coordinate reference frame.

A. Since net work and displacement are given, the net force in the displacement (x) direction can be readily obtained.

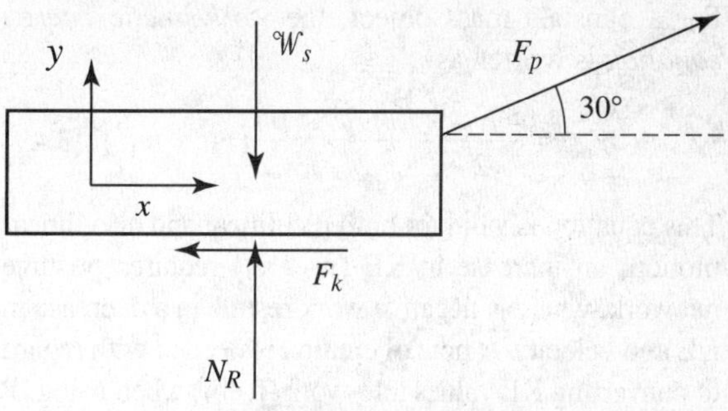

Figure 3.13

$$W_{net} = \Sigma F_X \, \Delta X$$

$$600.0 \text{ ft-lbf} = \Sigma F_x(300.0 \text{ ft}) \rightarrow \Sigma F_x = \frac{600.0 \text{ ft-lbf}}{300.0 \text{ ft}}$$

$$= 2.0 \text{ lbf}$$

Note that the work of pulling, F_p, is positive and the work of friction, F_k, is negative; therefore,

$$\Sigma F_x = F_{px} - F_k = F_p \cos 30° - \mu_k N_R$$
$$= 0.866F_p - 0.15\, N_R = 2.0 \text{ lbf}$$

$\Sigma F_y = 0$ required for sled to maintain contact with surface.

$$\Sigma F_y = F_p \sin 30° - \mathcal{W}_s + N_R = 0$$

$$0.5F_p - 65.0 \text{ lbf} + N_R = 0 \rightarrow N_R = 65.0 - 0.5F_p$$

Substitute for N_R in the equation for ΣF_x to obtain

$$0.866F_p - 0.15(65.0 - 0.5\, F_p) = 2.0 \text{ lbf}$$

$$\therefore 0.941F_p = 11.75 \text{ lbf} \rightarrow F_p = 12.49 \text{ lbf}$$

B. Substitute for F_p above to obtain the normal reaction:

$$N_R = 65.0 - 0.5(12.49) = 58.75 \text{ lbf}$$

$$\therefore F_k = 0.15(58.75 \text{ lbf}) = 8.81 \text{ lbf}$$

Principle of Work and Kinetic Energy

One of the most useful problem-solving methodologies for the dynamics section of the FE exam is the **principle of work and kinetic energy.** This principle is derived from Newton's second law and effectively states that the *net work done on a rigid body is equal to the change in kinetic energy.* For any process involving conservative (frictionless) and/or nonconservative external forces acting upon a single object from state 1 to state 2, the governing equation is as follows:

$$W_{net} = \Delta KE = KE_2 - KE_1 \qquad [3.48]$$

For a constant-mass object, the *work/kinetic energy equation* is written as

$$W_{net} = \frac{mv_2^2}{2} - \frac{mv_1^2}{2} = \frac{m}{2}(v_2^2 - v_1^2) \quad [3.49]$$

This equation is valid for both rectilinear and curvilinear motion; an increase in KE ($v_2 > v_1$) requires positive net work, whereas negative work results in a decrease in KE and velocity. A note of caution is needed with regard to converting KE values into work (ft-lbf) when using IP units. If initial and final velocities are known, net work can be computed directly without involving any forces or displacements. In most FE problems related to work/energy, however, it is necessary to determine forces and velocity (or KE) values at various stages of computation as illustrated in Example 3.12.

Example 3.12

A 0.25-kg cube initially at rest is projected from a compressed spring across a frictionless horizontal surface as shown in Figure 3.14. The cube then enters the 6.0-cm-radius circular loop and contains the minimum speed necessary at point C to allow it to barely maintain contact with the loop as it travels past the highest point, E. If the spring stiffness is 500.0 N/m, solve for the required initial deformation of the spring.

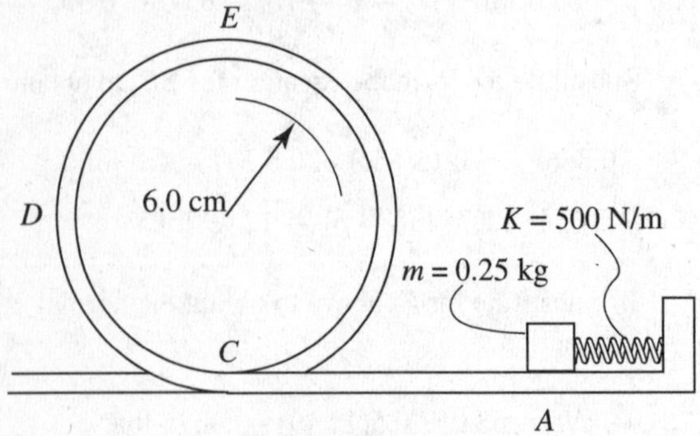

Figure 3.14

Solution:

The principle of work and kinetic energy is employed from the initial compressed position (point A) to the highest point E, where the object is assumed to have a negligible reaction force with the loop as a condition of minimum contact. The net work done on the cube is the difference in kinetic energy according to

$$W_{net} = KE_E - KE_A = \frac{1}{2}m(v_E^2 - v_A^2)$$

Since the cube is released from rest, $v_A = 0$ ($KE_A = 0$), and the net work done is simply the kinetic energy at E in this case:

$$W_{net} = \frac{1}{2}mv_E^2 = 0.125 \text{ kg}(v_E^2)$$

The net work done on the cube from A to E is the combination of the spring work and the gravity work:

$$W_{net} = W_s + W_g = \frac{1}{2}k(x_A^2 - x_B^2) + mg(h_A - h_E)$$

If the initial elevation is assumed to be zero, then $h_A = 0$ and $h_E = 2(6.0 \text{ cm}) = 0.12$ m. At point B, the spring is fully unloaded and undeformed $\rightarrow x_B = 0$. Substitute the above values into the work equation to obtain:

$$W_{net} = \frac{500.0 \text{ N/m}}{2}[x_A^2 - 0^2] + (0.25 \text{ kg})(9.81 \text{ m/s}^2)(0 - 0.12 \text{ m})$$

$$= 250.0 \text{ N/m}(x_A^2) - 0.29 \text{ N} \cdot \text{m} = 0.125 \text{ kg}(v_E^2)$$

At point E, the cube is clearly in circular motion with radius $R = 0.06$ m and reaction force $N_R = 0$. The FBD of the cube at E in Figure 3.15 shows the forces acting in the normal direction:

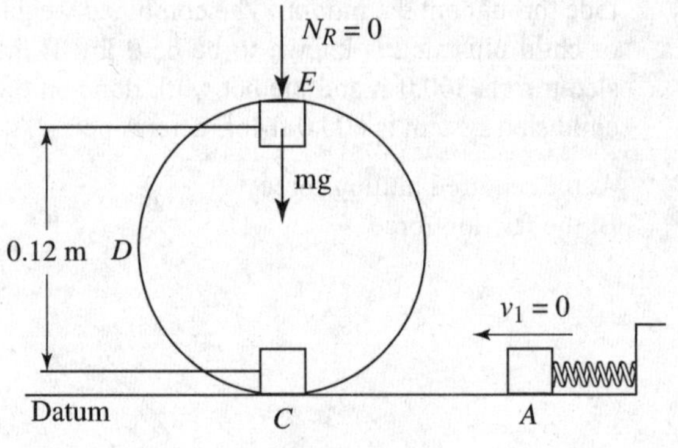

Figure 3.15

$$\Sigma F_n = \frac{mv_E^2}{R} = \frac{0.25\, v_E^2}{0.06 \text{ m}} = 4.17\, v_E^2 = mg + 0$$

$$4.17\, v_E^2 = (0.25 \text{ kg})(9.81 \text{ m/s}^2)$$

$$= 245 \text{ N} \rightarrow v_E = \sqrt{\frac{2.45}{4.17}} = 0.77 \text{ m/s}$$

Inserting the value of v_E into the work equation produces a solution for the spring deformation:

$$250.0 \text{ N/m}(x_A^2) = 0.125 \text{ kg}(0.77 \text{ m/s})^2 + 0.29 \text{ N} \cdot \text{m}$$

$$\rightarrow x_A^2 = \frac{(0.074 + 0.29) \text{ N} \cdot \text{m}}{250.0 \text{ N/m}}$$

$$\therefore x_A = \sqrt{\frac{0.364}{250.0}} = 0.038 \text{ m} = 3.8 \text{ cm}$$

Banking Angles

A frequently encountered FE exam topic for circular motion problems is the banking angles of roads or curved tracks. These angles are a very important consideration for vehicle safety in highway and/or public transportation design. Effectively, a **banking angle,** θ, with respect to a horizontal plane is the minimum angle required to keep a vehicle traveling at a *maximum rated speed* v_m from sliding outward, assuming that friction is negligible because of an icy or otherwise slippery road surface. If the radius of curvature R of a section of roadway is known, or if the path is circular, then Newton's second law analysis in the normal and vertical directions yields the *banking angle equation:*

$$v_m = \sqrt{gR \tan\theta}$$

or, equivalently,

$$\theta = \tan^{-1}\left(\frac{v_m^2}{gR}\right) \qquad [3.50]$$

where θ is measured in degrees.

Conservation of Energy

For motion of a rigid body in which only *conservative forces* (frictionless) are acting, the net work done on the body is independent of the path traveled and depends only upon the initial and final positions. Gravity work and ideal spring work are examples of conservative processes for which there is no friction energy loss. From the principle of work and kinetic energy equation (equation 3.49), it can readily be shown that, if gravity is the only type of work done on the particle or rigid body, *the change in kinetic energy* of the body or particle *is equal and opposite to the change in the potential energy.*

In essence, this requires that, if an object subjected to gravity force experiences only a kinetic energy increase from state 1 to state 2, there must be a loss of potential energy in an amount equal to the kinetic energy rise between the same two states. Energy is simply converted from one form to another, and no energy is lost from the object to the surrounding environment. The *conservation of energy equation* given below (equation 3.51) indicates that the sum of the potential and kinetic energy possessed by an object is constant for all states if only conservative (frictionless) forces are applied:

$$\mathrm{KE}_1 + \mathrm{PE}_1 = \mathrm{KE}_2 + \mathrm{PE}_2 = \ldots = \mathrm{KE}_n + \mathrm{PE}_n = \text{constant}$$

$$\Delta\mathrm{KE} = -\Delta\mathrm{PE}$$

$$\frac{1}{2}mv_1^2 + mgh_1 = \frac{1}{2}mv_2^2 + mgh_2 = \text{constant} \qquad [3.51]$$

For a rigid body or particle:

$$g(h_1 - h_2) = \frac{v_2^2 - v_1^2}{2}$$

With reference to equation 3.51, many FE dynamics problems involve a rigid body initially at rest ($v_1 = 0$) that experiences an elevation drop of ($h_1 - h_2$). The *final velocity* v_2 at the lower elevation h_2 is given (assuming no friction) by the equation

$$v_2 = \sqrt{2g(h_1 - h_2)} \qquad [3.52]$$

Note that, for free-fall (gravity) motion without air friction, equation 3.52 is often used to calculate terminal velocity.

Example 3.13

A 140.0-lbm ski jumper initially at rest begins to travel down the smooth ramp illustrated in Figure 3.16 from point A and attains a velocity of 65.0 mph at exit point B. Assuming that the skier experiences a normal reaction equal to 2.5 times his or her weight, determine:

A. the height h required to produce this stated speed
B. the radius of curvature ρ of the ramp at point B

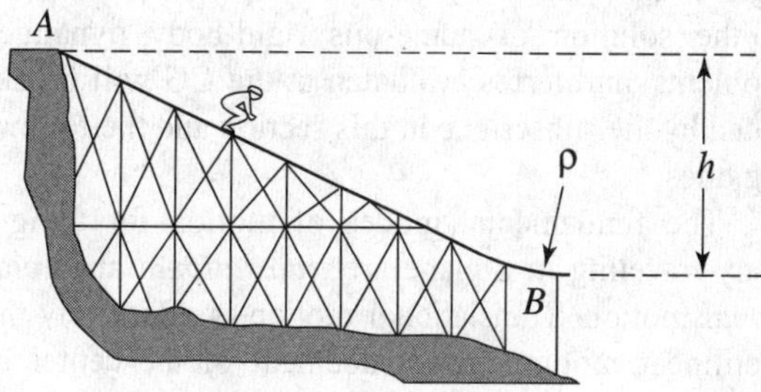

Figure 3.16

Solution:

A. Since gravity is the only work-producing force acting upon the skier if kinetic friction is considered negligible, the conservation of energy equation for terminal velocity (equation 3.52) may be employed, given that $v_B = 65.0$ mph $= 95.3$ ft/sec.

$$v_B = \sqrt{2g(h_A - h_B)} = \sqrt{2(32.2\ \text{ft/sec}^2)h} = 95.3\ \text{ft/sec}$$

$$\therefore h = \frac{(95.3)^2}{64.4} = 141.0\ \text{ft}$$

B. For the normal reaction N_R at B, it was stated that

$$N_R = 2.5\,\mathcal{W}_s = 2.5(140.0 \text{ lbf}) = 350.0 \text{ lbf}$$

Since the radius ρ of the ramp is desired, apply Newton's second law equation to the skier (free body) for circular motion in the normal direction:

$$\Sigma F_n = \frac{m v_B^{\,2}}{\rho} = N_R - \mathcal{W}_s$$

$$\frac{(140.0 \text{ lbm})(95.3 \text{ ft/sec})^2}{\rho} = (350.0 - 140.0) \text{ lbf}$$

$$\therefore \rho = \frac{(140)(9{,}082.1)\left(\frac{1}{32.2}\right) \text{ ft-lbf}}{210.0 \text{ lbf}} = 188.0 \text{ ft}$$

3.4 Rigid Body Motion in a Plane

The motion of rigid bodies in a two-dimensional plane is a commonly tested topic on the FE dynamics section. Typical problems involve rolling cylinders and wheels, rods within perpendicular slots, gears, rotating 3-D bodies, and so on. The *center of gravity* of the rigid body being analyzed is an important parameter in the solution of numerous rigid-body dynamics problems, and terms evaluated at the CG will be denoted by the subscript c in this section and the following ones.

The fundamental modes of motion for a rigid body traveling in a plane are *translational* and *rotational* motion. Translational motion is effectively the rectilinear motion or displacement of the center of gravity and is governed by Newton's second law equation:

$$\Sigma \mathbf{F} = m\mathbf{a}_c$$

Rotational motion is the spin of the body about an axis that normally passes through the CG or a parallel axis (discussed on page 87), and the magnitude of rotation is measured using the familiar terms *angular velocity* (ω) and *angular acceleration* (α). The applied torque or net moment for plane rigid-body motion is also typically measured with respect to the CG and may be determined by using the following equation:

$$\Sigma M_c = I_c\,\alpha \qquad [3.53]$$

where I_c is the mass moment of inertia, which is evaluated about a particular axis that passes through the CG of the object. The important concept of mass moment of inertia is reviewed in the next section.

Mass Moment of Inertia

The **mass moment of inertia** I for a three-dimensional rigid body is essentially a measure of the resistance of the body to angular acceleration. For any rigid body such as the one illustrated in Figure 3.17, mass moment of inertia is theoretically defined as the "second moment of mass" of all mass elements dm integrated throughout the entire mass m of the body:

$$I = \int_m r^2\,dm$$

where r represents the moment-arm distance from any mass element to the axis about which I is being evaluated. Recall that the units for mass moment are conventionally kg · m^2 or lbm-ft^2.

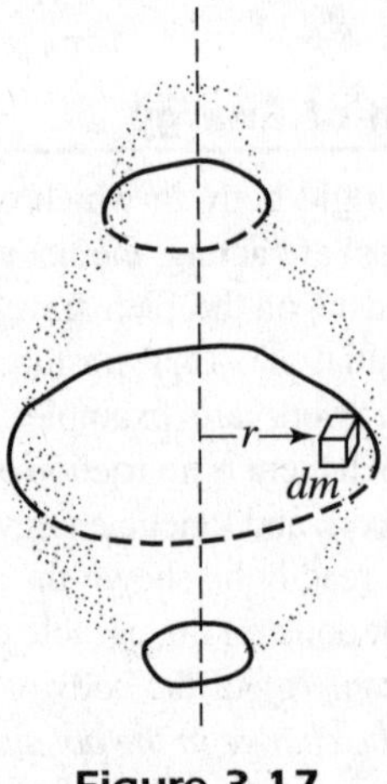

Figure 3.17

Clearly, performing the above integration for I is a tedious task, and therefore equations for the mass moments of inertia for various familiar shapes—cones, spheres, rectangular plates, disks, and so on—are provided in Table 3.1 for quick reference. The FE exam review pamphlet also contains this reference material for I. It is important to recognize that, for any given rigid-body geometry, the *formulas for I are directly dependent upon a specific axis for evaluating I,* and this axis is usually chosen perpendicular to the plane in which the forces act upon the body. For example, I_z is evaluated when forces are confined to an x-y plane. Since the mass m of the object is required to compute numerical values of I, the product of an object's density and volume must be calculated to obtain mass if it is not directly given on an FE problem.

For *composite bodies* or shapes, such as a cylindrical shaft connected to a circular plate (disk) at each end, the composite mass moment of inertia about a given axis is the algebraic *sum of the individual moments of inertia* of the component shapes about the same axis. This computation will usually require the use of the parallel axis theorem, which is reviewed in the next section.

Parallel Axis Theorem

Whenever the mass moment of inertia must be evaluated about an axis that does not pass directly through the CG of a rigid body but is required for a *parallel axis* that passes through an alternative location on the body, the key equation for use on FE problems is

$$I' = I_c + md^2 \qquad [3.54]$$

where I' = mass moment of inertia about a specified parallel axis,

d = perpendicular distance from the CG to a point on the parallel axis,

I_c = mass moment of inertia about the CG.

Example 3.14

The T-shaped pendulum pictured in Figure 3.18 consists of two thin rods, each having a weight of 7.0 lbf, and is hinged at point O. Find the mass moment of inertia of the combined pendulum about an axis passing through the pin at O.

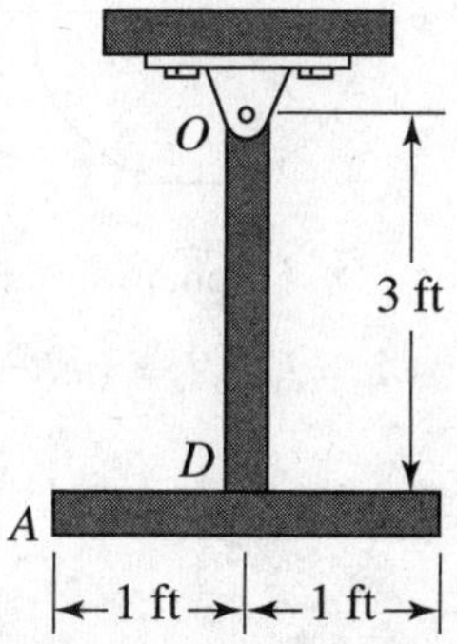

Figure 3.18

Solution:

The composite mass moment of inertia for the entire pendulum is the sum of the individual moments of inertia for rod OD and rod AB. Use Table 3.1 for mass moments of inertia for common geometries to obtain the equation for mass moment of inertia of a slender rod about an axis through one of its end points:

$$I_x' = \frac{ml^2}{3} = (I_O)_{\text{OD}} \quad \text{for rod OD}$$

$$(I_O)_{\text{OD}} = \frac{(30.0\ \text{lbm})(3.0\ \text{ft})^2}{3} = 90.0\ \text{lbm-ft}^2$$

For rod AB, compute the mass moment about point O by using the parallel axis theorem:

$$(I_O)_{AB} = (I_x)_{AB} + md^2$$

Since $d = 3.0$ ft from point D (the CG of AB) to the parallel axis through point O:

$$(I_O)_{AB} = \frac{ml^2}{12} + md^2$$
$$= \frac{(30.0\ \text{lbm})(2.0\ \text{ft})^2}{12} + (30.0)(3.0\ \text{ft})^2$$
$$= 280.0\ \text{lbm-ft}^2$$

∴ For the composite pendulum, the total moment of inertia I_O is summed as $I_O = 90.0 + 280.0 = 370.0$ lbm-ft^2.

Radius of Gyration

The **radius of gyration** of a rigid body of mass m is the *perpendicular distance* k from an axis passing through the CG to a point where the entire mass m can be concentrated to produce the same moment of inertia or gyration as the original body about this CG axis. Once I for a body of particular shape is obtained by using Table 3.1, the radius of gyration is readily computed from the relationship

$$I = mk^2 \qquad [3.55]$$

Then

$$\text{Radius of gyration} \rightarrow k = \sqrt{\frac{I}{m}}$$

Rotation of a Rigid Body About a Fixed Axis

The rotation of a rigid body within a two-dimensional plane about a fixed axis through a point that is not necessarily the CG of the body is a topic frequently presented on the FE exam. Figure 3.19 shows a rigid-body rotation within an x-y plane about an axis passing through point A, which is located at a distance r from the CG of the body.

If a constant net moment is applied, the body will experience a constant angular acceleration α according to the equation

$$\Sigma M_A = I_A\alpha \qquad [3.56]$$

Table 3.1 Centroids and Moments of Inertia for Various Geometries

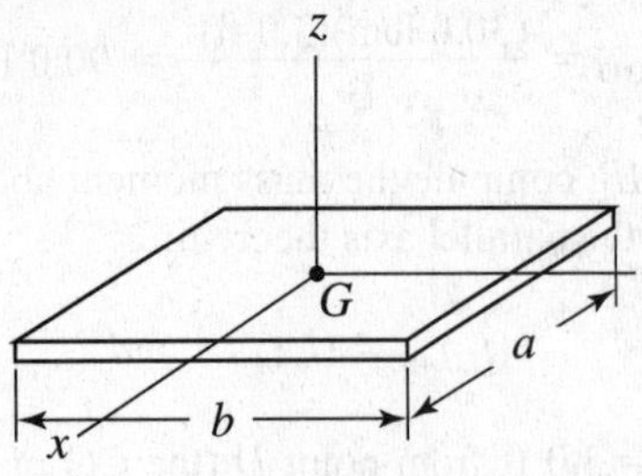

Thin plate

$I_x = \frac{1}{12}mb^2 \qquad I_y = \frac{1}{12}ma^2 \qquad I_z = \frac{1}{12}m(a^2 + b^2)$

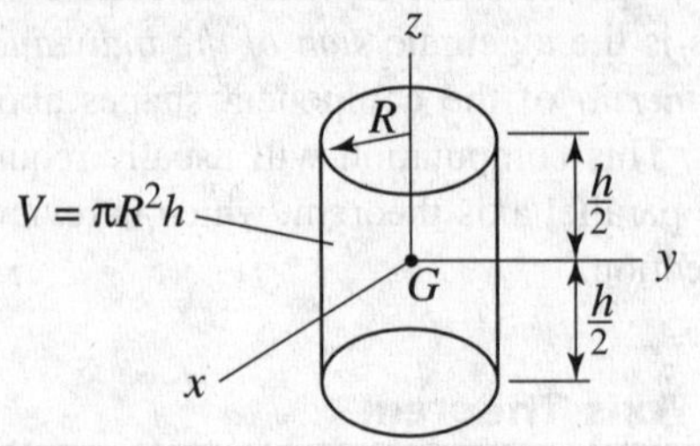

Cylinder

$I_x = I_y = \frac{1}{12}m(3R^2 + h^2) \qquad I_z = \frac{1}{2}mR^2$

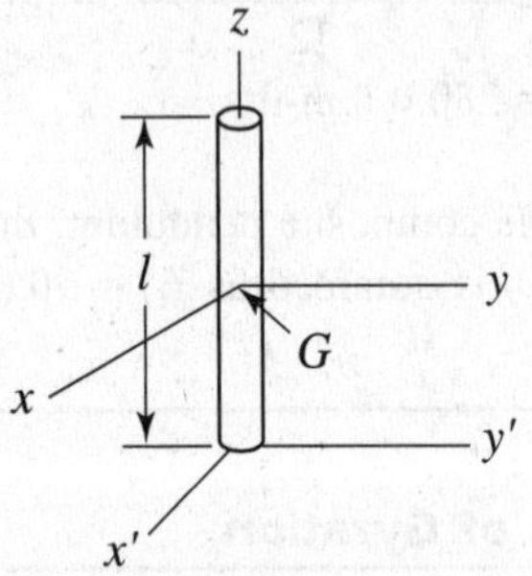

Slender rod

$I_x = I_y = \frac{1}{12}m\ell^2 \qquad I_{x'} = I_{y'} = \frac{1}{3}m\ell^2 \qquad I_z = 0$

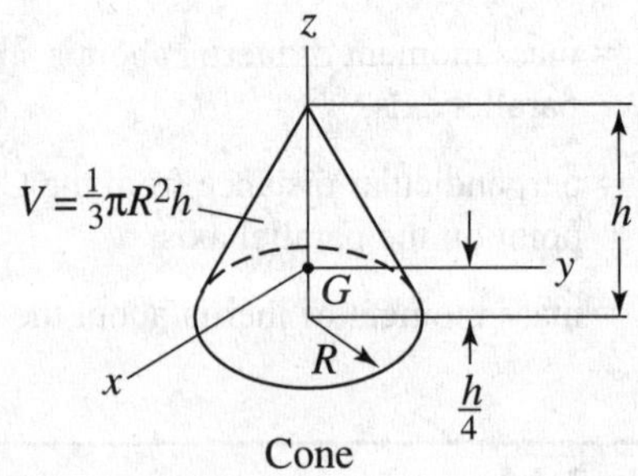

Cone

$I_x = I_y = \frac{3}{80}m(4R^2 + h^2) \qquad I_z = \frac{3}{10}mR^2$

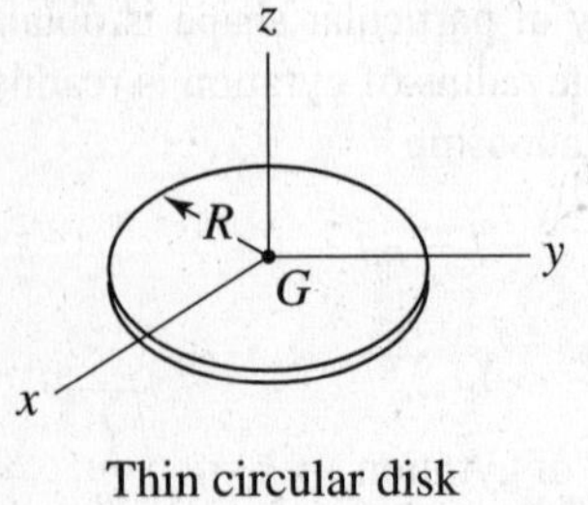

Thin circular disk

$I_x = I_y = \frac{1}{4}mR^2 \qquad I_z = \frac{1}{2}mR^2$

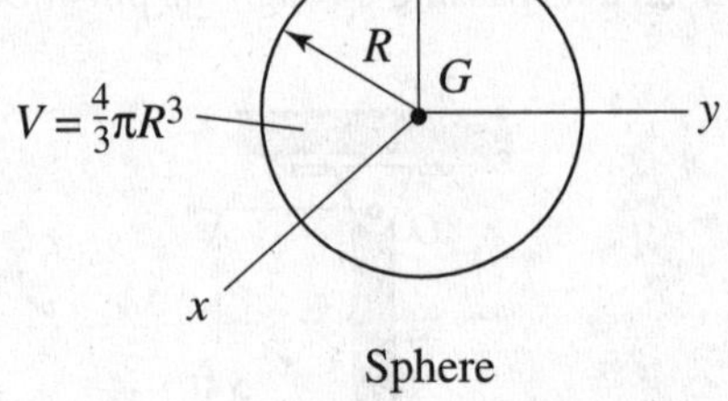

Sphere

$I_x = I_y = I_z = \frac{2}{5}mR^2$

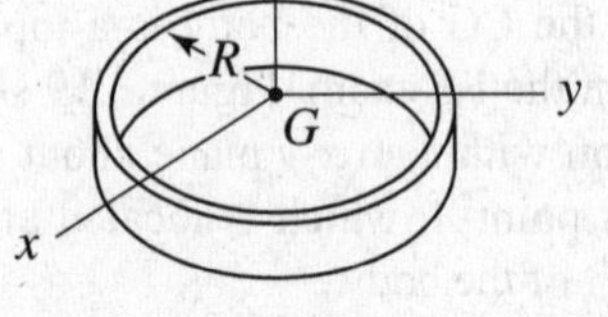

Thin ring

$I_x = I_y = \frac{1}{2}mR^2 \qquad I_z = mR^2$

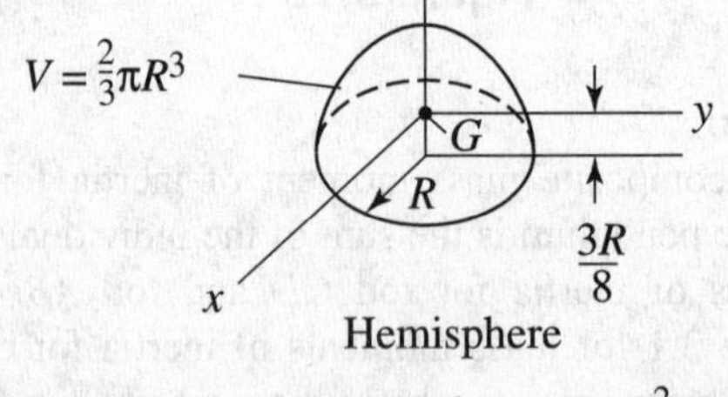

Hemisphere

$I_x = I_y = 0.259mR^2 \qquad I_z = \frac{2}{3}mR^2$

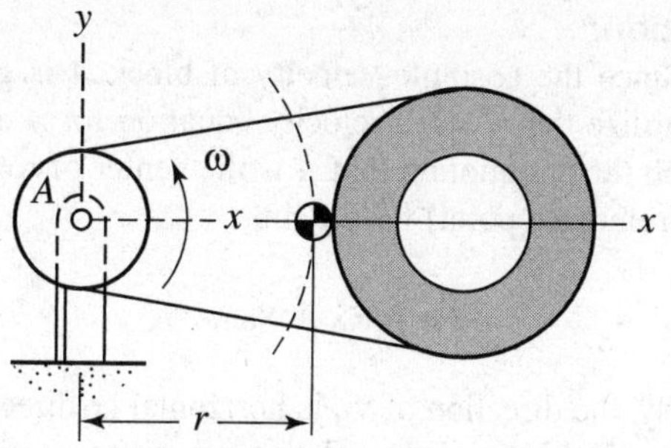

Figure 3.19

The above torque must be in a z-direction normal to the x-y plane, and the moment of inertia about a z-axis (the axis of rotation) through point A is obtained by using the parallel axis theorem:

$$I_A = I_c + mr^2 \qquad [3.57]$$

Since the motion of the CG is circular about point A, the acceleration of the CG with respect to A may be determined from tangential and normal acceleration equations. The net forces acting upon the rotating body in the x- and y-directions are then readily obtained:

$$a_{cx} = -r\omega^2 \rightarrow \Sigma F_x = -mr\omega^2$$
$$a_{cy} = r\alpha \rightarrow \Sigma F_y = mr\alpha \qquad [3.58]$$

Since the net moment shown above is assumed constant, then necessarily the *angular acceleration* α *is constant* and the angular velocity ω changes at a constant rate. The value of angular velocity at any time t is therefore given by

$$\omega(t) = \omega_0 + \alpha t \qquad [3.59]$$

where ω_0 is the initial angular velocity at $t = 0$, and ω is expressed in rad/s.

The velocity of the CG around the axis is entirely tangential and is determined by using the equation

$$v_c = r\,\omega \qquad [3.60]$$

Velocity and Acceleration: Absolute and Relative Motion

Rigid-body motion in a plane can be described by the simultaneous processes of *translation* and *rotation.* Many objects, such as automobile wheels, conveyor belts, and spinning baseballs, exhibit this type of motion, and the FE exam usually features at least one problem in this category. An understanding of the *relative motion* of two or more points on a rotating/translating rigid body is advantageous in developing the proper solution to various problems.

In Figure 3.20, point A is translating in a plane with an absolute velocity of $\mathbf{v_A}$ as shown. If A is considered to be the instantaneous center of rotation of the body, with all other points on the body having a common angular velocity ω about a perpendicular axis through A, an arbitrary point B can be chosen on the body that necessarily has circular motion as viewed from A. This *relative velocity of B with respect to A* is denoted by the vector $\mathbf{v_{B/A}}$, and the magnitude of the relative velocity is calculated as the product of the straight distance $r_{B/A}$ and the angular velocity ω:

$$\mathbf{v_{B/A}} = r_{B/A}\,\omega \qquad [3.61]$$

The relative velocity is then combined with the (absolute) translational velocity of A to produce the absolute velocity vector $\mathbf{v_B}$ at B:

$$\mathbf{v_B} = \mathbf{v_A} + \mathbf{v_{B/A}} \qquad [3.62]$$

The magnitude and direction of $\mathbf{v_B}$ are determined from the solution of the vector triangle illustrated in Figure 3.21 by using the law of cosines.

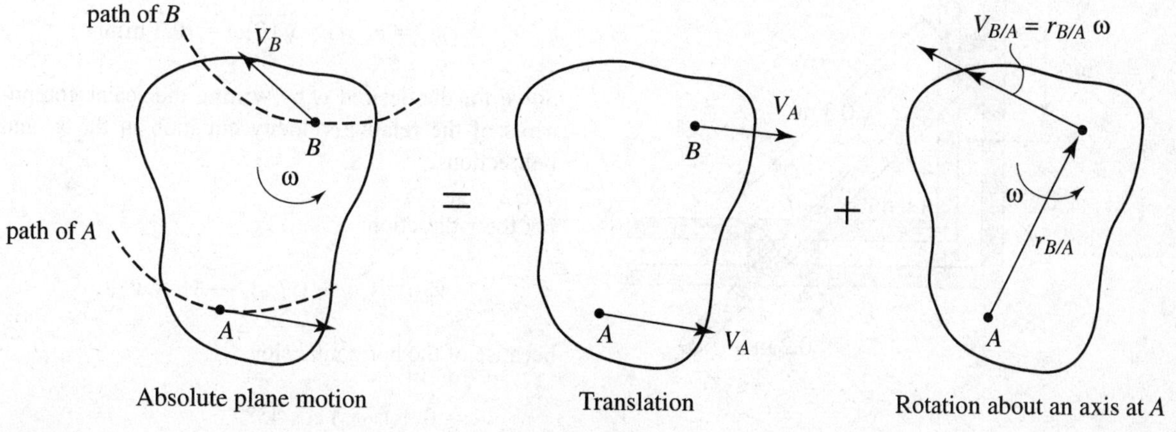

Figure 3.20

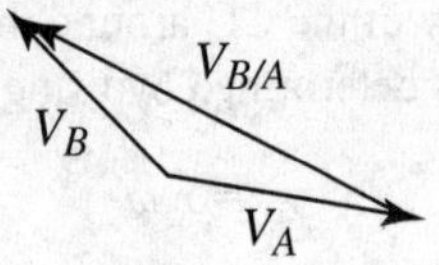

Figure 3.21

For *absolute and relative acceleration* of two points on a rigid body experiencing translational and rotational plane motion as described above, an equation similar to that used for relative velocity is employed for points A and B with the assumption that A is again the center of rotation.

$$\mathbf{a_B} = \mathbf{a_A} + \mathbf{a_{B/A}} \qquad [3.63]$$

If the absolute acceleration vector of A is known, the relative acceleration vector $\mathbf{a_{B/A}}$ is determined from the tangential and normal acceleration components $r_{B/A}\alpha$ and $r_{B/A}\omega^2$, respectively. Then a vector triangle is constructed to solve the absolute acceleration at B.

This methodology is useful in solving for the absolute acceleration of a point, B, on the circumference of a rolling wheel if the translational acceleration of the center of the wheel at point A is given, along with ω and α.

Example 3.15

The rigid link illustrated in Figure 3.22 moves within a vertical plane and is constrained by two blocks, A and B, that travel within the fixed perpendicular slots. If block A has an instantaneous velocity of 4.0 m/s vertically downward when the centerline of the link is 45° from the vertical, determine the angular velocity of the link at that position.

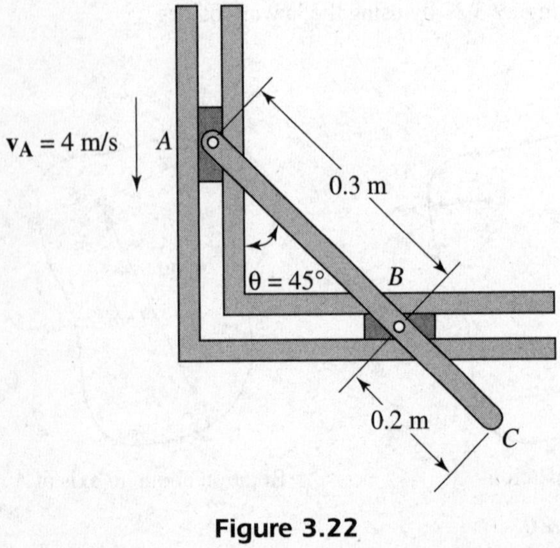

Figure 3.22

Solution:

Since the absolute velocity of block A is given, utilize the relative velocity equation for A and B on the assumption that A is the center of rotation (reference point) for the link:

$$\mathbf{v_B} = \mathbf{v_A} + \mathbf{v_{B/A}}$$

Clearly, the direction of $\mathbf{v_B}$ is horizontal (x-direction), and the direction of the relative velocity $\mathbf{v_{B/A}}$ is perpendicular to the centerline of the link, as shown in Figure 3.23, because of the circular motion of B about A. Therefore, it is necessary that $\mathbf{v_{B/A}}$ be directed at 45° from the positive x-direction as indicated in the figure.

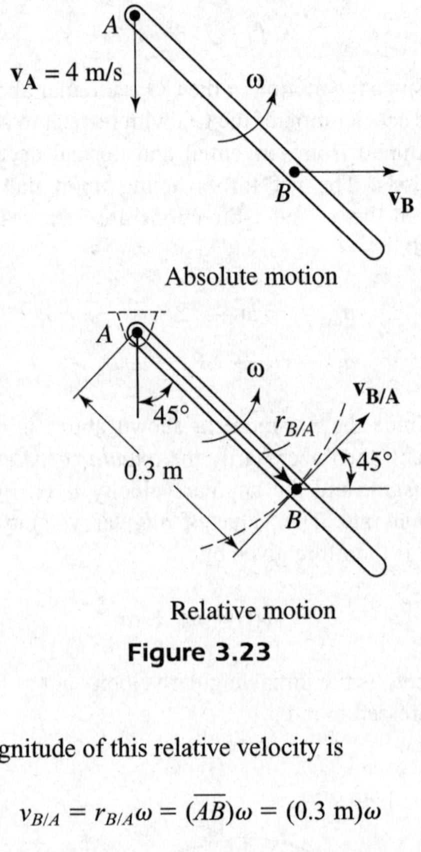

Figure 3.23

The magnitude of this relative velocity is

$$v_{B/A} = r_{B/A}\omega = (\overline{AB})\omega = (0.3 \text{ m})\omega$$

Solve for the desired ω by writing the scalar components of the relative velocity equation in the x- and y-directions.

For the x-direction:

$$v_{BX} = v_{AX} + (v_{B/A})_x \rightarrow v_B = v_{BX}$$

because of the horizontal slot

$$v_B = 0 + (v_{B/A})\cos 45°$$
$$= (0.3 \text{ m})\,\omega\,(0.707) = (0.212 \text{ m})\,\omega$$

For the y-direction:

$$v_{BY} = v_{AY} + (v_{B/A})_Y \rightarrow v_{AY} = v_A$$

because of the vertical slot

$$0 = -4.0 \text{ m/s} + (0.3 \text{ m})\omega \sin 45^\circ$$
$$= -4.0 + (0.212 \text{ m})\omega$$

$$\therefore \omega = \frac{4.0 \text{ m/s}}{0.212 \text{ m}} = 18.86 \text{ rad/s}$$

Note that the magnitude of the absolute velocity of B must be the same as that of A because of the 45° angle. Calculate v_B from the x-component equation above to check the result for ω:

$$v_B = (0.212 \text{ m})(18.86 \text{ rad/s}) = 3.998 \approx 4.0 \text{ m/s}$$

which verifies ω.

3.5 Vibrations

Mechanical *vibrations* problems involving linear spring/mass systems are frequently included on the FE exam. These problems typically involve single-degree-of-freedom systems that oscillate along a single direction (rectilinear motion). The following sections on free, damped, and torsional vibrations summarize the key concepts, equations, symbols, and problem applications for vibrations that are considered relevant to the FE exam.

The exhaustive mathematical derivations involving solutions of numerous ordinary differential equations are bypassed in order to focus on the interpretation of initial conditions and physical parameters involved in vibrations problems. This concentration should enable you to readily identify the appropriate end-use equations that allow for efficient and accurate solution methodologies.

Free Vibrations

This type of motion is characterized by an oscillation that occurs with a linear spring and mass system without any external force or excitation. The system is initially stretched beyond a static equilibrium position and then released. Typical free-vibration problems provide the value of the initial displacement (deformation), denoted by x_0, and require solutions for the amplitude, velocity, period, and/or natural frequency at a given time or position.

The key parameters for free vibrations are represented by the symbols and units given below:

- Spring constant, k: lb/in or N/m.
- Velocity, $\dot{x}$: in/sec, ft/sec, mm/sec, etc.
- Mass of object, m: lb, kg, etc.
- Natural circular frequency,

$$\omega_n = \sqrt{\frac{k}{m}} \text{ : rad/s} \quad [3.64]$$

- Period of vibration, $\tau = 2\pi\sqrt{\frac{m}{k}}$: s [3.65]
- Natural frequency

$$f_n = \frac{1}{\tau} = \frac{1}{2\pi}\sqrt{\frac{k}{m}} \text{ : rad/s} \quad [3.66]$$

- Displacement from equilibrium, $x(t)$: in, mm, ft, etc.
- Amplitude of vibration,

$$X = \sqrt{{x_0}^2 + \left[\frac{\dot{x}_0}{\omega_n}\right]^2} \text{ : in, mm, ft, etc.} \quad [3.67]$$

Governing equation for *displacement of free vibrations* without the presence of damping:

$$x(t) = X\cos(\omega_n t - \phi) \quad [3.68]$$

where ϕ is the phase angle calculated from

$$\phi = \tan^{-1}\left[\frac{\dot{x}_0}{x_0\omega_n}\right].$$

Damped Vibrations

The existence of a viscous force acting upon an oscillating system represents the condition of damped vibrations. For simplicity, the damping force F_d is regarded as the effect of damping resulting from the motion of a dashpot within a hydraulic cylinder. Key damping terms, symbols, and units are listed below:

- Damping constant, c: lbf-sec/ft, N · s/cm, etc.
- Critical damping constant, $c_c = 2m\omega_n$ (this is the condition of most rapid damping)
- Damping factor, $\xi = \frac{c}{c_c}$ ($\xi = 1$ represents critical damping) [3.69]
- Frequency of damped vibration,

$$\omega_d = \omega_n\sqrt{1 - \xi^2} \text{ : rad/s} \quad [3.70]$$

- Damping force $F_d = c\dot{x}$: lbf, N, etc.

Without derivation, the *displacement of a damped free vibration* is calculated from the following equation:

$$x(t) = Ce^{-\xi\omega_n t}\cos(\omega_d t - \phi) \quad [3.71]$$

where $\phi = \tan^{-1}\left(\frac{\dot{x}_0 + x_0\xi\omega_n}{x_0\omega_d}\right)$, $C = \frac{x_0}{\cos\phi}$.

Torsional Vibrations

In a previous section, it was shown that, for rotational motion of a rigid body, the next torque applied is proportional to the angular acceleration:

$$\Sigma M = I\alpha$$

Torsional vibration problems utilize this basic principle, and this type of oscillatory motion typically involves a rectangular plate or disk that experiences an initial angular displacement θ while attached to a cylindrical rod. In Figure 3.24 the angular displacement of the rigid body generates a twisting moment or torque within the rod according to the equation

$$\Sigma M = k_T\theta = I_0\ddot{\theta}, \qquad [3.72]$$

where k = *torsional stiffness* of the rod (N · m/rad or ft-lb/rad),

I_0 = mass moment of inertia of the oscillating body,

$\ddot{\theta}$ = the resulting angular acceleration (rad/s^2).

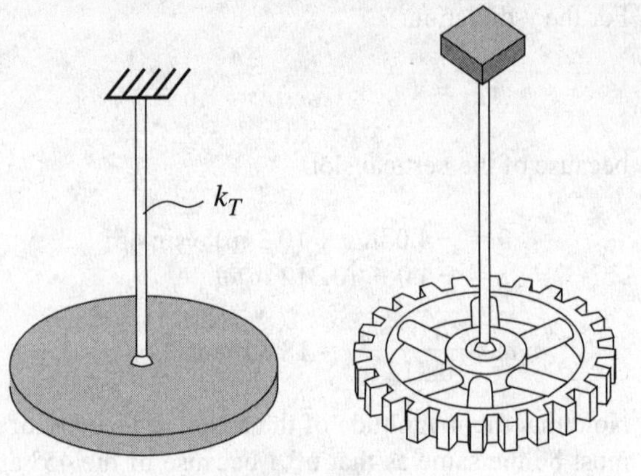

Figure 3.24

The *natural circular frequency* of a torsional vibration is given by

$$\omega_n = \sqrt{\frac{k_r}{I_0}}, \qquad [3.73]$$

and the *period* of the vibration is obtained from the equation

$$\tau = 2\pi\sqrt{\frac{I_0}{k}} \qquad [3.74]$$

PRACTICE PROBLEMS

Questions 1–3

The rectilinear motion of a particle is described by the equation

$$X(t) = 2t^3 - 16t^2 + 7$$

where X is measured in meters.

1. The acceleration of the particle when the velocity is 280 m/s is
   (A) 88.0 m/s^2
   (B) 3.1 m/s^2
   (C) 1.6 m/s^2
   (D) 120.0 m/s^2
2. The displacement at the elapsed time of 20.0 s will be
   (A) 1,607.0 m
   (B) −7.0 m
   (C) 1,600.0 m
   (D) 40.0 m
3. The minimum velocity during the first 50.0 s of motion has a value of
   (A) 2.7 m/s
   (B) 0 m/s
   (C) −1,340.0 m/s
   (D) −42.7 m/s

Questions 4 and 5

A young boy shoots an arrow having a mass of 150 g at an angle of 60° with respect to (above) a horizontal. The arrow is initially at 1.0 m above a zero-elevation datum and leaves the bow with a velocity of 7.0 m/s. Air resistance is considered negligible.

4. The maximum height attained by the arrow will be
   (A) 2.43 m
   (B) 2.88 m
   (C) 4.61 m
   (D) 1.88 m
5. The total speed of the arrow after 0.75 s of motion is nearly
   (A) 1.3 m/s
   (B) 7.1 m/s
   (C) 3.7 m/s
   (D) 4.8 m/s
6. An object having a mass of 3.0 slugs is subjected to a net force of 80.0 lbf. The magnitude of the resulting acceleration is
   (A) 26.7 ft/sec^2
   (B) 0.8 ft/sec^2
   (C) 859.7 ft/sec^2
   (D) 2.7 ft/sec^2
7. A 24″ truck wheel is rolling at 600 rpm along a highway pavement. If the wheel lug nuts are located 6″ from the center of rotation and have a mass of 0.5 lbm, the angular momentum of each lug about the center must be
   (A) 2.30 ft-lbf-sec
   (B) 7.85 ft-lbf-sec
   (C) 73.80 ft-lbf-sec
   (D) 0.24 ft-lbf-sec
8. Two boats experiencing rectilinear motion are approaching each other in a harbor. Boat A is traveling due south at 6 mph, while boat B has a constant speed of 10 mph in a direction 20° west of north as shown in the figure.

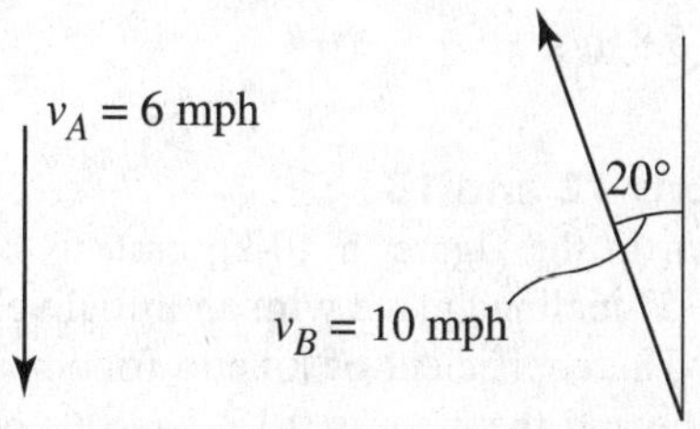

The magnitude and direction of the relative velocity of boat A as viewed from boat B should be

(A) 4.8 mph
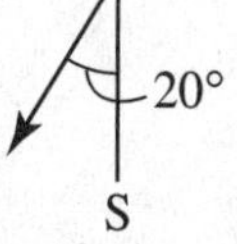

(B) 15.8 mph
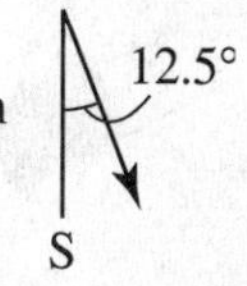

(C) 4.0 mph

(D) 16.0 mph
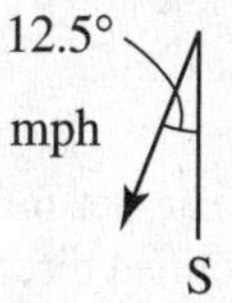

9. A bicycle racer enters a constant-radius curve on a flat track at a speed of 7.0 m/s. If the speed of the bicycle is increased at a constant rate of 1.5 m/s^2 along the curve and the total acceleration at the beginning of the curve is 1.7 m/s^2, the required radius of the curve is
   (A) 41.6 m
   (B) 60.0 m
   (C) 21.7 m
   (D) 76.5 m
10. A bowler rolls a 16.0-lbm ball at a single stationary pin having a mass of 3.0 lbm. If the ball strikes the pin with a speed of 9.0 ft/sec and the coefficient of restitution is 0.8, the

speed of the pin immediately after the collision is necessarily
(A) 7.2 ft/sec
(B) 1.5 ft/sec
(C) 13.6 ft/sec
(D) 2.1 ft/sec

11. A child having a mass of 30.0 kg jumps downward onto a trampoline at a speed of 4.0 m/s. If the average impulsive force of the trampoline is 800.0 N and it acts upon the child for 0.5 s in a vertically upward direction, the child's velocity immediately after the trampoline force has been applied should be
(A) 4.4 m/s
(B) 17.2 m/s
(C) 9.3 m/s
(D) 5.8 m/s

Questions 12 and 13

As shown in the figure, a 40-kg crate is projected down a 35° inclined plane with an initial velocity of 3.0 m/s. The coefficient of kinetic friction between the incline and the crate is 0.15, and this condition applies also to the horizontal surface. For simplicity of calculations, the length of the crate is considered small.

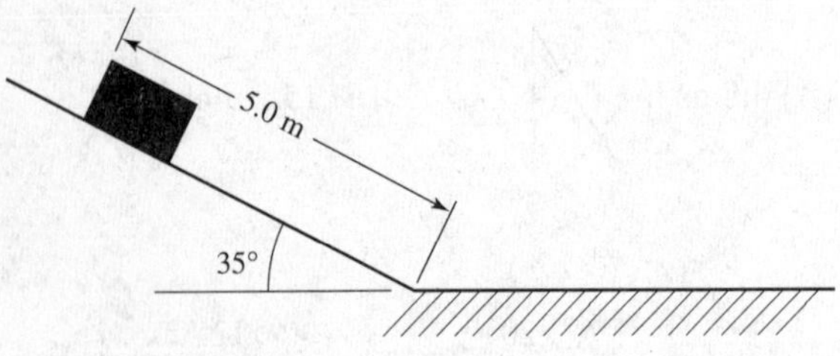

12. The net force acting upon the crate along the inclined direction is
(A) 18.1 N
(B) 176.9 N
(C) 273.3 N
(D) 29.9 N

13. The kinetic energy of the crate at the instant when it has displaced 1.0 m across the horizontal surface will be approximately
(A) 830 J
(B) 1,125 J
(C) 275 J
(D) 1,005 J

14. A 750-g rectangular block moves across the top of a smooth cylindrical surface with an initial velocity of V_0 m/s. The radius of curvature of the cylinder is 1.6 m, as shown in the figure, and the block begins to lose contact with the surface at the position where $\theta = 30°$. The value of V_0 required to satisfy the stated conditions is

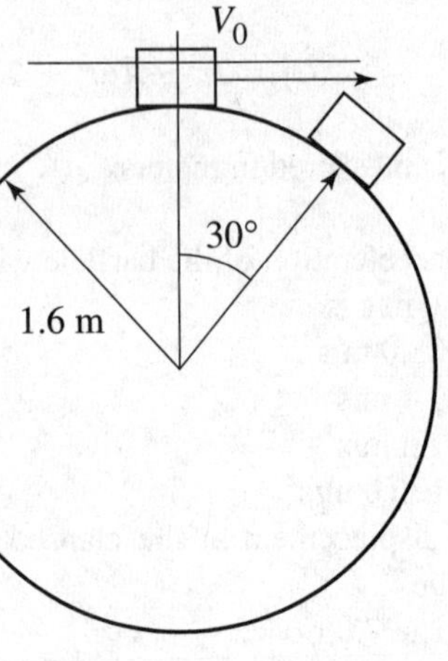

(A) 3.1 m/s
(B) 2.8 m/s
(C) 5.6 m/s
(D) 3.7 m/s

15. A cue ball strikes two billiard balls at rest simultaneously with a speed of 8.0 ft/sec. Immediately after the collision, the cue ball stops in place, while one of the other balls moves with a velocity of 5.0 ft/sec at 20° from the cue ball's line of action as diagrammed in the figure.

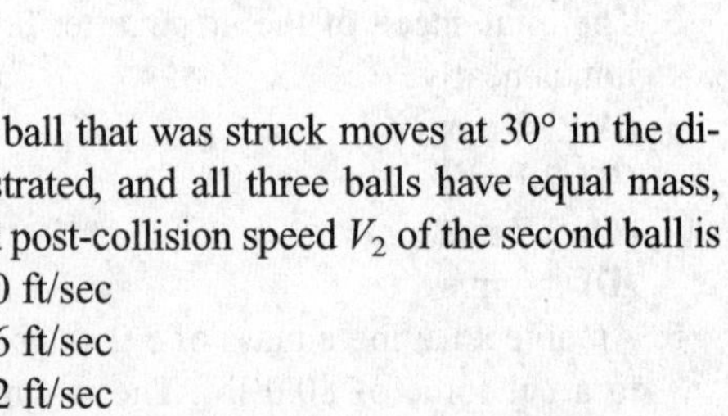

If the other ball that was struck moves at 30° in the direction illustrated, and all three balls have equal mass, the required post-collision speed V_2 of the second ball is
(A) 3.0 ft/sec
(B) 6.6 ft/sec
(C) 7.2 ft/sec
(D) 3.8 ft/sec

16. An overhead garage door is guided by two rollers that travel within the perpendicular channels as shown in the figure. When $\theta = 35°$, the velocity of the wheel at Q is 0.5 m/s upward.

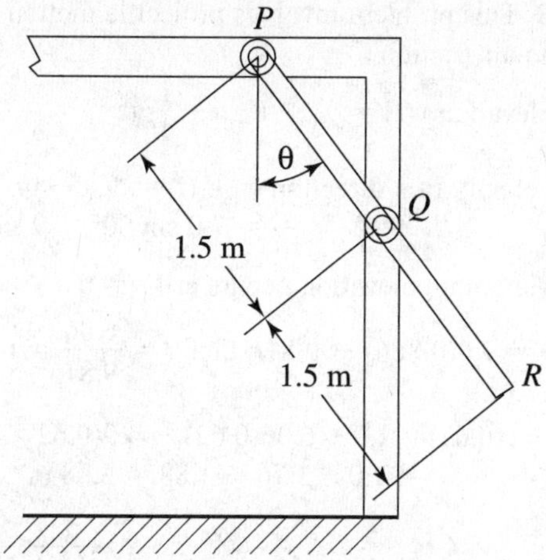

The angular velocity of the centerline PR of the door at this position is necessarily

(A) 3.60 rad/s
(B) 0.58 rad/s
(C) 0.33 rad/s
(D) 1.29 rad/s

17. As shown in the figure, a 125-kg package is initially suspended above an undeformed ideal spring having a stiffness of 3 kN/m. The package is then released from rest and begins traveling downward.

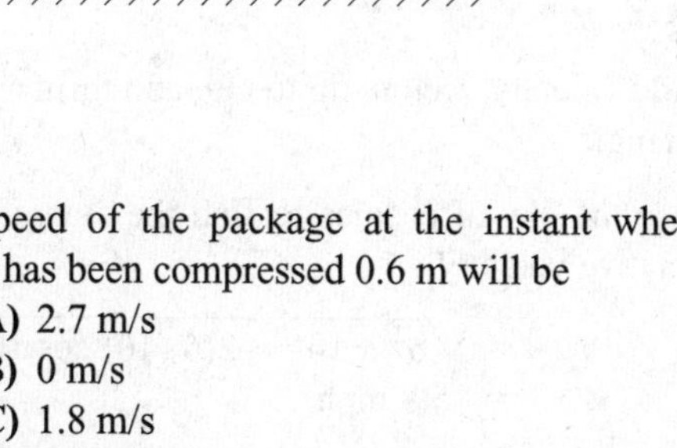

The speed of the package at the instant when the spring has been compressed 0.6 m will be

(A) 2.7 m/s
(B) 0 m/s
(C) 1.8 m/s
(D) 4.5 m/s

18. The pulley-belt drive system shown in the figure contains a pulley having a mass of 8.0 lbm and a radius of gyration of 6.0 in. At a given time, the angular acceleration of the pulley is known to be 3.0 rad/s^2.

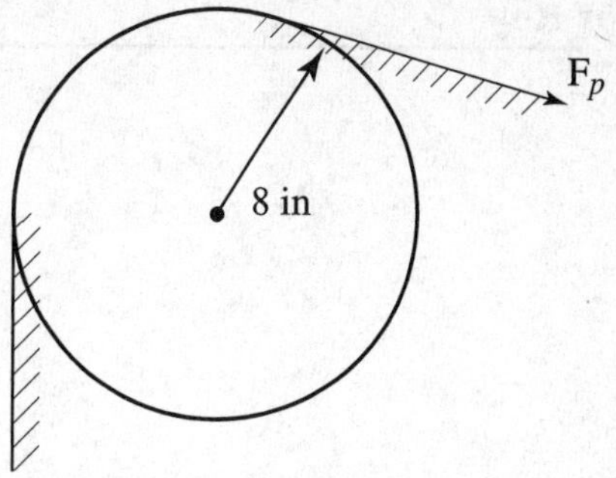

The force of the belt on the pulley at this instant is nearly

(A) 33.5 lbf
(B) 90.2 lbf
(C) 7.5 lbf
(D) 2.8 lbf

19. In the figure, the 16-kg cube is connected to a linear spring and moves without friction inside the chamber shown.

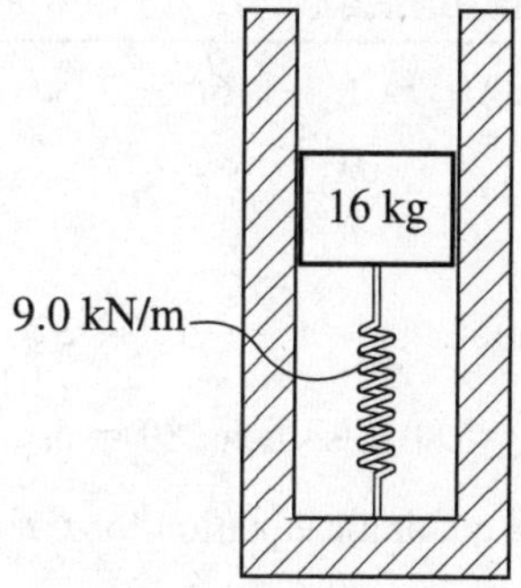

If the spring stiffness is 9.0 kN/m and the cube is given an initial downward velocity of 150 mm/s when the spring is compressed 4.0 mm, the amplitude of the resulting harmonic vibration should be

(A) 7.8 mm
(B) 14.1 mm
(C) 200.4 mm
(D) 55.2 mm

20. It is unlawful in most U.S. states to drop coins or other solid objects from skyscrapers or high outdoor platforms because of the dangerously high velocities attained. If air friction is considered negligible, the theoretical maximum speed of a coin thrown directly downward with an initial speed of 5.0 mph from an elevation of 800 ft above a reference datum will be

(A) 127.6 mph
(B) 165.4 mph
(C) 154.8 mph
(D) 143.9 mph

Answer Key

1. A
2. C
3. D
4. B
5. C
6. A
7. D
8. B
9. B
10. C
11. A
12. B
13. D
14. A
15. D
16. B
17. C
18. D
19. B
20. C

Answers Explained

1. A Given $X(t) = 2t^3 - 16t^2 + 7$

Velocity $V(t) = \dfrac{dX}{dt} = 6t^2 - 32t$

Acceleration $a(t) = \dfrac{dV}{dt} = 12t - 32$

When $V = 280$ m/s, then $280 = 6t^2 - 32t$.

Solve the quadratic equation for t: $t = 10$ s.

Then:

$$a(10) = 120 - 32 = 88.0 \text{ m/s}^2$$

2. C Displacement $\Delta X = X(t) - X_o$

At $t = 20.0$ s:

$$\Delta X = X(20) - 7 = (8{,}000 - 6{,}400 + 7) - 7 = 1{,}600.0 \text{ m}$$

3. D Minimum velocity occurs when $a = 0$.

$0 = 12t - 32$; then $t = 2.67$ s.

$$V(2.67) = 6(2.67)^2 - 32(2.67) = 42.77 - 85.44 = -42.7 \text{ m/s.}$$

4. B This problem involves projectile motion with no air friction.

Elevation $y(t) = y_o + V_{yo}t - \dfrac{1}{2}gt^2$

Velocity in y-direction $= V_y(t) = V_{yo} - gt = 7.0 \sin 60° - 9.81t$

Maximum elevation occurs at $V_y = 0$.

$0 = 7.0(0.866) - 9.81t$; then $t = \dfrac{6.06}{9.81} = 0.62$ s.

$$y(0.62) = 1.0 + 6.06(0.62) - 4.9(0.62)^2 = 1.0 + 3.76 - 1.88 = 2.88 \text{ m}$$

5. C Total speed of arrow is $V_T = \sqrt{V_x^2 + V_y^2}$

$V_x = 7.0 \cos 60° = 3.5$ m/s $=$ constant

$$V_y(0.75) = 6.06 - 9.81(0.75) = -1.30 \text{ m/s}$$
$$V_T = \sqrt{(3.5)^2 + (-1.3)^2} = 3.73 \text{ m/s}$$

6. A Here:

$$a = \frac{\Sigma F}{m} = \frac{80.0 \text{ lbf}}{3.0 \text{ sl}} = \frac{80.0}{3.0}\left(\frac{1.0 \text{ sl-ft/sec}^2}{\text{lbf}}\right) = 26.67 \text{ ft/sec}^2 \approx 26.7 \text{ ft/sec}^2$$

7. D Angular momentum $H = mr^2\dot{\theta}$

$$= 0.5\text{lbm}\left(\frac{6}{12}\text{ ft}\right)^2\dot{\theta}$$

$$\dot{\theta} = 600 \text{ rpm} \times \frac{2\pi}{60} = 62.8 \text{ rad/sec}$$

$$H = (0.5)(0.5)^2(62.8) = 7.85 \text{ lbm-ft}^2\text{/sec} = \frac{7.85}{32.2} = 0.24 \text{ ft-lbf-sec}$$

8. B Relative velocity of boat A with respect to boat B: $\mathbf{V}_{A/B} = \mathbf{V}_A + -\mathbf{V}_B$

Add velocity vectors tip to tail, and form a vector triangle.

Use the law of cosines to find the magnitude of relative velocity:

$$\mathbf{V}_{A/B} = \sqrt{6^2 + 10^2 - 2(6)(10)\cos 160°} = 15.8 \text{ mph}$$

Use the law of sines to find the direction of $\mathbf{V}_{A/B}$:

$\dfrac{\sin 160°}{15.8} = \dfrac{\sin a}{10.0}$; angle $a = 12.5°$ east of south.

9. B Use the tangential and normal (circular) coordinate system. Total acceleration magnitude is $a(t) = \sqrt{a_t^2 + a_n^2}$

Given $a_t = 1.5$, $a = 1.7$, and $V = 7.0$. Note that $a_n = \frac{V^2}{R}$. Then:

$$1.7 = \sqrt{(1.5)^2 + \left(\frac{V^2}{R}\right)^2}$$

$$\frac{V^2}{R} = \sqrt{(1.7)^2 - 2.25}$$

$$R = 60.0 \text{ m}$$

10. C Use conservation of linear momentum for impact:

$m_A V_A + m_B V_B = m_A V_A' + m_B V_B'$ (equation I)

Given $V_B = 0$, $V_A = +9.0$. Coefficient of restitution $e = 0.8$.

$V_B' - V_A' = e(V_A - V_B) = 0.8(9.0 - 0) = 7.2$ (equation II)

From equation I, $(16.0)(9.0) = 16V_A' + 3V_B'$ (equation III)

From equation II, $V_A' = V_B' - 7.2$. Substitute in equation II, and solve V_B' for the pin's postimpact velocity.

$144 = 16(V_B' - 7.2) + 3\ V_B'$; $19V_B' = 259.2$. Then:

$$V_B' = 13.6 \text{ ft/sec}$$

11. C Use the impulse/momentum equation in the vertical y-direction:

$\text{Imp}_y = mV_2 - mV_1$

$(-800.0 \text{ N})(0.5 \text{ s}) = 30.0 \text{ kg } (V_2 - 4.0)$. Note that the y-direction is positive downward.

$-400.0 \text{ N} \cdot \text{s} = 30.0V_2 - 120.0$; then:

$$V_2 = \frac{-400.0 + 120.0}{30.0} = -9.33 \text{ m/s upward}$$

12. B Establish an FBD of the block; external forces are gravity, friction, and normal reaction. The kinetic friction force acts opposite the block's motion along the incline. Take the positive direction as downward along the inclined plane.

$\Sigma F_I = W_I - F_{FI} = (40.0)(9.81) \sin 35° - 0.15N_R$. Normal reaction N_R balances the weight component in the normal direction.

$N_R = W \cos\theta = (40.0)(9.81) \cos 35° = 321.4$ N; then:

$$\Sigma F_I = 225.07 - 0.15(321.4) = 176.9 \text{ N}$$

13. D $KE_2 = KE_1 + W_{net\ 1\to 2}$, and $W_{net\ 1\to 2}$ is the work along the incline plus along the 1.0-m horizontal displacement.

$$KE_2 = \frac{1}{2}(40.0)(3.0)^2 + \left[\sum F_I(5.0 \text{ m}) + \sum F_X(1.0 \text{ m})\right]$$

$$= 180.0 \text{ N} \cdot \text{m} + (176.9 \text{ N})(5.0 \text{ m}) + [-0.15(40)(9.81)(1.0 \text{ m})]$$

$$KE_2 = 180.0 + 884.5 - 58.8 = 1{,}005.6 \text{ N} \cdot \text{m} \approx 1{,}006 \text{ J}$$

14. A Use tangential and normal coordinates for this circular-type motion. Draw an FBD of the block, and note that the block has no normal reaction ($N_R = 0$) when $\theta = 30°$.

Since $\Sigma F_n = \frac{mV^2}{R}$, let V_2 represent the velocity at the position when $\theta = 30°$. Use the FBD and substitute given values:

$$\sum F_n = \frac{(0.75 \text{ kg})V_2^2}{1.6 \text{ m}}$$

$$W \cos 30° = 0.469 \frac{\text{kg}}{\text{m}} V_2^2 \ (0.75 \text{ kg})(9.81 \text{ m/s}^2) \times (0.866) = 0.469 \frac{\text{kg}}{\text{m}} V_2^2$$

$$V_2 = \sqrt{\frac{(1.6 \text{ m})(6.37 \text{ N})}{0.75 \text{ kg}}} = 3.69 \text{ m/s}$$

Use the conservation of energy equation from the top of the cylinder to point 2 to solve V_o:

$KE_1 + PE_1 = KE_2 + PE_2$. Set $PE_2 = 0$, and let $KE_1 = \frac{1}{2}mV_o^2$.

$$PE_1 = mg(1.6 - 1.6 \cos 30°) = mg(0.214 \text{ m})$$

Then $0.5mV_o^2 + mg(0.214) = 0.5m\ (3.69 \text{ m/s})^2 + 0$, and

$$V_o = \sqrt{9.43 \text{ m}^2/\text{s}^2} = 3.1 \text{ m/s}$$

15. D Use the conservation of linear momentum for the system of three balls in the x-direction: $m_c V_c = m_1 V_{1x} + m_2 V_{2x} + m_c V_c' \rightarrow V_c' = 0$, and $m_c = m_1 = m_2$

$$m_c(8.0 \text{ ft/sec}) = m_1(5.0 \cos 20°) + m_2(V_2 \cos 30°)$$

$$8.0 = 4.7 + 0.866V_2, \text{ and}$$

$$V_2 = \frac{8.0 - 4.7}{0.866} = 3.8 \text{ ft/sec}$$

16. B Let a point C be located along a vertical line through point P that is the shortest perpendicular distance to point Q. Then, the given speed of point Q can be expressed as $V_Q = (CQ)\omega$, where distance $CQ = (1.5 \text{ m}) \sin 35° = 0.86$ m, and ω is the desired angular speed of centerline PR.

Then $0.5 \text{ m/s} = (0.86 \text{ m})\omega$, and

$$\omega = 0.58 \text{ rad/s}.$$

17. C Utilize the principle of work and kinetic energy to determine speed V_2 of the package. $W_{\text{net } 1\rightarrow 2} = KE_2 - KE_1$. Since $V_1 = 0$, $KE_1 = 0$.

The net work on the package is due to gravity and spring work.

$$W_{\text{net } 1\rightarrow 2} = (mg)(0.6 \text{ m}) + \frac{1}{2}k(X_1^2 - X_2^2)$$

$$= \frac{1}{2}mV_2^2$$

$$(125.0 \text{ kg})(9.81)(0.6 \text{ m}) + 0.5\,(3{,}000.0 \text{ N/m})[0 - (0.6 \text{ m})^2]$$

$$= \frac{125.0 \text{ kg}}{2}V_2^2$$

Simplify:

$$V_2 = \sqrt{\frac{195.7}{62.5}} = 1.8 \text{ m/s}$$

18. D Rigid-body rotation requires $\Sigma M = I\alpha$, where $I = mk^2$.

$$I = (8.0 \text{ lbm})(0.5 \text{ ft})^2 = 2.0 \text{ lbm-ft}^2$$

$$\sum M = (2.0 \text{ lbm-ft}^2)(30.0 \text{ rad/sec}^2)$$

$$= \frac{60.0}{32.2} = 1.86 \text{ ft-lbf}$$

Since $\Sigma M = rF_p = 1.86$:

$$F_p = \frac{1.86}{0.67 \text{ ft}} = 2.8 \text{ lbf}$$

19. B Amplitude $X = \sqrt{x_o^2 + \left(\frac{\dot{x}_o}{\omega_n}\right)^2}$, and

$$\omega_n = \sqrt{\frac{k}{m}} = \sqrt{\frac{9{,}000 \text{ N/m}}{16.0 \text{ kg}}} = 23.7 \text{ rad/s. Then:}$$

$$X = \sqrt{(0.004)^2 + \left(\frac{0.15 \text{ m/s}}{23.7 \text{ rad/s}}\right)^2}$$

$$= \sqrt{0.00016 + 0.000040} = 0.0141 \text{ m} = 14.1 \text{ mm}$$

20. C $W_{\text{net}} = KE_2 - KE_1$

$$mg(\Delta h) = \frac{1}{2}m(v_2^2 - v_1^2)$$

$$2g(800.0 \text{ ft}) = v_2^2 - \left(5 \text{ mph} \times \frac{88 \text{ ft/sec}}{60 \text{ mph}}\right)^2$$

$$51{,}520 \frac{\text{ft}^2}{\text{sec}^2} = v_2^2 - 53.77$$

$$v_2 = \sqrt{51{,}573.8} = 227.1 \text{ ft/sec} = 154.8 \text{ mph}$$

CHAPTER 4

Electric Circuits

Frederick F. Driscoll

Introduction

This chapter reviews the basic concepts of electrical engineering. It is divided into the nine sections listed below.

- Current, Voltage, and Power
- Resistance
- Direct-Current (DC) Circuit Analysis
- Inductance
- Capacitance
- Resistor-Capacitor (R-C) and Resistor-Inductor (R-L) Circuits
- Alternating-Current (AC) Circuit Analysis
- Operational Amplifiers
- Electric and Magnetic Fields

4.1 Current, Voltage, and Power

Our physical word may be interpreted in terms of matter and energy, both of which exist in a variety of forms. Matter undergoes change; energy either causes or is a result of the change. *Matter* has been defined as anything that occupies space and possesses mass. *Energy,* on the other hand, is the ability to do work. Although energy itself cannot be measured, its results can.

Matter exists either in a solid, a liquid, or a gaseous state. Since most electric components are solids, circuit analysis usually begins with an introduction to atomic structure or at least the properties of electric charge.

Electric Charge

One of the unique properties of an atom's electron is its negative **electric charge.** The charge of a single electron is the smallest electric charge that exists. For purposes of analysis it is more practical to group a large number of electrons together; hence the basic quantity of electric charge is the coulomb (C). One coulomb equals the accumulated charge of 6.24×10^{18} electrons and is represented by q or Q.

Note: It is conventional to use lower-case letters to represent values that vary with time and to use upper-case letters to represent values that do not vary with time.

Materials that are good conductors of electric current are composed of atoms with only one valence electron. Valence electrons are the electrons in an atom's outermost energy level. In a metal, valence electrons are not tightly bound to the nucleus of the atom and are said to be free or mobile. Good conductors, such as silver, copper, and aluminum, have high concentrations of free electrons. Materials such as air, glass, mica, and rubber have considerably fewer free electrons and are referred to as insulators.

Current

To understand **electric current,** consider a portion of a conductor as shown in Figure 4.1a. First consider the case where no outside energy except thermal energy is applied to the conductor. Thermal energy is always present because a temperature of absolute zero cannot be achieved. Under normal conditions, free electrons are said to be *uniformly distributed* and to have *random motion.*

Uniform distribution means that free electrons will not be concentrated in one particular location but will permeate throughout the material as a gas diffuses through a closed container. Thus at any instant any incremental volume of the same size will contain the same number of free electrons.

Random motion means that no specific direction can be assigned to the free electrons. Therefore the probability of finding a particular number of free electrons moving in one direction is the same as finding an equal number of free electrons moving in the opposite direction. Thus the net motion in any one direction is zero. For free electrons to have direction, energy other than thermal energy must be applied to one end of the conductor. When a positive charge is connected to one end of the conductor and a negative charge to the other, a potential difference is created between the ends of the conductor, as shown in Figure 4.1b. Since like charges repel and unlike charges attract, electrons will travel toward the positive end of the conductor and away from the negative end.

Even when the application of different charges to a conductor has caused the free electrons to move toward the positive charge, they do not move in a straight path. Instead, they follow a zigzag pattern similar to random motion. Unlike true random motion, however, there is now a definite drift toward the positive charge. This net motion of free electrons in one direction constitutes an electric current known as a *drift current.* This current depends on the rate at which the free electrons move. The term "rate" implies a quantity divided by time. It should be noted that "current" is a rate-of-flow term and not a velocity term. Thus, current depends, not on the speed of individual electrons, but rather on the net motion of a large number of free electrons.

The basic unit of current is the ampere (A). A definition of ampere is as follows: If 1 coulomb of charge passes through a cross-sectional area of a conductor in 1 second, there is 1 ampere of current.

$$1 \text{ ampere} = \frac{1 \text{ coulomb}}{1 \text{ second}} \qquad [4.1a]$$

This relationship may be expressed mathematically as

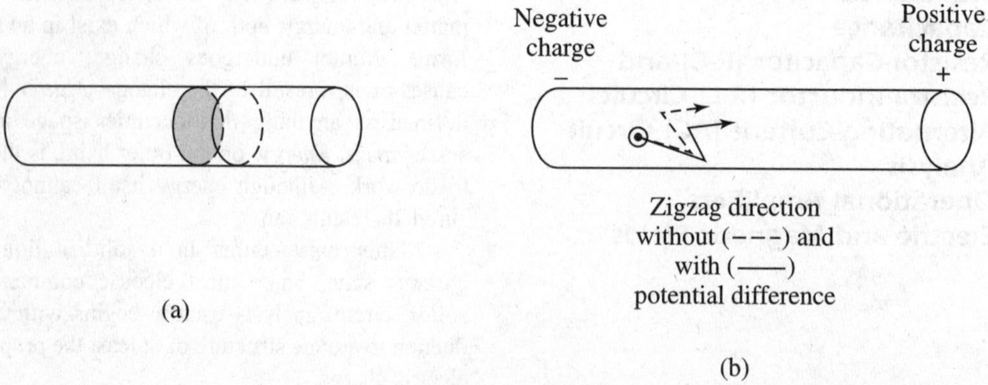

Figure 4.1

$$i = \frac{dq}{dt} \quad [4.1b]$$

where i is the instantaneous current, and dq/dt is the rate of change of charge with respect to time (coulombs per second).

An electron has a negative charge; it drifts from a negative terminal to a positive one. This principle is known as *electron flow.* The analysis of electric circuits is usually based, however, on the direction of current from an energy source's positive terminal through the circuit to the source's negative terminal. This is known as the **conventional current direction.**

Voltage

For an electric current to exist in a conductor, the ends of the conductor must be connected to different charges. Only then is it possible to have a movement of free electrons in a specific direction. A voltage exists between two points in a circuit whenever one point has a more positive charge than the other point. It is this charge difference or potential energy difference, known as **voltage,** that causes current.

Voltage is referred to as either a potential rise or a potential fall. A voltage rise or potential rise occurs when work is done on the charge by an element; an example is an energy source. A voltage drop or potential fall exists when work is done by the charge on an element; an example is a load. The distinction between potential rise and potential fall is established by polarity markings across an element as shown in Figure 4.2.

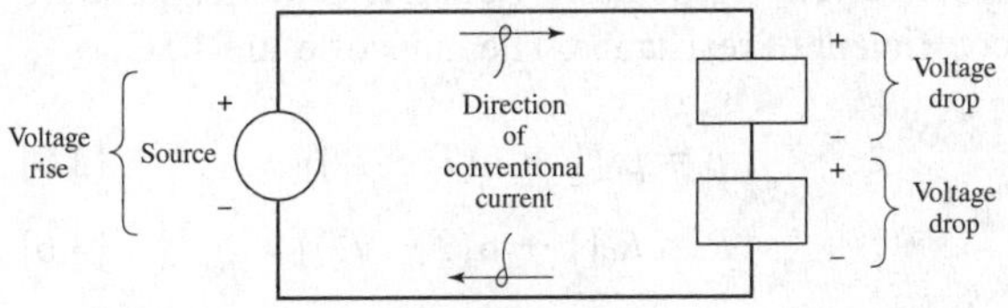

Figure 4.2

The basic unit of voltage, either a potential rise or a potential fall, is the volt (V). A definition of voltage is as follows: If 1 joule of energy is expended in moving 1 coulomb of charge from one point to another in an electric circuit, the voltage is 1 volt.

$$1 \text{ volt} = \frac{1 \text{ joule}}{1 \text{ coulomb}} \quad [4.2a]$$

The mathematical expression for voltage is

$$v = \frac{dw}{dq} \quad [4.2b]$$

where v is the instantaneous voltage and dw/dq is the change in energy with respect to change in charge.

Power

The goal of an electric circuit is to transfer energy from one point to another in order to accomplish useful work. Hence electric circuits are composed of (1) sources and (2) loads. The *source* supplies the electrical energy, while the *load* converts the energy into work to accomplish what the circuit or system has been designed for. The rate at which energy is transferred from the source to the load is called power. **Power** is defined as energy per unit time, and the basic unit of power is the watt (W).

$$1 \text{ watt} = \frac{1 \text{ joule}}{1 \text{ second}} \quad [4.3a]$$

Although power is defined as the transfer of 1 joule of electrical energy in 1 second, it may be determined from measured values of voltage and current.

$$\text{Power} = \text{voltage} \times \text{current} \quad [4.3b]$$

Using the symbols for voltage and current gives the expression

$$p = v \times i \quad [4.3c]$$

Summary of Symbols

The expressions of charge, current, voltage, energy, and power are summarized in Table 4.1.

Table 4.1 Summary of Expressions

Quantity	*Symbol*	*Unit*	*Equation*
Charge	q	coulomb	$q(t) = \int i(t)\,dt$
Current	i	ampere	$i(t) = dq/dt$
Voltage	v	volt	$v(t) = dw/dq$
Energy	w	joule	$w(t) = \int p(t)\,dt$
Power	p	watt	$p(t) = dw/dt$
			$p(t) = v(t) \cdot i(t)$

Electric Circuits

This chapter has summarized many concepts in the analysis of electric circuits that consist of energy sources and loads. The energy sources will be primarily voltage sources, and the loads will contain passive components or active devices along with passive components.

Passive components, which are capable only of storing or dissipating energy, consist of resistance, inductance (self and mutual), and capacitance. Resistance converts electrical energy into other energy forms. Self-inductance stores energy in a magnetic field, and mutual inductance transfers energy from one part of a circuit to another through a magnetic field. Capacitance stores energy in an electric field.

Operational amplifiers, introduced in Section 4.8, are one type of active device used in the design of electric circuits. This review concentrates primarily, however, on passive circuits.

4.2 Resistance

As previously mentioned, the application of potential energy to a conductor causes a net movement of free electrons in one direction. Even under the influence of potential energy, the path of a single electron is not straight but is a zigzag pattern similar to random motion. One cause of the zigzag pattern is collisions of the electron with other atoms. Since energy cannot be destroyed, the externally applied potential energy is transformed into kinetic energy of the electron.

When an electron collides with an atom, heat is produced in a thermodynamic process called *Joule heating*. The collisions, which simultaneously produce heat, also constitute an opposition to the flow of current. Opposition to current flow is **resistance,** as shown in Figure 4.3a. For circuit analysis, the primary characteristic of resistance is energy conversion (dissipation of heat or other forms of energy).

Every material used as a conductor has some degree of resistance. Some materials conduct electric charge more efficiently, that is, with less resistance and production of heat, than others. Copper, for example, is an excellent conductor, while steel is a good conductor but not an excellent one.

Resistance is a characteristic of that part of a device that transforms electrical energy into heat. Resistance is designated by the letter R and the symbol shown in Figures 4.3b and 4.3c. The basic unit of resistance is the ohm (Ω). A resistor (same letter and symbol designation) is the actual physical device that is inserted into a circuit or system to limit the flow of current. It produces a voltage drop and dissipates energy. A resistor may be classified as either fixed or variable. A *fixed* resistor is one whose value is constant, while a *variable* resistor is one whose value can be changed. The circuit symbols for a fixed and a variable resistor are shown in Figures 4.3b and 4.3c, respectively.

The resistance of a material with uniform cross section is given by the equation

$$R = \frac{\rho l}{A} \qquad [4.4]$$

where R = resistance (Ω),
ρ = resistivity ($\Omega \cdot$ m),
l = length of the material (m),
A = cross-sectional area (perpendicular to current flow) (m^2), and units of measurement are indicated in parentheses.

This equation is illustrated in Figure 4.3a.

Typical values of resistivity for various materials are listed in Table 4.2.

Table 4.2 Resistivities of Four Materials

Material	*Resistivity, ρ* ($\Omega \cdot$ m)
Silver	1.468×10^{-8}
Copper	1.72×10^{-8}
Aluminum	2.83×10^{-8}
Insulators	10^6 to 10^{16}

The resistivity of a material depends on the temperature. For most metals, resistivity increases with an increase in temperature. In Equations 4.5 and 4.6, ρ_0 and R_0 are the resistivity and resistance values, respectively, at temperature T_0 and α is the temperature coefficient of resistance. The units of α are 1/°C.

$$\rho = \rho_0[1 + \alpha(T - T_0)] \qquad [4.5]$$

$$R = R_0[1 + \alpha(T - T_0)] \qquad [4.6]$$

Ohm's Law

For a linear resistor, the voltage drop across a resistor is directly proportional to the current and is given by Ohm's law:

$$v(t) = i(t)R \qquad [4.7]$$

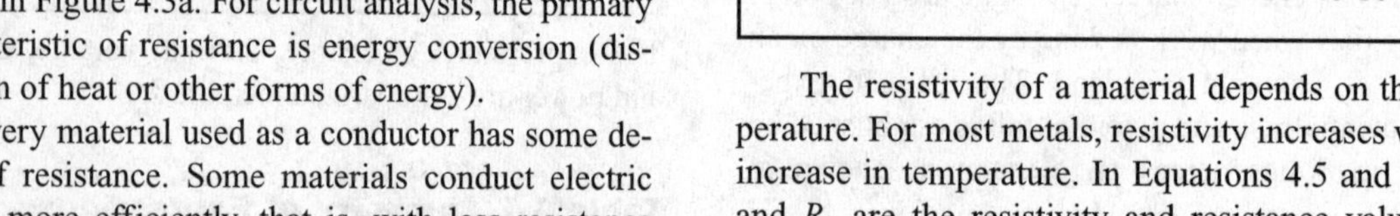

(a) Length of wire (b) Fixed resistor (c) Variable resistor

Figure 4.3

If the current and voltage do not vary with time, Ohm's law is usually written as follows:

$$V = IR \quad [4.8]$$

Power Dissipated by a Resistor

The average power dissipated by a resistor is determined by using the equation

$$P = VI = \frac{V^2}{R} = I^2R \quad [4.9]$$

The unit for power is the watt (joules per second).

Resistors in Series

Resistors connected in series have the same current through each element, as shown in Figure 4.4. The sum of the voltages across the resistors equals the source voltage. This relationship is known as *Kirchhoff's voltage law:*

$$V_T = V_1 + V_2 + V_3 \quad [4.10]$$

Applying Ohm's law to each term yields

$$IR_T = IR_1 + IR_2 + IR_3 \quad [4.11]$$

Dividing by $I \neq 0$ gives

$$R_T = R_1 + R_2 + R_3 \quad [4.12]$$

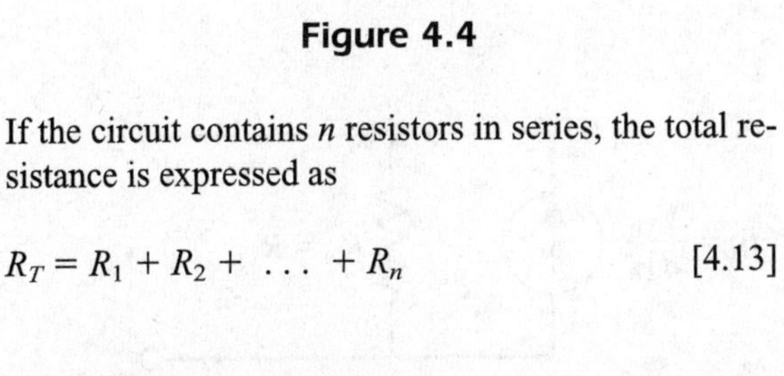

Figure 4.4

If the circuit contains n resistors in series, the total resistance is expressed as

$$R_T = R_1 + R_2 + \ldots + R_n \quad [4.13]$$

Resistors in Parallel

Two or more resistors are in parallel if they experience the same voltage drop. Figure 4.5 shows three resistors in parallel. Kirchhoff's current law states that the sum of the currents entering a node equals the sum of the currents leaving that node. Therefore, for the circuit of Figure 4.5:

$$I_T = I_1 + I_2 + I_3 \quad [4.14]$$

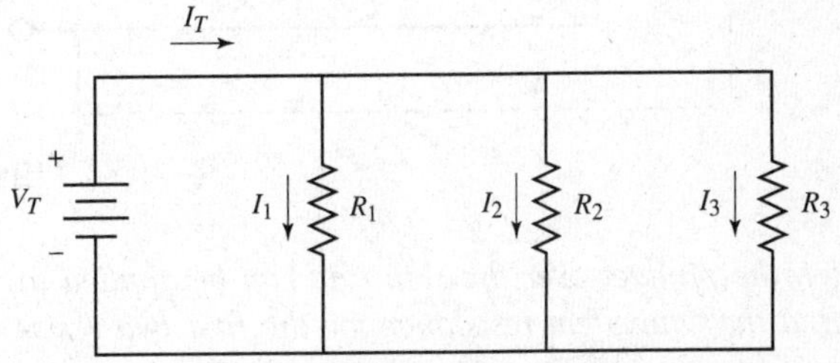

Figure 4.5

Since the voltage across each resistor is the same, equation 4.14 can be divided by V_T to obtain

$$\frac{I_T}{V_T} = \frac{I_1}{V_T} + \frac{I_2}{V_T} + \frac{I_3}{V_T} \quad [4.15]$$

where each term is the reciprocal of Ohm's law:

$$\frac{1}{R_T} = \frac{1}{R_1} + \frac{1}{R_2} + \frac{1}{R_3} \quad [4.16a]$$

Rearranging yields the equivalent resistance:

$$R_T = \frac{1}{\frac{1}{R_1} + \frac{1}{R_2} + \frac{1}{R_3}} \quad [4.16b]$$

Equations 4.16a and 4.16b may be expanded as follows to n resistors in parallel:

$$\frac{1}{R_T} = \frac{1}{R_1} + \frac{1}{R_2} + \ldots + \frac{1}{R_n} \quad [4.17a]$$

and

$$R_T = \frac{1}{\frac{1}{R_1} + \frac{1}{R_2} + \ldots + \frac{1}{R_n}} \quad [4.17b]$$

If there are only two resistors in parallel, the equivalent resistance can be determined by a *product over the sum rule:*

$$R_T = \frac{R_1R_2}{R_1 + R_2} \quad [4.18]$$

Note: The product over the sum rule is for only two resistors in parallel, but it can be used more than once. For example, if three resistors are connected in paral-

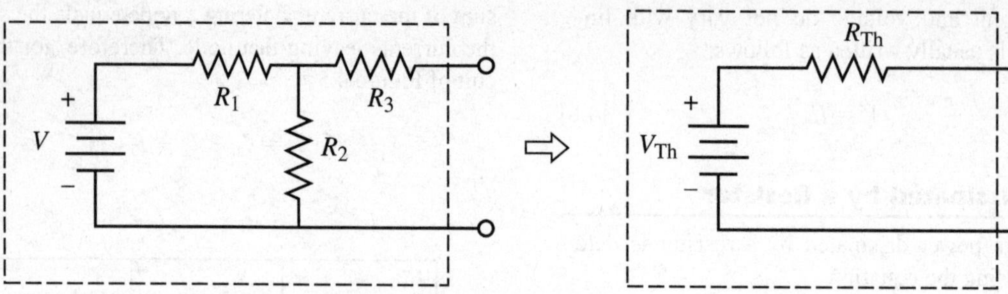

Figure 4.6

lel, the product over the sum rule can be applied to find the equivalent resistance for the first two resistors and that answer used with the third resistor and the product over the sum rule applied again.

Thévenin and Norton Equivalent Circuits

Thévenin Circuit

Any two terminals of a circuit may be represented by a series combination of a voltage source and a resistor. The value of the equivalent voltage source is the voltage appearing at the open-circuit terminals. The value of the equivalent resistance is equal to the resistance "seen" looking back into the network with all energy sources replaced by their internal resistances (ideal voltage sources have zero internal resistance, and ideal current sources have infinite internal resistance). This series combination of a voltage source, V_{Th}, and a resistor, R_{Th}, is known as a *Thévenin equivalent circuit* and is shown in Figure 4.6. Note that the equivalence exists only at the terminals.

Norton Circuit

Any two terminals of a circuit may be represented by a parallel combination of a current source and a resistor. The value of the equivalent current source is the short-circuit current appearing at the terminals. The value of the equivalent resistance is equal to the resistance "seen" looking back into the network with all energy sources replaced by their internal resistances (ideal voltage sources have zero internal resistance, and ideal current sources have infinite internal resistance). This parallel combination of a current source, I_N, and a resistor, R_N, is known as a *Norton equivalent circuit* and is shown in Figure 4.7a. Figure 4.7b shows equivalent circuits.

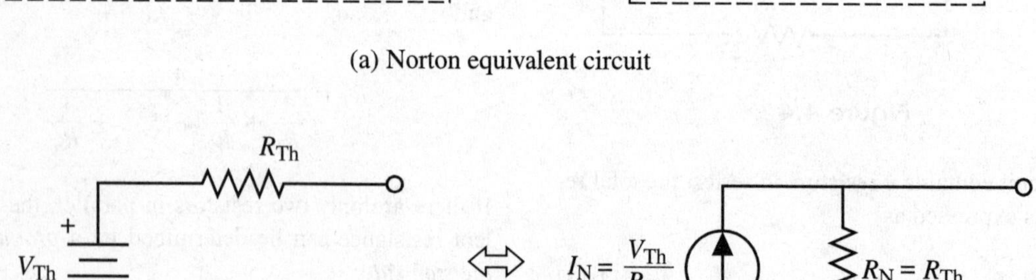

(a) Norton equivalent circuit

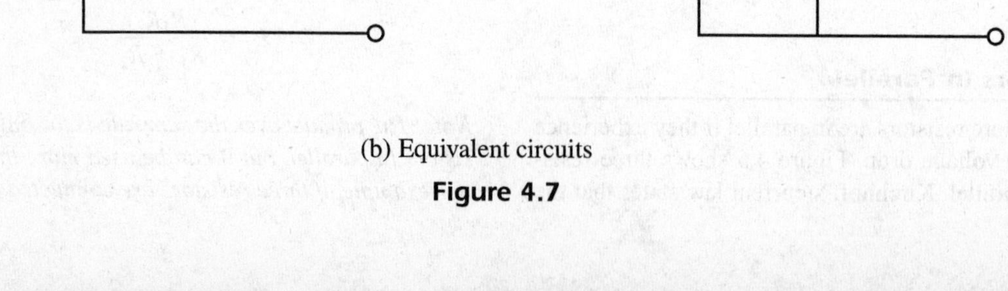

(b) Equivalent circuits

Figure 4.7

Example 4.1

What is the resistance of 2,000 m of copper wire that has a resistivity of $1.72 \times 10^{-8}\ \Omega \cdot \text{m}$ and a diameter of 4 mm?

A. 0.086 Ω
B. 2.74 Ω
C. 1.37 Ω
D. 3.24 Ω

Solution:

Apply equation 4.4 to obtain

$$R = \frac{\rho l}{A} = \frac{(1.72 \times 10^{-8}\ \Omega \cdot \text{m})(2{,}000\ \text{m})}{\frac{\pi}{4}(4 \times 10^{-3}\ \text{m})^2} = 2.74\ \Omega$$

Answer is B.

Example 4.2

For the circuit of Figure 4.8, what is the value of current I_T?

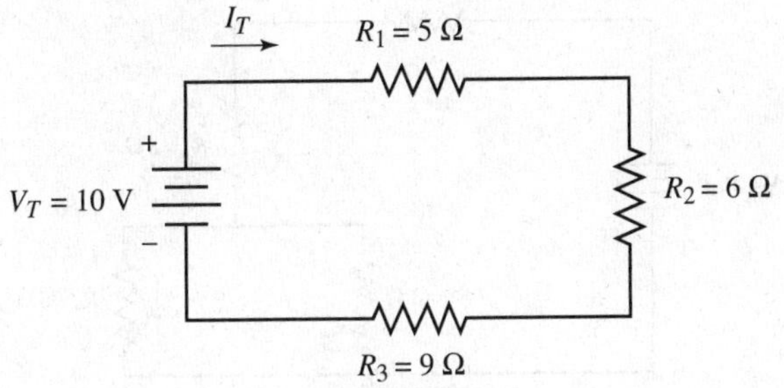

Figure 4.8

A. 1.5 A
B. 4.0 A
C. 2.0 A
D. 0.5 A

Solution:

Use equation 4.12 to solve for the total resistance "seen" by the voltage source:

$$R_T = R_1 + R_2 + R_3 = 20\ \Omega$$

Apply Ohm's law to obtain

$$I_T = \frac{10\ \text{V}}{20\ \Omega} = 0.5\ \text{A}$$

Answer is D.

Example 4.3

For the circuit of Figure 4.8, what is the value of the power dissipated by R_2?

A. 1.5 W
B. 4.0 W
C. 1.25 W
D. 3.0 W

Solution:

From the solution of Example 4.2, $I_T = 0.5$ A. Apply equation 4.9 to obtain

$$P = I_T^2 R_2 = (0.5\ \text{A})^2 \times 6\ \Omega = 1.5\ \text{W}$$

Answer is A.

Example 4.4

What is the equivalent resistance for the circuit of Figure 4.9?

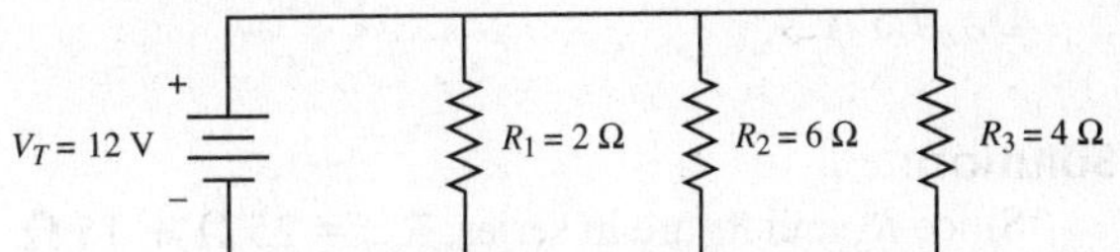

Figure 4.9

A. 1.24 Ω
B. 1.09 Ω
C. 0.24 Ω
D. 2.41 Ω

Solution:

For three resistors in parallel use equation 4.16b. Then:

$$R_T = \frac{1}{\frac{1}{2} + \frac{1}{6} + \frac{1}{4}} = 1.09\ \Omega$$

Answer is B.

Example 4.5

If a 9-V battery produces 10 A of current when a short circuit is placed across its terminals, what is the battery's internal resistance?

A. 1.11 Ω
B. 0.45 Ω
C. 0.90 Ω
D. 1.45 Ω

Solution:

Apply Ohm's law (equation 4.8):

$$R = \frac{V_T}{I} = \frac{9\ \text{V}}{10\ \text{A}} = 0.9\ \Omega$$

Answer is C.

Example 4.6

What is the value of I_T in the circuit of Figure 4.10?

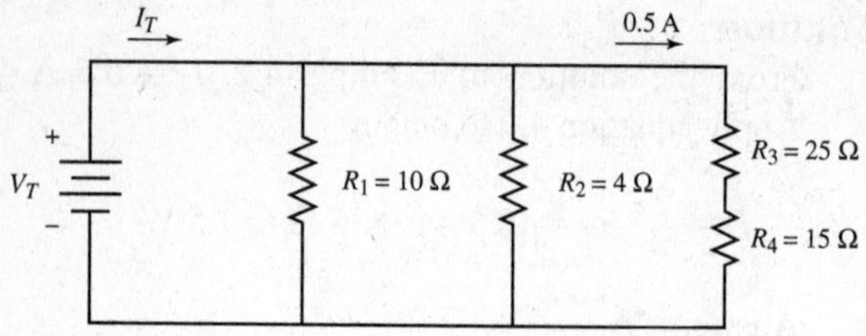

Figure 4.10

A. 0.5 A
B. 3.0 A
C. 2.5 A
D. 7.5 A

Solution:

Since R_3 and R_4 are in series, $R_{eq} = 25\ \Omega + 15\ \Omega = 40\ \Omega$. The voltage across this combination is $(0.5\text{ A})(40\ \Omega) = 20$ V. Since R_1 and R_2 are in parallel with this combination, 20 V appears across R_1 and R_2. Apply Ohm's law to obtain

$$I_1 = \frac{20\text{ V}}{10\ \Omega} = 2\text{ A} \qquad \text{and} \qquad I_2 = \frac{20\text{ V}}{4\ \Omega} = 5\text{ A}$$

Then apply Kirchhoff's current law, yielding:

$$I_T = I_1 + I_2 + I_3 = 2\text{ A} + 5\text{ A} + 0.5\text{ A} = 7.5\text{ A}$$

Answer is D.

Example 4.7

What are the The-venin equivalent voltage and resistance between terminals A and B of Figure 4.11?

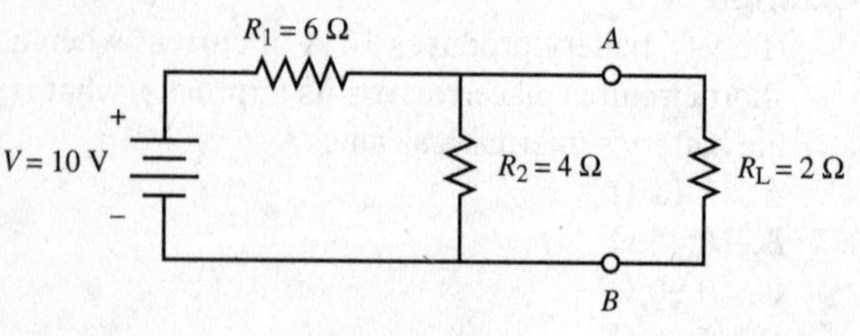

Figure 4.11

A. 10 V, 4.0 Ω
B. 4.0 V, 2.0 Ω
C. 6.0 V, 4.2 Ω
D. 4.0 V, 2.4 Ω

Solution:

Remove the 2-Ω-load resistor, and "look back" into the circuit toward the left. The voltage drop across the 4-Ω resistor is the The-venin equivalent voltage:

$$V_{\text{Th}} = \frac{4\ \Omega}{6\ \Omega + 4\ \Omega} \times 10\text{ V} = 4\text{ V}$$

This equation is known as the *voltage division law,* but the same answer can be determined by calculating the total current and using Ohm's law.

To determine the Thévenin equivalent resistance, replace the voltage source, V_T, by its internal resistance, 0 Ω. This puts the 6-Ω resistor in parallel with the 4-Ω resistor. Apply equation 4.18 to obtain

$$R_{\text{Th}} = \frac{6\ \Omega \times 4\ \Omega}{6\ \Omega + 4\ \Omega} = 2.4\ \Omega$$

Answer is D.

Example 4.8

What is the value of the current through the 6-Ω resistor in the circuit of Figure 4.12?

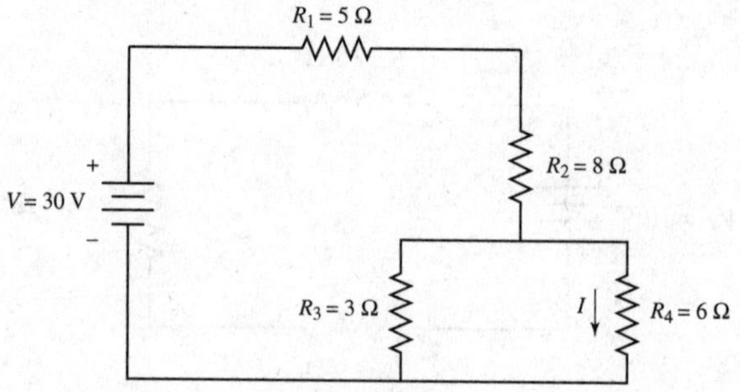

Figure 4.12

A. 2.0 A
B. $\frac{2}{3}$ A
C. 5.0 A
D. $\frac{4}{3}$ A

Solution:

To determine the total current drawn from the voltage source, determine the total resistance, R_T:

$$R_T = R_1 + R_2 + \frac{R_3 \times R_4}{R_3 + R_4}$$

$$= 5\ \Omega + 8\ \Omega + \frac{3\ \Omega \times 6\ \Omega}{3\ \Omega + 6\ \Omega} = 15\ \Omega$$

and the total current:

$$I_T = \frac{30\text{ V}}{15\ \Omega} = 2\text{ A}$$

The total current flows through the 5-Ω and 8-Ω resistors and then divides between the 3-Ω resistor and the 6-Ω resistor:

$$I_{6\Omega} = \frac{3\ \Omega}{3\ \Omega + 6\ \Omega} \times 2\ \text{A} = \frac{2}{3}\ \text{A}$$

The last equation is known as the *current division law.* The same result can be obtained by using Ohm's law and the equivalent resistance of the parallel combination of the 3-Ω and 6-Ω resistors.

Answer is B.

4.3 Direct-Current (DC) Circuit Analysis

This section applies Ohm's law and Kirchhoff's voltage and current laws to solve current and voltage in dc resistive circuits with more than one energy source.

Some circuits have two or more voltage sources, and one method to solve these problems is to apply Kirchhoff's voltage law and write a set of simultaneous linear equations. The unknown values are known as the loop currents. The rules of writing this set of equations are as follows:

1. Determine the number of loop currents by using the expression $(T - N) + 1$, where T is the total number of elements in the circuit and N is the number of nodes in the circuit.
2. Assign a loop current for each independent closed path.
3. Apply Kirchhoff's voltage law to each loop. If you are applying Kirchhoff's voltage law to one loop, and an element has two or more loop currents flowing through it, the total voltage drop across the element equals the sum (or difference) of the voltage drops due to the individual loop currents.

With reference to the circuit shown in Figure 4.13a, the three steps are as follows:

1. The circuit has six elements and four nodes; therefore it can be analyzed using three loop currents (I_A, I_B, and I_C).
2. A set of loop currents is shown in the figure.
3. Kirchhoff's voltage law is applied to each loop.

Now you have three simultaneous equations with three unknowns.

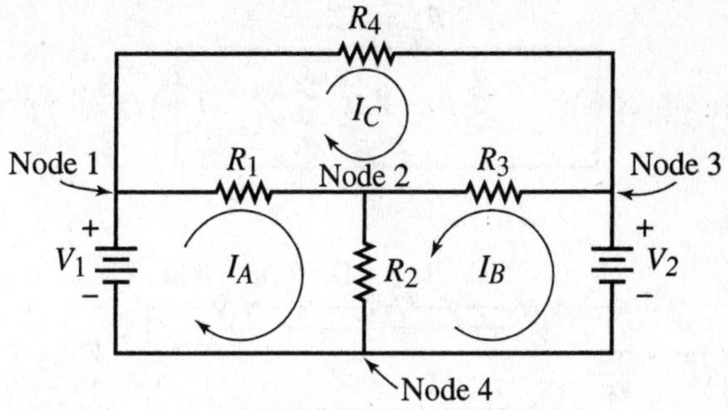

$$(R_1 + R_2) I_A + R_2 I_B - R_1 I_C = V_1$$

$$+ R_2 I_A + (R_2 + R_3) I_B + R_3 I_C = V_2$$

$$- R_1 I_A + R_3 I_B + (R_1 + R_3 + R_4) I_C = 0$$

(a)

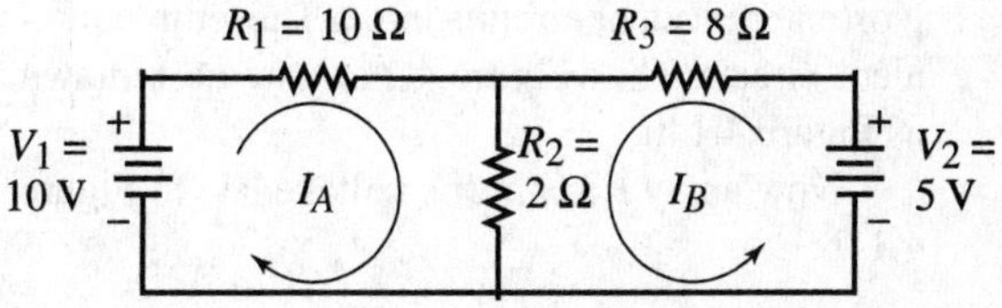

(b)

Figure 4.13

Example 4.9

What is the value of the current through R_1 in the circuit of Figure 4.13b?

A. 0.833 A
B. 0.345 A
C. 0.776 A
D. 1.33 A

Solution:

The set of equations is as follows:

Loop A: $(10\ \Omega + 2\ \Omega)I_A + (2\ \Omega)I_B = 10\ \text{V}$

Loop B: $(2\ \Omega)I_A + (8\ \Omega + 2\ \Omega)I_B = 5\ \text{V}$

Since R_1 has only one loop current flowing through it, only loop current I_A need be calculated.

$$I_A = \frac{\begin{vmatrix} 10 & 2 \\ 5 & 10 \end{vmatrix}}{\begin{vmatrix} 12 & 2 \\ 2 & 10 \end{vmatrix}} = \frac{100 - 10}{120 - 4} = \frac{90}{116} = 0.776\ \text{A}$$

Answer is C.

Example 4.10

What is the value of the current through the 4-Ω resistor in the circuit of Figure 4.14a?

A. 0.2 A
B. 4.0 A
C. 0.85 A
D. 1.5 A

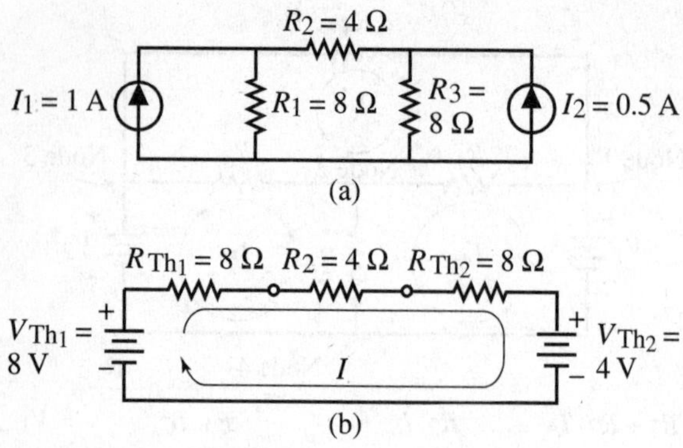

Figure 4.14

Solution:

This circuit can be solved by converting the Norton equivalent circuits into a Thévenin equivalent circuit. Thus Figure 4.14a may be redrawn as Figure 4.14b.

Now apply Kirchhoff's voltage law to Figure 4.14b:

$$I_{4\,\Omega} = \frac{V_{Th_1} - V_{Th_2}}{R_1 + R_2 + R_3} = \frac{8\text{ V} - 4\text{ V}}{8\ \Omega + 4\ \Omega + 8\ \Omega} = 0.2\text{ A}$$

Answer is A.

4.4 Inductance

The second passive element mentioned in Section 4.1 is **inductance.** The unique property of this element is that it stores energy in a *magnetic field.* Let us, then, examine some fundamental properties of a magnetic field.

Before 1819, electricity and magnetism were considered independent natural phenomena. However, in that year Hans Christian Oersted (1777–1851) observed an interaction between electricity and magnetism. Thus the new science of electromagnetism was born. Oersted's experiment showed that an electric current caused a magnetic compass needle to move. Because the wire through which the electric current flowed did not come into direct contact with the compass needle, Oersted concluded that the interaction must involve the surrounding space.

Whenever there is an interaction between two points in space with no visible contact between them, the surrounding space is called a field. The two important properties of a field are intensity (magnitude) and direction. In Oersted's experiment the current had an effect on the magnetic compass because of a field.

We now know that, whenever a current flows in a conductor, a magnetic field is created. The flow of current dictates both the intensity and the direction of the magnetic field. The larger the current value, the greater the intensity, **H**, of the magnetic field, which is a vector quantity. The direction of the magnetic field is determined by the *right-hand rule:* If the thumb of the right hand points in the direction of conventional current, the fingers of the right hand will curl around the conductor in the direction of the magnetic field. (See Figure 4.15a and b.)

Because it is a human trait to want to visualize every concept, it is convenient to have some way of depicting a field. Michael Faraday (1791–1867), a pioneer in the science of electromagnetism, suggested adopting "lines of force" to represent a magnetic field. Although these lines are imaginary, they are the best way to visualize a magnetic field.

For a current-carrying conductor, Figure 4.15a shows magnetic lines of force and their direction. The direction of the magnetic field is always perpendicular to the direction of current, and the field must always form a complete loop.

If a current-carrying conductor is wound in the form of a coil, not only will the magnetic lines of force encircle each infinitesimal portion of the conductor, but also they will add to produce a magnetic field surrounding the entire coil.

Up to this point, the discussion of the interaction between electricity and magnetism has dealt with the fact that the flow of current in a conductor produces a magnetic field about the conductor. Now consider another interaction between electricity and magnetism;

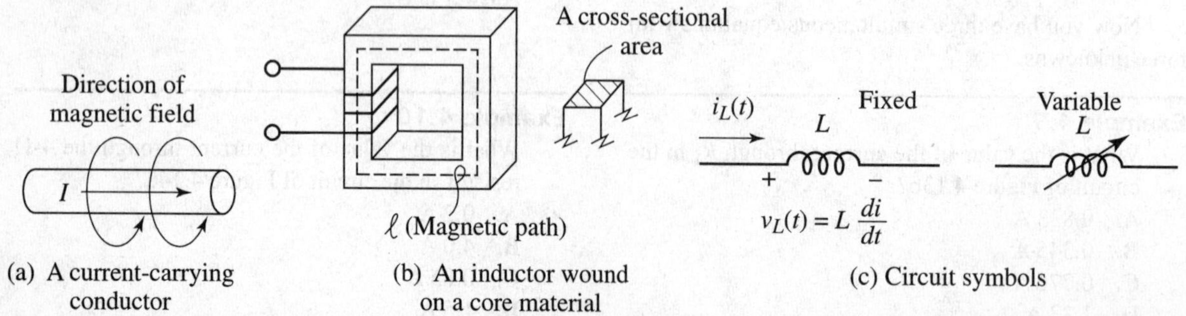

Figure 4.15

that is, a changing magnetic field surrounding a conductor induces a voltage in the conductor. This induced voltage is called a *self-induced voltage* because it is induced in the same conductor that is carrying the current.

Note that a voltage, not a current, is induced in the conductor. The existence of current depends on whether or not there is a complete circuit. (If the induced voltage occurs in another conductor, the principle is known as *mutual inductance.* Applications of mutual inductance are given in section 4.7.)

If the circuit is complete (a continuous path for current), the direction of the self-induced voltage is given by Lenz's law: *The direction of a self-induced voltage is such as to oppose the change in current.* For example, suppose that the current in a coil tends to increase; then the magnetic field about the coil increases, and the direction of the self-induced voltage, according to Lenz's law, is such as to oppose any change, thus inhibiting the increase.

On the other hand, when the current in a circuit tends to decrease, the magnetic field also decreases and the direction of the self-induced voltage tends to keep the current from decreasing. Thus, when the magnetic field is collapsing, it gives energy back to the circuit, temporarily acting as an energy source. This opposition to change in current is an effect of electromagnetic induction.

The circuit element that has the property of opposing any change in current in a circuit by storing energy in a magnetic field is called *self-inductance.* The basic unit for inductance, mutual or self, is the henry (H), named in honor of Joseph Henry. Inductance, the electrical property of storing energy in a magnetic field, is represented by the symbol L.

An *inductor* is the physical device connected into a circuit to store energy in a magnetic field. Inductors may be classified as fixed or variable; the circuit symbols for both types are shown in Figure 4.15c. A *fixed inductor* has a nonadjustable value and has either an air core or an iron core. A variable inductor has an iron core that can be moved within the coil to vary the magnetic field and thereby vary its inductance.

An inductor stores energy in a magnetic field. In terms of physical parameters, inductance is calculated by using the equation

$$L = \frac{\mu A N^2}{l} \qquad [4.19]$$

where μ = permeability of the magnetic material (H/m),
A = cross-sectional area of the path (m^2),
N = number of turns of the coil,
l = length of the path (m).

Values of permeability for various materials are listed in Table 4.3.

Table 4.3 Permeability Values for Four Materials

Material	*Permeability, μ* (H/m)
Air	1.257×10^{-6}
Iron	6.53×10^{-3}
Steel	8.80×10^{-3}
Permalloy	1.257×10^{-1}

Voltage/Current Relationship for an Inductor

The voltage across an inductor depends on the value of the inductor times the rate of change of current through the inductor. The equation is as follows:

$$v_L(t) = L\frac{di_L}{dt} \qquad [4.20]$$

Energy Stored in an Inductor

The energy stored by an inductor is given by the expression

$$Energy = \frac{1}{2}LI^2 \qquad [4.21]$$

Inductors in Series

Inductors connected in series combine in the same way as resistors in series; that is, for n inductors in series the equivalent inductance is as follows:

$$L_T = L_1 + L_2 + \dots + L_n \qquad [4.22]$$

Inductors in Parallel

Inductors connected in parallel combine in the same way as resistors in parallel.

$$L_{eq} = \frac{1}{\frac{1}{L_1} + \frac{1}{L_2} + \dots + \frac{1}{L_n}} \qquad [4.23]$$

If only two inductors are connected in parallel, the product over the sum rule can be used:

$$L_{eq} = \frac{L_1 L_2}{L_1 + L_2} \qquad [4.24]$$

Example 4.11

What is the equivalent inductance of the circuit shown in Figure 4.16?

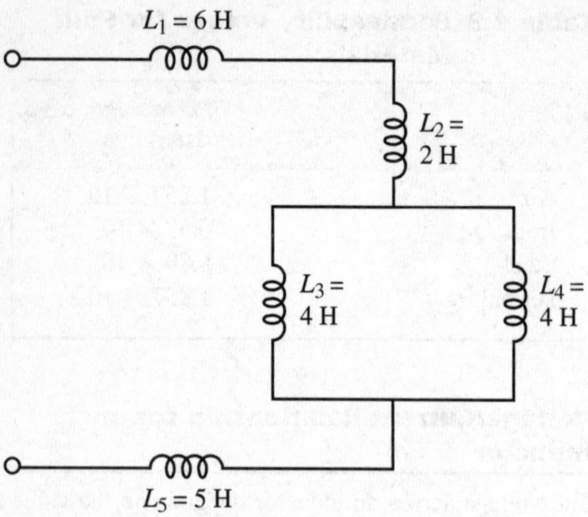

Figure 4.16

A. 13 H
B. 21 H
C. 12.5 H
D. 15 H

Solution:

Apply equations 4.22 and 4.24 to obtain

$$L_T = L_1 + L_2 + \frac{L_3 \times L_4}{L_3 + L_4} + L_5$$

$$= 6\text{ H} + 2\text{ H} + \frac{4\text{ H} \times 4\text{ H}}{4\text{ H} + 4\text{ H}} + 5\text{ H} = 15\text{ H}$$

Answer is D.

Example 4.12

The current waveform through a 1-H coil is shown in Figure 4.17. What is the voltage waveform? (Choose one of the waveforms given in Figure 4.18 as the answer.)

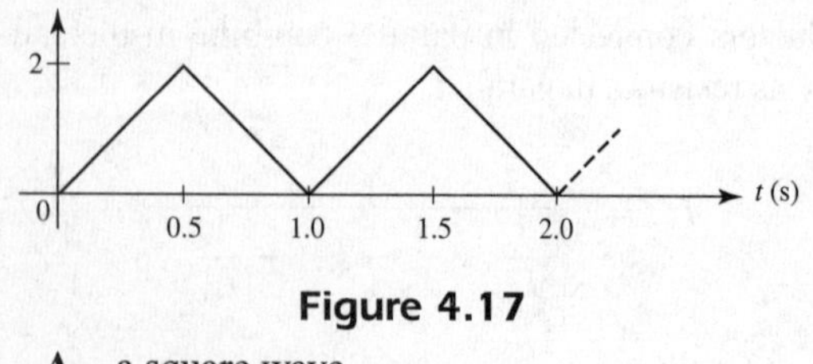

Figure 4.17

A. a square wave
B. a triangular wave
C. a pulse wave
D. a triangular wave with dc offset

Solution:

The waveform is periodic; that is, it repeats after 1 s. Determine the voltage waveform for the time intervals 0 to 0.5 s and 0.5 s to 1.0 s; the waveform repeats after 1 s. Since the current waveform is linear in each time interval, apply the equation of a straight line ($y = mx + b$) to determine the equation of current; then apply equation 4.20 for each time interval.

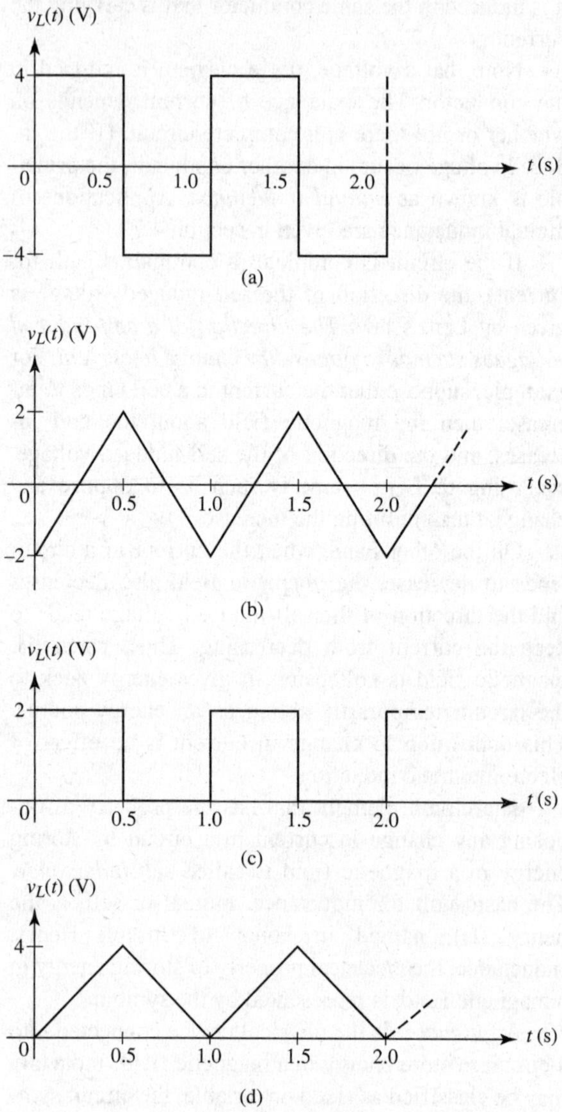

Figure 4.18

For the time interval 0 to 0.5 s:

$$i(t)_{0-0.5\text{ s}} = \frac{(2-0)\text{A}}{(0.5-0)\text{s}}t + 0 = 4\frac{\text{A}}{\text{s}} \times t$$

Apply equation 4.20 to obtain

$$v_L(t) = 1\text{ H} \times \frac{d}{dt}(4\frac{\text{A}}{\text{s}}t) = 4\text{ V}$$

For the time interval 0.5 s to 1.0 s:

$$i(t)_{0.5\text{ s}-1.0\text{ s}} = \frac{(0-2)\text{ A}}{(1-0.5)\text{ s}} \times t + 4\text{ A}$$

$$= -4\frac{\text{A}}{\text{s}} \times t + 4\text{ A}$$

Apply equation 4.20 to obtain

$$v_L(t) = 1\text{ H} \times \frac{d}{dt}\left(-4\,\frac{\text{A}}{\text{s}}\,t + 4\right) = -4\text{ V}$$

Plot the voltage values for each time interval; hence, the voltage waveform is a square wave.

Answer is A.

4.5 Capacitance

The third passive element mentioned in Section 4.1 is **capacitance.** Its properties are as unique as those of resistance and inductance. Whenever there is a difference of charge in a circuit, a voltage (or potential difference) exists. A *capacitor* stores energy in an *electric field,* which is the space between a positive and a negative charge. As in the case of a magnetic field, the "lines of force" concept may be used to visualize an electric field. Unlike the lines of force of a magnetic field, which form closed loops, the lines of force of an electric field always *begin and end* on charges.

Like the lines of force of a magnetic field, the lines of force of an electric field indicate both strength and direction, and electric field intensity, **E**, is a vector quantity. The greater the number of lines, the more intense the electric field. The strength of an electric field, measured from a point charge, is directly proportional to the charge and indirectly proportional to the distance squared. Thus the strength of an electric field is greatest closest to the charge and decreases as one moves away from it.

The direction of the electric field is the path that a positive charge would travel if placed in the field. Since a basic phenomenon of charge is that like charges repel and unlike charges attract, the direction of the lines of force is always *from the positive charge to the negative charge,* as shown in Figure 4.19a.

An electric field can be created in a circuit by placing two conducting plates in parallel and having one plate more positive than the other, as in Figure 4.19a. The material between the two plates is nonconducting, or insulating. This insulating material is called a *dielectric.* Some dielectrics in common use are air, Bakelite, ceramic, formica, glass, kraft paper, polyethylene, and Teflon.

Thus, capacitance is the property of storing energy in an electric field. The energy is stored between the parallel plates of a capacitor, which is a physical device having the property of capacitance. The unit for capacitance is the farad (F).

The capacitance for a pair of parallel plates such as those shown in Figure 4.19b is given by the equation

$$C = \frac{\varepsilon A}{d} \qquad [4.25]$$

where C = capacitance (F),
ε = dielectric constant (F/m),
A = area of each plate (m^2),
d = distance between plates (m).

The dielectric constants of several materials are listed in Table 4.4.

Table 4.4 Dielectric Constants of Six Materials

Material	*Dielectric Constant ε* (10^{-11} F/m)
Air	0.885
Pyrex	3.54
Mica	7.85
Mylar	4.16
Quartz	3.54
Tantalum dioxide	150

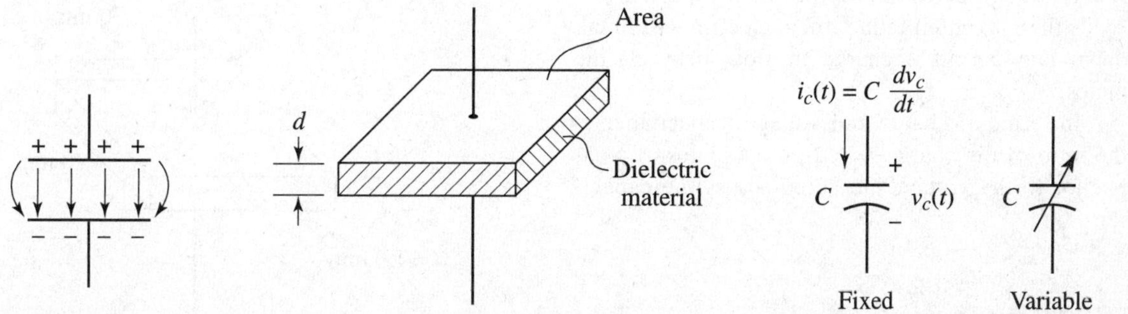

(a) Direction of electric field (b) Physical device (c) Circuit symbols for a capacitor

Figure 4.19

To examine how one plate of a capacitor can be made positive with respect to the other plate, consider a capacitor connected to a battery through a switch. When the switch is closed, electrons from the negative terminal of the battery collect on the bottom plate. To maintain equilibrium, an equal number of electrons leave the top plate and drift toward the positive terminal of the battery. While this is happening, the capacitor is said to be *charging.* This flow of charges will continue until the voltage across the capacitor equals the source voltage. When the capacitor voltage and applied voltage are equal, the capacitor is said to be *charged.*

The capacitor will remain in this charged condition even after the source is removed. For the capacitor to return to a neutral or uncharged state, an external path must be provided for the flow of charge. This external path may range from a short circuit (zero resistance) to a complicated network. While the capacitor is returning to a neutral (or uncharged) state, it is said to be *discharging.* Although a capacitor supplies energy to a circuit while it is discharging, it is not classified as an energy source because a capacitor cannot *transform* some other form of energy into electrical energy; it can only *store* energy.

Since the movement of charges in one direction constitutes an electric current, the current associated with a capacitor is present only when the capacitor is either charging or discharging, for only at these times is there a movement of electrons. It should be emphasized that charge flows, not *between* the plates of a capacitor, but only in the external circuit, although it is common to refer to the current in the capacitor or the capacitor current.

Capacitors may be classified as either fixed or variable. The circuit and letter symbols are shown in Figure 4.19c. A *fixed capacitor* has a nonadjustable value. A *variable capacitor* has one set of plates that are movable, thereby changing the value of the capacitance.

Both fixed and variable capacitors have maximum voltage ratings specified by the manufacturer. If the voltage across the plates of a capacitor exceeds the maximum rating, the dielectric will break down and permit a charge to flow between the plates.

In terms of charge and voltage, capacitance is the ratio of the charge stored on the plates of a capacitor to the voltage measured across the capacitor:

$$C = \frac{q_C(t)}{v_C(t)} \qquad [4.26]$$

Voltage/Current Relationship for a Capacitor

Capacitor current is the value of the capacitor times the time rate of change in voltage across the capacitor:

$$i_C(t) = C\frac{dv_C}{dt} \qquad [4.27]$$

Energy Stored in a Capacitor

The energy stored in a capacitor is given by the equation

$$\text{Energy} = \frac{1}{2}CV^2 \qquad [4.28]$$

Capacitors in Series

Capacitors connected in series combine in the same way as resistors in parallel:

$$C_{eq} = \frac{1}{\frac{1}{C_1} + \frac{1}{C_2} + \ldots + \frac{1}{C_n}} \qquad [4.29]$$

For two capacitors in series the product over the sum rule may be used:

$$C_{eq} = \frac{C_1 C_2}{C_1 + C_2} \qquad [4.30]$$

Capacitors in Parallel

Capacitors connected in parallel combine in the same way as resistors in series:

$$C_{eq} = C_1 + C_2 + \ldots + C_n \qquad [4.31]$$

Example 4.13

What is the value of capacitance for the capacitor shown in Figure 4.20 if the dielectric constant is 4.16×10^{-11} F/m?

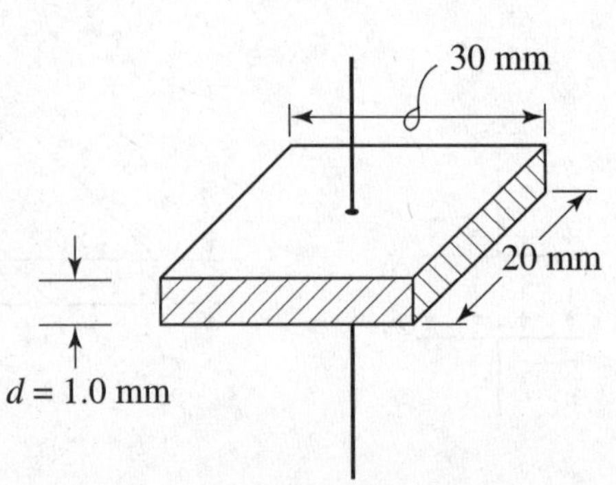

Figure 4.20

A. 0.25 μF
B. 25 pF
C. 2.5 μF
D. 4.1 nF

Solution:

Apply equation 4.25 to obtain

$$C = \frac{(4.16 \times 10^{-11}\text{F/m})(0.02\text{ m} \times 0.03\text{ m})}{0.001\text{ m}} = 25\text{ pF}$$

Answer is B.

Example 4.14

The charge on the plates of a 1.0-μF capacitor is 50 μC. What is the energy stored by the capacitor?

A. 1.25 mJ
B. 25 mJ
C. 5.5 mJ
D. 10.5 mJ

Solution:

Calculate the voltage across the capacitor by rearranging equation 4.26:

$$v_C(t) = \frac{q_C(t)}{C} = \frac{50\ \mu\text{C}}{1\ \mu\text{F}} = 50\text{ V}$$

Now apply equation 4.28:

$$\text{Energy} = \frac{1}{2}CV^2 = \frac{1}{2} \times 1\ \mu\text{F} \times (50\text{ V})^2 = 1.25\text{ mJ}$$

Answer is A.

Example 4.15

What is the total capacitance between terminals A and B for the circuit of Figure 4.21?

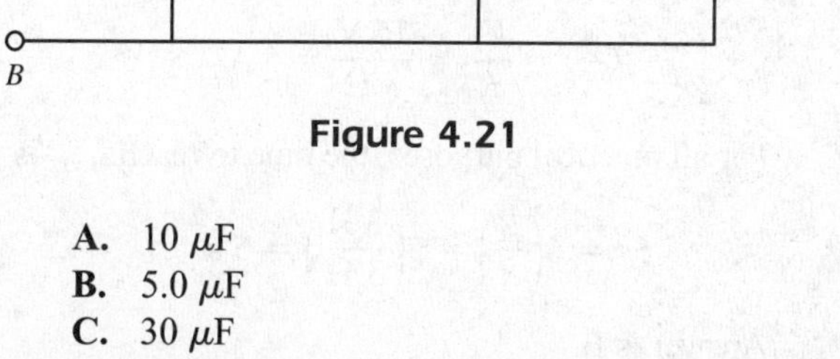

Figure 4.21

A. 10 μF
B. 5.0 μF
C. 30 μF
D. 60 μF

Solution:

For the parallel combination of C_3 and C_4, the equivalent capacitance is 30 μF. This capacitance value is in series with C_2; use equation 4.30:

$$C_{eq} = \frac{C_2 C_{3,4}}{C_2 + C_{3,4}} = \frac{60\ \mu\text{F} \times 30\ \mu\text{F}}{60\ \mu\text{F} + 30\ \mu\text{F}} = 20\ \mu\text{F}$$

Combine this equivalent capacitance value with C_1 to obtain 30 μF.

Answer is C.

4.6 Resistor-Capacitor (R-C) and Resistor-Inductor (R-L) Circuits

R-C Circuits

Figure 4.22 shows a resistor and a capacitor connected in series through a switch to a dc voltage source. When the switch is closed, the voltage across the capacitor increases exponentially. The rate of rise depends on the circuit's time constant, τ. The time constant $\tau = RC$ and is expressed in seconds. In one time constant, the voltage across the capacitor reaches 63.3% of its steady-state value. For all practical purposes the steady-state value is reached in 5τ. The value of resistance as "seen" by the capacitor is symbolized as R.

The equation for voltage across the capacitor, where the voltage increases or decreases exponentially is

$$v_C(t) = V_f + (V_i - V_f)e^{-t/\tau} \qquad [4.32]$$

where V_f is the maximum value that C will charge (or discharge) to, and V_i is the initial voltage across the capacitor.

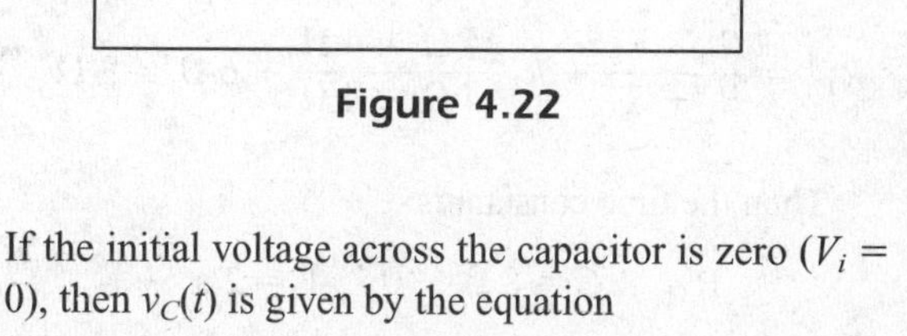

Figure 4.22

If the initial voltage across the capacitor is zero ($V_i = 0$), then $v_C(t)$ is given by the equation

$$v_C(t) = V_f(1 - e^{-t/\tau}) \qquad [4.33]$$

Example 4.16

Consider the circuit of Figure 4.22. The capacitor is initially uncharged, and the circuit values are $V_T = 10$ V, $R = 2\ \Omega$, and $C = 1/8$ F. What is the voltage across the capacitor 0.5 s after the switch is closed?

A. 5.52 V
B. 6.67 V
C. 7.54 V
D. 8.65 V

Solution:

The time constant for the circuit is

$$\tau = RC = 2 \times \frac{1}{8} = \frac{1}{4}\ \text{s}$$

Apply equation 4.33 to obtain

$$v_C(t) = 10\ \text{V} \times (1 - e^{-0.5/0.25}) = 8.65\ \text{V}$$

Answer is D.

Example 4.17

What is the time constant for the circuit of Figure 4.23?

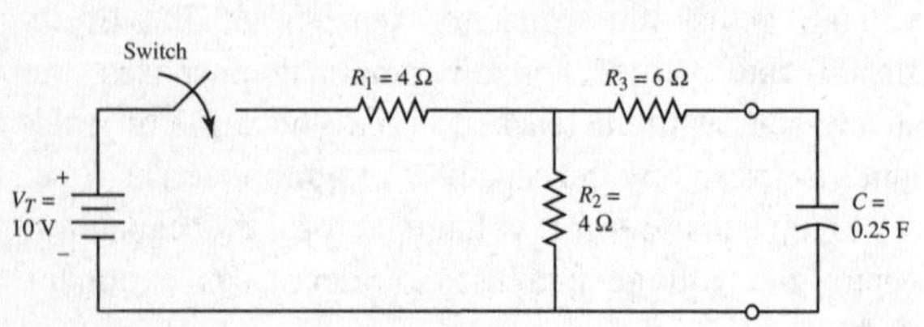

Figure 4.23

A. 2.0 s
B. 1.5 s
C. 4.5 s
D. 5.0 s

Solution:

Consider the capacitor as the load, and determine the The-venin equivalent resistance as "seen" looking back into the circuit from the capacitor. The equation is

$$R_{\text{Th}} = \frac{R_1 \times R_2}{R_1 + R_2} + R_3 \quad \frac{4\ \Omega \times 4\ \Omega}{4\ \Omega + 4\ \Omega} + 6\ \Omega = 8\ \Omega$$

Then the time constant is

$$\text{R}_{\text{Th}} \times C = 8\ \Omega \times 0.25\ \text{F} = 2\ \text{s}$$

Answer is A.

R-L Circuits

Figure 4.24 shows a resistor and an inductor connected in series through a switch to a dc voltage source. When the switch is closed, the inductor's magnetic field opposes any change in current; therefore current flow increases exponentially. The rate of increase in current depends on the circuit's time constant, τ. The time constant $\tau = L/R$ and is expressed in seconds. In one time constant, the current reaches 63.3% of its steady-state value. For all practical purposes the steady-state value is reached in 5τ.

The general equation for current through the inductor where the current increases or decreases exponentially is

$$i_L(t) = I_f + (i_I - I_f)e^{-t/\tau} \qquad [4.34]$$

where I_f is the maximum value of current that can exist in the inductor, $I_f = V_T/R$ for the circuit shown in Figure 4.24, and I_i is the initial condition that is the value of current through the inductor before the switch is closed. Note that the initial-condition value may be zero.

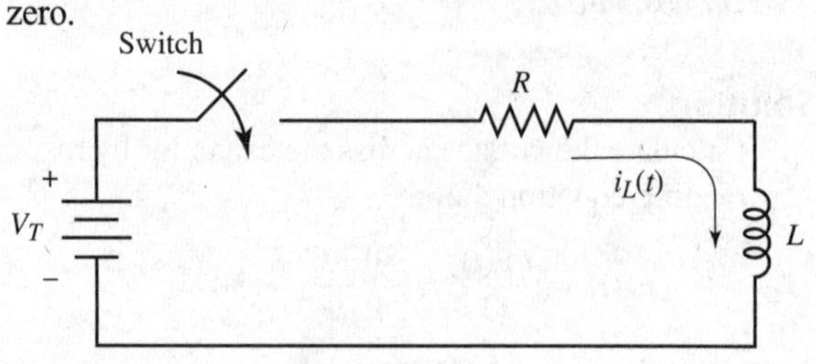

Figure 4.24

Example 4.18

For the circuit of Figure 4.24, let $V_T = 15$ V, $R = 3\ \Omega$, and $L = 3$ H. Find the maximum value of current through the inductor and the time to reach the final value. The initial condition is zero.

A. 5 A, 2 s
B. 5 A, 5 s
C. 3 A, 1 s
D. 2.67 A, 3 s

Solution:

The final or maximum value of current that can flow in the circuit of Figure 4.24 is given by the equation

$$I_{\text{max}} = \frac{V_T}{R} = \frac{15\ \text{V}}{3\ \Omega} = 5\ \text{A}$$

For all practical purposes, the time to reach I_{max} is

$$5\tau = 5\left(\frac{L}{R}\right) = 5\left(\frac{3\ \text{H}}{3\ \Omega}\right) = 5\ \text{s}.$$

Answer is B.

4.7 Alternating-Current (AC) Circuit Analysis

This section introduces ac voltage and current waveforms and ac circuit analysis. The analysis of ac circuits requires the use of complex numbers and complex algebra to solve the circuit problems. Therefore you may need to refer to Chapter 9, Mathematics, for a review of complex numbers.

Sinusoidal Waveform

In the United States commercially generated electrical energy is produced in the form of a periodic alternating voltage waveform, called a *sinusoidal waveform,* as shown in Figure 4.25, where T represents the period of the wave or the time for one complete cycle.

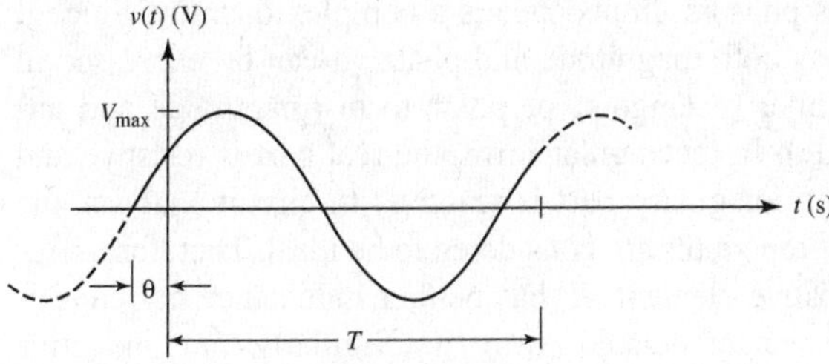

Figure 4.25

The reciprocal of the period is the frequency, f, of the wave, which is given by the equation

$$f = \frac{1}{T} \qquad [4.35a]$$

The unit of frequency is the hertz (Hz). This wave is periodic because it repeats every T seconds. The wave of Figure 4.25 can be expressed mathematically as

$$v(t) = V_{max} \sin(\omega t + \theta) \qquad [4.35b]$$

where $\omega = 2\pi f$ and has units of radians per second, and θ is the phase angle, expressed in radians.

Example 4.19

Write the equation for the sinusoidal voltage waveform shown in Figure 4.26.

A. $4(\sin 4t + 45°)$ V
B. $2(\sin 25.12t + \frac{\pi}{4})$ V
C. $8(\sin 25.25t + 22°)$ V
D. $4(\sin 12t + \frac{\pi}{8})$ V

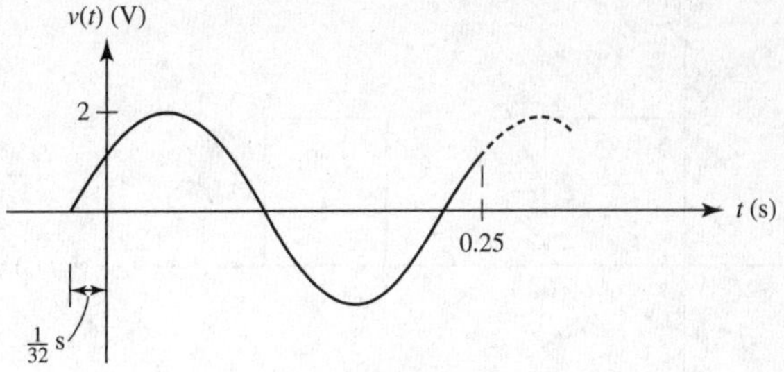

Figure 4.26

Solution:

Since the period, T, is 0.25 s, then the frequency, f, is 4 Hz ($f = 1/0.25$ s $= 4$ Hz), and $\omega = 2\pi(4) = 25.12$ rad/s. The phase angle is determined by converting 1/32 s to radians by setting up a ratio of $t/T = \theta/2\pi$:

$$\frac{\frac{1}{32}}{0.25} = \frac{\theta}{2\pi}$$

Solve for θ to obtain $\pi/4$ rad.

Hence the equation is

$$v(t) = 2\left(\sin 25.12t + \frac{\pi}{4}\right) \text{ volts}$$

Answer is B.

Average Values

The average value of a periodic waveform (either voltage or current) is given by equation 4.36a:

$$X_{eq} = \frac{1}{T}\int_0^T x(t)dt \qquad [4.36a]$$

where $x(t)$ is the waveform expression in the time domain, and T is the period of the waveform.

If the waveform is symmetrical about the time (x-axis), the average value is zero. Equation 4.36a states that the average value equals the area under the waveform divided by the period, or

$$X_{eq} = \frac{\text{area}}{\text{period}} \qquad [4.36b]$$

Equation 4.36b is useful when determining the average value for pulse, triangular, and other similarly shaped waveforms that are formed by straight lines only.

Example 4.20

For Figure 4.27, the maximum value is 2 V and the frequency is 4 Hz. What is the average value of the voltage?

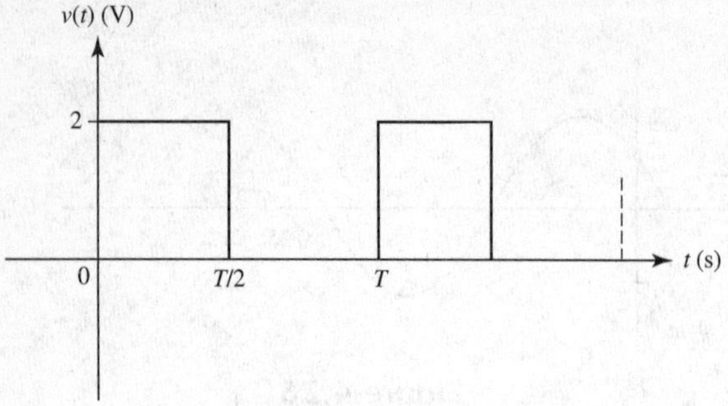

Figure 4.27

A. 1.0 V
B. 1.25 V
C. 2.15 V
D. 0.5 V

Solution:

Rearrange equation 4.35 to find the period of the wave:

$$T = \frac{1}{4} = 0.25 \text{ s} \quad \text{or} \quad \frac{T}{2} = 0.125 \text{ s}$$

Apply equation 4.36b to obtain

$$V_{avg} = \frac{2 \text{ V} \times 0.125 \text{ s}}{0.25 \text{ s}} = 1.0 \text{ V}$$

Answer is A.

Effective or RMS Values

An alternating voltage or current usually requires knowledge of its root mean square (rms) value. The rms value of voltage results in the same amount of heating effect to a load as a dc voltage of the same value would produce. Hence the effect is the same. The general equation for calculating rms values is as follows:

$$X_{\text{rms}} = \sqrt{\frac{1}{T}\int_0^T x^2(t)\, dt} \qquad [4.37]$$

Example 4.21

What is the rms value for the waveform shown in Figure 4.27? The amplitude is 2 V, and the period is 0.25 s.

A. 2 V
B. 2.5 V
C. $\sqrt{2}$ V
D. $2\sqrt{2}$ V

Solution:

Refer to Figure 4.27 and Example 4.20. The appropriate expression is

$$v(t) = \begin{cases} 2 \text{ V} & \text{for } 0 \le t \le 0.125 \text{ s} \\ 0 \text{ V} & \text{for } 0.125 \text{ s} < t < 0.25 \text{ s} \end{cases}$$

Apply equation 4.37 to obtain

$$v_{\text{rms}}(t) = \sqrt{\frac{1}{0.25}\left[\int_0^{0.125} 4\, dt + \int_{0.125}^{0.25} 0\, dt\right]} = \sqrt{2} \text{ V}$$

Answer is C.

Impedance

Impedance, Z, is defined as the opposition to ac current and is expressed in ohms (Ω). It is the ratio of total ac voltage to total ac current when both are expressed as phasors. Impedance is a complex quantity. Since it has both magnitude and phase, it can be expressed in either rectangular or polar form (magnitude and angle). In rectangular form, the real part is resistive and the imaginary part is reactive. In circuit analysis, the components are considered to be ideal. Therefore, a resistive element, R, has neither inductance nor capacitance associated with it. Similarly, an inductive element has neither resistance nor capacitance, and a capacitive element has neither resistance nor inductance. In rectangular form, impedance is expressed as

$$Z = R \pm jX \qquad [4.38]$$

where R is the resistance value, and X is the reactive value. Reactance may be either inductive or capacitive.

Inductive Reactance

The magnitude of inductive reactance is given by the expression

$$X_L = \omega L = 2\pi f L \qquad [4.39]$$

Thus inductive reactance depends on the value of L, the frequency, and the constant 2π.

Figure 4.28a shows a series R-L circuit driven by an ac voltage source. The phasor diagram and impedance expressions for this circuit are given in Figures 4.28b and 4.28c, respectively.

For an inductor, voltage leads current by 90°. Mathematically, this lead is represented by a $+j$ term. The impedance of an inductor is expressed as

$$Z_L = jX_L = j\omega L = j2\pi f L \qquad [4.40]$$

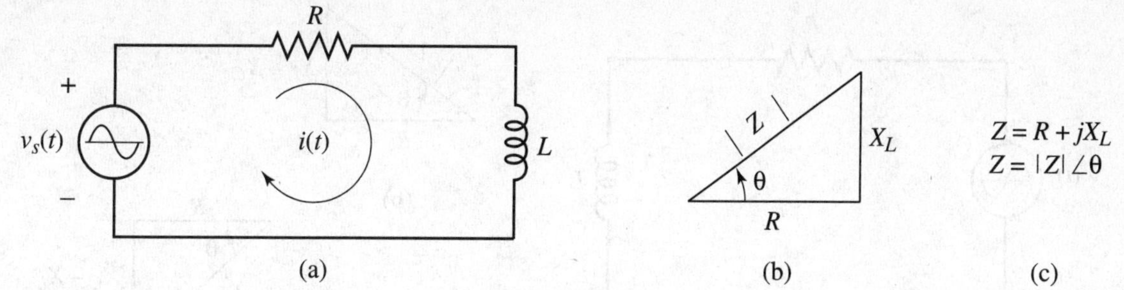

Figure 4.28

To find the equivalent impedance of a circuit, use the same rule as for resistors; that is, add impedances in series. For impedances in parallel, use the reciprocal rule.

Capacitive Reactance

The magnitude of capacitive reactance is given by the equation

$$X_C = \frac{1}{\omega C} = \frac{1}{2\pi fC} \qquad [4.41]$$

Thus capacitive reactance depends on the reciprocal of C, the frequency, and the constant 2π.

Figures 4.29a–c show a series R-C circuit driven by an ac voltage source, the phasor diagram, and the impedance expressions for this circuit.

For a capacitor, voltage lags current by 90°. A lag of 90° is represented by a $-j$ or $1/j$ term in an impedance formula. The impedance of a capacitor is expressed as

$$Z_C = -jX_C = \frac{-j}{\omega C} = \frac{-j}{2\pi fC} \qquad [4.42]$$

Series R-L-C Circuit

Figure 4.30a shows a series R-L-C circuit. The total impedance of this circuit is given by the equation

$$Z = R + jX_L - jX_C \qquad [4.43]$$

If the magnitude of the inductive reactance, X_L, is greater than the capacitive reactance, X_C, the phasor diagram will have a positive angle, as shown in Figure 4.30b. If, however, the magnitude of the capacitive reactance is greater than the inductive reactance, the phase angle will be negative, as shown in Figure 4.30c.

Parallel R-L-C Circuits

Figure 4.31 shows a parallel R-L-C circuit. The total impedance of this circuit is given by the equation

$$Z = \frac{1}{\frac{1}{R} + \frac{1}{jX_L} + jX_C} \qquad [4.44]$$

Example 4.22

What is the total impedance of the circuit shown in Figure 4.32?

A. 2.2 ∠48.7° kΩ
B. 6.4 ∠−36.6° kΩ
C. 5.19 ∠54.1° kΩ
D. 4.73 ∠62.3° kΩ

Solution:

First determine the equivalent inductance value for L_1 and L_2.

$$L_{eq} = L_1 + L_2 = 8\text{ H}$$

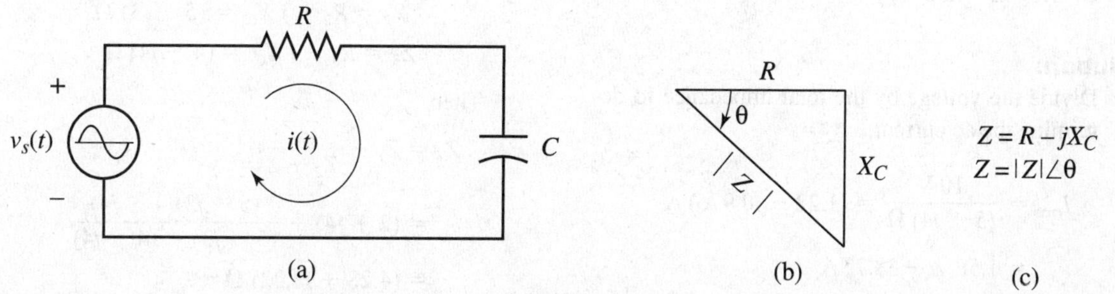

Figure 4.29

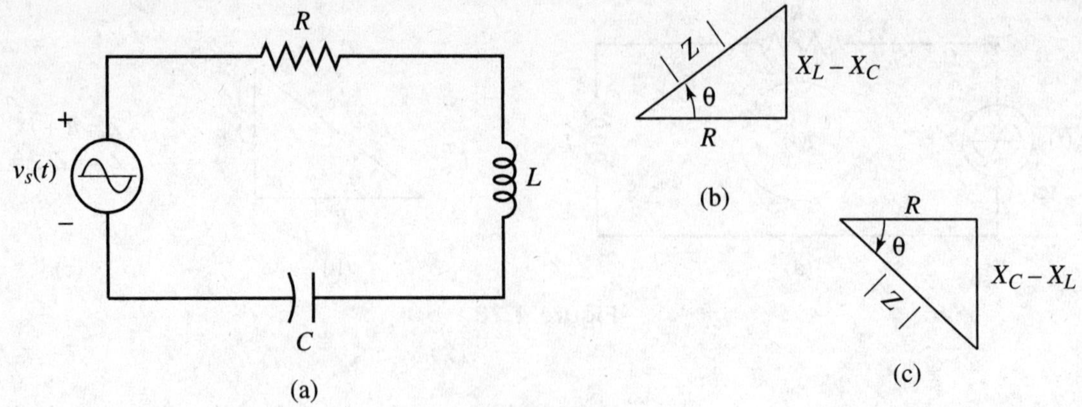

Figure 4.30

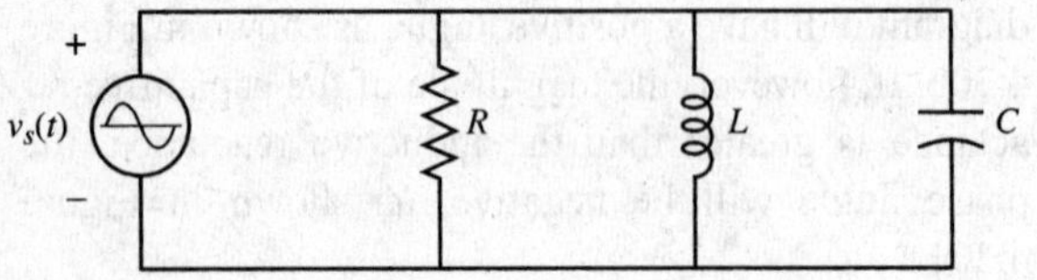

Figure 4.31

Therefore

$$X_{eq} = 2\pi f L_{eq} = 2\pi(400 \text{ Hz})(8 \text{ H}) = 20{,}106\ \Omega$$

and

$$X_C = \frac{1}{2\pi f C} = \frac{1}{2\pi(400 \text{ Hz})(0.025\ \mu\text{F})} = 15{,}915\ \Omega$$

The total reactance is $X_T = X_{eq} - X_C = 4.19$ kΩ, and the impedance is

$$Z = (2.2 + j\,4.19) \text{ k}\Omega = 4.73\ \angle 62.3° \text{ k}\Omega$$

Answer is D.

Example 4.23

What is the ac current in a circuit if the impedance is $(5 + j4)\ \Omega$ and the voltage source, V_{rms}, is 10 V?

A. $2.04\ \angle 38.7°$ A
B. $1.56\ \angle -38.7°$ A
C. $1.25\ \angle 54.3°$ A
D. $1.11\ \angle -42.6°$ A

Solution:

Divide the voltage by the total impedance to determine the ac current:

$$I_{\text{rms}} = \frac{10 \text{ V}}{(5 + j4)\ \Omega} = (1.22 - j0.976) \text{ A}$$

$$= 1.56\ \angle -38.7° \text{ A}$$

Answer is B.

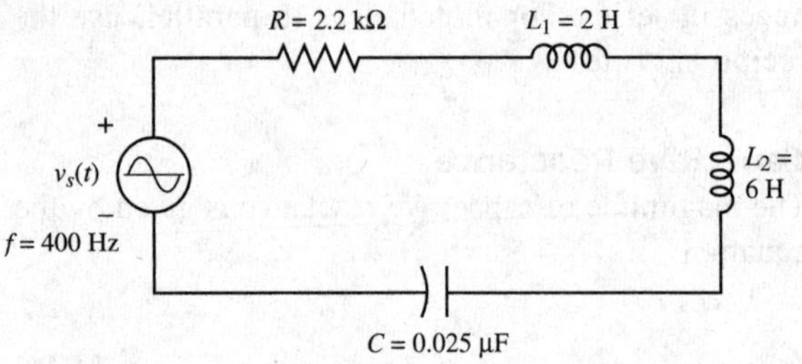

Figure 4.32

Example 4.24

What is the total impedance, Z_T, of the circuit shown in Figure 4.33?

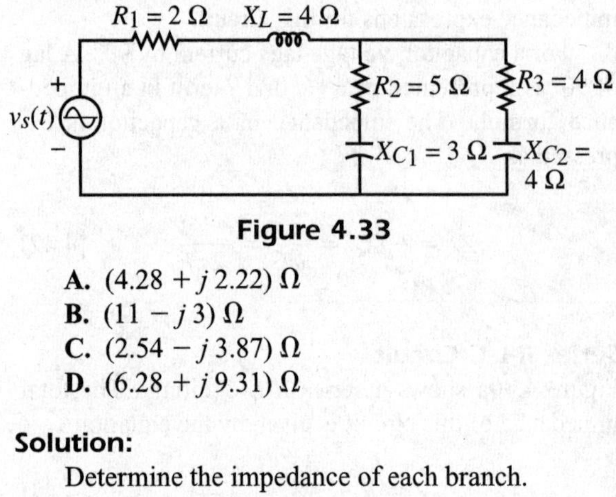

Figure 4.33

A. $(4.28 + j\,2.22)\ \Omega$
B. $(11 - j\,3)\ \Omega$
C. $(2.54 - j\,3.87)\ \Omega$
D. $(6.28 + j\,9.31)\ \Omega$

Solution:

Determine the impedance of each branch.

$$Z_1 = R_1 + j\,X_L = (2 + j4)\ \Omega$$
$$Z_2 = R_2 - j\,X_{C_1} = (5 - j3)\ \Omega$$
$$Z_3 = R_3 - j\,X_{C_2} = (4 - j4)\ \Omega$$

Then

$$Z_T = Z_1 + \frac{Z_2 Z_3}{Z_2 + Z_3}$$

$$= (2 + j4) + \frac{(5 - j3)(4 - j4)}{(5 - j3) + (4 - j4)}$$

$$= (4.28 + j2.22)\ \Omega$$

Answer is A.

Example 4.25

What is the total current, I_T, of the circuit shown in Figure 4.34?

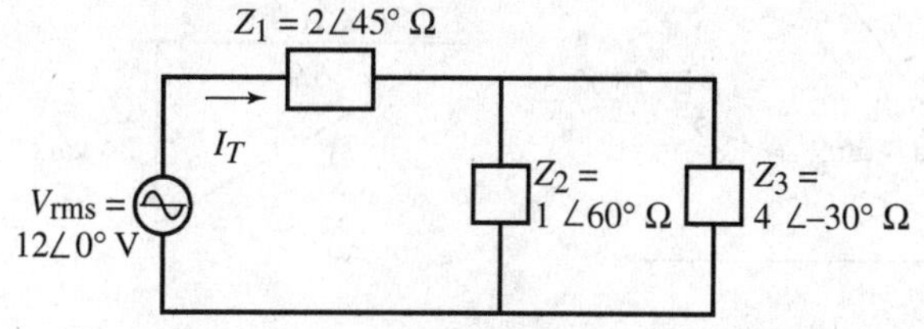

Figure 4.34

A. $(1 + j3)$ A
B. $(4 - j2)$ A
C. $4.04 \angle -45.3°$ A
D. $5.13 \angle 22.7°$ A

Solution:

The total impedance for the circuit is

$$Z_T = Z_1 + \frac{Z_2 Z_3}{Z_2 + Z_3}$$

$$= 2\angle 45° + \frac{(1\angle 60°)(4\angle -30°)}{1\angle 60° + 4\angle -30°} = 2.97\angle 45.3°\ \Omega$$

Then

$$I_T = \frac{12.0\angle 0°\ \text{V}}{2.97\angle 45.3°\ \Omega} = 4.04\angle -45.3°\ \text{A}$$

Answer is C.

Complex Power

The topic of this section is the product of voltage times current for ac circuits. For dc circuits, this product is the power dissipated by the resistance. For ac circuits that contain resistors as well as inductors and/or capacitors, the power dissipated by the resistance is known as the **real power;** but the product of voltage and current for the reactive elements, as well as the product of the total voltage and current, must be considered. The unit for power is the watt (W), and power is symbolized by the letter P.

The real power dissipated by an ac circuit is due to the resistance in the circuit and is given by the equation

$$P = V_{rms} I_{rms} \cos\theta \qquad [4.45]$$

where θ is the phase angle measured from V to I. The term $\cos\theta$ is referred to as the power factor, pf. Since $\cos\theta$ is positive for both positive and negative angles, the power factor is referred to as either leading (when the current leads the voltage) or lagging (when the current lags the voltage). For this analysis it is customary to use voltage as the reference. Therefore, for an inductive circuit the power factor is lagging, and for a capacitive circuit the power factor is leading.

The volt-ampere product for the reactive element(s) in the circuit is known as reactive power, is given the symbol Q, and has units of volt-amperes reactive (vars). The equation for reactive power is as follows:

$$Q = V_{rms} I_{rms} \sin\theta \qquad [4.46]$$

The complex power, S, for an ac circuit with both resistive and reactive elements is given by the expression

$$S = P \pm jQ \qquad [4.47]$$

and the units are volt-amperes (va). Volt-amperes represents a complex number, and the phase angle is either positive or negative depending on whether the circuit is capacitive or inductive, respectively, as shown in Figure 4.35.

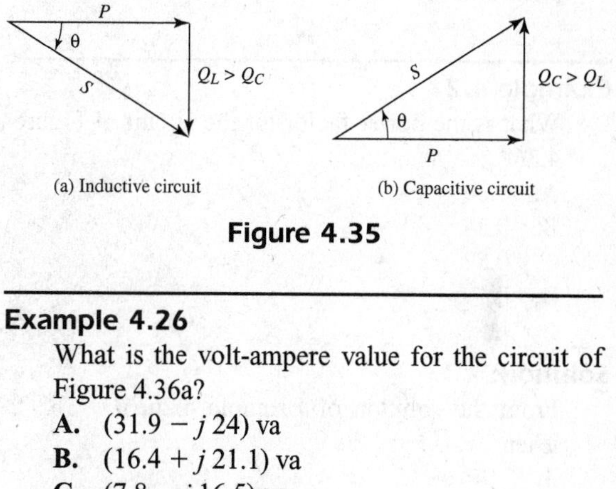

Figure 4.35

Example 4.26

What is the volt-ampere value for the circuit of Figure 4.36a?

A. $(31.9 - j\,24)$ va
B. $(16.4 + j\,21.1)$ va
C. $(7.8 - j\,16.5)$ va
D. $(21.1 + j\,16.4)$ va

Solution:

The current, I_{rms}, is given by the equation

$$I_{rms} = \frac{20\angle 60°\ \text{V}}{(8 + j6)\ \Omega} = 2\angle 23.1°\ \text{A}$$

The angle from V to I is $60° - 23.1° = 36.9°$. See Figure 4.36b. Apply equation 4.45 to obtain the real power:

$$P = (20)(2)\cos 36.9° = 31.9\ \text{W}$$

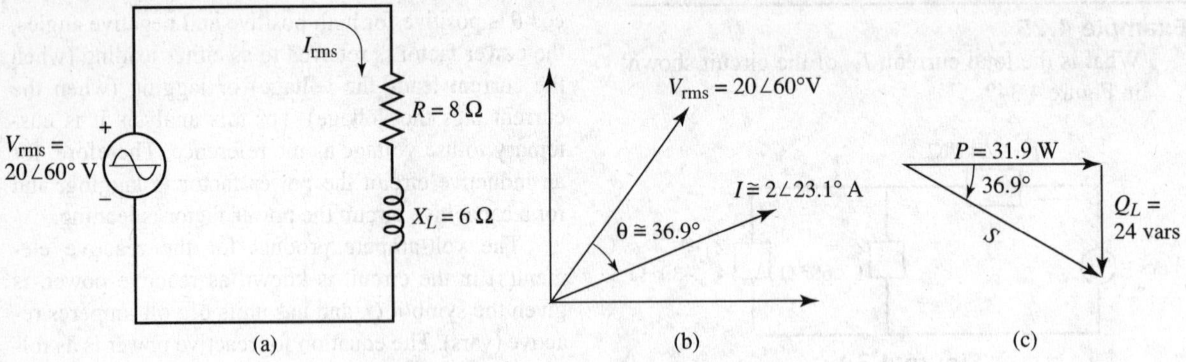

Figure 4.36

Then apply equation 4.46 to determine the reactive volt-amperes:

$$Q = (20)(2)\sin 36.9° = 24 \text{ vars}$$

Since the circuit is inductive, the power factor is lagging. Apply equation 4.47 to obtain

$$S = (31.9 - j24) \text{ va}$$

The triangle shown in Figure 4.36c is often referred to as a power triangle.

Answer is A.

Example 4.27

What is the power factor for the circuit of Figure 4.36?

A. 0.60
B. 0.34
C. 0.82
D. 0.79

Solution:

From the solution of Example 4.26, $\theta = 36.9°$. Then:

$$\text{Power factor} = \cos\theta = \cos 36.9° = 0.79$$

Answer is D.

Resonance

When a resistor, an inductor, and a capacitor are connected in series, there is a frequency at which $X_L = X_C$. At this frequency the circuit is said to be in resonance, and the frequency is called the series resonant frequency, f_0. At f_0, the impedance of the circuit is at a minimum and is equal to R. At resonance, the current is at a maximum; also, the voltage drops across, L and C are at a maximum. At frequencies below resonance, X_C is greater than X_L. At frequencies above resonance, X_L is greater than X_C. The resonant frequency, f_0, depends on the value of L and C and is given by the equation

$$\omega_0 = 2\pi f_0 = \frac{1}{\sqrt{LC}} \qquad [4.48]$$

where ω_0 is in radians per second and f_0 is in hertz. Since at resonance $X_L = X_C$, then

$$\omega_0 L = \frac{1}{\omega_0 C} \qquad [4.49]$$

and the impedance of the series circuit at resonance is given by the equation

$$Z = R \qquad [4.50]$$

A figure of merit to compare resonant circuits is known as the quality factor, Q. For a series resonant (tuned) circuit, the quality factor is expressed as

$$Q = \frac{\omega_0 L}{R} = \frac{1}{\omega_0 CR} \qquad [4.51]$$

Note: When analyzing a resonant circuit, the symbol Q represents the quality factor, not charge or reactive power.

Figure 4.37 shows how the current in a series circuit varies as the frequency is changed. The ratio of the resonant frequency to the quality factor is known as the bandwidth, BW. The equation for bandwidth is

$$\text{BW} = \frac{\omega_0}{Q} = \frac{R}{L} \text{ rad/s} \qquad [4.52a]$$

or

$$\text{BW} = \frac{R}{2\pi L} \text{ Hz} \qquad [4.52b]$$

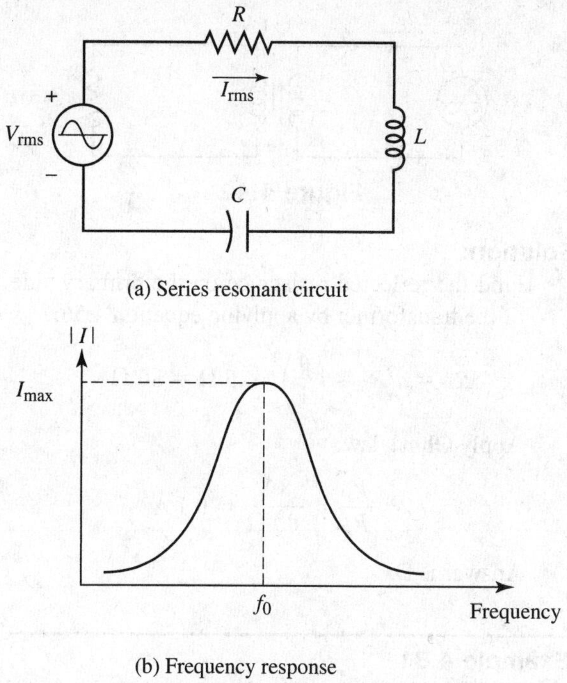

Figure 4.37

Figure 4.38 is a parallel *R-L-C* circuit. The frequency at which $X_L = X_C$ is also known as the resonant frequency and is given by equation 4.48. For this circuit, the voltage is a maximum at resonance, and the quality factor is expressed as

$$Q = \omega_0 RC = \frac{R}{\omega_0 L} \qquad [4.53]$$

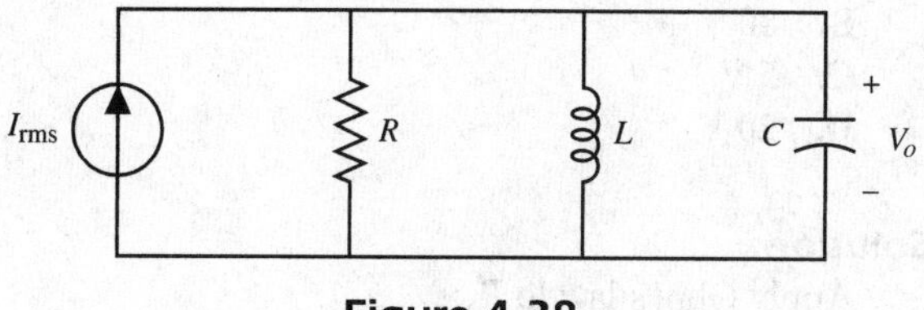

Figure 4.38

Example 4.28

What value of capacitance will cause the circuit of Figure 4.39 to have a resonant frequency of 1.2 MHz?

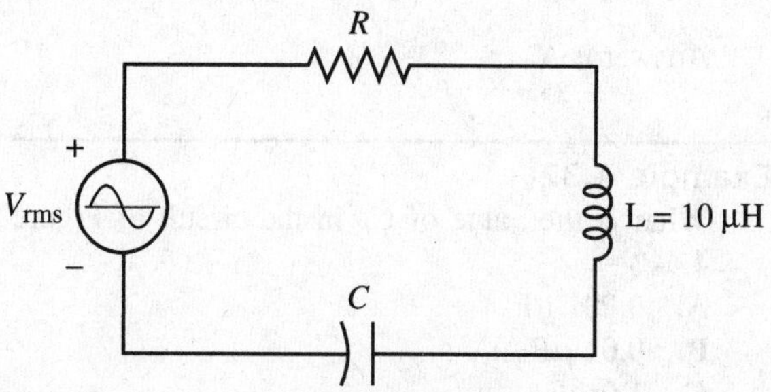

Figure 4.39

A. 0.054 μF
B. 0.00176 μF
C. 0.0034 μF
D. 0.012 μF

Solution:

Rearrange equation 4.48 to yield

$$C = \frac{1}{L(2\pi f_0)^2} = \frac{1}{(10 \times 10^{-6})(2\pi \times 1.2 \times 10^6)^2}$$
$$= 0.00176\ \mu\text{F}$$

Answer is B.

Example 4.29

If the capacitance in Figure 4.39 increases by a factor of 4, what happens to the resonant frequency?

A. It doubles.
B. It decreases by 50%.
C. It stays the same.
D. It increases by 50%.

Solution:

From equation 4.48:

$$f_0 = \frac{1}{2\pi\sqrt{L \times 4C}} = \frac{1}{4\pi\sqrt{LC}} = \frac{\frac{1}{2}}{2\pi\sqrt{LC}}$$

The resonant frequency is halved.

Answer is B.

Ideal Transformers

In Section 4.4, it is stated that any current-carrying conductor has a magnetic field associated with it. If the current is ac, the strength of the magnetic field is constantly increasing and decreasing. Likewise, if a changing magnetic field exists about the conductor, an ac voltage is induced in it. (A current exists in the conductor provided that a closed path exists.) The magnetic field is increased by winding the conductor in the form of a coil, thus creating the passive element of self-inductance.

If two coils are placed so that a changing magnetic field of one induces a voltage in the other, the two coils are connected through mutual induction. *Mutual inductance* between two coils is directly proportional to the number of magnetic lines of force that are common to both coils. The closer the coils are to one another, the greater the mutual inductance. Mutual inductance is increased further if both coils can be wound on a common iron core, as shown in Figure 4.40. If the coils are separated, mutual inductance is reduced. The circuit element that uses the principle of mutual inductance is the transformer.

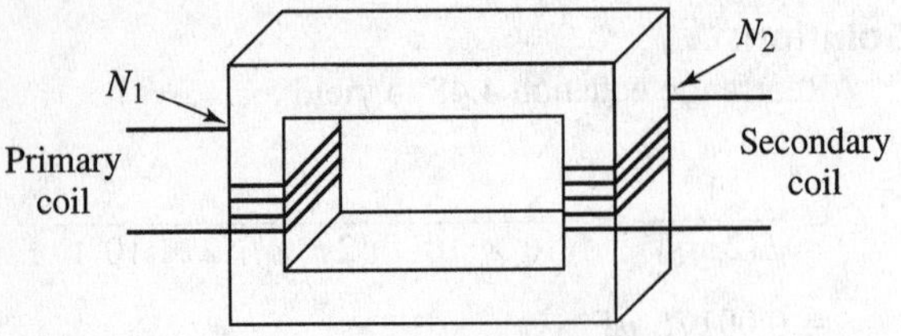

Figure 4.40

This review section deals with **ideal transformers** (those that have no losses). The iron-core transformers used in power and audio systems closely approximate the ideal. For the ideal transformer, reflected impedance, current ratio, and voltage ratio are quickly and easily calculated in terms of the number of turns on the primary and secondary coils, N_1 and N_2, respectively.

Figure 4.41 shows the schematic for an ideal transformer, and the equations for this device are as follows:

$$a = \frac{N_1}{N_2} \qquad [4.54]$$

where a represents the ratio of N_1 to N_2.

$$a = \left|\frac{V_P}{V_S}\right| = \left|\frac{I_S}{I_P}\right| \qquad [4.55]$$

$$Z_P = a^2 Z_S \qquad [4.56]$$

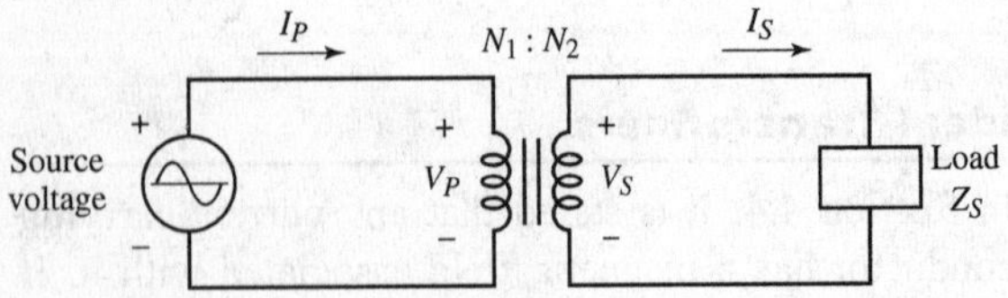

Figure 4.41

Note: Voltage is directly proportional to the turns ratio, and the current is inversely proportional to the turns ratio. Hence, for an ideal transformer the power on the primary side equals the power on the secondary side.

Example 4.30

For the circuit of Figure 4.42, what is the primary current?

A. 2.4 A
B. 1.6 A
C. 2.0 A
D. 0.1 A

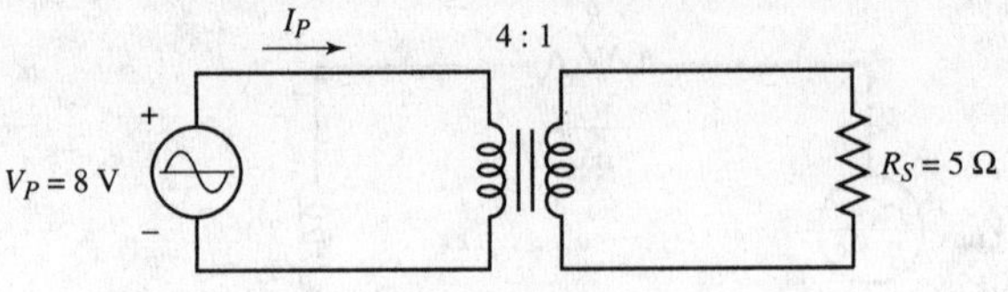

Figure 4.42

Solution:

Find the reflected resistance on the primary side of the transformer by applying equation 4.56:

$$R_P = a^2 R_S = \left(\frac{4}{1}\right)^2 \times 5\ \Omega = 80\ \Omega$$

Apply Ohm's law:

$$I_P = \frac{V_P}{R_P} = \frac{8\text{ V}}{80\ \Omega} = 0.1\text{ A}$$

Answer is D.

Example 4.31

What is the primary voltage in the circuit of Figure 4.43?

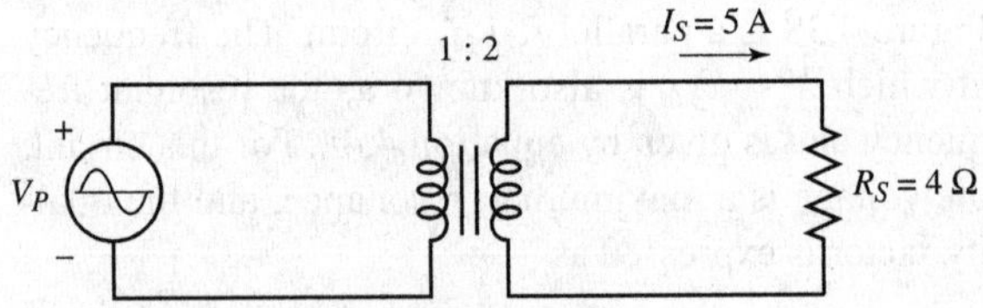

Figure 4.43

A. 10 V
B. 80 V
C. 5 V
D. 20 V

Solution:

Apply Ohm's law to R_S:

$$V_S = I_S R_S = (5\text{ A})(4\ \Omega) = 20\text{ V}$$

Rearrange equation 4.55 to obtain

$$V_P = a \times V_S = \left(\frac{1}{2}\right) \times 20\text{ V} = 10\text{ V}$$

Answer is A.

Example 4.32

What is the value of C_P in the circuit of Figure 4.44?

A. 0.001 μF
B. 0.01 μF
C. 1.0 μF
D. 10.0 μF

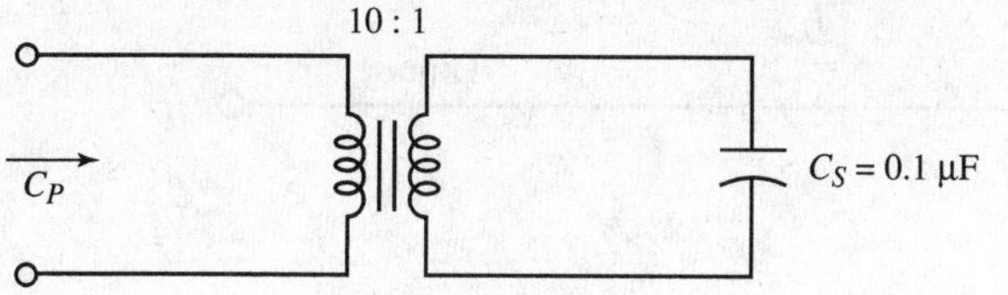

Figure 4.44

Solution:

Refer to equation 4.56, $Z_P = a^2 Z_S$. For a capacitor, this equation is as follows:

$$C_P = \frac{1}{a^2} \times C_S = \frac{1}{(10)^2} \times 0.1\ \mu\text{F} = 0.001\ \mu\text{F}$$

Remember that, for a capacitor, capacitive reactance is $X_C = 1/\omega C$.

Answer is A.

Polyphase Systems

Polyphase systems are used for the generation and distribution of large quantities of power. Some advantages of these systems are that induction motors have an inherent starting torque because the voltages are out of phase, total power is constant, the systems are more efficient, and for a fixed distance the line loss is less. Although polyphase systems may have any number of voltages not in phase, most polyphase systems are three phase. Three-phase (3-ϕ) motors are smaller than single-phase motors of the same horsepower, operate with less vibration, and have constant torque.

Figure 4.45 shows the waveforms produced from a three-phase generator. The waveforms are 120° out of phase with one another.

Figure 4.45

Figure 4.46a shows three single windings. These windings may be connected either in a wye (Y) connection (also called a star connection), as shown in Figure 4.46b, or in a delta (Δ) connection, as shown in Figure 4.46c. In the wye configuration, if the common connection is brought out (used), it is referred to as the neutral. In the delta configuration, there is no neutral. Generators are not connected in a delta configuration, but transformer windings are. For a wye connection, voltages may be specified as line-to-line or as line-to-neutral. For a delta connection, voltages are measured only line-to-line.

For a wye connection, the line current equals the corresponding phase current and is given by the equation

$$I_L = I_{Ph} = \frac{V_{Ph}}{Z_{Ph}} \qquad [4.57]$$

The line-to-line and phase voltages for a wye connection are 30° out of phase; the relationship between their magnitudes is expressed as

$$|V_L| = \sqrt{3}|V_{Ph}| \qquad [4.58]$$

The analysis of a delta configuration is similar to that for the wye connection. Any equation involving voltage or current for the wye has the same mathematical form as its counterpart for current or voltage for the delta. For a delta connection, the line-to-line and phase voltages are equal, and the equation is

$$V_L = V_{Ph} = I_{Ph}Z_{Ph} \qquad [4.59]$$

The line-to-line and phase currents for a delta connection are 30° out of phase; the relationship between their magnitudes is expressed as

$$|I_L| = \sqrt{3}|I_{Ph}| \qquad [4.60]$$

Example 4.33

A balanced delta-connected load is wired to a 208-V line-to-line system as shown in Figure 4.47. What is the magnitude of the line current?

A. 20.8 A
B. 18.0 A
C. 36.0 A
D. 12.0 A

Solution:

Rearrange equation 4.59 to obtain

$$I_{Ph} = \frac{V_{Ph}}{Z_{Ph}} = \frac{208\ \text{V}}{(6 - j8)\ \Omega} = 20.8\angle 53.1°\ \text{A}$$

Apply equation 4.60:

$$|I_L| = \sqrt{3}|I_{Ph}| = \sqrt{3} \times 20.8\ \text{A} = 36.0\ \text{A}$$

Answer is C.

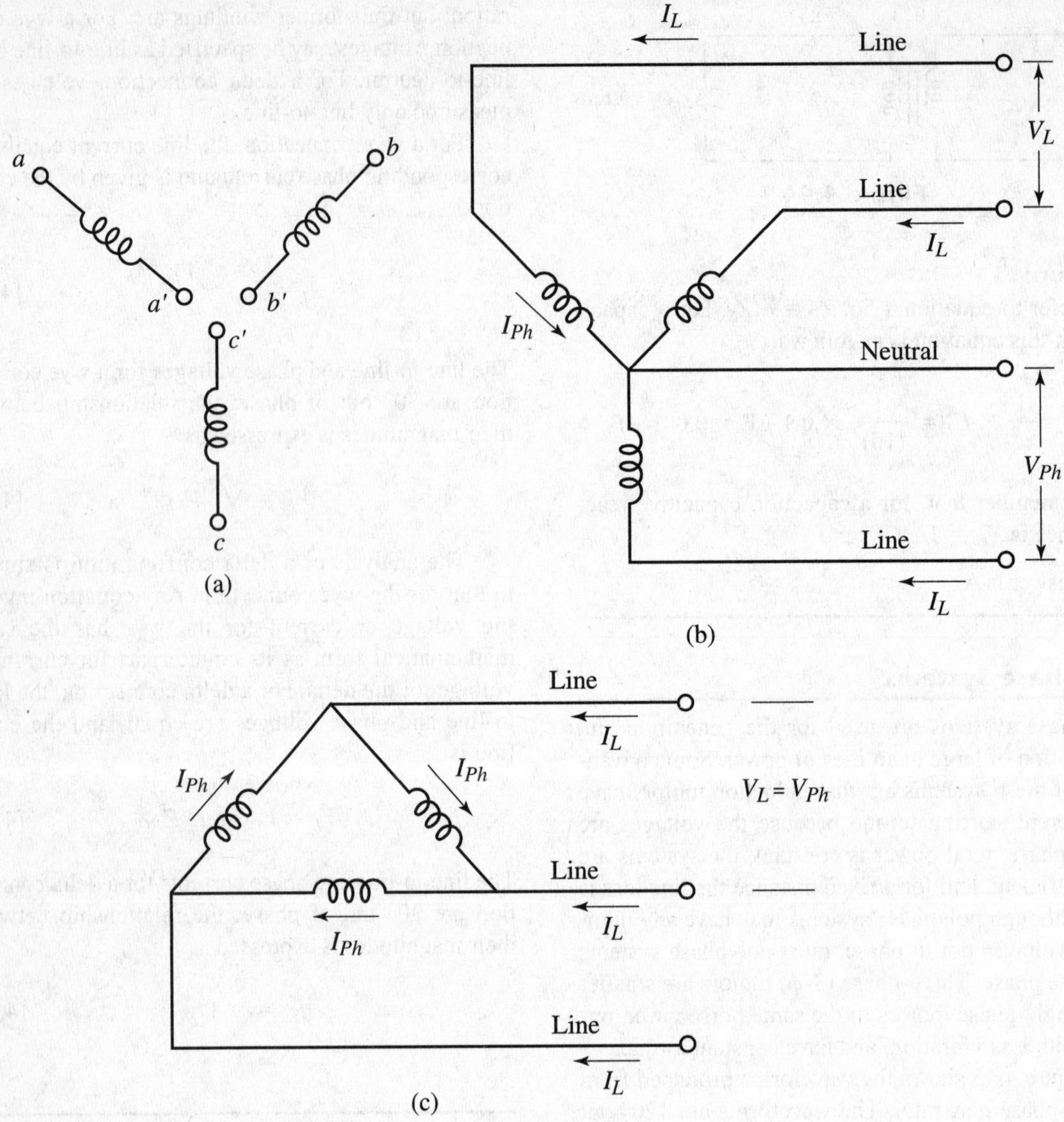

Figure 4.46

Example 4.34

If the load impedances in Figure 4.47 are connected in a wye configuration, what is the magnitude of the line current?

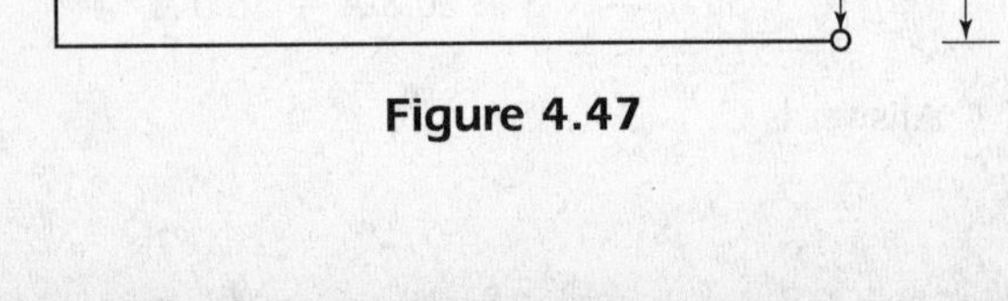

Figure 4.47

A. 20.8 A
B. 18.0 A
C. 36.0 A
D. 12.0 A

Solution:

Rearrange equation 4.58:

$$|V_{Ph}| = \frac{|V_L|}{\sqrt{3}} = \frac{208\text{ V}}{\sqrt{3}} = 120\text{ V}$$

Apply equation 4.57:

$$|I_L| = \frac{120\text{ V}}{(6 - j8)\ \Omega} = 12\text{ A}$$

Answer is D.

4.8 Operational Amplifiers

The operational amplifier (op amp), whose circuit symbol is shown in Figure 4.48, is a high-gain, direct-coupled amplifier with an open-loop gain, A_{OL}, of several hundred thousand. The differential input voltage, $E_d = v_1 - v_2$, is a small voltage, in the order of microvolts, that drives the amplifier. The output voltage, V_0, is the differential input voltage, E_d, times the open-loop gain:

$$V_0 = A_{OL} \times E_d = A_{OL} \times (v_1 - v_2) \quad [4.61]$$

where v_1 is the voltage measured at the noninverting input (+) terminal of the op amp with respect to ground, and v_2 is the voltage measured at the inverting input (−) terminal with respect to ground. For most op amps, the maximum output voltage swing is usually 1 or 2 volts less than the power supply's voltages, which are typically set at ± 15 volts. Therefore the maximum output voltage swing is ± 13 V.

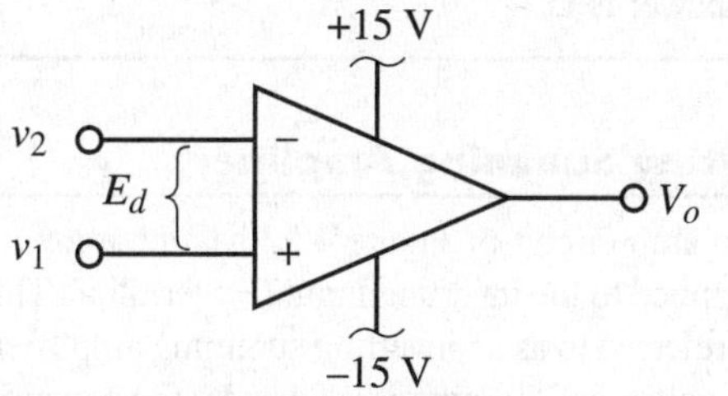

Figure 4.48

Example 4.35

What is a typical maximum input differential range for E_d if an op amp's open-loop gain is 250,000?

A. ± 60 μV
B. ± 52 μV
C. ± 30 μV
D. ± 45 μV

Solution:

Rearrange equation 4.61 to obtain

$$E_d = \frac{V_{OL}}{A_{OL}} = \frac{\pm 13 \text{ V}}{250 \times 10^3} = \pm 52 \ \mu\text{V}$$

Answer is B.

For most applications of op amps, an external resistor is connected between the output terminal and the op amp's (−) terminal. This type of circuit connection is called negative feedback. The advantage of negative feedback is that circuit performance can be expressed in terms of the op amp's closed-loop gain, A_{CL}, which depends only on the external resistors. By adding a negative-feedback circuit, designers can ignore the changes in A_{OL} from op amp to op amp as long as A_{OL} is at least 10 times larger than A_{CL}. This review considers circuits using the characteristics of an ideal op amp, which are summarized below, and negative feedback.

Ideal Op Amp Characteristics

1. The open-loop gain, A_{OL}, is infinite.
2. The differential input voltage, E_d, is zero.
3. The current drawn by either the (+) or the (−) input terminal is negligible.
4. The output impedance of the op amp is negligible.

Inverting Amplifiers

Figure 4.49 shows one of the most commonly used op amp circuits. The amplifier's closed-loop gain, A_{CL}, is set by the values of R_f and R_i according to the equation

$$A_{CL} = -\frac{R_f}{R_i} \quad [4.62]$$

where the minus sign indicates that the output and input voltage polarities are 180° out of phase. Therefore, the circuit is said to have a negative gain. The op amp circuit of Figure 4.49 can amplify both ac and dc signals.

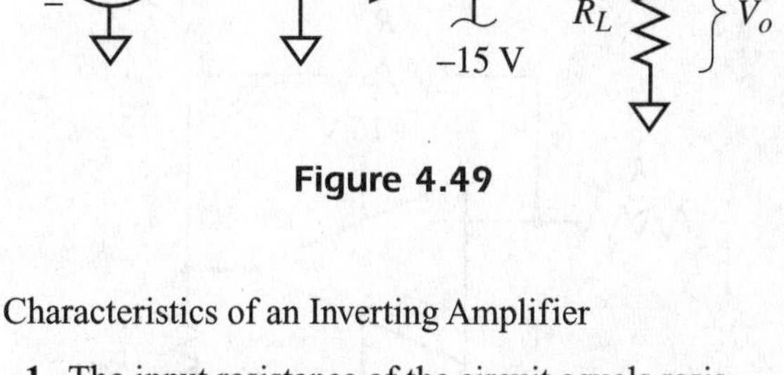

Figure 4.49

Characteristics of an Inverting Amplifier

1. The input resistance of the circuit equals resistance R_i.
2. The magnitude of the closed-loop gain is the ratio of R_f/R_i.
3. The output voltage will be the negative of the input signal.

Example 4.36

What must be the value of R_f in the circuit of Figure 4.50 for the magnitude of the closed-loop gain to be 15?

A. 7.5 kΩ
B. 1.5 kΩ
C. 150 kΩ
D. 75 kΩ

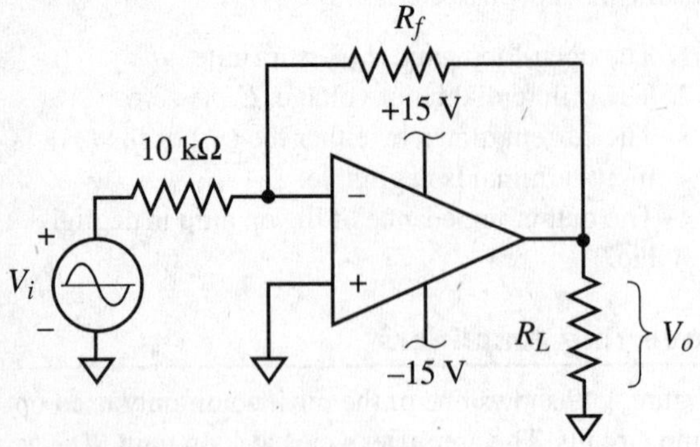

Figure 4.50

Solution:

Rearrange equation 4.62 to obtain

$$R_f = |A_{CL}| \times R_i = 15 \times 10\ \text{k}\Omega = 150\ \text{k}\Omega$$

Answer is C.

Noninverting Amplifier

The op amp circuit of Figure 4.51 has the input voltage applied to the noninverting input (+) terminal. Hence this circuit is referred to as a noninverting amplifier. The gain of this circuit is given by the equation

$$A_{CL} = 1 + \frac{R_f}{R_i} = \frac{R_f + R_i}{R_i} \qquad [4.63]$$

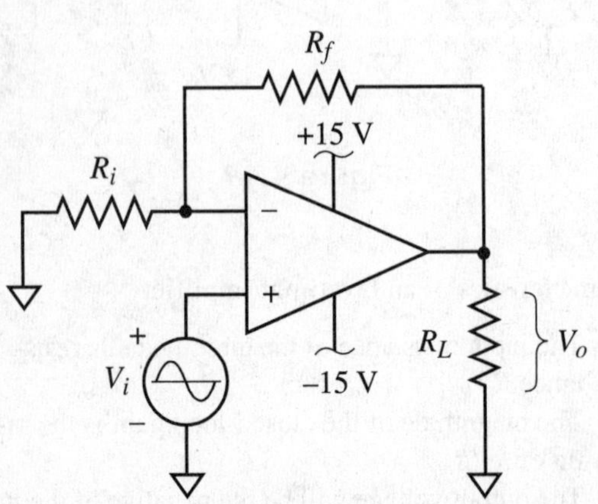

Figure 4.51

Characteristics of a Noninverting Amplifier

1. The input resistance of the circuit (as "seen" by the input voltage source) is infinite.
2. The magnitude of the closed-loop gain is 1 + R_f/R_i.
3. The output voltage will be in phase with the input signal.

Example 4.37

What is the gain of the op amp circuit of Figure 4.51 if R_i = 10 kΩ and R_f = 22 kΩ?

A. −2.2
B. 2.2
C. −3.2
D. 3.2

Solution:

Apply equation 4.63 to obtain

$$A_{CL} = 1 + \frac{22\ \text{k}\Omega}{10\ \text{k}\Omega} = 3.2$$

Answer is D.

Inverting Summing Amplifier

The op amp circuit of Figure 4.52 has three input voltages applied to the inverting input (−) terminal. This circuit is referred to as an inverting summing amplifier. The output voltage of this circuit is given by the equation

$$V_0 = -\left(\frac{R_f}{R_1} \times V_1 + \frac{R_f}{R_2} \times V_2 + \frac{R_f}{R_3} \times V_3\right) \qquad [4.64]$$

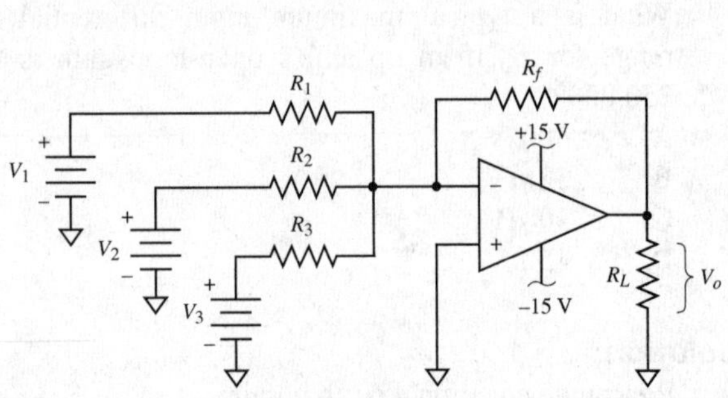

Figure 4.52

Example 4.38

What is the value of R_f in the circuit of Figure 4.53?

A. 16.66 kΩ
B. 45 kΩ
C. 33.33 kΩ
D. 4.62 kΩ

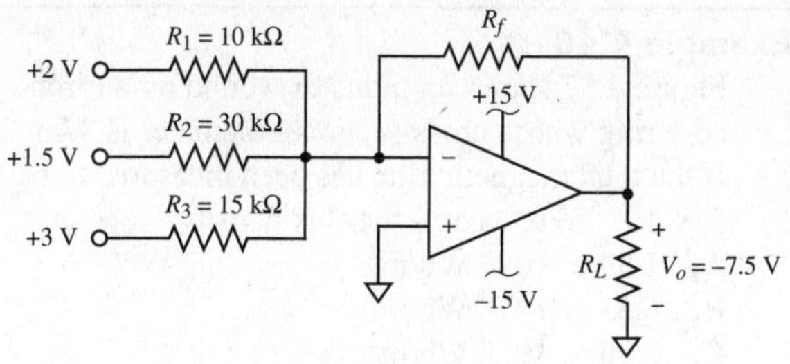

Figure 4.53

Solution:

Factor R_f from equation 4.64, and rearrange terms:

$$R_f = \frac{V_0}{-\left(\frac{V_1}{R_1} + \frac{V_2}{R_2} + \frac{V_3}{R_3}\right)}$$

$$= \frac{-7.5 \text{ V}}{-(0.2 + 0.05 + 0.2) \times 10^{-3}} = 16.66 \text{ k}\Omega$$

Answer is A.

4.9 Electric and Magnetic Fields

This section reviews some of the fundamental principles of electric and magnetic fields.

Electric Fields: Section 4.5 introduced the concept that like charges repel and unlike charges attract. Charles de Coulomb (1736–1806) first measured these attractions and repulsions and deduced the law that governs them. For charged objects whose size is much smaller than the distance between them (a concept known as point charges), Coulomb's law is expressed as

$$\mathbf{F} = \frac{1}{4\pi\,\varepsilon_0} \times \frac{q_1 q_2}{r^2} \qquad [4.65]$$

where **F** is the magnitude of the force that acts on the charges, q_1 and q_2 are the measures of charge on the objects, r is the distance between the charged objects, and ε_0 is known as the permittivity constant (for air $\varepsilon_0 = 8.854 \times 10^{-12}$ coulomb²/newton · meter² or farad per meter). Note that force, **F**, is a vector quantity. The direction of force can be determined by the direction that a positive point charge would move when released. If there are multiple point charges bound to an object, vector addition must be used to find the resultant force on the object.

In the vicinity of any point charge, there is an electric field, **E.** The units for **E** are newtons per coulomb (N/C) or volts per meter (V/m). The lines of force that constitute the electric field are lines of flux, Ψ. The direction of electric flux, by convention, is the direction in which a positive charge would move if released in the electric field. Figure 4.54 shows how to visualize the electric field between a positive and negative charge. The magnitude of the electric field intensity is given by the equation

$$\mathbf{E} = \frac{q_1}{4\pi\,\varepsilon_0\, r^2} \qquad [4.66]$$

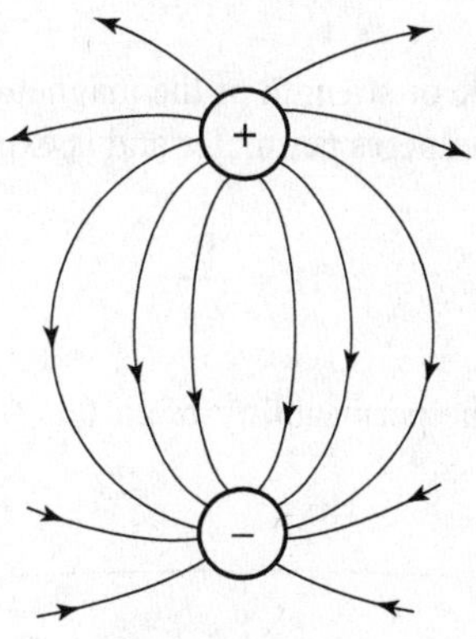

Figure 4.54

Example 4.39

Figure 4.55 shows point charges q_1 and q_2. What is the magnitude of the force acting on q_1? (Assume that $q_1 = -2.0 \times 10^{-6}$ C and $q_2 = +3.0 \times 10^{-6}$ C.)

A. 0.416 N
B. 1.254 N
C. 0.852 N
D. 2.357 N

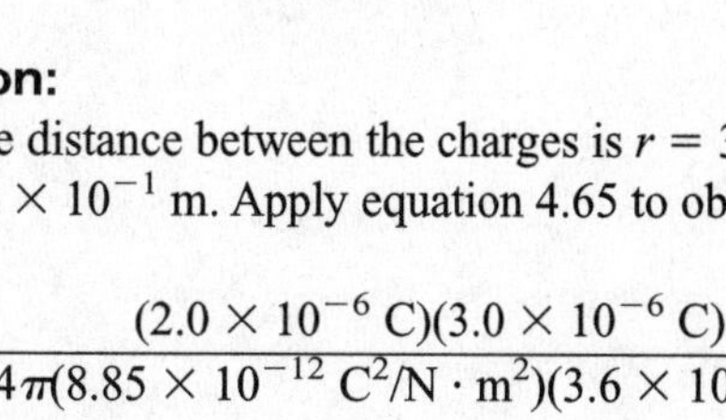

Figure 4.55

Solution:

The distance between the charges is $r = 36$ cm $= 3.6 \times 10^{-1}$ m. Apply equation 4.65 to obtain

$$|F| = \frac{(2.0 \times 10^{-6}\text{ C})(3.0 \times 10^{-6}\text{ C})}{4\pi(8.85 \times 10^{-12}\text{ C}^2/\text{N}\cdot\text{m}^2)(3.6 \times 10^{-1}\text{ m})^2}$$

$$= 0.416 \text{ N}$$

Answer is A.

Magnetic Fields: A magnetic field exists in the space around a magnet. The lines of magnetic flux, external to the magnet, are directed from the north to the south pole as shown in Figure 4.56. The total amount of magnetic flux is measured in webers (Wb) and is represented by the symbol ϕ. The magnitude of the flux density, **B** (weber/meter^2, or tesla (T)), is calculated by dividing the magnetic flux by an area perpendicular to it and is given by the equation

$$\mathbf{B} = \frac{\phi}{A} \qquad [4.67]$$

The magnitude or strength of the magnetic field, **H**, is measured in amperes per meter and is expressed as

$$\mathbf{H} = \frac{\mathbf{B}}{\mu_0} \qquad [4.68]$$

where μ_0 is the permeability of air ($\mu_0 = 4\pi \times 10^{-7}$ H/m).

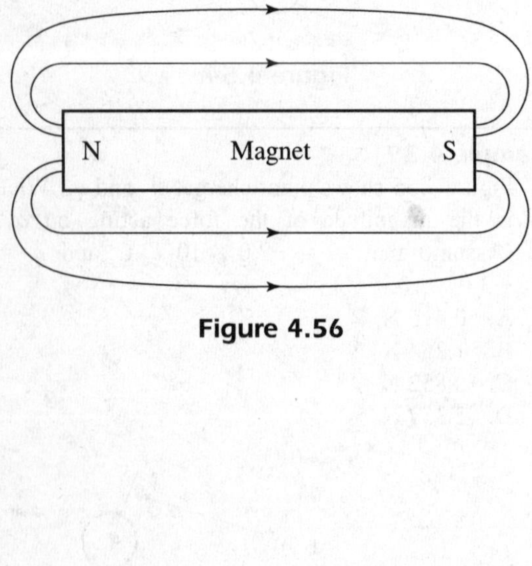

Figure 4.56

Example 4.40

Figure 4.57 shows an inductor wound on an iron-core ring whose cross-sectional diameter is 4 cm. If the total magnetic flux has been measured to be 5×10^{-5} Wb, what is the flux density?

A. 1.59×10^{-4} Wb/m^2
B. 6.53×10^{-4} Wb/m^2
C. 3.98×10^{-4} Wb/m^2
D. 2.75×10^{-4} Wb/m^2

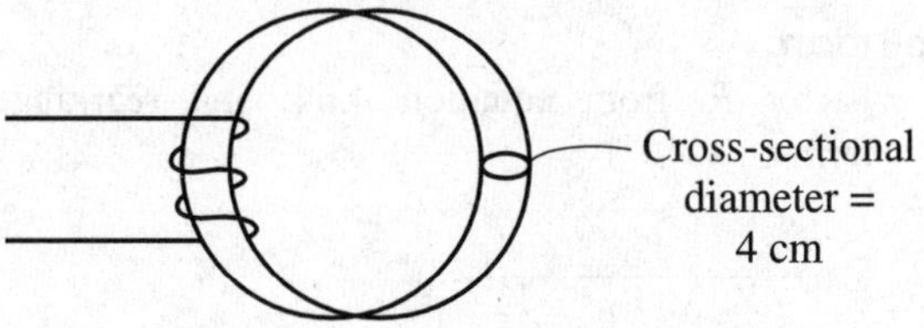

Figure 4.57

Solution:

Apply equation 4.67 to obtain

$$B = \frac{5 \times 10^{-5}\ \text{Wb}}{\frac{1}{4}\pi(0.04\ \text{m})^2} = 3.98 \times 10^{-4}\ \text{Wb/m}^2$$

Answer is C.

PRACTICE PROBLEMS

1. What is the resistance of 1,000 m of copper wire that has a resistivity of $1.72 \times 10^{-8}\ \Omega \cdot$ m and a diameter of 2 mm?
   (A) 6.97 Ω
   (B) 3.41 Ω
   (C) 5.47 Ω
   (D) 1.23 Ω
2. If the values given in Problem 1 are for a temperature at 25°C, what is the resistance of the wire at 75°C? The resistance temperature coefficient at 25°C is 0.0039/°C.
   (A) 6.54 Ω
   (B) 8.32 Ω
   (C) 4.07 Ω
   (D) 1.47 Ω
3. If the diameter of the wire in Problem 1 is increased by a factor of 10, what is the resistance of the 1,000 m of wire?
   (A) 69.7 mΩ
   (B) 54.7 mΩ
   (C) 92.1 mΩ
   (D) 0.033 Ω

Problems 4–7 are based on the following figure:

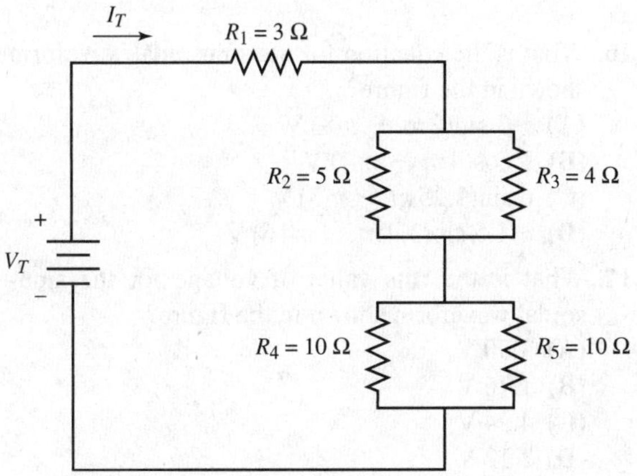

4. What is the total resistance for the circuit shown in the figure?
   (A) 15.3 Ω
   (B) 8.70 Ω
   (C) 12.8 Ω
   (D) 10.2 Ω
5. If current I_T in the figure is 1.5 A, what is V_T?
   (A) 15.3 V
   (B) 4.50 V
   (C) 10.6 V
   (D) 21.4 V
6. If current I_T in the figure is 1.5 A, what is the value of the current through R_3?
   (A) 0.66 A
   (B) 0.75 A
   (C) 0.83 A
   (D) 1.11 A
7. Consider that the parallel combination of R_4 and R_5 in the figure is the load. What are the Thévenin equivalent voltage and the resistance as "seen" by R_4 and R_5? (Assume $V_T = 10$ V.)
   (A) 5 V, 12 Ω
   (B) 10 V, 5.2 Ω
   (C) 5 V, 1.27 Ω
   (D) 10 V, 12 Ω

Problems 8 and 9 are based on the following figure:

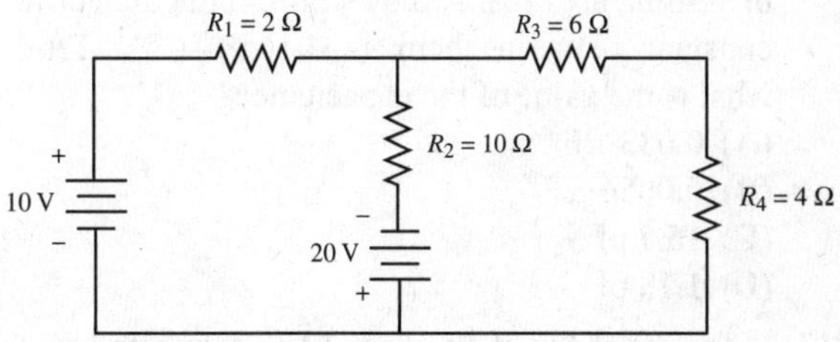

8. What is the value of current through R_2 in the circuit shown in the figure?
   (A) 2.0 A
   (B) 1.67 A
   (C) 2.43 A
   (D) 3.0 A
9. What is the value of power dissipated by R_4 in the figure?
   (A) 2.77 W
   (B) 1.83 W
   (C) 2.16 W
   (D) 0.73 W
10. The current through a 10-mH coil changes at the rate of 2 A/s. What voltage appears across the inductor?
   (A) 0.5 V
   (B) 20 mV
   (C) 50 mV
   (D) 0.2 V

11. What is the total energy stored in the circuit shown in the figure below?

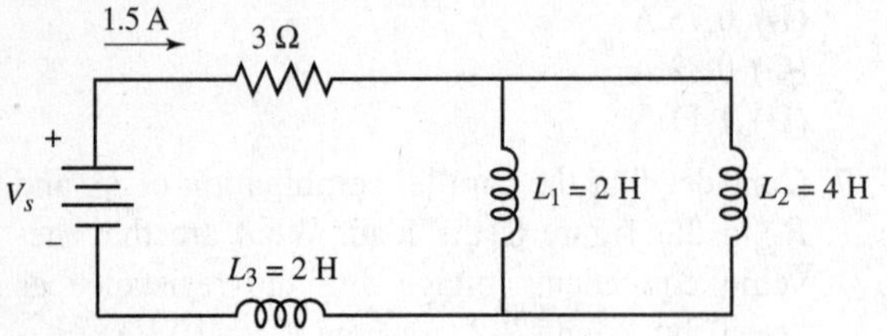

(A) 4.5 J
(B) 3.75 J
(C) 12.0 J
(D) 5.5 J

12. Two parallel circular disks, each with a diameter of 12 mm, are separated by 4 mm. If the dielectric constant between them is 4.16×10^{-11} F/m, what is the value of the capacitance?
(A) 0.033 μF
(B) 0.0054 μF
(C) 15.7 pF
(D) 1.18 pF

13. If the capacitor of Problem 12 is connected to a 12-V dc source, the charge on the plates of the capacitor is
(A) 14.1×10^{-12} C
(B) 64.8×10^{-8} C
(C) 20.3×10^{-12} C
(D) 128.6×10^{-8} C

14. If the initial current through the inductor in the figure below was 0 A, how long has the switch been closed?

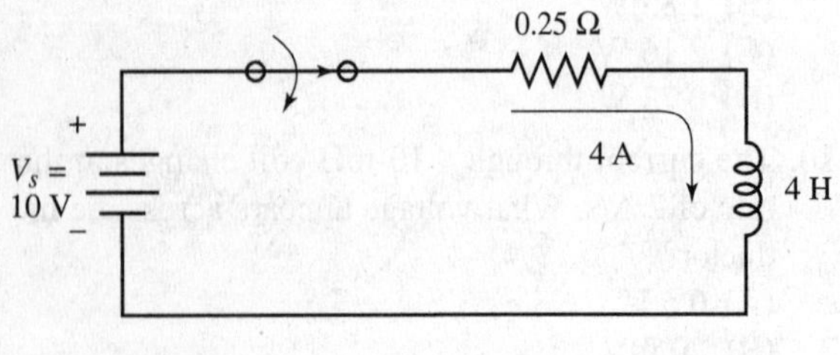

(A) 120 s
(B) 3.64 s
(C) 16.8 s
(D) 8.33 min

15. What is the capacitor voltage 5 s after the switch in the figure below is closed? The initial capacitor voltage is 2 V.

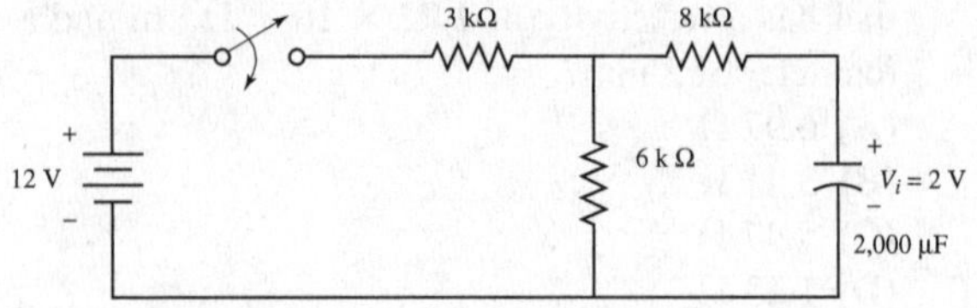

(A) 8.17 V
(B) 4.56 V
(C) 3.33 V
(D) 2.96 V

Problems 16 and 17 are based on the following figure:

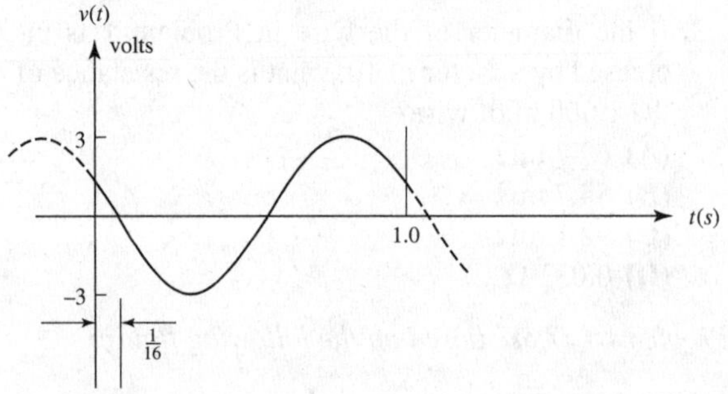

16. What is the equation for the sinusoidal waveform shown in the figure?
(A) $-3 \sin(2\pi t - \pi/8)$ V
(B) $3 \cos(4\pi t - \pi/4)$ V
(C) $6 \sin(1.25\pi t + \pi/3)$ V
(D) $-1.5 \sin(3.4\pi t - \pi/16)$ V

17. What is the rms value of voltage for the sinusoidal waveform shown in the figure?
(A) 3.00 V
(B) 1.76 V
(C) 4.24 V
(D) 2.12 V

18. What is the average value of voltage for the circuit shown in the figure below?

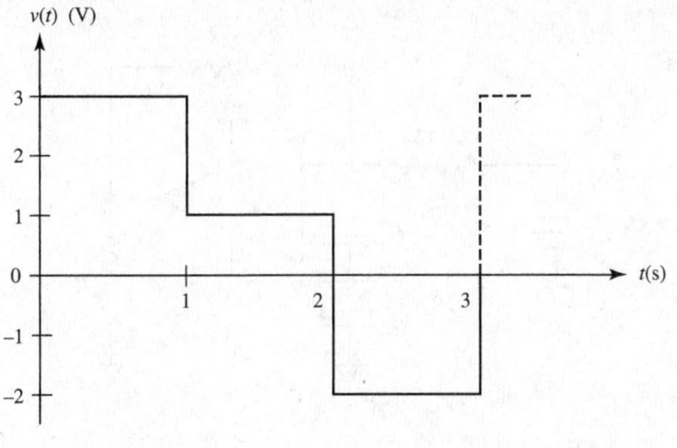

(A) 1.33 V
(B) 0.67 V
(C) 0.33 V
(D) 2.17 V

19. What is the total impedance, Z_T, of the circuit shown in the figure below?

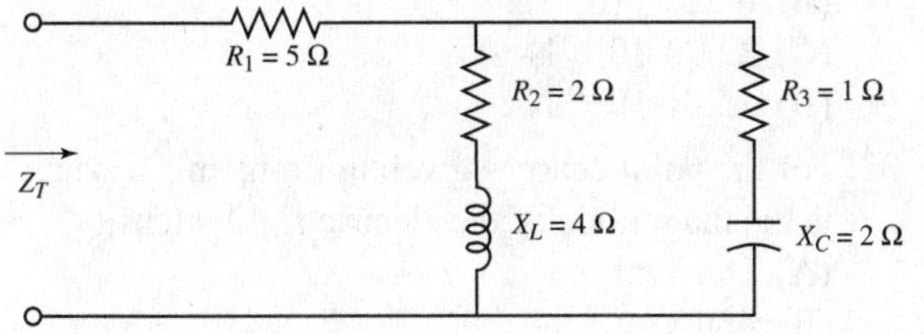

(A) 8.16 ∠ 15.1° Ω
(B) 7.47 ∠ −11.9° Ω
(C) (6.13 − j1.2) Ω
(D) (5.67 + j1.33) Ω

20. What is the value of the current if the impedance of a circuit is (4 − j2) Ω and the voltage source is 18 ∠ +30° V?
(A) 3.0 ∠ 30° A
(B) (4.32 − j2.08) A
(C) 5.12 ∠ −46° A
(D) (2.22 + j3.36) A

21. What is the value of current I_2 in the circuit shown in the figure below?

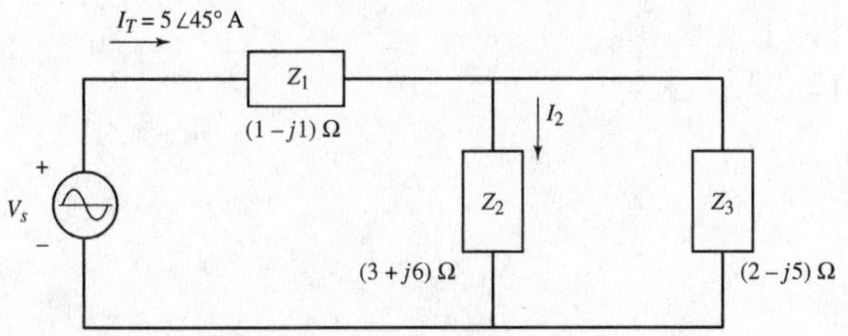

(A) (2.42 + j3.61) A
(B) 6.38 ∠ −23.5° A
(C) (4.35 − j2.99) A
(D) 2.67 ∠ +17.4° A

Problems 22–25 are based on the following figure:

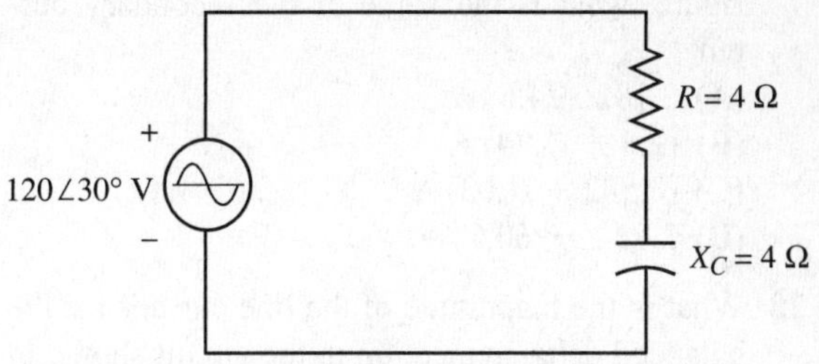

22. What is the power dissipated (the real power) by the circuit in the figure?
(A) 1.8 kW
(B) 3.2 kW
(C) 0.9 kW
(D) 2.7 kW

23. What is the power factor for the circuit in the figure?
(A) 0.866
(B) 0.258
(C) 0.707
(D) 0.512

24. If the frequency of the voltage source in the figure is 60 Hz, what value must an inductor connected in series have to make the circuit resonant?
(A) 0.088 H
(B) 402 mH
(C) 0.12 H
(D) 10.6 mH

25. A series resonant circuit has a Q value of 20 and a bandwidth of 15 kHz. What is the resonant frequency?
(A) 30.0 kHz
(B) 47.7 kHz
(C) 25.1 kHz
(D) 53.6 kHz

Problems 26 and 27 are based on the following figure:

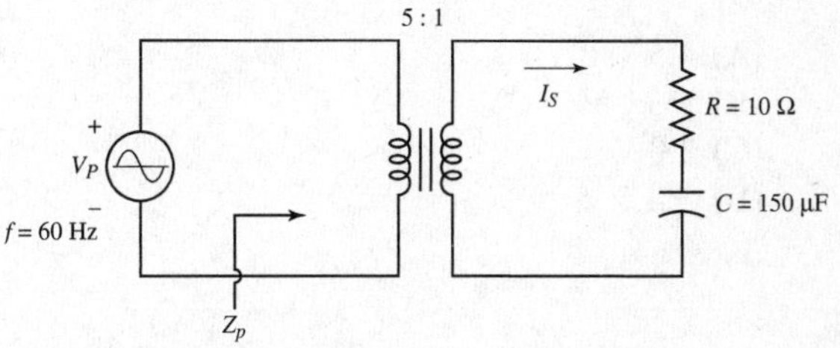

26. What is the impedance measured on the primary side of the transformer in the circuit shown in the figure?
(A) 508 ∠ −60.5° Ω
(B) (110 − j165) Ω
(C) (250 − j302) Ω
(D) 324 ∠ −42.5° Ω

27. If $V_{prms} = 120 \angle 0°$ V in the circuit shown in the figure, what is the value of the secondary current?
(A) $2.18 \angle 24.6°$ A
(B) $(2.4 - j1.34)$ A
(C) $(0.582 + j1.03)$ A
(D) $3.82 \angle -60.5°$ A

28. What is the magnitude of the line current for the balanced delta connection in the circuit shown in the figure below?

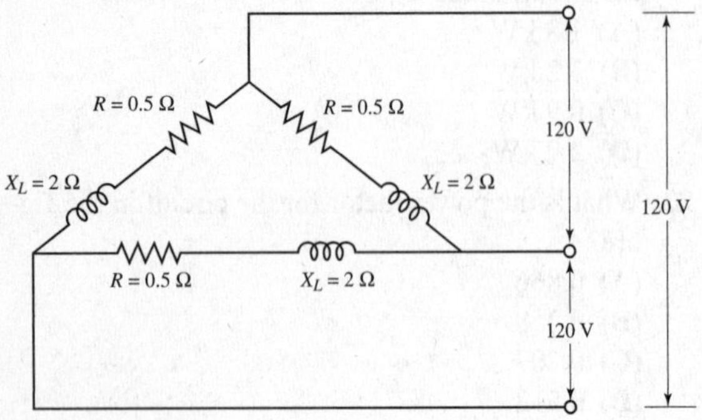

(A) 101 A
(B) 25.5 A
(C) 45.0 A
(D) 85.5 A

29. What is the output voltage, V_o, for the circuit shown in the figure below?

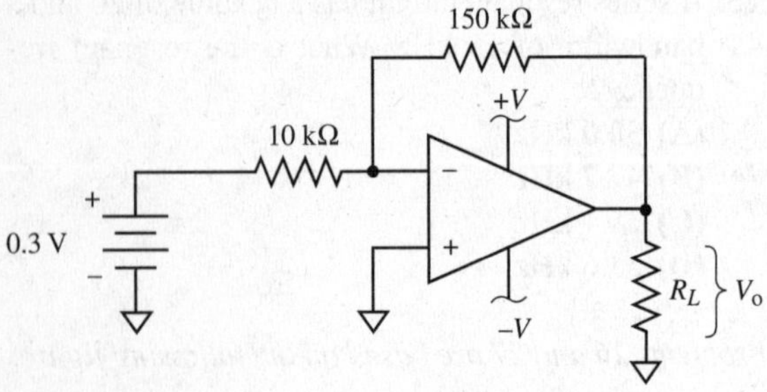

(A) 4.5 V
(B) −3.0 V
(C) 3.0 V
(D) −4.5 V

30. What is the output voltage, V_o, for the circuit shown in the figure below?

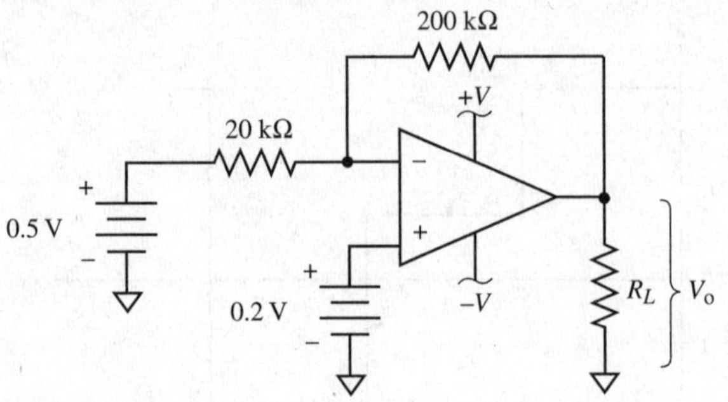

(A) −2.8 V
(B) −5.2 V
(C) 5.2 V
(D) 3.8 V

31. If two point charges, q_1 and q_2, are 2.0 m apart, what is the magnitude of the force acting on q_1?
(A) 0.84×10^{-6} N
(B) 6.52×10^{-6} N
(C) 3.6×10^{-6} N
(D) 1.2×10^{-6} N

32. For the point charges given in Problem 31, what is the magnitude of the electric field intensity?
(A) 164 V/m
(B) 460 V/m
(C) 1,200 V/m
(D) 90 V/m

Answer Key

1. C
2. A
3. B
4. D
5. A
6. C
7. B
8. C
9. D
10. B
11. B
12. D

13. A
14. C
15. C
16. A
17. D
18. B
19. B
20. D
21. C
22. A
23. C
24. D
25. B
26. A
27. C
28. A
29. D
30. A
31. C
32. D

Answers Explained

1. **C** Apply equation 4.4:

$$R = \frac{\rho l}{A} = \frac{(1.72 \times 10^{-8}\ \Omega \cdot \text{m})(1{,}000\ \text{m})}{\frac{\pi}{4}(2 \times 10^{-3}\text{m})^2}$$
$$= 5.47\ \Omega$$

2. **A** The resistance at 25°C is 5.47 Ω. Apply equation 4.6:

$$R = 5.47\ \Omega \times [1 + 0.0039/°\text{C} \times (75°\text{C} - 25°\text{C})] = 6.54\ \Omega$$

3. **B** Apply equation 4.4:

$$R = \frac{\rho l}{A} = \frac{(1.72 \times 10^{-8}\ \Omega \cdot \text{m})(1{,}000\ \text{m})}{\frac{\pi}{4}(20 \times 10^{-3}\ \text{m})^2}$$
$$= 54.7\ \text{m}\Omega$$

4. **D** Apply equation 4.18 to R_2 and R_3 and then again to R_4 and R_5. Then apply equation 4.12:

$$R_T = 3 + \frac{5 \times 4}{5 + 4} + \frac{10 \times 10}{10 + 10} = 10.2\ \Omega$$

5. **A** Apply Ohm's law; equation 4.8 yields

$$V_T = I_T \times R_T = (1.5\ \text{A})(10.2\ \Omega) = 15.3\ \text{V}$$

6. **C** Use the current division law:

$$I_3 = \frac{5\ \Omega}{5\ \Omega + 4\ \Omega} \times 1.5\ \text{A} = 0.83\ \text{A}$$

7. **B** When R_4 and R_5 are removed as the load, $I_T = 0$ A and

$$V_{\text{Th}} = V_T = 10\ \text{V}.$$

To solve for R_{Th}, replace V_T by 0 Ω; then

$$R_{\text{Th}} = 3\ \Omega + \frac{5\ \Omega \times 4\ \Omega}{5\ \Omega + 4\ \Omega} = 5.2\ \Omega$$

8. **C** Assume that both loop currents are chosen in a clockwise direction.

Loop *A*: Apply the Kirchhoff voltage law to the loop containing the two voltage sources and R_1 and R_2.

Loop *B*: Apply the Kirchhoff voltage law to the outside loop. (*Note:* Through R_1, loop currents I_A and I_B flow.) The set of simultaneous equations is:

$$12I_A + 2I_B = 30\ \text{V}$$
$$2I_A + 12I_B = 10\ \text{V}$$

Only loop current I_A flows through R_2; therefore only I_A has to be determined:

$$I_A = \frac{\begin{vmatrix} 30 & 2 \\ 10 & 12 \end{vmatrix}}{\begin{vmatrix} 12 & 2 \\ 2 & 12 \end{vmatrix}} = \frac{360 - 20}{144 - 4} = 2.43\ \text{A}$$

9. **D** Solve for loop current I_B:

$$I_B = \frac{\begin{vmatrix} 12 & 30 \\ 2 & 10 \end{vmatrix}}{\begin{vmatrix} 12 & 2 \\ 2 & 12 \end{vmatrix}} = \frac{120 - 60}{144 - 4} = 0.42\ \text{A}$$

Now apply equation 4.9:

$$P = I^2R_4 = (0.42\ \text{A})^2 \times 4\ \Omega = 0.73\ \text{W}$$

10. **B** Apply equation 4.20:

$$v_L = L\frac{di}{dt} = (10 \times 10^{-3}\ \text{H})(2\ \text{A/s}) = 20\ \text{mV}$$

11. B Calculate the total inductance by applying equations 4.24 and 4.22:

$$L_{eq} = \frac{L_1 L_2}{L_1 + L_2} + L_3 = \frac{2\text{ H} \times 4\text{ H}}{2\text{ H} + 4\text{ H}} + 2\text{ H}$$
$$= 3\frac{1}{3}\text{ H}$$

Apply equation 4.21:
Total energy stored $= \frac{1}{2} \times \frac{10}{3}\text{ H} \times (1.5\text{ A})^2 = 3.75\text{ J}$

12. D Apply equation 4.25:

$$C = \frac{(4.16 \times 10^{-11}\text{ F/m}) \times \frac{1}{4} \times \pi(0.012\text{ m})^2}{0.004\text{ m}}$$
$$= 1.18\text{ pF}$$

13. A Rearrange equation 4.26:

$$Q = C \times V = (1.18 \times 10^{-12}\text{ F})(12\text{ V})$$
$$= 14.1 \times 10^{-12}\text{ C}$$

14. C First determine the maximum value of current and the time constant:

$$I_{max} = \frac{V}{R} = \frac{10\text{ V}}{0.25\ \Omega} = 40\text{ A},$$
$$\tau = \frac{L}{R} = \frac{4\text{ H}}{0.25\ \Omega} = 16\text{ s}$$

Substitute into equation 4.34 with $I_i = 0$ A:

$$4 = 40(1 - e^{-t/16})$$

Solve for t:

$$t = 1.68\text{ s}$$

15. C Solve for the The-venin equivalent circuit values, using C as the load:

$$V_{Th} = \frac{6\ \Omega}{3\ \Omega + 6\ \Omega} \times 12\text{ V} = 8\text{ V},$$
$$R_{Th} = \frac{3\text{ k}\Omega \times 6\text{ k}\Omega}{3\text{ k}\Omega + 6\text{ k}\Omega} + 8\text{ k}\Omega = 10\text{ k}\Omega$$

Since V_{Th} is V_f and the resistance "seen" by C is $R_{Th} + 8\text{ k}\Omega = 10\text{ k}\Omega$:

$$\tau = R_T \times C = 10 \times 10^3\ \Omega \times 2{,}000 \times 10^{-6}\text{ F} = 20\text{ s}$$

Apply equation 4.32 with $V_i = 2$ V:

$$v_c(t) = 8 + (2 - 8)e^{-5/20} = 3.33\text{ V}$$

16. A The waveform in the figure can be expressed as a negative sine wave with a phase shift.

Solve for frequency, f: $f = \frac{1}{T} = \frac{1}{1\text{ s}} = 1$ Hz; then

$$\omega = 2\pi f = 2\pi\text{ rad/s}.$$

Set up a ratio to solve for the phase angle in radians per second:

$$\frac{\theta}{2\pi} = \frac{\frac{1}{16}}{1}$$
$$\theta = \frac{1}{16} \times 2\pi = \frac{\pi}{8}\text{ rad/s}$$

Substitute into equation 4.35(b):

$$v(t) = -3\sin\left(2\pi t - \frac{\pi}{8}\right)\text{ V}$$

17. D For sinuisoidal waveforms the rms value equals 0.707 of the peak voltage. Hence:

$$V_{rms} = 0.707V_{max} = 0.707(3\text{ V}) = 2.121\text{ V}$$

This value can also be determined by applying equation 4.37.

18. B Apply equation 4.36(b):

$$V_{avg} = \frac{(3\text{ V} \times 1\text{ s}) + (1\text{ V} \times 1\text{ s}) + (-2\text{ V} \times 1\text{ s})}{3\text{ s}}$$
$$= \frac{2}{3}\text{ V or } 0.67\text{ V}$$

19. B Apply this equation:

$$Z_T = Z_1 + \frac{Z_2 \times Z_3}{Z_2 + Z_3}$$

Substitute the circuit values:

$$Z_T = 5\ \Omega + \frac{(2 + j4)\ \Omega \times (1 - j2)\ \Omega}{(2 + j4)\ \Omega + (1 - j2)\ \Omega}$$
$$= (7.31 - j1.54)\ \Omega = 7.47\angle{-11.9°}\ \Omega$$

20. D Apply Ohm's law for ac circuits:

$$I_{rms} = \frac{V_s}{Z_T} = \frac{18\ \angle 30°\text{ V}}{(4 - j2)\ \Omega} = (2.22 + j3.36)\text{ A}$$

21. C Apply the current division law:

$$I_2 = \frac{Z_3}{Z_2 + Z_3} \times I_T$$
$$= \frac{(2 - j5)\ \Omega}{(3 + j6)\ \Omega + (2 - j5)\ \Omega} \times 5\angle 45°\ \text{A}$$
$$= 5.28\angle -34.5°\ \text{A} = (4.35 - j2.99)\ \text{A}$$

22. A Apply Ohm's law for ac circuits:

$$I_{\text{rms}} = \frac{120\angle 30°\ \text{V}}{(4 - j4)\ \Omega} = (5.49 + j20.5)\ \text{A}$$
$$= 21.2\angle 75°\ \text{A}$$

The phase angle from the voltage phasor to the current phasor is 30° to 75°, or 45°.

Apply equation 4.45:

$$P = V_{\text{rms}} \times I_{\text{rms}} \times \cos\theta = 120\ \text{V} \times 21.2\ \text{A} \times \cos(45°) = 1.8\ \text{kW}$$

23. C For the circuit shown:

$$pf = \cos\theta = \cos(45°) = 0.707$$

24. D At resonance, $X_L = X_C$. Since $X_C = 4\ \Omega$ for this problem and $X_L = 2\pi f L$, then

$$L = \frac{4\ \Omega}{2\pi \times 60\ \text{Hz}} = 10.6\ \text{mH}$$

25. B Rearrange equation 4.52(a) and solve for f_0:

$$f_0 = \frac{BW \times Q}{2\pi} = \frac{(15 \times 10^3\ \text{Hz})(20)}{2\pi}$$
$$= 47.7\ \text{kHz}$$

26. A From equation 4.56, $Z_p = a^2 Z_s$. For this problem $Z_s = R - jX_C$, where

$$X_C = \frac{1}{2\pi \times 60\ \text{Hz} \times 150 \times 10^{-6}\ \text{F}}$$
$$= 17.68\ \Omega$$

Therefore, $Z_s = R - jX_C = (10 - j17.68)\ \Omega$, and

$$Z_p = \left(\frac{5}{1}\right)^2 (10 - j17.68)\ \Omega = (250 - j442)\ \Omega$$
$$= 508\angle -60.5°\ \Omega$$

27. C Rearrange equation 4.55 to determine the secondary voltage:

$$V_s = \frac{V_p}{a} = \frac{120\angle 0°\ \text{V}}{5} = 24\angle 0°\ \text{V}$$

Apply Ohm's law:

$$I_s = \frac{V_s}{Z_s} = \frac{24\angle 0°\ \text{V}}{(10 - j17.68)\ \Omega}$$
$$= (0.582 + j1.03)\ \text{A}$$

28. A Rearrange equation 4.59:

$$I_{Ph} = \frac{V_{Ph}}{Z_{Ph}} = \frac{120\angle 0°\ \text{V}}{(0.5 + j2)\ \Omega} = 58.2\angle -76°\ \text{A}$$

Apply equation 4.60:

$$|I_L| = \sqrt{3} \times I_{Ph} = \sqrt{3} \times 58.2 = 101\ \text{A}$$

29. D The voltage gain for an inverting amplifier is given by equation 4.62:

$$A_{CL} = -\frac{150\text{k}\Omega}{10\text{k}\Omega} = -15$$

The output voltage is determined as follows:

$$V_o = A_{CL} \times \text{source voltage} = -15 \times 0.3\ \text{V}$$
$$= -4.5\ \text{V}$$

30. A Determine the output voltage due to each voltage source alone, and then add the results.

For the inverting amplifier:

$$V_{o1} = 0.5\ \text{V} \times \frac{-200\ \text{k}\Omega}{20\ \text{k}\Omega} = -5.0\ \text{V}$$

For the noninverting amplifier:

$$V_{o2} = 0.2\ \text{V} \times \frac{200\ \text{k}\Omega + 20\ \text{k}\Omega}{20\ \text{k}\Omega} = 2.2\ \text{V}$$

Total output voltage =

$$V_o = V_{o1} + V_{o2} = -5.0\ \text{V} + 2.2\ \text{V} = -2.8\ \text{V}$$

31. C Apply equation 4.65; the magnitude of the force is

$$F = \frac{(4 \times 10^{-8}\ \text{C})(4 \times 10^{-8}\ \text{C})}{4\pi(8.85 \times 10^{-12}\ \text{C/N·m})(2\ \text{m})^2}$$
$$= 3.6 \times 10^{-6}\ \text{N}$$

32. D Apply equation 4.66:

$$E = \frac{4 \times 10^{-8}\ \text{C}}{4\pi(8.85 \times 10^{-12}\ \text{C/N·m})(2\ \text{m})^2}$$
$$= 90\ \text{V/m}$$

CHAPTER

5

Engineering Economy

Thomas E. Hulbert, PE

Introduction

Engineering designs are subject to many levels of review. The design must meet the physical needs of the project, must utilize appropriate materials, must result in a structurally sound product, must be aesthetically pleasing, and must be economically feasible. If an engineering review indicates that the project meets all other criteria, the project must then be evaluated in financial terms. Beyond simply understanding the costs of materials, the engineer must have a firm grasp of labor costs, maintenance costs, insurance, interest, and depreciation. Also, he or she must be able to apply this knowledge to the project at hand.

The material in this chapter should serve as a general review for the Fundamentals of Engineering examination. Since you will be taking this examination with an open copy of the "National Council of Examiners for Engineering and Surveying Reference Handbook," the topics of this chapter follow the order of the book. Be sure to review this material before you attempt to solve the problems at the end of the chapter. If you feel that you need more in-depth instruction, refer to a textbook on the subject of engineering economy; three helpful references are listed in Section 5.14.

5.1 Fundamental Concepts

Engineering economy is based on two fundamental concepts: equivalence and money increase in value over time, that is, future value. **Equivalence** refers to the fact that various cost-benefit statements and differing cash-flow patterns may actually be equivalent, though not necessarily equal. **Future value** refers to the fact that money earns interest and thus increases its value over time. In engineering economics calculations, time is assumed to be one year, unless otherwise specified, and calculations are considered to have been made at the end of the year unless otherwise stated. Interest is the difference between the current value and the rate of increase of the future value.

For a simple illustration of equivalence, consider the following three alternatives:

Alternative A: Receive $100 today.
Alternative B: Receive $100 one year from today.
Alternative C: Receive $110 one year from today.

It is not too difficult to choose A over B. If you take into account inflation and the fact that the money cannot work for you during the intervening year, B represents a decrease in value. However, the choice between A and C is not clearly evident. If you choose C, you indicate that your minimum acceptable rate of return is 10% per year. If you choose A, your rate of return is indefinite—it may be greater or less than 10%. Some individuals may be indifferent toward the choice between A and C. For them, A and C are equally attractive or equivalent even though the two alternatives involve different amounts of money at different points in time and may not, in the final analysis, prove to be equal.

Another example of equivalence is the exchange of U.S. dollars into other currencies. In the exchange, only the exchange rate itself is considered, not the buying power of either currency. The amount of foreign currency received is equivalent to the amount of U.S. dollars, but it is not necessarily equal in purchasing power.

5.2 Nomenclature and Definitions

The following symbols are listed in the *NCEES FE Reference Handbook* and are those used in engineering economy problems and texts. The explanations of some symbols have been expanded for greater clarity.

- A Uniform amount per interest period
- B Benefit or savings derived from public projects
- BV Remaining value (book value) after the depreciation charge for the year
- C Initial value or present worth of all costs; the sum of costs in public works projects (see B above)
- d Combined interest rate per interest period
- D_j Depreciation in year j
- F Future worth, value, or amount
- f General inflation rate per interest period (treated same as i)
- G Uniform gradient amount per interest period
- i Interest rate per interest period (years unless otherwise stated)
- i_e Effective interest rate (annual)—used in engineering economy studies, unless otherwise stated
- m Number of compounding periods per year
- n Number of compounding periods or expected life of asset (usually years)
- P Present worth, value, or amount
- r Nominal annual interest rate or rate per annum
- S_n Expected salvage value in year n

5.3 Nominal and Effective (Nonannual Compounding) Interest Rates

The basis of engineering economics calculations is the same as that used by financial institutions in their calculation of interest.

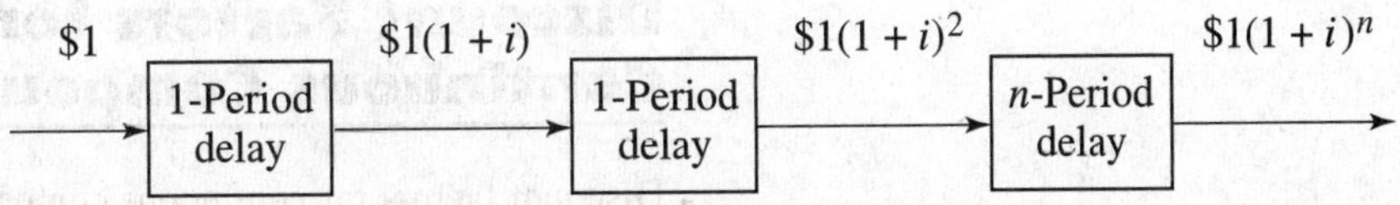

Note: Delays are normally expressed in years.

At the end of the first year there will be \$1(1 + i). At the end of the second year, there will be $\$1(1 + i)^2$. Therefore, at an interest rate of i, \$1 today is equivalent to $\$1(1 + i)^n$ received n years from today or at the end of n periods.

In many financial transactions, an annual nominal interest rate is specified, but the compounding process actually occurs several times throughout the year. For example, if a nominal interest rate of 12% per year is compounded semiannually, the effect is to pay a 6% interest rate per 6 months for two 6-month periods. If \$1,000 is invested under these conditions, it will become $\$1{,}000 \times 1.06^2 = \$1{,}123.60$. The effective interest rate is $(1.06^2 - 1) = 0.12360$ or 12.36%.

If the nominal interest rate is r per year compounded m times per year, the effective annual interest rate is

$$i_e = \left(1 + \frac{r}{m}\right)^m - 1$$

As a second example, suppose a finance company charges 1.5% per month compounded monthly. The nominal interest rate is 1.5% + 12 = 18%, but the effective interest rate is actually $(1.015)^{12} - 1 = 0.1956$ or 19.56%.

5.4 Cash-Flow Diagrams

The flow of money is shown on a diagram known as a cash-flow diagram (Figure 5.1). Money at present, or time = 0, has a present value, which is designated as P. Uniform annual receipts or disbursements are designated as A; and money in the future has a future value, which is designated as F.

Figure 5.2 illustrates the gradient—a linearly increasing amount of money starting at time = 0 with the gradient line at 0. The cash-flow diagrams are represented as follows:

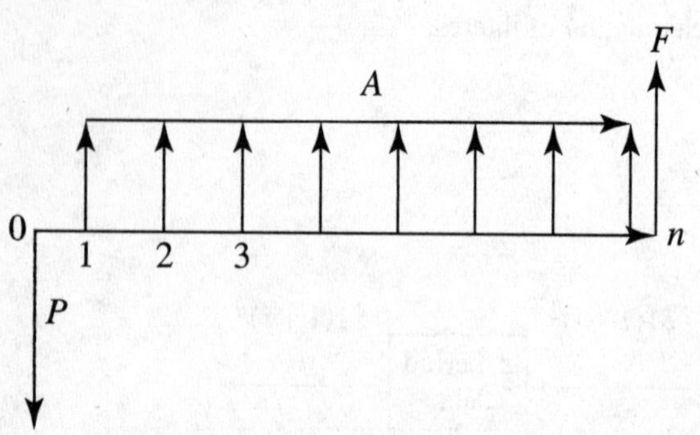

Figure 5.1 Cash-flow diagram

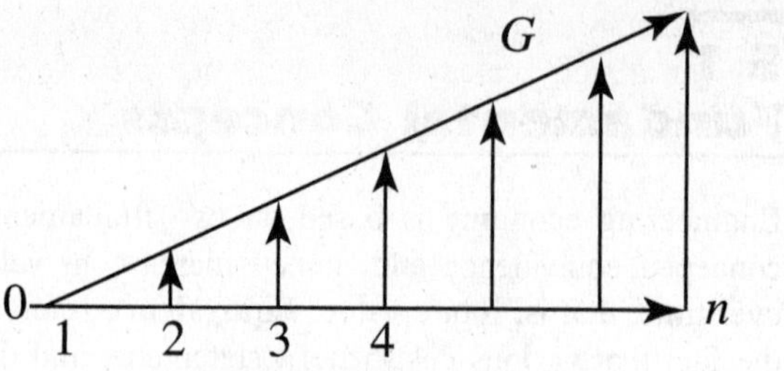

Figure 5.2 Gradient

5.5 Interest Formulas and Tables

The *NCEES FE Reference Handbook* includes the eight commonly used factors along with their original names, the current expression (symbol) for each factor, and the algebraic formula for each. You can solve problems either by searching a table or by using a calculator with the formulas. A complete set of the factor tables provided for the exams is included at the end of this chapter.

A portion of a factor table for 8% interest is shown below. The left column represents the time period, generally in years. The four factors and their respective values are shown in the matrix of the table.

Factor Table for i = 8.00%

n	*P/F*	*P/A*	*P/G*	*F/P*
1	0.9259	0.9259	0.0000	1.0800
2	0.8573	1.7833	0.8573	1.1664
3	0.7938	2.5771	2.4450	1.2597
4	0.7350	3.3121	4.6501	1.3605
5	0.6806	3.9927	7.3724	1.4693
6	0.6302	4.6229	10.5233	1.5869
·	·	·	·	·
·	·	·	·	·
·	·	·	·	·
30	0.0994	11.2578	103.4558	10.0627
40	0.0460	11.9246	126.0422	21.7245
50	0.0213	12.2335	139.5928	46.9016
60	0.0099	12.3766	147.3000	101.2571
100	0.0005	12.4943	155.6107	2,199.7613

5.6 Discount Factors for Continuous Compounding

Discount factors for continuous compounding are different from those for discrete compounding. Given the nominal interest rate, r, and the number of years, n, you can directly calculate the discounting factor, e^{rn}. For example:

$$(F/P, r\%, n) = e^{rn}$$

The totals from daily compounding closely approximate those from continuous compounding.

5.7 Depreciation Methods

The value of the client's existing assets—heavy equipment, machinery, and tools—is one of many factors entering into your analysis of the economic feasibility of a project. It is likely that some of these assets were placed in service years ago and will have already been partially, or even fully, depreciated. You must review the depreciation method used by your client, because in a challenger-defender analysis the depreciation method employed at the start must be continued.

In the accounting world, depreciation is an expense. In other words, it is a systematic write-off of an asset over time. The Internal Revenue Service Code specifies the available systems of depreciation and the lifetimes allotted to various types of physical assets. The taxpayer may choose from among a limited number of optional methods. The after-tax analysis reduces the rate of return. Since depreciation charges are not linear (except in straight-line depreciation), you must calculate their impact on the rate of return.

You must be familiar with various depreciation methods in order to tackle problems on the FE exam.

Before 1980

- **Straight-line depreciation** (*SL*) (necessary for current FE exam)

$$SL = \frac{FC - SV}{n}, \text{ same for every year}$$

$$= \left(\frac{\text{Last year [e.g., 10]}}{\text{Sum of digits of years, 1 to } n}\right)$$

$$\times \text{(First cost-salvage value)}$$

where FC = first cost,
SV = salvage value,
n = total number of years.

- **Sum of years' digits** *(SYD)*

Depreciation for first year

$$= \left(\frac{\text{Last year [e.g., 10]}}{\text{Sum of digits of years, 1 to } n}\right)$$

$$\times \text{(Capital cost} - \text{Salvage value)}$$

Example

Given an asset costing $120,000 with an estimated salvage value of $20,000 and a life of 10 years, calculate the depreciation write-off using the sum of years' digits method.

Solution:

Sum of years 1 to 10 = 55.

First-year depreciation = $\left(\frac{10}{55}\right)$(120,000 − 20,000) = $18,200.

Second-year depreciation = $\left(\frac{9}{55}\right)$(81,800) = $13,400, and so on.

Year-10 depreciation = $\left(\frac{1}{55}\right)$(Book value at end of year 9).

- **Fixed percentage declining balance** (*DDB*), usually double (2 times) the straight-line rate

DDB = (Book value at end of previous year) $\times \left(\frac{2}{N}\right)$, where $\frac{2}{N}$ is a constant factor based on the life, N, of the equipment or project.

DDB has to switch to the *SL* depreciation value when the depreciation charge for *DDB* becomes less than the depreciation charge for *SL*.

1980 and Beyond

Accelerated Cost Recovery System (ACRS) and Modified ACRS (MACRS)

Modified ACRS has been in effect since 1986. See the table below.

MACRS Factors Table

	Recovery Period (years)			
	3	*5*	*7*	*10*
Year	*Recovery Rate (years)*			
1	33.3	20.0	14.3	10.0
2	44.5	32.0	24.5	18.0
3	14.8	19.2	17.5	14.4
4	7.4	11.5	12.5	11.5
5		11.5	8.9	9.2
6		5.8	8.9	7.4
7			8.9	7.4
8			4.5	6.6
9				6.6
10				6.5
11				3.3

5.8 Bonds

Bonds are similar to stocks in that their values or prices fluctuate up and down with the market. Bonds, however, are somewhat more secure in that they have a par or purchase price that is guaranteed if the bonds are held to maturity. In return for the security, the interest is set at an unvarying rate, which the bond-owner earns as long as he or she holds the bonds.

Once a bond has been issued, its price is free to fluctuate; bond yield is influenced by bond price. The bond yield is computed on the basis of comparison of annual interest to current cost. You should set up cash flow diagrams to solve problems concerning bond yields.

Bonds are often issued to finance construction projects. The interest paid out to bondholders must be figured into the cost of the project.

5.9 Benefit-Cost Analysis

In a simple benefit-cost (B/C) analysis, the benefits (B) of a project should exceed the estimated costs (C). This calculation is based on a ratio of benefits to costs or of incremental benefits to the corresponding incremental costs. The higher the ratio (>1.0) or the larger the positive difference, the more attractive the project will be to the government or nonprofit agency funding the project. Benefit-cost analysis is used only in situations where no taxes are involved and where a rough estimate is adequate.

5.10 Capitalized Costs

Capitalized costs are the annualized expenditures, such as maintenance, replacement, and operating costs, necessary to keep an asset in service in perpetuity, or forever. To calculate capitalized costs, determine the annualized cost and divide by the interest rate:

$$\text{Capitalized costs} = P = \frac{A}{i}$$

where P = present sum
A = annual costs
i = interest rate

5.11 Inflation

In economic analysis you can treat inflation as simply another interest rate. To account for inflation, deflate future dollars by the general inflation rate. Alternatively, you can use the inflated interest rate, which includes both the influence of inflation and an inflation-free interest rate, in your calculations.

5.12 Methods of Analysis

- Present-worth analysis (when alternatives have the same lives)
  In comparing two alternatives, start with the initial investment at time = 0, then add or subtract the discounted values of all costs and revenues associated with each alternative. Select the one with the lowest present worth.
- Annualized cost analysis (when alternatives have different lives)
  Convert all costs and revenues to an annual cost (A), and sum them for each alternative. Choose the one with the lowest total annual cost.
- Rate-of-return analysis (when interest rate is unknown)
  The rate of return on an investment is the interest rate that makes the total annual worth of all revenues equal the total annual worth of all costs. Convert all cash flows to annual costs, and create an expression for revenues minus costs. Plug in values for interest (i) by trial and error. When the value switches signs (+ to −), linearly interpolate, using successive factor tables to determine the interest rate or rate of return.
- Rate of return on incremental investment
  Consider alternative designs or production methods to solve the problem. For example, suppose that a new machine must be purchased for production of a particular part, and that three machines are under consideration. To calculate the return on the incremental or added investment:
  1. List the alternatives in hierarchical order of capital cost (investment), beginning with the least costly alternative.
  2. Given revenues and costs for each, calculate a rate of return (or interest rate) for each alternative so as to make the present worth of that alternative equal to zero, using the factor P/A.
  3. Compare the rate of return for each alternative with the minimum acceptable rate of return for the enterprise.
  4. Eliminate from consideration any alternative that does not meet the minimum rate of return.
  5. Of the remaining alternatives, compare the one with the lowest investment to the one with the next higher investment by considering the incremental (or added) investments and the incremental revenues.

For each alternative, subtract the incremental investment from the incremental cost and calculate the rate of return.

6. Select the alternative that yields the highest return on added investment.

- Break-even analysis

On the same graph, plot the fixed and variable costs to produce a product and the revenues generated from the sale of that product. The intersection of the total cost (sum of fixed costs and variable A) and revenue lines is the break-even point. Profits are generated above the break-even point; losses below. See the example in Figure 5.3.

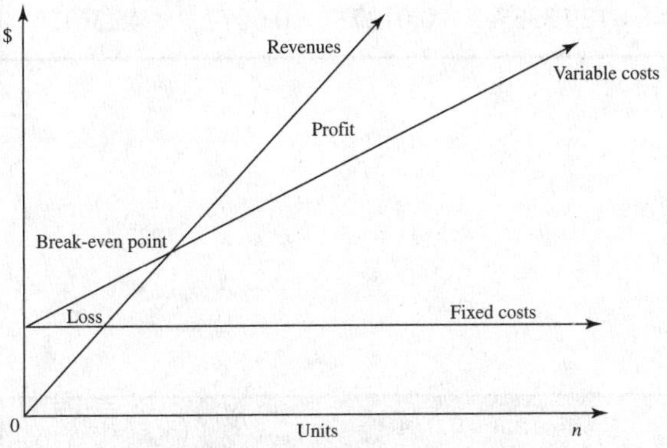

Figure 5.3 Break-even analysis

5.13 The Factors and the Factor Tables

Factors

(P/F) Present Worth given Future Worth
(P/A) Present Worth given Annual Cost/Revenue
(F/A) Future Worth given Annual Cost/Revenue
(A/P) Annual Cost/Revenue given Present Worth
(P/G) Present Worth given Gradient Value
(A/F) Annual Cost/Revenue given Future Worth
(F/P) Future Worth given Present Worth
(A/G) Annual Cost/Revenue given Gradient Value

Tables

i = 0.50%

n	P/F	P/A	P/G	F/P	F/A	A/P	A/F	A/G
1	0.9950	0.9950	0.0000	1.0050	1.0000	1.0050	1.0000	0.0000
2	0.9901	1.9851	0.9901	1.0100	2.0050	0.5038	0.4988	0.4988
3	0.9851	2.9702	2.9604	1.0151	3.0150	0.3367	0.3317	0.9967
4	0.9802	3.9505	5.9011	1.0202	4.0301	0.2531	0.2481	1.4938
5	0.9754	4.9259	9.8026	1.0253	5.0503	0.2030	0.1980	1.9900
6	0.9705	5.8964	14.6552	1.0304	6.0755	0.1696	0.1646	2.4855
7	0.9657	6.8621	20.4493	1.0355	7.1059	0.1457	0.1407	2.9801
8	0.9609	7.8230	27.1755	1.0407	8.1414	0.1278	0.1228	3.4738
9	0.9561	8.7791	34.8244	1.0459	9.1821	0.1139	0.1089	3.9668
10	0.9513	9.7304	43.3865	1.0511	10.2280	0.1028	0.0978	4.4589
11	0.9466	10.6770	52.8526	1.0564	11.2792	0.0937	0.0887	4.9501
12	0.9419	11.6189	63.2136	1.0617	12.3356	0.0861	0.0811	5.4406
13	0.9372	12.5562	74.4602	1.0670	13.3972	0.0796	0.0746	5.9302
14	0.9326	13.4887	86.5835	1.0723	14.4642	0.0741	0.0691	6.4190
15	0.9279	14.4166	99.5743	1.0777	15.5365	0.0694	0.0644	6.9069
16	0.9233	15.3399	113.4238	1.0831	16.6142	0.0652	0.0602	7.3940
17	0.9187	16.2586	128.1231	1.0885	17.6973	0.0615	0.0565	7.8803
18	0.9141	17.1728	143.6634	1.0939	18.7858	0.0582	0.0532	8.3658
19	0.9096	18.0824	160.0360	1.0994	19.8797	0.0553	0.0503	8.8504
20	0.9051	18.9874	177.2322	1.1049	20.9791	0.0527	0.0477	9.3342

i = 0.50% (Continued)

n	P/F	P/A	P/G	F/P	F/A	A/P	A/F	A/G
21	0.9006	19.8880	195.2434	1.1104	22.0840	0.0503	0.0453	9.8172
22	0.8961	20.7841	214.0611	1.1160	23.1944	0.0481	0.0431	10.2993
23	0.8916	21.6757	233.6768	1.1216	24.3104	0.0461	0.0411	10.7806
24	0.8872	22.5629	254.0820	1.1272	25.4320	0.0443	0.0393	11.2611
25	0.8828	23.4456	275.2686	1.1328	26.5591	0.0427	0.0377	11.7407
30	0.8610	27.7941	392.6324	1.1614	32.2800	0.0360	0.0310	14.1265
40	0.8191	36.1722	681.3347	1.2208	44.1588	0.0276	0.0226	18.8359
50	0.7793	44.1428	1,035.6966	1.2832	56.6452	0.0227	0.0177	23.4624
60	0.7414	51.7256	1,448.6458	1.3489	69.7700	0.0193	0.0143	28.0064
100	0.6073	78.5426	3,562.7934	1.6467	129.3337	0.0127	0.0077	45.3613

i = 1.00%

n	P/F	P/A	P/G	F/P	F/A	A/P	A/F	A/G
1	0.9901	0.9901	0.0000	1.0100	1.0000	1.0100	1.0000	0.0000
2	0.9803	1.9704	0.9803	1.0201	2.0100	0.5075	0.4975	0.4975
3	0.9706	2.9410	2.9215	1.0303	3.0301	0.3400	0.3300	0.9934
4	0.9610	3.9020	5.8044	1.0406	4.0604	0.2563	0.2463	1.4876
5	0.9515	4.8534	9.6103	1.0510	5.1010	0.2060	0.1960	1.9801
6	0.9420	5.7955	14.3205	1.0615	6.1520	0.1725	0.1625	2.4710
7	0.9327	6.7282	19.9168	1.0721	7.2135	0.1486	0.1386	2.9602
8	0.9235	7.6517	26.3812	1.0829	8.2857	0.1307	0.1207	3.4478
9	0.9143	8.5650	33.6959	1.0937	9.3685	0.1167	0.1067	3.9337
10	0.9053	9.4713	41.8435	1.1046	10.4622	0.1056	0.0956	4.4179
11	0.8963	10.3676	50.8067	1.1157	11.5668	0.0965	0.0865	4.9005
12	0.8874	11.2551	60.5687	1.1268	12.6825	0.0888	0.0788	5.3815
13	0.8787	12.1337	71.1126	1.1381	13.8093	0.0824	0.0724	5.8607
14	0.8700	13.0037	82.4221	1.1495	14.9474	0.0769	0.0669	6.3384
15	0.8613	13.8651	94.4810	1.1610	16.0969	0.0721	0.0621	6.8143
16	0.8528	14.7179	107.2734	1.1726	17.2579	0.0679	0.0579	7.2886
17	0.8444	15.5623	120.7834	1.1843	18.4304	0.0643	0.0543	7.7613
18	0.8360	16.3983	134.9957	1.1961	19.6147	0.0610	0.0510	8.2323
19	0.8277	17.2260	149.8950	1.2081	20.8109	0.0581	0.0481	8.7017
20	0.8195	18.0456	165.4664	1.2202	22.0190	0.0554	0.0454	9.1694
21	0.8114	18.8570	181.6950	1.2324	23.2392	0.0530	0.0430	9.6354
22	0.8034	19.6604	198.5663	1.2447	24.4716	0.0509	0.0409	10.0998
23	0.7954	20.4558	216.0660	1.2572	25.7163	0.0489	0.0389	10.5626
24	0.7876	21.2434	234.1800	1.2697	26.9735	0.0471	0.0371	11.0237
25	0.7798	22.0232	252.8945	1.2824	28.2432	0.0454	0.0354	11.4831
30	0.7419	25.8077	355.0021	1.3478	34.7849	0.0387	0.0277	13.7557
40	0.6717	32.8347	596.8561	1.4889	48.8864	0.0305	0.0205	18.1776
50	0.6080	39.1961	879.4176	1.6446	64.4632	0.0255	0.0155	22.4363
60	0.5504	44.9550	1,192.8061	1.8167	81.6697	0.0222	0.0122	26.5333
100	0.3697	63.0289	2,605.7758	2.7048	170.4814	0.0159	0.0059	41.3426

i = 1.50%

n	P/F	P/A	P/G	F/P	F/A	A/P	A/F	A/G
1	0.9852	0.9852	0.0000	1.0150	1.0000	1.0150	1.0000	0.0000
2	0.9707	1.9559	0.9707	1.0302	2.0150	0.5113	0.4963	0.4963
3	0.9563	2.9122	2.8833	1.0457	3.0452	0.3434	0.3284	0.9901
4	0.9422	3.8544	5.7098	1.0614	4.0909	0.2594	0.2444	1.4814
5	0.9283	4.7826	9.4229	1.0773	5.1523	0.2091	0.1941	1.9702
6	0.9145	5.6972	13.9956	1.0934	6.2296	0.1755	0.1605	2.4566
7	0.9010	6.5982	19.4018	1.1098	7.3230	0.1516	0.1366	2.9405
8	0.8877	7.4859	26.6157	1.1265	8.4328	0.1336	0.1186	3.4219
9	0.8746	8.3605	32.6125	1.1434	9.5593	0.1196	0.1046	3.9008
10	0.8617	9.2222	40.3675	1.1605	10.7027	0.1084	0.0934	4.3772
11	0.8489	10.0711	48.8568	1.1779	11.8633	0.0993	0.0843	4.8512
12	0.8364	10.9075	58.0571	1.1956	13.0412	0.0917	0.0767	5.3227
13	0.8240	11.7315	67.9454	1.2136	14.2368	0.0852	0.0702	5.7917
14	0.8118	12.5434	78.4994	1.2318	15.4504	0.0797	0.0647	6.2582
15	0.7999	13.3432	89.6974	1.2502	16.6821	0.0749	0.0599	6.7223
16	0.7880	14.1313	101.5178	1.2690	17.9324	0.0708	0.0558	7.1839
17	0.7764	14.9076	113.9400	1.2880	19.2014	0.0671	0.0521	7.6431
18	0.7649	15.6726	126.9435	1.3073	20.4894	0.0638	0.0488	8.0997
19	0.7536	16.4262	140.5084	1.3270	21.7967	0.0609	0.0459	8.5539
20	0.7425	17.1686	154.6154	1.3469	23.1237	0.0582	0.0432	9.0057
21	0.7315	17.9001	169.2453	1.3671	24.4705	0.0559	0.0409	9.4550
22	0.7207	18.6208	184.3798	1.3876	25.8376	0.0537	0.0387	9.9018
23	0.7100	19.3309	200.0006	1.4084	27.2251	0.0517	0.0367	10.3462
24	0.6995	20.0304	216.0901	1.4295	28.6335	0.0499	0.0349	10.7881
25	0.6892	20.7196	232.6310	1.4509	30.0630	0.0483	0.0333	11.2276
30	0.6398	24.0158	321.5310	1.5631	37.5387	0.0416	0.0266	13.3883
40	0.5513	29.9158	524.3568	1.8140	54.2679	0.0334	0.0184	17.5277
50	0.4750	34.9997	749.9636	2.1052	73.6828	0.0286	0.0136	21.4277
60	0.4093	39.3803	988.1674	2.4432	96.2147	0.0254	0.0104	25.0930
100	0.2256	51.6247	1,937.4506	4.4320	228.8030	0.0194	0.0044	37.5295

i = 2.00%

n	P/F	P/A	P/G	F/P	F/A	A/P	A/F	A/G
1	0.9804	0.9804	0.0000	1.0200	1.0000	1.0200	1.0000	0.0000
2	0.9612	1.9416	0.9612	1.0404	2.0200	0.5150	0.4950	0.4950
3	0.9423	2.8839	2.8458	1.0612	3.0604	0.3468	0.3268	0.9868
4	0.9238	3.8077	5.6173	1.0824	4.1216	0.2626	0.2426	1.4752
5	0.9057	4.7135	9.2403	1.1041	5.2040	0.2122	0.1922	1.9604
6	0.8880	5.6014	13.6801	1.1262	6.3081	0.1785	0.1585	2.4423
7	0.8706	6.4720	18.9035	1.1487	7.4343	0.1545	0.1345	2.9208
8	0.8535	7.3255	24.8779	1.1717	8.5830	0.1365	0.1165	3.3961
9	0.8368	8.1622	31.5720	1.1951	9.7546	0.1225	0.1025	3.8681
10	0.8203	8.9826	38.9551	1.2190	10.9497	0.1113	0.0913	4.3367
11	0.8043	9.7868	46.9977	1.2434	12.1687	0.1022	0.0822	4.8021
12	0.7885	10.5753	55.6712	1.2682	13.4121	0.0946	0.0746	5.2642
13	0.7730	11.3484	64.9475	1.2936	14.6803	0.0881	0.0681	5.7231
14	0.7579	12.1062	74.7999	1.3195	15.9739	0.0826	0.0626	6.1786
15	0.7430	12.8493	85.2021	1.3459	17.2934	0.0778	0.0578	6.6309
16	0.7284	13.5777	96.1288	1.3728	18.6393	0.0737	0.0537	7.0799

i = 2.00% (Continued)

n	*P/F*	*P/A*	*P/G*	*F/P*	*F/A*	*A/P*	*A/F*	*A/G*
17	0.7142	14.2919	107.5554	1.4002	20.0121	0.0700	0.0500	7.5251
18	0.7002	14.9920	119.4581	1.4282	21.4123	0.0667	0.0467	7.9681
19	0.6864	15.6785	131.8139	1.4568	22.8406	0.0638	0.0438	8.4073
20	0.6730	16.3514	144.6003	1.4859	24.2974	0.0612	0.0412	8.8433
21	0.6598	17.0112	157.7959	1.5157	25.7833	0.0588	0.0388	9.2760
22	0.6468	17.6580	171.3795	1.5460	27.2990	0.0566	0.0366	9.7055
23	0.6342	18.2922	185.3309	1.5769	28.8450	0.0547	0.0347	10.1317
24	0.6217	18.9139	199.6305	1.6084	30.4219	0.0529	0.0329	10.5547
25	0.6095	19.5235	214.2592	1.6406	32.0303	0.0512	0.0312	10.9745
30	0.5521	22.3965	291.7164	1.8114	40.5681	0.0446	0.0246	13.0251
40	0.4529	27.3555	461.9931	2.2080	60.4020	0.0366	0.0166	16.8811
50	0.3715	31.4236	642.3606	2.6916	84.5794	0.0318	0.0118	20.4420
60	0.3048	34.7609	823.6975	3.2810	114.0515	0.0288	0.0088	23.6961
100	0.1380	43.0984	1,464.7527	7.2446	312.2323	0.0232	0.0032	33.9863

i = 4.00%

n	*P/F*	*P/A*	*P/G*	*F/P*	*F/A*	*A/P*	*A/F*	*A/G*
1	0.9615	0.9615	0.0000	1.0400	1.0000	1.0400	1.0000	0.0000
2	0.9246	1.8861	0.9246	1.0816	2.0400	0.5302	0.4902	0.4902
3	0.8890	2.7751	2.7025	1.1249	3.1216	0.3603	0.3203	0.9739
4	0.8548	3.6299	5.2670	1.1699	4.2465	0.2755	0.2355	1.4510
5	0.8219	4.4518	8.5547	1.2167	5.4163	0.2246	0.1846	1.9216
6	0.7903	5.2421	12.5062	1.2653	6.6330	0.1908	0.1508	2.3857
7	0.7599	6.0021	17.0657	1.3159	7.8983	0.1666	0.1266	2.8433
8	0.7307	6.7327	22.1806	1.3686	9.2142	0.1485	0.1085	3.2944
9	0.7026	7.4353	27.8013	1.4233	10.5828	0.1345	0.0945	3.7391
10	0.6756	8.1109	33.8814	1.4802	12.0061	0.1233	0.0833	4.1773
11	0.6496	8.7605	40.3772	1.5395	13.4864	0.1141	0.0741	4.6090
12	0.6246	9.3851	47.2477	1.6010	15.0258	0.1066	0.0666	5.0343
13	0.6006	9.9856	54.4546	1.6651	16.6268	0.1001	0.0601	5.4533
14	0.5775	10.5631	61.9618	1.7317	18.2919	0.0947	0.0547	5.8659
15	0.5553	11.1184	69.7355	1.8009	20.0236	0.0899	0.0499	6.2721
16	0.5339	11.6523	77.7441	1.8730	21.8245	0.0858	0.0458	6.6720
17	0.5134	12.1657	85.9581	1.9479	23.6975	0.0822	0.0422	7.0656
18	0.4936	12.6593	94.3498	2.0258	25.6454	0.0790	0.0390	7.4530
19	0.4746	13.1339	102.8933	2.1068	27.6712	0.0761	0.0361	7.8342
20	0.4564	13.5903	111.5647	2.1911	29.7781	0.0736	0.0336	8.2091
21	0.4388	14.0292	120.3414	2.2788	31.9690	0.0713	0.0313	8.5779
22	0.4220	14.4511	129.2024	2.3699	34.2480	0.0692	0.0292	8.9407
23	0.4057	14.8568	138.1284	2.4647	36.6179	0.0673	0.0273	9.2973
24	0.3901	15.2470	147.1012	2.5633	39.0826	0.0656	0.0256	9.6479
25	0.3751	15.6221	156.1040	2.6658	41.6459	0.0640	0.0240	9.9925
30	0.3083	17.2920	201.0618	3.2434	56.0849	0.0578	0.0178	11.6274
40	0.2083	19.7928	286.5303	4.8010	95.0255	0.0505	0.0105	14.4765
50	0.1407	21.4822	361.1638	7.1067	152.6671	0.0466	0.0066	16.8122
60	0.0951	22.6235	422.9966	10.5196	237.9907	0.0442	0.0042	18.6972
100	0.0198	24.5050	563.1249	50.5049	1,237.6237	0.0408	0.0008	22.9800

i = 6.00%

n	P/F	P/A	P/G	F/P	F/A	A/P	A/F	A/G
1	0.9434	0.9434	0.0000	1.0600	1.0000	1.0600	1.0000	0.0000
2	0.8900	1.8334	0.8900	1.1236	2.0600	0.5454	0.4854	0.4854
3	0.8396	2.6730	2.5692	1.1910	3.1836	0.3741	0.3141	0.9612
4	0.7921	3.4651	4.9455	1.2625	4.3746	0.2886	0.2286	1.4272
5	0.7473	4.2124	7.9345	1.3382	5.6371	0.2374	0.1774	1.8836
6	0.7050	4.9173	11.4594	1.4185	6.9753	0.2034	0.1434	2.3304
7	0.6651	5.5824	15.4497	1.5036	8.3938	0.1791	0.1191	2.7676
8	0.6274	6.2098	19.8416	1.5938	9.8975	0.1610	0.1010	3.1952
9	0.5919	6.8017	24.5768	1.6895	11.4913	0.1470	0.0870	3.6133
10	0.5584	7.3601	29.6023	1.7908	13.1808	0.1359	0.0759	4.0220
11	0.5268	7.8869	34.8702	1.8983	14.9716	0.1268	0.0668	4.4213
12	0.4970	8.3838	40.3369	2.0122	16.8699	0.1193	0.0593	4.8113
13	0.4688	8.8527	45.9629	2.1329	18.8821	0.1130	0.0530	5.1920
14	0.4423	9.2950	51.7128	2.2609	21.0151	0.1076	0.0476	5.5635
15	0.4173	9.7122	57.5546	2.3966	23.2760	0.1030	0.0430	5.9260
16	0.3936	10.1059	63.4592	2.5404	25.6725	0.0990	0.0390	6.2794
17	0.3714	10.4773	69.4011	2.6928	28.2129	0.0954	0.0354	6.6240
18	0.3505	10.8276	75.3569	2.8543	30.9057	0.0924	0.0324	6.9597
19	0.3305	11.1581	81.3062	3.0256	33.7600	0.0896	0.0296	7.2867
20	0.3118	11.4699	87.2304	3.2071	36.7856	0.0872	0.0272	7.6051
21	0.2942	11.7641	93.1136	3.3996	39.9927	0.0850	0.0250	7.9151
22	0.2775	12.0416	98.9412	3.6035	43.3923	0.0830	0.0230	8.2166
23	0.2618	12.3034	104.7007	3.8197	46.9958	0.0813	0.0213	8.5099
24	0.2470	12.5504	110.3812	4.0489	50.8156	0.0797	0.0197	8.7951
25	0.2330	12.7834	115.9732	4.2919	54.8645	0.0782	0.0182	9.0722
30	0.1741	13.7648	142.3588	5.7435	79.0582	0.0726	0.0126	10.3422
40	0.0972	15.0463	185.9568	10.2857	154.7620	0.0665	0.0065	12.3590
50	0.0543	15.7619	217.4574	18.4202	290.3359	0.0634	0.0034	13.7964
60	0.0303	16.1614	239.0428	32.9877	533.1282	0.0619	0.0019	14.7909
100	0.0029	16.6175	272.0471	339.3021	5,638.3681	0.0602	0.0002	16.3711

i = 8.00%

n	P/F	P/A	P/G	F/P	F/A	A/P	A/F	A/G
1	0.9259	0.9259	0.0000	1.0800	1.0000	1.0800	1.0000	0.0000
2	0.8573	1.7833	0.8573	1.1664	2.0800	0.5608	0.4808	0.4808
3	0.7938	2.5771	2.4450	1.2597	3.2464	0.3880	0.3080	0.9487
4	0.7350	3.3121	4.6501	1.3605	4.5061	0.3019	0.2219	1.4040
5	0.6806	3.9927	7.3724	1.4693	5.8666	0.2505	0.1705	1.8465
6	0.6302	4.6229	10.5233	1.5869	7.3359	0.2163	0.1363	2.2763
7	0.5835	5.2064	14.0242	1.7138	8.9228	0.1921	0.1121	2.6937
8	0.5403	5.7466	17.8061	1.8509	10.6366	0.1740	0.0940	3.0985
9	0.5002	6.2469	21.8081	1.9990	12.4876	0.1601	0.0801	3.4910
10	0.4632	6.7101	25.9768	2.1589	14.4866	0.1490	0.0690	3.8713
11	0.4289	7.1390	30.2657	2.3316	16.6455	0.1401	0.0601	4.2395
12	0.3971	7.5361	34.6339	2.5182	18.9771	0.1327	0.0527	4.5957
13	0.3677	7.9038	39.0463	2.7196	21.4953	0.1265	0.0465	4.9402
14	0.3405	8.2442	43.4723	2.9372	24.2149	0.1213	0.0413	5.2731
15	0.3152	8.5595	47.8857	3.1722	27.1521	0.1168	0.0368	5.5945
16	0.2919	8.8514	52.2640	3.4259	30.3243	0.1130	0.0330	5.9046

i = 8.00% (Continued)

n	P/F	P/A	P/G	F/P	F/A	A/P	A/F	A/G
17	0.2703	9.1216	56.5883	3.7000	33.7502	0.1096	0.0296	6.2037
18	0.2502	9.3719	60.8426	3.9960	37.4502	0.1067	0.0267	6.4920
19	0.2317	9.6036	65.0134	4.3157	41.4463	0.1041	0.0241	6.7697
20	0.2145	9.8181	69.0898	4.6610	45.7620	0.1019	0.0219	7.0369
21	0.1987	10.0168	73.0629	5.0338	50.4229	0.0998	0.0198	7.2940
22	0.1839	10.2007	76.9257	5.4365	55.4568	0.0980	0.0180	7.5412
23	0.1703	10.3711	80.6726	5.8715	60.8933	0.0964	0.0164	7.7786
24	0.1577	10.5288	84.2997	6.3412	66.7648	0.0950	0.0150	8.0066
25	0.1460	10.6748	87.8041	6.8485	73.1059	0.0937	0.0137	8.2254
30	0.0994	11.2578	103.4558	10.0627	113.2832	0.0888	0.0088	9.1897
40	0.0460	11.9246	126.0422	21.7245	259.0565	0.0839	0.0039	10.5699
50	0.0213	12.2335	139.5928	46.9016	573.7702	0.0817	0.0017	11.4707
60	0.0099	12.3766	147.3000	101.2571	1,253.2133	0.0808	0.0008	11.9015
100	0.0005	12.4943	155.6107	2,199.7613	27,484.5157	0.0800		12.4545

i = 10.00%

n	P/F	P/A	P/G	F/P	F/A	A/P	A/F	A/G
1	0.9091	0.9091	0.0000	1.1000	1.0000	1.1000	1.0000	0.0000
2	0.8264	1.7355	0.8264	1.2100	2.1000	0.5762	0.4762	0.4762
3	0.7513	2.4869	2.3291	1.3310	3.3100	0.4021	0.3021	0.9366
4	0.6830	3.1699	4.3781	1.4641	4.6410	0.3155	0.2155	1.3812
5	0.6209	3.7908	6.8618	1.6105	6.1051	0.2638	0.1638	1.8101
6	0.5645	4.3553	9.6842	1.7716	7.7156	0.2296	0.1296	2.2236
7	0.5132	4.8684	12.7631	1.9487	9.4872	0.2054	0.1054	2.6216
8	0.4665	5.3349	16.0287	2.1436	11.4359	0.1874	0.0874	3.0045
9	0.4241	5.7590	19.4215	2.3579	13.5735	0.1736	0.0736	3.3724
10	0.3855	6.1446	22.8913	2.5937	15.9374	0.1627	0.0627	3.7255
11	0.3505	6.4951	26.3962	2.8531	18.5312	0.1540	0.0540	4.0641
12	0.3186	6.8137	29.9012	3.1384	21.3843	0.1468	0.0468	4.3884
13	0.2897	7.1034	33.3772	3.4523	24.5227	0.1408	0.0408	4.6988
14	0.2633	7.3667	36.8005	3.7975	27.9750	0.1357	0.0357	4.9955
15	0.2394	7.6061	40.1520	4.1772	31.7725	0.1315	0.0315	5.2789
16	0.2176	7.8237	43.4164	4.5950	35.9497	0.1278	0.0278	5.5493
17	0.1978	8.0216	46.5819	5.5045	40.5447	0.1247	0.0247	5.8071
18	0.1799	8.2014	49.6395	5.5599	45.5992	0.1219	0.0219	6.0526
19	0.1635	8.3649	52.5827	6.1159	51.1591	0.1195	0.0195	6.2861
20	0.1486	8.5136	55.4069	6.7275	57.2750	0.1175	0.0175	6.5081
21	0.1351	8.6487	58.1095	7.4002	64.0025	0.1156	0.0156	6.7189
22	0.1228	8.7715	60.6893	8.1403	71.4027	0.1140	0.0140	6.9189
23	0.1117	8.8832	63.1462	8.9543	79.5430	0.1126	0.0126	7.1085
24	0.1015	8.9847	65.4813	9.8497	88.4973	0.1113	0.0113	7.2881
25	0.0923	9.0770	67.6964	10.8347	98.3471	0.1102	0.0102	7.4580
30	0.0573	9.4269	77.0766	17.4494	164.4940	0.1061	0.0061	8.1762
40	0.0221	9.7791	88.9525	45.2593	442.5926	0.1023	0.0023	9.0962
50	0.0085	9.9148	94.8889	117.3909	1,163.9085	0.1009	0.0009	9.5704
60	0.0033	9.9672	97.7010	304.4816	3,034.8164	0.1003	0.0003	9.8023
100	0.0001	9.9993	99.9202	13,780.6123	137,796.1234	0.1000		9.9927

i = 12.00%

n	P/F	P/A	P/G	F/P	F/A	A/P	A/F	A/G
1	0.8929	0.8929	0.0000	1.1200	1.0000	1.1200	1.0000	0.0000
2	0.7972	1.6901	0.7972	1.2544	2.1200	0.5917	0.4717	0.4717
3	0.7118	2.4018	2.2208	1.4049	3.3744	0.4163	0.2963	0.9246
4	0.6355	3.0373	4.1273	1.5735	4.7793	0.3292	0.2092	1.3589
5	0.5674	3.6048	6.3970	1.7623	6.3528	0.2774	0.1574	1.7746
6	0.5066	4.1114	8.9302	1.9738	8.1152	0.2432	0.1232	2.1720
7	0.4523	4.5638	11.6443	2.2107	10.0890	0.2191	0.0991	2.5515
8	0.4039	4.9676	14.4714	2.4760	12.2997	0.2013	0.0813	2.9131
9	0.3606	5.3282	17.3563	2.7731	14.7757	0.1877	0.0677	3.2574
10	0.3220	5.6502	20.2541	3.1058	17.5487	0.1770	0.0570	3.5847
11	0.2875	5.9377	23.1288	3.4785	20.6546	0.1684	0.0484	3.8953
12	0.2567	6.1944	25.9523	3.8960	24.1331	0.1614	0.0414	4.1897
13	0.2292	6.4235	28.7024	4.3635	28.0291	0.1557	0.0357	4.4683
14	0.2046	6.6282	31.3624	4.8871	32.3926	0.1509	0.0309	4.7317
15	0.1827	6.8109	33.9202	5.4736	37.2797	0.1468	0.0268	4.9803
16	0.1631	6.9740	36.3670	6.1304	42.7533	0.1434	0.0234	5.2147
17	0.1456	7.1196	38.6973	6.8660	48.8837	0.1405	0.0205	5.4353
18	0.1300	7.2497	40.9080	7.6900	55.7497	0.1379	0.0179	5.6427
19	0.1161	7.3658	42.9979	8.6128	63.4397	0.1358	0.0158	5.8375
20	0.1037	7.4694	44.9676	9.6463	72.0524	0.1339	0.0139	6.0202
21	0.0926	7.5620	46.8188	10.8038	81.6987	0.1322	0.0122	6.1913
22	0.0826	7.6446	48.5543	12.1003	92.5026	0.1308	0.0108	6.3514
23	0.0738	7.7184	50.1776	13.5523	104.6029	0.1296	0.0096	6.5010
24	0.0659	7.7843	51.6929	15.1786	118.1552	0.1285	0.0085	6.6406
25	0.0588	7.8431	53.1046	17.0001	133.3339	0.1275	0.0075	6.7708
30	0.0334	8.0552	58.7821	29.9599	241.3327	0.1241	0.0041	7.2974
40	0.0107	8.2438	65.1159	93.0510	767.0914	0.1213	0.0013	7.8988
50	0.0035	8.3045	67.7624	289.0022	2,400.0182	0.1204	0.0004	8.1597
60	0.0011	8.3240	68.8100	897.5969	7,471.6411	0.1201	0.0001	8.2664
100	0.0000	8.3332	69.4336	83,522.2657	696,010.5477	0.1200	0.0000	8.3321

i = 18.00%

n	P/F	P/A	P/G	F/P	F/A	A/P	A/F	A/G
1	0.8475	0.8475	0.0000	1.1800	1.0000	1.1800	1.0000	0.0000
2	0.7182	1.5656	0.7182	1.3924	2.1800	0.6387	0.4587	0.4587
3	0.6086	2.1743	1.9354	1.6430	3.5724	0.4599	0.2799	0.8902
4	0.5158	2.6901	3.4828	1.9388	5.2154	0.3717	0.1917	1.2947
5	0.4371	3.1272	5.2312	2.2878	7.1542	0.3198	0.1398	1.6728
6	0.3704	3.4976	7.0834	2.6996	9.4423	0.2859	0.1059	2.0252
7	0.3139	3.8115	8.9670	3.1855	12.1415	0.2624	0.0824	2.3526
8	0.2660	4.0776	10.8292	3.7589	15.3270	0.2452	0.0652	2.6558
9	0.2255	4.3030	12.6329	4.4355	19.0859	0.2324	0.0524	2.9358
10	0.1911	4.4941	14.3525	5.2338	23.5213	0.2225	0.0425	3.1936
11	0.1619	4.6560	15.9716	6.1759	28.7551	0.2148	0.0348	3.4303
12	0.1372	4.7932	17.4811	7.2876	34.9311	0.2086	0.0286	3.6470
13	0.1163	4.9095	18.8765	8.5994	42.2187	0.2037	0.0237	3.8449
14	0.0985	5.0081	20.1576	10.1472	50.8180	0.1997	0.0197	4.0250
15	0.0835	5.0916	21.3269	11.9737	60.9653	0.1964	0.0164	4.1887
16	0.0708	5.1624	22.3885	14.1290	72.9390	0.1937	0.0137	4.3369

i = 18.00% (Continued)

n	*P/F*	*P/A*	*P/G*	*F/P*	*F/A*	*A/P*	*A/F*	*A/G*
17	0.0600	5.2223	23.3482	16.6722	87.0680	0.1915	0.0115	4.4708
18	0.0508	5.2732	24.2123	19.6731	103.7403	0.1896	0.0096	4.5916
19	0.0431	5.3162	24.9877	23.2144	123.4135	0.1881	0.0081	4.7003
20	0.0365	5.3527	25.6813	27.3930	146.6280	0.1868	0.0068	4.7978
21	0.0309	5.3837	26.3000	32.3238	174.0210	0.1857	0.0057	4.8851
22	0.0262	5.4099	26.8506	38.1421	206.3448	0.1848	0.0048	4.9632
23	0.0222	5.4321	27.3394	45.0076	244.4868	0.1841	0.0041	5.0329
24	0.0188	5.4509	27.7725	53.1090	289.4944	0.1835	0.0035	5.0950
25	0.0159	5.4669	28.1555	62.6686	342.6035	0.1829	0.0029	5.1502
30	0.0070	5.5168	29.4864	43.3706	790.9480	0.1813	0.0013	5.3448
40	0.0013	5.5482	30.5269	750.3783	4,163.2130	0.1802	0.0002	5.5022
50	0.0003	5.5541	30.7856	3,927.3569	1,813.0937	0.1800	0.0000	5.5428
60	0.0001	5.5553	30.8465	20,555.1400	114,189.6665	0.1800	0.0000	5.5526
100	0.0000	5.5556	30.8642	15,424,131.91	85,689,616.17	0.1800	0.0000	5.5555

5.14 References

The material in this chapter provides a brief overview of engineering economy in preparation for the FE exam. Candidates who have not had a formal course in this subject may wish to review in more detail by referring to one of the following textbooks:

Engineering Economy, 10th ed., DeGarmo, Sullivan, Bonadelli, and Wicks. Prentice-Hall, 1997. ISBN 0-13-382193-5.

Principles of Engineering Economic Analysis, 4th ed., White, Case, Pratt, and Agee. John Wiley, 1998. ISBN 0-471-11027-2.

Principles of Engineering Economy, 8th ed., Grant, Leavenworth, and Ireson. John Wiley, 1990. ISBN 0-471-63526-X.

PRACTICE PROBLEMS

1. Mr. Smith has taken a loan of $10,000 at an interest rate of 10% compounded annually, and plans to pay the money back in 20 equal installments, one each year.
   a. What should be the annual payment?
   (A) $1,200
   (B) $1,175
   (C) $1,320
   (D) $1,120
   b. What is the unpaid principal balance remaining after the eighteenth payment?
   (A) $11,751
   (B) $1,890
   (C) $2,050
   (D) $2,350
2. About how many years will be required for $10,000 invested at 5% per year compounded annually to double in value?
   (A) 5
   (B) 12
   (C) 15
   (D) 18
3. Mrs. DeMarco deposits $200 in a savings account at the beginning of each year. The account draws interest at 6% per year compounded annually. At the end of 15 years the value of the account will be
   (A) $4,230
   (B) $4,560
   (C) $4,982
   (D) $5,135
4. It is estimated that 50 acres of land will be required for future expansion 20 years after the construction of presently needed facilities. The purchase price of the land is $200 per acre at the present time. Uniform annual taxes are 2% of the purchase price. If money is worth 6% per year, what is the total future value in 20 years of the land and the tax payments?
   (A) $750 per acre
   (B) $788 per acre
   (C) $812 per acre
   (D) $852 per acre
5. A payment of $500 is made at the end of each of the next 12 years. What is the present worth of the payments at 6% interest compounded annually?
   (A) $3,973
   (B) $4,192
   (C) $4,281
   (D) $5,420
6. Let S be the future worth, P the principal invested, i the effective interest per compounding period, and n the number of compounding periods. In which of the following formulas are these quantities correctly related?
   (A) $S = P(1 + ni)$
   (B) $S = P(1 + ni)^{n-1}$
   (C) $S = P(1 + i)^n$
   (D) $S = P(1 + i)^{n-1}$
7. A company can manufacture a product with off-the-shelf hand tools. Fixed costs will be $1,000 for tools and $1.50 manufacturing cost per unit. As an alternative, an automated system will cost $15,000 with a $0.50 manufacturing cost per unit. With an annual anticipated volume of 5,000 units, the break-even point in years is
   (A) 2.0
   (B) 2.8
   (C) 3.6
   (D) 15.0
8. A sum of $400,000 is borrowed under an agreement to repay at the rate of $10,000 per month with interest on the unpaid balance compounding at 1% per month. If the first payment occurs at the end of the first month, the number of monthly repayments will be
   (A) 34
   (B) 40
   (C) 48
   (D) 52
9. Suppose that $10,000 is borrowed now at 15% interest per annum compounded annually. The first repayment of $3,000 is made 4 years from now. The amount that will then remain to be paid is
   (A) $7,000
   (B) $8,050
   (C) $13,000
   (D) $14,490
10. A machine is purchased for $20,000 and has an expected life of 7 years. At the end of 7 years, the salvage value is estimated to be $3,200. According to straight-line depreciation, what is the book value of the machine at the end of 4 years?
    (A) $8,000
    (B) $10,400
    (C) $12,800
    (D) $15,200
11. The maintenance costs associated with an investment are $2,000 per year for the first 10 years and $1,000 per year thereafter. The investment has an infinite life. With interest at 10% per annum, the present worth of the annual disbursements is most nearly
    (A) $14,000
    (B) $16,000
    (C) $18,000
    (D) $22,000

12. A small South American country experiences inflation of 20% per month. The effective annual inflation rate is
(A) 20%
(B) 240%
(C) 790%
(D) 2,400%

13. With interest of 8% per year compounded semiannually, the value of \$1,000 after 5 years is most nearly
(A) \$1,350
(B) \$1,400
(C) \$1,470
(D) \$1,480

14. A personal computer system costs \$18,000, and annual maintenance is \$900. After 3 years the salvage value of the system is \$3,000. If the interest rate is 8%, the equivalent uniform annual cost is
(A) \$6,960
(B) \$6,922
(C) \$7,288
(D) \$7,499

Answer Key

1. a. B
   b. C
2. B
3. D
4. B
5. B
6. C
7. B
8. D
9. D
10. B
11. B
12. C
13. D
14. A

Answers Explained

1. a. B

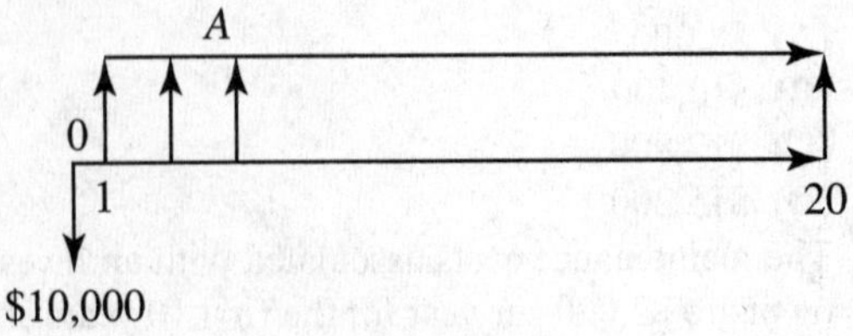

$A = \$10{,}000(A/P,\ 10\%,\ 20)$
$= \$10{,}000(0.1175) = \$1{,}175$
Annual payment = \$1,175

1. b. C

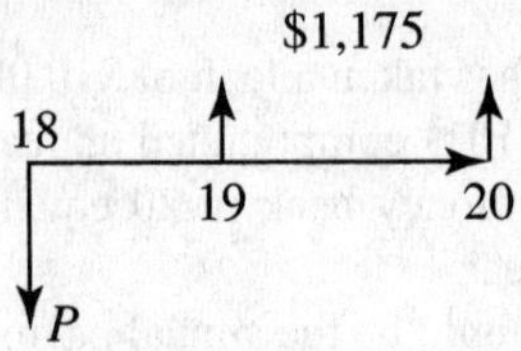

$P = \$1{,}175(P/A,\ 10\%,\ 2)$
$= \$1{,}175(1.736) = \$2{,}050$

2. B

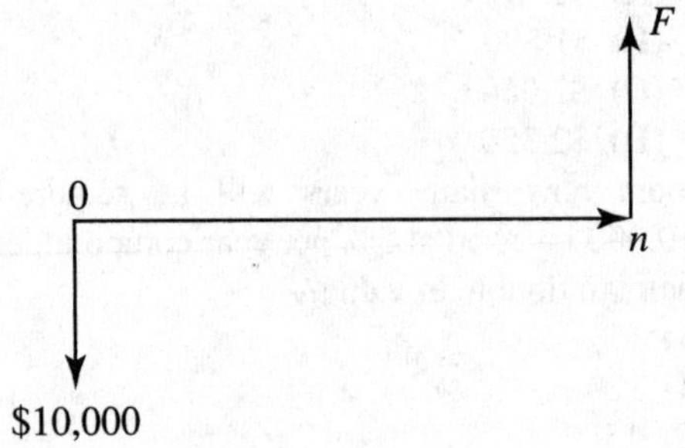

$F = \$10{,}000(F/P,\ 5\%,\ n)$
Answer is number where factor $(F/P,\ 6\%,\ n) = 2$.
Approx. 12 yr

3. D

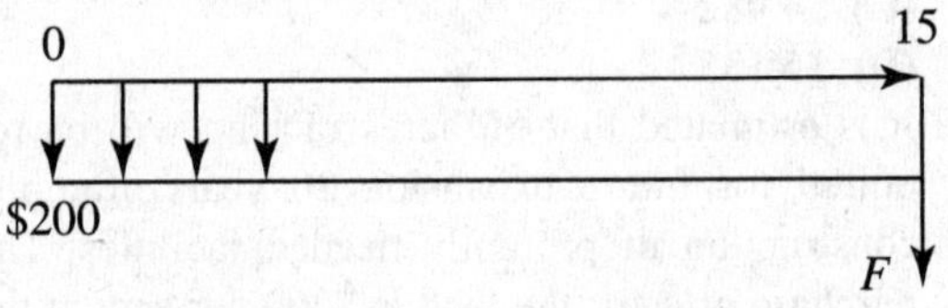

$F = \$200(F/A,\ 6\%,\ 15) + \$200(F/P,\ 6\%,\ 15)$
$= \$200(23.276) + \$200(2.3966)$
$= \$4{,}655.2 + \$479.3 = \$5{,}135$

4. B

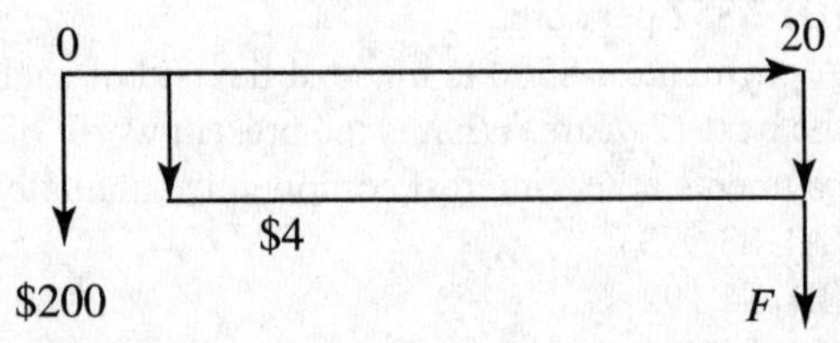

$F = \$200(F/P,\ 6\%,\ 20) + 4(F/A,\ 6\%,\ 20)$
$= \$200(3.207) + 4(36.786)$
$= \$788/\text{acre}$

5. B

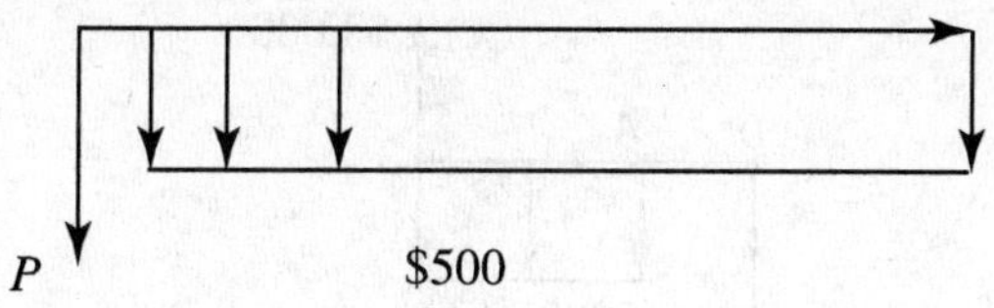

$P = \$500(P/A, 6\%, 12)$
$= \$500(8.3838) = \$4{,}192$

6. C

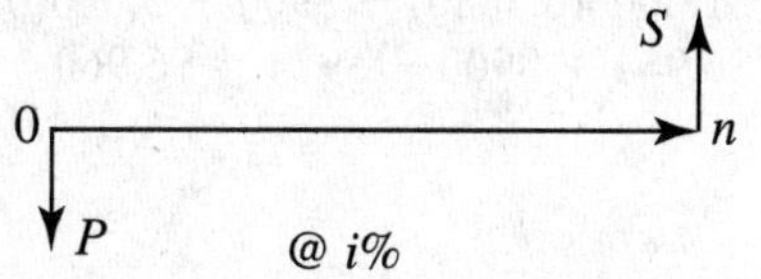

$S = P(1 + i)^n$

7. B

$\$1{,}000 + \$1.50x = \$0.50 + \$15{,}000$
$x = \$14{,}000$ @ 5,000/yr
$\$14{,}000/5{,}000 = 2.8$ yr

8. D

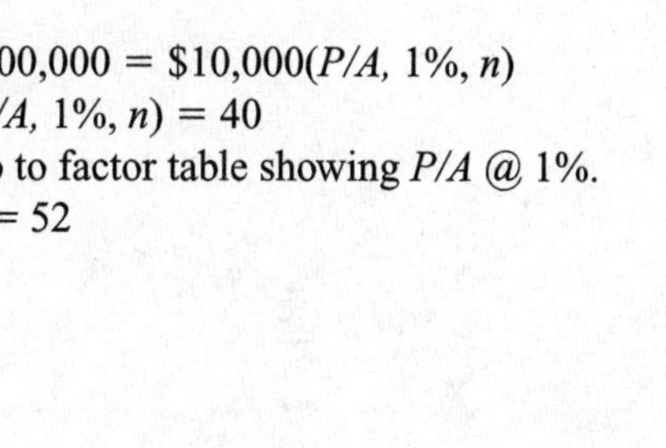

$\$400{,}000 = \$10{,}000(P/A, 1\%, n)$
$(P/A, 1\%, n) = 40$
Go to factor table showing P/A @ 1%.
$n = 52$

9. D

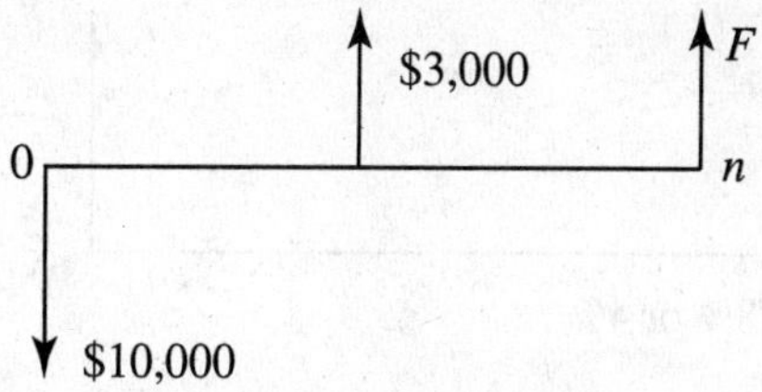

$F = \$10{,}000(F/P, 15\%, 4)$
$= \$10{,}000(1.749) = 17{,}490$
$- \; 3{,}000$
$\$14{,}490$

10. B

Year	*First Cost*	*Depreciation*	*Book Value*
1	$20,000	$2,400	$17,600
2	17,600	2,400	15,200
3	15,200	2,400	12,800
4	12,800	2,400	10,400

11. B

$P = \$2{,}000(P/A, 10\%, 10) + \$1{,}000$
$(P/A, 10, \infty)(P/F, 10, 10)$
$= \$2{,}000(6.1446) + \$1{,}000(10)(.3855)$
$= \$12{,}289 + \$3{,}855$
$= \$16{,}144$

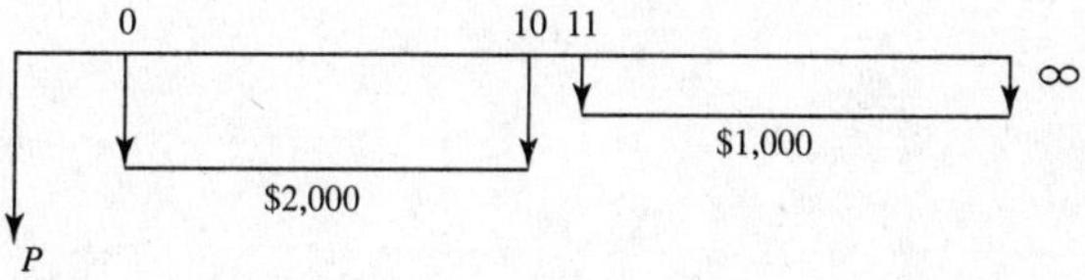

12. C

Effective inflation rate $= (1 + r/m)^m - 1$
$= (1 + 0.2)^{12} - 1 = 7.916$
$= 790\%$

13. D

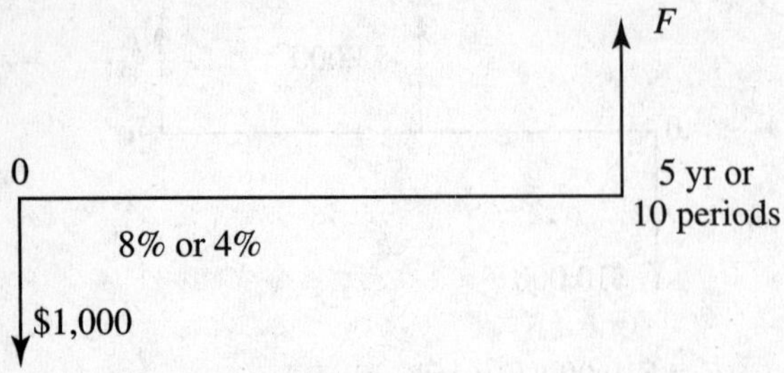

$$F = \$1{,}000(F/P, 4\%, 10)$$
$$= \$1{,}000(1.4802)$$
$$= \$1{,}480.20$$

14. A

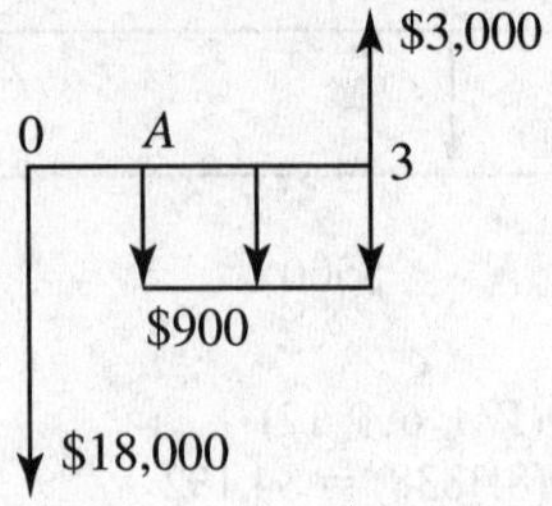

$$A = \$18{,}000(A/P, 8\%, 3) + \$900 - \$3{,}000(A/F, 8\%, 3)$$
$$= \$18{,}000(0.3880) + \$900 - 3{,}000(0.3080)$$
$$= \$6{,}984 + \$900 - \$924 = \$6{,}960$$

C H A P T E R

6 Ethics

Thomas E. Hulbert, PE

Introduction

Ethics, as defined by Webster's New World Dictionary, is the system or code of morals of a particular person, religion, group, or profession. Engineering, being a profession, has its own code of ethics adopted by the National Society of Professional Engineers (NSPE). All Professional Engineers are bound by this code.

6.1 Engineering and Ethics

All of the occupations known as professions require advanced education and training and involve intellectual skills. Traditionally, the professions have included law, medicine, theology, teaching, architecture, and engineering. For the most part, members of these professions are held in high esteem by the general public; they also have special responsibilities to the community. These professionals must keep their knowledge and skills current through continuing education, must participate in learned societies, must exercise professional judgment in their work, and must adhere to a professional code of ethics.

Seasoned members of a profession are best qualified to determine what training and what experience are necessary for new practitioners to enter their specific profession and its subspecialties. In this way the professions are self-regulating: professional boards and societies control the training and evaluation criteria by which new members are admitted and certified to practice. Once credentialed, however, professionals have independence in the workplace and are expected to exercise educated judgment.

Like all other professionals, engineers are highly trained and highly skilled, are bound by the licensing and ethical rules of their society, and exercise autonomy in the workplace. In addition, because the quality of engineering work can vitally affect public safety, engineers are often regulated by state statutes, which may include state codes of ethics as well.

The professional services of engineers are used by all levels of government, by independent agencies, by the developers of commercial projects, and by individuals. The work of engineers is crucial to the public welfare. Engineers influence public safety through their choices of siting, design, materials specification, and construction methods. To effectively serve the public, engineers must maintain a high level of current technical competence. They must follow the literature, attend lectures and classes, and participate in seminars to follow advances in their fields.

Technical expertise, however, does not guarantee appropriate service. Strict compliance with ethical guidelines is essential to public welfare. Unethical behavior is tantamount to professional incompetence. Engineers must, therefore, be honest and ethical in all their judgments and dealings.

6.2 NCEES Model Rules of Professional Conduct

A code of ethics is a set of guidelines, not a list of regulations. Behaving in an ethical manner is a matter of "doing what is right," not of rigidly following a set of specific rules. Thus, the engineering ethics code spells out the parameters of proper behavior for engineers when acting in their professional capacities. Basically, engineering ethics is universal ethics with specific reference to the demands on and the responsibilities of the professional engineer.

The National Council of Examiners for Engineering and Surveying (NCEES) has promulgated a set of "Model Rules of Professional Conduct." All engineers must know this code, understand it, and follow the guidance that it provides. You will find the code reproduced in the *NCEES FE Reference Handbook* at the exam. However, for purposes of the exam, as well as for your practice of engineering, knowledge of the code is not enough. You must be able to apply the principles of the code to practical problems and to unusual situations on the exam and in your professional life.

The Preamble

The Preamble, that is, the introduction, states the purpose of the code and briefly describes the model rules and the ways in which they must be applied.

- The "Model Rules of Professional Conduct" were developed to comply with one of the main purposes of state laws: to safeguard life, health, and property and to promote the public welfare. The rules simply translate this purpose of the state laws into a code for engineers. The rules are binding on all registered engineers and surveyors, who must maintain high standards of ethical and moral conduct.
- The practice of professional engineering is not a matter of right but is a privilege that must be earned. Once an engineer has, through training and registration, earned the privilege to practice the profession, he or she must perform services only in areas of his or her current competence and to the highest standards. The engineer must beware of false or boastful advertising and must be open, objective, and truthful in representation to the public.
- Conflict of interest is unethical.
- Unfair competition is unethical.

Obligations to Three Constituencies

According to the Model Rules of Professional Conduct, licensed professional engineers (the designating term is "registrants") have major obligations to three discrete constituencies in this order of importance: first to society; second to employers and clients; and third to other registrants.

I. Registrants' Obligations to Society

This section makes clear that public safety and public welfare are higher considerations than money making or meeting deadlines for clients or employers. It further requires registrants to be forthright in all their dealings with governmental authorities and with the public and to limit their professional activities to their areas of competence. It stresses that registrants must avoid conflicts of interest or the appearance of such conflicts.

a. Registrants bear responsibility for the public welfare during and as an outcome of the performance of their services. Even when they are engaged by clients, employers, or customers, first consideration is to public safety and the public welfare.

b. Registrants must think beyond the requirements of a specific project toward the long-term health and welfare of the public. For example: when any number of materials might meet the needs of a particular enterprise and even exceed safety standards for the job, the engineer should be mindful of long-term welfare and should give adequate consideration to using recycled or recyclable materials if available and equally applicable.

c. If a client or employer overrules an engineer's professional judgment in a manner that adversely affects the public's life, health, welfare, or property, the engineer must report the action to the authorities. The registrant must safeguard the public even if such action displeases the hiring body. Safety takes precedence over cost cutting; and if the engineer's professional judgment cannot prevail, he or she must "blow the whistle."

d. Registrants often find that they must submit professional reports or statements or give testimony at civil trials. These reports, statements, and testimonies must be complete, objective, and honest, including all relevant and pertinent information of which the registrant is aware.

e. Engineers are often asked for their professional opinions with regard to various proposals, projects, and actions. They must refrain from expressing public opinions unless they have adequate knowledge of all the facts, are competent in the particular field under question, and have completely evaluated the subject matter.

f. "Registrants shall issue no statements, criticisms, or arguments on technical matters which are inspired or paid for by interested parties, unless they explicitly identify the interested parties on whose behalf they are speaking and reveal any interest they have in the matters." The effect of this rule is to prohibit the giving of "paid endorsements" unless the engineer clearly identifies the sponsor.

g. Registrants must deal only with honest, ethical individuals and firms. Engineers must be careful to avoid associating their names with persons or businesses of unsavory or even dubious reputation.

h. If a registrant has reason to suspect another engineer or firm of violation of any one of these rules, the registrant is required to notify the state board and, if requested, to assist the board in making its determination of violation.

II. Registrants' Obligations to Employers and Clients

This section emphasizes that registrants should provide services and advice only in areas in which they are completely competent. A second theme in this section is a requirement for confidentiality on the part of registrants. Finally, the section returns to the need for avoiding conflicts of interest or even the appearance of such conflicts and urges full disclosure of all contacts that may imply conflict of interest.

a. The first statement in this section is so obvious that it needs no explanation. It reads in its entirety: "Registrants shall undertake assignments only when qualified by education or experience in the specific technical fields of engineering or land surveying involved."

b. Beyond not taking on assignments for which they are not fully qualified, registrants must not approve any plans or documents that deal with subject matter beyond their areas of competence. Furthermore, they must not sign or seal any plans or documents not prepared under their direct control and personal supervision, even if they are fully competent to do so. Registrants must sign and seal only work for which they can honestly assume responsibility.

c. While registrants may not approve plans drawn by engineers not under their supervision, they may assume coordination of entire projects in which each design segment is signed and sealed by a fully competent engineer who has been responsible for preparation of that design segment.

d. Like all other professionals, engineers must maintain confidentiality in their relationships with clients. Information given about a project is privileged information. A registrant must obtain prior consent from a client or employer before disclosing any data or other information about a project.

e. Obviously, registrants should not accept bribes. Furthermore, engineers must not accept gifts, money, or promises of future benefits from contractors or contractors' agents or from anyone else in a position to influence purchases, awards, or special treatment from these individuals. Even if the registrant would not be influenced by such gifts, the appearance of impropriety or conflict of interest would damage confidence.

f. "Full prior disclosure" is a phrase to keep in mind for the purpose of avoiding misunderstandings and misinterpretations. If there is any possibility of a potential conflict of interest or any circumstance that might appear to influence a registrant's judgment or quality of service, the registrant should tell the employer or client in advance. Full prior disclosure is a sure means for maintaining trust.

g. A general rule of thumb is that one cannot serve two masters. The application of the rule is that a registrant should not be paid by two parties for services with regard to the same project unless all parties know of and agree to the arrangement.

h. While it is possible for a registrant to work for more than one private party to the same project if all parties agree (as provided in rule g), this arrangement is absolutely prohibited if one of the parties is a governmental body. Because this rule is strictly enforced, you must familiarize yourself with its precise language. In its entirety the rule states: "Registrants shall not solicit or accept a professional contract from a governmental body on which a principal or officer of their organization serves as a member. Conversely, registrants serving as members, advisors, or employees of a governmental body or department, who are the principals or employees of a private concern, shall not participate in decisions with respect to professional services offered or provided by said concern to the governmental body which they serve."

III. Registrants' Obligations to Other Registrants

This section prohibits false advertising, bribery, and influence peddling, and damaging the reputation of other registrants.

a. Registrants must not brag or inflate their importance when soliciting or bidding for contracts. They must describe their qualifications accurately and state all aspects of previous experience and assignments clearly. In competing for commissions, registrants must not overstate their credentials to the detriment of the competition.

b. Gaining assignments through bribery is also a form of unfair competition. The rule is very specific in prohibiting political contributions for the purpose of influencing the granting of contracts.

c. Finally, innuendo or slander to denigrate a competitor is unprofessional and unethical. This final rule brings us back full circle to our original statement that engineering ethics is ethics with specific reference to engineering situations. You should recognize this rule as: "Thou shalt not bear false witness against thy neighbor."

6.3 Resources for Engineering Ethics

You will find that the World Wide Web is an excellent resource in your preparation for ethics problems on your exam. The rules are easy to understand; their application to real situations, however, may be ambiguous. The NSPE's Board of Ethical Review maintains a website at www.nspe.org. This website features numerous ethics case studies published by the board. The "ethics" button at the NSPE website offers links to the websites of Case Western Reserve University's Ethics Center, the National Institute for Engineering Ethics, and Texas A&M University ethics case studies. As you study previous cases and their determinations, you will develop skill in analyzing and solving problems on your own.

6.4 Problem-Solving Strategy for the FE/EIT Exam

The problems on the FE/EIT Exam reflect the problems an engineer faces in real life. On the surface, the rules of ethics seem clear. In practice, however, you will often find that circumstances do not fit neatly into a category, that words can be interpreted in more than one way, or that the facts of a case are not complete or may even be in conflict. In addition, it is not always easy to identify the greatest good.

The exam problems seek to determine how well you might analyze and solve actual problems that could arise in your work as an engineer.

Here is how you should approach the exam problems:

- Read the entire problem. Reread. Be sure you understand the facts and the question.
- Eliminate any choices that are obviously ridiculous or clearly unethical.
- Pay particular attention to the following: conflict of interest issues, contract or agreement disputes as governed by the code, and accuracy and proper representation of individual and professional information.

Now try the typical questions presented in Examples 6.1 and 6.2.

Example 6.1

An engineer who enjoys a fine reputation for his many years of work in modernizing and reconfiguring large public buildings and who is currently engaged in conversion of an old school into a condominium is asked by a neighbor to renovate her 80-year-old, 12-room colonial. The engineer should

A. hire workers experienced in home renovation and sign a contract with her to complete the job

B. sign a contract with the neighbor, explaining that his experience is with larger projects

C. turn down the job

D. sign a contract only if he is certain that the neighbor understands that he must devote most of his time to the larger project

Solution:

Consider the choices:

A. is not permitted. An engineer must be personally competent to oversee the job. Workers are not licensed to sign off on plans or product.

B. is not a good choice. Full disclosure of incompetence is not an option under the code.

C. is what the engineer must do. He must not accept an assignment for which he is not competent.

D. introduces a twist on conflict of interest —in this case, a conflict of time. The engineer has first responsibility to the client for whom he is already working.

Example 6.2

You are the engineer responsible for the design and installation of plumbing in a new public elementary school under construction. The project is running behind schedule and above budget. The latest catch is that the supplier has not delivered the specified backflow preventers. Although a strike at the manufacturer's plant has been settled, the backorder list is moving slowly. The engineer serving as coordinator of the project orders you to obtain less expensive backflow preventers that are readily available from another manufacturer. These backflow preventers are of lesser quality than those specified in the plans, have a history of occasional failure, and are likely to need earlier replacement. You should

A. order and install the available backflow preventers, but refuse to sign off on this portion of the job

B. order and install the available backflow preventers, informing the school board that this equipment may not last as long but will help the project stay on schedule and closer to budget

C. order and install the available backflow preventers and say nothing to the school board

D. wait for the specified backflow preventers and explain your action to the school board

Solution:

Again consider the choices:

A. may seem like a good course of action, but is not. If you are in charge of this segment of the job, you are responsible. If you order and install the backflow preventers, you must sign off. But these backflow preventers may fail and may contaminate the school's drinking water. Obviously, the health and safety of the schoolchildren are more important than the schedule or the budget.

B. is a copout. Full disclosure that the health and safety of the public may be jeopardized by your action is not an option; it is an ethical requirement.

C. is an obviously unethical action.

D. is the ethical course. Your coordinating engineer may be hard on you for a while. Health and safety, however, are your first considerations. The school board should appreciate your responsible choice.

6.5 Summary

The three major sections of the Model Rules of Professional Conduct address the three primary obligations of the engineer:

1. Obligation to society.
2. Obligation to employers and clients.
3. Obligation to other registrants.

The principles articulated in these sections define the appropriate behavior of professional engineers. While the meaning of the code is clear, questions may arise concerning its application to specific situations.

Therefore, in real life, you may have to make judgment calls. "Does this token gift from a prospective contractor constitute the appearance of undue influence?" "Is my expertise on this particular building material adequate for me to serve as a witness in a liability case?" "How do I weigh the risks against the benefits of a certain course of action?" "For this situation is the safety versus economics tradeoff an ethical one?"

On the exam, you will be asked questions to prove that you know the provisions of the code and that you can solve ethical problems that arise in the workplace.

PRACTICE PROBLEMS

1. What is the best word to complete the following sentence: "Engineers are to uphold the health, safety, and public ____________"?
   (A) trust
   (B) good
   (C) confidence
   (D) welfare
2. The order of ranking of ethical responsibility of the professional engineer, from highest to lowest importance, is
   (A) society as a whole, the client, the profession, oneself
   (B) oneself, the client, society as a whole, the profession
   (C) oneself, the client, the profession, society as a whole
   (D) the client, society as a whole, the profession, oneself
3. An engineer employed at a large manufacturing company has been involved in developing a new production technique. After several years, she decides to leave and to establish her own consulting practice. A competitor of her former employer contacts her and requests that she solve a similar manufacturing problem. All indications are that the original design she developed for her previous employer is also the best solution for the competitor. Can the engineer accept the assignment?
   (A) Yes, provided that she left her previous employer with no written nondisclosure agreement
   (B) No; information from the original employer would have to be used in the new design
   (C) Yes; consulting engineers work for competing companies and transfer of knowledge naturally occurs
   (D) No; this would constitute accepting money more than once for the same project
4. An engineer working for a large consulting firm has decided to establish his own business. Although the new business is several months from start-up, the engineer should
   (A) approach current colleagues to tell them of his new plans
   (B) discuss his plans with his current supervisor
   (C) resign immediately
   (D) start developing promotional literature while he has use of his current employer's computers
5. An engineer employed by a Big Three auto maker is responsible for redesigning the steering system. While working on the new design, she discovers a defect in the steering system currently in production. After a thorough statistical analysis, she concludes that the defect might contribute to fatalities. She should
   (A) first inform the company of the defect and then notify the National Transportation Safety Board to initiate an inquiry
   (B) send an anonymous tip to the consumer "hot line" on a national radio network
   (C) continue to follow the company policy of selecting the most cost-effective design
   (D) inform her supervisor and resign from the company if it does not implement a new design
6. An engineering firm is hired to develop plans for an office/retail complex. Prior to the bid date, several contractors ask the engineers for details about the plans and the project. The firm
   (A) cannot reveal information about the project that might prejudice any contractor against bidding on the job
   (B) should provide information to bidders in whom it has confidence to complete the contract
   (C) cannot reveal data or information, without consent of the client, unless required by law specifically to do so
   (D) can supply the requested information as long as it is accurate
7. The principal in an 18-month-old engineering firm has developed a promotional brochure for the firm. The brochure contains a "list of clients," implying that companies on the list are clients of the firm, and a "list of projects of the firm," implying that these projects were performed by the firm. All of the engineers have come from other firms. In fact, the client list is actually a list of the companies at which the engineers were previously employed. Similarly, the project list is a list of the projects performed by the firm's engineers at their previous places of employment. It is
   (A) unethical to produce a promotional brochure in which the new firm claims for itself projects done by its engineers at their former firms and claims their former firms as clients
   (B) acceptable to publish such lists since long-established business relationships exist among engineering firms, engineers, and their clients
   (C) ethical to take credit for projects performed by another firm or group of engineers so long as they are now members of the new firm
   (D) not misleading to refer to "projects of the firm" in the new firm's brochure because they were, after all, projects of the firm's members

8. A licensed professional engineer and land surveyor works 35 hours per week on a flex-time basis for a state governmental agency. In addition, he is associated with XYZ Engineering and Surveying as the PE in charge. He spends about 20 hours per week supervising engineering services at the firm plus an additional 12 hours of work on the weekends and is available for consultation 24 hours a day. XYZ has granted him 10% of the shares of the stock in the firm, and he receives 5% of the gross billings for his seal as extra compensation for taking charge of engineering. This agreement is contingent on the understanding that, if any of the three principals of XYZ becomes licensed as a PE, the agreement will become void, and the engineer will return the stock. Both organizations—the state governmental agency and XYZ—are aware that he is a dual employee and have no objections. If this arrangement comes to the attention of the Board of Ethical Review, the board will determine that
   (A) a flexible schedule is not sufficient grounds for dual employment
   (B) the engineer is stretching the role of responsible charge and cannot assume this role for two employers
   (C) it is acceptable and ethical to be involved with both the state governmental agency and XYZ Engineering and Surveying in the manner described
   (D) the engineer cannot work for a government agency and a private organization at the same time

Answer Key

1. D	5. A
2. A	6. C
3. B	7. A
4. B	8. C

Answers Explained

1. **D** The public good and the public welfare are practically synonymous; but since "public welfare is the term used in the Model Rules, it is the better choice.
2. **A** The code stresses that the order of responsibility is to society as a whole, the client or customer, and then to professional colleagues. The code makes no mention of self-interest. Obviously, then, that must come last.
3. **B** The code is very specific: "Registrants shall not reveal facts, data, or information obtained in a professional capacity. . . ." Even without a written nondisclosure agreement, the engineer is bound to maintain confidentiality.
4. **B** The code requires full disclosure and frankness with regard to possible future conflicts of interest. Current colleagues may be the second to know. There is no reason for the engineer to leave the job before the new business is in place so long as he does not use his current position as a springboard for lining up his own clients. Choice (D) represents a dishonest use of the employer's facilities and a form of unfair competition.
5. **A** Safety must come first. The engineer is required to report unsafe practices to the authorities. No company wants to expose itself to product liability lawsuits; but when an expensive recall might be involved, the company might well attempt to discount an alert engineer's fears. The engineer must first alert the company to the problem and cooperate in trying to find a solution consistent with maintaining the public welfare. However, if the company resists taking appropriate measures, the engineer must "blow the whistle."
6. **C** Choice (D) looks good, but (C) meets the confidentiality requirement. Both (A) and (B) additionally violate the requirement for fair dealing among contractors.
7. **A** Despite the mitigating language in some other choices, it should be obvious that (A) is the correct choice. The brochure constitutes false advertising at its worst.
8. **C** The problem does not say that XYZ Engineering and Surveying is doing any work for the state governmental agency, so there is no question of conflict of interest here. The engineer has two part-time jobs, which do not involve the same project, and both employers have agreed that this situation is acceptable.

C H A P T E R

7

Fluid Mechanics

Mohamad Metghalchi, Sc.D.

Robert M. Scott

Introduction

Fluid mechanics is the study of the changes that occur in a fluid that is subjected to forces. There are two major divisions within the field of fluid mechanics: fluid statics and fluid dynamics. **Fluid statics** is the study of the state of a fluid subjected to balanced forces such that the fluid remains in an equilibrium condition. **Fluid dynamics** is the study of fluid in motion and the interactions of the fluid with the objects it may encounter.

7.1 Definitions

As with any other field of study, fluid mechanics has a vocabulary of terms that must be understood before the basic principles can be introduced.

What Is a Fluid?

A **fluid** is a substance that will deform *continuously* when a shear stress is applied to it, no matter how small the shear stress is. A substance in a liquid or vapor phase is a fluid.

Control Volume

All of the principles of fluid mechanics are defined in relation to a control volume. The **control volume** is an arbitrary region in space defined by its boundaries, which may be stationary or moving. In general, material may cross a boundary of the control volume. Though the boundaries of a control volume are completely arbitrary, when possible they are chosen in a way that simplifies analysis.

Stress

The forces that act upon a fluid may be categorized as either body forces or surface forces. *Body forces* are forces that act on all fluid particles within the fluid and occur without physical contact. Examples include electromagnetic and gravitational forces. *Surface forces* are forces that are applied directly to the surface of the fluid through physical contact.

The total force per unit area acting on the fluid at any point within its volume is an important parameter, and has been given the name stress. The **stress** at any point P is defined as follows:

$$\sigma(P) = \lim_{\delta A \to 0} \frac{\delta \mathbf{F}}{\delta \mathbf{A}} \qquad [7.1]$$

where $\sigma(P)$ = the vector stress at point P,
$\delta\mathbf{A}$ = an infinitesimal area at point P,
$\delta\mathbf{F}$ = the force acting on infinitesimal area $\delta\mathbf{A}$.

Both the area and the force in equation 7.1 are vector quantities; that is, they have magnitude and direction. These quantities are usually expressed by three components with respect to some coordinate system.

In general, to describe the stress of a fluid at any point with respect to a coordinate system, nine components are required. For convenience, stress is often expressed in terms of two vector components, in relation to the differential area ($\delta\mathbf{A}$). The component normal (or perpendicular) to $\delta\mathbf{A}$ is the normal stress (σ_n), and the component along $\delta\mathbf{A}$ is the shear stress (τ).

In a stationary fluid, the normal stress is the fluid pressure, whose magnitude is independent of the direction of the differential area used. The shear stress is related to fluid motion.

7.2 Fluid Properties

The **fluid properties** are the fluid characteristics whose values are used to predict the reaction of a fluid that is subjected to applied forces. The list that follows does not include all the possible fluid properties, but it defines the terms used throughout this chapter.

Velocity

Velocity is the time rate of change of the position of a fluid particle. The velocity of a fluid is a vector field quantity. For each point within the volume that makes up the fluid, a value can be assigned to the magnitude and direction of the fluid velocity. The velocity of a fluid will appear in three forms throughout this chapter. These forms are as follows:

- Velocity ($\mathbf{V}$) = the vector quantity of fluid velocity at a given point in the fluid. Both magnitude and direction are associated with this quantity.
- Speed (V) = the magnitude of the vector velocity at a given point in the fluid.
- Average speed ($\bar{V}$) = the average fluid speed through a surface of a control volume.

Mach Number

The **Mach number** (M_a) is a dimensionless parameter used to describe fluid speed. It is defined as the ratio of fluid speed to the speed of sound:

$$M_a = \frac{V}{c} \qquad [7.2]$$

where M_a = Mach number (dimensionless),
V = fluid speed (ft/sec or m/s),
c = speed of sound (ft/sec or m/s).

For a perfect gas, the speed of sound is defined as

$$c = \sqrt{kRT} \qquad [7.3]$$

where c = speed of sound (ft/sec or m/s),
k = specific heat ratio (c_p/c_v),
R = gas constant (ft-lbf/lb mole-°R or kJ/kg · K),
T = absolute temperature of the gas (K or °R).

In equation 7.3:

$$R = \frac{\bar{R}}{M} \qquad [7.4]$$

where $\bar{R}$ = universal gas constant:
= 1,545 ft-lbf/lb mole-°R,
= 8.314 kJ/(mol · K),
M = molecular weight of the gas.

Example 7.1

What is the Mach number of a jet of oxygen gas at standard conditions (1 atm and 25°C) with a speed of 450 m/s? (Assume that for oxygen k = 1.40 and R = 0.260 kJ/kg · K.)

Solution:

Oxygen at standard condition can be modeled as a perfect gas; therefore, from equation 7.3, the speed of sound is as follows:

$$c = \sqrt{kRT}$$

$$= \sqrt{(1.40)\left(0.260\frac{\text{kj}}{\text{kg}\cdot\text{K}}\right)[(25+273)\text{K}]\left(\frac{1{,}000\ \text{N}\cdot\text{m}}{\text{kJ}}\right)\left(\frac{\frac{\text{kg}\cdot\text{m}}{\text{s}^2}}{\text{N}}\right)}$$

$$= 329.35\ \text{m/s}$$

Now determine the Mach number directly from equation 7.2:

$$M_a = \frac{V}{c}$$

$$= \frac{450 \text{ m/s}}{329.35 \text{ m/s}}$$

$$= 1.37$$

Acceleration

Acceleration is the time rate of change in the velocity of a fluid particle. Acceleration is also a vector field quantity, and can act to change either the magnitude or the direction of the velocity.

Pressure

There are two reference values for pressure to which all other values of pressure are related. **Gage pressure** is defined in reference to the ambient atmospheric pressure, and **absolute pressure** is defined in reference to true zero pressure. The two values for pressure are related by the equation:

$$p_a = p_g + p_{atm} \quad [7.5]$$

where p_a = absolute pressure (lbf/in^2 = psia or N/m^2 = kPa),
p_g = gage pressure (lbf/in^2 = psig or N/m^2 = kPa),
p_{atm} = ambient atmospheric pressure:
= 14.696 psia or 101.3 kPa at standard sea-level conditions.

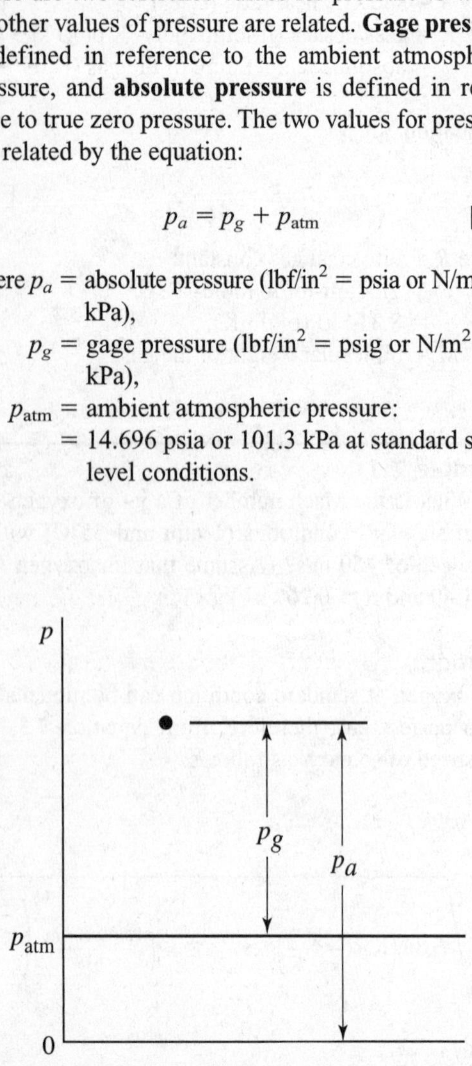

Figure 7.1 Definition of gage pressure.

Example 7.2

What will a pressure gauge read if the fluid in a vessel is at 200 psia? (Assume that the vessel is in an environment at standard sea-level pressure.)

Solution:

From equation 7.5:

$$p_g = p_a - p_{atm}$$
$$= 200 \text{ psi} - 14.7 \text{ psi}$$
$$= 185.3 \text{ psig}$$

Density

The **density** of a fluid (ρ) is the mass contained in one unit of volume. The density of a fluid at a given location is expressed as

$$\rho = \lim_{\Delta V \to 0} \left(\frac{\Delta m}{\Delta V} \right) \quad [7.6]$$

where ρ = fluid density (lbm/ft^3 or kg/m^3),
Δm = mass contained in infinitesimal volume ΔV (lbm or kg),
ΔV = infinitesimal volume (ft^3 or m^3).

Analysis of fluid systems is often simplified by assuming that the density is the same for every point within the volume of the fluid, as in incompressible flow analysis.

Specific Volume

The **specific volume** of a fluid (v) is the volume of space occupied by a unit mass of the fluid. It is the reciprocal of the density and is expressed as:

$$v = \frac{1}{\rho} \quad [7.7]$$

where v = specific volume ($\text{ft}^3\text{/lbm}$ or $\text{m}^3\text{/kg}$).

Specific Weight

The **specific weight** (γ) of a fluid is defined as the weight of a unit volume of fluid. It is related to the fluid density as follows:

$$\gamma = \rho g \quad [7.8]$$

where γ = specific weight (lbf/ft^3 or N/m^3),
g = acceleration due to gravity:
= 32.17 ft/sec^2 or 9.81 m/s^2 at sea level.

Specific Gravity

Specific gravity is a dimensionless expression for the density of a fluid. Its value is the ratio of the fluid density to the density of liquid water at 4°C:

$$SG = \frac{\rho}{\rho_{water}} = \frac{\gamma}{\gamma_{water}} \quad [7.9]$$

where $\rho_{water} = 1{,}000\ \text{kg/m}^3$,
$= 62.4\ \text{lbm/ft}^3$,
$\gamma_{water} = 9{,}810\ \text{N/m}^3$,
$= 62.4\ \text{lbf/ft}^3$.

Example 7.3

What is the density of an oil if its specific gravity is 0.86?

Solution:

From equation 7.9:

$$\rho = (SG)(\rho_{water})$$
$$= (0.86)(62.4\ \text{lbm/ft}^3)$$
$$= 53.7\ \text{lbm/ft}^3$$

Viscosity

When a shear force is applied to a fluid, fluid motion will occur. The magnitude of the fluid velocity is related to the magnitude of the shear stress. For most common fluids the shear stress within the fluid is directly proportional to the velocity gradient. **Viscosity** (μ) is the name given to the proportionality constant:

$$\tau_n(P) = \mu \frac{\partial \mathbf{V}}{\partial x_n} \quad [7.10]$$

where $\tau_n(P)$ = shear stress on a differential area normal to direction n,
μ = fluid viscosity (described below),
$\frac{\partial \mathbf{V}}{\partial x_n}$ = velocity gradient in direction n.

Fluids of this type are called *Newtonian fluids.* It should be recognized from equation 7.10 that, for a given shear stress, as the viscosity of a fluid increases, the magnitude of the velocity gradient decreases.

There are many fluids, such as toothpaste, blood, and many paints, that cannot be classified as Newtonian fluids. For many non-Newtonian fluids the shear stress can be related to the velocity gradient of the fluid through a power law relationship. Two examples of such non-Newtonian fluids are *psuedoplastic* fluids, for which the viscosity decreases as the velocity gradient increases, and *dilitant* fluids, for which the viscosity increases as the velocity gradient increases.

For a power law (non-Newtonian) fluid:

$$\tau_t(P) = K\left(\frac{\partial \mathbf{V}}{\partial \mathbf{X_i}}\right)^n \quad [7.11]$$

where K = consistency index,
n = power law index: $n < 1$ for a psuedoplastic fluid, $n > 1$ for a dilatant fluid.

Surface Tension

At the surface of any fluid, there is a force that tends to hold the surface together. This force is called the **surface tension** of the fluid, which is defined as the tensile force between two points on the surface of the fluid, per unit length of distance between the two points:

$$\sigma = \frac{F}{L} \quad [7.12]$$

where σ = surface tension,
F = force along the fluid surface,
L = length of the fluid surface.

Capillarity

Capillary action or **capillarity** is observed as the change in shape of a fluid's free surface when in contact with a solid wall. It is a result of the interaction of the surface tension and the general cohesive forces between the molecules of the liquid.

The curved fluid surface that generally forms as a result of capillary action is called a *meniscus,* shown in Figure 7.2(a). If the area of a free surface is large, then, rather than forming a complete meniscus, the edges of the surface will be curved as shown in Figures 7.2(b) and (c). Whether or not the surface forms a complete meniscus, the slope of the curve at the wall of the tube is called the *angle of contact,* (β). The angle of contact is an indication of the relationship between the surface tension and the cohesive forces of the liquid. If the angle is less than 90°, as in Figure 7.2(b), the surface tension is stronger than the cohesive forces; if the angle is greater than 90°, as in Figure 7.2(c), the cohesive forces are stronger than the surface tension.

When a small-diameter tube is placed in a fluid for which the surface tension is stronger than the molecular cohesive forces, the fluid level inside the tube will rise a certain distance, as shown in Figure 7.2(a). The height of this column is given by these equations:

$$h = \frac{4\sigma \cos \beta}{\rho d g} \quad [7.13]$$

and

$$h = \frac{4\sigma \cos \beta}{\gamma d} \quad [7.14]$$

where h and d are as shown in Figure 7.2(a).

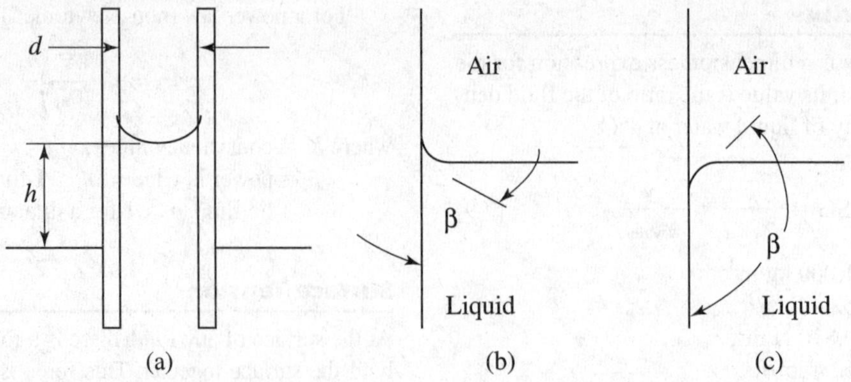

Figure 7.2 Illustration of a meniscus. (a) Meniscus in a small tube. (b) Surface tension dominates cohesive forces. (c) Cohesive forces dominate surface tension.

7.3 Fluid Statics

Fluid statics is the study of fluid systems with no fluid motion. The primary challenge of fluid statics is to determine the pressure distribution within a fluid.

Hydrostatic Pressure

When a fluid is not moving, the stress acting on each fluid particle becomes independent of the direction from which it is evaluated. In other words, for stress as defined in equation 7.1, the stress in a stationary fluid at some point has some value that is the same no matter in what direction the differential area (δA) is taken. This value is the **hydrostatic pressure** of the fluid at that point.

The hydrostatic pressure of a fluid is a function of height within the volume, regardless of the shape of the container. This is due to the fact that, at any point in a fluid, the fluid must support the weight of the fluid above it. For any two locations at the same height, the hydrostatic pressure will be the same. This is the principle behind the operation of two devices used to measure hydrostatic pressure, manometers and barometers.

For the control volume shown in Figure 7.3, the hydrostatic pressure at point B in the fluid is given by the equations:

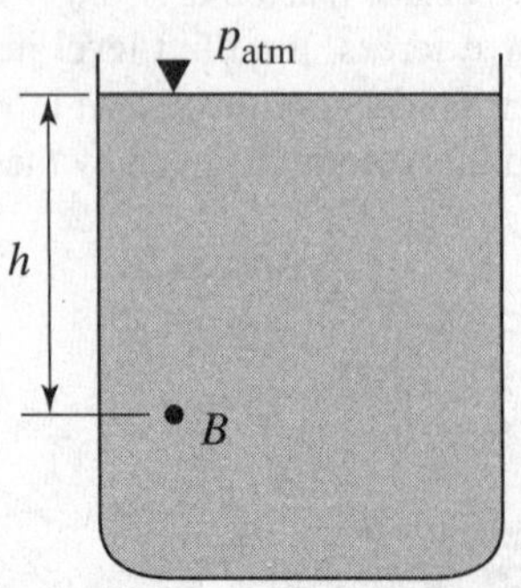

Figure 7.3 Hydrostatic pressure at point B.

$$p_g = \rho g h \quad \text{or} \quad p_g = \gamma h \qquad [7.15]$$

and

$$p_a = p_{atm} + \rho g h \qquad [7.16]$$

Example 7.4

The two vessels shown in the accompanying figure are filled with water ($\rho = 62.4$ lbm/ft^3). What is the hydrostatic pressure in each container at points A and B 2 feet below the surface of the water?

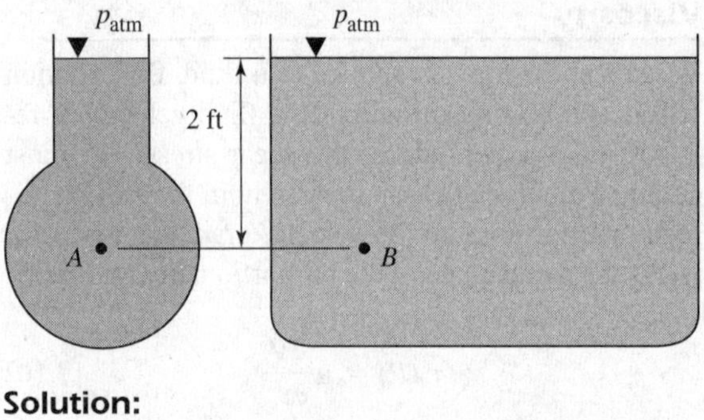

Solution:

Since the hydrostatic pressure in a fluid is a function of its depth only and is independent of the shape of the container, the pressure at point A will equal the pressure at point B.

From equation 7.15:

$$p_g = \rho g h$$

$$= \left(62.4\frac{\text{lbm}}{\text{ft}^3}\right)\left(32.17\frac{\text{ft}}{\text{sec}^2}\right) \times (2\text{ ft})\left(\frac{\text{ft}^2}{144\text{ in}^2}\right)\left(\frac{\text{lbf}}{32.17\frac{\text{lbm ft}}{\text{sec}^2}}\right)$$

$$= 0.866\text{ lbf/in}^2 = 0.866\text{ psig}$$

The term $\left(\frac{\text{lbf}}{32.17\frac{\text{lbm ft}}{\text{sec}^2}}\right)$ in the above solution represents a unit conversion between pounds mass and pounds feet. This is the inverse of the quantity g_c.

Manometry

A **manometer,** illustrated in Figure 7.4, is a device used to measure a pressure difference. It consists of a U-shaped tube with each end open to one of the two environments whose pressure we wish to compare.

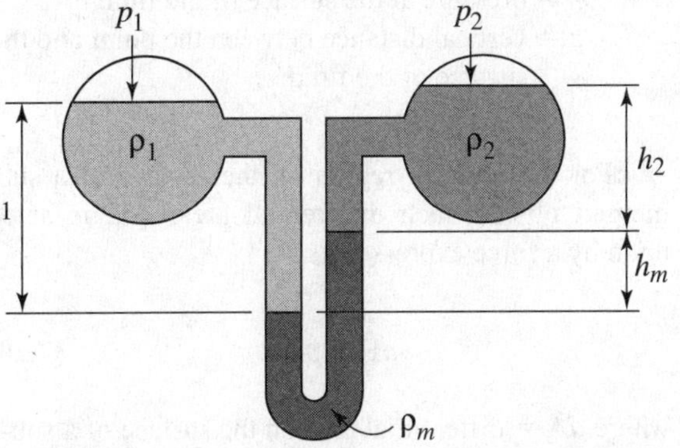

Figure 7.4 Diagram of a manometer, used to measure the difference in hydrostatic pressure between vessel 1 and vessel 2.

The difference in pressure between these two environments is related to the difference in height between the two legs of the manometer as follows:

$$p_1 - p_2 = \rho_m g h_m + (\rho_2 g h_2 - \rho_1 g h_1) \quad [7.17]$$

or

$$p_1 - p_2 = \gamma_m h_m + (\gamma_2 h_2 - \gamma_1 h_1) \quad [7.18]$$

If the density or specific weight of either fluid 1 or fluid 2 in Figure 7.4 is small compared to the density or specific weight of the manometer fluid, its contribution to equations 7.17 and 7.18 can be neglected. For example, if fluid 1 is air (density = 1.23 kg/m^3), fluid 2 is water (density = 1,000 kg/m^3), and the manometer fluid is oil (density = approx. 830 kg/m^3), then the effect of the air can be neglected, and equations 7.17 and 7.18 can be reduced to

$$p_1 - p_2 = \rho_m g h_m + \rho_2 g h_2 \quad [7.19]$$

and

$$p_1 - p_2 = \gamma_m h_m + \gamma_2 h_2 \quad [7.20]$$

If, however, the densities or specific weights of *both* fluids are small compared to the density or specific weight of the manometer fluid, equations 7.17 and 7.18 reduce to

$$p_1 - p_2 = \rho_m g h_m \quad [7.21]$$

and

$$p_1 - p_2 = \gamma_m h_m \quad [7.22]$$

When one end of the manometer is exposed directly to the atmosphere, the device is called an open manometer, illustrated in Figure 7.5. Equations 7.17 and 7.18 apply to an open manometer if p_2 is replaced with atmospheric pressure p_{atm}.

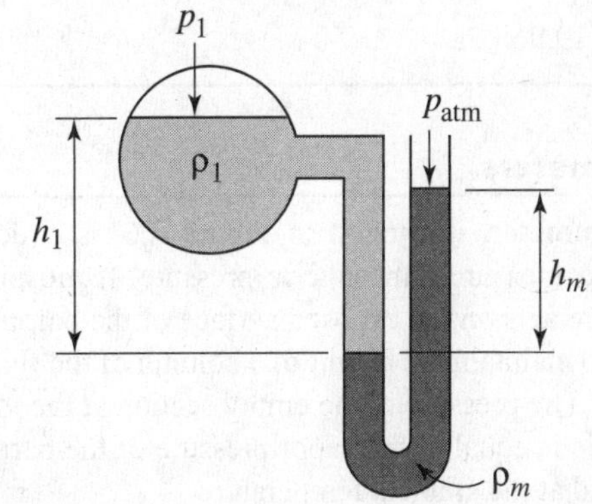

Figure 7.5 Diagram of an open manometer.

For the manometer shown in Figure 7.5, the pressure at the surface of fluid 1(p_1) is given by

$$p_1 = p_{atm} + \rho_m g h_m - \rho_1 g h_1 \quad [7.23]$$

and

$$p_1 = p_{atm} + \gamma_m h_m - \gamma_1 h_1 \quad [7.24]$$

Example 7.5

The open manometer shown in the accompanying figure is used to measure the pressure (p_1) in an air tank. The manometer fluid is mercury, which has a density of 13,550 kg/m^3. What is the pressure in the vessel?

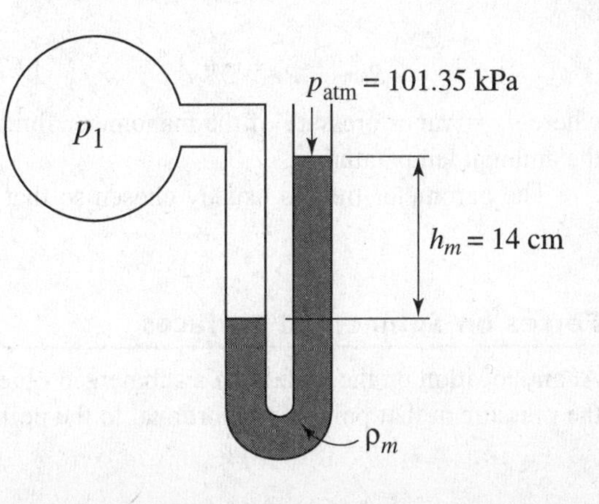

Solution:

The density of air is much smaller than the density of mercury, so the contribution of air can be neglected. From equation 7.23:

$$p_1 = p_{atm} + \rho_m g h_m$$

$$= 101.35\ \text{kPa} + \left(13{,}550\ \frac{\text{kg}}{\text{m}^3}\right)\left(9.81\ \frac{\text{m}}{\text{s}^2}\right)$$

$$(14\ \text{cm})\left(\frac{\text{m}}{100\ \text{cm}}\right)\left(\frac{\text{N}}{\frac{\text{kg}\cdot\text{m}}{\text{s}^2}}\right)\left(\frac{\text{kPa}}{1{,}000\ \frac{\text{N}}{\text{m}^2}}\right)$$

$$= 119.96\ \text{kPa}$$

Barometers

A **barometer,** illustrated in Figure 7.6, is a device used to measure atmospheric pressure. Atmospheric pressure acts on the exposed surface of the barometer fluid to maintain the height of a column of the fluid in a tube. The pressure in the empty section at the top of the tube is equal to the vapor pressure of the barometer fluid at the ambient temperature.

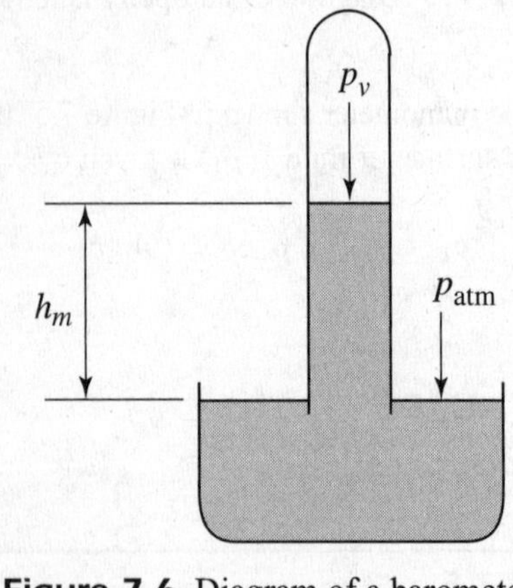

Figure 7.6 Diagram of a barometer.

The height of the fluid column is related to the atmospheric pressure as follows:

$$p_{atm} - p_v = \rho g h_m \qquad [7.25]$$

or

$$p_{atm} - p_v = \gamma h_m \qquad [7.26]$$

where p_v = vapor pressure of the manometer fluid at the ambient temperature.

The barometer fluid is usually chosen so that $p_v \approx 0$.

Forces on Submerged Surfaces

At any location on the surface of a submerged object, the pressure at that point is proportional to the point's distance below the surface. This pressure is determined as follows:

$$p = p_0 + \rho g z \qquad [7.27]$$

or

$$p = p_0 + \gamma z \qquad [7.28]$$

where p = pressure at the given location,
p_0 = pressure at the surface of the fluid,
z = vertical distance between the point and the surface of the fluid.

For an arbitrary region on the surface of a submerged object, each differential area, $d\mathbf{A}$, is acted upon by a force expressed as

$$d\mathbf{F} = p\, d\mathbf{A} \qquad [7.29]$$

where $d\mathbf{A}$ = differential area on the surface of a submerged object,
$d\mathbf{F}$ = force acting on $d\mathbf{A}$,
p = fluid pressure at the location of $d\mathbf{A}$.

The direction of the force is normal to and into the surface. If this force is integrated over a region, the total force acting on that region is obtained. If this region is a flat plate, as in the control volume shown in Figure 7.7, and the pressure at the surface of the fluid is zero, this force is expressed as follows:

$$\mathbf{F} = \mathbf{F}_x + \mathbf{F}_y \qquad [7.30]$$

$$|\mathbf{F}_x| = \frac{p_1 + p_2}{2} A_v \qquad [7.31]$$

$$|\mathbf{F}_y| = \rho g V_f \qquad [7.32]$$

where $\mathbf{F}$ = total force exerted on the plate by the fluid, directed normal into the surface of the plate,
$|\mathbf{F}_x|$ = magnitude of the horizontal component of $\mathbf{F}$,
$|\mathbf{F}_y|$ = magnitude of the vertical component of $\mathbf{F}$,
p_1 = gage pressure at the top edge of the plate,
p_2 = gage pressure at the bottom edge of the plate,
A_v = vertical projection of the plate area,
V_f = volume of fluid contained in the region bounded by the plate and the horizontal projection of the plate onto the free surface of the fluid.

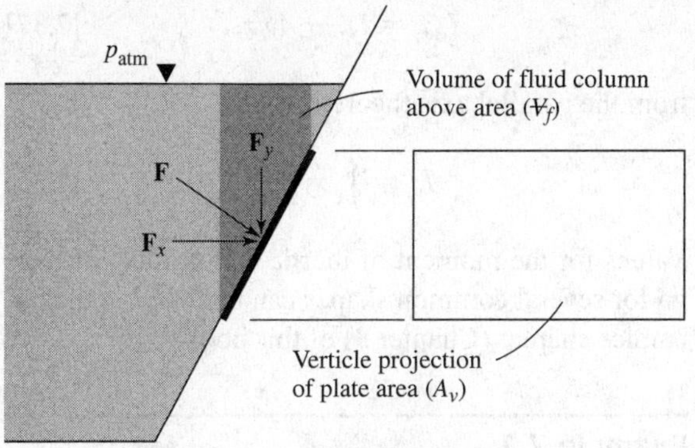

Figure 7.7 A flat-plate region of a submerged surface.

Equations 7.30 through 7.32 apply when the contribution of the atmospheric pressure to the force on a submerged surface is negligible. When this effect is not negligible, the gage pressures in equation 7.31 should be replaced with absolute pressures, and a surface-force term ($P_{atm}A_h$) should be added to equation 7.32. In this term, A_h is the horizontal projection of the submerged plate onto the free surface of the fluid.

Example 7.6

Find the total force acting on the submerged plate shown in the accompanying figure. Assume that the back side of the plate is also exposed to p_{atm}.

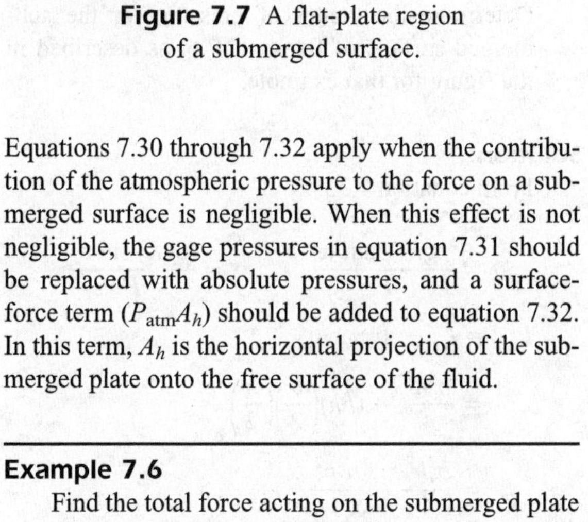

Solution:

The total force acting on the plate is directed normal to the plate, and into the plate, as shown in the figure. The magnitude of this force can be determined from equation 7.30:

$$\mathbf{F} = \mathbf{F}_x + \mathbf{F}_y$$

From equation 7.31:

$$|\mathbf{F}_x| = \frac{p_1 + p_2}{2} A_v$$

$$p_1 = \rho g h_1$$

$$= \left(1{,}000\ \frac{\text{kg}}{\text{m}^3}\right)\left(9.81\ \frac{\text{m}}{\text{s}^2}\right)(1.0\ \text{m}) \times \left(\frac{\text{N}}{\frac{\text{kb}\cdot\text{m}}{\text{s}^2}}\right)\left(\frac{\text{kPa}}{1{,}000\ \frac{\text{N}}{\text{m}^2}}\right)$$

$$= 9.81\ \text{kPa}$$

$$p_2 = \rho g h_2$$

$$h_2 = 1.0\ \text{m} + (1.2\ \text{m})\sin 60$$

$$= 2.04\ \text{m}$$

$$p_2 = \left(1{,}000\ \frac{\text{kg}}{\text{m}^3}\right)\left(9.81\ \frac{\text{m}}{\text{s}^2}\right)(2.04\ \text{m}) \times \left(\frac{\text{N}}{\frac{\text{kg}\cdot\text{m}}{\text{s}^2}}\right)\left(\frac{\text{kPa}}{1{,}000\ \frac{\text{N}}{\text{m}^2}}\right)$$

$$= 20.01\ \text{kPa}$$

$$A_v = (2.0\ \text{m})[(1.2\ \text{m})\sin 60]$$

$$= 2.08\ \text{m}^2$$

$$|\mathbf{F}_x| = \frac{9.81\ \text{kPa} + 20.01\ \text{kPa}}{2} \times (2.08\ \text{m}^2)\left(\frac{1{,}000\ \frac{\text{N}}{\text{m}^2}}{\text{kPa}}\right)$$

$$= 31{,}010\ \text{N}$$

From equation 7.33:

$$|\mathbf{F}_y| = \rho g V_f$$

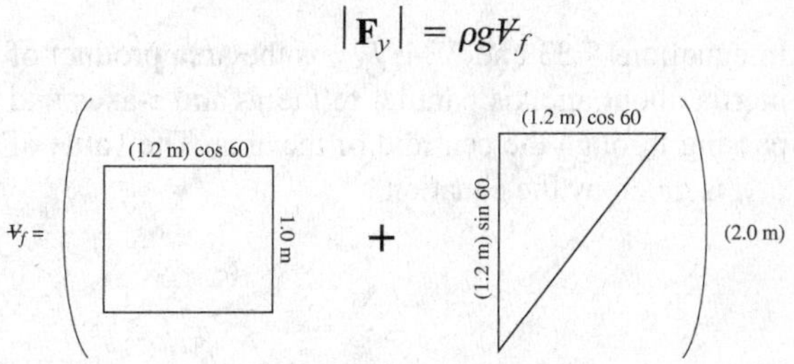

$$V_f = \left\{[(1.0\ \text{m})(1.2\ \text{m})\cos 60] + \frac{[(1.2\ \text{m})\cos 60][(1.2\ \text{m})\sin 60]}{2}\right\}(2.0\ \text{m})$$

$$= 1.82\ \text{m}^3$$

$$|\mathbf{F}_y| = \left(1{,}000\ \frac{\text{kg}}{\text{m}^3}\right)\left(9.81\ \frac{\text{m}}{\text{s}^2}\right)(1.82\ \text{m}^3)\left(\frac{\text{N}}{\frac{\text{kg}\cdot\text{m}}{\text{s}^2}}\right)$$

$$= 17{,}850\ \text{N}$$

The total force can be expressed as

$$|\mathbf{F}| = \sqrt{|\mathbf{F}_x|^2 + |\mathbf{F}_y|^2}$$
$$= \sqrt{(31{,}010\text{ N})^2 + (17{,}850\text{ N})^2}$$
$$= 35{,}780\text{ N}$$

The Center of Pressure

For a region on the surface of a submerged rigid body, the **center of pressure** is the location in this region through which a concentrated point force (**F** from the preceding section) will have the same effect on the submerged body as the distributed pressure force over the entire region. This definition is illustrated in Figure 7.8.

The coordinates' center of pressure relative to the centroid of the submerged area (y^* and z^*) is given by the following equations:

$$y^* = \frac{\rho g I_{y_c z_c} \sin\alpha}{F}, \qquad z^* = \frac{\rho g I_{y_c} \sin\alpha}{F} \qquad [7.33]$$

or

$$y^* \frac{\gamma I_{y_c z_c} \sin\alpha}{F}, \qquad z^* = \frac{\gamma I_{y_c} \sin\alpha}{F} \qquad [7.34]$$

where I_{y_c} = area moment of inertia about an axis parallel to the y-axis and passing through the centroid of the area. The value of I_{y_c} is given by the equation

$$I_{y_c} = I_y - A y_c^{\,2} \qquad [7.35]$$

from the parallel axis theorem, where

$$I_y = \int_A y^2\, dA \qquad [7.36]$$

In equations 7.33 and 7.34, $I_{y_c z_c}$ is the area product of inertia about an axis parallel to the y- and z-axes and passing through the centroid of the area. The value of $I_{y_c z_c}$ is given by the equation

$$I_{y_c z_c} = I_{yz} - A y_c z_c \qquad [7.37]$$

from the parallel axis theorem, where

$$I_{yz} = \int_A xy\, dA \qquad [7.38]$$

Values for the moment of inertia and product of inertia for several common shapes can be found in the dynamics chapter (Chapter 3) of this book.

Example 7.7

Determine the center of pressure for the submerged surface of Example 7.6, as described in the figure for that example.

Solution:

From equation 7.33:

$$y^* = \frac{\rho g I_{y_c z_c} \sin\alpha}{F}, \qquad z^* = \frac{\rho g I_{y_c} \sin\alpha}{F}$$

$$I_{y_c z_c} = I_{yz} - A y_c z_c$$
$$= \frac{b^2h^2}{4} - (bh)\left(\frac{b}{2}\right)\left(\frac{h}{2}\right)$$
$$= \frac{b^2h^2}{4} - \frac{b^2h^2}{4}$$
$$= 0$$
$$y^* = 0\text{ m}$$
$$I_{y_c} = I_y - A y_c^{\,2}$$
$$= \frac{b^3h}{3} - (bh)\left(\frac{b}{2}\right)^2$$
$$= \frac{b^3h}{3} - \frac{b^3h}{4}$$
$$= \frac{b^3h}{12}$$

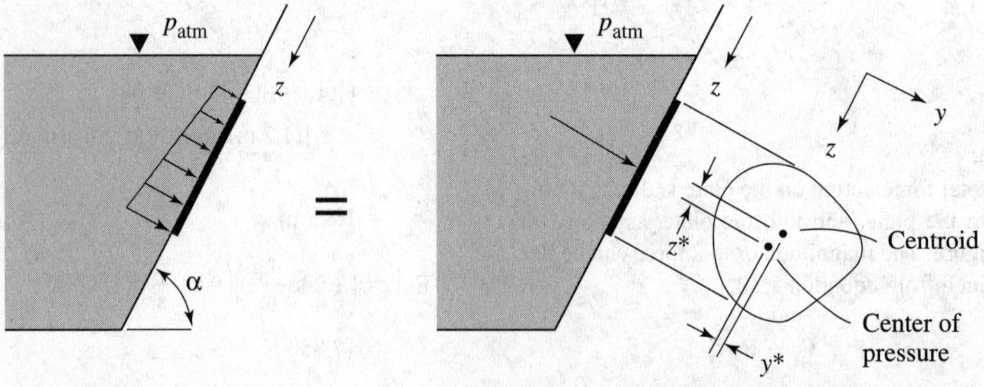

Figure 7.8 Distributed pressure force and equivalent point force on a submerged surface.

$$= \frac{(0.20\text{ m})^3(0.12\text{ m})}{12}$$

$$= 8 \times 10^{-5}\text{ m}^4$$

$$z^* = \frac{\left(1{,}000\ \frac{\text{kg}}{\text{m}^3}\right)\left(9.81\ \frac{\text{m}}{\text{s}^2}\right)(8 \times 10^{-5}\text{ m}^4)\sin 60}{36.06\text{ N}}$$

$$\times \left(\frac{\text{N}}{\frac{\text{kg}\cdot\text{m}}{\text{s}^2}}\right)$$

$$= 0.0188\text{ m}$$

$$= 1.88\text{ cm}$$

Archimedes' Principle and Buoyancy

Any object that is completely or partially submerged will experience a buoyant force. This is a force directed in a direction opposite to the weight of the object, which is the result of the total pressure force of the fluid acting on the submerged body.

According to **Archimedes' principle,** the magnitude of the buoyant force is equal to the weight of the fluid displaced by the object. If the object is floating on the surface of a fluid, it will displace a volume of the fluid that has the same weight as the object.

Example 7.8

A 25-kg cube is submerged in water ($\rho = 1{,}000$ kg/m^3), as shown in part (a) of the accompanying figure. What is the magnitude of the buoyant force acting on the cube?

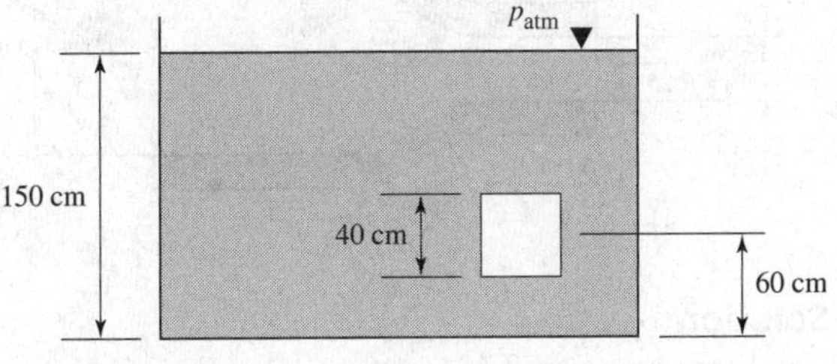

(a)

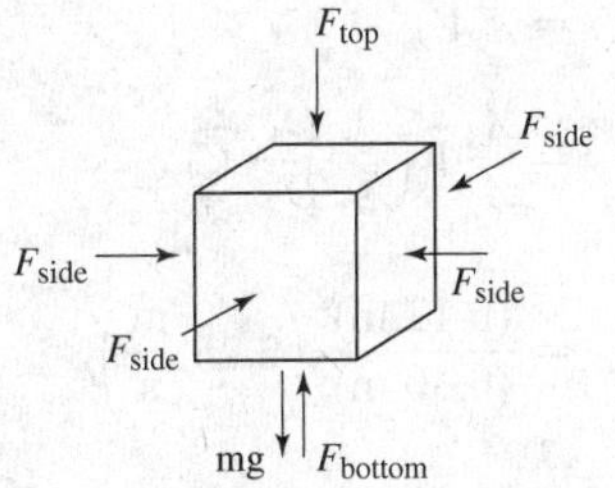

(b)

Solution:

From the free-body diagram in part (b) of the figure, it can be seen that the force acting on each side of the cube is counteracted by the force on the opposite side; therefore the total force acting on the cube must be directed vertically. Take forces directed up as positive; then the total resultant force is given by the equation

$$F_{total} = F_{bottom} - F_{top} - mg$$

Calculate the force on each face of the cube by multiplying the hydrostatic pressure on that face by the area of the face:

$$F_{bottom} = A_{bottom}(\rho g h)_{water}$$

$$= (40\text{ cm})^2\left(\frac{\text{m}}{100\text{ cm}}\right)^2\left[\left(1{,}000\ \frac{\text{kg}}{\text{m}^3}\right)\left(9.81\ \frac{\text{m}}{\text{s}^2}\right) \times (110\text{ cm})\left(\frac{\text{m}}{100\text{ cm}}\right)\left(\frac{\text{N}}{\frac{\text{kg}\cdot\text{m}}{\text{s}^2}}\right)\right]$$

$$= 1{,}727\text{ N}$$

$$F_{top} = A_{top}(\rho g h)_{water}$$

$$= (40\text{ cm})^2\left(\frac{\text{m}}{100\text{ cm}}\right)^2\left[\left(1{,}000\ \frac{\text{kg}}{\text{m}^3}\right)\left(9.81\ \frac{\text{m}}{\text{s}^2}\right) \times (70\text{ cm})\left(\frac{\text{m}}{100\text{ cm}}\right)\left(\frac{\text{N}}{\frac{\text{kg}\cdot\text{m}}{\text{s}^2}}\right)\right]$$

$$= 1{,}099\text{ N}$$

The weight of the cube is

$$mg = (25\text{ kg})\left(9.81\ \frac{\text{m}}{\text{s}^2}\right)\left(\frac{\text{N}}{\frac{\text{kg}\cdot\text{m}}{\text{s}^2}}\right)$$

$$= 245\text{ N}$$

The total force is

$$F_{total} = F_{bottom} - F_{top} - mg$$

$$= 1{,}727\text{ N} - 1{,}099\text{ N} - 245\text{ N}$$

$$= 383\text{ N}$$

As an alternative to the approach shown above, Archimedes' principle may be used to solve the problem. The cube will experience a buoyant force equal to the weight of the water it displaces:

$$F_{buoyant} = \rho_{water}V_{cube}g$$

$$= \left(1{,}000\ \frac{\text{kg}}{\text{m}^3}\right)(0.40\text{ m})^3\left(9.81\ \frac{\text{m}}{\text{s}^2}\right)\left(\frac{\text{N}}{\frac{\text{kg}\cdot\text{m}}{\text{s}^2}}\right)$$

$$= 628\text{ N}$$

The weight of the cube will counteract the buoyant force, so the total resultant force acting on the cube is

$$F_{total} = F_{buoyant} - mg$$

$$= 628\text{ N} - 245\text{ N}$$

$$= 383\text{ N}$$

7.4 Fluid Dynamics

Fluid dynamics is the study of fluid in motion and the interactions of the fluid with the objects it may encounter. The basic principles of mass and energy conservation and Newton's second law of motion are applied to fluid systems to allow prediction of the flow characteristics.

Conservation of Mass (the Continuity Equation)

In every fluid system, mass is conserved. This conservation can be stated in terms of a mass balance equation:

$$\left(\frac{dm}{dt}\right)_{cv} = \dot{m}_{in} - \dot{m}_{out} \qquad [7.39]$$

A common class of fluid problem is the steady-state problem, in which the values of all of the fluid properties within the control volume do not change with time. For a steady-state control volume:

$$\left(\frac{dm}{dt}\right)_{cv} = 0 \qquad [7.40]$$

so that

$$\dot{m}_{in} = \dot{m}_{out} \qquad [7.41]$$

For the arbitrary control volume shown in Figure 7.9, conservation of mass is expressed as

$$\dot{m}_1 = \dot{m}_2 \qquad [7.42]$$

where $\dot{m}_1$ = mass flow rate through cross-sectional area of control volume at point 1,
$\dot{m}_2$ = mass flow rate through cross-sectional area of control volume at point 2.

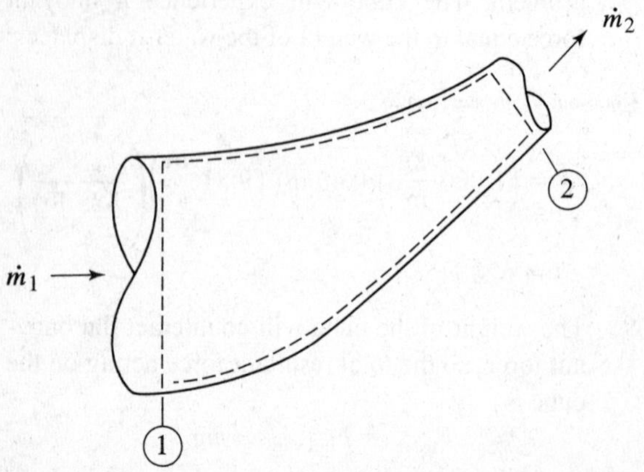

Figure 7.9 Conservation of mass in an arbitrary control volume.

Equivalent expressions of equation 7.42 are as follows:

$$\rho_1 A_1 \overline{V}_1 = \rho_2 A_2 \overline{V}_2 \qquad [7.43]$$

and

$$\rho_1 Q_1 = \rho_2 Q_2 \qquad [7.44]$$

where A_1 = cross-sectional area of control volume at point 1,
A_2 = cross-sectional area of control volume at point 2,
$\overline{V}_1$ = average fluid speed at point 1,
$\overline{V}_2$ = average fluid speed at point 2,
Q_1 = volumetric flow rate of fluid entering control volume at point 1,
Q_2 = volumetric flow rate of fluid entering control volume at point 2.

If the flow is incompressible, the value of density is constant, and conservation of mass, or **continuity equation,** can be expressed as:

$$Q = A_1 \overline{V}_1 = A_2 \overline{V}_2 \qquad [7.45]$$

Example 7.9

What is the average speed at section 2 for the diffuser shown in the accompanying figure? (Assume that the flow is incompressible.)

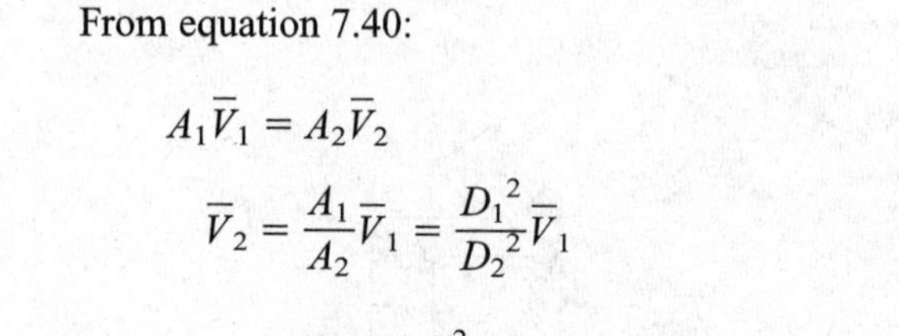

Solution:

From equation 7.40:

$$A_1 \overline{V}_1 = A_2 \overline{V}_2$$

$$\overline{V}_2 = \frac{A_1}{A_2}\overline{V}_1 = \frac{D_1^2}{D_2^2}\overline{V}_1$$

$$= \frac{(0.12\ \text{m})^2}{(0.30\ \text{m})^2}\left(2.25\ \frac{\text{m}}{\text{s}}\right)$$

$$= 0.36\ \text{m/s}$$

Impulse-Momentum Principle

Newton's second law of motion (**F** = *m***a**) can be applied to fluid systems through a principle known as the **impulse-momentum principle.** This principle is expressed mathematically for a control volume as follows:

$$\Sigma\left(\frac{d\mathbf{P}}{dt}\right)_{cv} = \Sigma\mathbf{F} \qquad [7.46]$$

where $\frac{d\mathbf{P}}{dt}$ = rate of momentum entering or leaving the control volume = $\dot{m}\mathbf{V}$,

$\Sigma\mathbf{F}$ = total external force acting on the control volume.

For a steady-state system, the change in momentum of a control volume can be expressed as

$$\left(\frac{d\mathbf{P}}{dt}\right)_{cv} = \left(\frac{d\mathbf{P}}{dt}\right)_{in} - \left(\frac{d\mathbf{P}}{dt}\right)_{out} = (\dot{m}\mathbf{V})_{in} - (\dot{m}\mathbf{V})_{out} \qquad [7.47]$$

so that

$$\Sigma\mathbf{F} = (\dot{m}\mathbf{V})_{in} - (\dot{m}\mathbf{V})_{out} \qquad [7.48]$$

The impulse-momentum principle can be applied to the case of a pipe bend, enlargement, or contraction to find the total force exerted on a fluid by such a device.

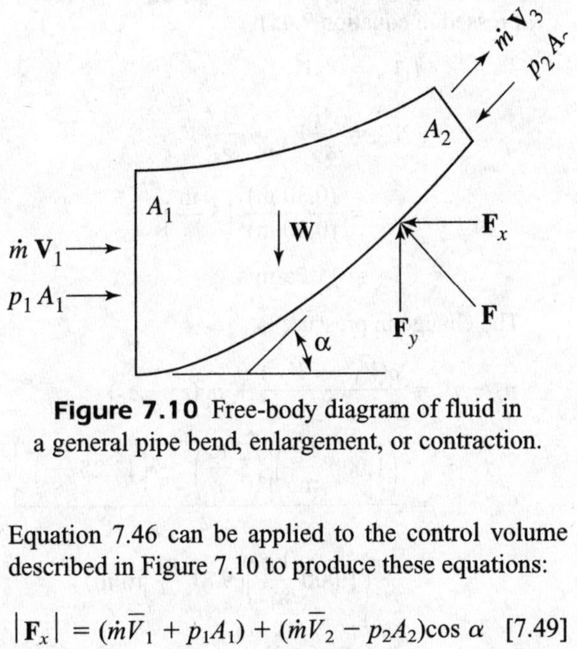

Figure 7.10 Free-body diagram of fluid in a general pipe bend, enlargement, or contraction.

Equation 7.46 can be applied to the control volume described in Figure 7.10 to produce these equations:

$$|\mathbf{F}_x| = (\dot{m}\overline{V}_1 + p_1A_1) + (\dot{m}\overline{V}_2 - p_2A_2)\cos\alpha \qquad [7.49]$$

$$|\mathbf{F}_y| = \mathbf{W} - (\dot{m}\overline{V}_2 - p_2A_2)\sin\alpha \qquad [7.50]$$

Example 7.10

For the control volume shown in Figure 7.10 with the parameters listed below, find the x- and y-components of the resultant force on the control volume.

$\rho = 1{,}000\ \text{kg/m}^3 \quad \overline{V}_1 = 4\ \text{m/s}$

$\mathcal{V}_{cv} = 1.25\ \text{m}^3 \quad p_1 = 12\ \text{kPa} \quad p_2 = 10\ \text{kPa}$

$\alpha = 40° \quad A_1 = 0.50\ \text{m}^2 \quad A_2 = 0.30\ \text{m}^2$

Solution:

From equation 7.49:

$$|\mathbf{F}_x| = (\dot{m}\overline{V}_1 + p_1A_1) + (\dot{m}\overline{V}_2 - p_2A_2)\cos\alpha$$

$$\dot{m} = \rho\overline{V}_1A_1 = \left(1{,}000\ \frac{\text{kg}}{\text{m}^3}\right)\left(4\ \frac{\text{m}}{\text{s}}\right)(0.50\ \text{m}^2) = 2{,}000\ \text{kg/s}$$

$$\overline{V}_2 = \frac{\overline{V}_1A_1}{A_2} = \frac{\left(4\frac{\text{m}}{\text{s}}\right)(0.50\ \text{m}^2)}{0.30\ \text{m}^2} = 6.67\ \text{m/s}$$

$$|\mathbf{F}_x| = \left[\left(2{,}000\ \frac{\text{kg}}{\text{s}}\right)\left(4\ \frac{\text{m}}{\text{s}}\right)\left(\frac{\text{N}}{\frac{\text{kg}\cdot\text{m}}{\text{s}^2}}\right) + (12{,}000\ \text{Pa})(0.50\ \text{m}^2)\left(\frac{\frac{\text{N}}{\text{m}^2}}{\text{Pa}}\right)\right]$$
$$+ \left[\left(2{,}000\ \frac{\text{kg}}{\text{s}}\right)\left(6.67\ \frac{\text{m}}{\text{s}}\right)\left(\frac{\text{N}}{\frac{\text{kg}\cdot\text{m}}{\text{s}^2}}\right) - (10{,}000\ \text{Pa})(0.30\ \text{m}^2)\left(\frac{\frac{\text{N}}{\text{m}^2}}{\text{Pa}}\right)\right]\cos 40$$
$$= (8{,}000\ \text{N} + 6{,}000\ \text{N}) + (13{,}333\ \text{N} - 3{,}000\ \text{N})\cos 40$$
$$= 21{,}915\ \text{N}$$

From equation 7.50:

$$|\mathbf{F}_y| = |\mathbf{W}| - (\dot{m}\overline{V}_2 - p_2A_2)\sin\alpha$$

$$|\mathbf{W}| = \rho\mathcal{V}_{cv}g = \left(1{,}000\ \frac{\text{kg}}{\text{m}^3}\right)(1.25\ \text{m}^3)\left(9.81\ \frac{\text{m}}{\text{s}^2}\right)\left(\frac{\text{N}}{\frac{\text{kg}\cdot\text{m}}{\text{s}^2}}\right) = 12{,}263\ \text{N}$$

$$|\mathbf{F}_y| = 12{,}263\ \text{N} - (13{,}333\ \text{N} - 3{,}000\ \text{N})\sin 40 = 5{,}621\ \text{N}$$

Conservation of Energy (the Bernoulli or Field Equation)

Where there is continuous flow, the idea of conservation of energy can be expressed using the Bernoulli equation. The **Bernoulli equation,** known also as the **field equation,** is an expression of the conservation of energy, neglecting frictional losses. It applies to changes in energy along the path of a fluid particle. The Bernoulli equation is expressed as:

$$\frac{p_1}{\gamma} + \frac{\overline{V}_1^2}{2g} + z_1 = \frac{p_2}{\gamma} + \frac{\overline{V}_2^2}{2g} + z_2 \quad [7.51]$$

Any real flow will experience frictional losses, which are not accounted for in the Bernoulli equation. Equation 7.51 can be modified to include the effect of frictional losses as follows:

$$\frac{p_1}{\gamma} + \frac{\overline{V}_1^2}{2g} + z_1 = \frac{p_2}{\gamma} + \frac{\overline{V}_2^2}{2g} + z_2 + h_f \quad [7.52]$$

Here, h_f is the major head loss, and its value is determined using empirical relationships. For flow in a horizontal pipe with constant cross-sectional area, equation 7.52 reduces to

$$h_f = \frac{p_1 - p_2}{\gamma} \quad [7.53]$$

Example 7.11

For the system described in Example 7.10, find the change in pressure between sections 1 and 2 using the Bernoulli equation. (Assume that frictional losses are negligible.)

Solution:

From equation 7.51:

$$\frac{p_1}{\rho} + \frac{\overline{V}_1^2}{2} = \frac{p_2}{\rho} + \frac{\overline{V}_2^2}{2}$$

$$p_2 - p_1 = \frac{(\overline{V}_1^2 - \overline{V}_2^2)\rho}{2}$$

$$= \frac{\left[\left(2.25\frac{\text{m}}{\text{s}}\right)^2 - \left(0.36\,\frac{\text{m}}{\text{s}}\right)^2\right]\left(1{,}000\,\frac{\text{kg}}{\text{m}^3}\right)}{2}$$

$$\times \left(\frac{\text{N}}{\frac{\text{kg}\cdot\text{m}}{\text{s}^2}}\right)\left(\frac{\text{kPa}}{1{,}000\,\frac{\text{N}}{\text{m}^2}}\right)$$

$$= 2.47\text{ kPa}$$

Example 7.12

Water enters the control volume shown in the accompanying figure with a speed of 5 m/s. Assuming that the flow is incompressible and that friction is negligible, find the change in pressure between sections 1 and 2.

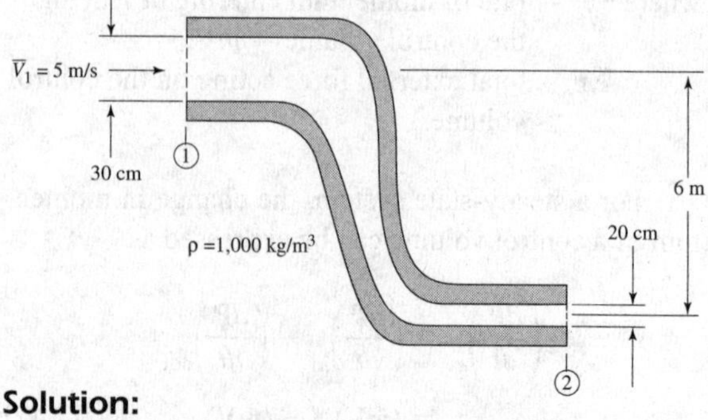

Solution:

From equation 7.51:

$$\frac{p_1}{\rho g} + \frac{\overline{V}_1^2}{2g} + z_1 = \frac{p_2}{\rho g} + \frac{\overline{V}_2^2}{2g} + z_2$$

$$p_2 - p_1 = \rho g\left[\left(\frac{\overline{V}_1^2 - \overline{V}_2^2}{2g}\right) + (z_1 - z_2)\right]$$

$$= \frac{\rho(\overline{V}_1^2 - \overline{V}_2^2)}{2} + \rho g(z_1 - z_2)$$

Calculate $\overline{V}_2$ using the continuity equation (as expressed in equation 7.45):

$$A_1\overline{V}_1 = A_2\overline{V}_2$$

$$\overline{V}_2 = \frac{A_1}{A_2}\overline{V}_1 = \frac{D_1^2}{D_2^2}\overline{V}_1$$

$$= \frac{(0.30\text{ m})^2}{(0.20\text{ m})^2}\left(5\,\frac{\text{m}}{\text{s}}\right)$$

$$= 11.25\text{ m/s}$$

The change in pressure is:

$$p_2 - p_1 = \frac{\rho(\overline{V}_1^2 - \overline{V}_2^2)}{2} + \rho g(z_1 - z_2)$$

$$= \frac{\left(1{,}000\,\frac{\text{kg}}{\text{m}^3}\right)\left[\left(5\,\frac{\text{m}}{\text{s}}\right)^2 - \left(11.25\,\frac{\text{m}}{\text{s}}\right)^2\right]}{2}$$

$$+ \left(1{,}000\,\frac{\text{kg}}{\text{m}^3}\right)\left(9.81\,\frac{\text{m}}{\text{s}^2}\right)(6\text{ m})$$

$$= \left(-50{,}781\,\frac{\text{kg}}{\text{m}\cdot\text{s}^2} + 41{,}880\,\frac{\text{kg}}{\text{m}\cdot\text{s}^2}\right)$$

$$\times \left(\frac{\text{N}}{\frac{\text{kg}\cdot\text{m}}{\text{s}^2}}\right)\left(\frac{\text{kPa}}{1{,}000\,\frac{\text{N}}{\text{m}^2}}\right)$$

$$= -8.90\text{ kPa}$$

Static Versus Stagnation Pressure

The pressure used in the Bernoulli equation is the **static pressure** of a fluid. It is the pressure that would be measured by a device that moves with the fluid. A stationary device that measures pressure in a moving fluid would read a different pressure, known as the **stagnation pressure.** A relationship between the static pressure and the stagnation pressure of a fluid can be derived from the Bernoulli equation:

$$\frac{p_0}{\rho} = \frac{p_s}{\rho} + \frac{V^2}{2} \qquad [7.54]$$

or

$$p_0 = p_s + \frac{1}{2}\rho V^2 \qquad [7.55]$$

where p_s = static pressure of the fluid,
p_0 = stagnation pressure of the fluid,
V = speed of the fluid at the point where the measurement is taken.

Grade Line (Hydraulic Gradient) and Energy Line

If a pipe is fitted with a series of open manometers along its length, the static fluid pressure at each location can be visualized. With flowing fluid, the pressure at each successive location will be lower, as shown in Figure 7.11. If an imaginary line is drawn through the meniscus of each manometer, that line is the **grade line** or **hydraulic gradient.**

Alternatively, the hydraulic gradient can be thought of as a plot of static pressure as a function of distance along the pipe. If the stagnation pressure rather than the static pressure of a fluid flowing through a pipe is plotted as a function of distance along the pipe, the line that results is the **energy line.**

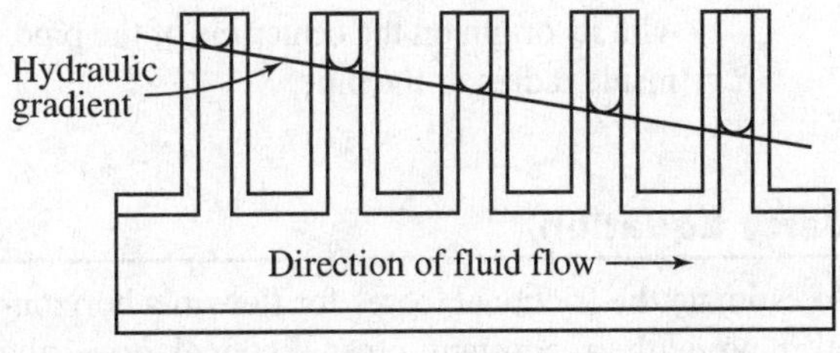

Figure 7.11 Description of the hydraulic gradient.

Reynolds Number

The **Reynolds number** (Re) is a nondimensional number used to characterize fluid flow. It is a ratio of the inertial forces to viscous forces acting on the fluid and is defined as follows:

$$\mathrm{Re} = \frac{\rho \overline{V} D}{\mu} \qquad [7.56]$$

or

$$\mathrm{Re} = \frac{\overline{V} D}{\nu} \qquad [7.57]$$

where ν = kinematic viscosity, defined as μ/ρ.

The parameter D used in equations 7.56 and 7.57 is a characteristic length. For flow in a tube the characteristic length is the pipe diameter. For flow over a flat plate, the characteristic length is the length of the plate in the direction of flow.

For a power-law non-Newtonian fluid, the Reynolds number is defined as

$$\mathrm{Re}' = \frac{\rho \overline{V}^{2-n} D^n}{K\left(\frac{3n+1}{4n}\right)^n 8^{n-1}} \qquad [7.58]$$

where K = consistency index,
n = power law index: $n < 1$ for a pseudoplastic fluid, $n > 1$ for a dilatant fluid.

Example 7.13

Find the Reynolds number for the water exiting the control volume of Example 7.12. Assume that the viscosity of water is $8 \times 10^{-3}\ \mathrm{N \cdot s/m^2}$.

Solution:

From equation 7.56:

$$\mathrm{Re} = \frac{\rho \overline{V} D}{\mu}$$

$$= \frac{\left(1{,}000\ \frac{\mathrm{kg}}{\mathrm{m}^3}\right)\left(11.25\ \frac{\mathrm{m}}{\mathrm{s}}\right)(0.20\ \mathrm{m})}{8 \times 10^{-3}\ \frac{\mathrm{N \cdot s}}{\mathrm{m}^2}}$$

$$= 281{,}250$$

Laminar Flow

As fluid flow begins from rest, the flow is highly organized. All streamlines are smooth and continuous, and all fluid particles move in a path parallel to the mean bulk flow. This type of flow, called **laminar flow,** generally occurs in fluid flows with low Reynolds numbers, or in fluids with high viscosity and/or low density flowing at low speed. In laminar flow, the fluid flow field can be thought of as a collection of fluid layers. In each layer, all fluid particles are moving with the same velocity, and there is no macroscopic mixing of fluid layers.

Turbulent Flow

As the flow rate is increased, the general character of the flow begins to change significantly. Random, three-dimensional fluctuations in flow velocity will begin to appear, superimposed over the local mean flow velocity. This type of flow, called **turbulent flow,** results in significant fluid mixing.

The lowest Reynolds number for which turbulent flow can be expected is called the *critical Reynolds number* (Re_c). For flow in a pipe, the value of Re_c is approximately 2,300. For pipe flow at Reynolds numbers greater than approximately 4,000, the flow is considered fully turbulent. The range of Reynolds numbers between these limits is the transitional region, where it is difficult to predict which type of flow will occur.

7.5 Internal Flow

In this section we consider fluid flowing through a closed pipe or duct. Experimental observation has shown that fluid particles adjacent to the walls of the pipe have zero velocity. This is called the *no-slip condition* (no fluid is slipping against the wall of the pipe). The maximum fluid velocity occurs along the centerline of the pipe.

The variation in fluid velocity is caused by the viscous forces within the fluid, or the shear force between fluid particles. The shear forces perform work against the moving fluid, reducing the fluid energy as it travels through the pipe. This loss of energy, often called *head loss* (h_f), is observed as a drop in fluid pressure in the pipe.

As fluid enters or leaves a pipe or other internal passage, the velocity profile in the passage, is a function of the fluid's location along the length of the passage and the geometry of the opening. Far from the entrance and exit, however, the velocity profile becomes uniform for any position along the length of the pipe, and independent of the entrance and exit geometry. Flow in this region is fully developed.

For fully developed laminar flow, illustrated in Figure 7.12, the velocity of a fluid particle in a pipe is a function of the radial location of that particle in the pipe and of the pressure drop through the tube ($\Delta p/L$). Some relationships for flow in a pipe are as follows:

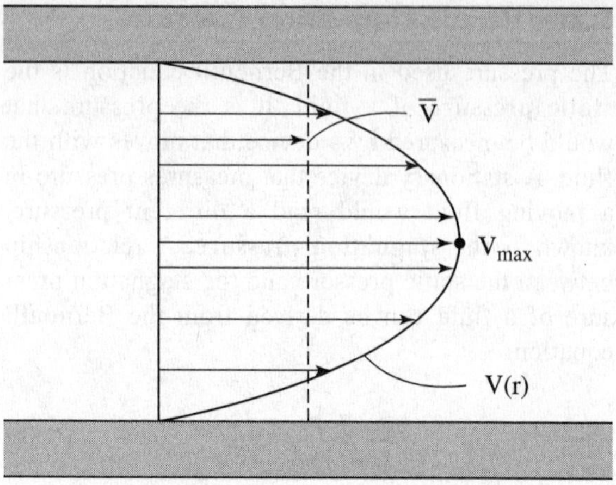

Figure 7.12 Fully developed laminar-flow velocity profile for flow in a pipe.

- Speed distribution:

$$V(r) = -\frac{R^2}{4\mu}\frac{\Delta p}{L}\left[1 - \left(\frac{r}{R}\right)^2\right] \qquad [7.59]$$

- Average speed:

$$\overline{V} = \frac{Q}{A} = -\frac{R^2}{8\mu}\frac{\Delta p}{L} \qquad [7.60]$$

- Maximum speed:

$$V_{max} = -\frac{R^2}{4\mu}\frac{\Delta p}{L} = 2\overline{V} \qquad [7.61]$$

- Volumetric flow rate:

$$Q = -\frac{\pi R^4}{8\mu}\frac{\Delta p}{L} \qquad [7.62]$$

- Shear stress distribution:

$$\tau(r) = \frac{r}{2}\frac{\Delta p}{L} \qquad [7.63]$$

and

$$\frac{\tau(r)}{\tau_w} = \frac{r}{R} \qquad [7.64]$$

where r = radial coordinate of a coordinate system with its origin on the centerline of the pipe,
R = inside radius of the pipe.

Darcy Equation

To estimate the frictional losses for flow in a horizontal pipe with a constant cross-sectional area, the Bernoulli equation (equation 7.51) reduces to

$$p_1 - p_2 = \rho g h_f = \gamma h_f \qquad [7.65]$$

The frictional head loss is estimated using the **Darcy equation:**

$$h_f = f\frac{L}{D}\frac{\overline{V}^2}{2g} \qquad [7.66]$$

For laminar flow:

$$f = \frac{64}{\text{Re}}$$

The friction factor (f) for transitional or turbulent flow can be found in the Moody or Stanton diagram, a copy of which is included at the end of this chapter. Another parameter required for use of the Moody diagram is the relative roughness (e/D). The roughness (e) of a pipe is a function of the material and the process by which the pipe is manufactured. Some examples of roughness values are given in Table 7.1.

Table 7.1 Roughness Values for Selected Materials

Material	*e* (ft)	*e* (mm)
Riveted steel	0.003–0.03	0.9–9.0
Concrete	0.001–0.01	0.3–3.0
Cast iron	0.00085	0.25
Galvanized iron	0.0005	0.15
Galvanized steel or wrought iron	0.000015	0.046
Drawn tubing	0.000005	0.0015

Example 7.14

Using the Darcy equation, calculate the head loss in a horizontal pipe of constant cross-sectional area if the inside diameter of the pipe is 6 in and its length is 200 ft. Water with a density of 62.4 lbm/ft^3 and a viscosity of 1.67×10^{-5} lbf-sec/ft^2 flows into the pipe at a speed of 2 ft/sec. The roughness of the pipe is 0.01 in. (Assume that the flow is incompressible.)

Solution:

To use the Darcy equation, first calculate the Reynolds number and relative roughness.

$$\text{Re} = \frac{\rho \overline{V} D}{\mu}$$

$$= \frac{\left(62.4\,\frac{\text{lbm}}{\text{ft}^3}\right)\left(2\,\frac{\text{ft}}{\text{sec}}\right)(6\text{ in})\left(\frac{\text{ft}}{12\text{ in}}\right)}{1.67 \times 10^{-5}\,\frac{\text{lbf-sec}}{\text{ft}^2}} \times \left(\frac{\text{lbf}}{32.17\,\frac{\text{lbm-ft}}{\text{sec}^2}}\right)$$

$$= 9{,}670$$

$$\frac{e}{D} = \frac{0.01\text{ in}}{6\text{ in}}$$

$$= 0.00167$$

Use the Moody diagram to determine that the friction factor is 0.024. Now use the Darcy equation to find the head loss.

$$h_f = f \cdot \frac{L}{D} \cdot \frac{\overline{V}^2}{2g}$$

$$= 0.024\left[\frac{200\text{ ft}}{6\text{ in}\left(\frac{\text{ft}}{12\text{ in}}\right)}\right]\left[\frac{\left(2\,\frac{\text{ft}}{\text{sec}}\right)^2}{2\left(32.17\,\frac{\text{ft}}{\text{sec}^2}\right)}\right]$$

$$= 0.596\text{ ft}$$

Hagen-Poiseuille Equation

Pressure loss for laminar flow in a circular pipe can be related to volumetric flow rate by using the **Hagen-Poiseuille equation:**

$$Q = \frac{\pi R^4\,\Delta p_f}{8\mu L} \qquad [7.67]$$

or

$$Q = \frac{\pi D^4\,\Delta p_f}{128\mu L} \qquad [7.68]$$

where Q = volumetric flow rate (ft^3/sec or m^3/s),
R = inside radius of the pipe,
D = inside diameter of the pipe,
Δp_f = pressure drop in the pipe due to frictional losses.

Head Losses in Pipe Bends, Enlargements, Contractions, Entrances, and Exits

Minor head losses (h_{fm}) occur any time that the size or direction of a pipe changes. The value of the minor head loss can be found by using the following equation:

$$h_{fm} = C\frac{\overline{V}^2}{2g} \qquad [7.69]$$

The loss coefficient (C) is determined by the geometry of the change and can vary greatly. A table is commonly used to determine the loss coefficient; Figure 7.13 gives the loss coefficients for some types of entrances and exits.

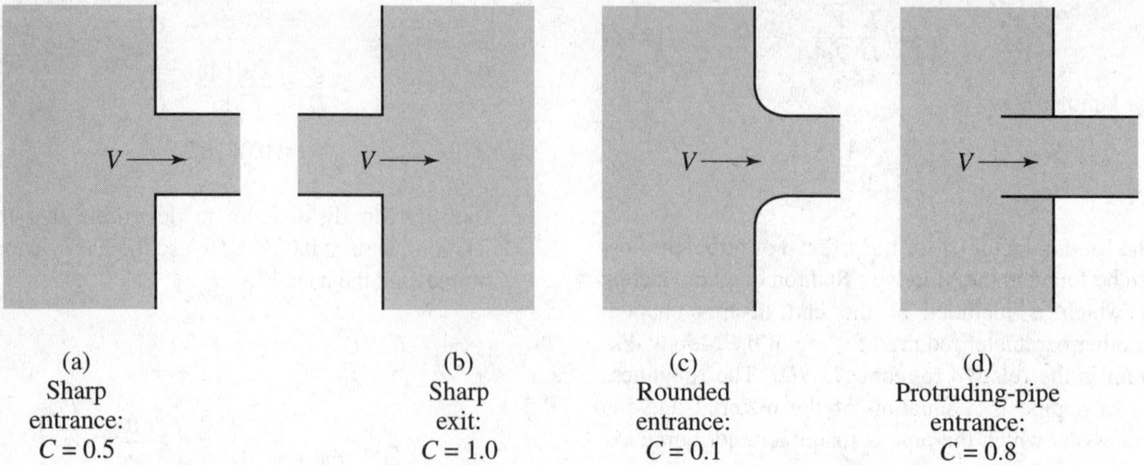

Figure 7.13 Loss coefficients for several types of pipe entrances and exits.

The Bernoulli equation is modified as follows to determine the change in energy of a fluid for flow through a pipe, including both major and minor head losses:

$$\frac{p_1}{\gamma} + \frac{\overline{V}_1^2}{2g} + z_1 = \frac{p_2}{\gamma} + \frac{\overline{V}_2^2}{2g} + z_2 + h_f + h_{fm} \quad [7.70]$$

Example 7.15

If an elbow with loss coefficient $C = 0.75$ is placed at the end of the pipe of Example 7.14, what is the minor head loss through the elbow?

Solution:

From equation 7.69:

$$h_{fm} = C\frac{\overline{V}^2}{2g}$$

$$= 0.75\left[\frac{\left(2\frac{\text{ft}}{\text{sec}}\right)^2}{2\left(32.17\frac{\text{ft}}{\text{sec}^2}\right)}\right]$$

$$= 0.047 \text{ ft}$$

Multiple-Path Pipeline

A common technique used to increase the capacity of a pipe is to add another pipe in parallel.

It is possible to predict how much fluid will flow through each path. The fluid pressures before and after the branch must be equal. Therefore, the flow will divide itself in such a way that the head losses through each path will be equal.

For the multiple-path pipeline shown in Figure 7.14:

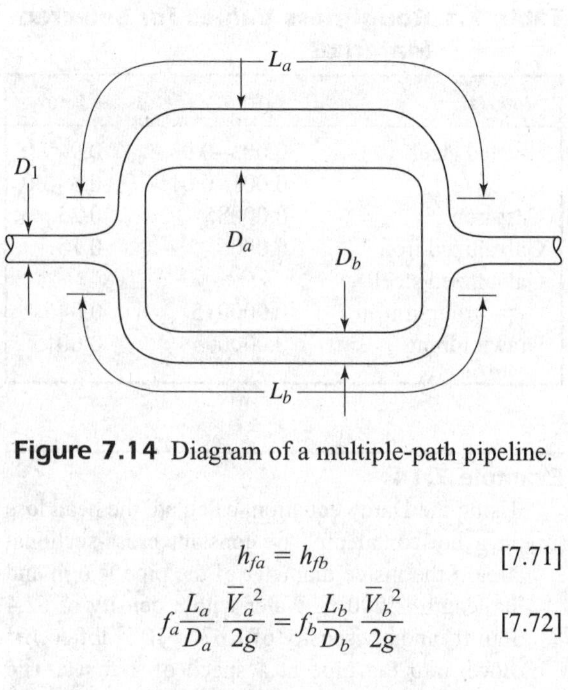

Figure 7.14 Diagram of a multiple-path pipeline.

$$h_{fa} = h_{fb} \quad [7.71]$$

$$f_a\frac{L_a}{D_a}\frac{\overline{V}_a^2}{2g} = f_b\frac{L_b}{D_b}\frac{\overline{V}_b^2}{2g} \quad [7.72]$$

From the continuity equation (equation 7.45):

$$\frac{\pi}{4}D_1^2\overline{V}_1 = \frac{\pi}{4}D_a^2\overline{V}_a + \frac{\pi}{4}D_b^2\overline{V}_b \quad [7.73]$$

When the flow rate of the fluid entering the control volume and the diameters and lengths of the pipes are known, equations 7.72 and 7.73 can be solved simultaneously to determine $\overline{V}_a$ and $\overline{V}_b$.

Example 7.16

For the multiple-path pipeline shown in the accompanying figure, what is the average speed through pipe A ($\overline{V}_A$)? (Assume that the friction factor in pipe A is equal to the friction factor in pipe B.)

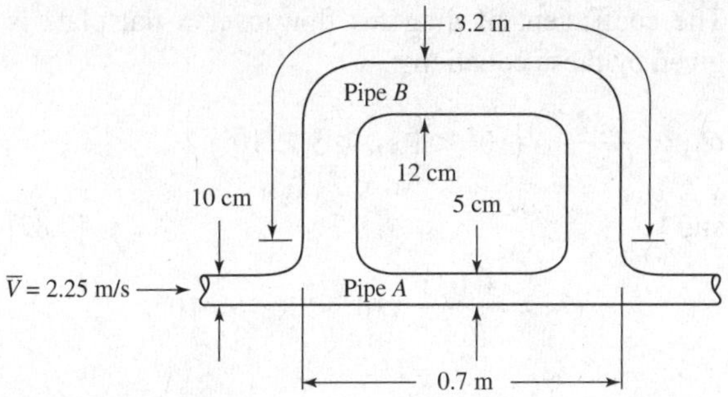

Solution:

From equation 7.72:

$$f_A \frac{L_A}{D_A} \frac{\overline{V}_A^2}{2g} = f_B \frac{L_B}{D_B} \frac{\overline{V}_B^2}{2g}$$

$$\frac{\overline{V}_A}{\overline{V}_B} = \sqrt{\frac{D_A}{D_B} \frac{L_B}{L_A}}$$

$$= \sqrt{\frac{5\text{ cm}}{12\text{ cm}} \frac{3.2\text{ m}}{0.7\text{ m}}}$$

$$= 1.38$$

From equation 7.73:

$$\overline{V}A = \overline{V}_A A_A + \overline{V}_B A_B$$

$$= \overline{V}_A A_A + \frac{\overline{V}_A}{1.38} A_B$$

$$= \overline{V}_A \left(A_A + \frac{A_B}{1.38} \right)$$

$$\overline{V}_A = \overline{V} \left(\frac{\frac{\pi D^2}{4}}{\frac{\pi D_A^2}{4} + \frac{\pi D_B^2}{4(1.38)}} \right)$$

$$= \overline{V} \left(\frac{D^2}{D_A^2 + \frac{D_B^2}{1.38}} \right)$$

$$= 2.25 \frac{\text{m}}{\text{s}} \left[\frac{(10\text{ cm})^2}{(5\text{ cm})^2 + \frac{(12\text{ cm})^2}{1.38}} \right]$$

$$= 1.74\text{ m/s}$$

Flow in Noncircular Ducts

Flow in noncircular ducts can be analyzed using the same techniques used for round ducts. All that is needed is to replace the tube diameter with a new parameter called the *hydraulic radius* (R_h) or *hydraulic diameter* (D_h). The equations for this parameter are as follows:

$$R_h = \frac{\text{cross-sectional area}}{\text{wetted perimeter}} \quad [7.74]$$

$$D_h = 4\left(\frac{\text{cross-sectional area}}{\text{wetted perimeter}}\right) = 4R_h \quad [7.75]$$

For instance, the Reynolds number for flow in a noncircular duct is expressed as:

$$\text{Re}_{D_h} = \frac{\rho \overline{V} D_h}{\mu} \quad [7.76]$$

Example 7.17

Find the hydraulic diameter of a rectangular duct 24 in wide and 15 in high.

Solution:

$$D_h = 4\left(\frac{\text{cross-sectional area}}{\text{wetted perimeter}}\right)$$

$$= 4\left[\frac{wh}{2(w+h)}\right]$$

$$= 4\left[\frac{(24\text{ in})(15\text{ in})}{2(24\text{ in} + 15\text{ in})}\right]$$

$$= 18.46\text{ in}$$

Open-Channel Flow

The relationships developed until now have been for flow inside a closed pipe. Most of these, such as the Darcy friction factor, have been determined through experimentation. As the basic geometry of the fluid system to be analyzed changes, we can expect to need new empirical relationships. Two such relationships for open-channel flow are Manning's equation and the Hazen-Williams equation.

Manning's equation:

$$\overline{V} = \frac{1}{n} R^{2/3} S^{1/2} \quad [7.77]$$

Hazen-Williams equation:

$$\overline{V} = 0.849 C R^{0.63} S^{0.54} \quad [7.78]$$

where n = Manning roughness coefficient,
C = Hazen-Williams roughness coefficent,
R = hydraulic radius of the channel (ft or m),
S = slope of the energy grade line (ft/ft or m/m).

7.6 External Flow

Often important in external flow analysis is the total drag force acting on the object of study. This drag is measured using a nondimensional coefficient of drag (C_D), which is defined as follows:

$$C_D = \frac{F_D}{\frac{1}{2}\rho V_\infty{}^2 A} \qquad [7.79]$$

where C_D = nondimensional coefficient of drag,
F_D = total drag force exerted on the object by the fluid,
ρ = density of the fluid,
V_∞ = speed of the fluid far from the object,
A = area over which the drag force is acting.

If the coefficient of drag is given, the drag force can be calculated using this equation:

$$F_D = \frac{C_D \rho V_\infty{}^2 A}{2} \qquad [7.80]$$

Uniform Flow over a Flat Plate

Flow over a flat plate demonstrates a concept important to the study of fluid dynamics, the boundary layer. As the fluid flow encounters the first edge of the plate, the vertical flow distribution is uniform, as shown in Figure 7.15.

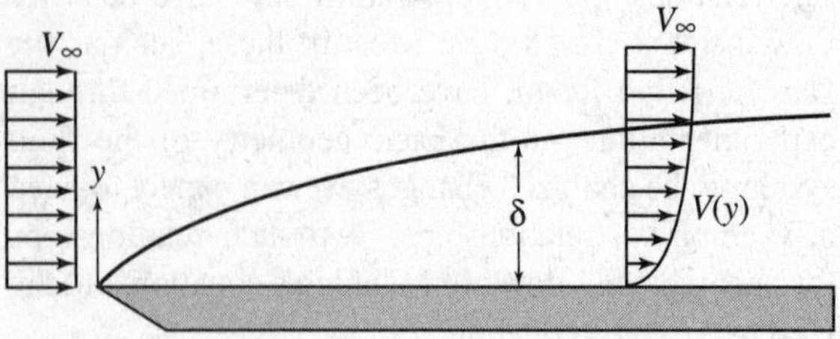

Figure 7.15 Flow over a flat plate.

As the flow progresses along the plate, the vertical distance above the plate at which fluid with a speed of V_∞ is first encountered increases. This distance is called the boundary layer thickness (δ). In the boundary layer, the fluid velocity and the shear stress in the fluid vary with distance above the surface of the plate.

The characteristic length used for uniform flow over a flat plate is the length of the plate. The Reynolds number for flow over a flat plate is expressed as follows:

$$\text{Re}_L = \frac{\rho V_\infty L}{\mu} \qquad [7.81]$$

The coefficient of drag for flow over a flat plate is given by these equations:

$$C_D = \frac{1.33}{\text{Re}_L^{0.5}} \quad (10^4 < \text{Re}_L < 5 \times 10^5)$$

and [7.82]

$$C_D = \frac{0.031}{\text{Re}_L^{1/7}} \quad (10^6 < \text{Re}_L < 10^9)$$

Example 7.18

A square plate with 50 cm on a side is placed in an airstream with a speed of 12 m/s.

A. What is the coefficient of drag for the plate?
B. What is the total drag force on the plate? (Assume that the density of air is 1.225 kg/m^3, and that the viscosity is 2×10^{-5} N · s/m^2.)

Solution:

A. From equation 7.81:

$$\text{Re}_L = \frac{\rho V_\infty L}{\mu} = \frac{\left(1.225\frac{\text{kg}}{\text{m}^3}\right)\left(12\,\frac{\text{m}}{\text{s}}\right)(0.50\text{ m})}{2 \times 10^{-5}\,\frac{\text{N}\cdot\text{s}}{\text{m}^2}}\left(\frac{\text{N}}{\frac{\text{kg}\cdot\text{m}}{\text{s}^2}}\right) = 3.67 \times 10^5$$

From equation 7.82:

$$C_D = \frac{1.33}{\text{Re}_L^{0.5}} = \frac{1.33}{(3.67 \times 10^5)^{0.5}} = 2.19 \times 10^{-3}$$

B. The total force is given by equation 7.80:

$$F_D = \frac{C_D \rho V_\infty{}^2 A}{2} = \frac{(2.19 \times 10^{-3})\left(1.225\,\frac{\text{kg}}{\text{m}^3}\right)\left(12\,\frac{\text{m}}{\text{s}}\right)^2(0.50\text{ m})^2}{2} \times \left(\frac{\text{N}}{\frac{\text{kg}\cdot\text{m}}{\text{s}^2}}\right) = 4.84 \times 10^{-2}\text{ N}$$

7.7 Devices

The principles of fluid mechanics discussed so far can be used to describe the operation of many industrial devices. A few examples follow.

Deflector and Blades

Many devices utilize the kinetic energy of a high-velocity fluid to produce power, which is commonly transmitted to a series of curved surfaces or blades. The impulse-momentum principle is used to describe their operation. We will neglect the viscous drag of the fluid at the blade surface; therefore, the fluid leaving the trailing edge of the blade will have the same speed as the fluid approaching the leading edge of the blade.

Fixed Blade

Figure 7.16 shows a fluid jet acting on a stationary blade. Since the blade does not move, the direction of the fluid stream that leaves the blade is determined by the angle of the trailing edge of the blade. The blade's reaction force is related to the change in momentum of the fluid. It is assumed that the speed of the fluid stream leaving the blade is equal to the speed of the fluid stream entering the blade.

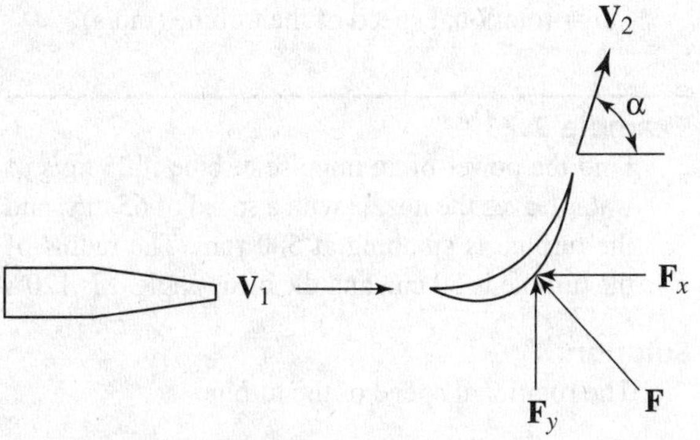

Figure 7.16 Fluid jet flowing over a stationary blade.

$$|\mathbf{V}_2| = |\mathbf{V}_1| \quad [7.83]$$

$$|\mathbf{F}_x| = \dot{m}(|\mathbf{V}_1| - |\mathbf{V}_2| \cdot \cos\alpha) \quad [7.84]$$

$$|\mathbf{F}_y| = \dot{m}|\mathbf{V}_2| \cdot \sin\alpha \quad [7.85]$$

where $|\mathbf{V}_1|$ = magnitude of the fluid velocity approaching the blade,

$|\mathbf{V}_2|$ = magnitude of the fluid velocity leaving the blade.

Example 7.19

Find the total reaction force on a fixed blade if 5 kg/s of water with a speed of 6 m/s enters the blade, and the blade angle α is 65°.

Solution:

From equation 7.84:

$$|\mathbf{F}_x| = \dot{m}(|\mathbf{V}_1| - |\mathbf{V}_2| \cdot \cos\alpha)$$

$$= \left(5\,\frac{\text{kg}}{\text{s}}\right)\left[6\,\frac{\text{m}}{\text{s}} - 6\,\frac{\text{m}}{\text{s}}(\cos 65)\right]\left(\frac{\text{N}}{\frac{\text{kg}\cdot\text{m}}{\text{s}^2}}\right)$$

$$= 17.32\text{ N}$$

From equation 7.85:

$$|\mathbf{F}_y| = \dot{m}|\mathbf{V}_2| \cdot \sin\alpha$$

$$= \left(5\,\frac{\text{kg}}{\text{s}}\right)\left(6\,\frac{\text{m}}{\text{s}}\right)\sin 65\left(\frac{\text{N}}{\frac{\text{kg}\cdot\text{m}}{\text{s}^2}}\right)$$

$$= 27.19\text{ N}$$

The magnitude of the reaction force is

$$|\mathbf{F}| = \sqrt{|\mathbf{F}_x|^2 + |\mathbf{F}_y|^2}$$

$$= \sqrt{(17.32\text{ N})^2 + (27.19\text{ N})^2}$$

$$= 32.23\text{ N}$$

Moving Blade

When the blade is moving in the same direction as the fluid jet, as is the case in the rotating portions of turbomachinery, the velocity of the blade affects the change in fluid momentum that occurs. This situation is illustrated in Figure 7.17.

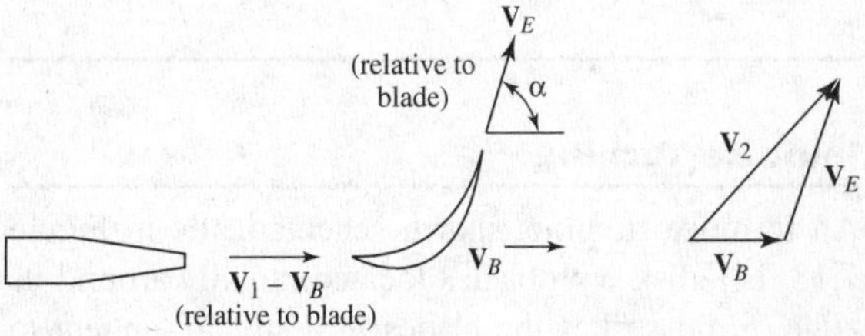

Figure 7.17 Fluid jet flowing over a moving blade.

The relationships between the velocities and the forces on the blade are given by the following equations:

$$\mathbf{V}_E = \mathbf{V}_1 - \mathbf{V}_B \quad [7.86]$$

$$\mathbf{V}_2 = \mathbf{V}_E + \mathbf{V}_B \quad [7.87]$$

$$|\mathbf{F}_x| = -\dot{m}(|\mathbf{V}_1| - |\mathbf{V}_B|)(1 - \cos\alpha) \quad [7.88]$$

$$|\mathbf{F}_y| = \dot{m}(|\mathbf{V}_1| - |\mathbf{V}_B|) \cdot \sin\alpha \quad [7.89]$$

where $\mathbf{V}_1$ = velocity of the fluid jet approaching the blade,
$\mathbf{V}_B$ = velocity of blade,
$\mathbf{V}_E$ = velocity of fluid leaving the blade, relative to the blade,
$\mathbf{V}_2$ = true velocity of fluid leaving the blade.

Example 7.20

Find the total reaction force on a moving blade if 5 kg/s of water with a speed of 6 m/s enters the blade, the blade is moving at a speed of 1.4 m/s, and the blade angle α is 65°.

Solution:

From equation 7.88:

$$|\mathbf{F}_x| = \dot{m}(|\mathbf{V}_1| - |\mathbf{V}_B|)(1 - \cos\alpha)$$

$$= \left(5\,\frac{\text{kg}}{\text{s}}\right)\left(6\,\frac{\text{m}}{\text{s}} - 1.4\,\frac{\text{m}}{\text{s}}\right)(1 - \cos 65)\left(\frac{\text{N}}{\frac{\text{kg}\cdot\text{m}}{\text{s}^2}}\right)$$

$$= 13.28\ \text{N}$$

From equation 7.89:

$$|\mathbf{F}_y| = \dot{m}(|\mathbf{V}_1| - |\mathbf{V}_B|)(\sin\alpha)$$

$$= \left(5\,\frac{\text{kg}}{\text{s}}\right)\left(6\,\frac{\text{m}}{\text{s}} - 1.4\,\frac{\text{m}}{\text{s}}\right)(\sin 65)\left(\frac{\text{N}}{\frac{\text{kg}\cdot\text{m}}{\text{s}^2}}\right)$$

$$= 20.85\ \text{N}$$

The magnitude of the reaction force is:

$$|\mathbf{F}| = \sqrt{|\mathbf{F}_x|^2 + |\mathbf{F}_y|^2}$$

$$= \sqrt{(13.28\ \text{N})^2 + (20.85\ \text{N})^2}$$

$$= 24.72\ \text{N}$$

Impulse Turbine

An **impulse turbine,** shown schematically in Figure 7.18, is a disk with blades located radially around its edge. Fluid strikes the blades in a stream tangent to the turbine. The reaction force of the fluid against the blades begins to turn the turbine around its axis, and this motion can be used to generate power.

The amount of power generated is related to the angle of blade deflection (α). Maximum power is generated at α = 180°. The turbine power is related to the mass flow rate of the fluid and to its velocity by the equation

$$\dot{W} = Q\rho(|\mathbf{V}_1 - \mathbf{V}_B|)(1 - \cos\alpha)|\mathbf{V}_B| \qquad [7.90]$$

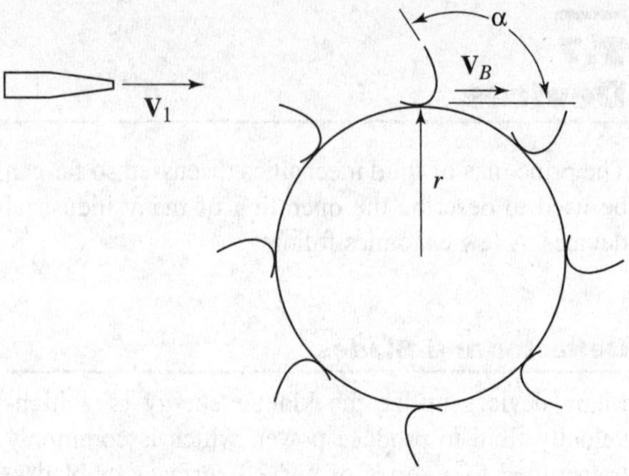

Figure 7.18 An impulse turbine.

Maximum power is expressed as

$$\dot{W}_{\text{max}} = Q\rho\left(\frac{|\mathbf{V}_1{}^2|}{4}\right)(1 - \cos\alpha) \qquad [7.91]$$

Or, when α = 180°:

$$\dot{W}_{\text{max}} = \frac{Q\rho|\mathbf{V}_1|^2}{2} \qquad [7.92]$$

The speed of the blade is related to the rotational speed of the turbine by the equation

$$|\mathbf{V}_B| = r\omega \qquad [7.93]$$

where r = radius of the turbine (ft or m),
ω = rotational speed of the turbine (rad/s).

Example 7.21

Find the power of an impulse turbine if 25 kg/s of water leaves the nozzle with a speed of 65 m/s, and the turbine is spinning at 500 rpm. The radius of the turbine is 50 cm, and the blade angle α is 120°.

Solution:

The rotational speed of the turbine is

$$\omega = \left(500\,\frac{\text{rev}}{\text{min}}\right)\left(\frac{2\pi\ \text{rad}}{\text{rev}}\right)\left(\frac{\text{min}}{60\ \text{s}}\right)$$

$$= 52.36\ \text{rad/s}$$

From equation 7.93, the blade velocity is

$$|\mathbf{V}_B| = r\omega$$

$$= (0.50\ \text{m})\left(52.36\,\frac{\text{rad}}{\text{s}}\right)$$

$$= 26.18\ \text{m/s}$$

From equation 7.90:

$$\dot{W} = \dot{m}(|\mathbf{V}_1 - \mathbf{V}_B|)(1 - \cos\alpha)|\mathbf{V}_B|$$

$$= \left(25\ \frac{\text{kg}}{\text{s}}\right)\left(65\ \frac{\text{m}}{\text{s}} - 26.18\ \frac{\text{m}}{\text{s}}\right)(1 - \cos 120)$$

$$\times \left(26.18\ \frac{\text{m}}{\text{s}}\right)\left(\frac{\text{N}}{\frac{\text{kg}\cdot\text{m}}{\text{s}^2}}\right)\left(\frac{\text{kW}}{1{,}000\ \frac{\text{N}\cdot\text{m}}{\text{s}}}\right)$$

$$= 38.11\ \text{kW}$$

Jet Propulsion

A fluid jet used for propulsion is an example of the practical use of the impulse-momentum principle. The momentum of the fluid jet leaving the control volume results in a force that acts on the control volume in a direction opposite to that of the fluid jet. In the system described in Figure 7.19, the potential energy of the fluid is converted to kinetic energy as the fluid flows out of the orifice. As the fluid is expelled, it leaves the system with a certain amount of momentum. As a result, a force is exerted on the control volume in the opposite direction to the flow out of the orifice. This force is given by the equation

$$F = Q\rho(\overline{V} - 0) \qquad [7.94]$$

or

$$F = \rho\overline{V}^2 A \qquad [7.95]$$

where F = force on the control volume,
$\overline{V}$ = average speed of the fluid through the nozzle,
A = cross-sectional area of the nozzle exit.

By applying the Bernoulli equation between the free surface and the outlet of this system, we calculate the force as follows:

$$\frac{p_1}{\gamma} + (z_2 + h) + \frac{0^2}{2g} = \frac{p_1}{\gamma} + z_2 + \frac{\overline{V}^2}{2g} \qquad [7.96]$$

$$\overline{V}^2 = 2gh \qquad [7.97]$$

$$F = 2\rho ghA \qquad [7.98]$$

Pumps

Pumps utilize mechanical energy to increase the energy of a fluid. The amount of energy that is added to the fluid per unit time is expressed as

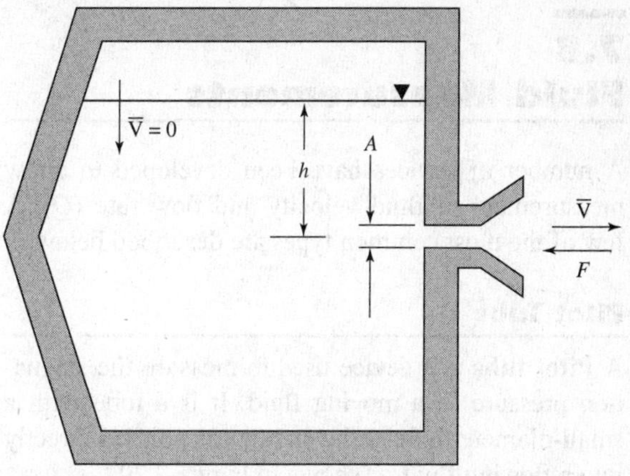

Figure 7.19 Jet of fluid exiting a container.

$$P = Q\gamma h \qquad [7.99]$$

where P = pump power (ft-lbf/sec or W),
Q = volumetric flow rate of fluid that is pumped (ft^3/sec or m^3/s),
h = change in fluid head (ft or m).

Because of inefficiencies in the pump, the amount of energy that must be supplied to the pump is somewhat greater than the amount of energy that is transferred to the fluid. The ratio of power transferred to the fluid to power supplied to the pump is the pump's efficiency (η). The amount of power that must be supplied to a pump can be found by using this equation:

$$P_{\text{req}} = \frac{Q\gamma h}{\eta} \qquad [7.100]$$

Example 7.22

A pump that is 63% efficient is required to lift 500 L/min of water from a stream into a tank that is 12 m above the surface of the stream. What is the minimum power input required for this pump?

Solution:

From equation 7.100:

$$P_{\text{req}} = \frac{Q\gamma h}{\eta}$$

$$= \frac{\left(500\ \frac{\text{L}}{\text{min}}\right)\left(9{,}810\ \frac{\text{N}}{\text{m}^3}\right)(12\ \text{m})}{0.63}$$

$$\times \left(\frac{\text{m}^3}{1{,}000\ \text{L}}\right)\left(\frac{\text{min}}{60\ \text{s}}\right)\left(\frac{\text{kW}}{1{,}000\ \frac{\text{N}\cdot\text{m}}{\text{s}}}\right)$$

$$= 1.56\ \text{kW}$$

7.8 Fluid Measurements

A number of devices have been developed to allow measurement of fluid velocity and flow rate (Q). A few of the most common types are described below.

Pitot Tube

A **Pitot tube** is a device used to measure the stagnation pressure of a moving fluid. It is a tube with a small-diameter hole at the end that is pointed directly into a flowing fluid, as shown in Figure 7.20.

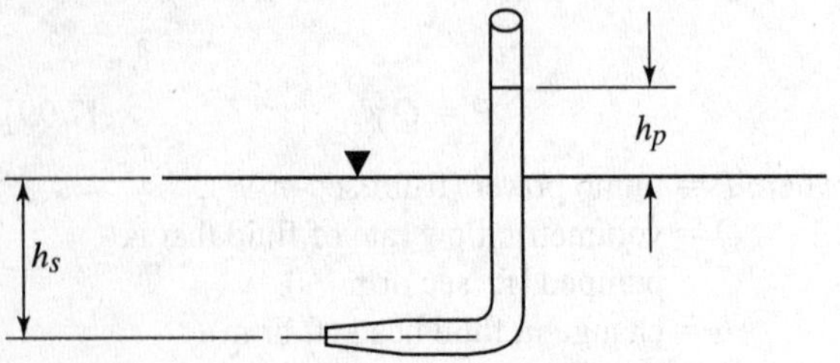

Figure 7.20 Illustration of a Pitot-tube flow-measurement device.

The speed of the fluid is computed from the stagnation pressure using one of these equations:

$$V = \sqrt{\frac{2(p_O - p_s)}{\rho}} \quad [7.101]$$

or

$$V = \sqrt{\frac{2g(p_O - p_s)}{\gamma}} \quad [7.102]$$

For the system shown in Figure 7.20, the static pressure and the stagnation pressure at the opening of the Pitot tube are given by the following relationships:

$$p_s = \rho g h_s + p_{\text{atm}} = \gamma h_s + p_{\text{atm}} \quad [7.103]$$

and

$$p_O = p_s + \rho g h_p \quad [7.104]$$

By combining equations 7.102 and 7.104, the fluid speed can be related directly to h_p:

$$h_p = \frac{V^2}{2g} \quad [7.105]$$

Although equation 7.101 was developed for an incompressible fluid, it may also be used with reasonable accuracy for a compressible fluid if the Mach number is less than approximately 0.3.

Example 7.23

A. For the Pitot tube shown in Figure 7.20, what is the stagnation pressure of the fluid if h_p = 13.6 cm and h_s = 8 cm? [Assume that the fluid is water (ρ = 1,000 kg/m^3), and that p_{atm} = 101.3 kPa.]

B. What is the fluid speed?

Solution:

A. From equation 7.103:

$$p_s = \rho g h_s + p_{\text{atm}}$$

$$= \left(1{,}000\,\frac{\text{kg}}{\text{m}^3}\right)\left(9.81\,\frac{\text{m}}{\text{s}^2}\right)(8\text{ cm})$$

$$\times\left(\frac{\text{m}}{100\text{ cm}}\right)\left(\frac{\text{N}}{\frac{\text{kg}\cdot\text{m}}{\text{s}^2}}\right)\left(\frac{\text{kPa}}{1{,}000\,\frac{\text{N}}{\text{m}^2}}\right) + 101.3\text{ kPa}$$

$$= 102.1\text{ Pa}$$

From equation 7.104:

$$p_O = p_s + \rho g h_p$$

$$= 102.1\text{ kPa} + \left(1{,}000\,\frac{\text{kg}}{\text{m}^3}\right)\left(9.81\,\frac{\text{m}}{\text{s}^2}\right)(13.6\text{ cm})$$

$$\times\left(\frac{\text{m}}{100\text{ cm}}\right)\left(\frac{\text{N}}{\frac{\text{kg}\cdot\text{m}}{\text{s}^2}}\right)\left(\frac{\text{kPa}}{1{,}000\,\frac{\text{N}}{\text{m}^2}}\right)$$

$$= 103.4\text{ kPa}$$

B. From equation 7.101:

$$V = \sqrt{\frac{2(p_O - p_s)}{\rho}}$$

$$= \sqrt{\frac{2(103.4\text{ kPa} - 102.1\text{ kPa})}{1{,}000\,\frac{\text{kg}}{\text{m}^3}}\left(\frac{1{,}000\,\frac{\text{N}}{\text{m}^2}}{\text{kPa}}\right)\left(\frac{\frac{\text{kg}\cdot\text{m}}{\text{s}^2}}{\text{N}}\right)}$$

$$= 1.61\text{ m/s}$$

Orifice Flow Meter

The **orifice flow meter,** illustrated in Figure 7.21, is a flat plate, with a small hole in the center, placed in a pipe. Pressure measurements are taken at fixed locations upstream and downstream of the orifice. The flow rate of the fluid is related to the difference in value between the upstream and downstream pressure measurements.

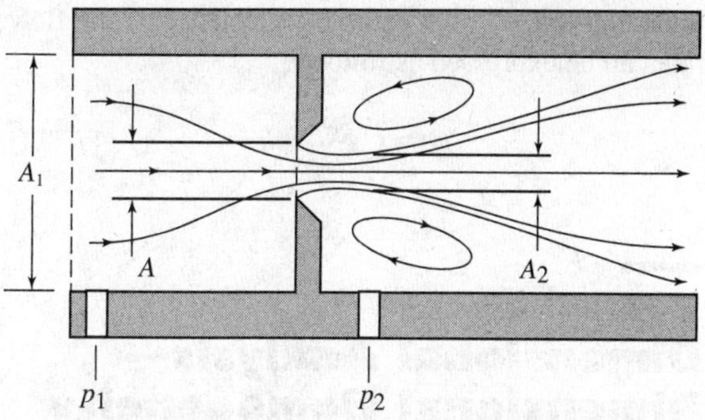

Figure 7.21 Diagram of an orifice flow meter.

The volumetric flow rate through an orifice flow meter is given by the following equation:

$$Q = CA\sqrt{2g\left[\left(\frac{p_1}{\gamma} + z_1\right) - \left(\frac{p_2}{\gamma} + z_2\right)\right]} \quad [7.106]$$

The flow meter coefficient (C) is given by the equation

$$C = \frac{C_v C_c}{\sqrt{1 - C_c^2\left(\frac{A}{A_1}\right)^2}} \quad [7.107]$$

The coefficients C_v and C_c are given in Table 7.2.

Table 7.2 Various Types of Orifices and Their Nominal Coefficient Values

	Sharp Edge	*Rounded*	*Short Tube*	*Borda*
	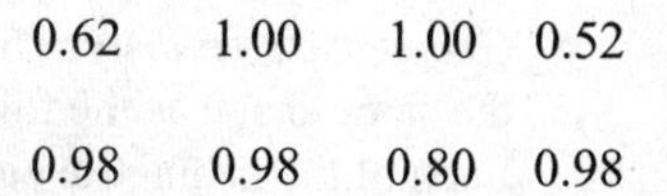			
Minimum value of				
C (meter coefficient)	0.61	0.98	0.80	0.51
C_c (coefficient of contraction)	0.62	1.00	1.00	0.52
C_v (coefficient of velocity)	0.98	0.98	0.80	0.98

An orifice flow meter provides a simple and efficient means to measure the flow rate. Unfortunately, however, this simplicity comes at a price; the sudden contraction of the flow produces large head losses.

Example 7.24

Water flows through a rounded orifice flow meter in a pipe having a 20-cm diameter. The orifice is in a horizontal section of the pipe and has an area of 0.03 m^2. The pressure just upstream of the orifice is 75 kPa, and the pressure just downstream is 15 kPa. What is the volumetric flow rate of the water?

Solution:

First determine the meter coefficient. From equation 7.107:

$$C = \frac{C_v C_c}{\sqrt{1 - C_c^2\left(\frac{A}{A_1}\right)^2}} = \frac{(0.98)(1.00)}{\sqrt{1 - (1.00)^2\left(\frac{0.03\ \text{m}^2}{\pi(0.25\ \text{m})^2}\right)}} = 1.065$$

Then use equation 7.106:

$$Q = CA\sqrt{2\left(\frac{p_1 - p_2}{\rho}\right)}$$

$$= (1.065)(0.03\ \text{m}^2) \times \sqrt{2\left[\left(\frac{75\ \text{kPa} - 15\ \text{kPa}}{1{,}000\ \frac{\text{kg}}{\text{m}^3}}\right)\right]\left(\frac{1{,}000\ \frac{\text{N}}{\text{m}^2}}{\text{kPa}}\right)\left(\frac{\frac{\text{kg}\cdot\text{m}}{\text{s}^2}}{\text{N}}\right)}$$

$$= 0.35\ \text{m}^3/\text{s}$$

Venturi Flow Meter

Like the orifice flow meter, the **venturi flow meter,** illustrated in Figure 7.22, uses a pressure drop across a flow restriction of known geometry to measure the flow rate.

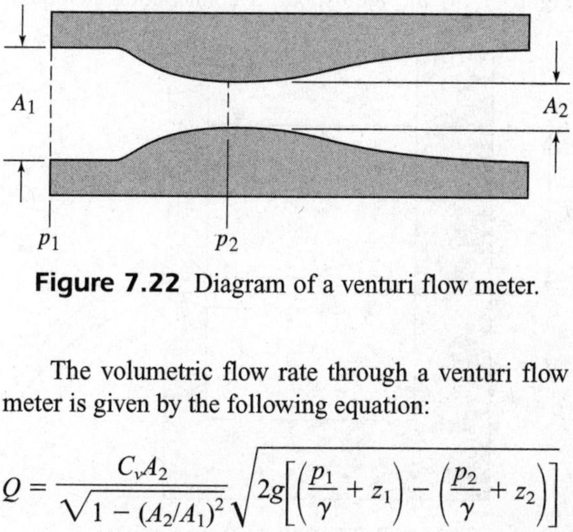

Figure 7.22 Diagram of a venturi flow meter.

The volumetric flow rate through a venturi flow meter is given by the following equation:

$$Q = \frac{C_v A_2}{\sqrt{1 - (A_2/A_1)^2}}\sqrt{2g\left[\left(\frac{p_1}{\gamma} + z_1\right) - \left(\frac{p_2}{\gamma} + z_2\right)\right]} \quad [7.108]$$

The coefficient of velocity (C_v) is obtained through experimentation.

The gradual contraction of the venturi flow meter largely reduces the head loss to the fluid stream. The shape of this device, however, is much more complicated to manufacture than is an orifice.

Submerged Orifice

The rate of flow through a submerged orifice, illustrated in Figure 7.23, is related to the hydrostatic pressure at each side of the orifice as shown in equation 7.106 or 7.107.

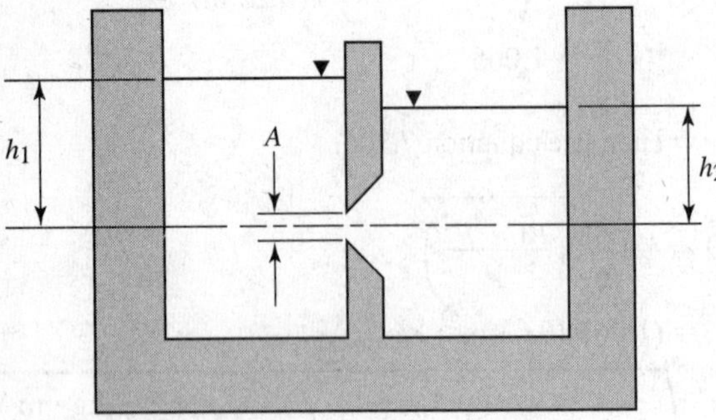

Figure 7.23 An orifice submerged below the surface of a fluid.

$$Q = C_c C_v A\sqrt{2g(h_1 - h_2)} \qquad [7.109]$$

or

$$Q = CA\sqrt{2g(h_1 - h_2)} \qquad [7.110]$$

Orifice Discharging into Atmosphere

If the fluid on the downstream side of an orifice discharges into the ambient atmosphere, as illustrated in Figure 7.24, the atmosphere's contribution to equations 7.108 and 7.109 can be neglected, and the flow rate can be expressed as follows:

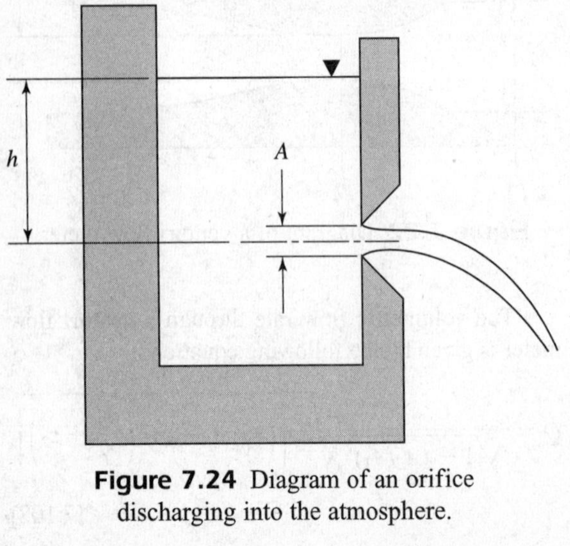

Figure 7.24 Diagram of an orifice discharging into the atmosphere.

$$Q = CA\sqrt{2gh} \qquad [7.111]$$

7.9 Dimensional Analysis—Dimensional Homogeneity

A dimensionally homogeneous relationship is one whose value is independent of the fundamental dimensions used (the units used to measure mass, length, or time). Dimensional homogeneity is assured for relationships that are placed in a dimensionless form. The *Buckingham PI* theorem tells how many dimensionless groups are required to describe a relationship. It states that, if the relationship has n independent variables, involving r different fundamental dimensions (mass, length, or time), then $n - r$ dimensionless groups are required.

7.10 Similitude

Model testing plays a large role in fluid dynamic analysis. The reason is that the equations of fluid flow are sufficiently complex that it is impracticable to solve them for all but the simplest flow conditions. Furthermore, testing of a full-size prototype is often prohibitively expensive.

We can be assured that the model we use for testing predicts accurately the fluid interaction of the full-scale prototype if we can prove that there is similarity between the two. Required are three kinds of similarity:

- *Geometric similarity:* The model must have the same shape as the full-scale prototype. Each of the geometric parameters that describe the shape and size of the model differs from the corresponding geometric parameter of the full-scale prototype by a constant scale factor.
- *Kinematic similarity:* The character of the fluid flow must be the same for the model and the full-scale prototype. In other words, the direction of flow of each fluid particle near the model must be the same as that of the fluid particle at the corresponding location near the full-scale prototype. The velocities of the two corresponding fluid particles must be related by a constant scale factor.

- *Dynamic similarity:* The forces that interact with the model must be similar to the forces that act on the full-scale prototype. For each force that acts on the full-scale prototype, there must be a corresponding force acting on the model. Each corresponding force must act in the same direction, through the corresponding location, and with a magnitude that differs by a constant scale factor. The model and the prototype must have geometric and kinematic similarity if dynamic similarity is to be achieved.

  Dynamic similarity is achieved when the following conditions are met:

$$\left[\frac{F_I}{F_p}\right]_p = \left[\frac{F_I}{F_p}\right]_m \quad \text{or} \quad \left[\frac{\rho\bar{V}^2}{p}\right]_p = \left[\frac{\rho\bar{V}^2}{p}\right]_m \qquad [7.112]$$

$$\left[\frac{F_I}{F_V}\right]_p = \left[\frac{F_I}{F_V}\right]_m \quad \text{or} \quad \left[\frac{\rho\bar{V}l}{\mu}\right]_p = \left[\frac{\rho\bar{V}l}{\mu}\right]_m \quad \text{or} \quad [\text{Re}]_p = [\text{Re}]_m \qquad [7.113]$$

$$\left[\frac{F_I}{F_G}\right]_p = \left[\frac{F_I}{F_G}\right]_m \quad \text{or} \quad \left[\frac{\bar{V}^2}{lg}\right]_p = \left[\frac{\bar{V}^2}{lg}\right]_m \quad \text{or} \quad [\text{Fr}]_p = [\text{Fr}]_m \qquad [7.114]$$

$$\left[\frac{F_I}{F_E}\right]_p = \left[\frac{F_I}{F_E}\right]_m \quad \text{or} \quad \left[\frac{\rho\bar{V}^2}{E}\right]_p = \left[\frac{\rho\bar{V}^2}{E}\right]_m \quad \text{or} \quad [\text{Ca}]_p = [\text{Ca}]_m \qquad [7.115]$$

$$\left[\frac{F_I}{F_T}\right]_p = \left[\frac{F_I}{F_T}\right]_m \quad \text{or} \quad \left[\frac{\rho l\bar{V}^2}{\sigma}\right]_p = \left[\frac{\rho l\bar{V}^2}{\sigma}\right]_m \quad \text{or} \quad [\text{We}]_p = [\text{We}]_m \qquad [7.116]$$

where F_I = inertia force,
F_p = pressure force,
F_V = viscous force,
F_G = gravity force,
F_E = elastic force,
F_T = surface-tension force,
l = characteristic length,
Re = Reynolds number,
Fr = Froude number,
Ca = Cauchy number,
E = modulus of elasticity,
σ = surface tension,
We = Weber number.

The subscript p refers to the full-scale prototype, and the subscript m refers to the model.

Example 7.25

If a one-fifth-scale boat model is to be tested in a tow tank, at what speed should the model be towed if a speed of 15 knots (7.72 m/s) is to be simulated?

Solution:

From equation 7.113:

$$\left[\frac{\rho\bar{V}l}{\mu}\right]_p = \left[\frac{\rho\bar{V}l}{\mu}\right]_m$$

$$\bar{V}_m = \left(\frac{\rho_p}{\rho_m}\right)\left(\frac{\mu_m}{\mu_p}\right)\left(\frac{l_p}{l_m}\right)\bar{V}_p$$

$$= (1)(1)\left(\frac{1}{5}\right)\left(7.72\ \frac{\text{m}}{\text{s}}\right)$$

$$= 1.54 \text{ m/s}$$

PRACTICE PROBLEMS

1. What is the Mach number of a fluid stream flowing at a velocity of 370 ft/sec? ($c = 1{,}080$ ft/sec)
   (A) 0.66 (B) 2.92
   (C) 0.34 (D) 3.4
2. What is the gage pressure of air in a vessel if the absolute pressure is 340 kPa, and the ambient atmospheric pressure is 101 kPa?
   (A) 441 kPa (B) 105 kPa
   (C) 340 kPa (D) 239 kPa
3. The specific weight of a fluid is:
   (A) the ratio of the density of the fluid to the density of water
   (B) the mass of the fluid per unit volume
   (C) the weight of the fluid per unit volume
   (D) the ratio of the weight of the fluid to the weight of water
4. The viscosity of a fluid:
   (A) relates an applied normal stress to the velocity gradient in the fluid
   (B) relates an applied shear stress to the velocity gradient in the fluid
   (C) appears constant for all values of the velocity gradient in a dilatant fluid
   (D) appears constant for all values of the velocity gradient in a pseudoplastic fluid
5. What is the pressure at a point 18,000 ft below the surface of the ocean?

   $(\gamma = 64.0 \text{ lb/ft}^3)$

   (A) 1,150,000 psig
   (B) 250 psig
   (C) 8,000 psig
   (D) 258,000 psig
6. In the figure, what is the absolute pressure (p_A) in vessel A?

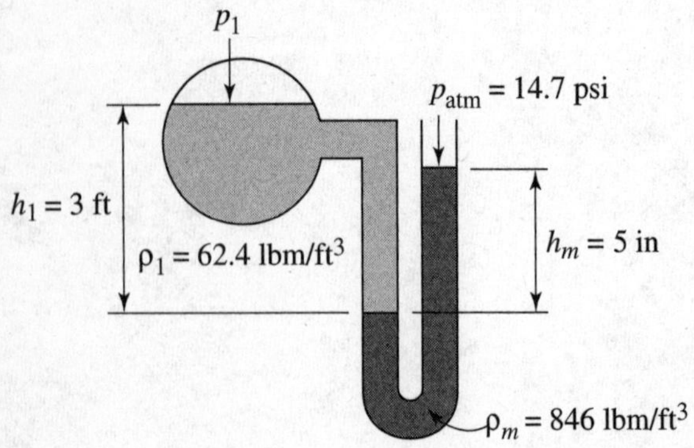

   (A) 15.8 psia (B) 18.4 psia
   (C) 13.6 psia (D) 11.0 psia
7. For the barometer shown in the figure, what is the atmospheric pressure if $h_m = 20$ cm, $\rho_m = 13{,}550$ kg/m^3, and $p_v = 0$ kPa?

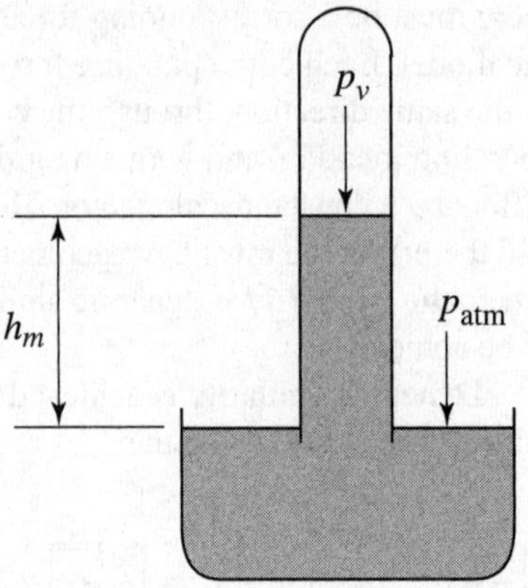

   (A) 128 kPa
   (B) 26.6 kPa
   (C) 4.36 kPa
   (D) 82.4 kPa
8. A cylindrical bar with a density of 41.6 lbm/ft^3 and a length of 3 ft floats in water ($\rho = 62.4$ lbm/ft^3) in such a way that the end surfaces of the bar are parallel to the surface of the water. How high will the top of the bar extend above the surface of the water?
   (A) 1 ft
   (B) 2 ft
   (C) 1.5 f
   (D) 0.5 ft
9. For steady flow of a compressible fluid in the expander shown in the figure, what is the density at the exit section (ρ_2)?

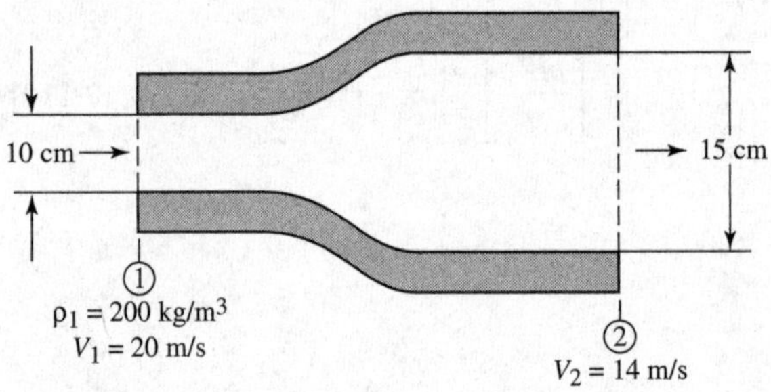

   (A) 190 kg/m^3
   (B) 62 kg/m^3
   (C) 642 kg/m^3
   (D) 127 kg/m^3

10. For the steady-state system shown in the figure, what is the force in the spring?

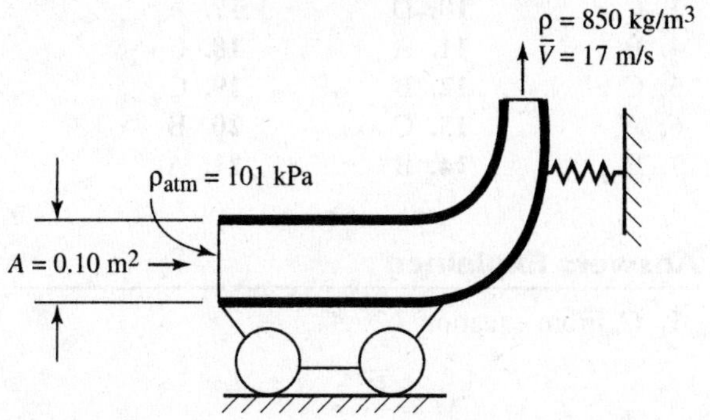

(A) 43,495 N
(B) 24,575 N
(C) 16,895 N
(D) 24,565 N

11. For the control volume shown in the figure, what is the change in pressure ($p_1 - p_2$) if the specific weight of the fluid is 9,810 N/m³? (Assume that frictional losses are negligible.)

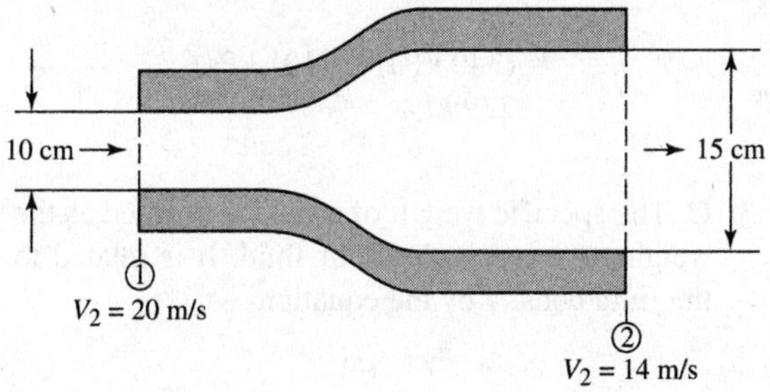

(A) −102 kPa
(B) −204 kPa
(C) 102 kPa
(D) 204 kPa

12. What is the stagnation pressure of water (ρ = 1,000 kg/m³) flowing with a velocity of 28 m/s if the static pressure is 300 kPa?
(A) −92 kPa
(B) 692 kPa
(C) 92 kPa
(D) 1,084 kPa

13. Water flows through a 20-cm-diameter pipe. If the critical Reynolds number is 2,300, what is the maximum value of the average velocity for which laminar flow can be assumed?
(A) 0.047 m/s
(B) 1.2 m/s
(C) 0.092 m/s
(D) 0.75 m/s

14. Water flows through a 17-cm-diameter horizontal pipe (f = 0.017) at a rate of 0.34 m³/s. What is the frictional head loss per meter of pipe length?
(A) 1.31 m
(B) 1.14 m
(C) 0.02 m
(D) 0.78 m

15. What is the minor head loss for the pipe entrance shown in the figure?

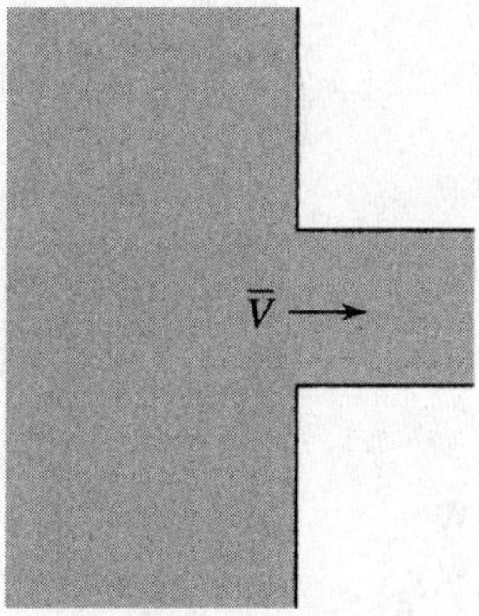

$\bar{V}$ = 165 m/s
C = 0.5

(A) 1.28 m
(B) 16.81 m
(C) 2,775 m
(D) 693.81 m

16. What is the hydraulic diameter of a square duct that measures 80 cm on a side?
(A) 2.4 m
(B) 1.2 m
(C) 0.80 m
(D) 0.40 m

17. What is the coefficient of drag for a flow of air (ρ = 1.225 kg/m³, μ = 1.8 × 10⁻⁵ N · s/m²) over a flat plate that is 93 cm long, if V_∞ = 86 m/s?
(A) 3.38 × 10^{-3}
(B) 5.70 × 10^{-3}
(C) 2.19 × 10^{-3}
(D) 8.27 × 10^{-3}

18. What is angle θ for the moving blade shown in the figure?

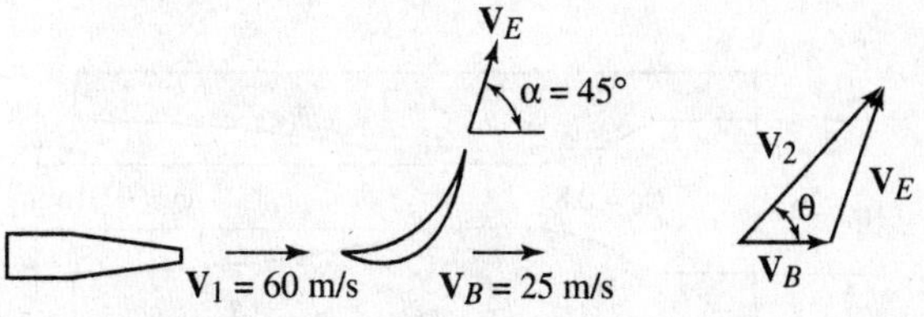

(A) 57.82°
(B) 63.55°
(C) 32.18°
(D) 26.45°

19. If 16 kg/s of water, traveling at 67 m/s, enters the impulse turbine shown in the figure, which has a 26-cm diameter and a blade angle α of 120°, what is the maximum power that can be generated?

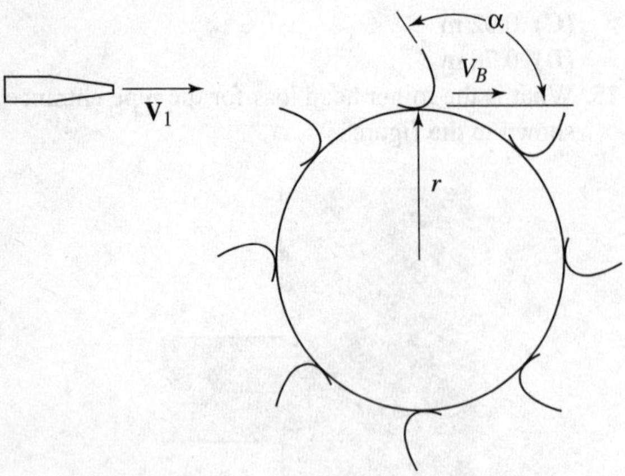

(A) 134 W
(B) 402 W
(C) 26.93 kW
(D) 8.98 kW

20. What is the pumping power required for the system shown in the figure? (Neglect friction in the pipes.)

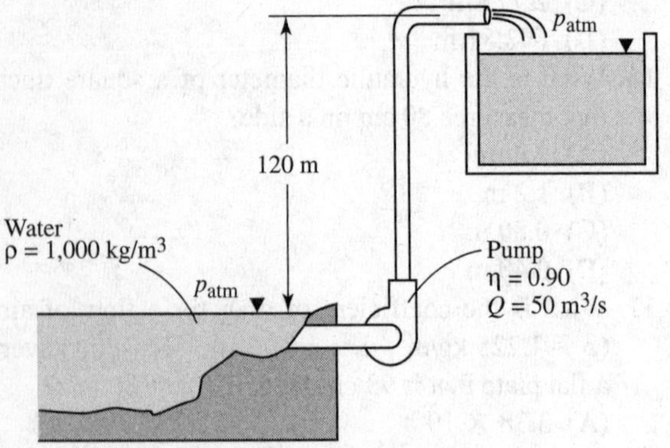

(A) 58,900 kW **(B)** 65,400 kW
(C) 82,300 kW **(D)** 53,000 kW

21. What is the volumetric flow rate (Q) of water ($\gamma = 9{,}810\ \text{N/m}^3$) for the venturi flow meter shown in the figure?

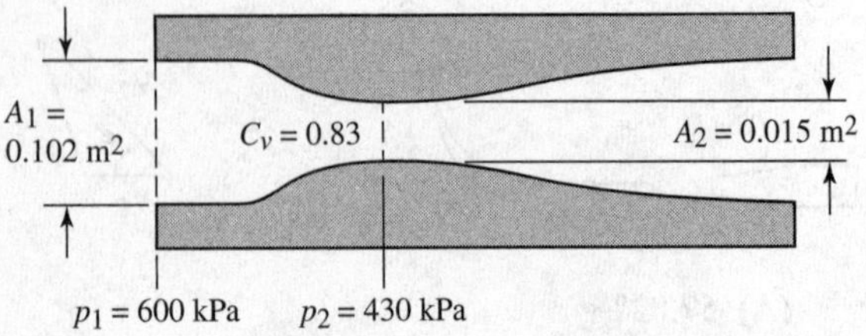

(A) 0.232 m³/s **(B)** 0.248 m³/s
(C) 0.733 m³/s **(D)** 0.467 m³/s

Answer Key

1. C	8. A	15. D
2. D	9. D	16. C
3. C	10. D	17. A
4. B	11. A	18. C
5. C	12. B	19. C
6. A	13. C	20. B
7. B	14. B	21. A

Answers Explained

1. C From equation 7.2:

$$M = \frac{\overline{V}}{c} = \frac{370\ \frac{\text{ft}}{\text{sec}}}{1{,}080\ \frac{\text{ft}}{\text{sec}}} = 0.343$$

2. D From equation 7.5:

$$p_a = p_g + p_{atm}$$

or

$$p_g = p_a - p_{atm} = (340\ \text{kPa}) - (101\ \text{kPa}) = 239\ \text{kPa}$$

3. C The specific weight of a fluid is defined as the weight of a unit volume of fluid. It is related to the fluid density by the equation

$$\gamma = \rho g$$

where γ = specific weight (lbf/ft³ or N/m³),
g = acceleration due to gravity (32.17 ft/sec² or 9.81 m/s² at sea level).
ρ = density

4. B It can be shown that the shear force in most common fluids can be expressed using equation 7.10:

$$\tau_{\mathbf{n}}(P) = \mu \frac{\partial \mathbf{V}}{\partial x_n}$$

Therefore choice **B** is correct. In a dilatant fluid, the viscosity appears to increase as the velocity gradient increases. In a pseudoplastic fluid, the viscosity appears to decrease as the velocity gradient increases.

5. C From equation 7.15: $p_g = \gamma h$

$$= \left(64.0\ \frac{\text{lbf}}{\text{ft}^3}\right)(18{,}000\ \text{ft})\left(\frac{\text{ft}^2}{144\ \text{in}^2}\right)$$
$$= 8{,}000\ \text{lbf/in}^2 \text{ or psig}$$

6. A From equation 7.23:

$$p_1 = p_{atm} + \rho_m g h_m - \rho_1 g h_1$$

Then

$$\rho_m g h_m = \left(846\ \frac{\text{lbm}}{\text{ft}^3}\right)\left(32.2\ \frac{\text{ft}}{\text{sec}^2}\right)(5\ \text{in}) \times \left(\frac{\text{lbf}}{32.2\ \frac{\text{lbm-ft}}{\text{sec}^2}}\right)\left(\frac{\text{ft}^3}{1{,}728\ \text{in}^3}\right)$$
$$= 2.45\ \text{lbf/in}^2$$

Also,

$$\rho_1 g h_1 = \left(62.4\ \frac{\text{lbm}}{\text{ft}^3}\right)\left(32.2\ \frac{\text{ft}}{\text{sec}^2}\right)(3\ \text{ft}) \times \left(\frac{\text{lbf}}{32.2\ \frac{\text{lbm-ft}}{\text{sec}^2}}\right)\left(\frac{\text{ft}^2}{144\ \text{in}^2}\right)$$
$$= 1.30\ \text{lbf/in}^2$$

so

$$p_1 = 14.7\ \frac{\text{lbf}}{\text{in}^2} + 2.45\ \frac{\text{lbf}}{\text{in}^2} - 1.30\ \frac{\text{lbf}}{\text{in}^2}$$
$$= 15.85\ \text{lbf/in}^2 \text{ or psia}$$

7. B From equation 7.25:

$$p_{atm} - p_v = \rho_m g h_m$$

Then

$$p_{atm} = \rho_m g h_m$$
$$= \left(13{,}550\ \frac{\text{kg}}{\text{m}^3}\right)\left(9.81\ \frac{\text{m}}{\text{s}^2}\right)(0.20\ \text{m}) \times \left(\frac{\text{N}}{\frac{\text{kg·m}}{\text{s}^2}}\right)\left(\frac{\text{kPa}}{1{,}000\frac{\text{N}}{\text{m}^2}}\right)$$
$$= 26.6\ \text{kPa}$$

8. A According to Archimedes' principle, an object floating in a fluid will displace an amount of fluid whose weight is equal to the weight of the object. The weight of the cylindrical bar is given by the equation

$$W_{bar} = m_{bar} g$$
$$= \rho_{bar} V_{bar} g$$
$$= \left(41.6\ \frac{\text{lbm}}{\text{ft}^3}\right)[(\pi R^2)(3\ \text{ft})]\left(32.2\ \frac{\text{ft}}{\text{sec}^2}\right) \times \left(\frac{\text{lbf}}{32.2\ \frac{\text{lbm-ft}}{\text{sec}^2}}\right)$$
$$= 392\ R^2\ \text{lbf/ft}^2$$

where R is the radius of the cylinder.

The weight of the fluid displaced is given by the equation

$$W_{disp} = m_{disp} g$$
$$= \rho_{water} V_{disp} g$$
$$= \left(62.4\ \frac{\text{lbm}}{\text{ft}^3}\right)[(\pi R^2)(L)]\left(32.2\ \frac{\text{ft}}{\text{sec}^2}\right)\left(\frac{\text{lbf}}{32.2\ \frac{\text{lbm-ft}}{\text{sec}^2}}\right)$$
$$= 196\ R^2 L\ \text{lbf/ft}^3$$

where L is the length of the displaced cylinder.

Find the value of L by setting the weight of the bar and the weight of the fluid equal to each other, and solving for L:

$$W_{bar} = W_{disp}$$
$$392\ R^2\ \frac{\text{lbf}}{\text{ft}^2} = 196\ R^2 L\ \frac{\text{lbf}}{\text{ft}^3}$$
$$L = \frac{392\ R^2\ \frac{\text{lbf}}{\text{ft}^2}}{196\ R^2\ \frac{\text{lbf}}{\text{ft}^3}}$$
$$= 2\ \text{ft}$$

This result is the amount of the bar that is submerged; therefore:

1 ft of bar will extend above
the surface of the water.

9. D From the principle of mass conservation, equation 7.43 gives:

$$\rho_1 A_1 \overline{V}_1 = \rho_2 A_2 \overline{V}_2$$

or

$$\rho_2 = \frac{\rho_1 A_1 \overline{V}_1}{A_2 \overline{V}_2}$$

$$= \left(200\,\frac{\text{kg}}{\text{m}^3}\right)\left(\frac{\frac{\pi(0.10\text{ m})^2}{4}}{\frac{\pi(0.15\text{ m})^2}{4}}\right)\left(\frac{20\,\frac{\text{m}}{\text{s}}}{14\,\frac{\text{m}}{\text{s}}}\right)$$

$$= 127\text{ kg/m}^3$$

10. D From application of the impulse-momentum principle and a summation of forces in the horizontal direction, the force in the spring is given by the equation

$$F_{\text{spring}} = \dot{m}\overline{V}$$

Also,

$$\dot{m} = \rho\overline{V}A$$

$$= \left(850\,\frac{\text{kg}}{\text{m}^3}\right)\left(17\,\frac{\text{m}}{\text{s}}\right)(0.10\text{ m}^2)$$

$$= 1{,}445\text{ kg/s}$$

so

$$F_{\text{spring}} = \left(1{,}445\,\frac{\text{kg}}{\text{s}}\right)\left(17\,\frac{\text{m}}{\text{s}}\right)\left(\frac{\text{N}}{\frac{\text{kg}\cdot\text{m}}{\text{s}^2}}\right)$$

$$= 24{,}565\text{ N}$$

11. A Use the Bernoulli equation (equation 7.51):

$$\frac{p_1}{\gamma} + \frac{\overline{V}_1^{\,2}}{2g} + z_1 = \frac{p_2}{\gamma} + \frac{\overline{V}_2^{\,2}}{2g} + z_2$$

or

$$p_1 - p_2 = \gamma\left[\frac{(\overline{V}_2^{\,2} - \overline{V}_1^{\,2})}{2g} + (z_2 - z_1)\right]$$

$$= \left(9{,}810\,\frac{\text{N}}{\text{m}^3}\right)\left[\frac{\left(14\,\frac{\text{m}}{\text{s}}\right)^2 - \left(20\,\frac{\text{m}}{\text{s}}\right)^2}{2\left(9.81\,\frac{\text{m}}{\text{s}^2}\right)} + 0\text{ m}\right]$$

$$\times\left(\frac{\text{kPa}}{1{,}000\,\frac{\text{N}}{\text{m}^2}}\right)$$

$$= -102\text{ kPa}$$

12. B From equation 7.55:

$$p_o = p_s + \frac{1}{2}\rho V^2$$

$$= (300\text{ kPa}) + \frac{1}{2}\left(1{,}000\,\frac{\text{kg}}{\text{m}^3}\right)\left(28\,\frac{\text{m}}{\text{s}}\right)^2\left(\frac{\text{N}}{\frac{\text{kg}\cdot\text{m}}{\text{s}^2}}\right)$$

$$\times\left(\frac{\text{kPa}}{1{,}000\,\frac{\text{N}}{\text{m}^2}}\right)$$

$$= 692\text{ kPa}$$

13. C From equation 7.56:

$$\text{Re} = \frac{\rho\overline{V}D}{\mu}$$

or

$$\overline{V} = \frac{\mu\text{Re}}{\rho D}$$

$$= \frac{\left(8\times10^{-3}\,\frac{\text{N}\cdot\text{s}}{\text{m}^2}\right)(2{,}300)}{\left(1{,}000\,\frac{\text{kg}}{\text{m}^3}\right)(0.20\text{ m})}\left(\frac{\frac{\text{kg}\cdot\text{m}}{\text{s}^2}}{\text{N}}\right)$$

$$= 0.092\text{ m/s}$$

14. B From equation 7.66: $h_f = f\left(\frac{L}{D}\right)\left(\frac{\overline{V}^2}{2g}\right)$

Find the average velocity through the pipe as follows:

$$\overline{V} = \frac{Q}{A}$$

$$= \frac{0.34\,\frac{\text{m}^3}{\text{s}}}{\pi\frac{(0.17\text{ m})^2}{4}}$$

$$= 14.98\text{ m/s}$$

Then

$$h_f = (0.017)\left[\frac{1\text{ m}}{0.17\text{ m}}\right]\left[\frac{\left(14.98\,\frac{\text{m}}{\text{s}}\right)^2}{2\left(9.81\,\frac{\text{m}}{\text{s}^2}\right)}\right]$$

$$= 1.14\text{ m}$$

15. D From equation 7.69: $h_{fm} = C\frac{\overline{V}^2}{2g}$

$$= (0.5)\frac{\left(165\,\frac{\text{m}}{\text{s}}\right)^2}{2\left(9.81\,\frac{\text{m}}{\text{s}^2}\right)}$$

$$= 693.81\text{ m}$$

16. C From equation 7.75:

$$D_h = 4\left(\frac{\text{cross-sectional area}}{\text{wetted perimeter}}\right) = 4\left(\frac{(0.80\text{ m})^2}{4(0.80\text{ m})}\right) = 0.80\text{ m}$$

17. A From equation 7.82:

$$C_D = \frac{1.33}{\text{Re}_L^{0.5}}\ (10^4 < \text{Re}_L < 5\times 10^5)$$

or

$$C_D = \frac{0.031}{\text{Re}_L^{1/7}}\ (10^6 < \text{Re}_L < 10^9)$$

The Reynolds number for this flow is given by equation 7.81:

$$\text{Re}_L = \frac{\rho V_\infty L}{\mu} = \frac{\left(1.225\ \frac{\text{kg}}{\text{m}^3}\right)\left(86\ \frac{\text{m}}{\text{s}}\right)(0.93\text{ m})}{\left(1.8\times 10^{-5}\ \frac{\text{N}\cdot\text{s}}{\text{m}^2}\right)} = 5.443\times 10^6$$

Therefore the second equation for the coefficient of drag is used:

$$C_D = \frac{0.031}{\text{Re}_L^{1/7}} = \frac{0.031}{(5.443\times 10^6)^{1/7}} = 3.381\times 10^{-3}$$

18. C If friction along the face of the blade is neglected, the velocity leaving the blade has the same magnitude as the velocity entering the blade, directed as shown in the diagram. Solve for angle θ as follows:

$$\mathbf{V}_{2x} = \mathbf{V}_B + \mathbf{V}_E \sin\alpha = 25\frac{\text{m}}{\text{s}} + \left(60\ \frac{\text{m}}{\text{s}}\right)\sin(45°) = 67.43\text{ m/s}$$

and

$$\mathbf{V}_{2y} = \mathbf{V}_E\cos\alpha = \left(60\ \frac{\text{m}}{\text{s}}\right)\cos(45°) = 42.43\text{ m/s}$$

Then:

$$\theta = \tan^{-1}\left(\frac{V_{2y}}{V_{2x}}\right) = \tan^{-1}\left(\frac{42.43\ \frac{\text{m}}{\text{s}}}{67.43\ \frac{\text{m}}{\text{s}}}\right) = 32.18°$$

19. C The maximum power that can be generated by the impulse turbine shown in the figure is given by equation 7.91:

$$\dot{W}_{\max} = Q\rho\left(\frac{|V_1^2|}{4}\right)(1-\cos\alpha) = \dot{m}\left(\frac{|V_1^2|}{4}\right)(1-\cos\alpha)$$

$$= \left(16\ \frac{\text{kg}}{\text{s}}\right)\left[\frac{\left(67\ \frac{\text{m}}{\text{s}}\right)^2}{4}\right][1-\cos(120°)] \times \left(\frac{\text{N}}{\frac{\text{kg}\cdot\text{m}}{\text{s}^2}}\right)\left(\frac{\text{kW}}{1{,}000\ \frac{\text{N}\cdot\text{m}}{\text{s}}}\right) = 26.93\text{ kW}$$

20. B Use the Bernoulli equation:

$$\frac{p_1}{\gamma} + \frac{\overline{V}_1^2}{2g} + z_1 + h_m = \frac{p_2}{\gamma} + \frac{\overline{V}_2^2}{2g} + z_2$$

In this case, $p_1 = p_2$ and $\overline{V}_1 = \overline{V}_2$, so

$$h_m = z_2 - z_1 = 120\text{ m}$$

The pumping power is then given by the equation

$$\dot{W} = \rho g h Q = \left(1{,}000\ \frac{\text{kg}}{\text{m}^3}\right)\left(9.81\ \frac{\text{m}}{\text{s}^2}\right)(120\text{ m})\left(50\ \frac{\text{m}^3}{\text{s}}\right) \times \left(\frac{\text{N}}{\frac{\text{kg}\cdot\text{m}}{\text{s}^2}}\right)\left(\frac{\text{kW}}{1{,}000\ \frac{\text{N}\cdot\text{m}}{\text{s}}}\right) = 58{,}860\text{ kW}$$

But this is the power required to pump the water. The pump will need somewhat more power to account for its irreversibilities:

$$\eta = \frac{\dot{W}}{\dot{W}_{\text{supplied}}}$$

$$\dot{W}_{\text{supplied}} = \frac{\dot{W}}{\eta} = \frac{58{,}860 \text{ kW}}{0.90} = 65{,}400 \text{ kW}$$

21. A The volumetric flow rate through a venturi flow meter is given by equation 7.108:

$$Q = \frac{C_v A_2}{\sqrt{1-(A_2/A_1)^2}}\sqrt{2g\left[\left(\frac{p_1}{\gamma}+z_1\right)-\left(\frac{p_2}{\gamma}+z_2\right)\right]}$$

$$= \frac{(0.83)(0.015 \text{ m}^2)}{\sqrt{1-\left(\dfrac{0.015 \text{ m}^2}{0.102 \text{ m}^2}\right)^2}}$$

$$\times \sqrt{2\left(9.81 \frac{\text{m}}{\text{s}^2}\right)\left[\left(\frac{(600 \text{ kPa})}{9{,}810 \frac{\text{N}}{\text{m}^3}}\right)\left(\frac{1{,}000 \frac{\text{N}}{\text{m}^2}}{\text{kPa}}\right)-\left(\frac{(430 \text{ kPa})}{9{,}810 \frac{\text{N}}{\text{m}^3}}\right)\left(\frac{1{,}000 \frac{\text{N}}{\text{m}^2}}{\text{kPa}}\right)\right]}$$

$$= 0.232 \text{ m}^3/\text{s}$$

MOODY (STANTON) DIAGRAM

	e, (ft)	e, (mm)
Riveted steel	0.003-0.03	0.9-9.0
Concrete	0.001-0.01	0.3-3.0
Cast iron	0.00085	0.25
Galvanized iron	0.0005	0.15
Commercial steel or wroght iron	0.00015	0.046
Drawn tubing	0.000005	0.0015

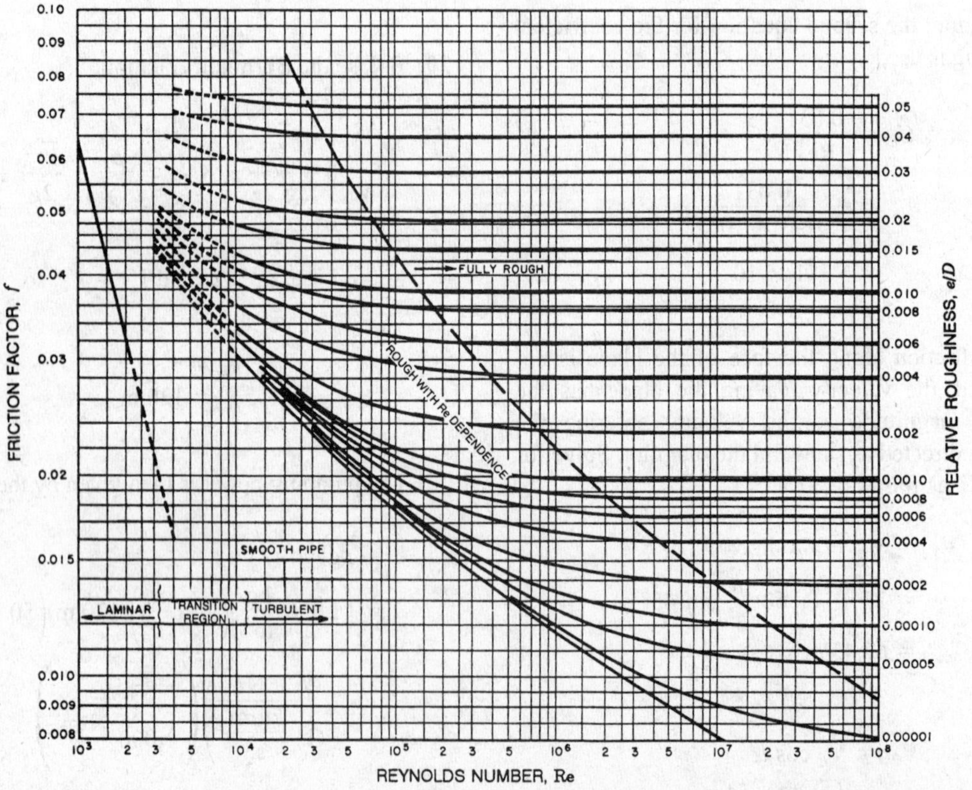

Reproduced from "Friction Factors for Pipe Flow," *MOODY DIAGRAM*, in *Trans. ASME 66*, 1944. Used with permission of ASME.

CHAPTER

8

Materials Science and Structure

Richard J. Murphy, Ph.D.

Introduction

This chapter is intended as a review of the important basic concepts in materials science. The presentation of the various content areas assumes that most of these topics have been covered in a full course in materials science. It may be useful to use the text from that course as a companion to the review presented here.

The chapter follows a conventional order of topics. It begins with atomic structure, followed by bonding, crystallography and phase equilibrium. After sections on ferrous metallurgy, solid solubility, diffusion, and corrosion, the various behaviors are covered: mechanical, magnetic, and electrical.

8.1 Atomic Structure

The atomic structure of an atom involves the spatial and energetic arrangement of the electrons in the atom. The nucleus is not included in the description of atomic structure. (It is important to remember that the term *atomic structure* refers to the arrangement of electrons in an atom, *not* the arrangement of atoms. Atom arrangement is what crystal structure is all about.)

For each atom, the number of electrons and the number of protons match the atomic number. The electrons are particles in constant motion around the nucleus. By virtue of their dual nature, they are also waves. Electrons possess energy that is due to their motion (mass and velocity) and their wavelengths. Because the wavelength of each electron must be an integral fraction of the path length of that electron around the nucleus, the energies of the electrons in an atom are not spread over a range of values; rather, they are limited to specific values with no possibility of intermediate energies. This characteristic is what is meant by quantization.

Later refinements of atomic theory expand many of the early concepts. The electrons occupy energy levels in such a way that no more than two electrons can have the same energy (occupy the same orbital), and those two must have different spins. This rule is called the **Pauli exclusion principle.** The gross quantization is designated by the principal quantum number n ($n = 1, \ldots, n$). The energy of each level (according to the Bohr atomic model) is given by equation 8.1:

$$E = -\frac{13.6Z^2}{n^2} \text{ eV} \qquad [8.1]$$

where Z is the atomic number and n is the principal quantum number of the energy level.

When electrons are excited from one energy level to another, energy is absorbed. The magnitude of the energy absorbed, that is, the difference between the two energy levels, is calculated by using equation 8.2:

$$\Delta E = E_2 - E_1 = -13.6Z^2\left(\frac{1}{2^2} - \frac{1}{1^2}\right)$$

$$= -\frac{13.6Z^2}{4} = -3.4Z^2 \text{ eV} \qquad [8.2]$$

The wavelength of radiation absorbed in this electron excitation can then be determined using equation 8.3:

$$\lambda = \frac{hc}{\Delta E} \qquad [8.3]$$

where h is Planck's constant and c is the velocity of light.

Within the energy level designated by each value of n, there is further quantization of energy, indicated by the letters s, p, d, and f in the order of increasing energy. These subquantizations are called orbitals (*not* orbits!). It is at this level that a connection is made between electron energy and spatial distribution. Energy levels with the designation s represent a spherically symmetric distribution of the probability of location of an electron, as shown in Figure 8.1a. The p levels are actually comprised of three separate, mutually perpendicular dumbbell-shaped probability distributions, each parallel to the x-, y-, or z-axis, as shown in Figure 8.1b. Each orbital can contain up to two and only two electrons. This is a restatement of the Pauli exclusion principle: each orbital can contain no more than two electrons, and those two electrons must have different spins.

This orbital notation can be used to identify the energy levels of each electron in any atom, as seen in Table 8.1. In each electron configuration, the magnitude of n is given first, followed by the designation of s and, if appropriate, of p and d. The number of electrons with each orbital designation (i.e., with this energy) is shown as a superscript. The sum of the superscripts is, therefore, the number of electrons in the atom.

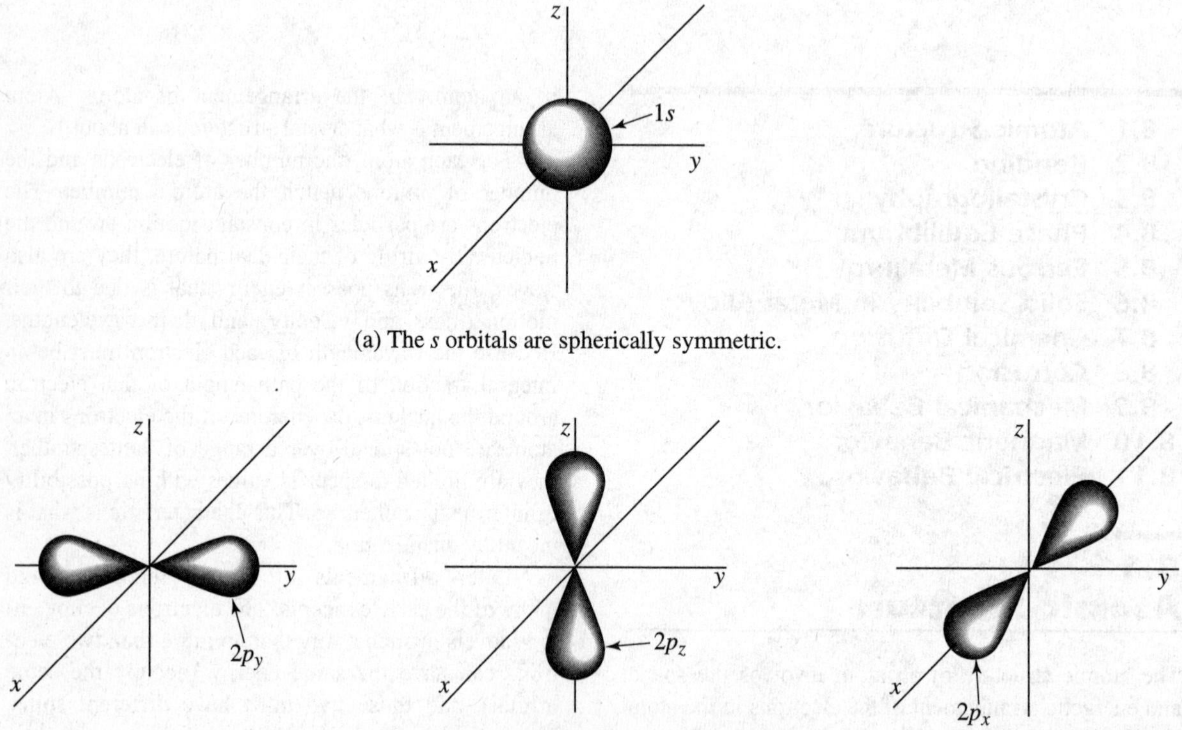

(a) The s orbitals are spherically symmetric.

(b) The p orbitals have a dumbbell shape

Figure 8.1 The shapes of (a) the s-orbital and (b) the three p-orbitals. (From Schaeffer et al. *The Science and Design of Engineering Materials*, 1994, McGraw-Hill. Reproduced with permission of the McGraw-Hill Companies.)

Table 8.1. The Electron Configurations of the First Thirty Elements

Element	*Atomic Number*	*Electron Configuration*
Hydrogen	1	$1s^1$
Helium	2	$1s^2$
Lithium	3	$1s^2 2s^1$
Beryllium	4	$1s^2 2s^2$
Boron	5	$1s^2 2s^2 2p^1$
Carbon	6	$1s^2 2s^2 2p^2$
Nitrogen	7	$1s^2 2s^2 2p^3$
Oxygen	8	$1s^2 2s^2 2p^4$
Fluorine	9	$1s^2 2s^2 2p^5$
Neon	10	$1s^2 2s^2 2p^6$
Sodium	11	$1s^2 2s^2 2p^6 3s^1$
Magnesium	12	$1s^2 2s^2 2p^6 3s^2$
Aluminum	13	$1s^2 2s^2 2p^6 3s^2 3p^1$
Silicon	14	$1s^2 2s^2 2p^6 3s^2 3p^2$
Phosphorus	15	$1s^2 2s^2 2p^6 3s^2 3p^3$
Sulfur	16	$1s^2 2s^2 2p^6 3s^2 3p^4$
Chlorine	17	$1s^2 2s^2 2p^6 3s^2 3p^5$
Argon	18	$1s^2 2s^2 2p^6 3s^2 3p^6$
Potassium	19	$1s^2 2s^2 2p^6 3s^2 3p^6 4s^1$
Calcium	20	$1s^2 2s^2 2p^6 3s^2 3p^6 4s^2$
Scandium	21	$1s^2 2s^2 2p^6 3s^2 3p^6 4s^2 3d^1$
Titanium	22	$1s^2 2s^2 2p^6 3s^2 3p^6 4s^2 3d^2$
Vanadium	23	$1s^2 2s^2 2p^6 3s^2 3p^6 4s^2 3d^3$
Chromium	24	$1s^2 2s^2 2p^6 3s^2 3p^6 4s^1 3d^5$
Manganese	25	$1s^2 2s^2 2p^6 3s^2 3p^6 4s^2 3d^5$
Iron	26	$1s^2 2s^2 2p^6 3s^2 3p^6 4s^2 3d^6$
Cobalt	27	$1s^2 2s^2 2p^6 3s^2 3p^6 4s^2 3d^7$
Nickel	28	$1s^2 2s^2 2p^6 3s^2 3p^6 4s^2 3d^8$
Copper	29	$1s^2 2s^2 2p^6 3s^2 3p^6 4s^1 3d^{10}$
Zinc	30	$1s^2 2s^2 2p^6 3s^2 3p^6 4s^2 3d^{10}$

8.2 Bonding

Material behavior is largely determined by the types of bonding that occur among the various atoms in the material. In some cases where molecules exist in the material, the more important bonds may be those among the molecules. Usually, the stronger bonding, called interatomic bonding, occurs between atoms. There are three types of interatomic bonding: covalent, ionic, and metallic. Each takes place because of special aspects of the structure of the atom.

Covalent Bonding

Consider the hydrogen atom. This atom has one electron of type *s*, designated as $1s^1$. Remember that the *s* orbital is a spherical cloud of probability of location; therefore, if that atom is in the vicinity of another hydrogen atom, the electron of the second atom can occupy the *s* orbital of the first atom because the two orbitals overlap to some extent. It can be shown by advanced calculations that the total energy of the pair of atoms, with both s orbitals sharing two electrons, is lower than the sum of the energies of the two atoms taken separately. This fact indicates that the two atoms would rather be together, that is, bonded, than apart. But the two atoms cannot overlap completely because of the strong repulsive force of the two nuclei. Therefore, the two atoms assume an equilibrium separation that balances the attractive and repulsive forces. The total energy curve representing this bonding event for two atoms is shown in Figure 8.2.

In this case, if a third hydrogen atom approached close enough to overlap the *s* orbitals of the first two atoms, it would provide a third electron to the *s* orbital. The Pauli exclusion principle states that an orbital can have no more than two electrons. Therefore, the third atom cannot enter into a bond relation with this pair and must move on. That is the reason why hydrogen gas exists as a diatomic molecule.

Covalent bonding can be defined as bonding that occurs between atoms with half-filled orbitals. For instance, chlorine has an atomic number of 17 and the atomic structure $1s^2 2s^2 2p^6 3s^2 3p^5$. Notice that each of the orbitals is filled with two electrons except one of the three 3*p* orbitals, which is half-filled. This is a covalent bonding orbital. It can bond with a half-filled orbital of any other atom, for example, another chlorine atom. This is the reason why chlorine gas exists as a diatomic molecule.

Carbon has only two half-filled orbitals, a configuration unfavorable for forming a three-dimen-

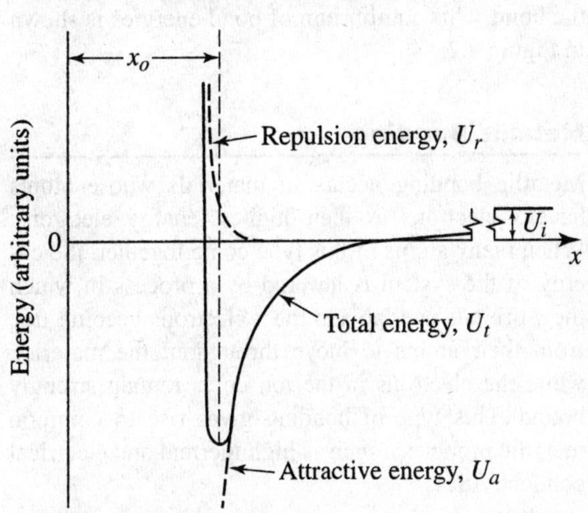

Figure 8.2 The energy versus atom separation curve for the bonding of two atoms or ions. (From Schaeffer et al. *The Science and Design of Engineering Materials*, 1994, McGraw-Hill. Reproduced with permission of the McGraw-Hill Companies.)

sional network of bonded carbon atoms. In an excited state, however, carbon atoms can possess four half-filled bonding orbitals, and thereby form covalent bonds with four neighbors that also have bonding orbitals. This is how diamond, silicon, methane, and carbon tetrachloride form, as well as the carbon-carbon bonds in polymers. This type of bond is very strong.

Ionic Bonding

Ionic bonding consists of electrostatic attraction between oppositely charged ions. Ions are atoms that have lost or gained electrons, giving them a positive or negative charge. Ions are formed most easily in atoms that have *s* electrons as the highest energy level or that are one or two electrons short of filling all the *p* orbitals. In the former case, the *s* electrons can be excited away from the atom, leaving a positively charged ion (cation), as in Na^+ and Ca^{2+}. In the latter case, the atom can attract and capture extra free electrons to completely fill the *p* orbitals, giving it a negative charge (anion), as in F^- and O^{2-}.

A measure of the ease with which atoms attract electrons to make negative ions is called **electronegativity.** The atoms on the far left of the Periodic Table, such as sodium and calcium, have low electronegativities and are considered electropositive; the atoms on the far right, such as fluorine and oxygen, have high electronegativities. When ions of opposite charge are present together, they can experience strong electrostatic attractive forces, which, in balance with the repulsive forces from nucleus-nucleus interaction, result in large net bonding energy. The larger the difference in electronegativity, the stronger the bond. This equilibrium of bond energies is shown in Figure 8.2.

Metallic Bonding

Metallic bonding occurs in materials whose atoms have *s* electrons as their highest energy electrons. When many atoms of this type come together, the energy of the system is lowered by a process in which the *s* orbitals overlap and the *s* electrons become free from their atoms to move throughout the material, while the electrons in the ion cores remain strongly bound. This type of bonding gives rise to common metallic properties such as high thermal and electrical conductivities.

It is not easy to compare the relative strengths of the three types of bonding. In general, however, average bond strengths increase in the order metallic, ionic, covalent. All three types are strong in comparison to the much weaker intermolecular bonds.

8.3 Crystallography

The arrangements of atoms in a solid material fall into two general classes:

1. Entirely periodic, predictable and reproducible
2. Quite random.

The first arrangement is characteristic of a crystal, while the second is found in amorphous solids, usually referred to as glasses. The arrangement of atoms in crystals is the subject of crystallography.

Bravais Lattices

The subject is simplified if one considers arrangements of points in space, called **lattices,** rather than of atoms. It has been shown that there are fourteen ways of arranging points in space so as to satisfy the symmetry and reproducible periodicity that a crystal requires. These arrangements are called the Bravais lattices. The three lattices that are important in structural metals are face-centered cubic (FCC), body-centered cubic (BCC), and simple hexagonal. The first two are common in metals with one atom per lattice point. The last is also common in the form of hexagonal close packed (HCP, simple hexagonal with two atoms per lattice point). These three lattices are shown in Figure 8.3. Expanding the lattice points until they touch as spheres in contact, much like the familiar Ping-Pong ball model, can provide another view of the cubic crystal.

The **coordination number** is the number of neighboring spheres each sphere contacts. In the FCC crystal that number is 12. This can be easily seen by constructing the close-packed plane, in which each sphere is in contact with six neighbors. When a similar plane is brought into contract with the first plane from above, three additional spheres come into contact, and, similarly, three are in contact from below ($6 + 3 + 3 = 12$).

For BCC, the coordination number, 8, is most easily determined by observing the eight corner spheres in contact with the body-centered sphere.

The distance between neighboring atoms is called the **nearest-neighbor distance.** For spheres in contact, it is represented as $2r$, where r is the radius of the sphere (representing the atomic radius). This nearest-neighbor distance can be written in terms of the lattice parameter, *a,* in the cubic system.

For FCC, $4r = a\sqrt{2}$, where $4r$ represents the face diagonal, as does $a\sqrt{2}$. Therefore:

$$2r = \frac{a\sqrt{2}}{2} = \frac{a}{\sqrt{2}}; \qquad r = \frac{a}{2\sqrt{2}} \qquad [8.4]$$

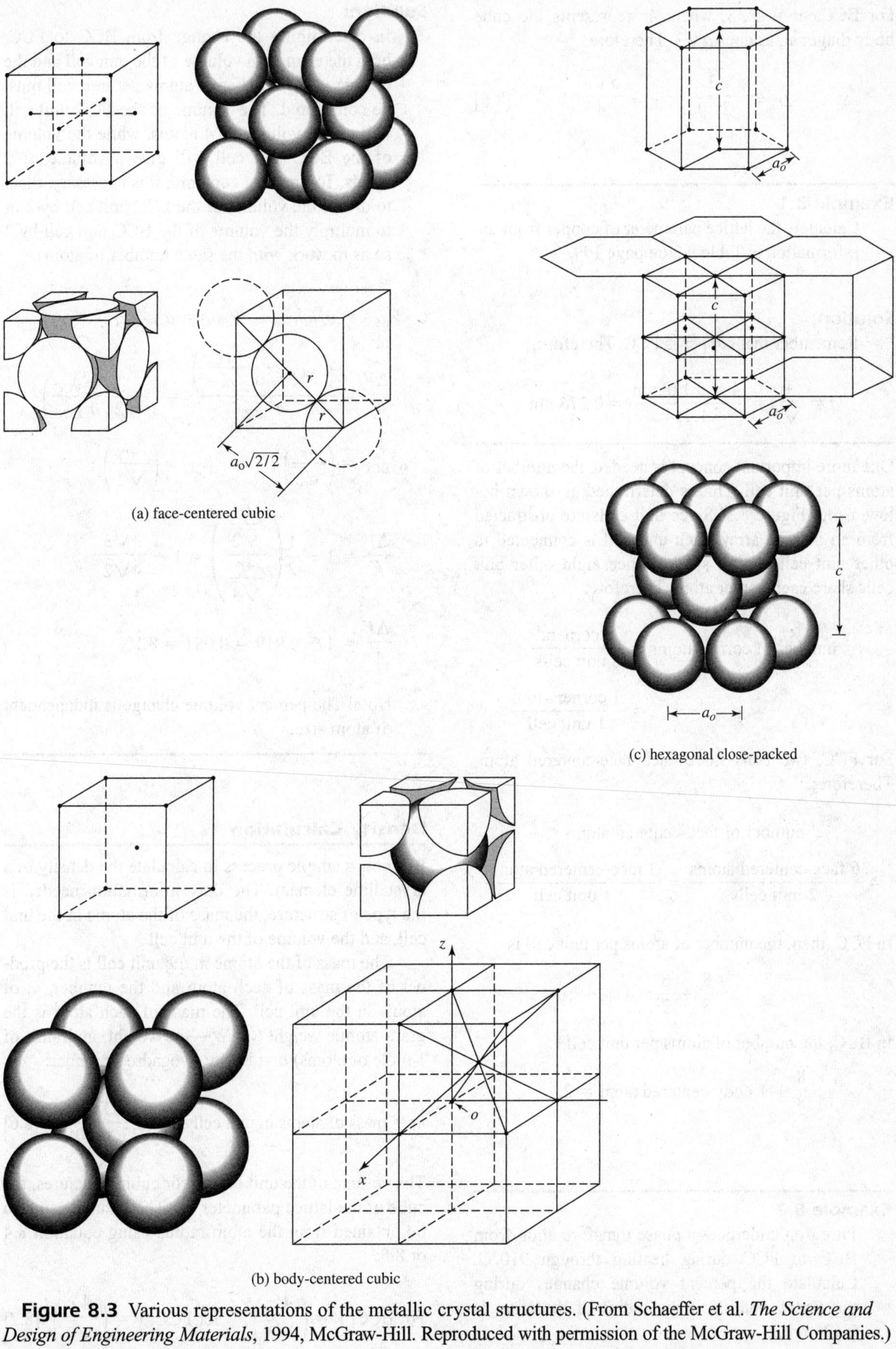

Figure 8.3 Various representations of the metallic crystal structures. (From Schaeffer et al. *The Science and Design of Engineering Materials*, 1994, McGraw-Hill. Reproduced with permission of the McGraw-Hill Companies.)

For BCC, $4r = a\sqrt{3}$, where $4r$ represents the cube body diagonal, as does $a\sqrt{3}$. Therefore:

$$2r = \frac{a\sqrt{3}}{2}; \qquad r = \frac{a\sqrt{3}}{4} \qquad [8.5]$$

Example 8.1

Calculate the lattice parameter of copper from the information in Table 8.2 on page 199.

Solution:

Remember that copper is FCC. Therefore:

$$a = \frac{4r}{\sqrt{2}} = \frac{4 \times 0.128 \text{ nm}}{1.414} = 0.276 \text{ nm}$$

One more important concept is needed, the number of atoms per unit cell. This is determined as shown below, using Figure 8.3. Since unit cells are abstracted from an infinite array, each unit cell is connected to other unit cells on all sides. Hence eight other unit cells share each corner atom. Therefore:

$$\text{number of corner atoms} = \frac{8 \text{ corners}}{8 \text{ unit cells}}$$

$$= \frac{1 \text{ corner atom}}{1 \text{ unit cell}}$$

For FCC, two cells share each face-centered atom. Therefore:

$$\text{number of face-centered atoms}$$

$$= \frac{6 \text{ face-centered atoms}}{2 \text{ unit cells}} = \frac{3 \text{ face-centered atoms}}{1 \text{ unit cell}}$$

In FCC, then, the number of atoms per unit cell is

$$\frac{8}{8} + \frac{6}{2} = 4.$$

In BCC, the number of atoms per unit cell is

$$\frac{8}{8} + 1 \text{ body-centered atom} = 2.$$

Example 8.2

Pure iron undergoes a phase transformation from BCC to FCC during heating through 910°C. Calculate the percent volume changes during the transformation if the radius of the atom is 0.124 nm.

Solution:

In determining the change from BCC to FCC, both the change in volume of the unit cell and the change in the number of atoms per unit cell must be considered. The volume of the FCC unit cell will give a volume of 4 atoms, while the volume of the BCC unit cell will give a volume of 2 atoms. To properly compare, it is necessary, then, to divide the volume of the FCC unit cell by 2 or to multiply the volume of the BCC unit cell by 2 so as to work with the same number of atoms.

$$V_{BCC} = a^3_{BCC}; \qquad V_{FCC} = a^3_{FCC};$$

$$\frac{\Delta V}{V} = \frac{a^3_{BCC} - \left(\frac{a^3_{FCC}}{2}\right)}{a^3_{BCC}} = 1 - \frac{1}{2}\left(\frac{a^3_{FCC}}{a^3_{BCC}}\right)$$

$$a^3_{BCC} = \left(\frac{4r}{\sqrt{3}}\right)^3; \qquad a^3_{FCC} = \left(\frac{4r}{\sqrt{2}}\right)^3;$$

$$\frac{\Delta V}{V} = 1 - \frac{1}{2}\left(\frac{\frac{4r}{\sqrt{2}}}{\frac{4r}{\sqrt{3}}}\right)^3 = 1 - \frac{3\sqrt{3}}{4\sqrt{2}}$$

$$\frac{\Delta V}{V} = 1 - 0.919 = 0.081 = 8.1\%$$

Note: The percent volume change is independent of atom size.

Density Calculation

It is now a simple process to calculate the density of a crystalline element. The only information needed is the type of structure, the mass of the atoms in the unit cell, and the volume of the unit cell.

The mass of the atoms in the unit cell is the product of the mass of each atom and the number, n, of atoms in the unit cell. The mass of each atom is the gram-atomic weight (GAW—the weight, in grams, of 1 mole of atoms) divided by Avogadro's number:

$$m = \text{mass of atoms in unit cell} = \frac{n \times \text{GAW}}{6.023 \times 10^{23}} \text{ g} \qquad [8.6]$$

The volume of the unit cell is, for cubic structures, the cube of the lattice parameter, a^3. The volume can also be obtained from the atom radius using equation 8.4 or 8.5:

$$\text{For BCC, } V = \left(\frac{4r}{\sqrt{3}}\right)^3; \quad \text{for FCC, } V = \left(\frac{4r}{\sqrt{2}}\right)^3 \qquad [8.7]$$

The equation for density is simply

$$\rho = \frac{M}{V}\ \text{gcm}^3 \qquad [8.8]$$

The crystal structures, atomic masses, atomic radii, and densities of four cubic crystals are given in Table 8.2.

Table 8.2 Data for Selected Crystals

Crystal	*Structure*	*Atomic Mass (amu)*	*Atomic Radius (nm)*	*Density (g/cm³)*
Cu	FCC	63.55	0.128	8.93
α-Fe	BCC	55.85	0.124	7.87
Mo	BCC	95.94	0.136	10.22
Al	FCC	26.98	0.143	2.7

Example 8.3

Calculate the density of aluminum from the data in Table 8.2.

Solution:

Aluminum is FCC. (You must know this. So also are copper, nickel, silver, gold, and austenitic stainless steel.) Therefore, there are 4 atoms per unit cell.

$$\text{density} = \frac{\text{mass of atoms in unit cell}}{\text{volume of unit cell}}$$

$$= \frac{4 \text{ atoms/unit cell} \times 26 \text{ g/mol}/6.024 \times 10^{23} \text{ atoms/mol}}{a^3 \text{ cm}^3/\text{unit cell}}$$

$$= 2.7 \text{ g/cm}^3$$

Atomic Packing Factor

The atomic packing factor (apf) is the volume of the atoms in a unit cell divided by the volume of the unit cell.

For FCC:

$$\text{apf} = \frac{4 \times \frac{4}{3}\pi r^3}{a^3} = \frac{4 \times \frac{4}{3}\pi r^3}{\left(\frac{4r}{\sqrt{2}}\right)^3} = \frac{\sqrt{2}\pi}{6} = 0.74 \qquad [8.9]$$

For BCC:

$$\text{apf} = \frac{2 \times \frac{4}{3}\pi r^3}{a^3} = \frac{2 \times \frac{4}{3}\pi r^3}{\left(\frac{4r}{\sqrt{3}}\right)^3} = \frac{\sqrt{3}\pi}{8} = 0.68 \qquad [8.10]$$

Miller Indices: The Language of Crystals

To describe the planes and directions in a cubic crystal, a special notation called the Miller indices has been developed. The method for determining the indices of a plane is as follows.

1. Construct the cubic unit cell using the rectangular coordinates system (x, y, z). Draw the plane of interest within the unit cell in such a way that it does not pass through the origin.
2. Note the intercepts with the x-, y-, and z-axes as integer or fractional multiples of the cell edge, and designate these numerical values as a, b, c, respectively.
3. Take the reciprocals of a, b, c, and call these values h, k, and l, respectively.
4. Enclose the reciprocals hkl in parentheses as a name for the plane.

For example, if a plane is parallel to the z-axis, the z-intercept, c, is ∞. Then the reciprocal, 1, is 0. (See Example 8.4.)

The method for determining the indices for crystallographic directions is somewhat different.

1. Construct the unit cell in an x-, y-, z-coordinate system. Draw the direction of interest within the unit cell in such a way that it passes through the origin.
2. Determine the x-, y-, z-coordinates of the point at which the direction intersects the cell away from the origin, and designate them as integer or fractional multiples of the length of the cube edge.
3. Enclose coordinates x, y, z in brackets as a name for the direction. For example, a cube edge is [100], [010], or [001].

Example 8.4

Determine the Miller indices of the plane and the direction shown in Figure 8.4.

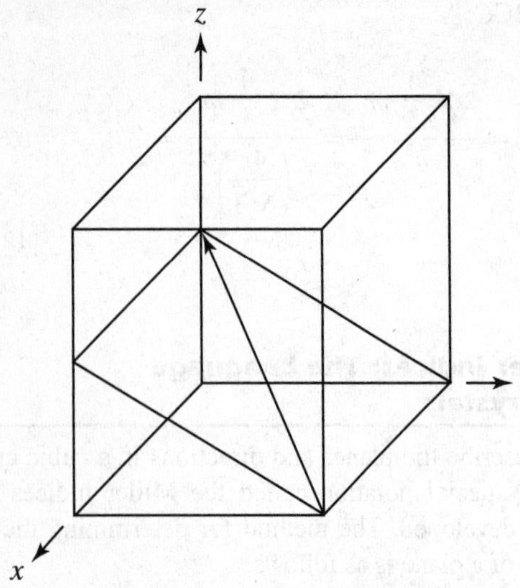

Figure 8.4 A sketch of a plane and a direction in a cubic unit cell.

Solution:

For the plane:

1. Construct a right-handed coordinate system using the edges of the unit cell. In this case the x-axis is pointing toward the viewer.
2. Select an origin that does not lie in the plane. In this case the origin can be the lower, back, left corner of the cell.
3. Note that the x-intercept is ∞; the y-intercept is 1; the z-intercept is $\frac{1}{2}$.
4. Take the reciprocals of these intercepts in order; the results are 0, 1, 2.
5. Since this is a plane, collect the reciprocals in parentheses without commas: (012).

For the direction:

1. Use the same construction as in step 1 for the plane.
2. Select the origin at the tail of the direction. In this case it is the lower, front, right corner.
3. Locate the point at which the head of the direction line intersects the unit cell, and write the coordinates of this point. In this case:

$$x = -1, y = -1, z = \frac{1}{2}.$$

4. Collect the coordinates in square brackets:

$$[\bar{1}\,\bar{1}\,\frac{1}{2}].$$

5. Clear fractions: $[\bar{2}\,\bar{2}\,1]$.

8.4 Phase Equilibrium

The relationship among phases in a material is strictly governed by the thermodynamic variables temperature, T, pressure, P, and phase composition (the relative amounts of components in solution within the phase). This relationship is summarized by the **equilibrium phase diagram,** which shows, at 1 atmosphere pressure, the conditions of temperature and alloy composition at which the various phases are stable or in equilibrium. For example, Figure 8.5 is the equilibrium phase diagram for the copper-nickel system. If you trace across the diagram at 1,000°C, you find only one phase, alpha, for all compositions. This is a solid region. At 1,200°C a traverse of the diagram begins with the liquid phase (designated as L), then enters the region containing liquid and alpha, and concludes with the alpha phase. This means that, in the copper-nickel system at 1,200°C, the liquid phase is stable over a range of compositions up to the boundary of the two-phase region called the liquidus. Also, it means that the alpha phase is stable over a range of compositions from pure nickel back to the boundary of the two-phase region, called the solidus; and that, within the two boundaries, the two phases, liquid and alpha, are in equilibrium. It is in this two-phase region that the **inverse lever rule** must be applied to gain information inside the region.

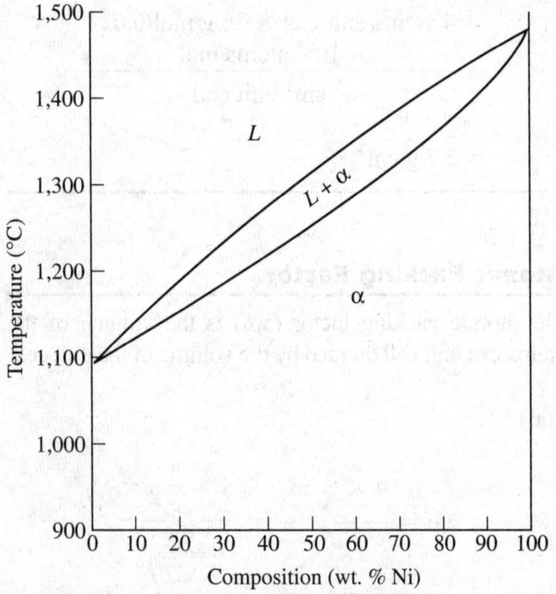

Figure 8.5 The copper-nickel equilibrium phase diagram.

The inverse Lever rule is used to determine the relative amounts of phases in a two-phase region. Now consider Figure 8.6. To analyze the copper-nickel system at 1,200°C, you draw a horizontal line, called a tie line, through the two-phase liquid-plus-solid region from one boundary to the next. The end points of the tie lines then indicate the compositions of the two phases that are in equilibrium. These compositions, called the phase compositions, are read by tracing down to the horizontal axis of the phase diagram.

If an alloy composition is chosen that falls within the end points of this tie line at 1,200°C, you know from the phase diagram that the alloy consists of two phases. You can determine the amounts of the phases in the alloy by applying the inverse lever rule. Label the alloy composition C_O, the composition of the solid C_S, and the composition of the liquid C_L; then the relationship for the fraction of liquid is given by equation 8.11:

$$f_L = \frac{C_S - C_O}{C_S - C_L} \quad [8.11]$$

Notice that the equation simply relates a segment of the tie line to the entire length of the tie line. The relationship is inverse in the sense that, if you are interested in the fraction of the phase on the left, you take the ratio of the right-hand segment of the tie line to the entire length of the tie line. If, however, you are seeking a fraction of the phase on the right, you take the left-hand end of the tie line and compare that to the entire length of the tie line.

This inverse lever rule can be used in any two-phase region in any phase diagram. It does not matter how complex the phase diagram; $f_L + f_S = 1$.

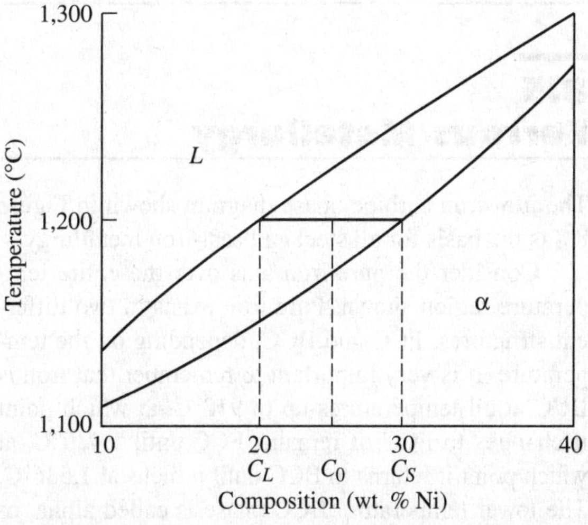

Figure 8.6 A portion of the copper-nickel equilibrium phase diagram.

Example 8.5

Consider an alloy containing 25 wt. % Ni that was heated to the liquid region and then slowly cooled to 1,200°C.

A. What phase(s) is (are) present?

B. If there is more than one phase, how much of each is present?

Solution:

A. This alloy is composed of two phases, liquid and solid.

B. Since the region involved is a two-phase region, first construct a tie line at the temperature in question. The left end gives the composition of the liquid phase, and the right end indicates the composition of the solid phase. The alloy composition falls within the line. According to equation 8.11, the combination of these three compositions will yield the weight fraction of the alloy that is liquid, f_L.

$$f_L = \frac{30 - 25}{30 - 20} = \frac{5}{10} = 50\%$$

Then the amount of solid is also 50%.

Some materials exhibit phase diagrams that are somewhat more complicated than the one in Figure 8.5. In some binary alloy systems, the addition of the second component lowers the melting point of the solvent at both ends of the phase diagram, so that the range of the liquid phase is extended downward in the middle, resulting in a phase diagram like that in Figure 8.7. This is called a **eutectic phase diagram** and is characterized by the feature that liquid is stable at temperatures below the melting points of both pure elements.

The important feature of the eutectic phase diagram is the horizontal line at which the liquid region becomes ever more narrow until it finally reaches a point. This line of constant temperature, called the eutectic temperature, connects three important points: the composition of the alpha phase, which is stable at this temperature; and the composition of the liquid phase. All three of these phases are in equilibrium. When the alloy passes through the eutectic temperature, the liquid phase of the eutectic composition changes into a two-phase solid mixture of alpha and beta, called the eutectic mixture or, simply, the eutectic. All the liquid is gone and has been replaced by the eutectic.

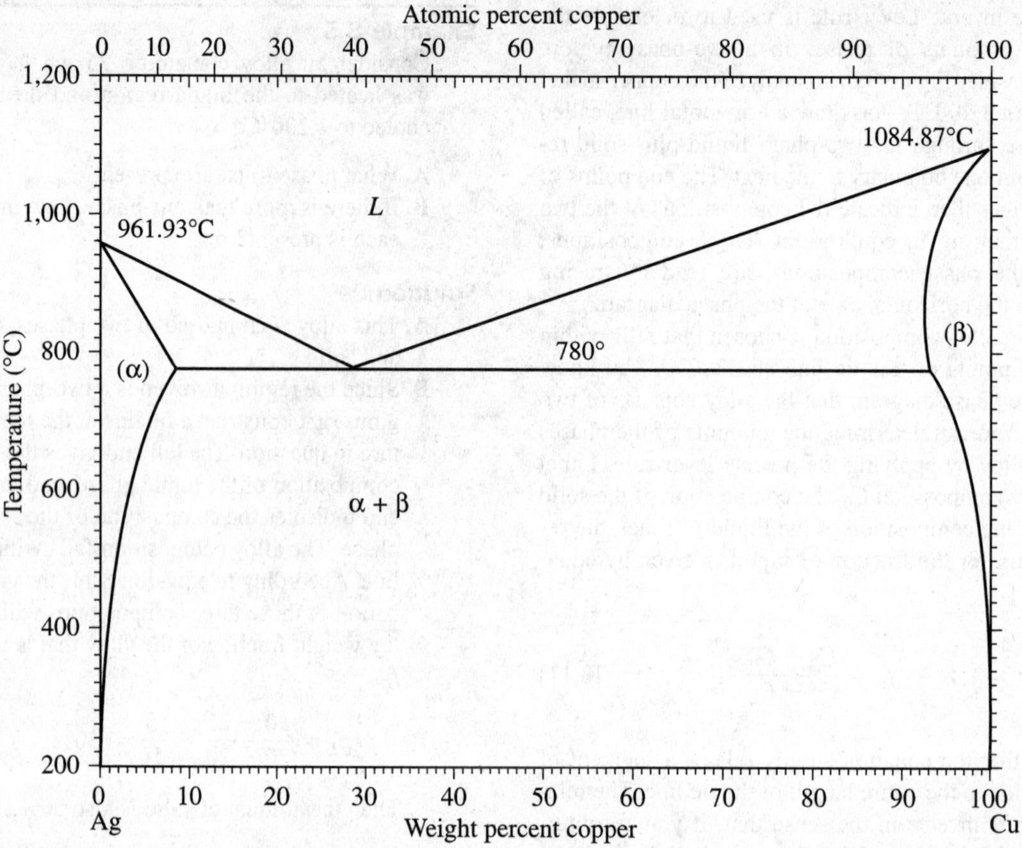

Figure 8.7 The copper-silver equilibrium phase diagram. (Used with permission of ASM International.)

The transformation of phases that occurs during the eutectic transformation is represented by equation 8.12.

$$L = \alpha + \beta \qquad [8.12]$$

Example 8.6

Using the phase diagram in Figure 8.7, consider an alloy of 20 wt. % Cu that has been slowly cooled from the liquid to 779°C. Calculate the fraction of the alloy that is eutectic.

Solution:

The amount of eutectic in the alloy at this temperature is equal to the amount of liquid in the alloy at 781°C, that is, just before the transformation to complete solid. To determine this amount of liquid, draw a tie line at 781°C in the liquid + alpha region. Sketch the vertical line representing the alloy composition of 20 wt. % Cu. Then use equation 8.11 to calculate the weight fraction of liquid. The amount of eutectic after solidification is the amount of liquid before solidification:

$$f_L = \frac{C_0 - C_\alpha}{C_L - C_\alpha} = \frac{20 - 9}{29 - 9} = \frac{11}{20} = 0.55 = 55\%$$

8.5 Ferrous Metallurgy

The iron-iron carbide phase diagram shown in Figure 8.8 is the basis for all steel and cast-iron metallurgy.

Consider the pure iron axis over the entire temperature region shown. Pure iron exists in two different structures, FCC and BCC, depending on the temperature. It is very important to remember that iron is BCC at all temperatures up to 912°C, at which point it changes to FCC. It remains FCC until 1,430°C, at which point it returns to BCC until it melts at 1,536°C. The lower temperature BCC phase is called alpha, or ferrite; the FCC phase is called gamma, or austenite; and the high-temperature BCC phase is called delta.

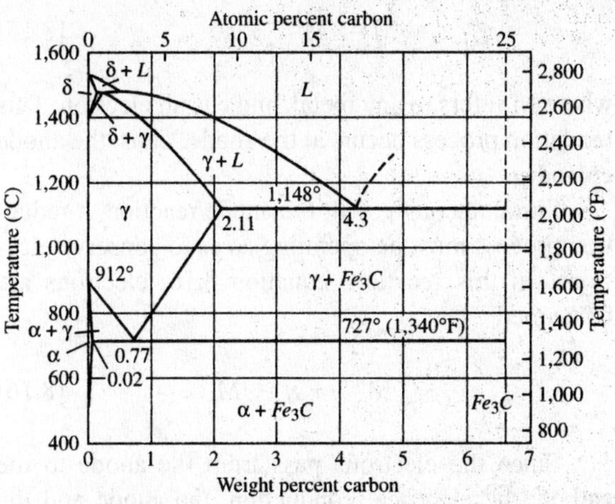

Figure 8.8 The iron-iron carbide equilibrium phase diagram. (Used with permission of ASM International.)

The phase diagram shows the degree of solubility of carbon in each of these phases. Notice that the ferrite region is very narrow, indicating low solubility of carbon, and that the austenite region is quite wide (up to 2 wt. % C max), indicating quite high solubility. The phase that occurs at 6.67 wt. % C is called Fe_3C, or cementite, and has virtually no solubility width; it exists only at 6.67 wt. % C.

To review the simple heat treatments available in the Fe-Fe_3C system, consider first an alloy containing 0.77 wt. % C. When heated above the eutectoid temperature, 727°C, the alloy is single-phase austenite. This part of the process is called austenitization. When the alloy is slowly cooled to the eutectoid temperature, the austenite undergoes a phase transformation to form a two-phase mixture of ferrite and cementite, called pearlite. When the transformation is complete, so that the microstructure is completely pearlitic, the alloy may continue to cool below 727°C. This heat treatment, called normalization, involves austenitization followed by air-cooling.

An alloy that contains less carbon than 0.77 wt. % is called a hypoeutectiod steel. These alloys are austenitized by heating above the A_3 temperature. The A_3 line is the boundary separating the austenite region from the ferrite plus austenite region. For any alloy, this boundary is the A_3 temperature. When they are slowly cooled below the A_3 temperature, ferrite called primary ferrite forms in the austenite. When the alloy crosses the A_1 temperature, the eutectoid temperature, the remaining austenite transforms to pearlite. The final microstructure, then, is ferrite and pearlite. The inverse lever rule determines the relative amounts of the two constituents. If the alloy is low carbon, say 0.2 wt. %, the final microstructure is nearly all ferrite with very little pearlite.

On the other hand, when austenite is cooled sufficiently fast to avoid the formation of pearlite, martensite will form below a threshold called the martensite start temperature. The martensite is a nonequilibrium phase whose chief virtue is its potentially high hardness. The hardness of martensite increases with carbon content, usually up to 0.8 wt. % C.

8.6 Solid Solubility in Metal Alloys

Solute atoms can reside in the solvent lattice, to some extent, in either of two ways: substitutionally or interstitially.

Substitutional solute atoms replace solvent atoms on their lattice sites. The extent varies according to thermodynamic and other factors. For instance, copper and nickel atoms can completely exchange with each other in the FCC lattice and are thus considered completely soluble. Copper and silver, on the other hand, can tolerate only limited exchange, and are thus considered only slightly soluble.

Interstitial solute atoms occupy positions between the solvent atoms in the solvent lattice. For this reason, interstitial solutes are limited to small atoms such as carbon, hydrogen, and nitrogen. The extent of solubility is also limited because only a small fraction of the interstitial sites can be occupied.

A vacancy is a vacant lattice site, that is, no atom is occupying the site. Every metal has an equilibrium concentration of vacancies that increases exponentially with increasing temperature up to the melting point.

8.7 Chemical Diffusion

At any temperature above absolute zero, atoms are vibrating in their lattice positions. An atom can change position by moving to a neighboring vacancy or, in the case of an interstitial solute atom, a neighboring interstitial site. The process is a simple jump from one site to the next. By this chemical diffusion process, atoms can move through the material.

Fick's first law gives the rate of atom motion in terms of rate of mass transfer:

$$J = -D\frac{dc}{dx} \quad [8.13]$$

where $\frac{dc}{dx}$ is the concentration gradient of the solution (the variation of the amount of solute, c, with distance), $J = \frac{1}{A}\frac{dm}{dt}$ is the mass flux in the x-direction (the mass of atoms moving through a section of area A), and D is the diffusion constant of the diffusing solute/solvent system.

The magnitude of D indicates a material system's rate of diffusion and is an exponential function of temperature, since the rate of atom jumping increases greatly with increasing temperature as the amplitude of atom vibration increases. The variation with temperature is given by equation 8.14:

$$D = D_0 \exp \frac{-Q}{RT} \qquad [8.14]$$

Here, D_0, the diffusion constant, and Q, the activation energy, are material constants for any given solute/solvent combination. R is the universal gas constant, expressed in the units of Q; and T is absolute temperature. The higher the activation energy, the lower the diffusion coefficient, D, and the greater its dependence on temperature.

Since interstitial atoms, such as hydrogen and carbon, are small and always have unoccupied interstitial sites as neighbors, the activation energy is lower and the diffusion rate is higher by several orders of magnitude than for substitutional solutes, principally because the chance of a neighboring site being vacant in the substitutional case is quite low.

Table 8.3 lists diffusion constants and activation energies for three systems.

Table 8.3. Diffusion Constants and Activation Energies for Some Systems

Diffusion System	*D_0 (m^2/sec)*	*Q (kJ/mol)*
C in α-Fe (BCC)	3.9×10^{-7}	80
C in γ-Fe (FCC)	7×10^{-6}	131
Cu in Al	6.5×10^{-5}	136

Since Q is given here in kilojoules per mole, the value of R should be 8.31 J/mol · K.

8.8 Corrosion

In this section the basic elements of galvanic corrosion of metals are discussed. The process by which metals lose mass is called **oxidation.** In this process, metal atoms lose one or more electrons and become metal ions as expressed in equation 8.15:

$$M \rightarrow M^{n+} + n\bar{e} \qquad [8.15]$$

where M refers to any metal, and $\bar{e}$ is an electron. This oxidation process occurs at the anode. Thus, the anode corrodes.

Simultaneously with the anode reaction, a reduction process must be operating so as to conserve electrons. In this reaction, equation 8.16, electrons are consumed:

$$M^{n+} + n \rightarrow M \qquad [8.16]$$

Since the electrons pass from the anode to the cathode by electrical conduction, the anode and the cathode must be electrically connected.

Typical anode reactions are as follows:

$$\begin{aligned} &Cu \rightarrow Cu^{2+} + 2e^- \\ &Ni \rightarrow N^+ + e^- \\ &Al \rightarrow Al^{3+} + 3e^- \\ &H_2 \rightarrow 2H^+ + 2e^- \end{aligned} \qquad [8.17]$$

Typical cathode reactions are these:

$$\begin{aligned} &Cu^{2+} + 2e^- \rightarrow Cu \\ &Ni^+ + e^- \rightarrow Ni \\ &Al^{3+} + 3e^- \rightarrow Al \\ &2H^+ + 2e^- \rightarrow H_2 \end{aligned} \qquad [8.18]$$

Corrosion can be viewed, then, as an electrochemical reaction consisting of the combination of an oxidation and a reduction process. Two half-cell reactions, like those shown above, can be combined to form a complete reaction. For example:

$$\begin{aligned} &Zn^{2+} + 2e^- \rightarrow Zn \quad \text{Anode} \\ &2H^+ + 2e^- \rightarrow H_2 \quad \text{Cathode} \end{aligned}$$

By reversing the direction of the anode reaction to represent oxidation, and then combining the two half-cell reactions, a complete reaction can be obtained. For example:

$$\begin{aligned} &Zn + 2HCl \rightarrow ZnCl_2 + H_2 \\ &\text{or} \\ &Zn + 2H^+ \rightarrow Zn^{2+} + H_2 \end{aligned} \qquad [8.19]$$

In the first reaction zinc is the anode and is oxidized, and hydrogen in hydrogen chloride is reduced to be liberated as hydrogen gas at the surface of the

Table 8.4 Standard EMF Series

	Electrode Reaction	*Standard Electrode Potential, V^0 (V)*
↑	$Au^3 + 3e^- \rightarrow Au$	+1.420
	$O_2 + 4H^+ + 4e^- \rightarrow 2H_2O$	+1.229
	$Pt^{2+} + 2e^- \rightarrow Pt$	~ +1.2
	$Ag^+ + e^- \rightarrow Ag$	+0.800
Increasingly inert	$Fe^{3+} + e^- \rightarrow Fe^{2+}$	+0.771
(cathodic)	$O_2 + 2H_2O + 4e^- \rightarrow 4(OH^-)$	+0.401
	$Cu^{2+} + 2e^- \rightarrow Cu$	+0.340
	$2H^+ + 2e^- \rightarrow H_2$	0.000
	$Pb^{2+} + 2e^- \rightarrow Pb$	−0.126
	$Sn^{2+} + 2e^- \rightarrow Sn$	−0.136
	$Ni^{2+} + 2e^- \rightarrow Ni$	−0.250
	$Co^{2+} + 2e^- \rightarrow Co$	−0.277
	$Cd^{2+} + 2e^- \rightarrow Cd$	−0.403
	$Fe^{2+} + 2e^- \rightarrow Fe$	−0.440
Increasingly active	$Cr^{3+} + 3e^- \rightarrow Cr$	−0.744
(anodic)	$Zn^{2+} + 2e^- \rightarrow Zn$	−0.763
	$Al^{3+} + 2e^- \rightarrow Al$	−1.662
	$Mg^{2+} + 2e^- \rightarrow Mg$	−2.363
	$Na^+ + e^- \rightarrow Na$	−2.714
↓	$K^+ + e^- \rightarrow K$	−2.924

metal conductor, which acts as the cathode. In some corrosion cells, the cathode half-cell reaction can be the plating out of metal ions onto the metal cathode. In most cases, however, the cathode half-cell reaction involves water and hydrogen. Some typical cathode reactions are as follows:

$$\begin{aligned} O_2 + 4H^+ + 4e^- &\rightarrow 2H_2O \quad pH < 7 \\ O_2 + 2H_2O + 4e^- &\rightarrow 4(OH^-) \quad pH \geq 7 \\ 2H^+ + 2e^- &\rightarrow H_2 \quad pH < 7 \end{aligned} \quad [8.20]$$

To determine the relative tendency of an anode-cathode pair to corrode, a concept of electrode potential is used. In the standard Emf Series shown in Table 8.4, the electrode potentials of the reduction half-cell reactions of various metals are listed with the hydrogen gas electrode serving as a reference of 0 volt. When two dissimilar metals are placed in contact, the one that is lower in the table is the anode and corrodes. Care should be taken to avoid using in service dissimilar metals that will be in electrical contact.

8.9 Mechanical Behavior

The Stress-Strain Curve

The response of a material to applied stress or applied strain is called mechanical behavior. For crystalline structural materials, that is, all metals and many ceramics, this behavior is of two types: linear elastic and plastic. Each type is characterized by the properties that relate the applied stress to the response variable, whatever it may be.

The most common of these relations is between stress and strain, and the relevant properties are measured on the uniaxial stress-strain curve. Keep in mind that stress, σ, in this case is defined as follows:

$$\sigma = \frac{\text{load}}{\text{area}} \quad [8.21]$$

where load is the applied load in the axial direction, and, for engineering stress, area is the original area; for true stress, area is the instantaneous area.

Strain, ε, is defined here as:

Engineering strain: $$\varepsilon = \frac{\Delta L}{L_0} \quad [8.22]$$

where ΔL is the change in length, and L_0 is the original or gauge length of the sample. Also:

True strain: $$\varepsilon = \ln\frac{L}{L_0} \quad [8.23]$$

where L_0 is the original length, and L is the instantaneous length.

An example of the engineering stress-strain curve for a typical engineering alloy is shown in Figure 8.9. From it some very important properties can be determined. The elastic modulus, the yield strength, the ultimate tensile strength, and the fracture strain are all clearly exhibited in an accurately constructed stress-strain curve. The elastic modulus, E (Young's modulus), is the slope of the elastic portion of the curve (the steep, linear region) because E is the proportionality constant relating stress and strain during elastic deformation: $\sigma = E\varepsilon$. The 0.2% offset yield strength is the stress value, $\sigma_{0.2\%ys}$ of the intersection of a line (called the offset) constructed parallel to the elastic portion of the curve but offset to the right by a strain of 0.002. It represents the onset of plastic deformation. The ultimate tensile strength is the engineering stress value, or σ_{uts}, at the maximum of the engineering stress-strain curve. It represents the maximum load, for that original area, that the sample can sustain without undergoing the instability of necking, which will lead inexorably to fracture. The fracture strain is the engineering strain value at which fracture occurred. However, a lot more information is contained in a stress-strain curve.

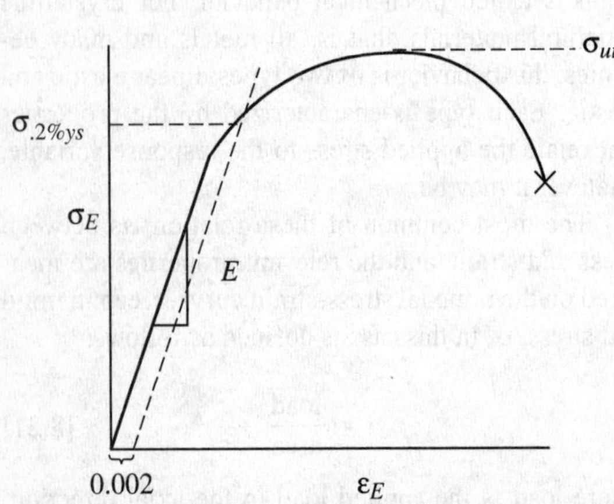

Figure 8.9 An example of the engineering stress-strain curve for a typical engineering alloy.

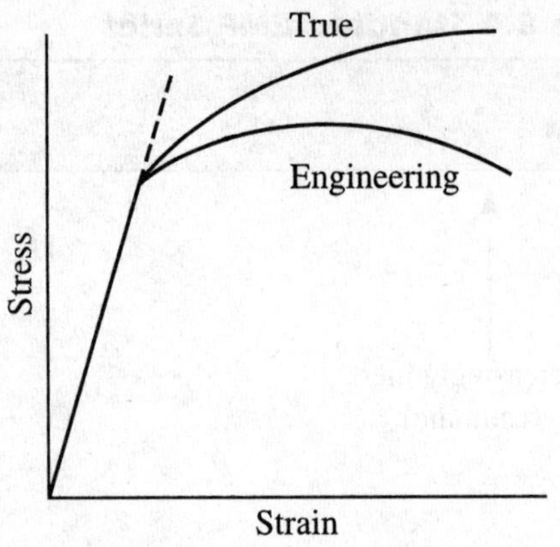

Figure 8.10 The true stress-strain curve and the engineering stress-strain curve for the same material.

At the outset, though, a clear distinction must be made between a true stress-true strain curve and an engineering stress-engineering strain curve. The difference is shown in Figure 8.10, in which are plotted, on the same axes, the true stress-strain curve and the engineering stress-strain curve for the same material. The difference is also evident in the definitions of true stress-true strain and engineering stress-engineering strain. The engineering stress is the load borne by the sample divided by a constant, the original area. The true stress is the load borne by the sample divided by a variable, the instantaneous area. Note that the true stress always rises in the plastic region, whereas the engineering stress rises and then falls after going through a maximum.

The maximum represents a significant difference between the engineering stress-strain curve and the true stress-strain curve. In the engineering stress-strain curve, this point indicates the beginning of necking. The ultimate tensile strength is the maximum load measured in the tension test divided by the original area.

Hardness

Since hardness is a measure of a material's resistance to permanent indentation, load in relation to indentation depth is a measure of strength. Strong materials have high hardnesses and vice versa.

Plastic Deformation of Crystalline Materials

The mechanism for plastic deformation in a crystalline material is the motion of dislocations through the crystal in response to shear stress of an adequate level. The magnitude of the stress required for this process is a measure of the ease of dislocation motion in that material. The yield strength of a crystalline material, then, can be viewed as the stress required to begin dislocation motion.

If there is an ease to dislocation motion, significant amounts of plastic deformation can be achieved and the material is considered to be **ductile.** If, however, there is so much resistance to dislocation motion that plastic deformation cannot occur without the stress rising to the fracture level, then the material is considered to be **brittle.** Being strong or hard is usually associated with being brittle; ductility is associated with being less strong.

Since the yield strength of a material has been defined as the stress at which plastic deformation begins, it follows that any means by which dislocation motion can be impeded will raise the stress required to initiate plastic deformation, and thereby raise the strength of the material. The various processes that accomplish this purpose are called strengthening mechanisms.

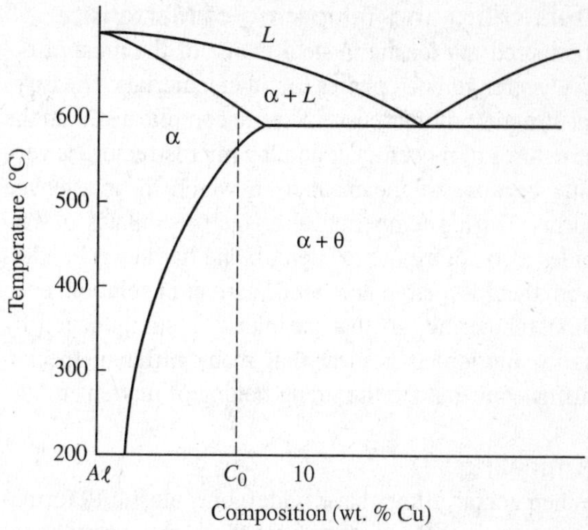

Figure 8.11 The aluminum-rich portion of the aluminum-copper equilibrium phase diagram.

Strengthening Mechanisms

Strain Hardening

One of the most common mechanisms for strengthening a crystalline material is strain hardening. In this case, dislocation motion itself becomes responsible for impeding dislocation motion. This mechanism involves two concurrent actions: the intersection of dislocations during motion impedes further motion, and the multiplication of dislocations during motion increases the rate of intersection. Therefore, in strain hardening, as plastic strain (dislocation motion) increases, the stress required to continue the motion must also increase. This result can be observed in the positive slope of the plastic region of the true stress-true strain curve shown in Figure 8.10.

Solid Solution Strengthening

Dislocations are more difficult to move through the lattice of a crystalline solid solution than through the lattice of the pure crystal. The resistance to motion increases with solute content. Although there is a significant variation in the degree to which various solutes contribute to the strengthening effect, most solutes serve to increase this effect. Therefore, in general, the purest crystals have lowest strength (neglecting strain hardening).

Second-Phase Strengthening

Dislocation motion is further impeded by small particles of one or more additional phases. The dislocations have difficulty passing through the particles and therefore must bow out between them in order to continue to move. Thus, the distance between these particles determines strength; as interparticle spacing decreases, strength increases.

A very common use of second-phase strengthening is the precipitation hardening of a group of aluminum alloys known as heat-treatable alloys. The phase diagram of an aluminum-copper alloy of this type is shown in Figure 8.11. The dashed line, C_0, indicates the particular alloy that is suited to precipitation hardening treatment. When this alloy is heated into the single-phase alpha region, the alloy becomes a solid solution, single phase. When cooled into the alpha plus theta region, the theta phase precipitates out of solution as a dispersion throughout the matrix. When the alpha solution is cooled slowly, large particles of theta form; when the alpha is cooled rapidly to room temperature, formation of theta is suppressed. Finally, if the supercooled alpha is reheated to a relatively low temperature, the theta will nucleate and grow as a very fine dispersion within the alpha matrix. This fine dispersion with small interparticle spacing will contribute significantly to the strength of the aluminum alloy.

The designation of this second-phase strengthening heat treatment is T6.

Grain Refinement

Fine-grained polycrystals are stronger than coarse-grained polycrystals because the limited volume of crystal in a small grain impedes dislocation motion. Higher stress is required in the small (fine) grain for the same amount of dislocation motion as in a large (coarse) grain.

An ASTM numbering scheme quantifies grain size. A grain size is designated by a number from 1 to 10; the larger the number, the smaller the size. The quantitative relationship is given by equation 8.24:

$$N = 2^{n-1} \qquad [8.24]$$

where N is the average number of grains per square inch at 100× magnification, and n is the ASTM grain-size number.

Quenching and Tempering of Martensite

Tempered martensite in steel is one of the most effectively strengthened phases found in materials. The crystal structure of martensite is more complicated than the structures of most metals and the microstructure is very fine because of the manner in which the martensite forms. During tempering, the fine precipitates of carbides also contribute to strength and hardness. In addition, there is a large amount of carbon in solution, even after tempering, so that the phase is strengthened by solid solution. It is clear that many different mechanisms contribute to the strengthening of martensite.

Annealing

When metal alloys have undergone plastic deformation, the length of dislocations in the crystals increases in proportion to the amount of plastic strain. Since the dislocations also possess elastic strain energy in proportion to their length, as dislocation length increases, so does the total energy of the metal. This increase in elastic strain energy is called stored energy of plastic deformation.

When a plastically deformed piece of metal is heated to a temperature above half its melting point, in degrees Kelvin (one-half the absolute melting temperature of the material), the stored energy of plastic deformation drives a process in which new grains are formed in the midst of the deformed grains. These new grains have the same dislocation distribution as was present before the plastic deformation and, therefore, have the original strength and hardness. Each new grain grows outward to consume all the deformed material, replacing it with new grains. In this way the annealed piece is returned to its original strength and ductility by a process called recrystallization. It is one of the most common annealing processes.

Cold Working versus Hot Working

When a metal alloy is plastically deformed at a temperature above half its absolute melting point, recrystallization occurs simultaneously with plastic deformation. In this situation, referred to as hot working, strain hardening cannot occur during the deformation. On the other hand, plastic deformation carried out at a temperature below between one-third to one-half the absolute melting point, referred to as cold working, is accompanied with the usual strain hardening.

8.10 Magnetic Behavior

The magnetic behavior of materials is divided generally into three groups: diamagnetic, paramagnetic, and ferromagnetic. When an uninformed person refers to a material being nonmagnetic, he or she is referring, without distinction, to the first two types of behavior. When a material is said to be magnetic, its behavior is ferromagnetic.

In all materials, the electrons in the atoms have magnetic moments because of their motions about the atoms and about their own axes of spin. Each of these motions produces a small magnetic moment that, with no applied magnetic field, is canceled. When a magnetic field is applied, however, one type of material experiences alignment of electron magnetic moments to oppose the applied field. This behavior is **diamagnetism.** In another type of material, the weak permanent magnetic moments of the atoms align with the applied magnetic field. This behavior is **paramagnetism.** Both of these magnetic responses to a magnetic field are *nonpermanent* and *weak.* When the applied field falls to zero, the net magnetic moment of the material also becomes zero. Copper and silver are diamagnetic, while aluminum and titanium are paramagnetic.

In certain metals (iron, cobalt, and nickel) and their alloys, a quite different behavior, **ferromagnetism,** is observed. In these metals, the magnetic moments from electron spin align themselves within the atom and from atom to atom, resulting in a *strong* magnetic moment in the absence of an applied magnetic field. If all the moments of all the atoms aligned themselves across a bar of such a material, the result would be a permanent magnet, with a north and a south pole.

In some of these materials, however, the bar divides itself into domains. Each domain would contain aligned atoms and possess north and south poles, but these would exactly cancel the north and south poles of neighboring domains. The *bar* would thus have no *net* moment, even though each domain was permanently aligned. When a magnetic field is applied, however, the domain boundaries reposition themselves to create a net magnetic moment to align with the applied field. Now, if the material is a hard magnet, the domains do not return to their original sizes and shapes. This bar will then be a strong permanent magnet. If the material is a soft magnet, the domains will reposition themselves when the applied field is removed so that again there is no *net* magnetic moment.

In most materials, the difference between hard and soft magnets is microstructural. The microstructural effect is in the ease of motion of the domain wall boundaries, called Bloch walls.

Thus, an electromagnet is a soft magnet, meaning that the applied field can control the net magnetic moment. A permanent magnet is a hard magnet in that the net magnetic moment is always present because the domain boundaries are prevented by the microstructure from moving.

To test a material for magnetic behavior, a permanent magnet is used as a test magnet. If the test magnet is attracted to the material, the material is ferromagnetic. If no attraction occurs, the material is either paramagnetic or diamagnetic. Those two types cannot be distinguished by feel.

A ferromagnetic material loses its ferromagnetic behavior and becomes paramagnetic when heated above the Curie temperature. For iron this is 768°C, just below the BCC (α) − FCC (γ) transformation temperature, 912°C. In steel, the FCC (γ) phase, austenite, can be stable below 768°C. In such cases, the paramagnetic behavior is related to the structure, not to the temperature; stable austenite, even at low temperature, will be paramagnetic rather than ferromagnetic.

8.11 Electrical Behavior

The electrical behavior of materials is divided among four types: metals (conductors), insulators, semiconductors, and superconductors.

Metals

Metal atoms are held together by metallic bonding, a very complicated process that has an important consequence—high electrical conductivity. The bonding mechanism produces free electrons, which are not bound to any particular atom in the solid—hence the term *free.* It is these free electrons that give rise to high electrical conductivity. The governing law of conductivity is Ohm's law:

$$V = IR \quad [8.25]$$

where V is voltage in volts, I is current in amperes, and R is resistance in ohms. Since R is dependent on the cross-sectional area and length of the conductor, it is not a material property. This is shown in the relation

$$R = \frac{\rho L}{A} \quad [8.26]$$

where ρ is the resistivity, in ohm-meters, of the material and is thus a material property. The conductivity of a material, σ, is the reciprocal of ρ:

$$\sigma = \frac{1}{\rho}\ (\text{ohm-meter})^{-1} \quad [8.27]$$

If conductivity is considered as the motion of charged carriers, electrons for example, the conductivity of a conductor is given by equation 8.28:

$$\sigma = \eta |e| \mu \quad [8.28]$$

where η is the number of charge carriers per unit volume (free electrons in metals), $|e|$ is the electron charge, and μ is the charge mobility.

In the case of metals, the carrier concentration, η, remains constant, while the mobility, μ, decreases, as the temperature increases because of the increase in the frequency of collisions of the electrons with the increasing amplitude of atom vibration. This relationship results in the rule that, for metals, *resistivity increases as temperature increases.* In fact, that rule becomes the basis for definition of a metal.

Insulators

In some materials, such as diamond, usually involving covalent bonding, the electrons are bound to their atoms. Hence, there are no free electrons and so η in equation 8.28 is nearly zero. The result is negligible conductivity or very high resistivity. These materials will act as insulators.

Semiconductors

In some materials, called semiconductors, the electrons are bound; but with increases in temperature and/or applied voltage, the electrons can be excited into allowed but unoccupied energy states. In such states, the electrons can act as free conduction electrons. For every excitation event, there is produced a vacant bound state that is abandoned when the electron is excited to the conduction state. Other bound electrons can then migrate into the vacant bound state (called a hole), giving rise to electron mobility or conduction. However, in this case, convention assigns positive current to hole motion, even though electrons are moving. The situation can be compared to a moving line of chairs with one chair vacant. If a person moves into the vacant chair when it arrives next to him, the person (electron) will be moving, say, from left to right, while the vacant chair (hole) will be moving from right to left.

In an intrinsic semiconductor such as pure silicon, the number of free electrons and the number of holes are always equal. This is a very important concept.

With these semiconductors, in equation 8.28 the term η, the carrier concentration, increases with increasing temperature because of the increasing number of excited electrons. The increase is very much larger than the decrease in mobility, so the net result is an increase in conductivity. Therefore, *conductivity increases* and *resistivity decreases* with increasing temperature. This is the basis for the definition of an intrinsic semiconductor; this definition is the converse of the metal definition.

In microelectronics, extrinsic semiconductors are the common ones. In these, impurity atoms, called dopants, control the carrier concentration. Selected solute atoms in silicon, for example, can be fully positively ionized at room temperature to provide one free conduction electron per dopant atom. In this case the free electron concentration remains roughly constant and equal to the dopant concentration. Since, in this case, the dopant atoms contribute *electrons* to the conduction process, the semiconductor is called an *n*-type (*n* for negative or electron conduction). If, however, another type of dopant that can be fully negatively ionized at room temperature is dissolved in silicon, it will capture one bound electron, thus creating one hole, per dopant atom. In this case the doped silicon is *p*-type (*p* for positive or hole conduction). In the former case the dopant atoms are called donors, and in the latter case they are called acceptors. Remember:

Dopant Type	Extrinsic Behavior
Donors	*n*-type
Acceptors	*p*-type

When a *p*-type semiconductor is electronically joined to an *n*-type semiconductor, a *p*-*n* junction is formed. This junction, called a diode, passes current proportional to the voltage when in forward bias; but when the voltage is reversed, in reverse bias, the diode passes only a small constant current. This behavior is the basis for the operation of a solid-state rectifier.

Superconductors

A limited group of materials, composed of metals and ceramics, displays a very complicated behavior called superconductivity. When these materials are cooled below a critical temperature, T_c, resistivity drops nearly to zero for all temperatures below T_c, as shown in Figure 8.12. The range of T_c extends from a low near 1 K for some niobium alloys to a high approaching 200 K for some of the newer ceramics.

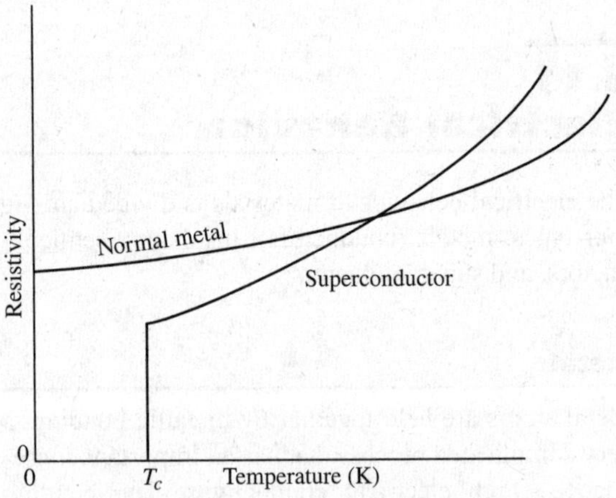

Figure 8.12 Resistivity versus temperature for a superconducting alloy.

PRACTICE PROBLEMS

1. In regard to corrosion, which of the following is NOT true?
   (A) The cathode loses mass.
   (B) Oxidation occurs at the anode.
   (C) The anode and cathode must be electrically connected.
   (D) Water usually plays an important role.
2. During the tension deformation of a metal test bar, necking occurs when
   (A) plastic deformation begins.
   (B) the ultimate tensile strength is reached.
   (C) strain hardening ceases to operate.
   (D) the heat of deformation causes recrystallization.
3. Which of the following is NOT related to recrystallization?
   (A) hot working
   (B) cold working
   (C) elastic modulus
   (D) melting temperature
4. The temperature above which a ferromagnetic material must be heated to lose its ferromagnetism is called the
   (A) Curie temperature.
   (B) saturation point.
   (C) transition temperature.
   (D) critical temperature.
5. Which of the following does NOT involve dislocations?
   (A) fracture strain
   (B) Young's modulus
   (C) 0.2% offset yield strength
   (D) ductile-brittle transition temperature
6. What is the diffusion coefficient of carbon in iron at 700°C?
   (A) 4.5×10^{-13} m²/s
   (B) 1.97×10^{-11} m²/s
   (C) 3.8×10^{-10} m²/s
   (D) 6.44×10^{-13} m²/s
7. Consider the phase diagram shown in Figure 8.7. If the alloy containing 50 wt. % Cu is slowly cooled to just below the eutectic temperature, what fraction is eutectic?
   (A) 34.4%
   (B) 65.6%
   (C) 50.6%
   (D) 77.1%
8. Consider the phase diagram shown in Figure 8.5. At 1,300°C an alloy contains 50% liquid in equilibrium with 50% solid. What is the composition of the alloy?
   (A) 45% Ni
   (B) 58% Ni
   (C) 51% Ni
   (D) 25% Ni
9. The volume of the unit cell of molybdenum, calculated by using the information in Table 8.2, is
   (A) 0.057 nm³.
   (B) 0.011 nm³.
   (C) 0.317 nm³.
   (D) 0.031 nm³.
10. A ferromagnetic material must
    (A) be a permanent magnet.
    (B) contain iron.
    (C) have ionic bonding.
    (D) have a large saturation magnetization.
11. Given the following data regarding nickel: structure is FCC; atomic mass is 58.71 amu; atomic radius is 0.125 nm, what is the theoretical density of this metal?
    (A) 8.9 g/cm³
    (B) 6.2 g/cm³
    (C) 2.7 g/cm³
    (D) 5.1 g/cm³
12. What are the indices of the direction along the face diagonal of a cubic crystal?
    (A) $\langle 111 \rangle$
    (B) $\langle 110 \rangle$
    (C) $\{111\}$
    (D) $\{110\}$
13. The diffusion rate of carbon in iron at 1,000°C is
    (A) 2.6×10^{-9} m²/s
    (B) 1.8×10^{-12} m²/s
    (C) 2.93×10^{-11} m²/s
    (D) 7.3×10^{-11} m²/s
14. As the temperature increases,
    (A) the resistivity of a metal decreases.
    (B) the diffusion coefficient of a solute decreases.
    (C) the conductivity of an intrinsic semiconductor increases.
    (D) the resistivity of a superconductor approaches 0.
15. A semiconductor with donor impurities
    (A) conducts by hole migration.
    (B) is an *n*-type semiconductor.
    (C) is an intrinsic semiconductor.
    (D) acts as a rectifier.
16. Heat treating of steel most frequently involves which of the following?
    (A) martensite
    (B) pearlite
    (C) ferrite
    (D) spherodite
17. At room temperature low-carbon steel is almost completely
    (A) martensite.
    (B) pearlite.
    (C) ferrite.
    (D) spherodite.

18. If the ASTM grain-size number increases from 3 to 9, by what factor does the number of grains in a 100× field of view change?
(A) 64
(B) −49
(C) 27
(D) −9
19. The strengthening process involving the formation of fine distribution of a second phase is called
(A) quench and temper.
(B) solid solution strengthening.
(C) precipitation hardening.
(D) case hardening.
20. In a ferromagnetic alloy, easy migration of domain boundaries usually results in
(A) permanent magnetism.
(B) good conductivity.
(C) a very weak net magnetic moment.
(D) superconductivity at low temperatures.

Answer Key

1. A
2. B
3. C
4. A
5. B
6. B
7. B
8. B
9. D
10. D
11. A
12. B
13. C
14. C
15. B
16. A
17. C
18. A
19. C
20. C

Answers Explained

1. **A** Reduction occurs at the cathode. The half-cell reaction is $M^{n+} + \text{ne} \rightarrow M$. This is characterized by the plating of metal ions from the electrolyte or the generation of hydrogen gas from dissolved hydrogen ions in the electrolyte.

2. **B** Necking is associated with the maximum value in the engineering stress-strain curve. The engineering stress coordinate of this maximum is defined as the ultimate tensile stress.

3. **C** Hot working is associated with plastic deformation carried out at temperatures above approximately one-half of the melting point in kelvin units. In this temperature range, recrystallization occurs whether the metal was worked below and then heated to this temperature or was worked above this temperature. Recrystallization has nothing to do with elastic deformation or the attendant property elastic modulus.

4. **A** This is the definition of the Curie temperature.

5. **B** Dislocation motion is the cause of plastic deformation. Fracture strain and ductile-brittle transition both involve dislocations because the type of fracture, ductile or brittle, depends on whether or not dislocations are able to move in crystalline materials. Young's modulus, on the other hand, pertains to elastic deformation and hence does not involve dislocations. It involves only the force-separation interaction from the interatomic or intermolecular bonding.

6. **B** Use the equation $D = D_O e^{-\frac{Q}{RT}}$, and choose the values for D_O and Q. At 700°C, iron is BCC. From Table 8.3, $D_O = 3.9 \times 10^{-7}$ m²/s and $Q =$ 80 kJ/mol. Then:

$$D_{700C} = 3.9 \times 10^{-7} e^{-\frac{80{,}000}{8.31 \cdot 973}} \text{ m}^2/\text{s}$$
$$= 1.97 \times 10^{-11} \text{ m}^2/\text{s}$$

7. **B** In Figure 8.7, the eutectic composition is 28 wt. % Cu, and the composition of the copper-rich phase is 92 wt. % Cu. Use the inverse Lever rule given in equation 8.11; then the fraction of the alloy that is eutectic is

$$f_{\text{eut}} = \frac{92 - 50}{92 - 28} = \frac{42}{64} = 65.6\%$$

8. **B** In Figure 8.5, the composition of liquid and solid at 1,300°C are 47 wt. % Ni and 64 wt. % Ni respectively. Use the lever rule to give equation 8.11:

$$0.5 = \frac{64 - x}{64 - 47}$$

$$x = 55.5 \text{ wt. \% Ni}$$

9. **D** Molybdenum is BCC. For this crystal structure, the lattice parameter, a, is related to the body diagonal by the equation

$$4r = a\sqrt{3}$$

or

$$a = \frac{4r}{\sqrt{3}}$$

Also, volume = a^3. Then

$$V = \left(\frac{4 \cdot 0.136}{\sqrt{3}}\right)^3 = 0.031 \text{ nm}^3$$

10. **D** A ferromagnetic material exhibits a large magnetic response to an applied magnetic field. The response need not be permanent; it may last only as long as the field is applied, or it may last long after the applied field is removed. Cobalt and nickel are ferromagnetic.

11. **A** The designation FCC indicates 4 atoms per unit cell, so the mass of the atoms in the nickel unit cell is given by the equation

$$\frac{4 \cdot 58.71}{6.023 \times 10^{23}} = 3.90 \times 10^{-22} \text{ g}$$

The volume of the unit cell is a^3. In terms of atom radius, $a = \frac{4r}{\sqrt{2}}$. Therefore, the volume is

$$V = \left(\frac{4r}{\sqrt{2}}\right)^3 = 0.044 \text{ nm}^3$$

Then, since density is mass divided by volume:

$$\rho = \frac{3.90 \times 10^{-22} \text{ g}}{0.044 \text{ nm}^3} = 8.9 \text{ g/cm}^3$$

12. **B** The arrow in the figure below represents the face diagonal of a cubic unit cell. To obtain the indices, determine the coordinates of the point at which one end of the arrow intersects the unit cell while the other end is at the origin. In this case, the coordinates are $1a$, $1a$, $0a$. Now, collect the coefficients of a in angle brackets: in this case, <110>, since it represents any or all of the face diagonals.

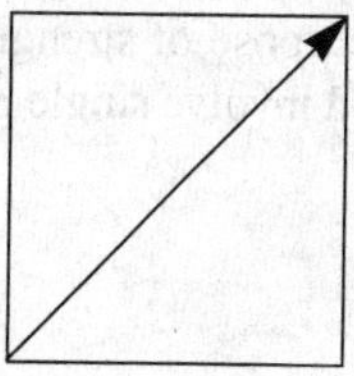

13. **C** Apply the same method as in Problem 6, but use the FCC values in Table 8.3, since iron is FCC at temperatures above 912°C. The equation is

$$D = D_0 e^{-\frac{Q}{RT}}$$

Then, since $D_0 = 7 \times 10^{-6}$ m²/s and $Q = 131$ kJ/mol:

$$D_{1{,}000°C} = 7 \times 10^{-6}\, e^{-\frac{131{,}000}{8.31 \cdot 1273}} \text{ m}^2\text{/s}$$
$$= 2.93 \times 10^{-11} \text{ m}^2\text{/s}$$

14. **C** As the temperature increases, the number of conductive electrons in the conduction bond increases. Therefore, the conductivity increases by equation 8.28.

15. **B** An extrinsic semiconductor with donor impurities is an n-type semiconductor, since conduction is by free electrons excited into the conduction band.

16. **A** The most common purpose for heat-treating steel is the formation of martensite, the very hard and strong phase in iron-carbon alloys.

17. **C** At room temperature low-carbon steel is ferrite and cementite. However, the lever law, applied at this temperature range for low-carbon steel, would yield ferrite as the overwhelming majority phase.

18. **A** The equation is $N = 2^{n-1}$; therefore, for $n = 3$, $N = 4$, and for $n = 9$, $N = 256$. The number of grains per square inch in a 100× field of view increases from 4 to 256, an increase by a factor of 64.

19. **C** Age hardening, also known as precipitation hardening, involves the formation of a second phase by precipitation during an aging heat treatment for the purpose of strengthening. The other processes listed involve single phases only.

20. **C** When ferromagnetic domain boundaries migrate easily, the result is the partitioning of the piece into regions with a cancelling or almost cancelling of magnetic moments. The net magnetic moment in this case is therefore very weak.

CHAPTER 9

Mathematics

David E. Stevens

Introduction

The intent of this chapter is to review some of the important mathematical topics that an engineer may encounter in the design and analysis of a physical system. The major topics include algebra, trigonometry, complex numbers, analytic geometry, linear algebra, vectors, sequences and series, probability, statistics, differential and integral calculus, and differential equations.

9.1 Straight Lines

Assigned to each point P in the coordinate plane is an ordered pair (a,b), called the **rectangular coordinates of the point.** The x-coordinate a is the directed distance from the y-axis to point P, and the y-coordinate b is the directed distance from the x-axis to point P, as shown in Figure 9.1.

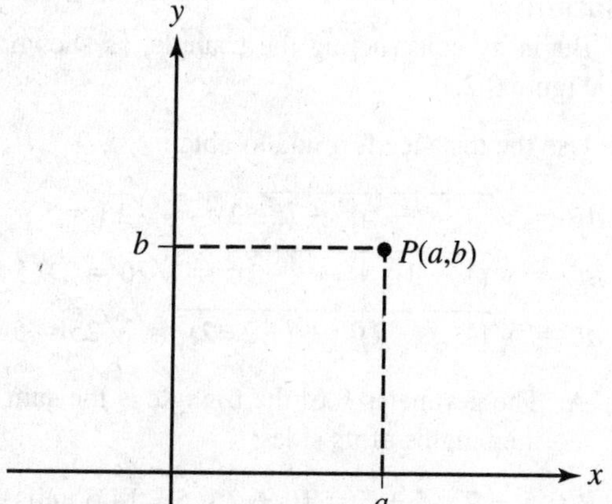

Figure 9.1

The distance between two points $P(x_1,y_1)$ and $Q(x_2,y_2)$ in the coordinate plane is given by the **distance formula:**

$$PQ = \sqrt{(x_1 - x_2)^2 + (y_1 - y_2)^2}$$

The rectangular coordinates of the midpoint M of a line segment joining points $P(x_1,y_1)$ and $Q(x_2,y_2)$ in the coordinate plane are given by the **midpoint formula:**

$$M\left(\frac{x_1 + x_2}{2}, \frac{y_1 + y_2}{2}\right)$$

The **slope** m of a nonvertical line through distinct points $P(x_1,y_1)$ and $Q(x_2,y_2)$, where $x_1 \neq x_2$, is

$$m = \frac{y_2 - y_1}{x_2 - x_1}$$

If $x_1 = x_2$, the line is vertical and its slope is undefined. There are three important forms for the equation of a straight line:

1. *Slope-intercept form:* $y = mx + b$, where m is the slope and b is the y-intercept.
2. *General form:* $Ax + By = C$, where A, B, and C are real numbers.
3. *Point-slope form:* $y - y_1 = m(x - x_1)$, where m is the slope and (x_1,y_1) is a point on the line.

Two distinct lines with slopes m_1 and m_2 are **parallel** if and only if $m_1 = m_2$, and are **perpendicular** if and only if $m_1 = -\dfrac{1}{m_2}$.

Example 9.1

A triangle has vertices at points $A(-2,2)$, $B(3,2)$, $C(1,-2)$ in the coordinate plane.

A. Find the perimeter of the triangle.
B. Find the area of the triangle.

Solution:

Begin by constructing the triangle, as shown in Figure 9.2.

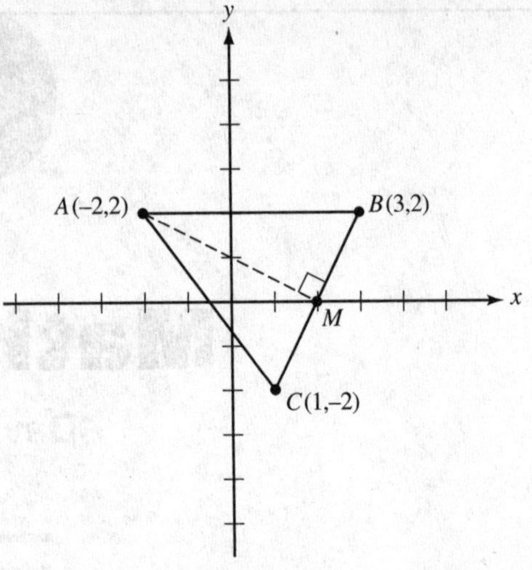

Figure 9.2

Use the distance formula to obtain

$$AB = \sqrt{[3 - (-2)]^2 + (2-2)^2} = \sqrt{25} = 5$$

$$BC = \sqrt{(1 - 3)^2 + (-2-2)^2} = \sqrt{20} = 2\sqrt{5}$$

$$AC = \sqrt{[1 - (-2)]^2 + (-2-2)^2} = \sqrt{25} = 5$$

A. The perimeter P of the triangle is the sum of the lengths of its sides:

$$P = 5 + 2\sqrt{5} + 5 = 10 + 2\sqrt{5} \approx 14.5 \text{ units}$$

B. Since $AB = AC$, this triangle is isosceles with $\overline{BC}$ the nonequal side. To find the area of this triangle, recall from geometry that the altitude to the nonequal side of an isosceles triangle bisects that side. Thus, if $\overline{AM}$ is the altitude to base $\overline{BC}$, then M is the midpoint of $\overline{BC}$. By the midpoint formula, the coordinates of midpoint M are

$$M\left(\frac{1 + 3}{2}, \frac{-2 + 2}{2}\right) = M(2,0)$$

and, by the distance formula, the length of altitude $\overline{AM}$ is

$$AM = \sqrt{[(2 - (-2)]^2 + (0 - 2)^2} = \sqrt{20} = 2\sqrt{5}$$

The area of triangle ABC is half the product of its base and altitude:

$$\text{Area} = \frac{1}{2}(BC)(AM) = \frac{1}{2}(2\sqrt{5})(2\sqrt{5}) = 10 \text{ square units}$$

As an alternative method for finding the area of this triangle, let $\overline{CN}$ be the altitude to base $\overline{AB}$. Since $\overline{AB}$ is a horizontal line segment, $CN = 4$. Hence:

$$\text{Area} = \frac{1}{2}(AB)(CN) = \frac{1}{2}(5)(4) = 10 \text{ square units}$$

Example 9.2

In each case, find the equation of a line that satisfies the given conditions.

A. Passes through points $(-2,-3)$ and $(2,1)$
B. Passes through point $(2,1)$ and is perpendicular to $3x - 5y = 10$

Solution:

A. The slope of the line that passes through points $(-2,-3)$ and $(2,1)$ is

$$m = \frac{1-(-3)}{2-(-2)} = \frac{4}{4} = 1$$

Using the point-slope form for the equation of a straight line with $(x_1,y_1) = (-2,-3)$ as the fixed point and $m = 1$ as the slope, find the equation of this line:

$$y - y_1 = m(x - x_1)$$
$$y + 3 = x + 2$$
$$y = x - 1$$

B. Determine the slope of line $3x - 5y = 10$ by writing it in slope-intercept form:

$$y = \frac{3}{5}x - 2$$

Hence, the slope of line $3x - 5y = 10$ is $\frac{3}{5}$. Therefore, the slope of a line perpendicular to this line is

$$m = -\frac{5}{3}$$

Use the point-slope form for the equation of a straight line with fixed point $(x_1,y_1) = (2,1)$ and slope $m = -\frac{5}{3}$ to find the desired equation:

$$y - y_1 = m(x - x_1)$$
$$y - 1 = -\frac{5}{3}(x - 2)$$
$$y = -\frac{5}{3}x + \frac{13}{3}$$

9.2 Quadratic Equations

An equation of the form $ax^2 + bx + c = 0$, where a, b, and c are real numbers with $a \neq 0$, is called a **quadratic equation in standard form.** The roots of this equation are given by **the quadratic formula:**

$$x = \frac{-b \pm \sqrt{b^2 - 4ac}}{2a}$$

In this formula, the quantity $b^2 - 4ac$ is called the **discriminant.** It indicates the nature of the roots of the quadratic equation:

1. Two distinct real roots if $b^2 - 4ac > 0$
2. Two complex conjugate roots if $b^2 - 4ac < 0$
3. One real root of multiplicity 2 if $b^2 - 4ac = 0$

Example 9.3

Solve each quadratic equation for x.

A. $x^2 + 6x = 18$ **B.** $x^2 + 5 = 2x$

Solution:

A. Before identifying a, b, and c, write $x^2 + 6x = 18$ in standard form:

$$x^2 + 6x - 18 = 0$$

Now, $a = 1$, $b = 6$, and $c = -18$. By the quadratic formula,

$$x = \frac{-6 \pm \sqrt{6^2 - 4(1)(-18)}}{2(1)} = \frac{-6 \pm \sqrt{108}}{2}$$
$$= -3 \pm 3\sqrt{3}$$

Hence, the two real roots of this equation are $-3 + 3\sqrt{3} \approx 2.20$ and $-3 - 3\sqrt{3} \approx -8.20$.

B. Begin by writing $x^2 + 5 = 2x$ in standard form:

$$x^2 - 2x + 5 = 0$$

Therefore, $a = 1$, $b = -2$, and $c = 5$. By the quadratic formula,

$$x = \frac{-(-2) \pm \sqrt{(-2)^2 - 4(1)(5)}}{2(1)}$$
$$= \frac{2 \pm \sqrt{-16}}{2} = 1 \pm 2i$$

Thus, the roots of this equation are the complex conjugates $1 + 2i$ and $1 - 2i$.

9.3 Conic Sections

If the graph of a **general quadratic equation in two unknowns:**

$$Ax^2 + Bxy + Cy^2 + Dx + Ey + F = 0$$

exists and is not degenerate, then its graph is:

1. A *circle* if $A = C$ and $B = 0$.
2. A *parabola* if the discriminant $B^2 - 4AC = 0$.
3. An *ellipse* (or a circle, see definition 1) if the discriminant $B^2 - 4AC < 0$.
4. A *hyperbola* if the discriminant $B^2 - 4AC > 0$.

A **circle** is the set of all points P in a plane that lie a fixed distance (radius) from a given point (center), as shown in Figure 9.3.

A **tangent** to a circle is a line with an endpoint not within the circle that intersects the circle in one

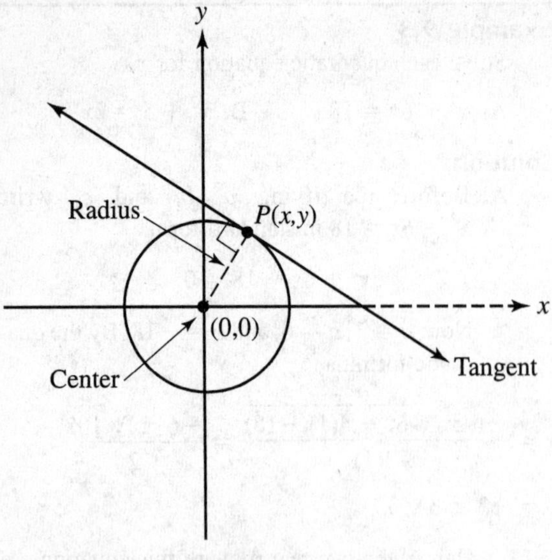

Figure 9.3

and only one point. Every tangent to a circle is perpendicular to a radius drawn to the point of tangency. The standard-form equation of a circle with center at the origin and radius r is

$$x^2 + y^2 = r^2$$

A **parabola** is the set of all points P in a plane that are equidistant from a fixed line (directrix) and a fixed point (focus) not on the line. In Figure 9.4, $PQ = PF$.

The standard-form equation of a parabola with its vertex at the origin and a vertical axis of symmetry is

$$x^2 = 4py$$

The parabola opens upward if $p > 0$, and opens downward if $p < 0$. The standard-form equation of a parabola with its vertex at the origin and a horizontal axis of symmetry is

$$y^2 = 4px$$

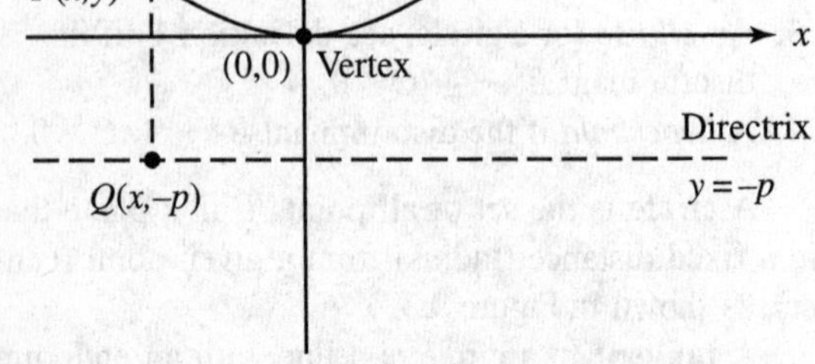

Figure 9.4

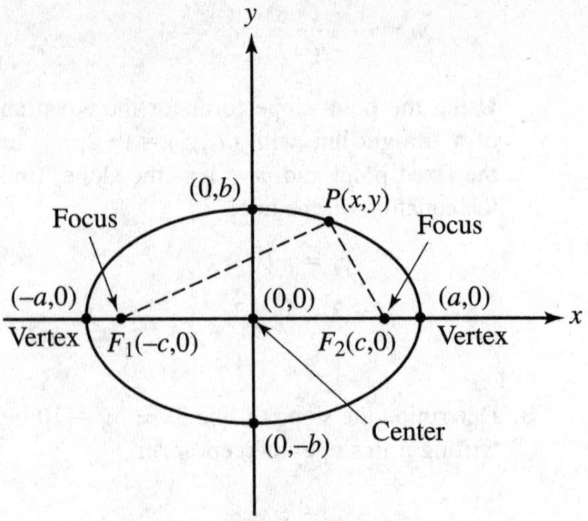

Figure 9.5

The parabola opens right if $p > 0$, and opens left if $p < 0$.

An **ellipse** is the set of all points P in a plane, the sum of whose distances from two fixed points (foci) is a constant that is equal to the length of the major axis of the ellipse. In Figure 9.5, $PF_1 + PF_2 = 2a$.

The standard-form equation of an ellipse with its center at the origin is

$$\frac{x^2}{a^2} + \frac{y^2}{b^2} = 1$$

If $a > b$, the vertices of the ellipse lie on the x-axis. If $b > a$, the vertices of the ellipse lie on the y-axis. For an ellipse, the center-to-focus distance is given by

$$c = \sqrt{|a^2 - b^2|}$$

A **hyperbola** is the set of all points P in a plane, the difference of whose distances from two fixed points (foci) is a constant that is equal to the length of the transverse axis of the hyperbola. In Figure 9.6, $PF_1 - PF_2 = 2a$.

The standard-form equation of a hyperbola with its center at the origin is

$$\frac{x^2}{a^2} - \frac{y^2}{b^2} = 1$$

if its vertices are on the x-axis, and

$$\frac{y^2}{a^2} - \frac{x^2}{b^2} = 1$$

if its vertices are on the y-axis. For a hyperbola, the center-to-focus distance is given by

$$c = \sqrt{a^2 + b^2}$$

The graph of the equation $xy = k$ (k is a constant) is also a hyperbola. Its center is at the origin, and its asymptotes are the x- and y-axes.

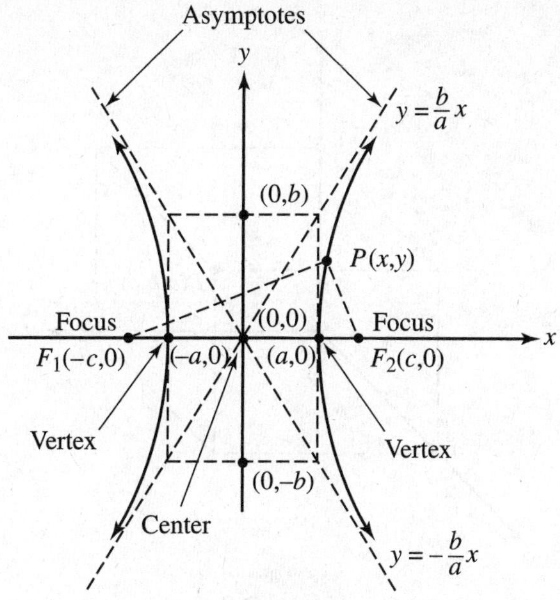

Figure 9.6

If the center (or vertex) of a conic section is translated from the origin to another point (h, k) in the coordinate plane, then the standard-form equation of the conic section is adjusted by replacing x with $x - h$ and y with $y - k$.

Example 9.4

Classify the graph of each general quadratic equation in two unknowns as a circle, a parabola, an ellipse, or a hyperbola.

A. $4x^2 - 4xy + y^2 - 5\sqrt{5}x + 5 = 0$
B. $8y^2 + 6xy - 9 = 0$

Solution:

A. In the general quadratic equation $4x^2 - 4xy + y^2 - 5\sqrt{5}x + 5 = 0$, $A = 4$, $B = -4$, and $C = 1$. Since the discriminant $B^2 - 4AC = 0$, the graph of this equation is a parabola.

B. In the general quadratic equation $8y^2 + 6xy - 9 = 0$, $A = 8$, $B = 6$, and $C = 0$. Since the discriminant $B^2 - 4AC = 36 > 0$, the graph of this equation is a hyperbola.

Example 9.5

Determine the coordinates of (1) the vertices and (2) the foci for the conic section defined by each equation.

A. $16x^2 + 9y^2 = 144$ **B.** $16x^2 - 9y^2 = 144$

Solution:

A. Divide both sides of this equation by 144:

$$\frac{x^2}{3^2} + \frac{y^2}{4^2} = 1$$

(1) This is the standard-form equation of an ellipse with its center at the origin and vertices on the y-axis (since $4 > 3$). Hence, the coordinates of the vertices are $(0,4)$ and $(0,-4)$.

(2) The center-to-focus distance is $c = \sqrt{4^2 - 3^2} = \sqrt{7}$. Therefore, the coordinates of the foci are $(0, \sqrt{7}) \approx (0, 2.646)$ and $(0, -\sqrt{7}) \approx (0, -2.646)$.

B. Divide both sides of this equation by 144:

$$\frac{x^2}{3^2} - \frac{y^2}{4^2} = 1$$

(1) This is the standard-form equation of a hyperbola with center at the origin and vertices on the x-axis (since the x^2-term is positive). Hence, the coordinates of the vertices are $(3, 0)$ and $(-3, 0)$.

(2) The center-to-focus distance is $c = \sqrt{3^2+4^2} = 5$. Therefore, the coordinates of the foci are $(5, 0)$ and $(-5, 0)$.

Example 9.6

In each case, determine the general quadratic equation of the conic section with the given characteristics.

A. Parabola: vertex at the origin and focus at $(-2, 0)$
B. Hyperbola: asymptotes along the x- and y-axes and passes through point $(3, 2)$

Solution:

A. A parabola with vertex at the origin and focus on the x-axis has the form $y^2 = 4px$, with $(p, 0)$ the coordinates of the focus. Since the x-coordinate of the focus is given to be -2, the general quadratic equation of this parabola is found by replacing p with -2 in the equation $y^2 = 4px$:

$$y^2 = -8x \quad \text{or} \quad y^2 + 8x = 0$$

B. A hyperbola with asymptotes along the x- and y-axes has the form $xy = k$. Since this hyperbola passes through point $(3, 2)$, $k = xy = 6$. The general quadratic equation of this hyperbola is found by replacing k with 6 in the equation $xy = k$:

$$xy = 6 \quad \text{or} \quad xy - 6 = 0$$

Example 9.7

A tangent to the circle with center $C(1,-2)$ and radius 3 passes through point $P(5, -5)$.

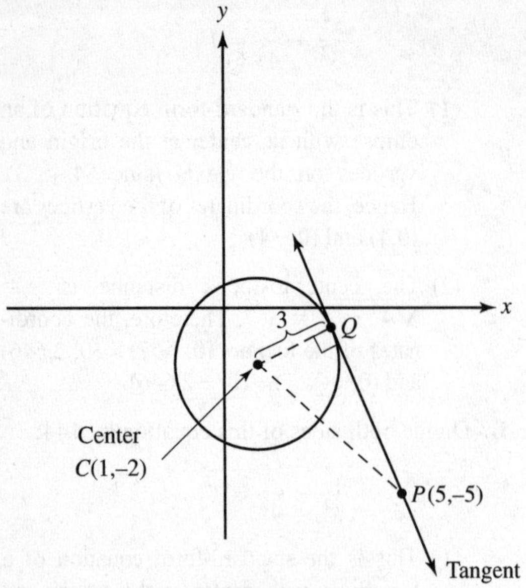

Figure 9.7

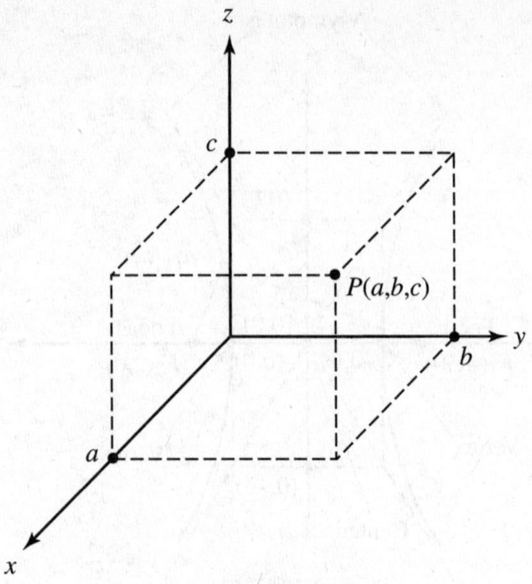

Figure 9.8

A. Find the equation of the circle.
B. Find the distance from point P to a point of tangency Q on the circle.

Solution:

A. The equation of a circle with radius 3 and center at the origin is $x^2 + y^2 = 9$. Hence, by a translation of axis, the equation of a circle with center at $C(1, -2)$ and radius 3 is

$$(x - 1)^2 + (y + 2)^2 = 9$$

B. Since every tangent to a circle is perpendicular to a radius drawn to the point of tangency Q, the triangle formed by points C, P, and Q must be a right triangle with hypotenuse CP, as shown in Figure 9.7.

Since the radius of the circle is 3, $CQ = 3$, and, by the distance formula, $CP = 5$. Hence, by the Pythagorean theorem

$$(PQ)^2 = (CP)^2 - (CQ)^2 = 5^2 - 3^2 = 16$$

implying that the distance from point P to the point of tangency Q is $PQ = 4$.

9.4 Spheres

Assigned to each point P in space is an ordered triple (a,b,c), called the **rectangular coordinates** of the point. The x-coordinate a is the directed distance from the yz-plane to point P, the y-coordinate b is the directed distance from the xz-plane to point P, and the z-coordinate c is the directed distance from the xy-plane to point P, as shown in Figure 9.8.

The distance between two points $P(x_1,y_1,z_1)$ and $Q(x_2,y_2,z_2)$ in space is given by the **distance formula:**

$$PQ = \sqrt{(x_2 - x_1)^2 + (y_2 - y_1)^2 + (z_1 - z_2)^2}$$

A sphere is a surface in space, each point of which is at a given fixed distance (radius) from a given fixed point (center). The standard-form equation of a sphere with center at (h,k,m) and radius r is

$$(x - h)^2 + (y - k)^2 + (z - m)^2 = r^2$$

The general-form equation of a sphere is

$$x^2 + y^2 + z^2 + Ax + By + Cz + D = 0$$

where A, B, C, and D are real numbers.

Example 9.8

A sphere with center $(1,-3,2)$ passes through point $(4,1,2)$.

A. Find the radius of the sphere.
B. Find the general-form equation of the sphere.

Solution:

A. The radius r of the sphere is the distance from its center to a point on the sphere. By the distance formula,

$$r = \sqrt{(4 - 1)^2 + [1 - (-3)]^2 + (2 - 2)^2} = \sqrt{25} = 5$$

B. The standard-form equation of a sphere with center $(1,-3,2)$ and radius 5 is given by

$$(x-1)^2+(y+3)^2+(z-2)^2=25$$

Its general-form equation is found by expanding and simplifying its standard-form equation:

$$x^2+y^2+z^2-2x+6y-4z-11=0$$

9.5 Logarithms

The **logarithmic function with base b** is defined by

$$y=\log_b x \quad \text{if and only if} \quad x=b^y \text{ for } x>0$$

A base-10 logarithm, written as $\log x$, is called a **common logarithm.** A base-e ($e \approx 2.718...$) logarithm, written as $\ln x$, is called a **natural logarithm.** To change from one logarithmic base to another, use the **change of base formula:**

$$\log_b x=\frac{\log_a x}{\log_a b},\ a>0,\ a\neq 1$$

Four **logarithmic identities** hold for all bases b, with $b>0$ and $b\neq 1$:

1. $\log_b 1=0$
2. $\log_b b=1$
3. $b^{\log_b u}=u,\ u>0$
4. $\log_b b^u=u$

If $b>0$, $b\neq 1$, then, for positive real numbers x and y, there are three **properties of logarithms:**

1. $\log_b xy=\log_b x+\log_b y$
2. $\log_b \frac{x}{y}=\log_b x-\log_b y$
3. $\log_b x^n=n\log_b x$

Example 9.9

Evaluate $\log_4 24$ using:

A. common logarithms **B.** natural logarithms

Solution:

A. Use the change of base formula with $a=10$, $b=4$, and the common logarithm key on a calculator:

$$\log_4 24=\frac{\log 24}{\log 4}\approx 2.29$$

B. Use the change of base formula with $a=e$, $b=4$, and the natural logarithm key on a calculator:

$$\log_4 24=\frac{\ln 24}{\ln 4}\approx 2.29$$

Example 9.10

Simplify each expression.

A. $e^{2\ln(x+1)}$ **B.** $\log_2 16^{x-2}$

Solution:

A. Apply logarithmic property 3, and use the fact that $b^{\log_b u}=u$, for $u>0$:

$$e^{2\ln(x+1)}=e^{\ln(x+1)^2}=(x+1)^2$$

provided that $x>-1$.

B. Begin by applying the properties of exponents and matching the base of the exponential expression to the base of the logarithm:

$$\log_2 16^{x-2}=\log_2 (2^4)^{x-2}=\log_2 2^{4x-8}$$

Now, since $\log_b b^u=u$ for any permissible base b and any real number u,

$$\log_2 16^{x-2}=\log_2 2^{4x-8}=4x-8$$

Example 9.11

Use the properties of logarithms to write each expression as a single logarithm.

A. $\log_6 50+2\log_6 4-3\log_6 2$
B. $\ln(x^2-1)-2\ln(x+1)$

Solution:

A. Begin with property 3 and then apply the other two logarithmic properties:

$$\begin{aligned}\log_6 50+2\log_6 4-3\log_6 2&=\log_6 50+\log_6 4^2-\log_6 2^3\\&=\log_6 50+\log_6 16-\log_6 8\\&=\log_6\frac{(50)(16)}{8}\\&=\log_6 100\end{aligned}$$

B. Assuming that $x>1$, begin with property 3 and then apply property 2, reducing the fraction to lowest terms:

$$\begin{aligned}\ln(x^2-1)-2\ln(x+1)&=\ln(x^2-1)-\ln(x+1)^2\\&=\ln\frac{x^2-1}{(x+1)^2}\\&=\ln\frac{x-1}{x+1}\end{aligned}$$

Example 9.12

Solve each equation for x.

A. $4e^{2x-1}=100$ **B.** $2-\log x=\log 3$

Solution:

A. Begin by dividing both sides of the equation by 4 to isolate the exponential expression on one side:

$$e^{2x-1} = 25$$

Now, take the natural logarithm of each side, apply log property 3, and solve for x:

$$\ln e^{2x-1} = \ln 25$$
$$(2x - 1)\ln e = \ln 25$$
$$x = \frac{1 + \ln 25}{2} \approx 2.109$$

B. Begin by grouping the logarithms on one side of the equation and then condense them into a single logarithm by applying the properties of logarithms:

$$2 - \log x = \log 3$$
$$\log 3 + \log x = 2$$
$$\log 3x = 2$$

Now, change to exponential form and solve for x:

$\log 3x = 2$ if and only if $10^2 = 3x$

implying that $x = \frac{100}{3}$.

9.6 Triangle Trigonometry

The interior angles of a polygon are usually measured in radians or degrees. The relationship between **radian measure** and **degree measure** is as follows:

$$\pi \text{ radians} = 180 \text{ degrees}$$

The **sum of the interior angles of an *n*-sided polygon** is

$$(n - 2)180° \quad \text{or} \quad (n - 2)\pi$$

An angle whose measure is less than 90° ($\pi/2$ radians) is called an **acute angle,** and an angle whose measure is between 90° and 180° is an **obtuse angle.** If an angle measures 90°, it is called a **right angle.** The Pythagorean theorem states that in any right triangle

$$x^2 + y^2 = r^2$$

as shown in Figure 9.9.

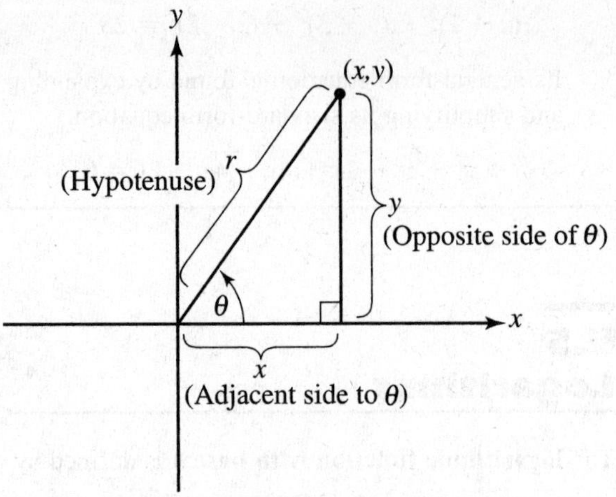

Figure 9.9

For Figure 9.9, there are six **trigonometric functions:**

1. $\sin\theta = \frac{y}{r} = \frac{\text{opp}}{\text{hyp}}$
2. $\cos\theta = \frac{x}{r} = \frac{\text{adj}}{\text{hyp}}$
3. $\tan\theta = \frac{y}{x} = \frac{\text{opp}}{\text{adj}}$
4. $\csc\theta = \frac{r}{y} = \frac{\text{hyp}}{\text{opp}}$
5. $\sec\theta = \frac{r}{x} = \frac{\text{hyp}}{\text{adj}}$
6. $\cot\theta = \frac{x}{y} = \frac{\text{adj}}{\text{opp}}$

Figure 9.10 shows in which quadrants the trigonometric functions are positive:

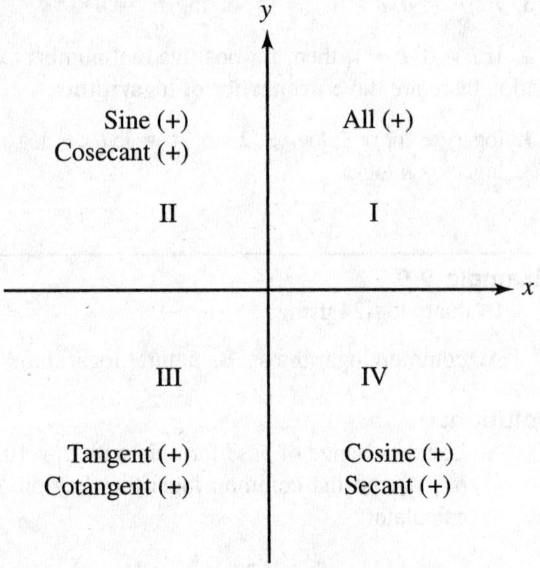

Figure 9.10

The **inverse trigonometric functions** are defined as follows:

1. $\sin^{-1} k$, with $-1 \le k \le 1$, denotes the angle between $-90°$ and $90°$ whose sine is k.
2. $\cos^{-1} k$, with $-1 \le k \le 1$, denotes the angle between $0°$ and $180°$ whose cosine is k.

3. $\tan^{-1} k$ denotes the angle between $-90°$ and $90°$ whose tangent is k.

The **law of sines** states that in a given triangle the ratio of the length of the side to the sine of the angle opposite that side has the same constant value:

$$\frac{a}{\sin A} = \frac{b}{\sin B} = \frac{c}{\sin C}$$

The **law of cosines** states that the square of the length of any side of a triangle is the sum of the squares of the other two sides minus twice the product of those two sides and the cosine of the angle between them:

$$a^2 = b^2 + c^2 - 2bc \cos A$$

If a and b are any two sides of a triangle and θ is the angle between those two sides, then the **area** A of the triangle is

$$A = \frac{ab \sin \theta}{2}$$

Example 9.13

Given that $\sin \theta = \frac{3}{5}$, find $\cos \theta$ if:

A. θ is acute. **B.** θ is obtuse.

Solution:

If $\sin \theta = \frac{3}{5}$, then, by the definition of sine, $y = 3$ and $r = 5$. Hence, by the Pythagorean theorem, $x^2 + 3^2 = 5^2$, implying that $x = \pm 4$.

A. If θ is acute, then θ is in quadrant I, where $\cos \theta > 0$. Hence:

$$\cos \theta = \frac{x}{r} = \frac{4}{5}$$

B. If θ is obtuse, then θ is in quadrant II, where $\cos \theta < 0$. Hence:

$$\cos \theta = \frac{x}{r} = \frac{-4}{5} = -\frac{4}{5}$$

Example 9.14

Given a right triangle with legs of lengths 5 meters and 12 meters, find:

A. the length of the hypotenuse
B. the angle (in radians) opposite the longer leg

Solution:

A. If z is the length of the hypotenuse, then, by the Pythagorean theorem,

$$z^2 = 5^2 + 12^2$$

implying that the length of the hypotenuse is $z = 13$ m.

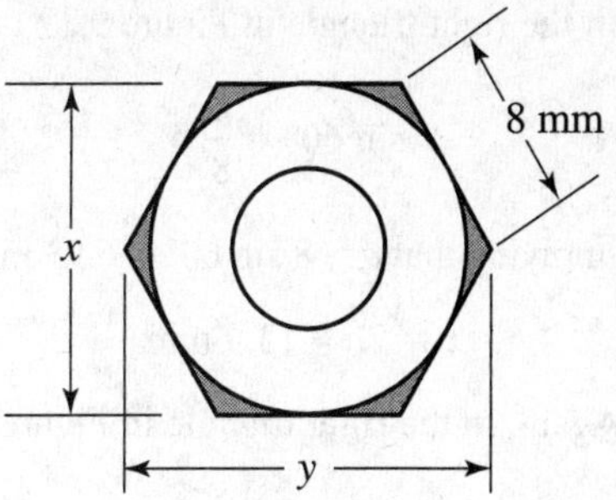

Figure 9.11

B. If θ is the angle opposite the longer leg, then, by the definition of tangent,

$$\tan \theta = \frac{\text{opp}}{\text{adj}} = \frac{12}{5}$$

To find θ, use the inverse tangent key on a calculator set in radian mode:

$$\theta = \tan^{-1}\frac{12}{5} \approx 1.176 \text{ rad}$$

Example 9.15

Each side of a hexagonal nut is 8 mm long, as shown in Figure 9.11.

A. Find distance x. **B.** Find distance y.

Solution:

A. Since a hexagonal nut has six sides, the sum of its interior angles is $(6 - 2)180° = 720°$. Therefore, each interior angle measures $720°/6 = 120°$, implying that triangle ABC is isosceles with $\theta = 60°$, as shown in Figure 9.12.

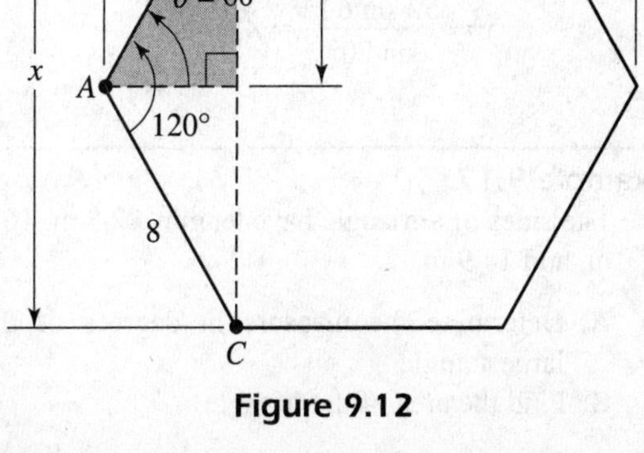

Figure 9.12

In the right triangle in Figure 9.12,

$$\sin 60° = \frac{a}{8}$$

implying that $a = 8 \sin 60° \approx 6.93$ mm. Thus:

$$x = 2a \approx 13.9 \text{ mm}$$

B. Again, in the right triangle in Figure 9.12,

$$\cos 60° = \frac{b}{8}$$

implying that $b = 8 \cos 60° = 4$ mm. Therefore:

$$y = 2b + 8 = 16 \text{ mm}$$

Example 9.16

Two angles of a triangle measure 62° and 48°. The length of the side opposite the unknown angle is 52 cm.

A. Find the measure of the unknown angle.
B. Find the lengths of the unknown sides.

Solution:

A. The sum of the interior angles of a triangle is 180°. Hence, if θ is the unknown angle, then

$$\theta = 180° - (62° + 48°) = 70°$$

B. Let x and y be the sides opposite the angles that measure 48° and 62°, respectively. To find these unknown sides, apply the law of sines by matching each side with the sine of the angle opposite that side:

$$\frac{52}{\sin 70°} = \frac{x}{\sin 48°} = \frac{y}{\sin 62°}$$

Hence:

$$x = \frac{52 \sin 48°}{\sin 70°} \approx 41.1 \text{ cm}$$

and

$$y = \frac{52 \sin 62°}{\sin 70°} \approx 48.9 \text{ cm}$$

Example 9.17

The sides of a triangle have lengths 22.5 m, 16.2 m, and 14.9 m.

A. Determine the measure in degrees of the largest angle.
B. Find the area of the triangle.

Solution:

A. The largest angle in a triangle is always opposite its longest side. Hence, the largest angle is opposite the side of length 22.5 m. If θ is the largest angle, then, by the law of cosines,

$$22.5^2 = 16.2^2 + 14.9^2 - 2(16.2)(14.9) \cos \theta$$

Solving for $\cos \theta$ gives

$$\cos \theta = \frac{22.5^2 - 16.2^2 - 14.9^2}{-2(16.2)(14.9)}$$

The inverse cosine function in conjunction with a calculator set in degree mode shows that θ is obtuse:

$$\theta = \cos^{-1}\left[\frac{22.5^2 - 16.2^2 - 14.9^2}{-2(16.2)(14.9)}\right] \approx 92.6°$$

B. From part **A,** the angle between the sides of lengths 16.2 m and 14.9 m is 92.6°. Thus, the area A of this triangle is

$$A = \frac{ab \sin \theta}{2} = \frac{(16.2)(14.9)\sin 92.6°}{2} \approx 121 \text{ m}^2$$

9.7 Analytic Trigonometry

Below is a list of the most frequently used trigonometric identities. For additional trigonometric identities, refer to the *Fundamentals of Engineering Reference Handbook.*

1. $\sin \theta \csc \theta = 1$
2. $\cos \theta \sec \theta = 1$
3. $\tan \theta \cot \theta = 1$
4. $\tan \theta = \dfrac{\sin \theta}{\cos \theta}$
5. $\cot \theta = \dfrac{\cos \theta}{\sin \theta}$
6. $\sin^2\theta + \cos^2\theta = 1$
7. $1 + \tan^2\theta = \sec^2\theta$
8. $1 + \cot^2\theta = \csc^2\theta$
9. $\cos(\alpha \pm \beta) = \cos \alpha \cos \beta \mp \sin \alpha \sin \beta$
10. $\sin(\alpha \pm \beta) = \sin \alpha \cos \beta \pm \cos \alpha \sin \beta$
11. $\sin 2\theta = 2 \sin \theta \cos \theta$
12. $\cos 2\theta = \cos^2\theta - \sin^2\theta = 2 \cos^2\theta - 1 = 1 - 2 \sin^2\theta$

Example 9.18

Given that $\sin \theta = \frac{3}{5}$ and θ is acute, find:

A. $\sin 2\theta$ **B.** $\cos(\theta + \pi)$

Solution:

From Example 9.13, if $\sin \theta = \frac{3}{5}$ and θ is acute, then $\cos \theta = \frac{4}{5}$.

A. Use trigonometric identity 11; then

$$\sin 2\theta = 2 \sin\theta \cos\theta = 2\left(\frac{3}{5}\right)\left(\frac{4}{5}\right) = \frac{24}{25}$$

B. Use trigonometric identity 9; then

$$\cos(\theta + \pi) = \cos\theta \cos\pi - \sin\theta \sin\pi$$
$$= \left(\frac{4}{5}\right)(-1) - \left(\frac{3}{5}\right)(0) = -\frac{4}{5}$$

Example 9.19

Simplify each expression to a single trigonometric function or a constant.

A. $\cos\theta \tan^2\theta + \cos\theta$ **B.** $\dfrac{\cos^2\theta}{1 - \sin\theta} - \sin\theta$

Solution:

A. Begin by factoring out $\cos\theta$ and then applying trigonometric identities 7 and 2:

$$\cos\theta \tan^2\theta + \cos\theta = \cos\theta(\tan^2\theta + 1)$$
$$= \cos\theta \sec^2\theta$$
$$= (\cos\theta \sec\theta)\sec\theta$$
$$= (1)\sec\theta$$
$$= \sec\theta$$

B. Begin by subtracting fractions and then apply trigonometric identity 6:

$$\frac{\cos^2\theta}{1 - \sin\theta} - \sin\theta = \frac{\cos^2\theta - \sin\theta(1 - \sin\theta)}{1 - \sin\theta}$$
$$= \frac{\cos^2\theta - \sin\theta + \sin^2\theta}{1 - \sin\theta}$$
$$= \frac{1 - \sin\theta}{1 - \sin\theta}$$
$$= 1$$

provided that $1 - \sin\theta \neq 0$

Example 9.20

Write each expression as a first power of the cosine function.

A. $\cos^2\theta$ **B.** $\sin^4\theta$

Solution:

A. Use identity 12, $\cos 2\theta = 2\cos^2\theta - 1$, to solve for $\cos^2\theta$:

$$\cos 2\theta = 2\cos^2\theta - 1$$
$$2\cos^2\theta = 1 + \cos 2\theta$$
$$\cos^2\theta = \frac{1}{2}(1 + \cos 2\theta)$$

B. Use identity 12, $\cos 2\theta = 1 - 2\sin^2\theta$, to solve for $\sin^2\theta$:

$$\cos 2\theta = 1 - 2\sin^2\theta$$
$$2\sin^2\theta = 1 - \cos 2\theta$$
$$\sin^2\theta = \frac{1}{2}(1 - \cos 2\theta)$$

Now, express $\sin^4\theta$ in terms of the cosine function:

$$\sin^4\theta = \sin^2\theta \sin^2\theta$$
$$= \frac{1}{2}(1 - \cos 2\theta)\frac{1}{2}(1 - \cos 2\theta)$$
$$= \frac{1}{4}(1 - 2\cos 2\theta + \cos^2 2\theta)$$

Finally, using the results of part **A**, replace $\cos^2 2\theta$ with $\frac{1}{2}(1 + \cos 4\theta)$:

$$\sin^4\theta = \frac{1}{4}\left[1 - 2\cos 2\theta + \frac{1}{2}(1 + \cos 4\theta)\right]$$
$$= \frac{1}{4}\left(\frac{3}{2} - 2\cos 2\theta + \frac{1}{2}\cos 4\theta\right)$$
$$= \frac{1}{8}(3 - 4\cos 2\theta + \cos 4\theta)$$

9.8 Complex Numbers

The **imaginary unit** i is defined by

$$i = \sqrt{-1}$$

where $i^2 = -1$.

A complex number z in **rectangular form** is written as

$$z = ai + b$$

where a and b are real numbers and i is the imaginary unit, as shown in the complex plane in Figure 9.13.

A complex number z in **polar form** is given by

$$z = re^{i\theta} = r(\cos\theta + i\sin\theta)$$

where $a = r\cos\theta$, $b = r\sin\theta$, $r = \sqrt{a^2 + b^2}$, and $\tan\theta = \frac{b}{a}$, as shown in Figure 9.13.

The **complex conjugate** of $z = a + bi$ is $\bar{z} = a - bi$. The product $z\bar{z}$ is the nonnegative real number $a^2 + b^2$.

DeMoivre's theorem is used to raise a complex number z in polar form to an integer power:

$$z^k = r^k e^{ik\theta} = r^k(\cos k\theta + i\sin k\theta)$$

If $z = re^{i\theta} = r(\cos\theta + i\sin\theta)$, with $z \neq 0$ and n a positive integer, then z has exactly n distinct nth roots $w_0, w_1, w_2, \ldots, w_{n-1}$, which are given by the ***n*th root formula:**

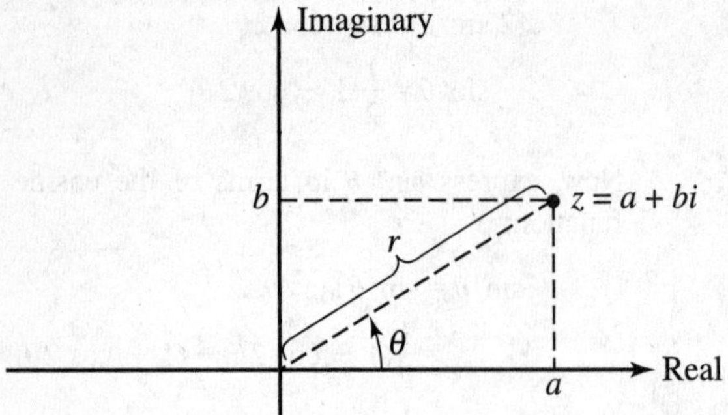

Figure 9.13

$$w_k = r^{1/n}e^{i(\theta+2\pi k)/n} = r^{1/n}\left[\cos\left(\frac{\theta + 2\pi k}{n}\right) + i\sin\left(\frac{\theta + 2\pi k}{n}\right)\right], \text{ for } k = 0, 1, 2, \ldots, n-1$$

Example 9.21

In each case, convert the given complex number to the indicated form.

A. $3 + 3i$ to polar form
B. $4.47e^{5.82i}$ to rectangular form

Solution:

A. For $3 + 3i$, $a = 3$ and $b = 3$. Thus:

$$r = \sqrt{a^2 + b^2} = \sqrt{3^2 + 3^2} = \sqrt{18} = 3\sqrt{2} \approx 4.24$$

Since $3 + 3i$ lies in quadrant I in the complex plane, θ must be a first-quadrant angle that satisfies the equation $\tan\theta = \frac{b}{a} = \frac{3}{3} = 1$. Hence,

$$\theta = \tan^{-1} 1 = \frac{\pi}{4} \approx 0.785$$

Thus, $3 + 3i = 3\sqrt{2}\, e^{(\pi/4)i} \approx 4.24e^{0.785i}$.

B. To express $4.47e^{5.82i}$ in rectangular form, use a calculator set in radian mode:

$$4.47e^{5.82i} = 4.47(\cos 5.82 + i \sin 5.82) \approx 4.00 - 2.00i$$

Example 9.22

In each case, given that $z_1 = 3 + 5i$ and $z_2 = 1 - 5i$, perform the indicated operation.

A. z_1z_2 **B.** $\frac{z_1}{z_2}$

Solution:

A. To find the product of two complex numbers in rectangular form, multiply each part of the first complex number by each part of the second complex number:

$$\begin{aligned} z_1z_2 &= (3 + 5i)(1 - 5i) \\ &= 3 - 15i + 5i - 25i^2 \\ &= 28 - 10i \end{aligned}$$

B. To find the quotient of two complex numbers in rectangular form, multiply by the complex conjugate of the denominator to obtain division by a nonnegative real number:

$$\begin{aligned} \frac{z_1}{z_2} &= \frac{3 + 5i}{1 - 5i} = \frac{(3 + 5i)(1 + 5i)}{(1 - 5i)(1 + 5i)} \\ &= \frac{-22 + 20i}{26} \\ &\approx -0.846 + 0.769i \end{aligned}$$

Example 9.23

In each case, given that $z_1 = 5e^{0.3i}$ and $z_2 = 3e^{2.5i}$, perform the indicated operation and write the answer in rectangular form:

A. z_1z_2 **B.** $z_1 + z_2$

Solution:

A. To multiply (or divide) complex numbers in polar form, add (or subtract) exponents:

$$z_1z_2 = (5e^{0.3i})(3e^{2.5i}) = 15e^{(0.3i+2.5i)} = 15e^{2.8i}$$

Now, convert to rectangular form:

$$15e^{2.8i} = 15(\cos 2.8 + i \sin 2.8) \approx -14.1 + 5.02i$$

B. To find the sum (or difference) of two complex numbers in polar form, convert the numbers to rectangular form and then add (or subtract) the real and imaginary parts of these numbers, separately. Hence:

$$\begin{aligned} z_1 + z_2 &= 5e^{0.3i} + 3e^{2.5i} \\ &= 5(\cos 0.3 + i \sin 0.3) + 3(\cos 2.5 + i \sin 2.5) \\ &= (5 \cos 0.3 + 3 \cos 2.5) + i\,(5 \sin 0.3 + 3 \sin 2.5) \\ &\approx 2.37 + 3.27i \end{aligned}$$

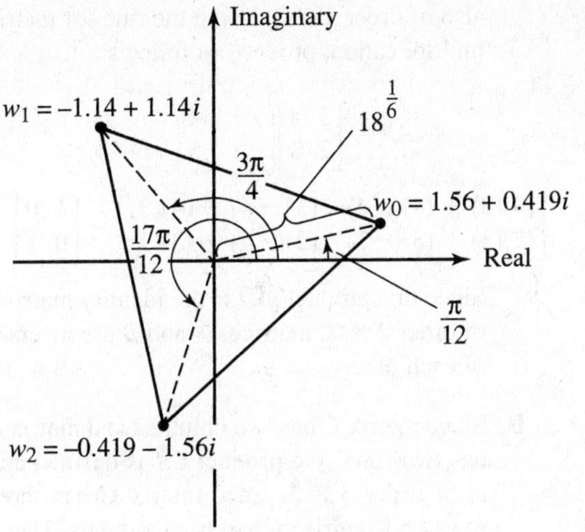

Figure 9.14

Example 9.24

In each case, given that $z = 3 + 3i$, find the indicated power or roots and write the answer in rectangular form.

A. z^4 **B.** the three cube roots of z

Solution:

A. From Example 9.21**A**, $z = 3 + 3i = 3\sqrt{2}e^{(\pi/4)i}$. Hence, by DeMoivre's theorem:

$$z^4 = (3\sqrt{2}e^{(\pi/4)i})^4 = (3\sqrt{2})^4 e^{4(\pi/4)i} = 324e^{\pi i}$$

Now, convert this answer to rectangular form:

$$324e^{\pi i} = 324(\cos \pi + i \sin \pi) = -324 + 0i = -324$$

B. Again, from Example 9.21**A**, $z = 3 + 3i = 3\sqrt{2}e^{(\pi/4)i}$. Hence, by the nth root formula, this complex number has three distinct cube roots given by

$$w_k = (3\sqrt{2})^{1/3} e^{i[(\pi/4)+2\pi k]/3}$$

for $k = 0, 1,$ and 2. Hence, the three cube roots are

$$w_0 = (3\sqrt{2})^{1/3} e^{i(\pi/12)} = 18^{1/6}\left(\cos \frac{\pi}{12} + i \sin \frac{\pi}{12}\right)$$
$$\approx 1.56 + 0.419i$$

$$w_1 = (3\sqrt{2})^{1/3} e^{i(3\pi/4)} = 18^{1/6}\left(\cos \frac{3\pi}{4} + i \sin \frac{3\pi}{4}\right)$$
$$\approx -1.14 + 1.14i$$

$$w_2 = (3\sqrt{2})^{1/3} e^{i(17\pi/12)} = 18^{1/6}\left(\cos \frac{17\pi}{12} + i \sin \frac{17\pi}{12}\right)$$
$$\approx -0.419 - 1.56i$$

Figure 9.14 shows the three cube roots of $3 + 3i$ in the complex plane.

Note that w_0, w_1, and w_2 form the vertices of an *equilateral triangle.* In general, the nth roots of a complex number form the vertices of a regular n-sided polygon in the complex plane.

9.9 Matrices

A **matrix** is a rectangular array of numbers enclosed by a pair of brackets. Each number in the matrix is called an *element.* Consider matrix A with m *rows* and n *columns:*

$$A = \begin{bmatrix} a_{11} & a_{12} & \cdots & a_{1j} & \cdots & a_{1n} \\ a_{21} & a_{22} & \cdots & a_{2j} & \cdots & a_{2n} \\ \vdots & \vdots & \vdots & \vdots & \vdots & \vdots \\ a_{i1} & a_{i2} & \cdots & a_{ij} & \cdots & a_{in} \\ \vdots & \vdots & \vdots & \vdots & \vdots & \vdots \\ a_{m1} & a_{m2} & \cdots & a_{mj} & \cdots & a_{mn} \end{bmatrix}$$

This matrix is of *order* $m \times n$ and can be denoted more compactly by writing $A = [a_{ij}]$, where a_{ij} stands for the element in the ith row, jth column. Two matrices $A = [a_{ij}]$ and $B = [b_{ij}]$ are equal if both are of order $m \times n$ and $a_{ij} = b_{ij}$ for all $i = 1, 2, 3, \ldots, m$ and $j = 1, 2, 3, \ldots, n$.

A **square matrix** is a matrix of order $n \times n$. The elements $a_{11}, a_{22}, \ldots, a_{nn}$ are called its *main diagonal elements.* A square matrix of order $n \times n$, with the digit 1 along its main diagonal and zeros elsewhere, is called an **identity matrix** of order $n \times n$. The **inverse** of a square matrix A of order $n \times n$ is denoted by A^{-1}. The product of a square matrix A and its inverse A^{-1} is the identity matrix I:

$$AA^{-1} = A^{-1}A = I$$

The **transpose** of matrix A, denoted by A^T, is formed by switching the rows of matrix A with its columns.

Three rules are used to add, subtract, and multiply matrices (matrix division is undefined):

1. **Matrix addition:** If $A = [a_{ij}]$ and $B = [b_{ij}]$ are matrices of order $m \times n$, then the sum $A + B$ is a matrix of order $m \times n$ defined by $A + B = [a_{ij} + b_{ij}]$.
2. **Scalar multiplication:** If $A = [a_{ij}]$ is a matrix of order $m \times n$ and k is a real number, then the scalar multiple kA is a matrix of order $m \times n$ defined by $kA = [ka_{ij}]$.

3. **Matrix multiplication:** If $A = [a_{ij}]$ is a matrix of order $m \times n$ and $B = [b_{ij}]$ is a matrix of order $n \times p$, then the product AB is a matrix of order $m \times p$ defined by using a row times column procedure; that is, $AB = [c_{ij}]$, where $c_{ij} = a_{i1}b_{1j} + a_{i2}b_{2j} + \ldots + a_{in}b_{nj}$.

Example 9.25

In each case, given the matrices $A = \begin{bmatrix} 2 & 5 \\ -3 & 0 \\ 1 & 4 \end{bmatrix}$ and $B = \begin{bmatrix} 4 & 6 \\ -2 & -5 \\ 0 & 3 \end{bmatrix}$, perform the indicated operation.

A. $2A - B$ **B.** $A^T + B^T$

Solution:

A. Using the rules for scalar multiplication and matrix addition, proceed as follows:

$$2A - B = 2A + (-1)B = 2\begin{bmatrix} 2 & 5 \\ -3 & 0 \\ 1 & 4 \end{bmatrix} + (-1)\begin{bmatrix} 4 & 6 \\ -2 & -5 \\ 0 & 3 \end{bmatrix}$$

$$= \begin{bmatrix} 4 & 10 \\ -6 & 0 \\ 2 & 8 \end{bmatrix} + \begin{bmatrix} -4 & -6 \\ 2 & 5 \\ 0 & -3 \end{bmatrix} = \begin{bmatrix} 0 & 4 \\ -4 & 5 \\ 2 & 5 \end{bmatrix}$$

B. First, find the transpose matrices A^T and B^T by switching rows and columns:

$$A^T = \begin{bmatrix} 2 & -3 & 1 \\ 5 & 0 & 4 \end{bmatrix}, \text{ and } B^T = \begin{bmatrix} 4 & -2 & 0 \\ 6 & -5 & 3 \end{bmatrix}$$

Now, use the rule for matrix addition to obtain the sum of the transposes:

$$A^T + B^T = \begin{bmatrix} 2 & -3 & 1 \\ 5 & 0 & 4 \end{bmatrix} + \begin{bmatrix} 4 & -2 & 0 \\ 6 & -5 & 3 \end{bmatrix} = \begin{bmatrix} 6 & -5 & 1 \\ 11 & -5 & 7 \end{bmatrix}$$

Example 9.26

Given the matrices $A = \begin{bmatrix} 3 & 4 \\ 2 & 3 \end{bmatrix}$, $B = \begin{bmatrix} 3 & -4 \\ -2 & 3 \end{bmatrix}$, and $C = \begin{bmatrix} 2 & -1 \\ 3 & 4 \\ 0 & -2 \end{bmatrix}$, find each product.

A. AB **B.** CA

Solution:

A. Since matrices A and B are square matrices of order 2×2, the product AB is defined and is also of order 2×2. Using the rule for matrix multiplication, proceed as follows:

$$AB = \begin{bmatrix} 3 & 4 \\ 2 & 3 \end{bmatrix}\begin{bmatrix} 3 & -4 \\ -2 & 3 \end{bmatrix} =$$

$$\begin{bmatrix} (3)(3) + (4)(-2) & (3)(-4) + (4)(3) \\ (2)(3) + (3)(-2) & (2)(-4) + (3)(3) \end{bmatrix} = \begin{bmatrix} 1 & 0 \\ 0 & 1 \end{bmatrix}$$

Since this product yields the identity matrix I of order 2×2, matrices A and B are inverses of each other.

B. Since matrix C has two columns and matrix A has two rows, the product CA is defined and is of order 3×2, since matrix C has three rows and matrix A has two columns. Using the rule for matrix multiplication, proceed as follows:

$$CA = \begin{bmatrix} 2 & -1 \\ 3 & 4 \\ 0 & -2 \end{bmatrix}\begin{bmatrix} 3 & 4 \\ 2 & 3 \end{bmatrix} =$$

$$\begin{bmatrix} (2)(3) + (-1)(2) & (2)(4) + (-1)(3) \\ (3)(3) + (4)(2) & (3)(4) + (4)(3) \\ (0)(3) + (-2)(2) & (0)(4) + (-2)(3) \end{bmatrix} = \begin{bmatrix} 4 & 5 \\ 17 & 24 \\ -4 & -6 \end{bmatrix}$$

Note that the number of columns in matrix A is *not* the same as the number of rows in matrix C. Hence, the product AC is not defined. Unlike multiplication of real numbers, matrix multiplication, in general, is not commutative; that is, $AC \neq CA$.

9.10 Determinants and Inverses of Matrices

A **determinant** of order n contains n^2 elements arranged in n rows and n columns and enclosed by two vertical bars. The **minor** of an element a_{ij} in a determinant is denoted by M_{ij}, and represents the determinant that remains after deleting the row and column in which the element a_{ij} appears. The **cofactor** of an element a_{ij} in a determinant, denoted by C_{ij}, differs from M_{ij} at most in sign and is given by $C_{ij} = (-1)^{i+j}M_{ij}$.

The value of an nth-order determinant is a sum found by multiplying each element in any row or column by its corresponding cofactor, and then adding the products. This sum is called the **expansion of the determinant** by the specified row or column. The expansion of a second-order determinant by any row or column is

$$\begin{vmatrix} a_{11} & a_{12} \\ a_{21} & a_{22} \end{vmatrix} = a_{11}a_{22} - a_{12}a_{21}$$

The inverse of an $n \times n$ matrix A can be found by using the **inverse formula:**

$$A^{-1} = \frac{\text{adj}(A)}{|A|}$$

where adj(A) is the *adjoint* of matrix A, obtained by replacing each element in the transpose matrix A^T with the value of its corresponding cofactor. If $|A| = 0$, then matrix A does not have an inverse.

A **system of n linear equations in n variables** $(x_1, x_2, \dots, x_n)$, with each equation written in the form $a_1x_1 + a_2x_2 + \dots + a_nx_n = k$, may be represented by the matrix equation

$$AX = K$$

where A is an $n \times n$ matrix containing the coefficients of the variables, X is an $n \times 1$ matrix containing the variables, and K is an $n \times 1$ matrix containing the constants on the right-hand sides of the equations. The **solution** of the $n \times n$ linear system of equations is given by $X = A^{-1}K$, provided that matrix A has an inverse.

Example 9.27

In each case, given the determinant $|A| = \begin{vmatrix} 1 & 3 & -2 \\ 3 & 0 & 1 \\ -1 & 2 & -4 \end{vmatrix}$, determine the value of (1) the minor and (2) the cofactor of the given element.

A. a_{31} **B.** a_{23}

Solution:

A. (1) To find M_{31}, the minor of element a_{31}, delete the third row and first column of $|A|$ and evaluate the remaining determinant:

$$M_{31} = \begin{vmatrix} 3 & -2 \\ 0 & 1 \end{vmatrix} = (3)(1) - (-2)(0) = 3$$

(2) The cofactor C_{31} of a_{31} is given by

$$C_{31} = (-1)^{3+1}M_{31} = M_{31} = 3$$

B. (1) To find M_{23}, the minor of element a_{23}, delete the second row and third column of $|A|$ and evaluate the remaining determinant:

$$M_{23} = \begin{vmatrix} 1 & 3 \\ -1 & 2 \end{vmatrix} = (1)(2) - (3)(-1) = 5$$

(2) The cofactor C_{23} of a_{23} is given by

$$C_{23} = (-1)^{2+3}M_{23} = -M_{23} = -5$$

Example 9.28

Evaluate each determinant.

A. $|A| = \begin{vmatrix} 1 & 3 & -2 \\ 3 & 0 & 1 \\ -1 & 2 & -4 \end{vmatrix}$ **B.** $|B| = \begin{vmatrix} 1 & -2 & 3 & -1 \\ 0 & 2 & 0 & 3 \\ 0 & 4 & 0 & -2 \\ 2 & 0 & 0 & 4 \end{vmatrix}$

Solution:

A. Since element $a_{22} = 0$, it is best to expand about the second row or second column. Choose the second row:

$$|A| = 3C_{21} + 0C_{22} + 1C_{23} = 3C_{21} + 1C_{23}$$

Now,

$$C_{21} = (-1)^{2+1}\begin{vmatrix} 3 & -2 \\ 2 & -4 \end{vmatrix} = 8$$

and

$$C_{23} = (-1)^{2+3}\begin{vmatrix} 1 & 3 \\ -1 & 2 \end{vmatrix} = -5$$

Hence:

$$|A| = 3C_{21} + 1C_{23} = 3(8) + 1(-5) = 19$$

B. Since the third column of this determinant contains three zeros, it is best to expand about this column:

$$|B| = 3C_{13} + 0C_{23} + 0C_{33} + 0C_{43} = 3C_{13}$$

Now,

$$C_{13} = (-1)^{1+3}\begin{vmatrix} 0 & 2 & 3 \\ 0 & 4 & -2 \\ 2 & 0 & 4 \end{vmatrix} = \begin{vmatrix} 0 & 2 & 3 \\ 0 & 4 & -2 \\ 2 & 0 & 4 \end{vmatrix}$$

Since the first column of this third-order determinant contains two zeros, it is best to expand about this column:

$$C_{13} = 2(-1)^{3+1}\begin{vmatrix} 2 & 3 \\ 4 & -2 \end{vmatrix} = -32$$

Hence:

$$|B| = 3C_{13} = 3(-32) = -96$$

Example 9.29

Find the inverse of each matrix.

A. $A = \begin{bmatrix} 3 & 4 \\ 2 & 3 \end{bmatrix}$ **B.** $\begin{bmatrix} 1 & 2 & -3 \\ 2 & 3 & -4 \\ -1 & 0 & 3 \end{bmatrix}$

Solution:

A. The inverse of matrix A is given by $A^{-1} = \frac{\text{adj}(A)}{|A|}$. Begin by finding the determinant:

$$|A| = \begin{vmatrix} 3 & 4 \\ 2 & 3 \end{vmatrix} = (3)(3) - (4)(2) = 1$$

To find adj(A), form A^T and then replace each element in A^T with its corresponding cofactor:

$$A^T = \begin{bmatrix} 3 & 2 \\ 4 & 3 \end{bmatrix} \text{ implies adj}(A) = \begin{bmatrix} 3 & -4 \\ -2 & 3 \end{bmatrix}$$

Hence:

$$A^{-1} = \frac{\text{adj}(A)}{|A|} = \frac{\begin{bmatrix} 3 & -4 \\ -2 & 3 \end{bmatrix}}{1} = \begin{bmatrix} 3 & -4 \\ -2 & 3 \end{bmatrix}$$

To verify this inverse, show that $AA^{-1} = A^{-1}A = \begin{bmatrix} 1 & 0 \\ 0 & 1 \end{bmatrix}$, the identity matrix of order 2×2.

B. The inverse of matrix B is defined by $B^{-1} = \frac{\text{adj}(B)}{|B|}$. For the determinant, expand about the third row:

$$|B| = -1(-1)^{3+1}\begin{vmatrix} 2 & -3 \\ 3 & -4 \end{vmatrix} + 3(-1)^{3+3}\begin{vmatrix} 1 & 2 \\ 2 & 3 \end{vmatrix} = -4$$

To find adj(B), form B^T and then replace each element in B^T with its corresponding cofactor:

$$B^T = \begin{bmatrix} 1 & 2 & -1 \\ 2 & 3 & 0 \\ -3 & -4 & 3 \end{bmatrix} \text{ implies adj}(B) = \begin{bmatrix} 9 & -6 & 1 \\ -2 & 0 & -2 \\ 3 & -2 & -1 \end{bmatrix}$$

Hence:

$$B^{-1} = \frac{\text{adj}(B)}{|B|} = -\frac{1}{4}\begin{bmatrix} 9 & -6 & 1 \\ -2 & 0 & -2 \\ 3 & -2 & -1 \end{bmatrix} = \begin{bmatrix} -\frac{9}{4} & \frac{3}{2} & -\frac{1}{4} \\ \frac{1}{2} & 0 & \frac{1}{2} \\ -\frac{3}{4} & \frac{1}{2} & \frac{1}{4} \end{bmatrix}$$

To check, show that $BB^{-1} = B^{-1}B = \begin{bmatrix} 1 & 0 & 0 \\ 0 & 1 & 0 \\ 0 & 0 & 1 \end{bmatrix}$, the identity matrix of order 3×3.

Example 9.30

Solve each system of linear equations by using the inverse method.

A. $3x + 4y = 6$
$2x + 3y = 5$

B. $x + 2y - 3z = -1$
$2x + 3y - 4z = 2$
$-x + 3z = 5$

Solution:

A. Let

$$A = \begin{bmatrix} 3 & 4 \\ 2 & 3 \end{bmatrix}, \quad X = \begin{bmatrix} x \\ y \end{bmatrix}, \quad \text{and} \quad K = \begin{bmatrix} 6 \\ 5 \end{bmatrix}$$

Then, by the rules for matrix multiplication and equality of matrices, the matrix equation $AX = K$ is equivalent to the given system of linear equations:

$$\begin{bmatrix} 3 & 4 \\ 2 & 3 \end{bmatrix}\begin{bmatrix} x \\ y \end{bmatrix} = \begin{bmatrix} 6 \\ 5 \end{bmatrix}$$

The solution of this matrix equation is $X = A^{-1}K$, provided that A^{-1} exists. Use the results of Example 9.29**A** to find X:

$$\begin{bmatrix} x \\ y \end{bmatrix} = \begin{bmatrix} 3 & 4 \\ 2 & 3 \end{bmatrix}^{-1}\begin{bmatrix} 6 \\ 5 \end{bmatrix} = \begin{bmatrix} 3 & -4 \\ -2 & 3 \end{bmatrix}\begin{bmatrix} 6 \\ 5 \end{bmatrix} = \begin{bmatrix} -2 \\ 3 \end{bmatrix}$$

Hence, the solution of this 2×2 system of linear equations is $x = -2$ and $y = 3$.

B. Let

$$B = \begin{bmatrix} 1 & 2 & -3 \\ 2 & 3 & -4 \\ -1 & 0 & 3 \end{bmatrix}, \quad X = \begin{bmatrix} x \\ y \\ z \end{bmatrix}, \quad \text{and} \quad K = \begin{bmatrix} -1 \\ 2 \\ 5 \end{bmatrix}$$

Then, by the rules for matrix multiplication and equality of matrices, the matrix equation $BX = K$ is equivalent to the given system of linear equations:

$$\begin{bmatrix} 1 & 2 & -3 \\ 2 & 3 & -4 \\ -1 & 0 & 3 \end{bmatrix}\begin{bmatrix} x \\ y \\ z \end{bmatrix} = \begin{bmatrix} -1 \\ 2 \\ 5 \end{bmatrix}$$

The solution of this matrix equation is $X = B^{-1}K$, provided that B^{-1} exists. Use the results of Example 9.29**B** to find X:

$$\begin{bmatrix} x \\ y \\ z \end{bmatrix} = \begin{bmatrix} 1 & 2 & -3 \\ 2 & 3 & -4 \\ -1 & 0 & 3 \end{bmatrix}^{-1}\begin{bmatrix} -1 \\ 2 \\ 5 \end{bmatrix} = \begin{bmatrix} -\frac{9}{4} & \frac{3}{2} & -\frac{1}{4} \\ \frac{1}{2} & 0 & \frac{1}{2} \\ -\frac{3}{4} & \frac{1}{2} & \frac{1}{4} \end{bmatrix}\begin{bmatrix} -1 \\ 2 \\ 5 \end{bmatrix} = \begin{bmatrix} 4 \\ 2 \\ 3 \end{bmatrix}$$

Hence, the solution of this 3×3 system of linear equation is $x = 4$, $y = 2$, and $z = 3$.

9.11 Vectors

A **vector** is a directed line segment in space that represents a force, a velocity, or a displacement. The *basic vectors,* denoted by the boldface letters **i, j,** and **k,** are directed line segments in the rectangular coordinate system from the origin (0,0,0) to points (1,0,0), (0,1,0), and (0,0,1), respectively. The *position vector* of a point in space, denoted by $\overrightarrow{OP} = x\mathbf{i} + y\mathbf{j} + z\mathbf{k}$, is a directed line segment from the origin

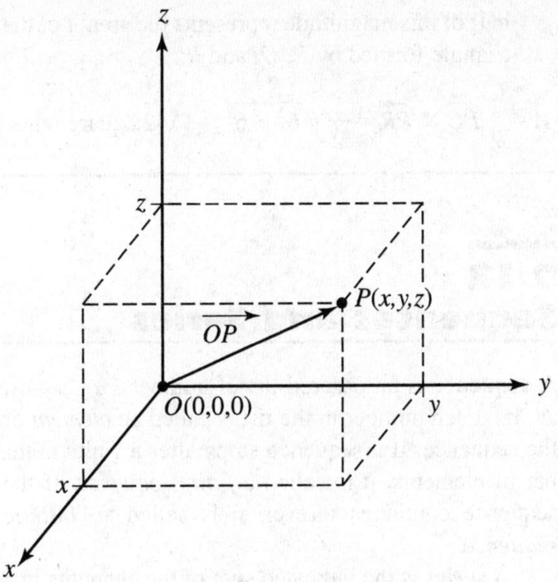

Figure 9.15

$O(0,0,0)$ to a point $P(x,y,z)$ in space, as shown in Figure 9.15.

The vector **A** from $P_1 = (x_1,y_1,z_1)$ to $P_2 = (x_2,y_2,z_2)$ is given by

$$\overrightarrow{P_1P_2} = \mathbf{A} = a_x\mathbf{i} + a_y\mathbf{j} + a_z\mathbf{k}$$

where $a_x = x_2 - x_1$, $a_y = y_2 - y_1$, and $a_z = z_2 - z_1$.

The **magnitude** (or length) of $\mathbf{A} = a_x\mathbf{i} + a_y\mathbf{j} + a_z\mathbf{k}$ is denoted by $|\mathbf{A}|$, and defined by

$$|\mathbf{A}| = \sqrt{(a_x)^2 + (a_y)^2 + (a_z)^2}$$

A vector whose magnitude is 1 is called a **unit vector.** If $\mathbf{A} = a_x\mathbf{i} + a_y\mathbf{j} + a_z\mathbf{k}$, then $\mathbf{A}/|\mathbf{A}|$ is a unit vector in the direction of **A**.

For the vectors $\mathbf{A} = a_x\mathbf{i} + a_y\mathbf{j} + a_z\mathbf{k}$ and $\mathbf{B} = b_x\mathbf{i} + b_y\mathbf{j} + b_z\mathbf{k}$, and scalar (real number) c, the following operations can be performed:

1. **Addition and subtraction:** $\mathbf{A} \pm \mathbf{B} = (a_x \pm b_x)\mathbf{i} + (a_y \pm b_y)\mathbf{j} + (a_z \pm b_z)\mathbf{k}$
2. **Scalar multiplication:** $c\mathbf{A} = ca_x\mathbf{i} + ca_y\mathbf{j} + ca_z\mathbf{k}$
3. **Dot product:** $\mathbf{A} \bullet \mathbf{B} = a_xb_x + a_yb_y + a_zb_z = |\mathbf{A}|\,|\mathbf{B}| \cos\theta$,

   where θ is the angle between **A** and **B.** Nonzero vectors **A** and **B** are perpendicular if and only if $\mathbf{A} \bullet \mathbf{B} = 0$.
4. **Cross product:** $\mathbf{A} \times \mathbf{B} = \begin{vmatrix} \mathbf{i} & \mathbf{j} & \mathbf{k} \\ a_x & a_y & a_z \\ b_x & b_y & b_z \end{vmatrix} = |\mathbf{A}|\,|\mathbf{B}|\,\mathbf{n} \sin\theta$,

   where **n** is a unit vector perpendicular to the plane formed by **A** and **B** by the *right-hand rule;* that is, **n** points the way your right thumb points when your fingers curl through the angle θ from **A** to **B.** Nonzero vectors **A** and **B** are parallel if and only if $\mathbf{A} \times \mathbf{B} = 0$. The magnitude of $\mathbf{A} \times \mathbf{B}$ is the area of a parallelogram determined by **A** and **B.**

Example 9.31

Given that $\mathbf{A} = 3\mathbf{i} - 6\mathbf{j} + 2\mathbf{k}$, find:

A. the magnitude of **A**
B. a unit vector in the direction of **A**

Solution:

A. The magnitude of $\mathbf{A} = 3\mathbf{i} - 6\mathbf{j} + 2\mathbf{k}$ is

$$|\mathbf{A}| = \sqrt{(3)^2 + (-6)^2 + (2)^2} = \sqrt{49} = 7$$

B. A unit vector in the direction of $\mathbf{A} = 3\mathbf{i} - 6\mathbf{j} + 2\mathbf{k}$ is

$$\frac{\mathbf{A}}{|\mathbf{A}|} = \frac{3\mathbf{i} - 6\mathbf{j} + 2\mathbf{k}}{7} = \frac{3}{7}\mathbf{i} - \frac{6}{7}\mathbf{j} + \frac{2}{7}\mathbf{k}$$

Example 9.32

Given that $\mathbf{A} = 10\mathbf{i} + 11\mathbf{j} - 2\mathbf{k}$ and $\mathbf{B} = 5\mathbf{i} + 12\mathbf{j}$, find:

A. $\mathbf{A} \bullet \mathbf{B}$
B. the angle θ (in degrees) between **A** and **B**

Solution:

A. To find the dot product of two given vectors, multiply their corresponding **i-**, **j-**, and **k-**components and add the results:

$$\mathbf{A} \bullet \mathbf{B} = (10)(5) + (11)(12) + (-2)(0) = 182$$

B. The magnitudes of **A** and **B** are

$$|\mathbf{A}| = \sqrt{(10)^2 + (11)^2 + (-2)^2} = 15$$

and

$$|\mathbf{B}| = \sqrt{(5)^2 + (12)^2} = 13$$

Now, use the dot product formula $\mathbf{A} \bullet \mathbf{B} = |\mathbf{A}|\,|\mathbf{B}| \cos\theta$ and the results from part **A** to obtain the angle θ between **A** and **B:**

$$\theta = \cos^{-1}\left(\frac{\mathbf{A} \bullet \mathbf{B}}{|\mathbf{A}|\,|\mathbf{B}|}\right) = \cos^{-1}\left[\frac{182}{(25)(13)}\right] = 21.0°$$

Example 9.33

Given that $\mathbf{A} = -8\mathbf{i} - 2\mathbf{j} - 4\mathbf{k}$ and $\mathbf{B} = 2\mathbf{i} + 2\mathbf{j} + \mathbf{k}$, find:

A. $\mathbf{A} \times \mathbf{B}$ **B.** $\mathbf{B} \times \mathbf{A}$

Solution:

A. Use the determinant formula for cross products; then

$$\mathbf{A}\times\mathbf{B}=\begin{vmatrix}\mathbf{i} & \mathbf{j} & \mathbf{k}\\ -8 & -2 & -4\\ 2 & 2 & 1\end{vmatrix}$$

$$=\mathbf{i}\begin{vmatrix}-2 & -4\\ 2 & 1\end{vmatrix}-\mathbf{j}\begin{vmatrix}-8 & -4\\ 2 & 1\end{vmatrix}+\mathbf{k}\begin{vmatrix}-8 & -2\\ 2 & 2\end{vmatrix}$$

$$= 6\mathbf{i} - 12\mathbf{k}$$

B. Use the determinant formula for cross products; then

$$\mathbf{B}\times\mathbf{A}=\begin{vmatrix}\mathbf{i} & \mathbf{j} & \mathbf{k}\\ 2 & 2 & 1\\ -8 & -2 & -4\end{vmatrix}$$

$$=\mathbf{i}\begin{vmatrix}2 & 1\\ -2 & -4\end{vmatrix}-\mathbf{j}\begin{vmatrix}2 & 1\\ -8 & -4\end{vmatrix}+\mathbf{k}\begin{vmatrix}2 & 2\\ -8 & -2\end{vmatrix}$$

$$= -6\mathbf{i} + 12\mathbf{k}$$

Note that the cross-product operation is not commutative; that is, $\mathbf{A}\times\mathbf{B}\neq\mathbf{B}\times\mathbf{A}$. In general, for cross products, $\mathbf{A}\times\mathbf{B} = -(\mathbf{B}\times\mathbf{A})$.

Example 9.34

Given points $P(1,-1,0)$, $Q(2,1,-1)$, and $R(-1,1,2)$, find:

A. a vector perpendicular to the plane formed by P, Q, and R

B. the area of the triangle with vertices P, Q, and R

Solution:

A. By the definition of cross product, $\overrightarrow{PQ}\times\overrightarrow{PR}$ is a vector perpendicular to the plane formed by P, Q, and R. Begin by writing $\overrightarrow{PQ}$ and $\overrightarrow{PR}$ in component form:

$$\overrightarrow{PQ} = (2-1)\mathbf{i} + [1-(-1)]\mathbf{j} + (-1-0)\mathbf{k} = \mathbf{i} + 2\mathbf{j} - \mathbf{k}$$

$$\overrightarrow{PR} = (-1-1)\mathbf{i} + [1-(-1)]\mathbf{j} + (2-0)\mathbf{k} = -2\mathbf{i} + 2\mathbf{j} + 2\mathbf{k}$$

Hence:

$$\overrightarrow{PQ}\times\overrightarrow{PR}=\begin{vmatrix}\mathbf{i} & \mathbf{j} & \mathbf{k}\\ 1 & 2 & -1\\ -2 & 2 & 2\end{vmatrix}$$

$$=\mathbf{i}\begin{vmatrix}2 & -1\\ 2 & 2\end{vmatrix}-\mathbf{j}\begin{vmatrix}1 & -1\\ -2 & 2\end{vmatrix}+\mathbf{k}\begin{vmatrix}1 & 2\\ -2 & 2\end{vmatrix}$$

$$= 6\mathbf{i} + 6\mathbf{k}$$

B. The magnitude of $\overrightarrow{PQ}\times\overrightarrow{PR}$ is the area of the parallelogram determined by P, Q, and R. Hence, half of this magnitude represents the area A of the triangle formed by P, Q, and R:

$$A = \frac{1}{2}|\overrightarrow{PQ}\times\overrightarrow{PR}| = \frac{1}{2}\sqrt{6^2+6^2} = 3\sqrt{2} \text{ square units}$$

9.12 Sequences and Series

A **sequence** is an ordered list of numbers: a_1, a_2, a_3, ... , a_n. Each number in the list is called an *element* of the sequence. If a sequence stops after a finite number of elements, it is called a *finite sequence.* If the sequence continues forever, it is called an *infinite sequence.*

A **series** is the indicated sum of the elements in a sequence: $a_1 + a_2 + a_3 + ... + a_n$. Each number in a series is called a *term* of the series. The terms of a series are identical to the elements in its corresponding sequence.

An **arithmetic sequence** is a sequence in which every element after the first is obtained by adding a fixed number d to the preceding element. The constant d is called the *common difference* of the sequence. The nth element a_n of an arithmetic sequence is given by

$$a_n = a_1 + (n-1)d$$

where a_1 is the first element and d is the common difference of the sequence. The sum S_n of an arithmetic series with n terms is given by

$$S_n = n\left(\frac{a_1+a_n}{2}\right) = \frac{n}{2}[2a_1 + (n-1)d]$$

where a_1 is the first term, a_n is the last term, and d is the common difference of the series.

A **geometric sequence** is a sequence in which every element after the first is obtained by multiplying the preceding element by a fixed nonzero number r. The constant r is called the *common ratio* of the sequence. The nth element a_n of a geometric sequence is given by

$$a_n = a_1 r^{n-1}$$

where a_1 is the first element and r is the common ratio of the sequence. The sum S_n of a geometric series with n terms is given by

$$S_n = \frac{a_1(1-r^n)}{1-r} = \frac{a_1 - ra_n}{1-r}$$

where a_1 is the first term, a_n is the last term, and r is the common ratio ($r \neq 1$).

If $|r| < 1$ in an infinite geometric series, then the series *converges* and has the finite sum

$$S = \frac{a_1}{1 - r}$$

where a_1 is the first term and r is the common ratio. If $|r| \geq 1$ in an infinite geometric series, then the series *diverges* and has no finite sum.

The **Taylor series** generated by a function f at $x = a$ is given by

$$f(x) = f(a) + f'(a)(x - a) + \frac{f''(a)}{2!}(x - a)^2$$

$$+ \ldots + \frac{f^n(a)}{n!}(x - a)^n + \ldots$$

where $f^k(a)$ represents the kth derivative of f at $x = a$. (For a discussion of derivatives, see Section 9.15.) When $a = 0$, the Taylor series is called a **Maclaurin series.**

Example 9.35

In each case, find the 15th element of the given sequence.

A. 23, 17, 11, 5, ... **B.** $2, -1, \frac{1}{2}, -\frac{1}{4}, \ldots$

Solution:

A. This sequence is an arithmetic sequence with first element $a_1 = 23$ and common difference $d = -6$. Hence, the nth element of this sequence is

$$a_n = a_1 + (n - 1)d = 23 + (n - 1)(-6) = 29 - 6n$$

To find the 15th element a_{15}, replace n with 15:

$$a_{15} = 29 - 6(15) = -61$$

B. This sequence is a geometric sequence with first element $a_1 = 2$ and common ratio $r = -1/2$. Hence, the nth element of this sequence is

$$a_n = a_1 r^{n-1} = 2\left(-\frac{1}{2}\right)^{n-1}$$

To find the 15th element a_{15}, replace n with 15:

$$a_{15} = 2\left(-\frac{1}{2}\right)^{15-1} = 2\left(-\frac{1}{2}\right)^{14} = \frac{1}{8{,}192}$$

Example 9.36

In each case, find the sum of the given series.

A. $\sum_{i=1}^{40}(4i - 3)$ **B.** $\sum_{i=1}^{10} 5(-2)^{i-1}$

Solution:

A. Since the summation variable i starts at 1 and ends at 40, the number of terms in this series is $n = 40$. Begin by writing this series in expanded form:

$$\sum_{i=1}^{40}(4i - 3) = 1 + 5 + 9 + \ldots + 157$$

This is an arithmetic series with common difference $d = 4$, first term $a_1 = 1$, and last term $a_{40} = 157$. Thus the sum of this series is

$$S_{40} = 40\left(\frac{a_1 + a_{40}}{2}\right) = 40\left(\frac{1 + 157}{2}\right) = 3{,}160$$

B. Since the summation variable i starts at 1 and ends at 10, the number of terms in this series is $n = 10$. Begin by writing this series in expanded form:

$$\sum_{i=1}^{10} 5(-2)^{i-1} = 5 - 10 + 20 - 40 + \ldots - 2{,}560$$

This is a geometric series with common ratio $r = -2$ and first term $a_1 = 5$. Thus the sum of this series is

$$S_{10} = \frac{a_1(1 - r^{10})}{1 - r} = \frac{5[1 - (-2)^{10}]}{1 - (-2)} = -1{,}705$$

Example 9.37

In each case, determine whether the infinite geometric series converges or diverges. If the series converges, find its sum.

A. $\sum_{n=0}^{\infty}\left(\frac{3}{2}\right)^n$ **B.** $\sum_{i=1}^{\infty}(-1)^{i+1}\left(\frac{1}{2}\right)^i$

Solution:

A. Write the series in expanded form:

$$\sum_{n=0}^{\infty}\left(\frac{3}{2}\right)^n = 1 + \frac{3}{2} + \frac{9}{4} + \frac{27}{8} + \ldots$$

This is an infinite geometric series with first term $a_1 = 1$ and common ratio $r = 3/2$. Since $|r| \geq 1$, the series diverges and has no finite sum.

B. Write the series in expanded form:

$$\sum_{i=1}^{\infty}(-1)^{i+1}\left(\frac{1}{2}\right)^i = \frac{1}{2} - \frac{1}{4} + \frac{1}{8} - \frac{1}{16} + \ldots$$

This is an infinite geometric series with $a_1 = \frac{1}{2}$ and common ratio $r = -\frac{1}{2}$. Since $|r| < 1$, the infinite geometric series converges and the sum of the series is

$$S = \frac{a_1}{1-r} = \frac{\frac{1}{2}}{1-\left(-\frac{1}{2}\right)} = \frac{1}{3}$$

Example 9.38

In each case, find the Taylor (Maclaurin) series generated by the given function f at $x = 0$.

A. $f(x) = e^x$ **B.** $f(x) = \cos x$

Solution:

A. Begin by finding the derivatives of $f(x) = e^x$:

$$f'(x) = e^x,\quad f''(x) = e^x,\quad f'''(x) = e^x,\quad \ldots,\quad f^{(n)}(x) = e^x$$

For $x = 0$, $e^x = 1$. Hence, the Taylor (Maclaurin) series generated by $f(x) = e^x$ at $x = 0$ is

$$f(0) + f'(0)x + \frac{f''(0)}{2!}x^2 + \frac{f'''(0)}{3!}x^3 + \ldots + \frac{f^{(n)}(0)}{n!}x^n + \ldots$$

$$= 1 + x + \frac{x^2}{2!} + \frac{x^3}{3!} + \ldots + \frac{x^n}{n!}$$

$$= \sum_{k=0}^{\infty} \frac{x^k}{k!}$$

B. The function and its derivatives are as follows:

$$f(x) = \cos x, \qquad f'(x) = -\sin x,$$

$$f''(x) = -\cos x, \qquad f'''(x) = \sin x,$$

$$\vdots \qquad\qquad \vdots$$

$$f^{(2n)}(x) = (-1)^n \cos x, \qquad f^{(2n+1)}(x) = (-1)^{n+1} \sin x$$

for $x = 0$, $\cos x = 1$, and $\sin x = 0$. Therefore, the Taylor (Maclaurin) series generated by $f(x) = \cos x$ and $x = 0$ is

$$f(0) + f'(0)x + \frac{f''(0)}{2!}x^2 + \frac{f'''(0)}{3!}x^3 + \ldots + \frac{f^{(n)}(0)}{n!}x^n + \ldots$$

$$= 1 - \frac{x^2}{2!} + \frac{x^4}{4!} - \frac{x^6}{6!} + \ldots + (-1)^n \frac{x^{2n}}{(2n)!} + \ldots$$

$$= \sum_{k=0}^{\infty} \frac{(-1)^k x^{2k}}{(2k)!}$$

9.13 Probability and Counting Techniques

The set of all outcomes of a random experiment is called its **sample space,** and each outcome in the sample space is referred to as an **element.** If S is a finite sample space of a random experiment in which all elements of S are equally likely to occur, and E is an event associated with the experiment, then the **probability of event E,** denoted by $P(E)$, is defined by

$$P(E) = \frac{n(E)}{n(S)}$$

where $n(E)$ is the number of elements in E, and $n(S)$ is the number of elements in S.

The notation $P(A \cup B)$ represents the probability that event A *or* B occurs, while the notation $P(A \cap B)$ represents the probability that events A *and* B occur. The notation $P(B|A)$ represents the probability that event B occurs, given that event A occurs.

The following rules are often used to find the probability that a certain event occurs:

1. **Additive rule:** $P(A \cup B) = P(A) + P(B) - P(A \cap B)$
2. **Multiplicative rule:** $P(A \cap B) = P(A) \cdot P(B|A)$

If a random experiment consists of k procedures in which the ith procedure may be performed in n_i ways ($i = 1, 2, 3, \ldots, k$), then the first procedure, followed by the second procedure, followed by the third procedure, ... , followed by the kth procedure may be performed in

$$n_1 \cdot n_2 \cdot n_3 \cdot \ldots \cdot n_k \text{ ways}$$

This fundamental principle of counting is called the **multiplication principle.**

Other counting procedures involve *permutations* and *combinations.* A **permutation** is an arrangement of a set of n distinct objects in a given order. The number of permutations of n distinct objects taken r at a time, where $r \leq n$, is denoted by $P(n, r)$ and is given by

$$P(n, r) = \frac{n!}{(n-r)!}$$

The selection of r objects from a set of n distinct objects *without* regard to order is called a **combination** of n objects taken r at a time. The number of combinations of n distinct objects taken r at a time, with $r \leq n$, is denoted by $C(n, r)$ and is given by

$$C(n, r) = \frac{n!}{r!(n-r)!}$$

The notation $n!$ (read as n factorial) represents the product of all consecutive integers from 1 up to and including n. Zero factorial (0!) is defined to be equal to 1.

Example 9.39

A random experiment consists of first tossing a coin and observing whether it lands showing heads (H) or tails (T), and then rolling a die and observing which number (1 to 6) appears on its top face. Find the probability of:

A. tossing a head and rolling an even number
B. tossing a head or rolling an even number

Solution:

A. The sample space S for this random experiment is

$$S = \{H1, H2, H3, H4, H5, H6, T1, T2, T3, T4, T5, T6\}$$

Therefore, $n(S) = 12$. If E is the event of tossing a head and rolling an even number, then

$$E = \{H2, H4, H6\}$$

Hence, $n(E) = 3$, and

$$P(E) = \frac{n(E)}{n(S)} = \frac{3}{12} = \frac{1}{4}$$

The *multiplicative rule* may also be used to find the probability of tossing a head *and* rolling an even number. Let A be the event of tossing a head, and B be the event of rolling an even number. Since the occurrence of event A has no impact on the odds of occurrence of event B, $P(B|A) = P(B)$. Therefore,

$$P(A \cap B) = P(A) \bullet P(B|A) = P(A) \bullet P(B) = \frac{1}{2} \bullet \frac{1}{2} = \frac{1}{4}$$

a probability that agrees with the preceding result.

B. From the sample space S given in part **A**, if E is the event of tossing a head *or* rolling an even number, then

$$E = \{H1, H2, H3, H4, H5, H6, T2, T4, T6\}$$

Hence, $n(E) = 9$, and

$$P(E) = \frac{n(E)}{n(S)} = \frac{9}{12} = \frac{3}{4}$$

The *additive rule* may also be used to find the probability of tossing a head *or* rolling an even number. Let A be the event of tossing a head, and B be the event of rolling an even number. Using the results from part **A** gives

$$P(A \cup B) = P(A) + P(B) - P(A \cap B) = \frac{1}{2} + \frac{1}{2} - \frac{1}{4} = \frac{3}{4}$$

Example 9.40

At a track meet, eight contestants are entered in the 100-yard dash. Find the number of possible orders of finish for:

A. all eight contestants
B. the first three positions

Solution:

The order in which the contestants finish the race matters. Hence, this is a permutation problem.

A. The number of permutations of eight distinct objects is

$$P(8, 8) = \frac{8!}{(8-8)!} = \frac{8!}{0!} = 40{,}320 \text{ orders}$$

B. The number of eight distinct objects taken three at a time is

$$P(8, 3) = \frac{8!}{(8-3)!} = \frac{8!}{5!} = 336 \text{ orders}$$

Example 9.41

In a certain poker game, five cards are dealt to a player from a standard deck of 52 cards.

A. How many different poker hands can be dealt?
B. What is the probability of being dealt a poker hand that includes exactly three aces?

Solution:

The order in which the five cards are dealt does not matter. Hence, this is a combination problem. A standard deck of 52 cards has four suits (hearts, diamonds, clubs, spades), and each suit contains 13 cards (2, 3, 4, 5, 6, 7, 8, 9, 10, jack, queen, king, ace).

A. The number of possible poker hands that can be dealt is the number of combinations of 52 objects taken five at a time:

$$C(52, 5) = \frac{52!}{5!(52-5)!} = \frac{52!}{5!\,47!} = 2{,}598{,}960 \text{ hands}$$

B. The number of ways of being dealt three aces from the four aces in the deck is

$$C(4, 3) = \frac{4!}{3!(4-3)!} = \frac{4!}{3!\,1!} = 4 \text{ ways}$$

The number of ways of being dealt the remaining two cards from the 48 non-ace cards is

$$C(48, 2) = \frac{48!}{2!(48-2)!} = \frac{48!}{2!\,46!} = 1{,}128 \text{ ways}$$

Thus, by the *multiplication principle,* a hand consisting of exactly three aces can be dealt in

$$[C(4, 3)][C(48, 2)] = (4)(1128) = 4{,}512 \text{ ways}$$

If E is the event of being dealt a poker hand that includes exactly three aces, then $n(E) = 4{,}512$. From part **A,** $n(S) = 2{,}598{,}960$. Hence:

$$P(E) = \frac{n(E)}{n(S)} = \frac{4{,}512}{2{,}598{,}960} \approx 0.0017$$

9.14 Statistics

The central tendency of a sample set of data taken from a population is measured by the *mode, median,* or *mean.* The **sample mode** is the value that occurs with greatest frequency in the sample. If the sample data are arranged in increasing order of magnitude, then the **sample median** is defined as the value of the middle item when the number of items is *odd,* and the average value of the middle two items when the number of items is *even.* The **sample mean** is denoted by $\bar{x}$, and defined by

$$\bar{x} = \sum_{i=1}^{n} \frac{x_i}{n}$$

where n is the number of items in the sample.

Just as there are many measures of central tendency, there are also many measures of the spread or dispersion of the sample data. The simplest measure of dispersion is the **range,** which is defined as the difference between the maximum value and the minimum value in the sample data set. The measure of dispersion most often used for n samples from a population is the **sample standard deviation,** which is denoted by s and defined by

$$s = \sqrt{\sum_{i=1}^{n} \frac{(x_i - \bar{x})^2}{n-1}}$$

The quantity s^2 is called the **sample variance.**

Example 9.42

A manufacturer is interested in determining the lifetime of a certain type of battery. The items in a sample, designated by hours of life, are as follows:

125, 118, 142, 120, 125, 131, 128, 127

A. Find the (1) sample mode, (2) median, and (3) mean.

B. Find the (1) sample range, (2) standard deviation, and (3) variance.

Solution:

A. (1) The value that occurs with greatest frequency in the sample is 125. Hence, the mode of this sample is 125 hr.

(2) To determine the sample median of these eight items, arrange the data in increasing order of magnitude:

118, 120, 125, 125, 127, 128, 131, 142

The sample median is 126, the average value of the fourth and fifth items.

(3) The sample mean is

$$\bar{x} = \sum_{i=1}^{n} \frac{x_i}{n} =$$

$$\frac{125 + 118 + 142 + 120 + 125 + 131 + 128 + 127}{8}$$

$$= 127 \text{ hr}$$

B. (1) The range of the sample is the difference between the maximum value (142) and the minimum value (118):

$$142 - 118 = 24 \text{ hr}$$

(2) To determine the sample standard deviation, begin by computing $(x_i - \bar{x})^2$, the square of the difference from the sample mean for each of the eight items:

$$(125 - 127)^2 = (-2)^2 = 4, \quad (118 - 127)^2 = (-9)^2 = 81,$$

$$(142 - 127)^2 = (15)^2 = 225, \quad (120 - 127)^2 = (-7)^2 = 49,$$

$$(125 - 127)^2 = (-2)^2 = 4, \quad (131 - 127)^2 = (4)^2 = 16,$$

$$(128 - 127)^2 = (1)^2 = 1, \quad (127 - 127)^2 = (0)^2 = 0$$

Hence, the sample standard deviation is

$$s = \sqrt{\sum_{i=1}^{n} \frac{(x_i - \bar{x})^2}{n-1}}$$

$$= \sqrt{\frac{4 + 81 + 225 + 49 + 4 + 16 + 1 + 0}{8 - 1}}$$

$$= \sqrt{\frac{380}{7}} \approx 7.37 \text{ hr}$$

(3) The sample variance is the square of the standard deviation:

$$s^2 = \left(\sqrt{\frac{380}{7}}\right)^2 = \frac{380}{7} \approx 54.3$$

9.15 Derivatives

The derivative of $y = f(x)$ with respect to x is defined as the limit of the ratio $\frac{\Delta y}{\Delta x}$ as Δx approaches zero ($\Delta x \to 0$). A physical interpretation of the derivative is the *instantaneous velocity* of a moving particle. A geometric interpretation of the derivative is the *slope of the tangent* to the curve.

The most common notations for the derivative of a function $y = f(x)$ with respect to x are $D_x y$, y', $f'(x)$, and $\frac{dy}{dx}$. The derivative of its derivative is called the second derivative of $y = f(x)$ and is denoted by $D_x^2 y$, y'', f'', or $\frac{d^2y}{dx^2}$. Similarly, the derivative of the second derivative is called the third derivative, and so on for derivatives of any order.

In the following **rules for differentiation,** c is a constant, x is the independent variable, u and v are functions of x, and n is a rational exponent:

1. Derivative of a constant: $D_x(c) = 0$
2. Derivative of the independent variable: $D_x(x) = 1$
3. Derivative of a power of the independent variable: $D_x(x^n) = nx^{n-1}$
4. Derivative of a constant times a function: $D_x(c\,u) = c\,D_x u$
5. Derivative of a sum or difference of two functions: $D_x(u \pm v) = D_x u \pm D_x v$
6. Derivative of a product of two functions: $D_x(u \cdot v) = u \cdot D_x v + v \cdot D_x u$
7. Derivative of a quotient of two functions: $D_x(\frac{u}{v}) = \dfrac{v \cdot D_x u - u \cdot D_x v}{v^2}$
8. Derivative of a power of a function: $D_x(u^n) = nu^{n-1} \cdot D_x u$

The following is a list of the most frequently used **derivative formulas.** For additional derivative formulas, refer to the *Fundamentals of Engineering Reference Handbook.*

1. $D_x(e^u) = e^u \cdot D_x u$
2. $D_x(\ln u) = \frac{1}{u} \cdot D_x u$
3. $D_x(\sin u) = \cos u \cdot D_x u$
4. $D_x(\cos u) = -\sin u \cdot D_x u$
5. $D_x(\tan u) = \sec^2 u \cdot D_x u$
6. $D_x(\cot u) = -\csc^2 u \cdot D_x u$
7. $D_x(\sec u) = \sec u \tan u \cdot D_x u$
8. $D_x(\csc u) = -\csc u \cot u \cdot D_x u$
9. $D_x(\sin^{-1} u) = \dfrac{1}{\sqrt{1-u^2}} \cdot D_x u$
10. $D_x(\tan^{-1} u) = \dfrac{1}{1+u^2} \cdot D_x u$

Derivatives may be used to evaluate limits in the indeterminate forms 0/0 and ∞/∞ by applying **L'Hôpital's rule:** If $f(x) \to 0$ and $g(x) \to 0$ as $x \to a$, or if $f(x) \to \infty$ and $g(x) \to \infty$ as $x \to a$, then

$$\lim_{x \to a} \frac{f(x)}{g(x)} = \lim_{x \to a} \frac{f'(x)}{g'(x)}$$

provided that the latter limit exists.

If y is defined as an implicit function of x by an equation of the form $F(x, y) = 0$, then $D_x y$ may be found by a method called **implicit differentiation:** Differentiate the equation $F(x, y) = 0$ term by term with respect to x, regarding y as a function of x, and then solve the resulting equation for $D_x y$.

The concept of the derivative of a function of one variable may be extended to the concept of the *partial derivatives* of a function of two or more variables:

1. The **partial derivative of $z = f(x, y)$ with respect to x** is the ordinary derivative of z when y is held constant, and is usually denoted by z_x, $f_x(x, y)$, $\frac{\partial z}{\partial x}$, or $\frac{\partial f}{\partial x}$.
2. The **partial derivative of $z = f(x, y)$ with respect to y** is the ordinary derivative of z when x is held constant, and is usually denoted by zy, $fy(x, y)$, $\frac{\partial z}{\partial y}$, or $\frac{\partial f}{\partial y}$.

Example 9.43

For a model rocket rising vertically, the height s (in feet) at time t (in seconds) is given by

$$s = 120t - 16t^2.$$

A. Find the instantaneous velocity v of the rocket at any time t.

B. Find the greatest height the rocket attains.

Solution:

A. The instantaneous velocity v at any time t is the derivative $D_t s$. To find $D_t s$, apply differentiation rules 4 and 5, then rules 2 and 3:

$$v = D_t s = 120\,D_t(t) - 16D_t(t^2)$$
$$= 120(1) - 16(2t)$$
$$= 120 - 32t$$

B. The rocket attains its greatest height when its velocity $v = 0$. Substituting $v = 0$ into the velocity equation from part **A,** solve for t:

$$0 = 120 - 32t \quad \text{implies} \quad t = 3.75 \text{ sec}$$

To find the maximum height (s_{max}), substitute $t = 3.75$ into the height equation:

$$s_{max} = 120(3.75) - 16(3.75)^2 = 225 \text{ ft}$$

Example 9.44

In each case, find the slope of the tangent to the given curve at the point where $x = 1$.

A. $y = e^{-3x} + 2\sin^3 x$
B. $y = 2x\tan^{-1}x - \ln(x^2 + 1)$

Solution:

A. The required slope is the value of the derivative D_xy at $x = 1$. To find D_xy, begin by applying differentiation rules 4 and 5:

$$D_xy = D_x(e^{-3x}) + 2\,D_x(\sin^3 x)$$

For $D_x(e^{-3x})$, apply derivative formula 1, and for $D_x(\sin^3 x) = D_x(\sin x)^3$, apply differentiation rule 8 with derivative formula 3:

$$D_xy = e^{-3x}D_x(-3x) + 2\,[3(\sin x)^2 \bullet D_x(\sin x)]$$
$$= e^{-3x}(-3) + 2\,[3\,(\sin x)^2 \bullet \cos x \bullet D_xx]$$
$$= -3e^{-3x} + 6\sin^2 x\cos x$$

Substitute $x = 1$ into this derivative formula, and use a calculator set in radian mode to find the slope of the tangent to the curve at this point:

$$-3e^{-3(1)} + 6\sin^2(1)\cos(1) \approx 2.146$$

B. To find D_xy for $y = 2x\tan^{-1}x - \ln(x^2 + 1)$, begin by applying differentiation rules 4 and 5:

$$D_xy = 2\,D_x(x\tan^{-1}x) - D_x[\ln(x^2 + 1)]$$

For $D_x(x\tan^{-1}x)$, apply differentiation rule 6 and derivative formula 10, and for $D_x[\ln(x^2 + 1)]$, apply derivative formula 2:

$$D_xy = 2\,[x \bullet D_x(\tan^{-1}x) + \tan^{-1}x \bullet D_x(x)] - \frac{1}{x^2 + 1} \times D_x(x^2 + 1)$$

$$= 2\left(\frac{x}{1 + x^2} + \tan^{-1}x\right) - \frac{2x}{x^2 + 1}$$

$$= 2\tan^{-1}x$$

Substitute $x = 1$ into this derivative formula, and use a calculator set in radian mode to find the slope of the tangent to the curve at this point:

$$2\tan^{-1}(1) \approx 1.571$$

Example 9.45

Use L'Hôpital's rule to evaluate each limit.

A. $\lim\limits_{x\to 0}\left(\dfrac{1 - \cos x}{3x^2}\right)$ **B.** $\lim\limits_{x\to 0}(x\ln x)$

Solution:

A. Since $\cos x \to 1$ as $x \to 0$, the quotient $(1 - \cos x)/(3x^2)$ takes the indeterminate form 0/0, which is a form for L'Hôpital's rule:

$$\lim_{x\to 0}\left(\frac{1 - \cos x}{3x^2}\right) = \lim_{x\to 0}\left[\frac{D_x(1 - \cos x)}{D_x(3x^2)}\right] = \lim_{x\to 0}\left(\frac{\sin x}{6x}\right)$$

Since $\sin x \to 0$ as $x \to 0$, the quotient $(\sin x)/(6x)$ still takes on the indeterminate form 0/0. Hence, apply L'Hôpital's rule again:

$$\lim_{x\to 0}\left(\frac{\sin x}{6x}\right) = \lim_{x\to 0}\left[\frac{D_x(\sin x)}{D_x(6x)}\right] = \lim_{x\to 0}\left(\frac{\cos x}{6}\right) = \frac{1}{6}$$

Therefore, $\lim\limits_{x\to 0}\left(\dfrac{1 - \cos x}{3x^2}\right) = \dfrac{1}{6}$

B. Since $\ln x \to -\infty$ as $x \to 0$, the product $x\ln x$ takes on the indeterminate form $0 \bullet \infty$, which is *not* a form for L'Hôpital's rule. However, rewrite this product as a quotient:

$$\lim_{x\to 0}(x\ln x) = \lim_{x\to 0}\left(\frac{\ln x}{x^{-1}}\right)$$

Now, as $x \to 0$, the quotient $(\ln x)/x^{-1}$ takes on the indeterminate form ∞/∞, which is a form for L'Hôpital's rule:

$$\lim_{x\to 0}\left(\frac{\ln x}{x^{-1}}\right) = \lim_{x\to 0}\left[\frac{D_x(\ln x)}{D_x(x^{-1})}\right] = \lim_{x\to 0}\left(\frac{1/x}{-1/x^2}\right) =$$
$$\lim_{x\to 0}(-x) = 0$$

Therefore, $\lim\limits_{x\to 0}(x\ln x) = 0$.

Example 9.46

For the circle defined by the equation $x^2 + y^2 - 4x + 2y - 20 = 0$, find:

A. D_xy **B.** the equation of the line normal to the circle at (6,2)

Solution:

A. Use implicit differentiation, and differentiate each term with respect to x, treating y as a function of x:

$$D_x(x^2) + D_x(y^2) - D_x(4x) + D_x(2y) - D_x(20) = D_x(0)$$

$$2x + 2yD_xy - 4 + 2D_xy = 0$$

Now, solve the last equation for D_xy:

$$D_xy = \frac{4-2x}{2y+2} = \frac{2-x}{y+1}$$

B. The slope of the tangent to the circle at (6,2) is found by replacing x with 6 and y with 2 in the derivative formula from part **A.** Hence, the slope of the tangent is $-4/3$. The normal to the circle at (6,2) is a line that is *perpendicular* to the tangent at the point of tangency. Hence, the slope of the normal is 3/4. Use the *point-slope form* of a line to find the equation of the line normal to the circle at (6,2):

$$y - y_1 = m(x - x_1)$$

$$y - 2 = \frac{3}{4}(x - 6)$$

$$y = \frac{3}{4}x - \frac{5}{2}$$

Example 9.47

In each case, find the partial derivatives of the given function with respect to each of the independent variables.

A. $z = x^2 + 5xy + 3y^2$ **B.** $z = e^{x^2y}$

Solution:

A. To find the partial derivative of $z = x^2 + 5xy + 3y^2$ with respect to x, use the basic differentiation rules with the assumption that y is constant:

$$\frac{\partial z}{\partial x} = \frac{\partial(x^2)}{\partial x} - \frac{\partial(5xy)}{\partial x} + \frac{\partial(3y^2)}{\partial x} = 2x + 5y$$

To find the partial derivative of $z = x^2 + 5xy + 3y^2$ with respect to y, use the basic differentiation rules with the assumption that x is constant:

$$\frac{\partial z}{\partial y} = \frac{\partial(x^2)}{\partial y} - \frac{\partial(5xy)}{\partial y} + \frac{\partial(3y^2)}{\partial y} = 5x + 6y$$

B. To find the partial derivative of $z = e^{x^2y}$ with respect to x, use derivative formula 1 with the assumption that y is constant:

$$\frac{\partial z}{\partial x} = e^{x^2y}\frac{\partial(x^2y)}{\partial x} = 2xye^{x^2y}$$

To find the partial derivative of $z = e^{x^2y}$ with respect to y, use derivative formula 1 with the assumption that x is constant:

$$\frac{\partial z}{\partial y} = e^{x^2y}\frac{\partial(x^2y)}{\partial y} = x^2e^{x^2y}$$

9.16 Maxima, Minima, and Points of Inflection

The **maximum value** of a function is the value that is greater than any other value of that function immediately preceding or following. In Figure 9.16, A is a maximum.

The **minimum value** of a function is the value that is less than any other value of that function immediately preceding or following. In Figure 9.16, B is a minimum. A **point of inflection** on a curve is a point at which the curve changes from concave upward to concave downward, or vice versa. In Figure 9.16, C is a point of inflection.

To find the maximum and minimum values of $y = f(x)$, first find the *critical values* of the function by solving the equation $f'(x) = 0$. Then, for each critical value a, determine the sign of $f''(a)$:

1. Maximum at $x = a$ if $f'(a) = 0$ and $f''(a) < 0$
2. Minimum at $x = a$ if $f'(a) = 0$ and $f''(a) > 0$

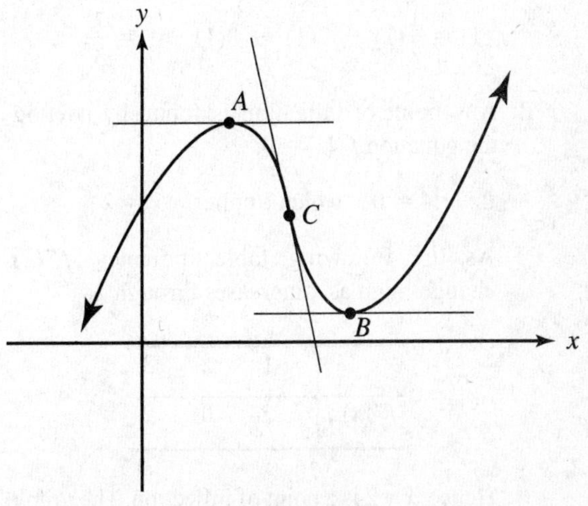

Figure 9.16

To find the points of inflection on the graph of $y = f(x)$, first find the roots of the equation $f'(x) = 0$. If $x = a$ is a root of this equation and if $f''(x)$ changes sign as x increases through a, then $x = a$ is a point of inflection.

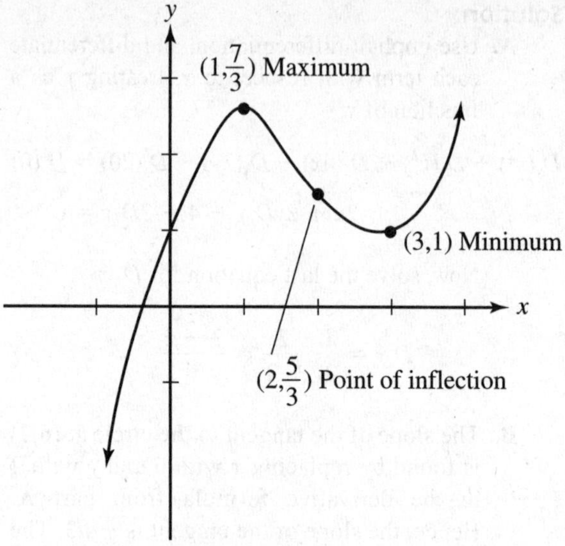

Figure 9.17

Example 9.48

Examine the function $f(x) = \frac{1}{3}x^3 - 2x^2 + 3x + 1$ for:

A. maxima and minima **B.** point of inflection

Solution:

A. Using the rules for differentiation, find $f'(x)$ and $f''(x)$:

$f'(x) = x^2 - 4x + 3$ and $f''(x) = 2x - 4$

The critical values are found by solving the equation $f'(x) = 0$:

$$f'(x) = x^2 - 4x + 3 = 0$$

which implies $x = 3$ or $x = 1$

Now, determine the sign of $f''(3)$ and $f''(1)$:

$$f''(3) = 2(3) - 4 = 2 > 0$$

and $f''(1) = 2(1) - 4 = -2 < 0$

Since $f''(3) > 0$, this function has a *minimum value* at $x = 3$ and the minimum value is

$$f(3) = \frac{1}{3}(3)^3 - 2(3)^2 + 3(3) + 1 = 1$$

Since $f''(1) < 0$, this function has a *maximum value* at $x = 1$ and the maximum value is

$$f(1) = \frac{1}{3}(1)^3 - 2(1)^2 + 3(1) + 1 = \frac{7}{3}$$

B. Any point of inflection is found by solving the equation $f''(x) = 0$:

$2x - 4 = 0$ which implies $x = 2$

As the following table indicates, $f''(x)$ changes sign as x increases through 2.

x	1	2	3
$f''(x)$	−2	0	2

Hence, $x = 2$ is a point of inflection. The graph of this function is shown in Figure 9.17.

Example 9.49

A rectangular beam with dimensions x and y is cut from a circular log of diameter 12 cm, as shown in Figure 9.18. The strength S of the beam is proportional to its width x and to the square of its depth y: $S = kxy^2$.

A. Find the width x of the strongest beam that can be cut from this log.

B. Find the depth y of the strongest beam that can be cut from this log.

Solution:

A. Refer to Figure 9.18, and apply the Pythagorean theorem:

$$y^2 = 12^2 - x^2$$

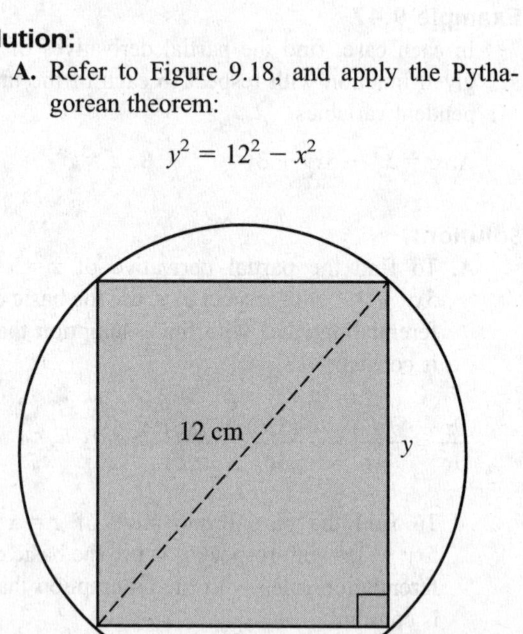

Figure 9.18

Replace y^2 with $12^2 - x^2$ in the strength formula $S = kxy^2$:

$$S = kx(12^2 - x^2) = 144kx - kx^3$$

To find the width x of the beam with the maximum strength (the strongest beam) that can be cut from this log, solve the equation $D_xS = 0$ for x:

$$D_xS = 144k - 3kx^2 = 0 \quad \text{implies} \quad x = 4\sqrt{3} \approx 6.93 \text{ cm}$$

B. To determine the depth y of the strongest beam that can be cut from this log, replace x with 4 in the equation $y^2 = 12^2 - x^2$:

$$y^2 = 12^2 - (4\sqrt{3})^2 = 96 \quad \text{implies} \quad y = 4\sqrt{6} \approx 9.80 \text{ cm}$$

9.17 Indefinite Integrals

The inverse operation of differentiation is called **integration.** The **indefinite integral** of $f(x)$ is denoted by $\int f(x)dx$ and is defined by

$$\int f(x)\,dx = F(x) + C$$

where C is called the *integration constant* and $D_x[F(x)] = f(x)$.

In the following **integration rules,** k is a constant, x is the independent variable, u and v are functions of x, and n is a rational exponent.

1. Integral of a constant: $\int k\,dx = kx + C$
2. Integral of a power of the independent variable: $\int x^n dx = \frac{x^{n+1}}{n+1} + C \quad \text{if } n \neq -1$
3. Integral of a constant times a function: $\int ku\,dx = k\int u\,dx$
4. Integral of a sum or difference of two functions: $\int (u \pm v)\,dx = \int u\,dx \pm \int v\,dx$

The following **integral formulas** are inversions of the differentiation rules and derivative formulas in Section 9.15. Formula 2, called *integration by parts,* is the inversion of the formula for differentiation of a product. For additional integral formulas, refer to the *Fundamentals of Engineering Reference Handbook.*

1. $\int u^n\,du = \frac{u^{n+1}}{n+1} + C \quad \text{if } n \neq -1$
2. $\int u\,dv = uv - \int v\,du$
3. $\int e^u\,du = e^u + C$
4. $\int \frac{1}{u}\,du = \ln|u| + C$
5. $\int \cos u\,du = \sin u + C$
6. $\int \sin u\,du = -\cos u + C$
7. $\int \sec^2 u\,du = \tan u + C$
8. $\int \csc^2 u\,du = -\cot u + C$
9. $\int \sec u \tan u\,du = \sec u + C$
10. $\int \csc u \cot u\,du = -\csc u + C$
11. $\int \frac{1}{\sqrt{1-u^2}}\,du = \sin^{-1} u + C$
12. $\int \frac{1}{1+u^2}\,du = \tan^{-1} u + C$

Example 9.50

Find the equation of the curve that passes through point (3,4) and whose slope of the tangent to the curve is given by

A. $\frac{dy}{dx} = 2x - 4$ **B.** $\frac{dy}{dx} = -\frac{x}{y}$

Solution:

A. Begin by writing the slope of the tangent to the curve in differential form by treating $\frac{dy}{dx}$ as a fraction and multiplying both sides by dx:

$$dy = (2x - 4)dx$$

Now, using the rules for integration, integrate each side of this equation and combine the integration constants on the right-hand side:

$$\int dy = \int (2x - 4)\,dx$$

$$\text{which implies} \quad y = x^2 - 4x + C$$

The equation $y = x^2 - 4x + C$ represents a family of parabolas each having $2x - 4$ as the slope of the tangent to the curve. Since the required parabola passes through point (3,4), substitute $x = 3$ and $y = 4$ into the equation $y = x^2 - 4x + C$ to find that $C = 7$.

Hence, the equation of the curve that satisfies the given conditions is $y = x^2 - 4x + 7$.

B. Separating variables, write the slope of the tangent to the curve in differential form:

$$y\,dy = -x\,dx$$

Using the rules for integration, integrate each side of this equation separately:

$$\int y\,dy = \int -x\,dx \quad \text{which implies} \quad \frac{y^2}{2} = -\frac{x^2}{2} + C$$

Multiply both sides of the equation by 2, and collect the variable terms on the left-hand side to obtain the equivalent equation $x^2 + y^2 = 2C$, which is a family of circles each having $-x/y$ as the slope of the tangent to the curve. Since the required circle passes through point (3,4), substitute $x = 3$ and $y = 4$ into the equation $x^2 + y^2 = 2C$ to find that $2C = 25$.

Hence, the equation of the curve that satisfies the given conditions is $x^2 + y^2 = 25$.

Example 9.51

Use substitution to evaluate each integral.

A. $\int \frac{3}{4x-1}\,dx$ **B.** $\int \frac{1}{4+x^2}\,dx$

Solution:

A. Let $u = 4x - 1$; then $du = 4dx$, which implies that $dx = (1/4)du$. Substitute these quantities into the given integral:

$$\int \frac{3}{4x-1}\,dx = 3\int \frac{dx}{4x-1} = 3\int \frac{(1/4)du}{u} = \frac{3}{4}\int \frac{du}{u}$$

To evaluate this integral, use integral formula 4 with $u = 4x - 1$. Hence,

$$\int \frac{3}{4x-1}\,dx = \frac{3}{4}\ln|4x-1| + C$$

B. Factor out 4 from the denominator to obtain

$$\int \frac{1}{4+x^2}\,dx = \frac{1}{4}\int \frac{dx}{1+(x^2/4)}$$

Let $u^2 = x^2/4$; then $u = x/2$. Thus, $du = (1/2)\,dx$, which implies that $dx = 2du$. Substitute these quantities into the given integral to obtain

$$\int \frac{1}{4+x^2}\,dx = \frac{1}{4}\int \frac{dx}{1+(x^2/4)} = \frac{1}{4}\int \frac{2du}{1+u^2} = \frac{1}{2}\int \frac{du}{1+u^2}$$

To evaluate this integral, use integral formula 12 with $u = x/2$. Hence:

$$\int \frac{1}{4+x^2}\,dx = \frac{1}{2}\tan^{-1}\frac{x}{2} + C$$

Example 9.52

Use integration by parts (integral formula 2) to evaluate each integral.

A. $\int x \sin 3x\,dx$ **B.** $\int \ln 4x^2\,dx$

Solution:

A. Using the integration by parts formula, $\int u\,dv = uv - \int v\,du$, let

$$u = x \quad\text{and}\quad dv = \sin 3x\,dx$$

To find du, differentiate both sides of $u = x$, and to find v, integrate both sides of $dv = \sin 3x\,dx$ using integral formula 6:

$$du = dx \quad\text{and}\quad v = -\frac{1}{3}\cos 3x$$

Substitute these quantities into the integration by parts formula, and then apply integral formula 5, to evaluate the given integral:

$$\int x\sin 3x\,dx = -\frac{1}{3}x\cos 3x + \frac{1}{3}\int \cos 3x\,dx$$

$$= -\frac{1}{3}x\cos 3x + \frac{1}{9}\sin 3x + C$$

B. Using the integration by parts formula, $\int u\,dv = uv - \int v\,du$, let

$$u = \ln 4x^2 \quad\text{and}\quad dv = dx$$

To find du, differentiate both sides of $u = \ln 4x^2$ using derivative formula 2, and to find v, integrate both sides of $dv = dx$:

$$du = \frac{1}{4x^2}\bullet 8x\,dx = \frac{2}{x}dx \quad\text{and}\quad v = x$$

Substitute these quantities into the integration by parts formula to find that

$$\int \ln 4x^2\,dx = x\ln 4x^2 - 2\int dx = x\ln 4x^2 - 2x + C$$

9.18 Definite Integrals

The **definite integral** of $f(x)$ from a to b is denoted by the symbol $\int_a^b f(x)\,dx$ and is defined by

$$\int_a^b f(x)\,dx = \lim_{\delta\to 0}\sum_{k=1}^{n} f(\xi_k)\Delta x_k$$

where ξ_k are points in the interval (a,b). The function f is called the *integrand,* and a and b are the *lower limit* and *upper limit,* respectively. A physical interpretation of the definite integral is the *work done* by a variable force. A geometric interpretation of the definite integral is the *area under a curve.* The **fundamental theorem of integral calculus** connects the two concepts of the indefinite integral and the definite integral:

$$\int_a^b f(x)\,dx = F(x)\,\Big|_a^b = F(b) - F(a)$$

where F is any particular integral of $f(x)$.

Definite integrals are used to find the area between two curves, the volume of a solid of revolution, and the centroid (center of gravity) of an area. The **area between two curves** is found by using either a vertical strip with width dx or a horizontal strip with width dy:

1. By using a vertical strip: $A = \int_a^b$ (length of strip) dx, where the left-hand and right-hand boundaries for the vertical strip are from $x = a$ to $x = b$
2. By using a horizontal strip: $A = \int_c^d$ (length of strip) dy, where the lower and upper boundaries for the horizontal strip are from $y = c$ to $y = d$

The **volume of a solid of revolution** is found by using either a vertical disk with thickness dx or a horizontal disk with thickness dy:

1. By using a vertical disk: $V = \pi \int_a^b$ (radius of disk)^2 dx, where the left-hand and right-hand boundaries for the vertical disk are from $x = a$ to $x = b$
2. By using a horizontal disk: $V = \pi \int_c^d$ (radius of disk)^2 dy, where the lower and upper boundaries for the horizontal disk are from $y = c$ to $y = d$

The coordinates of the **centroid of an area** A are denoted by $(\overline{x}, \overline{y})$ and given by

$$(\overline{x}, \overline{y}) = \left(\frac{M_y}{A}, \frac{M_x}{A}\right)$$

where M_y and M_x are the *first moments* with respect to the y-axis and x-axis, respectively. The first moments are defined as follows:

$$M_y = \int_a^b x(\text{length of vertical strip})\,dx,$$

where the left-hand and right-hand boundaries for the vertical strip are from $x = a$ to $x = b$ and

$$M_x = \int_c^d y(\text{length of horizontal strip})\,dy$$

where the lower and upper boundaries for the horizontal strip are from $y = c$ to $y = d$.

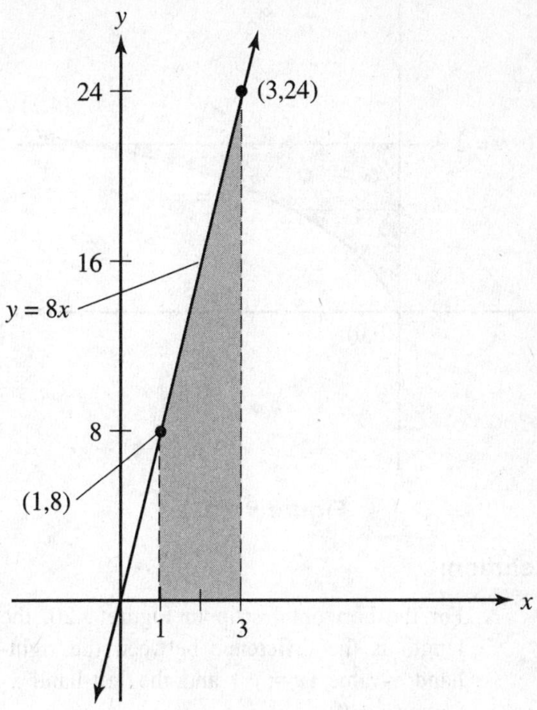

Figure 9.19

Example 9.53

Consider the definite integral $\int_1^3 8x\,dx$.

A. Evaluate this integral.

B. Give a geometric interpretation of this integral.

Solution:

A. Use the fundamental theorem of integral calculus to evaluate the integral:

$$\int_1^3 8x\,dx = 4x^2\,\Big|_1^3 = 4(3)^2 - 4(1)^2 = 32$$

B. Geometrically, this definite integral represents the area under the curve $y = 8x$ from $x = 1$ to $x = 3$. A sketch of this area is shown in Figure 9.19.

To verify this answer, use the formula for the area of a trapezoid:

$$A = \frac{1}{2}h(b_1 + b_2) = \frac{1}{2}(2)(8 + 24) = 32 \text{ square units}$$

which agrees with the value of the definite integral found in part **A.**

Example 9.54

Find the area of the shaded region in Figure 9.20:

A. by using a horizontal strip

B. by using a vertical strip

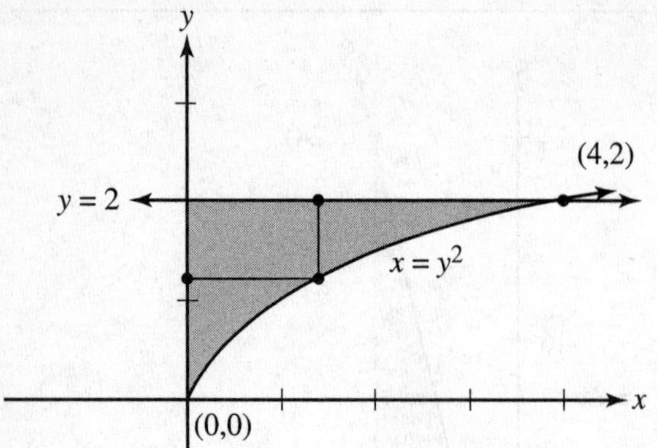

Figure 9.20

Solution:

A. For the horizontal strip in Figure 9.20, the length is the difference between the right-hand x-value ($x = y^2$) and the left-hand x-value ($x = 0$):

$$\text{length of strip} = y^2 - 0 = y^2$$

The lower and upper boundaries for the horizontal strip are from $y = 0$ to $y = 2$. The area of the shaded region is given by the area formula:

$$A = \int_c^d (\text{length of strip})\, dy$$

$$A = \int_0^2 y^2 dy = \frac{y^3}{3}\bigg|_0^2 = \left(\frac{8}{3}\right) - (0) = \frac{8}{3} \text{ square units}$$

B. For the vertical strip in Figure 9.20, the length is the difference between the upper y-value ($y = 2$) and the lower y-value ($y = \sqrt{x} = x^{1/2}$):

$$\text{length of strip} = 2 - x^{1/2}$$

The left-hand and right-hand boundaries of the vertical strip are from $x = 0$ to $x = 4$. The area of the shaded region is given by the area formula:

$$A = \int_a^b (\text{length of strip})\, dx$$

$$= \int_0^4 (2 - x^{1/2})\, dx = 2x - \frac{2x^{3/2}}{3}\bigg|_0^4$$

$$= \left(8 - \frac{16}{3}\right) - (0) = \frac{8}{3} \text{ square units}$$

which agrees with the answer found in part A.

Example 9.55

Find the volume generated by revolving the shaded area in Figure 9.20:

A. about the y-axis **B.** about the x-axis

Solution:

A. If the shaded area in Figure 9.20 is revolved about the y-axis, then the length of the horizontal strip becomes the radius of a horizontal disk. Hence:

$$\text{radius of disk} = y^2 - 0 = y^2$$

The lower and upper boundaries for the horizontal disk are from $y = 0$ to $y = 2$. Thus, the volume generated by revolving the shaded region about the y-axis is given by the volume formula:

$$V = \pi \int_c^d (\text{radius of disk})^2\, dy$$

$$= \pi \int_0^2 (y^2)^2\, dy = \pi \int_0^2 y^4\, dy = \pi\left(\frac{y^5}{5}\right)\bigg|_0^2$$

$$= \frac{32\pi}{5} \text{ cubic units}$$

B. If the shaded area in Figure 9.20 is revolved about the x-axis, then the volume that is generated is a cylinder with a hollowed-out middle. To find this volume, determine the volume of the cylinder and subtract from it the volume of the hollowed-out portion, which can be determined by using a vertical disk:

$$V = \pi r^2 h - \pi \int_a^b (\text{radius of disk})^2\, dx$$

The radius of a vertical disk in the hollowed-out portion is the difference between its upper y-value ($y = \sqrt{x} = x^{1/2}$) and its lower y-value ($y = 0$):

$$\text{radius of disk} = x^{1/2} - 0 = x^{1/2}$$

Thus, the volume of this region is

$$V = \pi(2)^2(4) - \pi \int_0^4 (x^{1/2})^2\, dx = 16\pi - \pi \int_0^4 x\, dx$$

$$= 8\pi \text{ cubic units}$$

Example 9.56

For the area in Figure 9.20, find:

A. the first moments with respect to the y-axis and x-axis

B. the coordinates of the centroid of the area

Solution:

A. The first moment with respect to the y-axis is

$$M_y = \int_0^4 x(2 - x^{1/2})\,dx = \int_0^4 (2x - x^{3/2})dx$$

$$= x^2 - \frac{2x^{5/2}}{5}\Big|_0^4 = \frac{16}{5}$$

and the first moment with respect to the x-axis is

$$M_x = \int_0^2 y(y^2 - 0)\,dy = \int_0^2 y^3\,dy = \frac{y^4}{4}\Big|_0^2 = 4$$

B. From Example 9.54, the area of this region is 8/3 square units. Use this fact and the results from part **A** to find the centroid:

$$(\bar{x}, \bar{y}) = \left(\frac{M_y}{A}, \frac{M_x}{A}\right) = \left(\frac{16/5}{8/3}, \frac{4}{8/3}\right) = \left(\frac{6}{5}, \frac{3}{2}\right)$$

9.19 Differential Equations

An equation involving derivatives (or differentials) of one or more unknown functions is called a **differential equation.** Its *order* is the order of the highest derivative appearing in the equation, and its *degree* is the power to which the derivative of highest order is raised. The *solution* of the equation is a functional relation between the variables involved, not containing derivatives or differentials, that satisfies the differential equation.

Any differential equation that may be written in the derivative form

$$\frac{dy}{dx} = f(x, y)$$

or in the differential form

$$M\,dx + N\,dy = 0$$

where M and N are functions of x and y only, is called **a differential equation of the first order and first degree.** This kind of differential equation usually appears as either a *separable-type* or a *linear-type* equation.

1. **Separable type:** An equation that can be written in the form $X\,dx = Y\,dy$, where X is a function of x only and Y is a function of y only. The solution is obtained by direct integration.
2. **Linear type:** An equation that can be written in the form $\frac{dy}{dx} + Py = Q$, where P and Q are functions of x only. The solution is given by the **linear formula**

$$y\,e^{\int P dx} = \int Qe^{\int P dx}\,dx + C$$

Any differential equation that can be written in the form $y'' + ay' + by = X$, where the coefficients a and b are constants and X is 0 or is a function of x only, is called a **linear differential equation of the second order with constant coefficients.** This kind of differential equation appears as either a *homogeneous-type* or a *nonhomogeneous-type* equation.

1. **Homogeneous type:** An equation in which $X = 0$. The solution of the equation depends on the character of the roots of its *auxiliary equation,* $m^2 + am + b = 0$, as indicated in Table 9.1. The auxiliary equation is formed by replacing the kth derivative with m^k and replacing y with 1.

TABLE 9.1

Roots of Auxiliary Equation	*Solution of Differential Equation*
Real and distinct roots; m_1, m_2	$y = c_1e^{m_1x} + c_2e^{m_2x}$
Real repeated root; r	$y = c_1e^{rx} + c_2xe^{rx}$
Conjugate imaginary roots; $a \pm bi$	$y = e^{ax}(c_1 \cos bx + c_2 \sin bx)$

2. **Nonhomogeneous type:** An equation in which $X \neq 0$. The solution is $y = y_c + y_p$, where y_c is called the *complementary solution* or *homogeneous solution* (i.e., the general solution of the corresponding homogeneous equation) and y_p is the *particular solution* of the given nonhomogeneous equation. If X is of the form e^{ax}, sin bx, cos bx, or a polynomial in x, then y_p may be found by the *method of undetermined coefficients.* The procedure in this method is to assume for y_p an expression based on X and its derivatives, and containing certain undetermined coefficients, as indicated in Table 9.2.

To find the values of the undetermined coefficients ($A, B, A_0, A_1, \ldots, A_m$), substitute the assumed form of y_p into the differential equation and equate coefficients of corresponding types.

TABLE 9.2

For X =	*Assume y_p =*
$a_0x^m + a_1x^{m-1} + \ldots + a_m$ ($a_1, a_2, \ldots,$ or a_m may be 0)	$A_0x^m + A_1x^{m-1} + \ldots + A_m$ if 0 is not a root of the auxiliary equation; $x(A_0x^m + A_1x^{m-1} + \ldots + A_m)$ if 0 is a root of the auxiliary equation
ce^{ax}	Ae^{ax} if a is not a root of the auxiliary equation; Axe^{ax} if a is a root of the auxiliary equation; Ax^2e^{ax} if a is a repeated root of the auxiliary equation
$c_1 \sin bx + c_2 \cos bx$ (c_1 or c_2 may be 0)	$A \sin bx + B \cos bx$ if bi is not a root of the auxiliary equation; $x(A \sin bx + B \cos bx)$ if bi is a root of the auxiliary equation

Example 9.57

Solve each differential equation of the first order and first degree.

A. $\frac{dy}{dx} = 2xy$ **B.** $\frac{dy}{dx} + \frac{3y}{x} = 5x$, with $y(2) = 0$

Solution:

A. This equation may be treated as a separable type by writing it in the form

$$\frac{dy}{y} = 2x\,dx$$

or as a linear type, with $P = -2x$ and $Q = 0$, by writing it in the form

$$\frac{dy}{dx} - 2x \cdot y = 0$$

To solve this equation, use either approach.

Separable: Begin by integrating both sides of $(dy)/y = 2x\,dx$:

$$\ln y = x^2 + C$$

Rewriting this expression in exponential form, solve for y:

$$y = e^{x^2+C} = e^{x^2} \cdot e^C = C_1e^{x^2}$$

Hence, the solution of this differential equation is $y = C_1e^{x^2}$.

Linear: Begin by evaluating $e^{\int P(x)dx}$ with $P = -2x$:

$$e^{\int -2x\,dx} = e^{-x^2}$$

Now, use the linear formula, with $Q = 0$, to obtain

$$y\,e^{-x^2} = \int 0 \cdot e^{-x^2}\,dx + C = C$$

Multiply both sides of this equation by e^{x^2} to obtain $y = Ce^{x^2}$, which agrees with the answer obtained by using the separable approach.

B. Although this equation is *not* separable, it is linear in y with $P = 3/x$ and $Q = 5x$. Use the properties of logarithms to help evaluate $e^{\int P(x)dx}$:

$$e^{\int (3/x)dx} = e^{3\ln x} = e^{\ln x^3} = x^3$$

Now, use the linear formula, with $Q = 5x$, to obtain

$$yx^3 = \int (5x)x^3\,dx + C \quad \text{which implies} \quad yx^3 = x^5 + C$$

Applying the initial conditions, $y(2) = 0$, solve for C:

$$(0)(2)^3 = (2)^5 + C \quad \text{implies} \quad C = -32$$

Hence, the solution of this differential equation is $yx^3 = x^5 - 32$ or

$$y = x^2 - \frac{32}{x^3}$$

Example 9.58

Solve each homogeneous linear differential equation of the second order.

A. $y'' + 8y' + 16 = 0$ **B.** $\frac{d^2x}{dt^2} + 4x = 0$

Solution:

A. Find the roots of the corresponding auxiliary equation, $m^2 + 8m + 16 = 0$, by factoring and setting the individual factors equal to 0:

$$(m + 4)(m + 4) = 0$$

implies $m = -4$ is a repeated root

Hence, by Table 9.1, the general solution of this differential equation is

$$y = c_1e^{-4x} + c_2xe^{-4x}$$

B. By the quadratic formula, the roots of the corresponding auxiliary equation, $m^2 + 4 = 0$, are $m = 0 \pm 2i$. Hence, by Table 9.1, the general solution of this differential equation is

$$x = e^{0t}(c_1 \cos 2t + c_2 \sin 2t) = c_1 \cos 2t + c_2 \sin 2t$$

Example 9.59

Solve each nonhomogeneous linear differential equation of the second order.

A. $y'' + y' - 2y = 4x^2$ **B.** $y'' - 2y' - 3y = 8e^{3x}$

Solution:

A. To find y_c for this nonhomogeneous differential equation, solve the corresponding homogeneous equation, $y'' + y' - 2y = 0$. Its auxiliary equation, $m^2 + m - 2 = 0$, which may be written as $(m + 2)(m - 1) = 0$, has real distinct roots $m = -2$ and $m = 1$. Hence:

$$y_c = c_1e^{-2x} + c_2e^x$$

Referring to Table 9.2, for $X = 4x^2$ with 0 not a root of the auxiliary equation, assume

$$y_p = Ax^2 + Bx + C$$

which implies

$$y'_p = 2Ax + B \quad \text{and} \quad y''_p = 2A$$

where A, B, and C are undetermined coefficients. Substitute these values of y''_p, y'_p, and y_p into the given differential equation to obtain

$$2A + (2Ax + B) - 2(Ax^2 + Bx + C) = 4x^2$$

Equating coefficients of the x^2, x, and constant terms on the left-hand and right-hand sides of this equation yields a system of three equations with three unknowns:

$$-2A = 4,\ 2A - 2B = 0, \text{ and } 2A + B - 2C = 0$$

Solve this system of equations to find that $A = -2$, $B = -2$, and $C = -3$. Hence:

$$y_p = -2x^2 - 2x - 3$$

The solution of the nonhomogeneous linear differential equation is $y = y_c + y_p$:

$$y = c_1e^{-2x} + c_2e^x - 2x^2 - 2x - 3$$

B. To find y_c for $y'' - 2y' - 3y = 8e^{3x}$, take the corresponding homogeneous equation, $y'' - 2y' - 3y = 0$, form the auxiliary equation, $m^2 - 2m - 3 = 0$, and find its roots. Since this auxiliary equation has real distinct roots $m = 3$ and $m = -1$,

$$y_c = c_1e^{3x} + c_2e^{-x}$$

The right-hand member X for this differential equation is $8e^{3x}$ with $a = 3$. Since 3 is also a singular root of the auxiliary equation, assume that

$$y_p = Axe^{3x}$$

where A is an undetermined coefficient, as indicated in Table 9.2. Hence:

$$y'_p = 3Axe^{3x} + Ae^{3x} \quad \text{and} \quad y''_p = 9Axe^{3x} + 6Ae^{3x}$$

Substitute these values of y''_p, y'_p, and y_p into the given differential equation to obtain

$$9Axe^{3x} + 6Ae^{3x} - 2(3Axe^{3x} + Ae^{3x}) - 3Axe^{3x} = 8e^{3x}$$

The xe^{3x}-terms drop out, leaving $4Ae^{3x} = 8e^{3x}$, which implies $A = 2$. Hence:

$$y_p = 2xe^{3x}$$

The solution of the nonhomogeneous linear differential equation is $y = y_c + y_p$:

$$y = c_1e^{3x} + c_2e^{-x} + 2xe^{3x}$$

Example 9.60

A weight attached to a spring moves up and down, so that the equation of motion is $\frac{d^2x}{dt^2} + 4x = 0$, where x is the displacement, in feet, of the weight from its equilibrium position at any time t. Suppose that at $t = 0$ sec the displacement is x

= 1 ft [$x(0) = 1$] and the velocity is $v = dx/dt$ = 6 ft/sec [$x'(0) = 6$]. Find:

A. x in terms of t, the equation of motion
B. the amplitude, period, and phase shift of this motion

Solution:

A. From Example 9.58**B**, the general solution of this differential equation is

$$x = c_1 \cos 2t + c_2 \sin 2t$$

Using the initial condition $x(0) = 1$, determine c_1:

$$1 = c_1 \cos 0 + c_2 \sin 0 \quad \text{implies} \quad c_1 = 1$$

To determine c_2 from the given initial conditions, first find the derivative x':

$$x' = -2c_1 \sin 2t + 2c_2 \cos 2t$$

Now, use the initial condition $x'(0) = 6$ with the fact that $c_1 = 1$ to determine c_2:

$$6 = -2(1) \sin 0 + 2c_2 \cos 0 \quad \text{implies} \quad c_2 = 3$$

Hence, the equation of motion is given by

$$x = \cos 2t + 3 \sin 2t$$

B. To determine the amplitude, period, and phase shift from an equation of the form $x = c_1 \cos \omega t + c_2 \sin \omega t$, transform it into the form

$$x = A \sin(\omega t + \phi)$$

where $A = \sqrt{c_1{}^2 + c_2{}^2}$, and $\phi = \tan^{-1}\frac{c_1}{c_2}$, with $\sin \phi = \frac{c_1}{A}$ and $\cos \phi = \frac{c_2}{A}$. When the equation of motion is written in this form, the amplitude, period, and phase shift are easily found:

$$\text{amplitude} = A, \quad \text{period} = \frac{2\pi}{\omega}, \quad \text{phase shift} = \frac{\phi}{\omega}$$

For $x = \cos 2t + 3 \sin 2t$, note that $c_1 = 1$, $c_2 = 3$, and $\omega = 2$. Thus:

$$A = \sqrt{1^2 + 3^2} = \sqrt{10} \approx 3.162$$

$$\text{and} \quad \phi = \tan^{-1}\frac{1}{3} \approx 0.3218$$

Hence, the equation of motion is equivalent to

$$x = 3.162 \sin(2t + 0.3218)$$

Thus, the amplitude is 3.162 ft, the period is π sec, and the phase shift is 0.1609 ft, as shown in Figure 9.21.

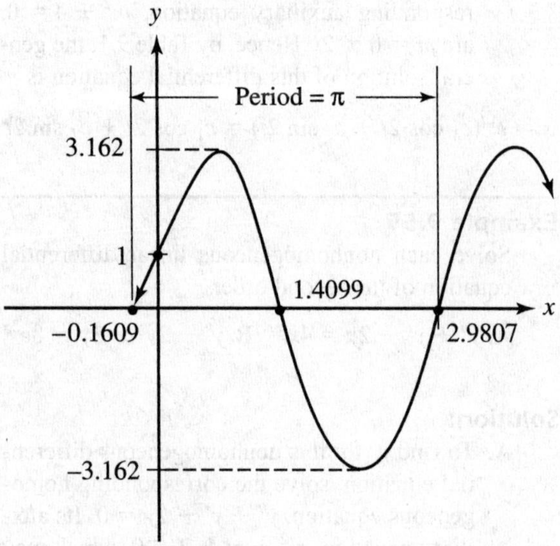

Figure 9.21

PRACTICE PROBLEMS

1. Find the approximate perimeter of a triangle whose vertices are points $A(-2,1)$, $B(1,3)$, and $C(4,-3)$ in the coordinate plane.
   - **(A)** 17.5 units
   - **(B)** 14.3 units
   - **(C)** 18.0 units
   - **(D)** 21.3 units

2. Find the equation of a line that passes through points $(4,-1)$ and $(2,5)$ in the coordinate plane.
   - **(A)** $y = -2x + 9$
   - **(B)** $y = -3x + 11$
   - **(C)** $y = -3x + 9$
   - **(D)** $y = -2x + 12$

3. Solve the equation $x(2x - 3) = 5$ for x.
   - **(A)** -1
   - **(B)** 5/2
   - **(C)** 3
   - **(D)** both (A) and (B)

4. Classify the graph of the equation $x^2 + xy + y^2 - 6 = 0$ as a
   - **(A)** circle
   - **(B)** parabola
   - **(C)** ellipse
   - **(D)** hyperbola

5. Find the coordinates of the foci for the hyperbola whose equation is given by $9y^2 - 4x^2 = 36$.
   - **(A)** $(\pm\sqrt{13},0)$
   - **(B)** $(0, \pm\sqrt{13})$
   - **(C)** $(0, \pm 2)$
   - **(D)** $(\pm 3,0)$

6. Determine the equation of an ellipse with center $(0,0)$, foci $(\pm 2,0)$, and major axis of length 6.
   - **(A)** $5x^2 + 9y^2 = 45$
   - **(B)** $9x^2 + 5y^2 = 45$
   - **(C)** $x^2 + 9y^2 = 4$
   - **(D)** $5x^2 + y^2 = 20$

7. Find the equation of a circle that is tangent to the y-axis and whose center is at point $(-2,5)$ in the coordinate plane.
   - **(A)** $x^2 + y^2 + 10x - 4y + 16 = 0$
   - **(B)** $x^2 + y^2 - 10y + 25 = 0$
   - **(C)** $x^2 + y^2 + 4x - 10y + 50 = 0$
   - **(D)** $x^2 + y^2 + 4x - 10y + 25 = 0$

8. Find the radius of a sphere whose equation is $x^2 + y^2 + z^2 - 4x + 2y - 4 = 0$.
   - **(A)** 2
   - **(B)** 5
   - **(C)** 3
   - **(D)** 4

9. Evaluate $\log_2 12$ to four significant digits.
   - **(A)** 2.654
   - **(B)** 3.585
   - **(C)** 3.841
   - **(D)** 4.372

10. Simplify the exponential expression $e^{2 \ln x}$.
    - **(A)** $2x$
    - **(B)** 2^x
    - **(C)** x^2
    - **(D)** $x/2$

11. Express $3 \ln x - \ln 2 + 2 \ln 4$ as a single logarithm with a coefficient of 1.
    - **(A)** $\ln 8x^3$
    - **(B)** $\ln 16x$
    - **(C)** $\ln 8x$
    - **(D)** $\ln (x^3/32)$

12. Find the approximate solution of the equation $4e^{-7x} = 15$.
    - **(A)** -0.2981
    - **(B)** -1.672
    - **(C)** 2.570
    - **(D)** -0.1888

13. Given that $\sin \theta = 3/5$ and θ is obtuse, find $\tan \theta$.
    - **(A)** $-4/5$
    - **(B)** 4/5
    - **(C)** 3/5
    - **(D)** $-3/4$

14. The two legs of a right triangle measure 12 cm and 18 cm. Find the approximate measure of the smallest angle in the triangle.
    - **(A)** 28.8°
    - **(B)** 33.7°
    - **(C)** 31.6°
    - **(D)** 37.1°

15. When a helicopter is 1.2 km above one end of an island, the angle of depression to the other end of the island is 22.7°. Find the approximate length of the island.
    - **(A)** 1.89 km
    - **(B)** 2.87 km
    - **(C)** 2.25 km
    - **(D)** 3.17 km

16. Two angles in an oblique triangle measure 32° and 47°. If the side opposite the unknown angle is 12.5 m, find the approximate length of the smallest side of the triangle.
    - **(A)** 6.75 m
    - **(B)** 6.25 m
    - **(C)** 7.45 m
    - **(D)** 5.85 m

17. Three sides of an oblique triangle measure 196 ft, 212 ft, and 92 ft. Find the approximate measure of the smallest angle.

(A) 32.1°
(B) 28.3°
(C) 21.9°
(D) 25.7°

18. Given that $\sin\theta = 3/5$ and θ is acute, find $\cos 2\theta$.

(A) 7/25
(B) −7/25
(C) −4/5
(D) 4/5

19. Express $(\sin x + \cos x)^2 + (\sin x - \cos x)^2$ as a constant.

(A) 0
(B) 1
(C) 2
(D) 3

20. Express $\cos^2 3x$ in terms of the first power of the cosine function.

(A) $(1 - \cos 6x)/2$
(B) $(1 + \cos 6x)/2$
(C) $(1 + \sin 3x)/2$
(D) $(1 - \cos 3x)/2$

21. Express the complex number $2.65 + 7.91i$ in polar form.

(A) $8.34e^{1.25i}$
(B) $8.34e^{-1.25i}$
(C) $5.88e^{1.25i}$
(D) $5.88e^{-1.25i}$

22. Express the quotient $(1 - 2i)/(1 + 2i)$ in rectangular form.

(A) $0.6 - 0.8i$
(B) $-0.6 + 0.8i$
(C) $0.6 + 0.8i$
(D) $-0.6 - 0.8i$

23. Express the product $(5e^{(17\pi/12)i})(\sqrt{2} + i\sqrt{2})$ in polar form.

(A) $10e^{(2\pi/3)i}$
(B) $e^{(5\pi/3)i}$
(C) $-10e^{(\pi/3)i}$
(D) $10e^{(5\pi/3)i}$

24. Express the power $(1 + i)^8$ in rectangular form.

(A) 16
(B) $8i$
(C) $1 - i$
(D) −6

25. Given the matrices $A = \begin{bmatrix} -1 & 1 \\ 1 & -1 \end{bmatrix}$ and $B = \begin{bmatrix} 5 & 5 \\ -2 & 2 \end{bmatrix}$, find $3A - 2B$.

(A) $\begin{bmatrix} -2 & 8 \\ 3 & -2 \end{bmatrix}$

(B) $\begin{bmatrix} -13 & -7 \\ 7 & 1 \end{bmatrix}$

(C) $\begin{bmatrix} -10 & -3 \\ 5 & 1 \end{bmatrix}$

(D) $\begin{bmatrix} 13 & -7 \\ 7 & 0 \end{bmatrix}$

26. Given the matrices in Problem 25, find BA.

(A) $\begin{bmatrix} 1 & 0 \\ 0 & 1 \end{bmatrix}$

(B) $\begin{bmatrix} 0 & 0 \\ 0 & 0 \end{bmatrix}$

(C) $\begin{bmatrix} 0 & 1 \\ 1 & 0 \end{bmatrix}$

(D) $\begin{bmatrix} 1 & 1 \\ 1 & 1 \end{bmatrix}$

27. For the matrix $A = \begin{bmatrix} 1 & 0 & 2 \\ 2 & -3 & 4 \\ -3 & 1 & 9 \end{bmatrix}$, find the minor of element a_{11}.

(A) −31
(B) 12
(C) 0
(D) −45

28. Evaluate the determinant of the matrix in Problem 27.

(A) −31
(B) 12
(C) 0
(D) −45

29. Find the inverse of the matrix $A = \begin{bmatrix} 1 & 4 \\ 2 & 3 \end{bmatrix}$.

(A) $\frac{1}{2}\begin{bmatrix} -1 & 7 \\ 2 & -1 \end{bmatrix}$

(B) $\frac{1}{3}\begin{bmatrix} -3 & -1 \\ 2 & 4 \end{bmatrix}$

(C) $\frac{1}{5}\begin{bmatrix} -3 & 4 \\ 2 & -1 \end{bmatrix}$

(D) $\begin{bmatrix} -3 & 3 \\ 2 & 1 \end{bmatrix}$

30. Solve this system of equations:

$$x - y + z = -3$$
$$2x + y = 1$$
$$y - 3z = 7$$

(A) $x = 0, y = -11, z = 2$
(B) $x = 0, y = 1, z = -2$
(C) $x = 1, y = -1, z = 0$
(D) $x = 0, y = 2, z = -6$

31. Find the magnitude of vector $\mathbf{A} = \mathbf{i} - 2\mathbf{j} + 3\mathbf{k}$.

(A) $\sqrt{14}$
(B) $\sqrt{10}$
(C) $\sqrt{6}$
(D) 4

32. For the vectors $\mathbf{A} = 2\mathbf{i} + \mathbf{j} + \mathbf{k}$ and $\mathbf{B} = -4\mathbf{i} + 3\mathbf{j} + \mathbf{k}$, find the dot product $\mathbf{A} \cdot \mathbf{B}$.

(A) 12
(B) 6
(C) 4
(D) -4

33. For the vectors in Problem 32, find the cross product $\mathbf{A} \times \mathbf{B}$.

(A) $\mathbf{i} + 6\mathbf{j} + 5\mathbf{k}$
(B) $-2\mathbf{i} + 5\mathbf{j} - 9\mathbf{k}$
(C) $-2\mathbf{i} - 6\mathbf{j} + 10\mathbf{k}$
(D) $\mathbf{i} - 6\mathbf{j}$

34. Find the area of a triangle with vertices $P(2,-2,1)$, $Q(3,-1,2)$, and $R(3,-1,1)$.

(A) 4 square units
(B) $\sqrt{2}/2$ square units
(C) $\sqrt{2}$ square units
(D) 8 square units

35. Find the tenth element of the arithmetic sequence $11, 4, -3, -10, \ldots$.

(A) -52
(B) -106
(C) -99
(D) -58

36. Find the sum of the arithmetic series $\sum_{i=1}^{58}(7 - 5i)$.

(A) $-8{,}149$
(B) 946
(C) $-2{,}369$
(D) $-9{,}980$

37. Find the sum of the infinite geometric series $\sum_{i=2}^{\infty}(-0.2)^i$.

(A) 1
(B) 1/15
(C) 1/45
(D) 1/30

38. Find the Taylor (Maclaurin) series generated by $f(x) = \sin x$ at $x = 0$.

(A) $x + \frac{x^3}{3!} + \frac{x^5}{5!} + \ldots + \frac{x^{2n-1}}{(2n-1)!}$
(B) $1 - \frac{x^2}{2!} + \frac{x^4}{4!} - \ldots + (-1)^{n+1}\frac{x^{2n-2}}{(2n-2)!}$
(C) $x - \frac{x^3}{3!} - \frac{x^5}{5!} - \ldots - \frac{x^{2n-1}}{(2n-1)!}$
(D) $x - \frac{x^3}{3!} + \frac{x^5}{5!} - \ldots + (-1)^{n+1}\frac{x^{2n-1}}{(2n-1)!}$

39. Find the probability of obtaining a head and an ace when tossing a fair coin and then selecting one card from a standard deck of playing cards.

(A) 1/13
(B) 1/46
(C) 1/108
(D) 1/26

40. A family of five has bought seats to a baseball game. In how many ways can they be seated in the five seats?

(A) 90
(B) 120
(C) 156
(D) 96

41. Nine equally qualified students, five boys and four girls, apply for three scholarships. Find the probability that two girls receive scholarships.

(A) 5/14
(B) 1/2
(C) 5/8
(D) 2/3

42. Find the sample mean for the following data: 13, 19, 12, 15, 16, 12, 15, 19, 14, 15.

(A). 15
(B) 14.6
(C) 14
(D) 15.1

43. A rock thrown vertically upward from the surface of the moon reaches a height of $s = 24t - 0.8t^2$ m in t s. Find the velocity v at any time t.

(A) $v = 16 - 1.4t$ m/s
(B) $v = 24 - 1.6t$ m/s
(C) $v = 22 + 1.8t$ m/s
(D) $v = -13 - 1.9t$ m/s

44. Find the equation of the tangent to the curve $y = x^2 - 3x + 4$ at $x = 2$.

(A) $y = x + 2$
(B) $y = 2x - 1$
(C) $y = x$
(D) $y = -x$

45. Evaluate $\lim_{x\to 0}\left(\frac{\cos x - 1}{\cos 2x - 1}\right)$.

(A) 1/2
(B) 1/3
(C) 2/3
(D) 1/4

46. Find the equation of the normal to the circle $x^2 + y^2 = 25$ at (3, −4).

(A) $y = \frac{4}{3}x - 6$
(B) $y = -\frac{2}{3}x - 6$
(C) $y = -\frac{4}{3}x + 8$
(D) $y = -\frac{4}{3}x$

47. For $z = x^2y^2 + e^{2x}y^3$, find $\partial z/\partial x$.

(A) $xy^2 + 2e^x$
(B) $2xy^2 + 2e^{2x}y^3$
(C) $2xy + 2e^xy^3$
(D) $2x + y^3$

48. Determine a point of inflection for the graph of $y = x^3 + 6x^2$.

(A) (−2,16)
(B) (0,0)
(C) (−1,5)
(D) (2,32)

49. Find the dimensions of the rectangle with greatest area that can be cut from a semicircle of radius 6 cm.

(A) 3 cm by 4 cm
(B) $6\sqrt{2}$ cm by $3\sqrt{2}$ cm
(C) $\sqrt{2}$ cm by $6\sqrt{2}$ cm
(D) $6\sqrt{2}$ cm by $6\sqrt{2}$ cm

50. Find the equation of the curve that passes through point (1,2) and whose slope of the tangent to the curve is given by $dy/dx = 4x - 6$.

(A) $y = x^2 + 1$
(B) $y = 2x^2 - 6x + 6$
(C) $y = 2x^2 - 6x$
(D) $y = 2x^2 + 6x + 1$

51. Evaluate $\int \frac{4}{2x - 1}dx$.

(A) $(2x - 1)^2 + C$
(B) $x^2 + C$
(C) $\ln(2x - 1) + C$
(D) $\ln(2x - 1)^2 + C$

52. Evaluate $\int x \sin 2x\, dx$.

(A) $x \cos 2x + C$
(B) $-\frac{1}{2}x^2 \sin 2x + C$
(C) $-\frac{1}{2}x \cos 2x + \frac{1}{4} \sin 2x + C$
(D) $x \cos 2x + \cos 2x + C$

53. Evaluate $\int_0^3 \frac{5x\, dx}{\sqrt{1 + x^2}}$.

(A) $5\sqrt{10} - 5$
(B) 2
(C) $\sqrt{8} - 3$
(D) 0

54. Find the area in the first quadrant bounded by $y^2 = 4x$ and $x = 4$.

(A) 32/3 square units
(B) 16 square units
(C) 8/3 square units
(D) 24 square units

55. Find the volume of the solid generated by revolving about the x-axis the area described in Problem 54.

(A) 16π cubic units
(B) 8π cubic units
(C) 32π cubic units
(D) 48π cubic units

56. Find the first moment with respect to the x-axis of the area described in Problem 54.

(A) 2
(B) 4
(C) 8
(D) 16

57. Solve the differential equation $\frac{dy}{dx} + \frac{y}{x} = 2$.

(A) $y = cx$
(B) $y = \frac{1}{x} + c$
(C) $y = 3x + c$
(D) $y = x + \frac{c}{x}$

58. Solve the differential equation $y'' - y' - 6y = 0$.

(A) $y = c_1e^{3x} + c_2$
(B) $y = c_1e^{3x} + c_2e^{-2x}$
(C) $y = c_1e^{-3x} + c_2e^{-2x}$
(D) $y = c_1e^{-5x} + c_2e^{-x}$

59. Solve the differential equation $y'' + 4y' = 10 \sin 2x$.

(A) $y = c_1 + c_2e^{-4x} + \sin 2x - \cos 2x$
(B) $y = c_1 + c_2e^{-4x} - 0.5 \sin 2x - \cos 2x$
(C) $y = c_1 + c_2e^{-4x}$
(D) $y = c_1 + c_2e^{-4x} + \cos 2x$

60. A weight attached to a spring moves up and down, so that the equation of motion is $\frac{d^2x}{dt^2} + 64x = 0$, where x is the displacement (in feet) of the weight from its equilibrium position at any time t. Suppose that at $t = 0$ sec the displacement is 3 in $[x(0) = 1/4]$ and the velocity is 1 ft/sec $[x'(0) = 1]$. Find the approximate amplitude of the motion.

(A) 1 ft
(B) 0.280 ft
(C) 0.119 ft
(D) 0.521 ft

Answer Key

1. A	13. D	25. B	37. D	49. B
2. B	14. B	26. B	38. D	50. B
3. D	15. B	27. A	39. D	51. D
4. C	16. A	28. D	40. B	52. C
5. B	17. D	29. C	41. A	53. A
6. A	18. A	30. B	42. A	54. A
7. D	19. C	31. A	43. B	55. C
8. C	20. B	32. D	44. C	56. D
9. B	21. A	33. C	45. D	57. D
10. C	22. D	34. B	46. D	58. B
11. A	23. D	35. A	47. B	59. B
12. D	24. A	36. A	48. A	60. B

Answers Explained

1. **A** The length of the sides of the triangle are as follows: $AB = \sqrt{3^2 + 2^2} = \sqrt{13}$, $BC = \sqrt{3^2 + 6^2} = \sqrt{45}$, and $AC = \sqrt{6^2 + 4^2} = \sqrt{52}$. Hence:

Perimeter $P = \sqrt{13} + \sqrt{45} + \sqrt{52} \approx 17.5$ units.

2. **B** Slope $m = \frac{-1 - 5}{4 - 2} = -3$. Hence:

$$y - 5 = -3(x - 2) \quad \text{or} \quad y = -3x + 11$$

3. **D** The given equation is equivalent to $2x^2 - 3x - 5 = 0$ or $(2x - 5)(x + 1) = 0$. Hence, $x = \frac{5}{2}$ or -1.

4. **C** The discriminant $B^2 - 4AC = 1^2 - 4(1)(1) = -3 < 0$. Hence, the graph is an ellipse.

5. **B** The center of this hyperbola is at the origin, and its vertices are on the y-axis with $c = \sqrt{2^2 + 3^2} = \sqrt{13}$. Hence, the coordinates of the foci are $(0, \pm\sqrt{13})$.

6. **A** Using $c = \sqrt{|a^2 - b^2|}$ with $a = 3$ and $c = 2$ implies $b = \pm\sqrt{5}$. Hence, the equation of the ellipse is

$$(x^2/9) + (y^2/5) = 1 \quad \text{or} \quad 5x^2 + 9y^2 = 45$$

7. **D** The equation of the circle is

$$(x + 2)^2 + (y - 5)^2 = 2^2$$
or $$x^2 + y^2 + 4x - 10y + 25 = 0$$

8. **C** Complete the squares to rewrite the equation as $(x - 2)^2 + (y + 1)^2 + (z - 0)^2 = 9$. Hence, the radius of the sphere is $\sqrt{9}$ or 3.

9. **B** To four significant digits, $\log_2 12 = \frac{\ln 12}{\ln 2} \approx 3.585$.

10. **C** Simplify as follows: $e^{2\ln x} = e^{\ln x^2} = x^2$.

11. **A** Rewrite as

$$\ln x^3 - \ln 2 + \ln 4^2 = \ln\left(\frac{4^2 x^3}{2}\right) = \ln 8x^3$$

12. **D** The equation $e^{-7x} = \frac{15}{4}$ implies

$$-7x = \ln\left(\frac{15}{4}\right)$$

or $$x = \frac{\ln\left(\frac{15}{4}\right)}{-7} \approx -0.1888$$

13. **D** That θ is obtuse implies

$$\cos\theta = -\sqrt{1 - \sin^2\theta}$$
$$= -\sqrt{1 - \left(\frac{3}{5}\right)^2} = -\frac{4}{5}$$

Hence:

$$\tan\theta = \frac{\sin\theta}{\cos\theta} = \frac{3/5}{-4/5} = -\frac{3}{4}$$

14. B That $\tan\theta = \frac{12}{18}$ implies $\theta = \tan^{-1}\left(\frac{12}{18}\right) \approx 33.7°$.

15. B Since $\tan 22.7° = 1.2/x$, then $x = \frac{1.2}{\tan 22.7°} \approx 2.87$ km.

16. A By the law of sines, $\frac{12.5}{\sin 101°} = \frac{x}{\sin 32°}$. Hence, $x = \frac{12.5 \sin 32°}{\sin 101°} \approx 6.75$ m.

17. D By the law of cosines,

$$92^2 = 196^2 + 212^2 - 2(196)(212)\cos\theta$$

Hence:

$$\theta = \cos^{-1}\left(\frac{92^2 - 196^2 - 212^2}{-2(196)(212)}\right) \approx 25.7°$$

18. A That θ is acute implies

$$\cos\theta = \sqrt{1 - \sin^2 x} = \sqrt{1 - \left(\frac{3}{5}\right)^2} = \frac{4}{5}$$

Hence:

$$\cos 2\theta = \cos^2\theta - \sin^2\theta = \left(\frac{4}{5}\right)^2 - \left(\frac{3}{5}\right)^2 = \frac{7}{25}$$

19. C Here:

$$(\sin x + \cos x)^2 = \sin^2 x + 2\sin x\cos x + \cos^2 x = 1 + 2\sin x\cos x$$

and

$$(\sin x - \cos x)^2 = \sin^2 x - 2\sin x\cos x + \cos^2 x = 1 - 2\sin x\cos x$$

Hence, the sum of these two expressions is 2.

20. B In terms of the first power of the cosine function,

$$\cos^2 3x = \frac{1}{2}(1 + \cos[2(3x)]) = \frac{1 + \cos 6x}{2}$$

21. A Since $r = \sqrt{2.65^2 + 7.91^2} \approx 8.34$ and $\theta = \tan^{-1}\left(\frac{7.91}{2.65}\right) \approx 1.25$ rad, then $2.65 + 7.91i \approx 8.34e^{1.25i}$.

22. D The rectangular form is as follows:

$$\frac{1-2i}{1+2i} \cdot \frac{1-2i}{1-2i} = \frac{1 - 4i + 4i^2}{1 - 4i^2} = \frac{-3-4i}{5} = -0.6 - 0.8i$$

23. D Since $\sqrt{2} + i\sqrt{2} = 2e^{(\pi/4)i}$, then:

$$(5e^{(17\pi/12)i})(2e^{(\pi/4)i}) = 10e^{[(17\pi/12)+(\pi/4)]i} = 10e^{(5\pi/3)i}$$

24. A In rectangular form,

$$(1+i)^8 = (\sqrt{2}\,e^{(\pi/4)i})^8 = 16e^{2\pi i} = 16$$

25. B
$$3A - 2B = \begin{bmatrix} -3 & 3 \\ 3 & -3 \end{bmatrix} + \begin{bmatrix} -10 & -10 \\ 4 & 4 \end{bmatrix} = \begin{bmatrix} -13 & -7 \\ 7 & 1 \end{bmatrix}$$

26. B
$$BA = \begin{bmatrix} 5 & 5 \\ -2 & -2 \end{bmatrix}\begin{bmatrix} -1 & 1 \\ 1 & -1 \end{bmatrix} = \begin{bmatrix} -5+5 & 5-5 \\ 2-2 & -2+2 \end{bmatrix} = \begin{bmatrix} 0 & 0 \\ 0 & 0 \end{bmatrix}$$

27. A
$$\begin{vmatrix} -3 & 4 \\ 1 & 9 \end{vmatrix} = -27 - 4 = -31$$

28. D Expand about the first row; then:

$$|A| = 1\begin{vmatrix} -3 & 4 \\ 1 & 9 \end{vmatrix} + 2\begin{vmatrix} 2 & -3 \\ -3 & 1 \end{vmatrix} = -31 + 2(-7) = -45$$

29. C $|A| = 3 - 8 = -5$, $A^T = \begin{bmatrix} 1 & 2 \\ 4 & 3 \end{bmatrix}$, and $\text{adj}(A) = \begin{bmatrix} 3 & -4 \\ -2 & 1 \end{bmatrix}$. Hence:

$$A^{-1} = \frac{\text{adj}(A)}{|A|} = \frac{1}{5}\begin{bmatrix} -3 & 4 \\ 2 & -1 \end{bmatrix}$$

30. B
$$\begin{bmatrix} x \\ y \\ z \end{bmatrix} = \begin{bmatrix} 1 & -1 & 1 \\ 2 & 1 & 0 \\ 0 & 1 & -3 \end{bmatrix}^{-1}\begin{bmatrix} -3 \\ 1 \\ 7 \end{bmatrix} = \frac{1}{7}\begin{bmatrix} 3 & 2 & 1 \\ -6 & 3 & -2 \\ -2 & 1 & -3 \end{bmatrix}\begin{bmatrix} -3 \\ 1 \\ 7 \end{bmatrix} = \begin{bmatrix} 0 \\ 1 \\ -2 \end{bmatrix}$$

Hence, the solution of the system of equations is $x = 0$, $y = 1$, and $z = -2$.

31. A $|\mathbf{A}| = \sqrt{1^2 + (-2)^2 + 3^2} = \sqrt{14}$.

32. D $\mathbf{A} \cdot \mathbf{B} = (2)(-4) + (1)(3) + (1)(1) = -4$.

33. C $\mathbf{A} \times \mathbf{B} = \begin{vmatrix} \mathbf{i} & \mathbf{j} & \mathbf{k} \\ 2 & 1 & 1 \\ -4 & 3 & 1 \end{vmatrix}$

$$= \mathbf{i}\begin{vmatrix} 1 & 1 \\ 3 & 1 \end{vmatrix} - \mathbf{j}\begin{vmatrix} 2 & 1 \\ -4 & 1 \end{vmatrix} + \mathbf{k}\begin{vmatrix} 2 & 1 \\ -4 & 3 \end{vmatrix}$$

$$= -2\mathbf{i} - 6\mathbf{j} + 10\mathbf{k}$$

34. B $\overrightarrow{PQ} = \mathbf{i} + \mathbf{j} + \mathbf{k}$ and $\overrightarrow{PR} = \mathbf{i} + \mathbf{j}$. Hence:

$$\overrightarrow{PQ} \times \overrightarrow{PR} = \begin{vmatrix} \mathbf{i} & \mathbf{j} & \mathbf{k} \\ 1 & 1 & 1 \\ 1 & 1 & 0 \end{vmatrix} = -\mathbf{i} + \mathbf{k}.$$

Therefore:

$$\text{Area} = \frac{1}{2}|\overrightarrow{PQ} \times \overrightarrow{PR}| = \frac{\sqrt{2}}{2} \text{ square units}$$

35. A In the given sequence,

$$a_{10} = 11 + (10 - 1)(-7) = -52$$

36. A $S_{58} = \frac{58}{2}[2(2) + 57(-5)] = -8{,}149$

37. D $S = \frac{0.04}{1 - (-0.2)} = \frac{1}{30}$

38. D Here, $f(x) = \sin x$, $f'(x) = \cos x$, $f''(x) = -\sin x$, $f'''(x) = -\cos x$, etc. Hence:

$$\sin x = f(0) + f'(0)x + \frac{f''(0)}{2!}x^2 + \frac{f'''(0)}{3!}x^3 + \cdots$$

$$= x - \frac{x^3}{3!} + \frac{x^5}{5!} - \cdots$$

39. D $P(\text{head and ace}) = P(\text{head}) \cdot P(\text{ace})$

$$= \frac{1}{2} \bullet \frac{1}{13} = \frac{1}{26}$$

40. B The number of possibilities is $5! = 120$.

41. A $P(2 \text{ girls}) = \frac{[C(4,2) \bullet C(5,1)]}{C(9,3)}$

$$= \frac{(6)(5)}{84} = \frac{5}{14}$$

42. A Here,

$$\bar{x} = \frac{13 + 19 + 12 + 15 + 16 + 12 + 15 + 19 + 14 + 15}{10}$$

$$= 15$$

43. B At any time t, $v = \frac{ds}{dt} = 24 - 1.6t$ m/s.

44. C Here, $\frac{dy}{dx} = 2x - 3$. At $x = 2$ and $y = 2$, $\frac{dy}{dx} = 1$. Hence:

$$y - 2 = 1(x - 2) \quad \text{or} \quad y = x$$

45. D By L'Hôpital's rule,

$$\lim_{x \to 0}\left(\frac{\cos x - 1}{\cos 2x - 1}\right) = \lim_{x \to 0}\left(\frac{-\sin x}{-2 \sin 2x}\right)$$

$$= \lim_{x \to 0}\left(\frac{-\cos x}{-4 \cos 2x}\right) = \frac{1}{4}$$

46. D Use implicit differentiation: $2x + 2y\frac{dy}{dx} = 0$ implies $\frac{dy}{dx} = \frac{-x}{y}$. At $(3,-4)$, $\frac{dy}{dx} = \frac{3}{4}$. Hence, the slope of the normal is $\frac{-4}{3}$. Thus, the equation of the normal is

$$y + 4 = -\frac{4}{3}(x - 3) \quad \text{or} \quad y = -\frac{4}{3}x$$

47. B For the given equation,

$$\frac{\partial z}{\partial x} = (2x)y^2 + (2e^{2x})y^3 = 2xy^2 + 2y^3e^{2x}$$

48. A Here, $y'' = 6x + 12 = 0$ implies $x = -2$ and $y = 16$. Since y'' changes sign as x increases through -2, $(-2,16)$ is a point of inflection.

49. B The equation of the semicircle is $y = \sqrt{36 - x^2}$. Hence, the area A of the inscribed rectangle is $A = 2x\sqrt{36 - x^2}$. Then:

$$\frac{dA}{dx} = \frac{-2x^2}{(36 - x^2)^{1/2}} + 2(36 - x^2)^{1/2} = 0$$

which implies $x = 3\sqrt{2}$ and $y = 3\sqrt{2}$. Therefore, the dimensions of the rectangle with greatest area are $6\sqrt{2}$ cm by $3\sqrt{2}$ cm.

50. **B** Here, $dy = (4x - 6)dx$ implies $y = 2x^2 - 6x + C$. If $x = 1$ and $y = 2$, then $C = 6$. Hence, $y = 2x^2 - 6x + 6$.

51. **D** Here, $\int \frac{4}{2x-1}dx = 2\ln|2x - 1| + C$

$$= \ln(2x-1)^2 + C$$

52. **C** Use integration by parts with $u = x$, $du = dx$, $dv = \sin 2x\,dx$, and $v = -\frac{1}{2}\cos 2x$:

$$\int x \sin 2x\,dx = -\frac{1}{2}x\cos 2x + \frac{1}{2}\int \cos 2x\,dx$$

$$= -\frac{1}{2}x\cos 2x + \frac{1}{4}\sin 2x + C$$

53. **A** Here, $5\int_0^3 x(1 + x^2)^{-1/2}\,dx = \frac{5}{2}\int u^{-1/2}\,du = 5(1 + x^2)^{1/2}\Big|_0^3 = 5\sqrt{10} - 5$.

54. **A** Area $= \int_0^4 2x^{1/2}\,dx = \frac{4}{3}x^{3/2}\Big|_0^4 = \frac{32}{3}$ square units.

55. **C** Volume $= \pi\int_0^4 (2x^{1/2})^2\,dx$

$$= \pi\int_0^4 4x\,dx$$

$$= \pi(2x^2)\Big|_0^4 = 32\pi \text{ cubic units.}$$

56. **D** $M_x = \int_0^4 y\left(4 - \frac{1}{4}y^2\right)dy = \int_0^4 (4y - \frac{1}{4}y^3)\,dy$

$$= 2y^2 - \frac{1}{16}y^4\Big|_0^4 = 16.$$

57. **D** The given equation is linear in y with integrating factor $e^{\int(1/x)\,dx} = e^{\ln x} = x$. Hence:

$$yx = \int 2x\,dx + c \quad \text{or} \quad y = x + \frac{c}{x}$$

58. **B** The solutions of the auxiliary equation $m^2 - m - 6 = 0$ are 3 and -2. Hence, $y = c_1e^{3x} + c_2e^{-2x}$.

59. **B** The solutions of the auxiliary equation $m^2 + 4m = 0$ are 0 and -4. Hence, $y_c = c_1 + c_2e^{-4x}$. Substitute $y_p = A\sin 2x + B\cos 2x$ into $y'' + 4y' = 10\sin 2x$ to obtain

$$-4A\sin 2x - 4B\cos 2x + 4(2A\cos 2x - 2B\sin 2x) = 10\sin 2x$$

which implies $A = -\frac{1}{2}$ and $B = -1$. Hence:

$$y = c_1 + c_2e^{-4x} - 0.5\sin 2x - \cos 2x$$

60. **B** The solutions of the auxiliary equation $m^2 + 64 = 0$ are $\pm 8i$. Hence, $x = c_1\cos 8t + c_2\sin 8t$ with $x(0) = \frac{1}{4}$, and $x' = -8c_1\sin 8t + 8c_2\cos 8t$ with $x'(0) = 1$ implies $c_1 = \frac{1}{4}$ and $c_2 = \frac{1}{8}$.

Therefore, $x = \frac{1}{4}\cos 8t + \frac{1}{8}\sin 8t$, and amplitude of motion $=$

$$\sqrt{\left(\frac{1}{4}\right)^2 + \left(\frac{1}{8}\right)^2} \approx 0.280 \text{ ft}$$

CHAPTER

10

Mechanics of Materials

Masoud Olia, Ph.D., PE

Introduction

Mechanics of materials is the branch of mechanics that relates external loads applied to a body in equilibrium to internal forces and the subsequent deformation of the body. In this chapter the concepts of stress and strain and their relationship are introduced. The deformation of axially loaded members is presented. The torsion and the bending of structural members are analyzed. Structures under combined loading, as well as the design of columns, are discussed.

10.1 Normal Stress

Consider a bar with constant cross-sectional area (prismatic) under the action of a constant force that is applied at the centroid of the bar. The stress is defined as the load, P, divided by the area (load per unit area), A, and is called normal stress, denoted by σ. If the bar is in tension, the stress is called tensile stress; if the bar is compressed, the stress is called compressive stress. Stress has units of pounds per square inch (lb/in^2 or psi) in the English system and newtons per square meter (N/m^2) or pascals (Pa) in the metric system.

$$\sigma = \frac{P}{A}$$

$$\sigma_t = \text{tensile stress } (+) \qquad [10.1]$$

$$\sigma_c = \text{compressive stress } (-)$$

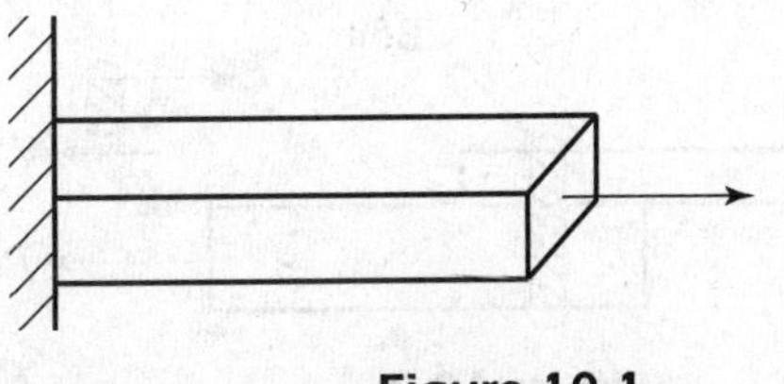

Figure 10.1

Example 10.1

For the composite bar shown below, determine the normal stress in each section.

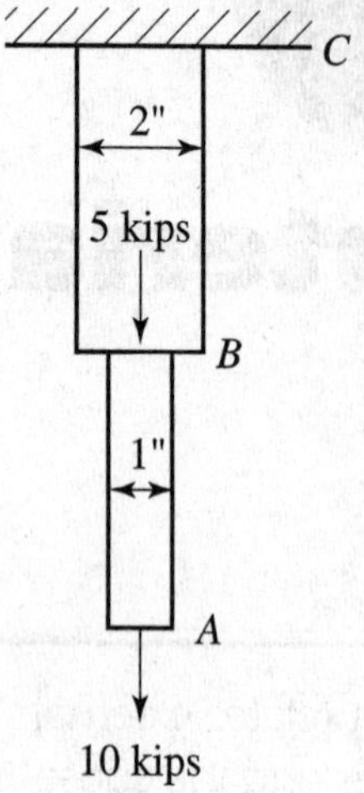

Figure 10.2

Solution:

$$\sigma_{AB} = \frac{10}{\frac{\pi}{4}(1)^2} = 12.73 \text{ ksi (tensile)}$$

$$\sigma_{BC} = \frac{15}{\frac{\pi}{4}(2)^2} = 4.77 \text{ ksi (tensile)}$$

10.2 Shear Stress

If two plates are bolted or glued to each other, the stress parallel to the area of contact, A_s, is called the shear stress and is denoted by τ.

$$\tau = \frac{V}{A_s} \qquad [10.2]$$

where V = shear load,

A_s = shear area.

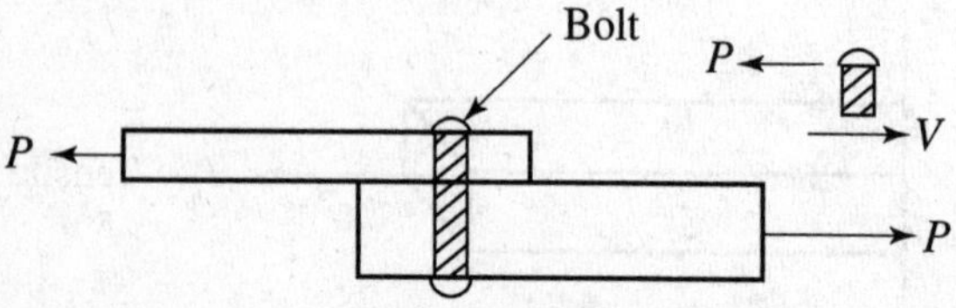

Figure 10.3

Example 10.2

If the allowable shearing stress in the bolt shown below is 350 MPa, determine the minimum diameter of the bolt.

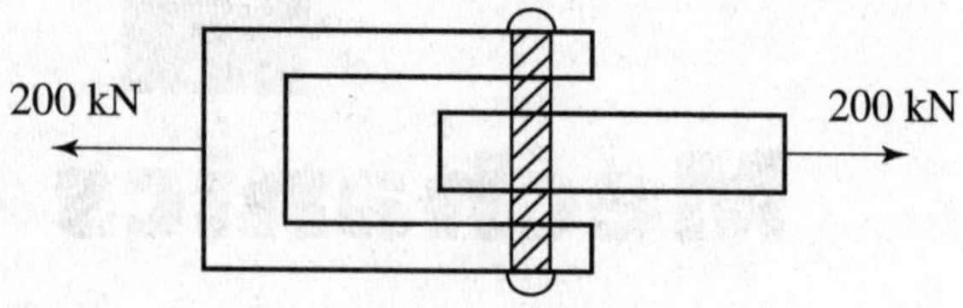

Figure 10.4

Solution:

This is a case of double shear.

$$V = \frac{P}{2} = \frac{200}{2} = 100 \text{ kN}$$

$$\tau = \frac{V}{A_s}, \ A_s = \frac{V}{\tau_{\text{all}}} = \frac{100 \times 10^3}{350 \times 10^6} = 2.857 \times 10^{-4}$$

$$d = \sqrt{\frac{4A_s}{\pi}} = \sqrt{\frac{4(2.857 \times 10^{-4})}{\pi}} = 0.01907 \text{ m}$$

10.3 Normal Strain

Consider again a prismatic bar under the action of a tensile load. The initial length of the bar is l, and after the load is applied the bar elongates by δ. Normal strain is defined as the ratio of change in length to initial length and is denoted by ε. If the bar is in tension, the strain is called tensile strain. If the bar is in compression, the strain is called compressive strain. Note that strain is dimensionless.

$$\varepsilon = \frac{\delta}{\ell}$$

ε_t = tensile strain [10.3]

ε_c = compressive strain

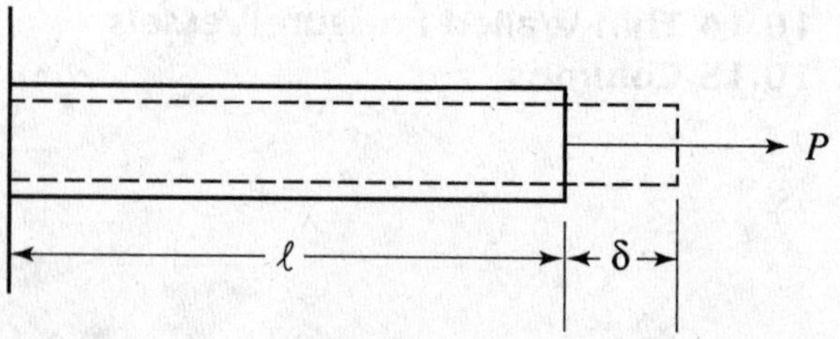

Figure 10.5

10.4 Shear Strain

Consider the stress element under the action of the shear stresses shown in the drawing below. The shear stress on each side (face) must be the same in order for the stress element to remain in equilibrium. Shear strain, denoted by γ, is defined as the change in the angle between two sides of the stress element from the 90-degree initial angle. Shear strain is a measure of distortion of the element under the action of shear stresses. Shear strain is dimensionless, and its unit must be radians.

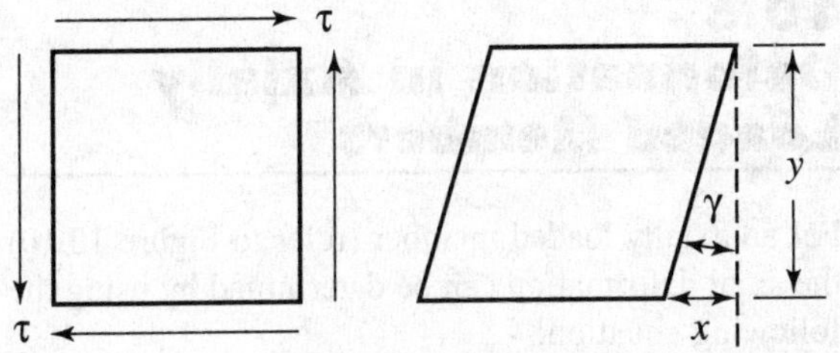

Figure 10.6

$$\tan \gamma \approx \gamma = \frac{x}{y} \qquad [10.5]$$

10.5 The Relationship of Stress and Strain

The relationship of elastic stress to elastic strain is based on a law known as Hooke's law:

$$\sigma = E\varepsilon \qquad [10.6]$$

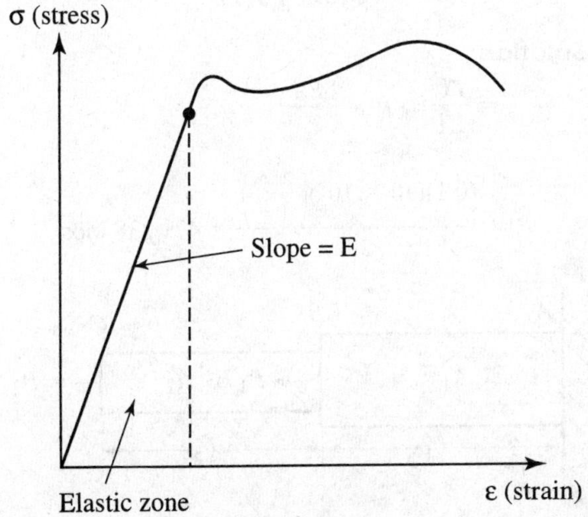

Figure 10.7

Here, E is a material property known as the modulus of elasticity or Young's modulus. For example, E for structural steel is about 30×10^6 psi or 200 GPa. If the relationship between stress and strain is represented graphically, then E is the slope of the straight line in the linear zone.

Hooke's law can be applied to a member in pure shear (i.e., a shaft being twisted) and relates shear stress, τ, to shear strain, γ:

$$\tau = G\gamma \qquad [10.7]$$

where G is a material property known as modulus of rigidity.

Example 10.3

For the rectangular block shown below, $G = 500$ MPa. If the lower plate is fixed and the upper plate moves through 0.7 mm as a result of applied force P, determine the value of force P.

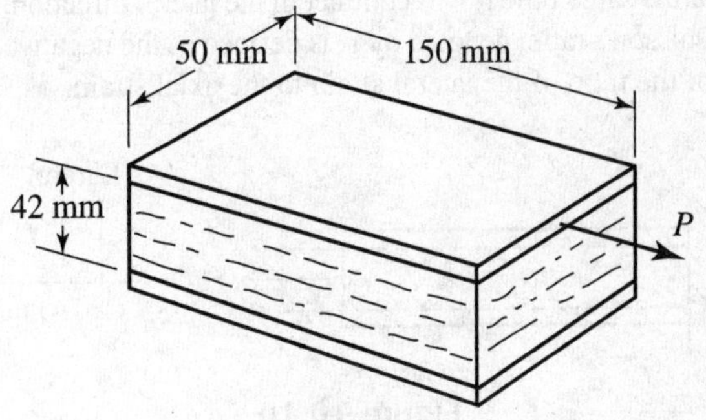

Figure 10.8

Solution:

$$\gamma = \frac{0.7 \text{ mm}}{42 \text{ mm}} = 0.0166 \text{ rad}$$

$$\tau = G\gamma = (500 \text{ MPa})(0.0166) = 8.3 \text{ MPa}$$

$$\tau = \frac{V}{A} = \frac{P}{A} \Rightarrow P = \tau A$$

$$P = (8.3 \times 10^6)(0.05 \times 0.15) = 62{,}250 \text{ N}$$

10.6 Thermal Strain

If a bar is constrained, as the temperature changes the bar will deform. The strain due to change in temperature is called thermal strain.

$$\varepsilon_T = \alpha \Delta T \qquad [10.8]$$

Here, α is the coefficient of thermal expansion, with units of 1/°F or 1/°C, and is defined as the strain

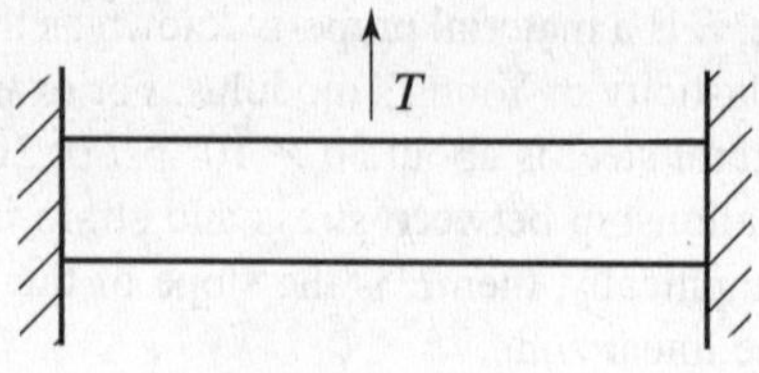

Figure 10.9

due to a 1-degree change in temperature. Note that α, like E and G, is a material property.

10.7 Poisson's Ratio

Consider a bar under the action of a load. The direction of the load is axial direction, and perpendicular to the axial direction is lateral direction. When the load is applied, the bar will elongate in the axial direction, but at the same time it will contract in the lateral direction. Poisson's ratio, denoted by ν, is defined as the negative of the ratio of the lateral strain to the axial strain.

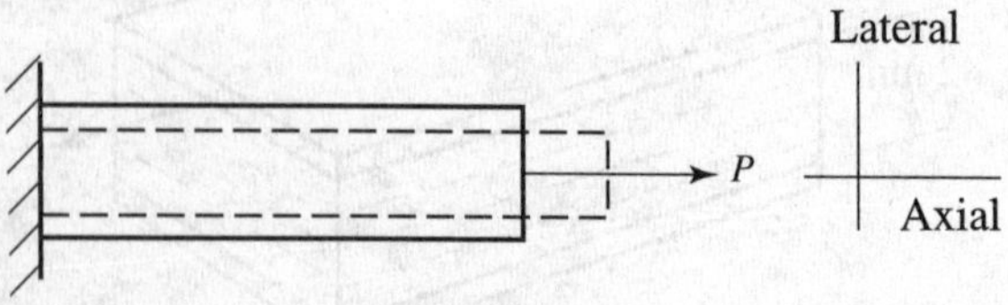

Figure 10.10

$$\nu = -\frac{\varepsilon_{\text{lateral}}}{\varepsilon_{\text{axial}}} \qquad [10.9]$$

The three properties E, G, and ν are related to each other as follows:

$$G = \frac{E}{2(1+\nu)} \qquad [10.10]$$

Example 10.4

The plastic rod shown below is 150 mm long and 12 mm in diameter. Determine the change in length and the change in diameter that occur when a 400-N load is applied if, for the plastic, E =2.5 GPa and ν = 0.4.

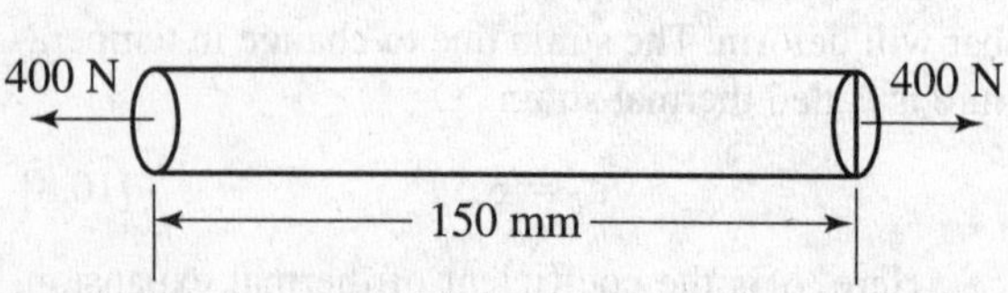

Figure 10.11

Solution:

$$\sigma = E\varepsilon_{\text{axial}}$$

$$\varepsilon_{\text{axial}} = \frac{\sigma}{E} = \frac{P}{EA} = \frac{400}{\frac{\pi}{4}(0.012)^2(2.5 \times 10^9)} = 0.0044$$

$$\delta = \ell\varepsilon_{\text{axial}} = 0.666\text{-mm increase in length}$$

$$\varepsilon_{\text{lateral}} = -\nu\varepsilon_{\text{axial}} = -0.4(0.0044) = -0.00177$$

$$\Delta d = d\varepsilon_{\text{lateral}} = (12\text{ mm})(-0.00177)$$

$$\Delta d = -0.0213\text{-mm decrease in diameter}$$

10.8 Deformation in Axially Loaded Members

For an axially loaded member (refer to Figure 10.10) the axial deformation can be determined by using the following equation:

$$\delta = \frac{P\ell}{EA} \qquad [10.11]$$

Example 10. 5

The circular steel rod (E = 30 × 10^6 psi) shown in Figure 10.12, which is 2 inches in diameter, is loaded axially. Determine the load P that causes a deformation of 0.1 in in the rod.

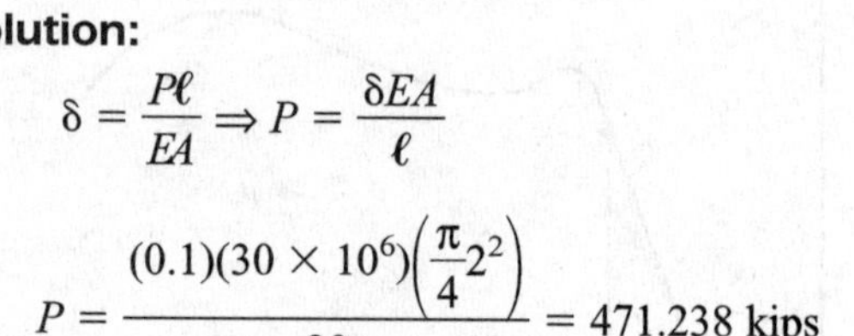

Figure 10.12

Solution:

$$\delta = \frac{P\ell}{EA} \Rightarrow P = \frac{\delta EA}{\ell}$$

$$P = \frac{(0.1)(30 \times 10^6)\left(\frac{\pi}{4}2^2\right)}{20} = 471.238 \text{ kips}$$

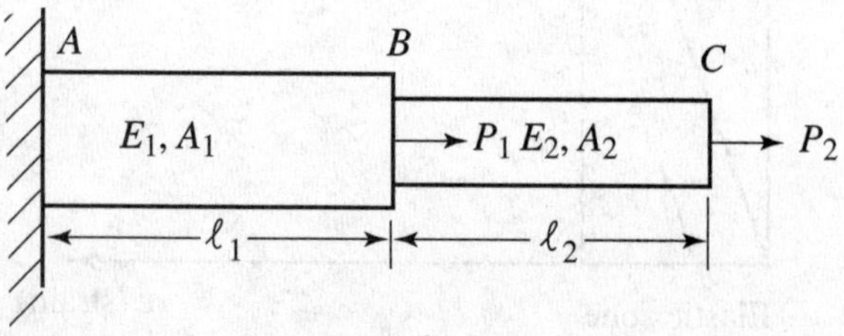

Figure 10.13

For a composite structure (stepped shaft), the summation form of the equation can be used to determine the total axial deformation.

$$\delta = \Sigma \frac{P\ell}{EA} \qquad [10.12]$$

Example 10.6

Using Figure 10.13, determine the total elongation of the stepped shaft for the following values:

$P_1 = 10$ kips, $P_2 = 5$ kips

$E_1 = E_2 = 30 \times 10^6$ psi

$d_1 = 2$ in, $d_2 = 1$ in

$\ell_1 = 20$ in, $\ell_2 = 15$ in

Solution:

$$\delta = \Sigma \frac{P\ell}{EA} = \left(\frac{P\ell}{EA}\right)_{AB} + \left(\frac{P\ell}{EA}\right)_{BC}$$

$$\delta = \left(\frac{(15 \times 10^3)(20)}{(30 \times 10^6)\left(\frac{\pi}{4}2^2\right)}\right) + \left(\frac{(5 \times 10^3)(15)}{(30 \times 10^6)\left(\frac{\pi}{4}1^2\right)}\right)$$

$$= 0.006366 \text{ in}$$

10.9 Torsion

If a straight bar with constant circular cross section (i.e., shaft) is fixed at one end and is twisted by a torque at the other end, such a member is said to be in pure torsion.

When the shaft is twisted, shear stresses are developed throughout the shaft as a result. The shear stress varies as a function of radial distance, r, and is maximum at the surface when r is maximum (i.e., $r = c$).

$$\tau = \frac{Tr}{J}, \quad \tau_{max} = \frac{Tc}{J} \qquad [10.13]$$

Here, J is called the polar moment of inertia; for a circular cross section (shaft) $J = \pi d^4/32$ or $J =$

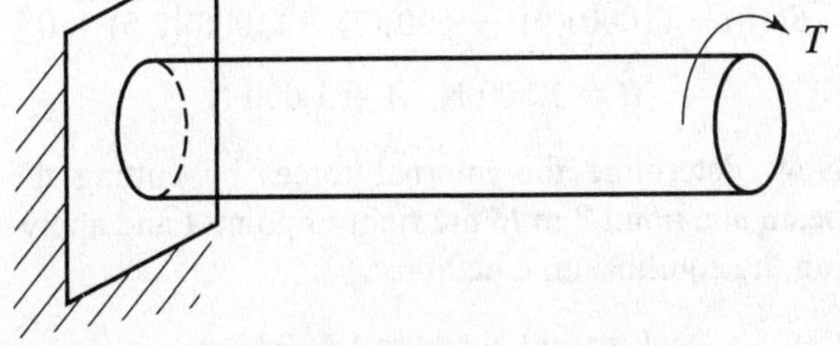

Figure 10.14

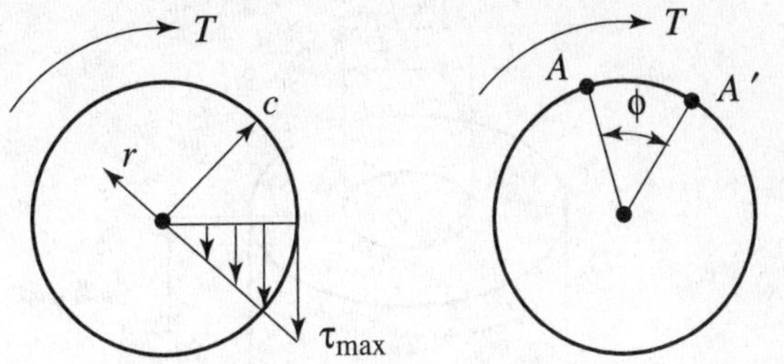

Figure 10.15

$\pi c^4/2$ and has units of inch^4 or meter^4. (Refer to Table 2 in Chapter 11 for formulas to determine J.)

Twisting will also cause the shaft to deform (distortion). The angle of twist, (ϕ), for a shaft of length L, under the action of torque T, is given by the equation

$$\phi = \frac{TL}{GJ} \qquad [10.14]$$

Here G is the shear modulus (material property), and ϕ is dimensionless and should be expressed in radians.

Note that for a hollow shaft the polar moment of inertia, J, is given by

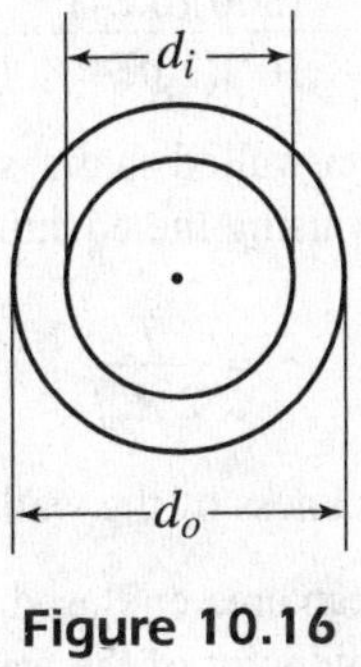

Figure 10.16

$$J = \frac{\pi(d_o^{\,4} - d_i^{\,4})}{32}, \quad J = \frac{\pi(c_o^{\,4} - c_i^{\,4})}{2} \qquad [10.15]$$

where d_o and c_o are the outside diameter and radius, respectively, and d_i and c_i are the inside diameter and radius, respectively.

Example 10.7

For the hollow cylinder shown in Figure 10.17, determine the torque, T, that causes a maximum shearing stress of 400 MPa.

Solution:

$$J = \frac{\pi(d_o^{\,4} - d_i^{\,4})}{32} = \frac{\pi(2^4 - 1.5^4)}{32}$$

$$J = 1.074 \text{ cm}^4 = 1.074 \times 10^{-8} \text{ m}^4$$

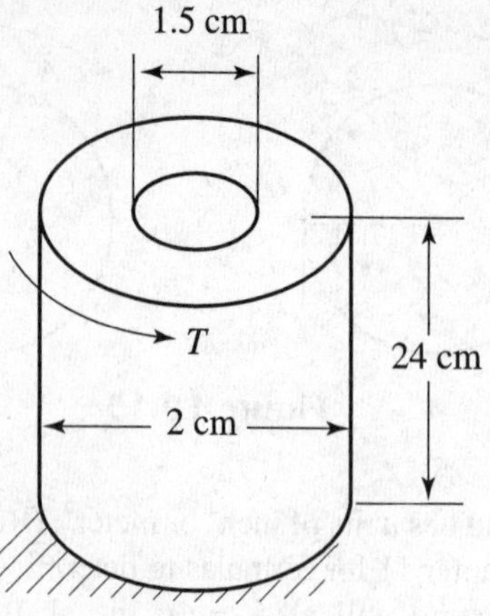

Figure 10.17

$$\tau_{max} = \frac{Tc_o}{J} \Rightarrow T = \frac{\tau_{max}J}{c_o}$$

$$T = \frac{(400 \times 10^6)(1.074 \times 10^{-8})}{0.01} = 429.6 \text{ N}\cdot\text{m}$$

Example 10.8

Using Figure 10.17, determine the angle of twist for $T = 500$ N · m and $G = 100$ GPa.

Solution:

$$\phi = \frac{TL}{GJ} = \frac{(500)(0.24)}{(100 \times 10^9)(1.074 \times 10^{-8})} = 0.11 \text{ rad}$$

For hollow, thin-walled shafts, shear stress can be determined by using the equation

$$\tau = \frac{T}{2A_m t} \qquad [10.16]$$

where t = thickness of the wall,

A_m = total mean area enclosed by the shaft measured to the midpoint of the wall.

10.10 Bending

A beam is defined as a long, prismatical structure designed to support loads at various points along the member. In most cases, the loads are applied perpendicularly to the axis of the beam and cause only shear and bending in the beam.

Internal Forces

Consider the simply supported beam shown in Figure 10.18.

If the beam is cut at a certain section, it is observed that, for the left or right section to be in

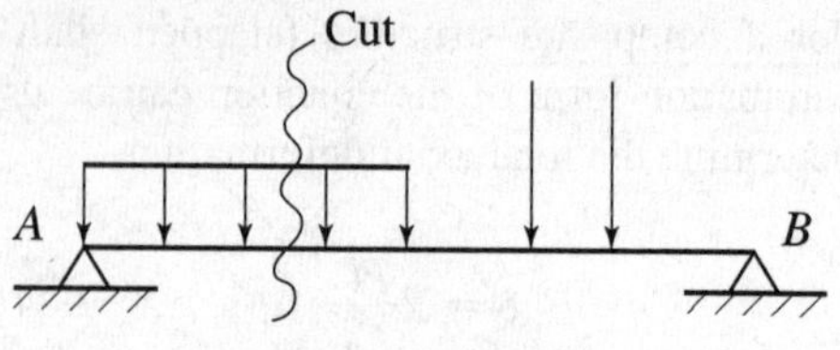

Figure 10.18

equilibrium, a shear load, V, and a bending moment, M, must be present at that section. The shear load and the bending moment are called internal forces. Note in Figure 10.19 that the directions of V and M for the left and right sections of the beam are indicated by the sign conventions used for positive shear and positive moment.

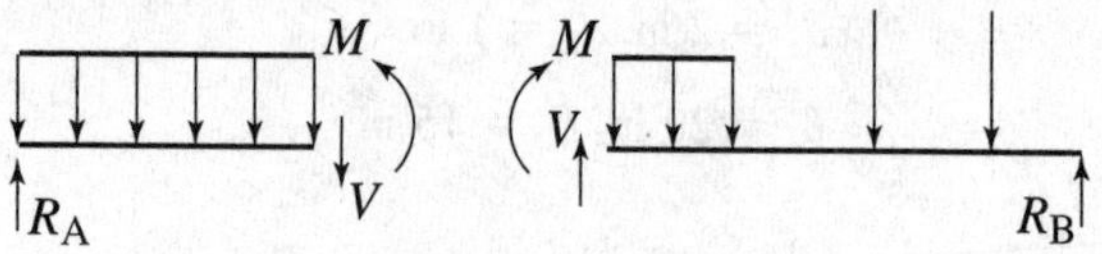

Figure 10.19

To determine the internal forces, do the following:

1. *Determine the reactions at the supports.*
2. *Cut the section where the internal forces are to be calculated, and draw the free-body diagram.*
3. *Use equilibrium equations to determine the internal forces.*

Note that the result is the same regardless of the section (right or left) used.

Example 10.9

For the beam shown below, determine the shear force and the bending moment at a point 2 m to the right of point A.

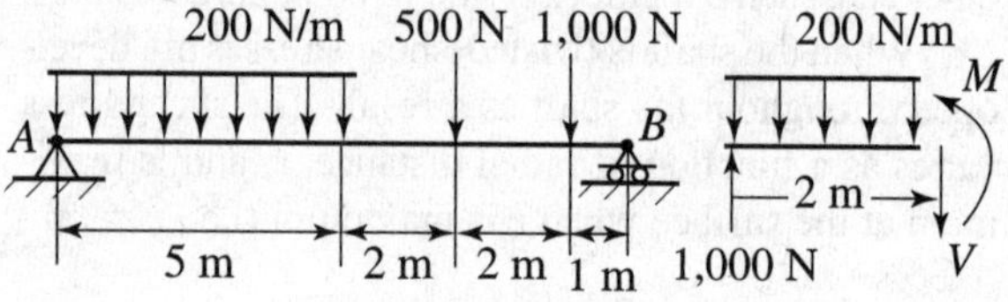

Figure 10.20

Solution:

First, calculate the reactions:

$$\Sigma M_A = 0$$

$$B(10) - (1000)(9) - (500)(7) - (1000)(2.5) = 0$$

$$B = 1{,}500 \text{ N}, \; A = 1{,}000 \text{ N}$$

Now, determine the internal forces by cutting the beam at a point 2 m to the right of point A and applying the equilibrium equations:

$$V = 600 \text{ N}, \; M = 1{,}600 \text{ N}\cdot\text{m}$$

Shear and Bending-Moment Diagrams

Since determination of maximum shear and bending moment is important in design, it is more convenient to plot shear and bending moment along the beam than to cut many sections to calculate these values. The graphs obtained are called the shear diagram and the bending-moment diagram, respectively.

Drawing Shear and Bending-Moment Diagrams

The following relations hold:

$$\frac{dV}{dx} = -w, \qquad \int_{V_1}^{V_2} dV = -\int_{x_1}^{x_2} w dx \quad [10.17]$$

where w is the distributed load acting on the beam.
Net shear force = −(area under distributed load from x_1 to x_2)

$$\frac{dM}{dx} = V, \qquad \int_{M_1}^{M_2} dM = -\int_{x_1}^{x_2} V dx \quad [10.18]$$

Net bending moment = (area under shear load from x_1 to x_2)

Example 10.10

Draw the shear and bending-moment diagrams for the beam shown.

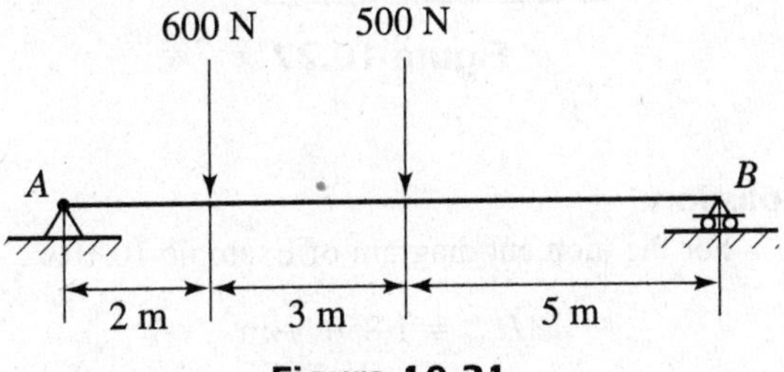

Figure 10.21

Solution:

First, determine the reactions.

$$\Sigma M_A = 0$$

$$B(10) - 500(5) - 600(2) = 370 \text{ N.}$$

$$\Sigma F_y = 0$$

$$A + B - 500 - 600 = 0$$

$$A = 730 \text{ N}$$

Then draw the diagrams.

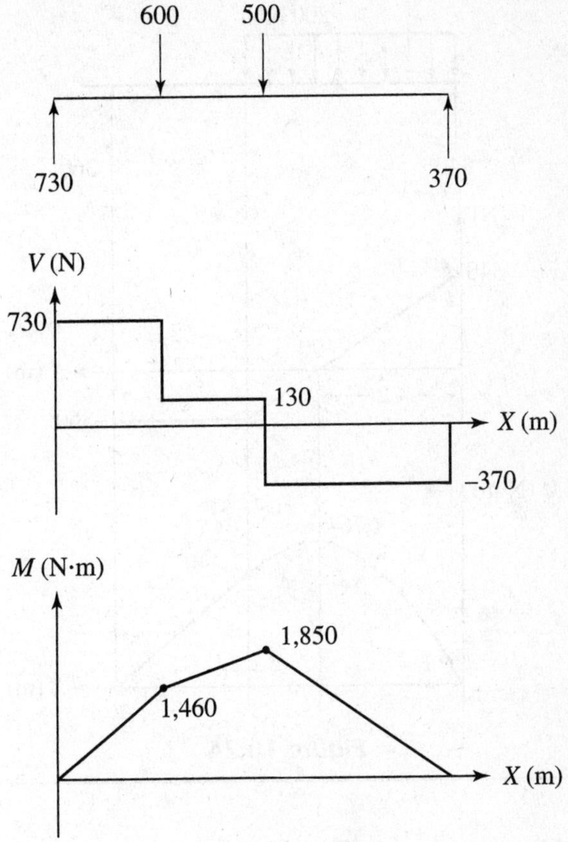

Figure 10.22

Example 10.11

Draw the shear and bending-moment diagrams for the beam shown.

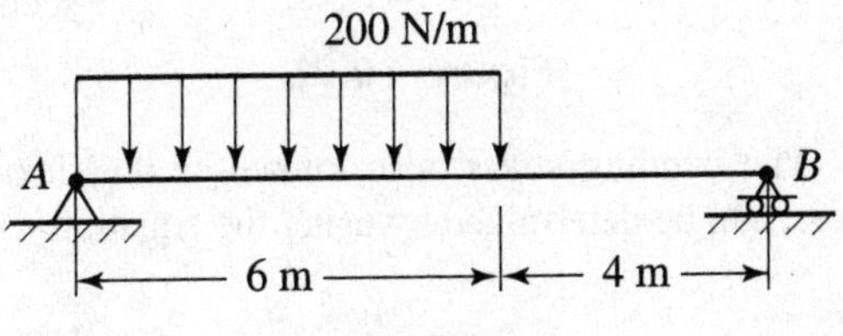

Figure 10.23

Solution:

First, determine the reactions.

$$\Sigma M_A = 0$$

$$B(10) - (200)(6)(3) = 0 \Rightarrow B = 360 \text{ N}$$

$$\Sigma F_y = 0$$

$$A + B - 200(6) = 0$$

$$A = 840 \text{ N}$$

Then draw the diagrams.

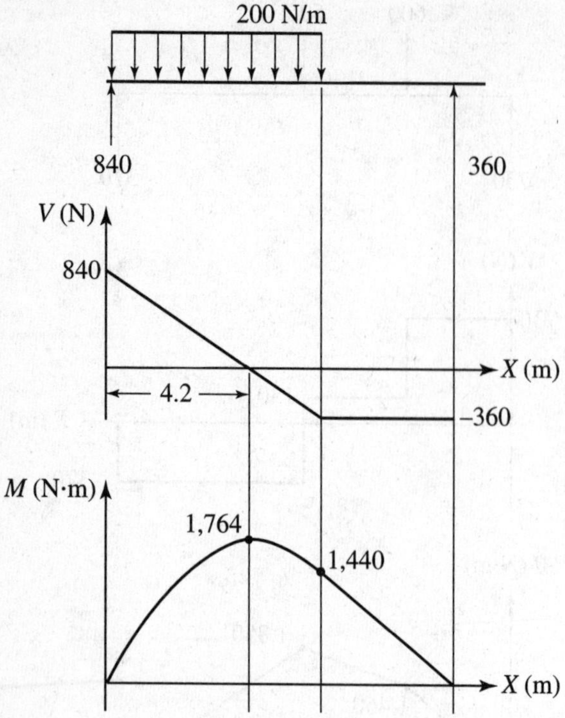

Figure 10.24

Stresses Due to Bending

Consider a prismatic beam that is bent under the action of applied loads, as shown below.

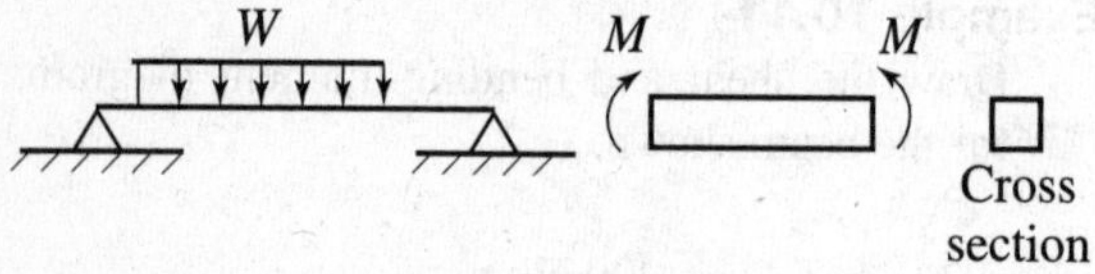

Figure 10.25

The bending stress, also known as the flexural stress, can be determined by using the equation

$$\sigma = \frac{My}{I} \qquad [10.19]$$

where σ = bending (flexural) stress,
M = bending moment at a given point,
y = distance from the centroid (neutral axis) to the point where the stress is to be calculated,
I = area moment of inertia with respect to the axis of bending through the centroid.

The maximum bending stress can be determined by using the equation

$$\sigma_{\max} = \frac{Mc}{I} \qquad [10.20]$$

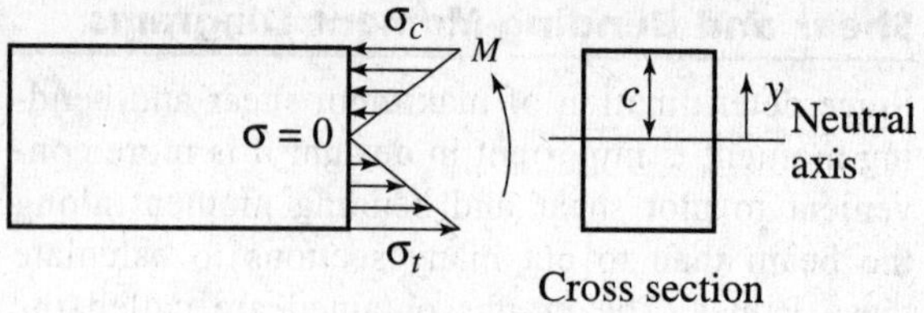

Figure 10.26

where c is the perpendicular distance from the neutral axis to a point farthest away from the neutral axis (top or bottom fiber).

Note that the stress distribution along the cross section is linear and the stress is zero at the centroid (neutral axis).

Example 10.12

Determine the maximum bending stress for the beam and loading of Example 10.10 with the cross section shown below.

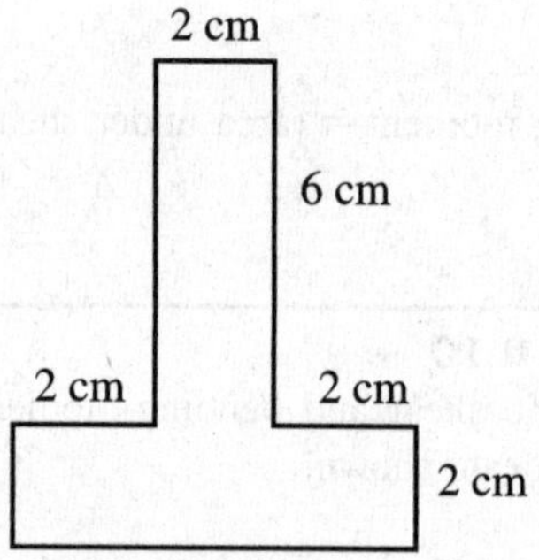

Figure 10.27

Solution:

For the moment diagram of Example 10.10,

$$M_{\max} = 1{,}850 \text{ N}\cdot\text{m}$$

To determine the maximum bending stress, first determine the area moment of inertia with respect to the neutral axis (refer to Example 11.24 in Chapter 11):

$$I = 100 \text{ cm}^4$$

Then calculate the maximum stress:

$$\sigma_{\max} = \frac{M_{\max}C}{I} = \frac{(1{,}850)(0.05)}{100 \times 10^{-8}} = 92.5 \text{ MPa}$$

Note that this is the maximum compressive stress that occurs at the top fiber.

10.11 Transverse Shear Stress

The stress developed in a structure as a result of a shear force, V, is called transverse shear stress and is denoted by τ.

$$\tau = \frac{VQ}{It} \qquad [10.21]$$

where V = shear force at a given point,

Q = first moment of area with respect to the neutral axis $= \Sigma y A = \int y dA$,

I = area moment of inertia with respect to the neutral axis,

t = thickness of beam at position y for which the shear stress is calculated.

Note that the shear stress is zero at the top and bottom fibers (free surfaces) and is maximum at the neutral axis.

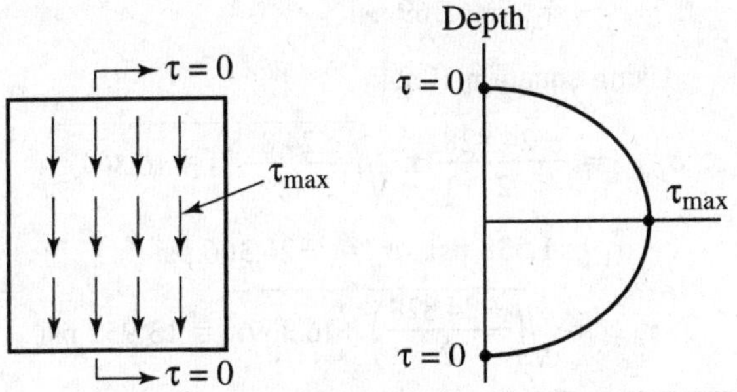

Figure 10.28

For the rectangular cross sections:

$$\tau_{max} = \frac{3V}{2A} \qquad [10.22]$$

where A = cross-sectional area.

For the solid circular cross sections:

$$\tau_{max} = \frac{4V}{3A} \qquad [10.23]$$

Example 10.13

Determine the maximum transverse shear stress for a 40 × 60-cm rectangular beam with the loading of Example 10.11.

Solution:

For the shear diagram of Example 10.11, the maximum shear load V = 840 N.

Since the cross section of the beam is rectangular, equation 10.22 can be used to determine the maximum transverse shear stress:

$$\tau_{max} = \frac{3V}{2A} = \frac{3\,(840)}{2\,(0.24)} = 5250 \text{ Pa}$$

10.12 Combined Loading

Consider a structural member subjected to some combination of axial, bending, and torsional loads.

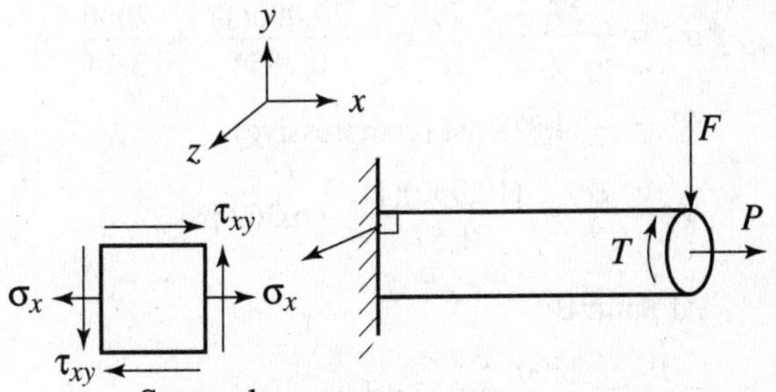

Figure 10.29

To determine the maximum stresses (normal and shear), first locate the point where the stresses are most severe. For a cantilever beam, this point is located at the fixed support. Once the stresses due to different loads are calculated, they can be represented on a very small element (stress element) and then maximum normal and shear stresses can be determined. The maximum normal stresses are called principal stresses, and the planes at which these stresses occur are called principal planes.

Example 10.14

Determine the normal and shearing stresses at points A and B in the figure below.

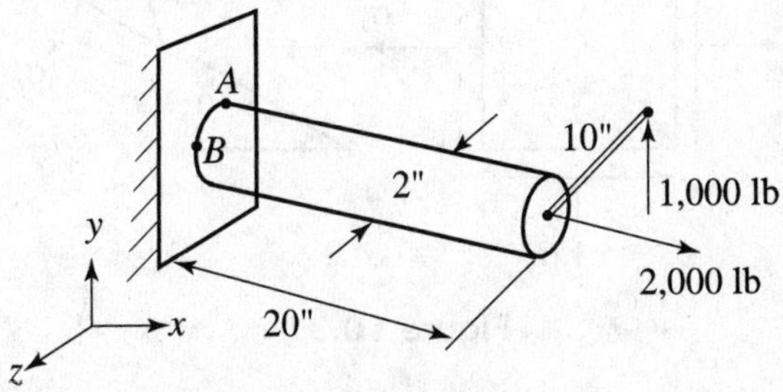

Figure 10.30

Solution:

$$T = M_x = -1{,}000(10) = -10{,}000 \text{ lb} \cdot \text{in}$$

$$M_z = 1{,}000\ (20) = 20{,}000 \text{ lb} \cdot \text{in}$$

$$V_y = 1{,}000 \text{ lb}$$

$$P_x = 2{,}000 \text{ lb}$$

$$I = \frac{\pi}{4}(1)^4 = 0.7954 \text{ in}^4$$

$$J = 2I = 1.57 \text{ in}^4$$

$$A = \frac{\pi}{4}(2)^2 = 3.14 \text{ in}^2$$

At point A:

$$\sigma_A = -\frac{M_z\, c}{I_z} + \frac{P_x}{A} = -\frac{20{,}000(1)}{0.7854} + \frac{2000}{3.14}$$

$$= -24{,}828 \text{ psi (compressive)}$$

$$\tau_A = \frac{Tc}{J} = \frac{(10{,}000)(1)}{1.57} = 6{,}369 \text{ psi}$$

At point B:

$$\sigma_B = \frac{P_x}{A} = \frac{2000}{3.14} = 637 \text{ psi}$$

$$\tau_B = \frac{Tc}{J} - \frac{4\ V_y}{3A} = \frac{(10{,}000)(1)}{1.57} - \frac{4(1{,}000)}{3(3.14)}$$

$$= 5{,}944 \text{ psi}$$

10.13 Principal and Maximum Shear Stresses

To determine the principal stresses and maximum shear stress and their planes:

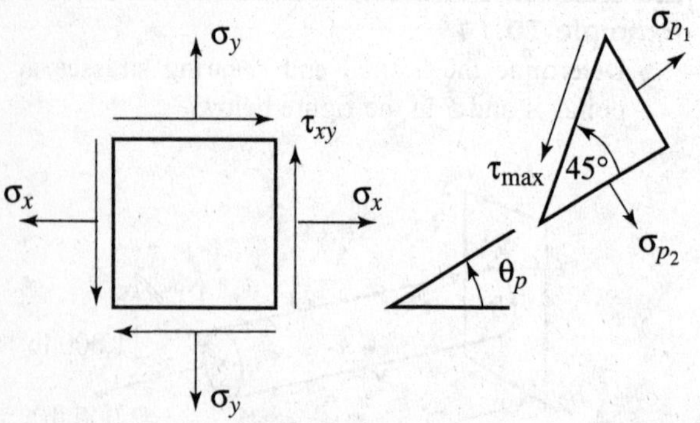

Figure 10.31

use the following equations:

$$\sigma_{p_1,p_2} = \sigma_{\max,\min} = \frac{\sigma_x + \sigma_y}{2} \pm \sqrt{\left(\frac{\sigma_x - \sigma_y}{2}\right)^2 + \tau_{xy}^{\ 2}}$$

$$\tan 2\theta_p = \frac{2\tau_{xy}}{\sigma_x - \sigma_y} \qquad [10.24]$$

$$\tau_{\max} = \frac{\sigma_{\max} - \sigma_{\min}}{2} = \sqrt{\left(\frac{\sigma_x - \sigma_y}{2}\right)^2 + \tau_{xy}^{\ 2}}$$

$$\tan 2\theta_s = -\frac{\sigma_x - \sigma_y}{2\tau_{xy}}$$

Also note that

$$\theta_p = \theta_s \pm 45 \qquad [10.25]$$

Example 10.15

Determine the principal and maximum shear stresses of Example 10.14 for point A.

Solution:

$$\sigma_x = -24{,}828 \text{ psi}, \ \sigma_y = 0$$

$$\tau_{xy} = 6{,}369 \text{ psi}$$

Using equation 10.24:

$$\sigma_{p_1,p_2} = \frac{-24{,}828}{2} \pm \sqrt{\left(\frac{-24{,}828}{2}\right)^2 + (6{,}369)^2}$$

$$\sigma_1 = 1{,}538 \text{ psi}, \ \sigma_2 = -26{,}366 \text{ psi}$$

$$\tau_{\max} = \sqrt{\left(\frac{-24{,}828}{2}\right)^2 + (6{,}369)^2} = 13{,}952 \text{ psi}$$

10.14 Thin-Walled Pressure Vessels

Cylindrical and spherical pressure vessels are used in industry for boilers or storage tanks. The term "thin-wall" refers to a tank for which the ratio of inner radius to thickness is equal to or larger than 10 ($r_i/t \geq 10$).

Cylindrical Vessels

For a cylinder of inner radius r and thickness t that is under pressure P, circumferential (hoop) and longitudinal stresses are developed in the vessel.

$$\sigma_{circ} = \sigma_{hoop} = \sigma_1 = \frac{Pr}{t} \qquad [10.26]$$

$$\sigma_{long} = \sigma_2 = \frac{Pr}{2t} \qquad [10.27]$$

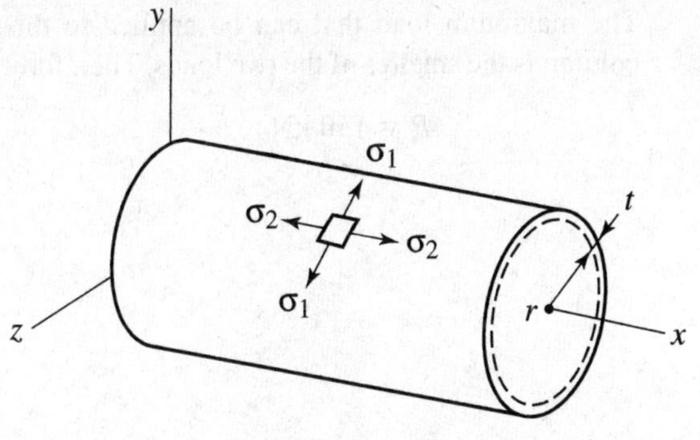

Figure 10.32

Example 10.16

A cylindrical pressure vessel has an inner radius of 2 m and a thickness of 3 cm. Determine the maximum internal pressure this vessel can sustain so that its circumferential stress component will not exceed 120 MPa.

Solution:

$$\sigma_1 = \frac{Pr}{t} \Rightarrow P = \frac{\sigma_1 t}{r}$$

$$P = \frac{(120 \times 10^6)(0.03)}{2} = 1.8 \text{ MPa}$$

Spherical Vessels

For a thin-walled spherical vessel subjected to inside pressure P:

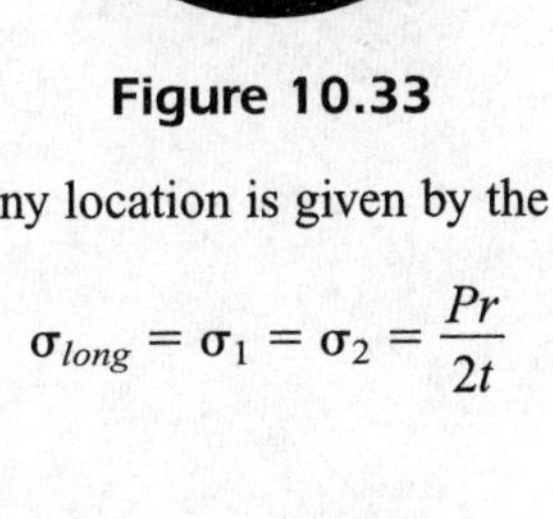

Figure 10.33

the stress at any location is given by the equation

$$\sigma_{long} = \sigma_1 = \sigma_2 = \frac{Pr}{2t} \qquad [10.28]$$

10.15 Columns

A column is defined as a long, slender member that is loaded axially in compression. In designing a column, the following rules must be followed:

1. *The normal stress due to the applied load should not exceed the allowable stress.*
2. *The axial deformation should not exceed the allowable deformation.*
3. *The load applied must be less than the critical load that causes buckling.*

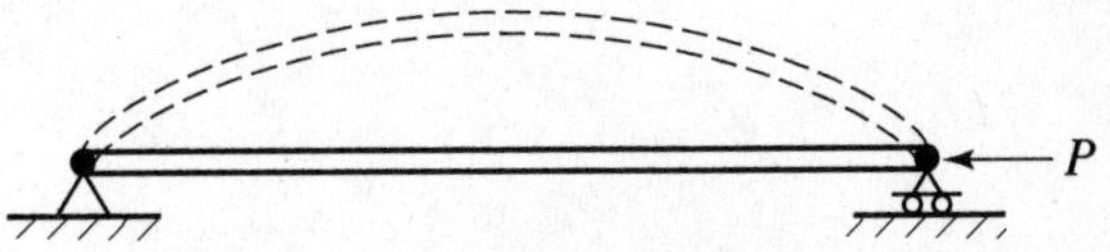

Figure 10.34

If a column is pinned at both ends, the smallest critical load P is given by the equation

$$P_{cr} = \frac{\pi^2 EI}{L^2} \qquad [10.29]$$

Equation 10.29 is known as *Euler's formula.* For other end conditions, the equation

$$P_{cr} = \frac{\pi^2 EI}{L_e^2} \qquad [10.30]$$

can be used. Here, L_e is called the *effective length* and is shown in Figure10.35 for four end conditions.

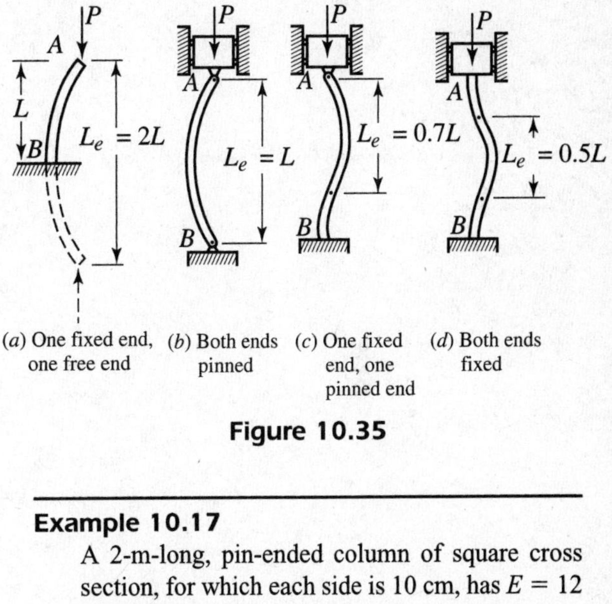

(*a*) One fixed end, one free end (*b*) Both ends pinned (*c*) One fixed end, one pinned end (*d*) Both ends fixed

Figure 10.35

Example 10.17

A 2-m-long, pin-ended column of square cross section, for which each side is 10 cm, has $E = 12$ GPa and $\sigma_{all} = 15$ MPa. Determine the maximum allowable load that can be applied.

Solution:

Use Euler's formula.

$$I = \frac{(.1)^4}{12} = 8.3 \times 10^{-6} \text{ m}^4$$

$$P_{cr} = \frac{\pi^2 EI}{L^2} = \frac{(3.14)^2(12 \times 10^9)(8.3 \times 10^{-6})}{2^2}$$

$$= 246.74 \text{ kN}$$

Now determine the load based on allowable stress.

$$\sigma = \frac{P}{A} \Rightarrow P = \sigma A$$

$$P = (15 \times 10^6)(0.1)^2 = 150 \text{ kN}$$

The maximum load that can be applied to this column is the smaller of the two loads. Therefore:

$$P = 150 \text{ kN}$$

PRACTICE PROBLEMS

1. Determine the normal stress in section AB.

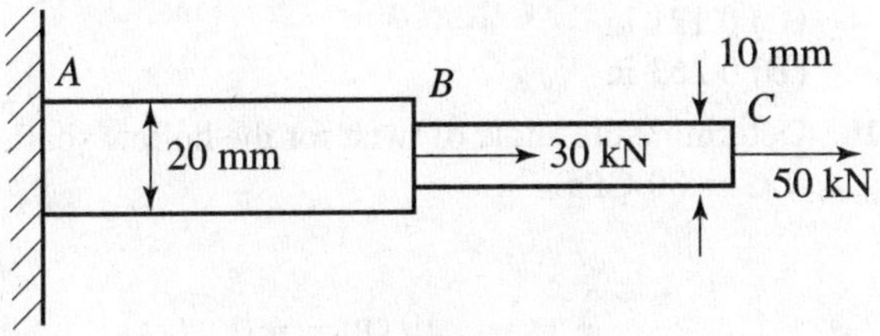

Figure 10.36

(A) 0.095 MPa
(B) 0.255 MPa
(C) 0.159 MPa
(D) 2.6 MPa

2. Determine the normal stress in link AB if AB has a cross-sectional area of 400 mm^2.

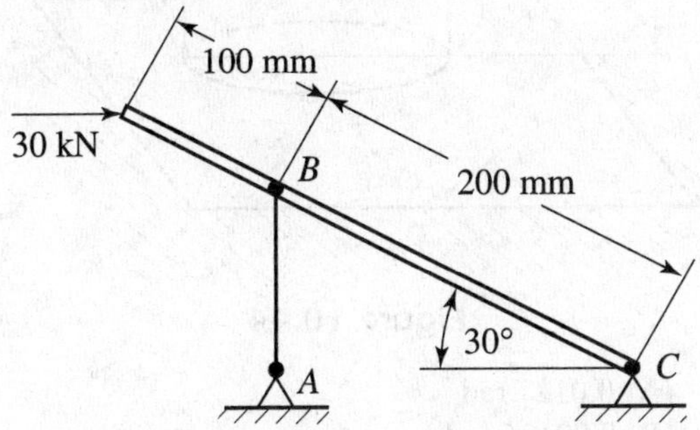

Figure 10.37

(A) 0.065 MPa
(B) 0.075 MPa
(C) 0.113 MPa
(D) 0.05 MPa

3. If the allowable shear stress for the bolts is 10 ksi, determine the minimum required diameter of each bolt.

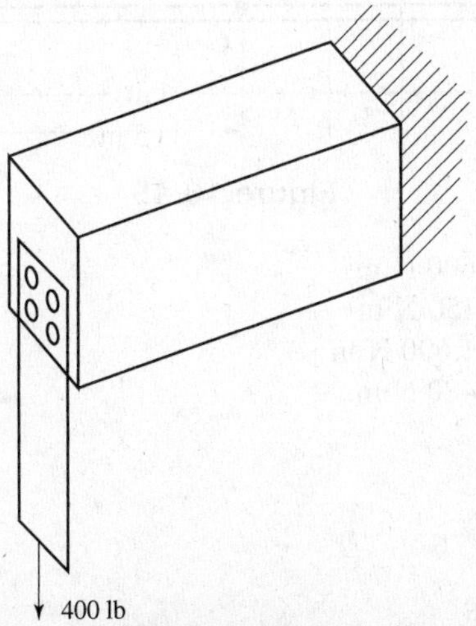

Figure 10.38

(A) 0.2 in
(B) 0.225 in
(C) 0.3in
(D) 0.113 in

4. If member AB elongates 10 mm as a result of the applied load, determine the normal strain in AB.

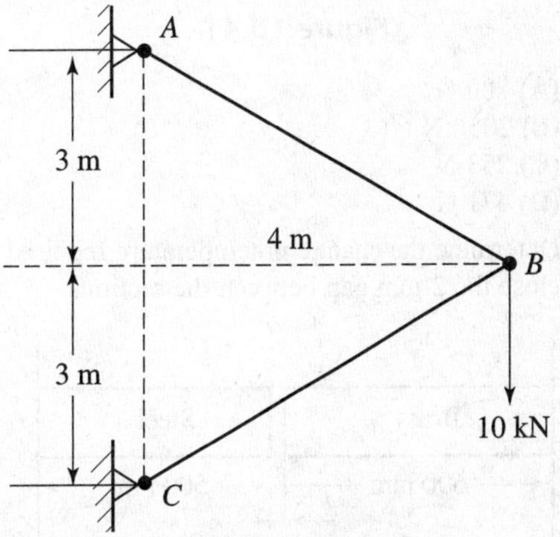

Figure 10.39

(A) 0.0033
(B) 0.002
(C) 0.0025
(D) 0.001

5. Determine the approximate vertical displacement of plate A. Each pad has cross-sectional dimensions of 30×30 mm and $G = 3$ MPa.

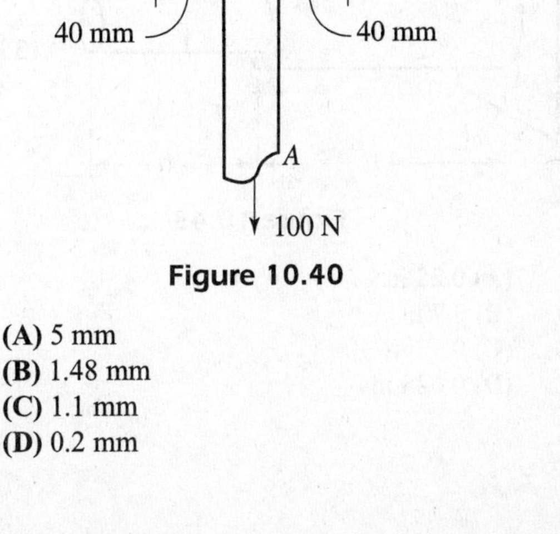

Figure 10.40

(A) 5 mm
(B) 1.48 mm
(C) 1.1 mm
(D) 0.2 mm

6. Determine the load required to decrease the diameter of the rod by 0.003 mm if $E = 4$ GPa and $\nu = 0.3$.

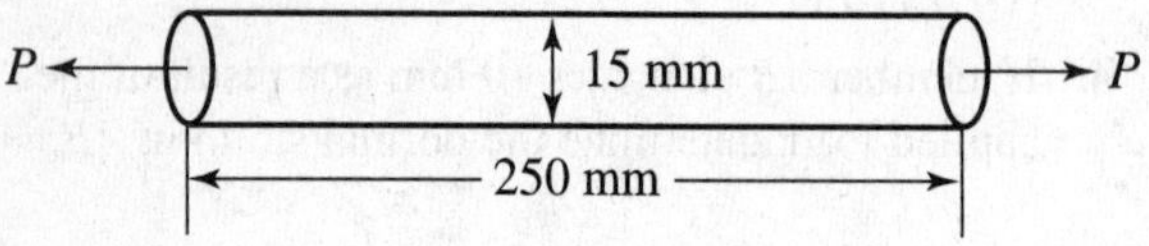

Figure 10.41

(A) 800 N
(B) 205 kN
(C) 253 N
(D) 471 N

7. Determine the change in temperature required to close the 2-mm gap between the sections.

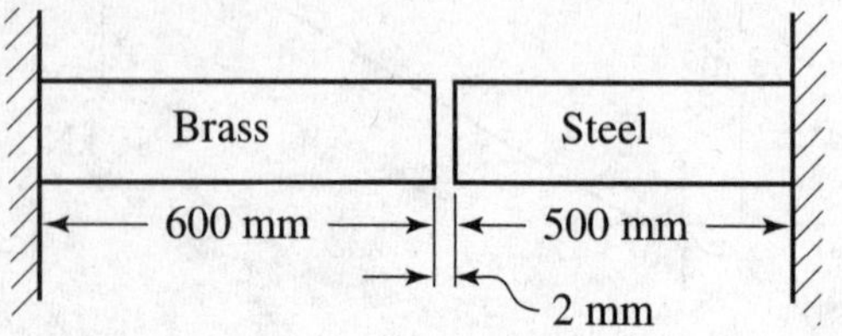

Brass
$E = 100$ GPa
$\alpha = 21 \times 10^{-6}$ 1/°C

Steel
$E = 200$ GPa
$\alpha = 12 \times 10^{-6}$ 1/°C

Figure 10.42

(A) 108 C°
(B) 55 C°
(C) 85 C°
(D) 20 C°

8. Determine diameter d if the deflection of point C is 0.014 in and $E = 30 \times 10^6$ psi for both sections.

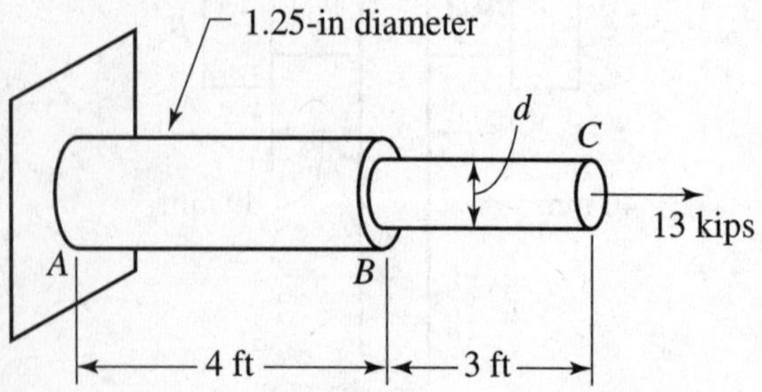

Figure 10.43

(A) 0.25 in
(B) 0.7 in
(C) 0.37 in
(D) 0.625 in

9. If the allowable shear stress is 900 KPa, determine the required diameter of a solid shaft under the action of a 1,500-N · m torque.
(A) 0.209 in
(B) 0.0091 in
(C) 0.121 in
(D) 0.263 in

10. Determine the angle of twist for the hollow shaft if $G = 80$ GPa.

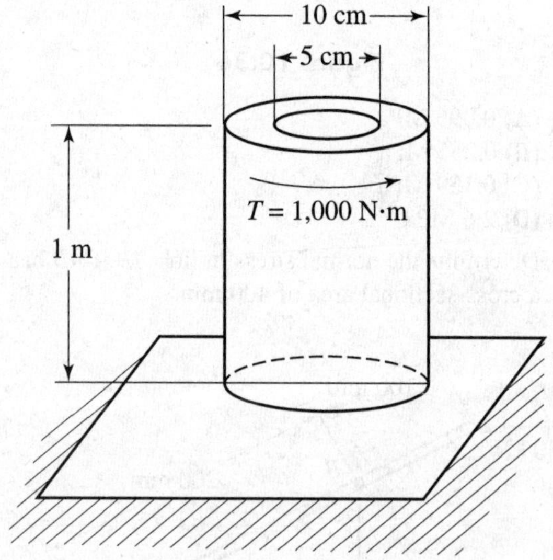

Figure 10.44

(A) 0.0127 rad
(B) 0.00136 rad
(C) 0.001 rad
(D) 0.52 rad

11. Determine the bending moment at the center (point C) of the beam.

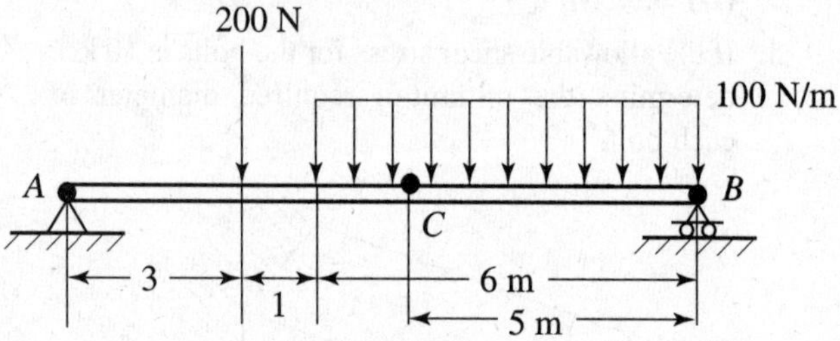

Figure 10.45

(A) 600 N·m
(B) 350 N·m
(C) 1,600 N·m
(D) 480 N·m

12. Determine the maximum magnitude of the bending moment in the beam. The bending moment at each end of the beam is zero, and there are no concentrated couples along the beam.

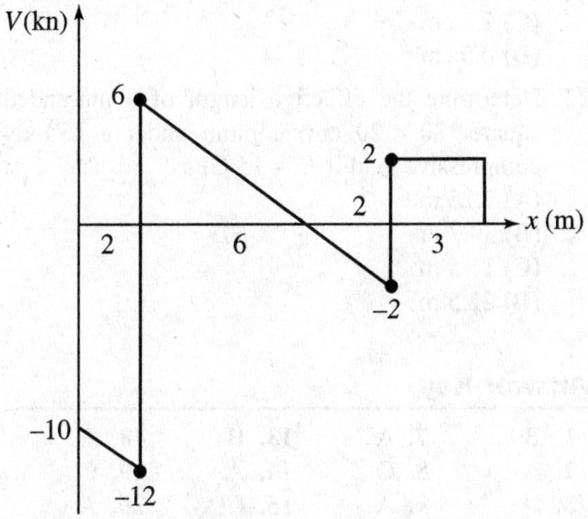

Figure 10.46

(A) 18 kN · m
(B) 6 kN · m
(C) 22 kN · m
(D) 4 kN · m

13. If the allowable bending stress is 5 ksi, determine *h*.

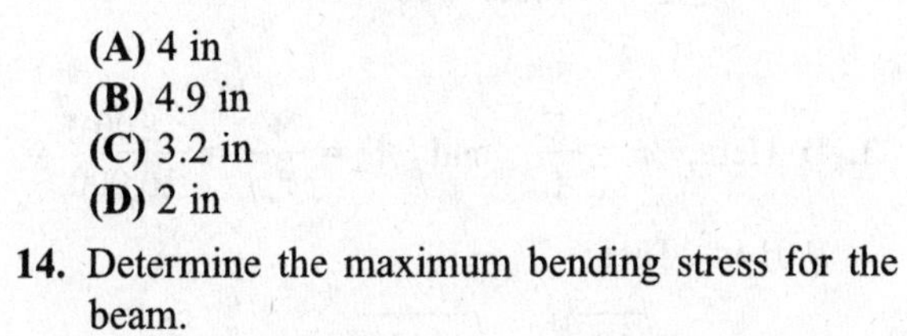

Figure 10.47

(A) 4 in
(B) 4.9 in
(C) 3.2 in
(D) 2 in

14. Determine the maximum bending stress for the beam.

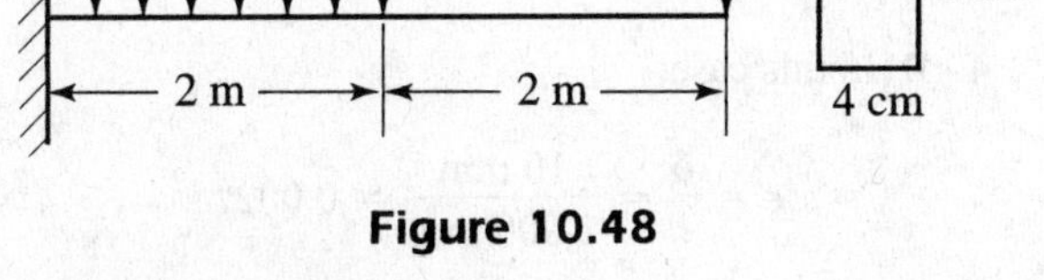

Figure 10.48

(A) 66.7 MPa
(B) 50 MPa
(C) 25.2 MPa
(D) 5.55 Mpa

15. If the allowable bending stress is 10 ksi, determine the diameter of the shaft loaded as shown.

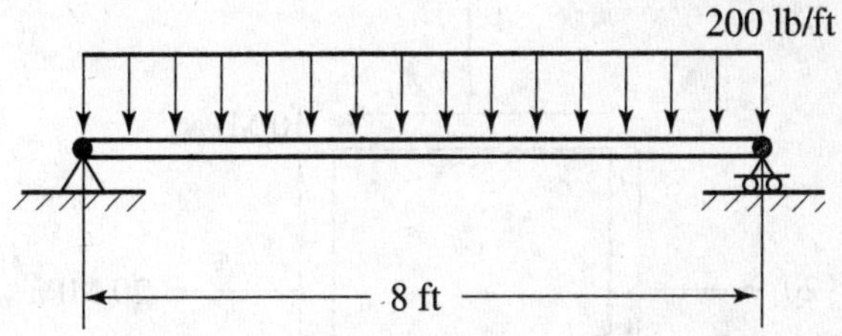

Figure 10.49

(A) 1.17 in
(B) 3.5 in
(C) 2.7 in
(D) 2.35 in

16. Determine the maximum transverse shear stress for the beam.

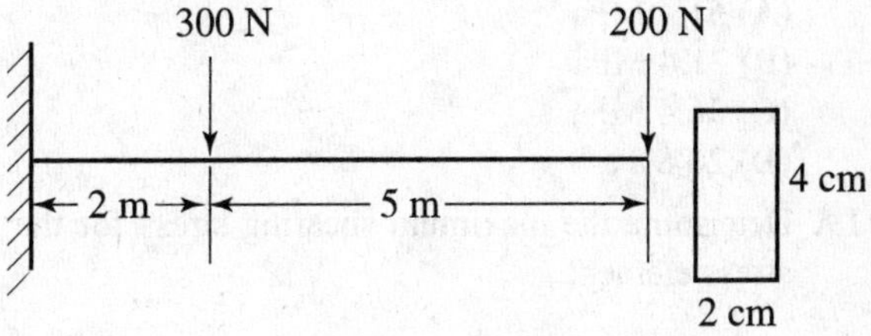

Figure 10.50

(A) 0.94 MPa
(B) 0.625 MPa
(C) 0.375 MPa
(D) 0.833 MPa

17. Determine the normal stress at point *A* for the shaft.

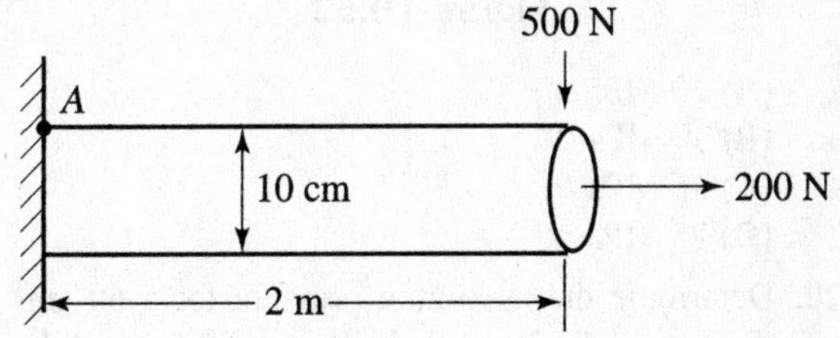

Figure 10.51

(A) 25.46 MPa
(B) 10.18 MPa
(C) 10.16 MPa
(D) 10.21 MPa

18. Determine the maximum tensile stress for the stress element.

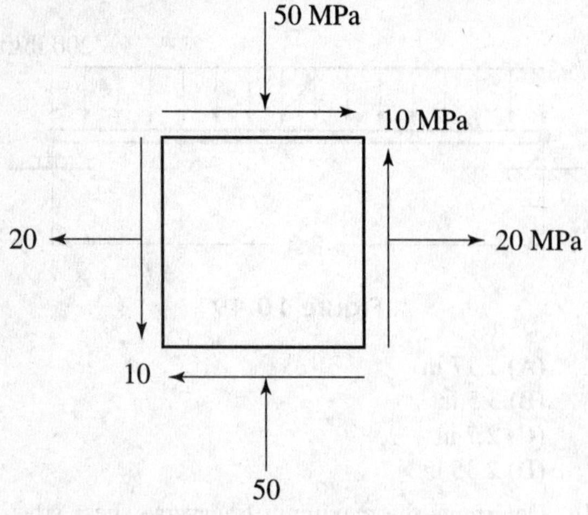

Figure 10.52

(A) 51.4 MPa
(B) 21.4 MPa
(C) 36.4 MPa
(D) 20 MPa

19. Determine the maximum shearing stress for the stress element.

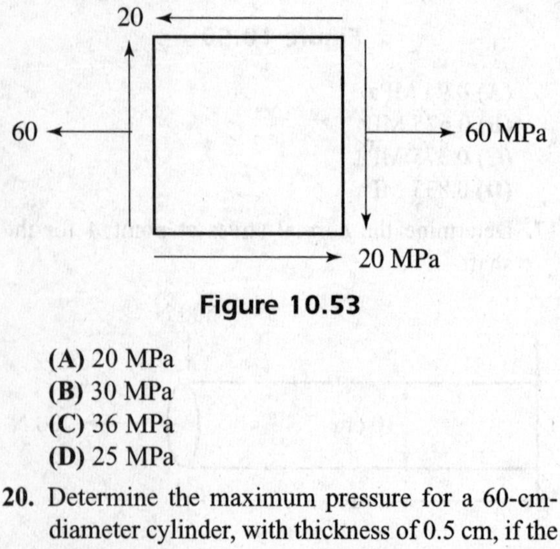

Figure 10.53

(A) 20 MPa
(B) 30 MPa
(C) 36 MPa
(D) 25 MPa

20. Determine the maximum pressure for a 60-cm-diameter cylinder, with thickness of 0.5 cm, if the allowable tensile stress is 150 MPa.
(A) 2.5 MPa
(B) 1.25 MPa
(C) 5 MPa
(D) 1.2 MPa

21. Determine the thickness of a 100-cm-diameter sphere under a pressure of 600 KPa if the allowable stress is 150 MPa.
(A) 2 cm
(B) 1 cm
(C) 1.5 cm
(D) 0.5 cm

22. Determine the effective length of a pin-ended square (20 × 20 cm) column under a 150-kN compressive load if $E = 15$ GPa.
(A) 7.25 m
(B) 39.7 m
(C) 11.5 m
(D) 22.5 m

Answer Key

1. B	7. A	13. B	18. A
2. A	8. C	14. A	19. C
3. D	9. A	15. C	20. A
4. B	10. B	16. A	21. B
5. B	11. B	17. D	22. C
6. D	12. C		

Answers Explained

1. **B** $P_{AB} = 80$ kN in tension, and

$$\sigma_{AB} = \frac{P_{AB}}{A_{AB}} = \frac{80}{\frac{\pi}{4}(0.02)^2} = 254.6 \text{ MPa}$$

2. **A** Draw an FBD of member *BC*, and take the moment about point *C*: $\Sigma M_c = 0$. Then $F_{AB} = 25.98$ kN, and

$$\sigma_{AB} = \frac{F_{AB}}{A_{AB}} = \frac{25.98}{400 \times 10^{-6}} = 0.065 \text{ MPa}$$

3. **D** Here, $\tau = \frac{V}{A_s}$, and $A_s = \frac{V}{\tau_{all}} = \frac{100}{10{,}000} = 0.01 \text{ in}^2$. Then:

$$d = \sqrt{\frac{4A_s}{\pi}} = \sqrt{\frac{4(.01)}{\pi}} = 0.1128 \text{ in}$$

4. **B** In this case:

$$\epsilon = \frac{\delta}{l} = \frac{10 \text{ mm}}{5{,}000 \text{ mm}} = 0.002$$

5. B This is a case of double shear. $V = \frac{100}{2} =$ 50 N, and

$$\tau = \frac{V}{A} = \frac{50}{900 \times 10^{-6}} = 0.055 \text{ MPa}$$

Also:

$$\tau = G\gamma$$

$$\gamma = \frac{\tau}{G} = \frac{0.055}{3} = 0.0185 \text{ rad}$$

Then:

$$y = (40 \text{ mm})(0.0185 \text{ rad}) = 0.74 \text{ mm}$$

6. D In this case:

$$\epsilon_{\text{lateral}} = \frac{0.003}{15} = 0.0002 \quad \text{and}$$

$$\epsilon_{\text{axial}} = \frac{\epsilon_{\text{lateral}}}{v} = \frac{0.0002}{0.3} = 0.00066$$

Also:

$$\epsilon_{\text{axial}} = \frac{\sigma}{E} = \frac{P}{EA}$$

$$P = EA\epsilon_{\text{axial}} = 471 \text{ N}$$

7. A Here: $\delta = \Sigma\alpha l\,\Delta T$

$$\Delta T = \frac{\delta}{\Sigma\alpha l}$$

$$= \frac{2}{(21 \times 10^{-6})(600) + (12 \times 10^{-6})(500)}$$

$$= 108\text{C}°$$

8. C In this case:

$$\delta = \Sigma\frac{Pl}{EA} \quad \text{and}$$

$$0.04 = \frac{13{,}000}{30 \times 10^{6}}\left(\frac{48}{\frac{\pi}{4}(1.25)^2} + \frac{36}{\frac{\pi}{4}(d)^2}\right)$$

Then $d = 0.93$ in.

9. A For a solid shaft, $\tau = \frac{16\,T}{\pi\,d^3}$. Then:

$$d = \sqrt[3]{\frac{16\,T}{\pi\tau}} = \sqrt[3]{\frac{16(1{,}500)}{\pi(840{,}000)}} = 0.209 \text{ in}$$

10. B For the hollow shaft, $J = \frac{\pi}{32}(0.1^4 - 0.05^4) =$ $9.2 \times 10^{-6}\text{ m}^4$. Then:

$$\phi = \frac{TL}{GJ} = \frac{(1{,}000)(1)}{(80 \times 10^9)(9.2 \times 10^{-6})}$$

$$= 0.00136 \text{ rad}$$

11. B First, determine the reactions:

$$B = 480 \text{ N} \qquad A = 320 \text{ N}$$

Cut the beam at point *C*, and use either the left or the right side of the beam:

$$\Sigma M_C = 0 \quad \text{and} \quad M_C = 1{,}150 \text{ N·m}$$

12. C The area under the shear diagram is equal to the net bending moment, so $M_{\text{max}} = 22$ kN·m

13. B In this case:

$$\sigma_{\text{max}} = \frac{M_{\text{max}}C}{I} \qquad 5{,}000 = \frac{40{,}000\left(\frac{h}{2}\right)}{\frac{1}{12}(2)\,h^3}$$

Then $h = 4.9$ in.

14. A The maximum moment will occur at the support and is equal to 1,600 N·m, so

$$\sigma_{\text{max}} = \frac{M_{\text{max}}C}{I} = \frac{(1{,}600)(0.03)}{\frac{1}{12}(0.04)(0.06)^3}$$

$$= 66.7 \text{ MPa}$$

15. C The maximum moment will occur at the center of the shaft and is equal to 1,600 lb-ft = 19,200 lb-in. Then:

$$\sigma_{\text{max}} = \frac{M_{\text{max}}C}{I} = \frac{(19{,}200)\left(\frac{d}{2}\right)}{\frac{\pi}{64}d^4}$$

and $d = 2.7$ in.

16. A The maximum shear load $V = 500$ N. For a rectangular cross section:

$$\tau = \frac{3V}{2A} = \frac{3(500)}{2(0.02)(0.04)} = 0.94 \text{ MPa}$$

17. D At point *A*:

$$\sigma_A = \frac{Mc}{I} + \frac{P}{A} = \frac{(1{,}000)(0.05)}{\frac{\pi}{64}(0.1)^4} + \frac{200}{\frac{\pi}{4}(0.1)^2} = 10.21 \text{ MPa}$$

18. A For the stress element:

$$\sigma_{p_1,p_2} = \frac{20-50}{2} \pm \sqrt{\left[\frac{20-(-50)}{2}\right]^2 + (10)^2} \sigma_{max} = 51.4 \text{ MPa}$$

19. C Here,

$$\tau_{max} = \sqrt{\left(\frac{60-0}{2}\right)^2 + (-20)^2} = 36 \text{ MPa}$$

20. A For the cylinder:

$$\sigma_1 = \frac{Pr}{t}$$

$$P = \frac{\sigma_1 t}{r} = \frac{(150 \times 10^6)(0.005)}{0.3} = 2.5 \text{ MPa}$$

21. B For the sphere:

$$\sigma = \frac{Pr}{2t}$$

$$t = \frac{Pr}{2\sigma} = \frac{600 \times 10^3\,(0.5)}{2(15 \times 10^6)} = 0.01 \text{ m} = 1 \text{ cm}$$

22. C Here, $P_{cr} = \frac{\pi^2 EI}{L_e^2}$. Then:

$$L_e = \sqrt{\frac{\pi^2 EI}{P_{cr}}} = 11.47 \text{ m}$$

CHAPTER 11

Statics

Masoud Olia, Ph.D., PE

Introduction

Statics is the study of rigid bodies at rest. For a body to be at rest, the forces acting on the body have to balance each other. In this chapter, presentation of the concepts of static equilibrium of particles and rigid bodies is followed by discussion of the determination of external and internal forces for structures such as trusses and frames. Moments of inertia, centroids of plane areas, and basic concepts of friction are also discussed. The following is a complete list of this chapter's contents:

11.1 Forces

A **force** is considered as a push or a pull exerted by one body on another. Force is a vector quantity, which has both magnitude and direction. Forces are classified as external, internal, concentrated, or distributed, as shown in Figure 11.1.

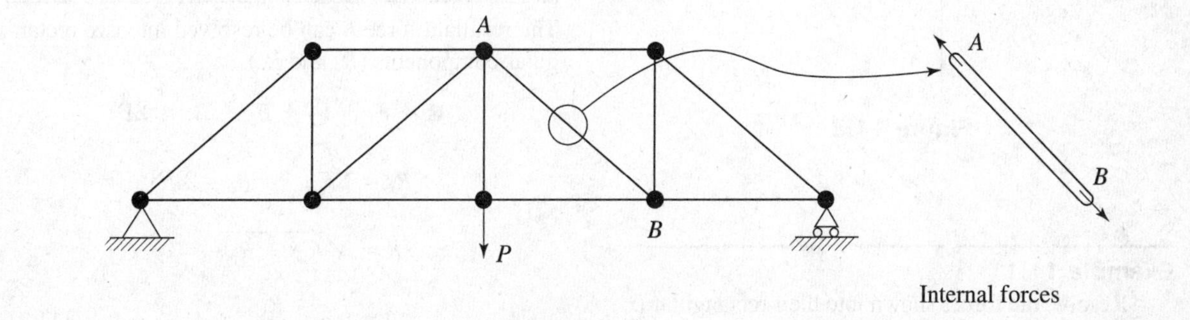

Figure 11.1

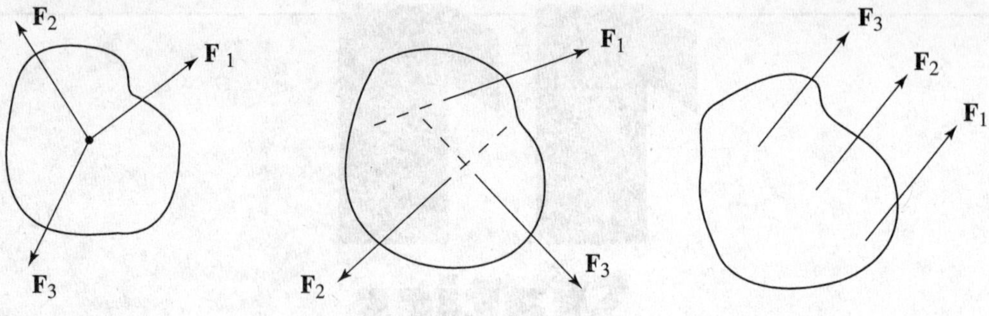

Figure 11.2

A force system can be classified as concurrent or nonconcurrent. If all the forces acting on a body pass through the same point, the force system is called concurrent. If all the forces acting on the body do not pass through a common point, the force system is nonconcurrent.

Resolution of a Force (2-D)

A force can be resolved along any two arbitrary axes. It is more convenient and efficient, however, to resolve a force along the *x*- and *y*-axes (Cartesian or rectangular coordinates system). The appropriate equations are as follows:

$$F_x = F\cos\theta, \qquad F_y = F\sin\theta \qquad [11.1]$$

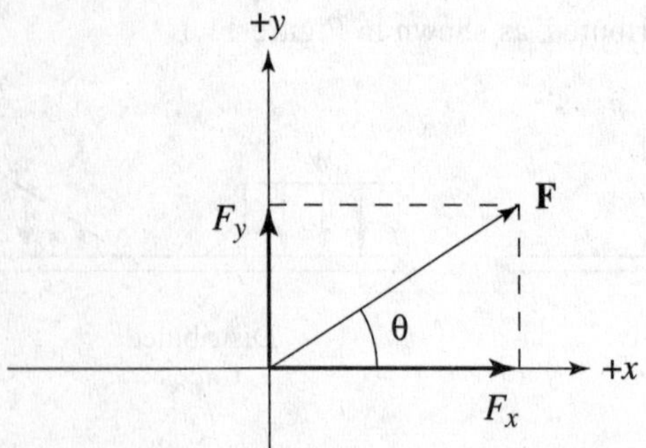

Figure 11.3

Example 11.1

Resolve the forces shown into their rectangular (*x* and *y*) components.

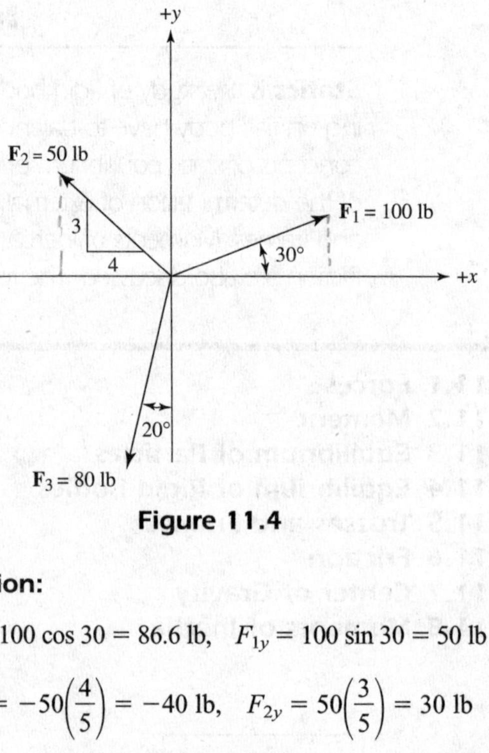

Figure 11.4

Solution:

$$F_{1x} = 100\cos 30 = 86.6 \text{ lb}, \quad F_{1y} = 100\sin 30 = 50 \text{ lb}$$

$$F_{2x} = -50\left(\frac{4}{5}\right) = -40 \text{ lb}, \quad F_{2y} = 50\left(\frac{3}{5}\right) = 30 \text{ lb}$$

$$F_{3x} = -80\sin 20 = -27.36 \text{ lb}, \quad F_{3y} = -80\cos 20 = -75.17 \text{ lb}$$

Resultant of a Concurrent Force System (2-D)

The resultant force *R* can be resolved into two rectangular components (R_x and R_y).

$$\mathbf{R} = \mathbf{F}_1 + \mathbf{F}_2 + \mathbf{F}_3 + \ldots = \Sigma\mathbf{F}$$

$$R_x = \Sigma F_x, \qquad R_y = \Sigma F_y$$

$$R = \sqrt{R_x^{\,2} + R_y^{\,2}}$$

$$\theta = \tan^{-1}\frac{R_y}{R_x} \qquad [11.2]$$

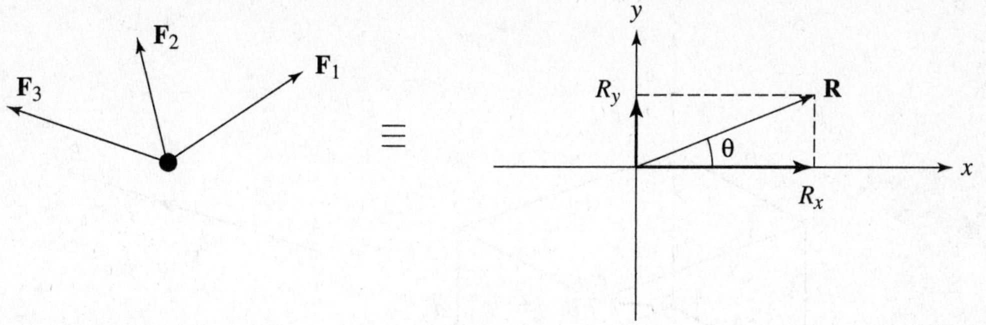

Figure 11.5

Example 11.2

Find the resultant of the forces shown.

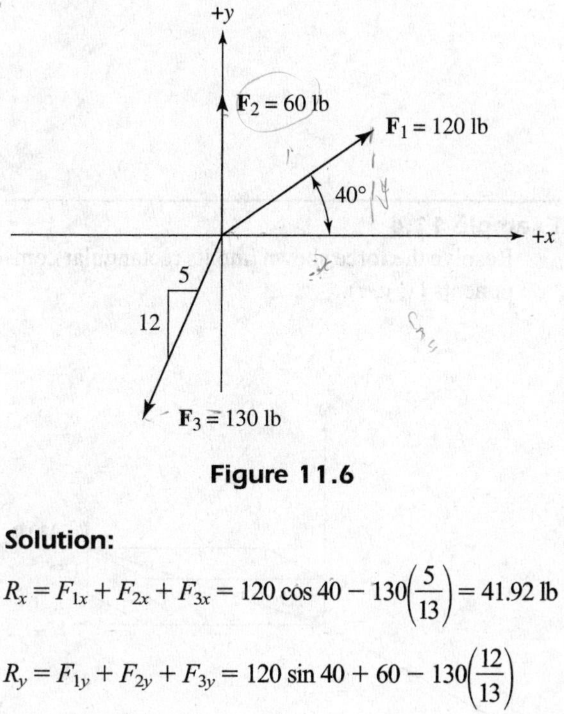

Figure 11.6

Solution:

$R_x = F_{1x} + F_{2x} + F_{3x} = 120 \cos 40 - 130\left(\frac{5}{13}\right) = 41.92 \text{ lb}$

$R_y = F_{1y} + F_{2y} + F_{3y} = 120 \sin 40 + 60 - 130\left(\frac{12}{13}\right)$

$= 17.13 \text{ lb}$

$R = \sqrt{41.92^2 + 17.13^2} = 45.28 \text{ lb}$

$\theta = \tan^{-1} \frac{17.13}{41.92} = 22.42°$

Resolution of a Force (3-D)

To resolve a force into its components (F_x, F_y, F_z), two methods are available.

Method 1. If the angles between the force (**F**) and the axes (x, y, z) are known (see Figure 11.7), then

$$F_x = F \cos \theta_x,\ F_y = F \cos \theta_y,\ F_z = F \cos \theta_z \quad [11.3]$$

Also, there is a relation between these angles such that

$$\cos^2 \theta_x + \cos^2 \theta_y + \cos^2 \theta_z = 1 \quad [11.4]$$

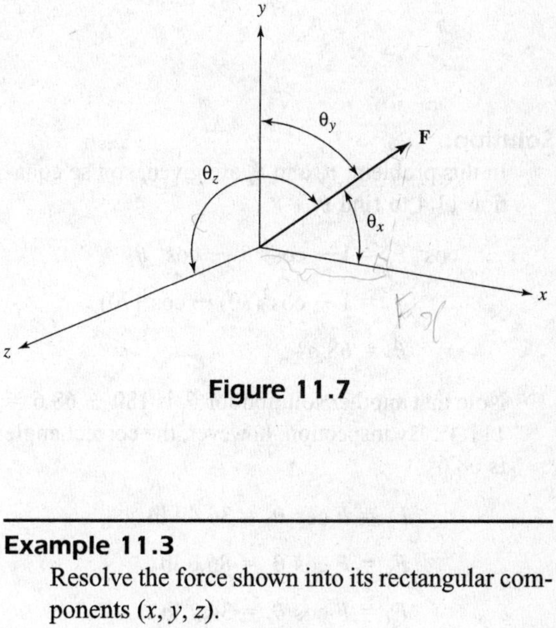

Figure 11.7

Example 11.3

Resolve the force shown into its rectangular components (x, y, z).

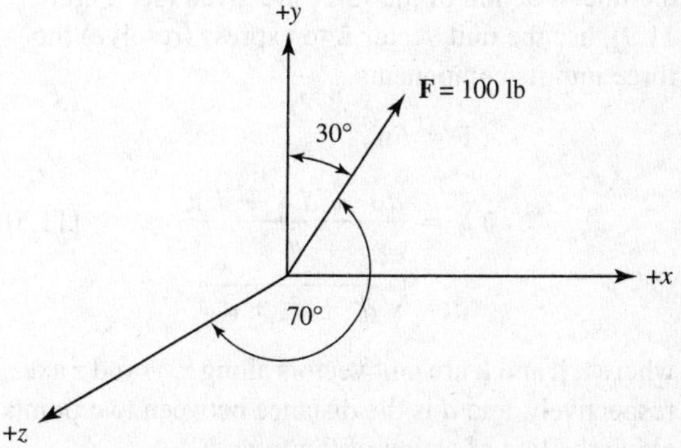

Figure 11.8

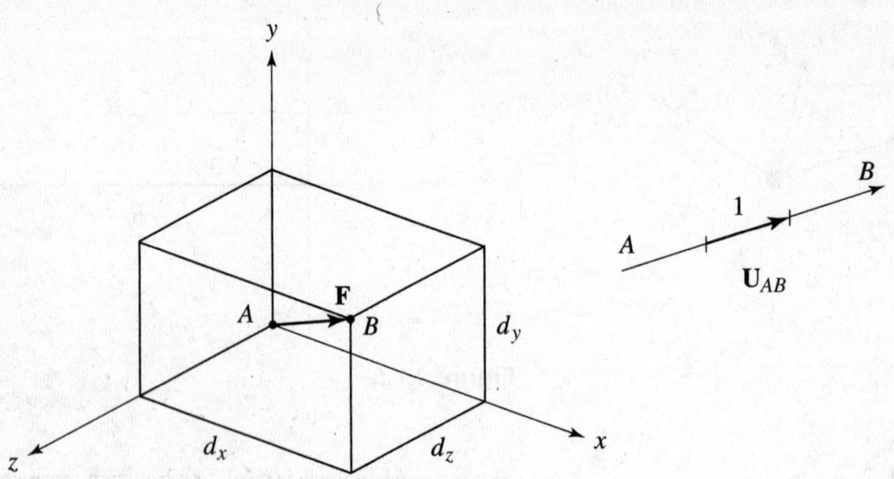

Figure 11.9

Solution:

In this problem, θ_y and θ_z are given, so use equation 11.4 to find θ_x.

$$\cos^2 \theta_x = 1 - \cos^2 \theta_y - \cos^2 \theta_z$$

$$= 1 - \cos^2(30) - \cos^2(70)$$

$$\theta_x = 68.6°$$

Note that another solution for θ_x is $180 - 68.6 = 111.4°$. By inspection, however, the correct angle is 68.6°.

$$F_x = F \cos \theta_x = 36.47 \text{ lb}$$

$$F_y = F \cos \theta_y = 86.6 \text{ lb}$$

$$F_x = F \cos \theta_z = 34.2 \text{ lb}$$

Method 2. If the coordinates of two points along the line of action of the force are given (see Figure 11.9), use the unit vector $\hat{\mathbf{u}}$ to express (resolve) the force into its components.

$$\mathbf{F} = F\hat{\mathbf{u}}_{AB}$$

$$\hat{\mathbf{u}}_{AB} = \frac{d_x\widehat{\mathbf{i}} + d_y\widehat{\mathbf{j}} + d_z\widehat{\mathbf{k}}}{d} \qquad [11.5]$$

$$d = \sqrt{d_x^2 + d_y^2 + d_z^2}$$

where **i, j,** and **k** are unit vectors along *x, y,* and *z* axes, respectively, and *d* is the distance between two points along the line of action of the force **F**.

Example 11.4

Resolve the force shown into its rectangular components (*x, y, z*).

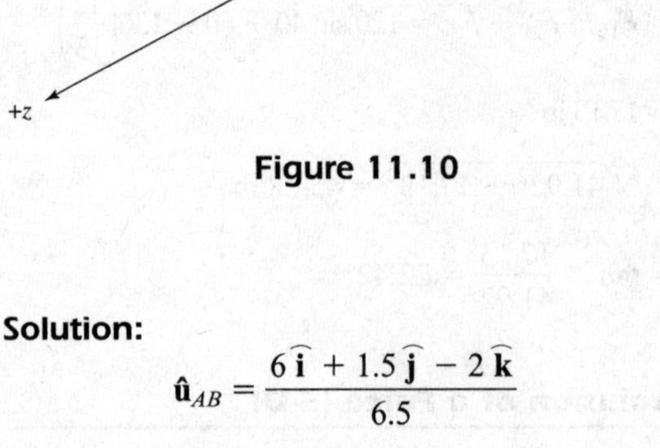

Figure 11.10

Solution:

$$\hat{\mathbf{u}}_{AB} = \frac{6\,\widehat{\mathbf{i}} + 1.5\,\widehat{\mathbf{j}} - 2\,\widehat{\mathbf{k}}}{6.5}$$

$$\mathbf{F} = 130\hat{\mathbf{u}}_{AB}$$

$$= 120\,\widehat{\mathbf{i}} + 30\widehat{\mathbf{j}} - 40\,\widehat{\mathbf{k}}$$

where **i, j,** and **k** are unit vectors along *x, y,* and *z* axes, respectively.

Resultant of a Concurrent Force System (3-D)

This is similar to the two-dimensional case except that there is a third component (R_z). The equations are as follows:

$$R_x = \Sigma F_x, \quad R_y = \Sigma F_y, \quad R_z = \Sigma F_z$$

$$R = \sqrt{R_x^2 + R_y^2 + R_z^2} \qquad [11.6]$$

Example 11.5

Determine the resultant of the forces shown.

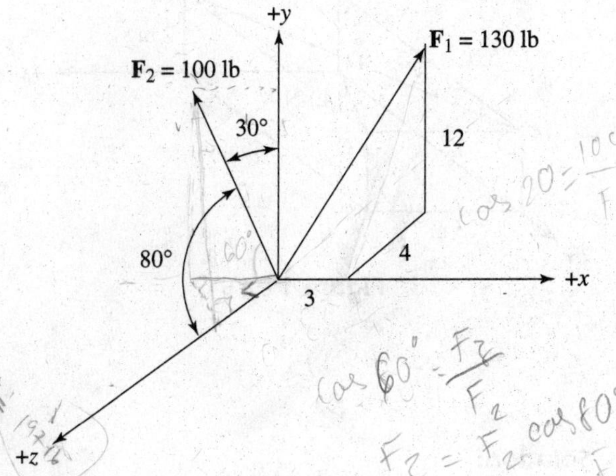

Figure 11.11

Solution:

$$\cos^2 \theta_x = 1 - \cos^2 \theta_y - \cos^2 \theta_z$$
$$= 1 - \cos^2(30) - \cos^2(80)$$
$$\theta_x = 62° \text{ and also } \theta_x = 180° - 62° = 118°$$

From the figure, the correct angle is 118°.

$$F_{2x} = F_x \cos \theta_x = -46.9 \text{ lb}$$
$$F_{2y} = F_2 \cos \theta_y = 86.6 \text{ lb}$$
$$F_{2z} = F \cos \theta_z = 34.2 \text{ lb}$$
$$\hat{\mathbf{u}}_{AB} = \frac{3\,\hat{\mathbf{i}} + 12\,\hat{\mathbf{j}} - 4\,\hat{\mathbf{k}}}{13}$$
$$\mathbf{F}_1 = 130\,\hat{\mathbf{u}}_{AB}$$
$$= 30\,\hat{\mathbf{i}} + 120\,\hat{\mathbf{j}} - 40\,\hat{\mathbf{k}}$$
$$R_x = \Sigma F_x = 30 - 46.9 = -16.9 \text{ lb}$$
$$R_y = \Sigma F_y = 120 + 86.9 = 206.9 \text{ lb}$$
$$R_z = \Sigma F_z = -40 + 34.2 = -5.8 \text{ lb}$$
$$R = \sqrt{(-16.9)^2 + 206.9^2 + (-5.8)^2} = 207.6 \text{ lb}$$

To specify the direction of the resultant force, determine the angles that the resultant forms with the axes.

$$\cos \theta_x = \frac{R_x}{R} = \frac{-16.9}{207.6} \Rightarrow \theta_y = 94.66°$$

$$\cos \theta_y = \frac{R_y}{R} = \frac{206.9}{207.6} \Rightarrow \theta_x = 4.7°$$

$$\cos \theta_z = \frac{R_z}{R} = \frac{-5.8}{207.6} \Rightarrow \theta_z = 91.6°$$

11.2 Moment

The **moment** of a force is the measure of tendency of a rigid body to rotation about an axis. Moment is divided into two parts, moment of a single force and moment of a couple.

Moment of a Single Force

The moment of a single force can be about (1) a point or (2) an axis.

1. The moment of a force about a point is the product of the force and the perpendicular distance from the point to the line of action of the force. Therefore the magnitude of the moment about point A is expressed by the equation

$$M_A = Fd \qquad [11.7]$$

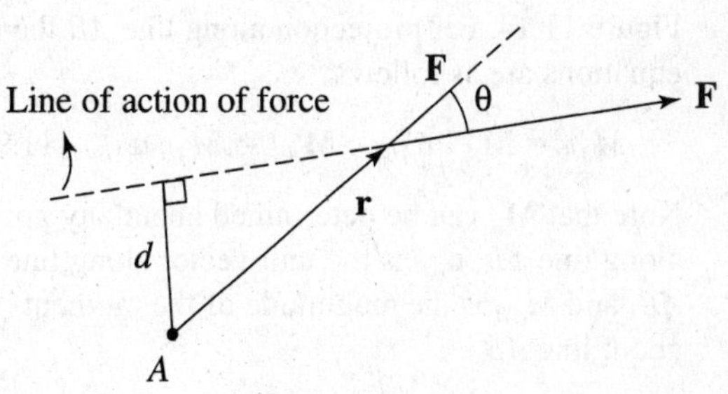

Figure 11.12

Moment can also be determined vectorially, and is given by the equation

$$\mathbf{M}_A = \mathbf{r} \times \mathbf{F} \qquad [11.8]$$

Where **r** is the position vector from the point to anywhere along the line of action of the force.

Example 11.6

Find the moment of the force shown about point A, using both the scalar and the vector approach.

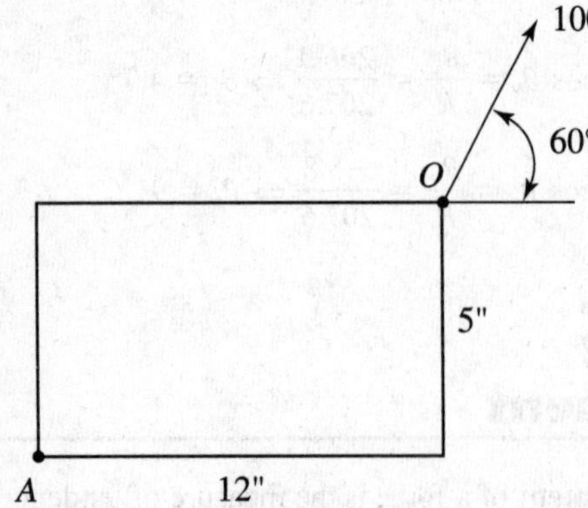

Figure 11.13

Solution:

Scalar approach:

CCW + :

$$M_A = -100 \cos 60(5) + 100 \sin 60(12) = 789.2 \text{ lb-in}$$

Therefore, the magnitude of the moment about A is 789.2 lb-in and its direction is counterclockwise.

Vector approach:

$$\mathbf{M}_A = \mathbf{r}_{AO} \times \mathbf{F} = (12\,\hat{i} + 5\,\hat{j}) \times (50\,\hat{i} + 86.6\,\hat{j})$$

$$= 789.2\,\hat{k}$$

2. The moment of a force about an axis is the projection of the moment along that axis, shown in Figure 11.14. For projection along line AB the equations are as follows:

$$M_{AB} = \mathbf{M}_A \cdot \mathbf{u}_{AB}, \quad \mathbf{M}_{AB} = M_{AB}\,\mathbf{u}_{AB} \quad [11.9]$$

Note that $\mathbf{M}_A$ can be determined about any point along line AB, $\mathbf{u}_{AB}$ is the unit vector along line AB, and M_{AB} is the magnitude of the moment about line AB.

Example 11.7

Determine, for the figure shown, the magnitude of the moment of the 140-N force about line AB.

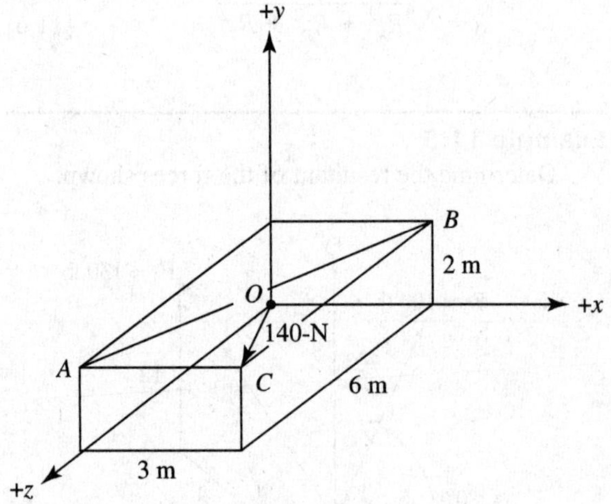

Figure 11.15

Solution:

$$\mathbf{M}_A = \mathbf{r}_{AO} \times \mathbf{F} = (-2\,\hat{\mathbf{j}} - 6\,\hat{\mathbf{k}}) \times (60\,\hat{\mathbf{i}} + 40\,\hat{\mathbf{j}} + 250\,\hat{\mathbf{k}})$$

$$= -360\,\hat{\mathbf{j}} + 120\,\hat{\mathbf{k}}$$

$$M_{AB} = \mathbf{M}_A \cdot \mathbf{u}_{AB} = (-360\,\hat{\mathbf{j}} + 120\,\hat{\mathbf{k}}) \cdot \left(\frac{3\,\hat{\mathbf{i}} - 6\,\hat{\mathbf{k}}}{\sqrt{45}}\right)$$

$$= -107.33\ N \cdot m$$

Moment of a Couple

Two equal and parallel forces that have noncollinear lines of actions and are opposite in sense form a **couple** (Figure 11.6). The moment of a couple is the product of the force and the shortest distance between the two forces. Note in the equation below that the

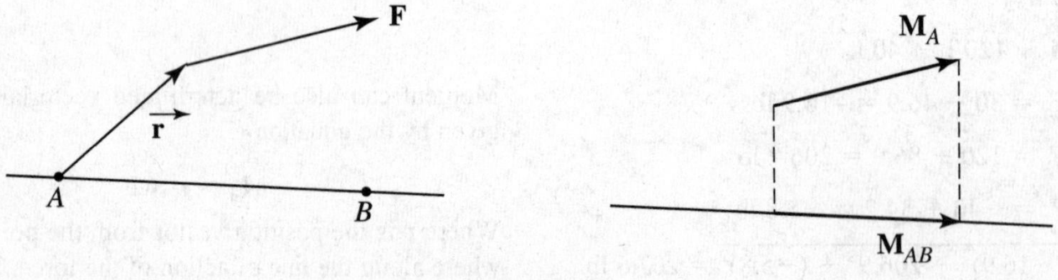

Figure 11.14

moment of a couple is the same with respect to any point in space.

$$M = Fd$$

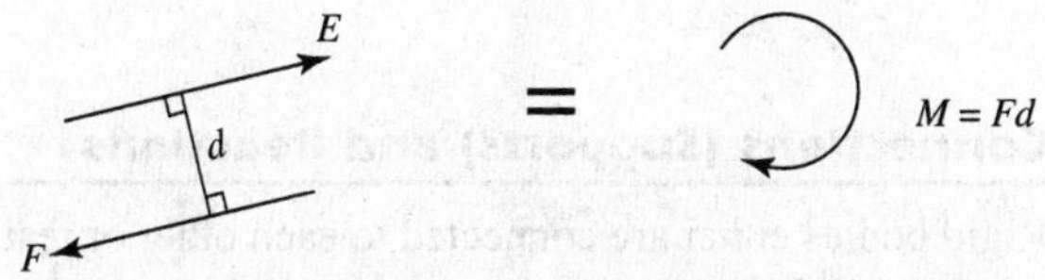

Figure 11.16

Example 11.8

Determine the resultant of the couple shown.

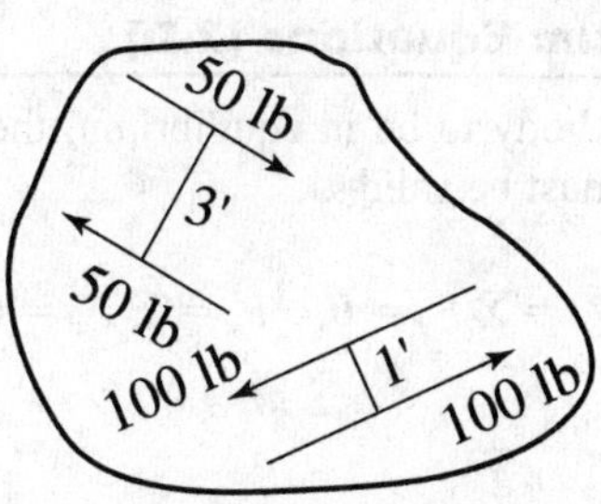

Figure 11.17

Solution:

CCW + :

$$M = (100)(1) - (50)(3) = -50 \text{ lb-ft}$$

Therefore, the resultant moment (couple) is clockwise.

11.3 Equilibrium of Particles

Two-Dimensional Case

For a particle to be in equilibrium (at rest), the resultant of the forces acting on the particle must be equal to zero (i.e., there is no translation).

$$R_x = \Sigma F_x = 0, \quad R_y = \Sigma F_y = 0 \quad [11.10]$$

Example 11.9

Two cables are tied together at C and loaded as shown. Determine the tension in each cable.

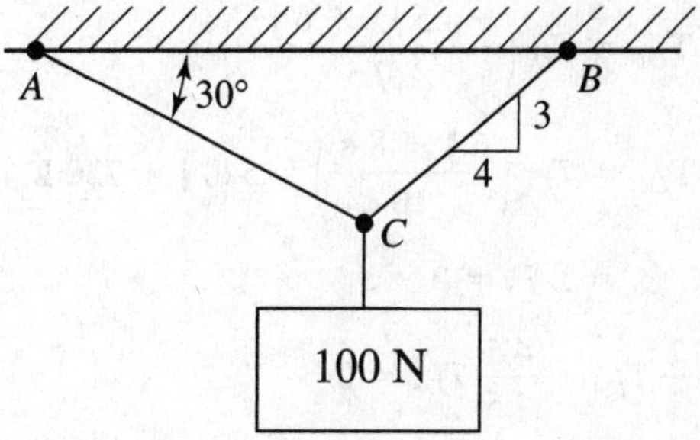

Figure 11.18

Solution:

$$R_x = \Sigma F_x = \frac{4}{5}T_{BC} - T_{AC}\cos 30 = 0$$

$$R_y = \Sigma F_y = \frac{3}{5}T_{BC} + T_{AC}\sin 30 - 100 = 0$$

Solve simultaneously for the tensions:

$$T_{AC} = 87 \text{ N} \quad \text{and} \quad T_{BC} = 94.17 \text{ N}$$

Three-Dimensional Case

This is the same as the two-dimensional case except that there is a component in the z-direction.

$$R_x = \Sigma F_x = 0,\ R_y = \Sigma F_y = 0,\ R_z = \Sigma F_z = 0 \ [11.11]$$

Example 11.10

A load W is supported by three cables as shown. Determine the magnitude of load W if the tension in cable CD is 900 N.

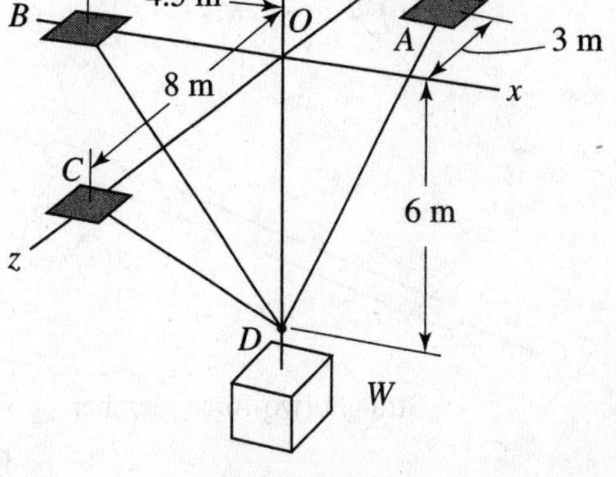

Figure 11.19

Solution:

It is given that $T_{DC} = 900$ N. Then:

$$\mathbf{T}_{DA} = T_{DA}\left(\frac{2\,\hat{\mathbf{i}} + 6\,\hat{\mathbf{j}} - 3\,\hat{\mathbf{k}}}{7}\right),$$

$$\mathbf{T}_{DB} = T_{DB}\left(\frac{-4.5\,\hat{\mathbf{i}} + 6\,\hat{\mathbf{j}}}{7.5}\right),$$

$$\mathbf{T}_{DC} = T_{DC}\left(\frac{6\,\hat{\mathbf{j}} + 8\,\hat{\mathbf{k}}}{10}\right) = 540\,\hat{\mathbf{j}} + 720\,\hat{\mathbf{k}}$$

$$R_x = \Sigma F_x = 0$$

$$\frac{2}{7}T_{DA} - \frac{4.5}{7.5}T_{DB} = 0$$

$$R_y = \Sigma F_y = 0$$

$$\frac{6}{7}T_{DA} + \frac{6}{7.5}T_{DB} + 540 - W = 0$$

$$R_z = \Sigma F_z = 0$$

$$-\frac{3}{7}T_{DA} + 720 = 0$$

Solve simultaneously for W:

$$W = 2{,}652 \text{ N}$$

11.4 Equilibrium of Rigid Bodies

Two-Force Members

If a member is under the action of only two forces (at different points on the body), the member is called a **two-force member.** For a straight two-force member, the force must act along the axis of the member (tension or compression).

If the force member is not straight, the force must act along the diagonal line connecting the two points where the two forces are acting.

Connections (Supports) and Reactions

Rigid bodies either are connected to each other or rest on surfaces. In most cases it is necessary to determine the resulting reactions for different supports. To find the number and type of reaction for a given support, determine whether the point of connection can translate or rotate. If the point cannot translate, a **force reaction** along the line of translation (x, y, or z) is required. If the point cannot rotate, a **moment reaction** about that axis is required.

Equilibrium Equations (2-D)

For a rigid body to be in equilibrium, the following equations must be valid.

$$R_x = \Sigma F_x = 0, \quad R_y = \Sigma F_y = 0 \qquad [11.12]$$
$$\Sigma M = 0$$

In equation 11.12 the moment can be taken about any point on the body. Note that for a two-dimensional case there are three equilibrium equations, so there cannot be more than three unknowns for a given free-body diagram (FBD).

Straight two-force member

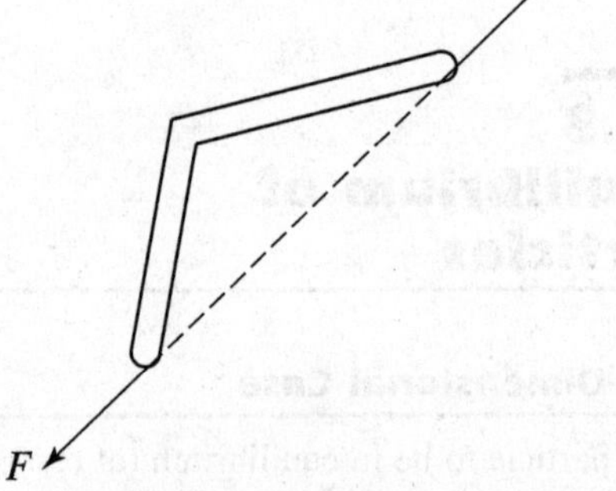

Nonstraight two-force member

Figure 11.20

Table 11.1. Supports for Rigid Bodies

Connections (Supports)	Reactions	Number of Unknowns
Hinge, pin 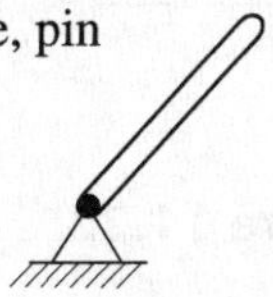	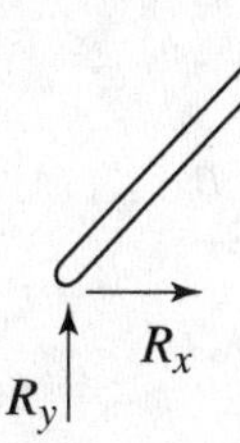	2
Rough surface 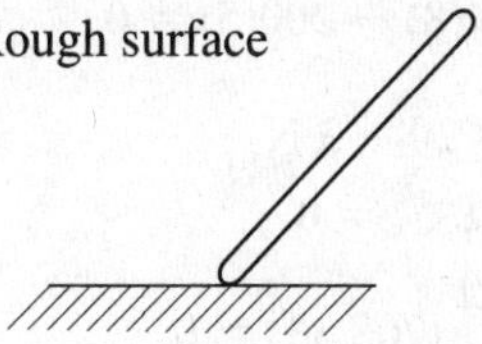	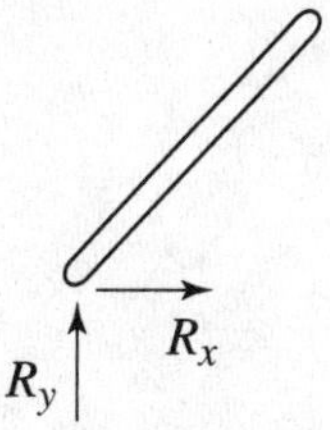	2
Roller, rocker smooth surface 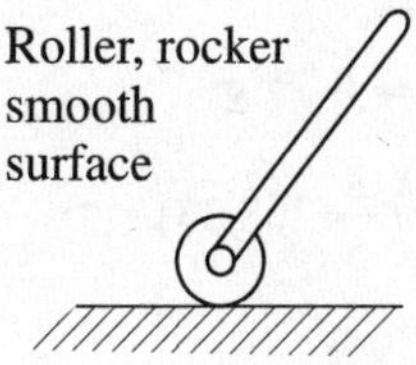	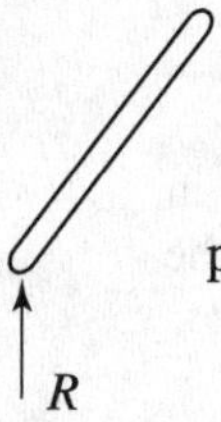 Reaction perpendicular to surface	1
Fixed 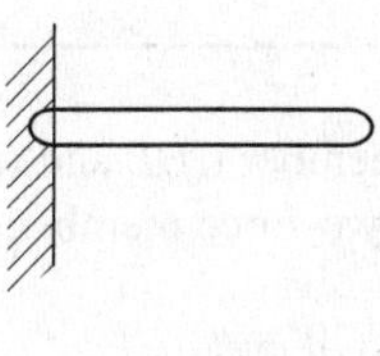	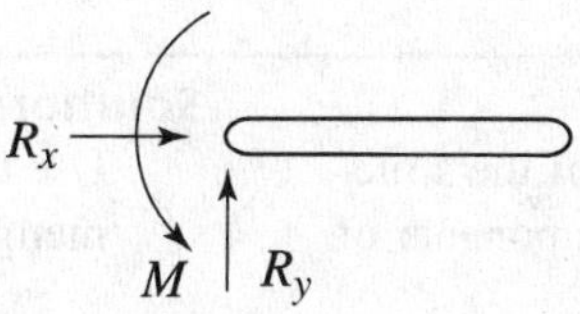	3
Ball and socket joint 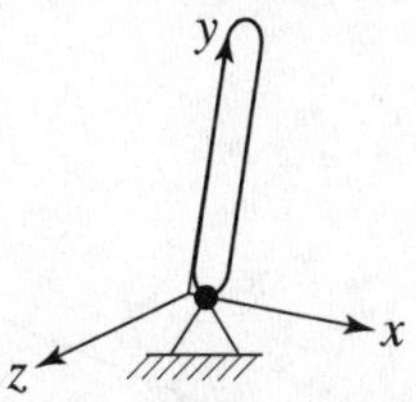	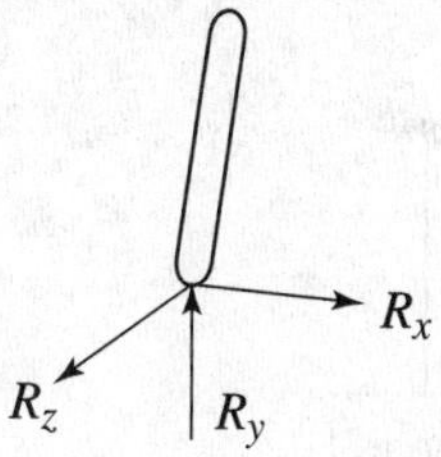	3
Fixed 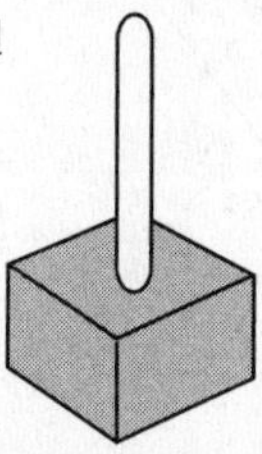	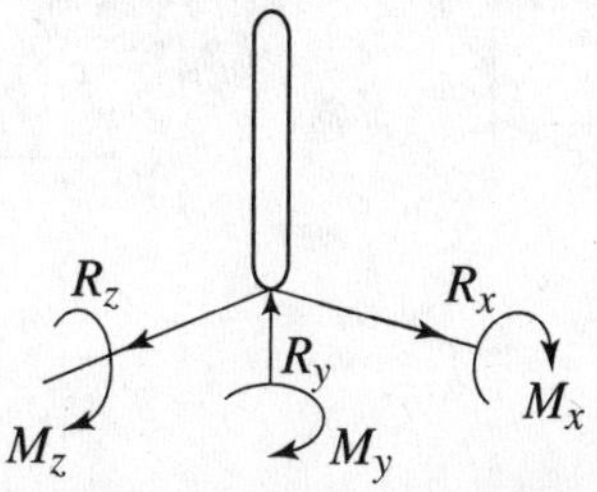	6

Example 11.11

For the beam and loading shown, determine the reaction at each support.

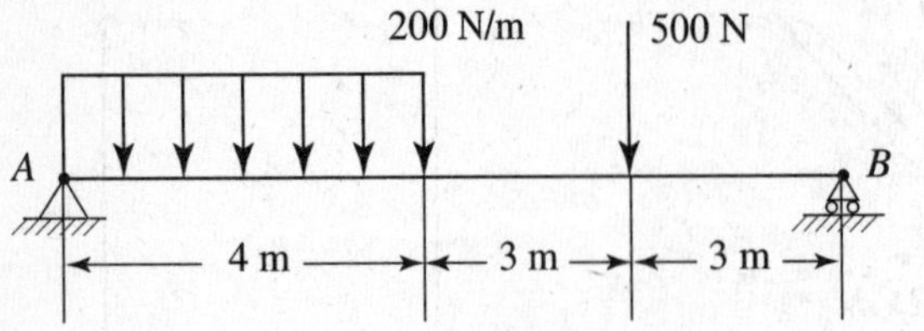

Figure 11.21

Solution:

$\Sigma M_A = 0 \quad CCW+:$

$B(10) - 500(7) - 800(2) = 0$; then $B = 510$ lb

$R_x = \Sigma F_x = 0, \quad A_x = 0$

$R_y = \Sigma F_y = 0,$

$A_y + 510 - 500 - 800 = 0 \Rightarrow A_y = 790$ N

Example 11.12

For the figure shown, determine the tension in cable BC and the reaction at A (neglect the weight of beam AB).

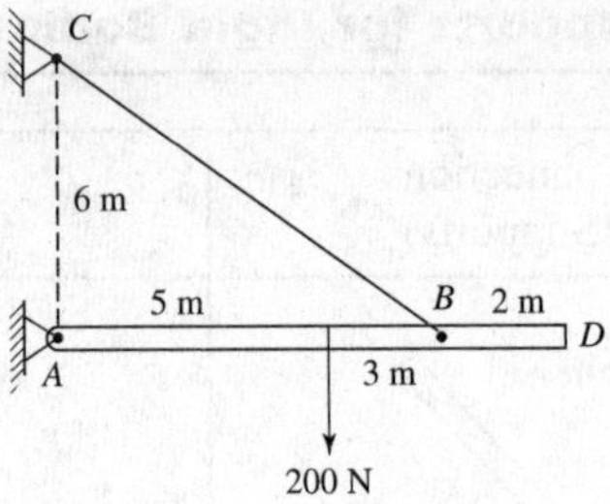

Figure 11.22

Solution:

$\Sigma M_A = 0$

$\frac{3}{5} T_{BC}(8) - 200(5) = 0$

$T_{BC} = 208.33$ N

$R_x = \Sigma F_x = 0$

$A_x - \frac{4}{5}(208.33) = 0$

$A_x = 166.66$ N

$R_y = \Sigma F_y = 0$

$A_y - 200 + \frac{3}{5}(208.33) = 0$

$A_y = 75$ N

Example 11.13

Determine the force in member BD of the structure shown. Also determine the components of reaction at point C.

Solution:

Use the FBD of member CDE and recognize that member BD is a two-force member. Then:

$\Sigma M_C = 0 \quad CCW+:$

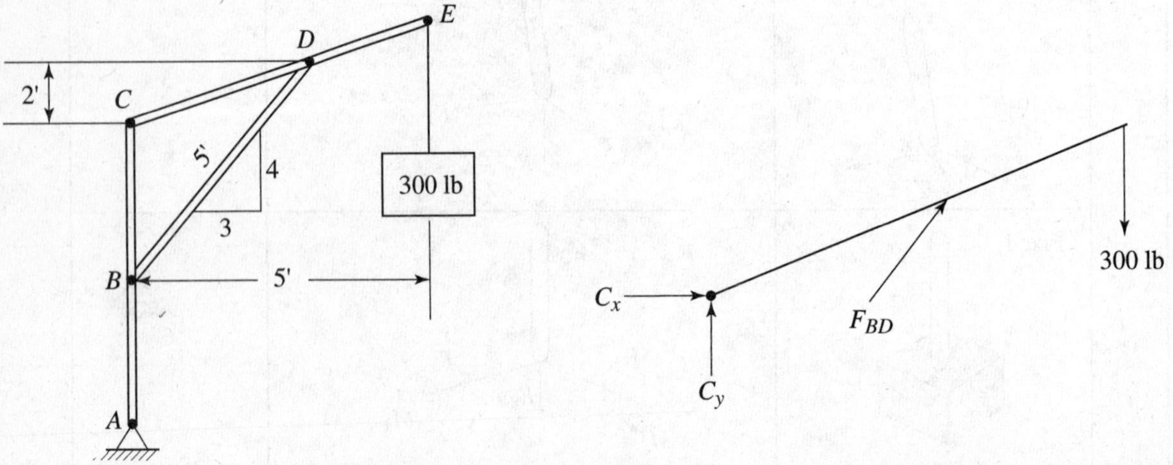

Figure 11.23

$$-\frac{3}{5}F_{BD}(2) + \frac{4}{5}F_{BD}(3) - 300(5) = 0$$

$$F_{BD} = 1{,}250 \text{ lb}$$

$$R_x = \Sigma F_x = 0$$

$$C_x + \frac{3}{5}(1{,}250) = 0$$

$$C_x = -750 \text{ lb}$$

$$R_y = \Sigma F_y = 0$$

$$C_y - 300 + \frac{4}{5}(1{,}250) = 0$$

$$C_y = -700 \text{ lb}$$

Equilibrium Equations (3-D)

In this case there are six equilibrium equations (three force equations and three moment equations).

$$R_x = \Sigma F_x = 0, \quad R_y = \Sigma F_y = 0, \quad R_z = \Sigma F_z = 0$$

$$\Sigma M_x = 0, \quad \Sigma M_y = 0, \quad \Sigma M_z = 0 \quad [11.13]$$

Example 11.14

In the figure, a plate weighing 135 N is supported by two cables (*CD* and *BE*) and a ball and socket joint at *A*. Determine the tension in each cable.

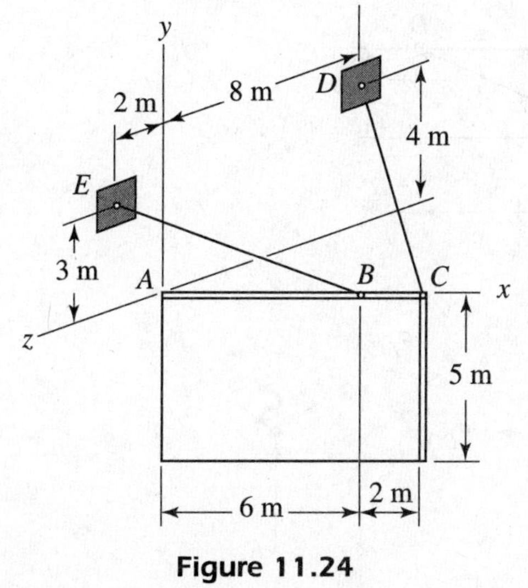

Figure 11.24

Solution:

$$\mathbf{T}_{CD} = T_{CD}\left(\frac{-8\hat{\mathbf{i}} + 4\hat{\mathbf{j}} - 8\hat{\mathbf{k}}}{12}\right)$$

$$\mathbf{T}_{BE} = T_{BE}\left(\frac{-6\hat{\mathbf{i}} + 3\hat{\mathbf{j}} + 2\hat{\mathbf{k}}}{7}\right)$$

$$\Sigma M_A = 0$$

$$8\hat{\mathbf{i}} \times T_{CD}\left(\frac{-8\hat{\mathbf{i}} + 4\hat{\mathbf{j}} - 8\hat{\mathbf{k}}}{12}\right) + 6\hat{\mathbf{i}}$$

$$\times\, T_{BE}\left(\frac{-6\hat{\mathbf{i}} + 3\hat{\mathbf{j}} + 2\hat{\mathbf{k}}}{7}\right) + (4\hat{\mathbf{i}} - 2.5\hat{\mathbf{j}})$$

$$\times\, (-135\hat{\mathbf{j}}) = 0$$

$$\left(\frac{16}{3}T_{CD} - \frac{12}{7}T_{BE}\right)\hat{\mathbf{j}} + \left(\frac{8}{3}T_{CD} + \frac{18}{7}T_{BE} - 540\right)\hat{\mathbf{k}} = 0$$

Set each parenthesis equal to zero, and solve for the tensions:

$$T_{BE} = 157.5 \text{ N}, \qquad T_{CD} = 50.63 \text{ N}$$

11.5 Trusses and Frames

Trusses

A collection of rigid bodies that are pin connected to each other at their ends to form a new rigid body is known as a *truss*. Each member of a truss is a straight two-force body. The main objective is to determine the internal forces in some or all members of a truss. Each member can be in tension (T) or compression (C), depending on the loading or configuration of the truss.

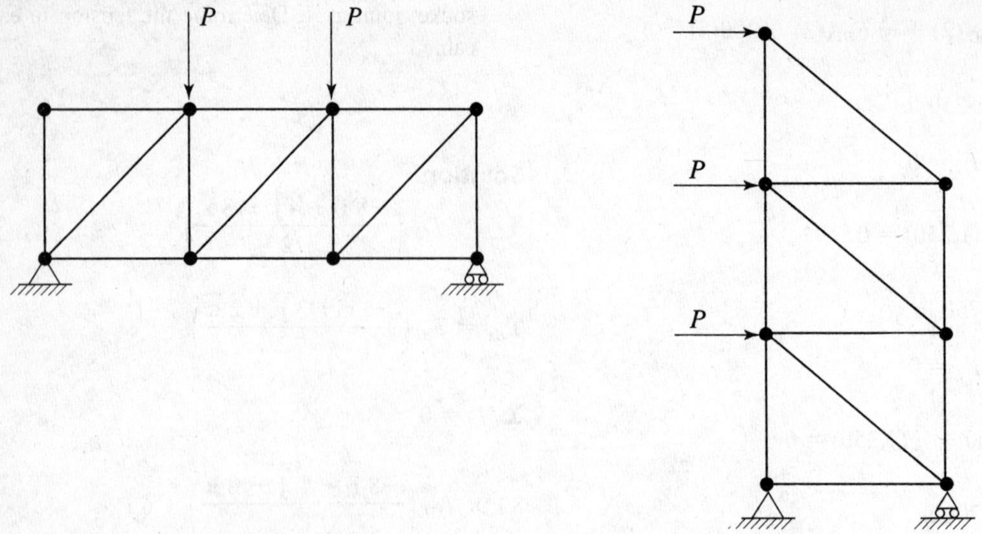

Figure 11.25

Generally two methods are available to determine internal forces in a given truss, the method of joints and the method of sections.

Method of Joints

To use this method, draw the FBD of the joint and apply the two-dimensional equilibrium equations for particles. Note that for a given joint there cannot be more than two unknowns.

$$R_x = \Sigma F_x = 0, \quad R_y = \Sigma F_y = 0$$

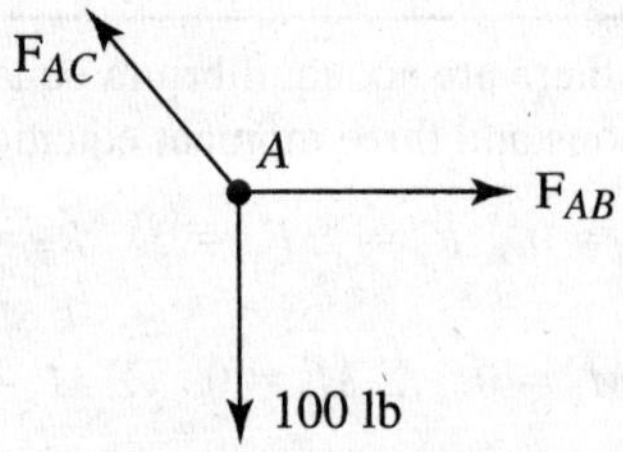

Figure 11.26

Example 11.15

Using the method of joints, determine the force in each member of the truss shown.

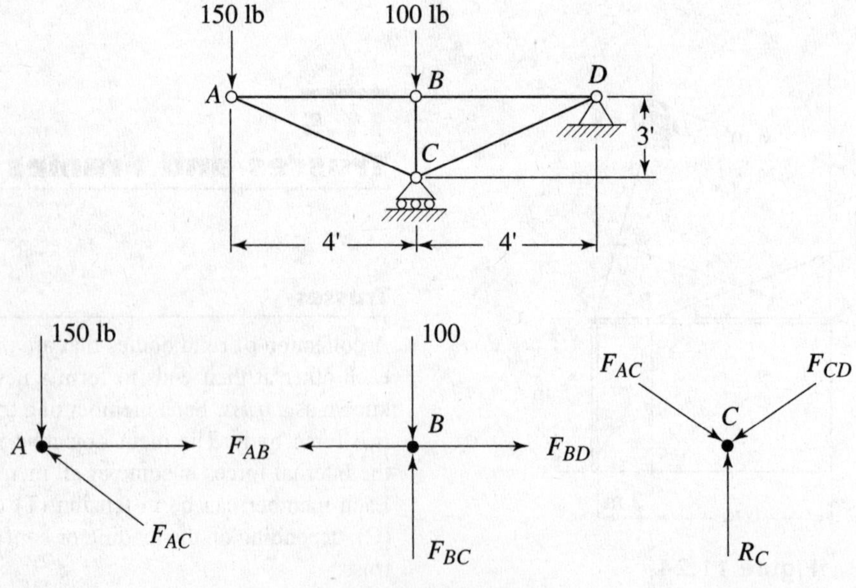

Figure 11.27

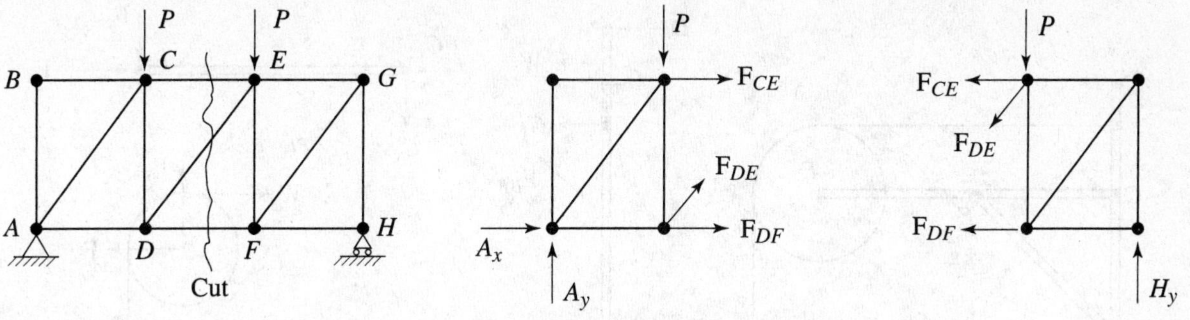

Figure 11.28

Solution:

Using Figure 11.27:

Joint A:

$$\Sigma F_y = 0 \Rightarrow -150 - \frac{3}{5}F_{AC} = 0$$

$$F_{AC} = 250 \text{ lb C}$$

$$\Sigma F_x = 0 \Rightarrow F_{AB} - \frac{4}{5}(250) = 0$$

$$F_{AB} = 200 \text{ lb T}$$

Joint B:

$$\Sigma F_x = 0 \Rightarrow F_{BD} = 200 \text{ lb T}$$

$$\Sigma F_x = 0 \Rightarrow F_{BC} = 100 \text{ lb T}$$

Joint C:

$$\Sigma F_x = 0 \Rightarrow F_{CD} = 250 \text{ lb C}$$

Method of Sections

This method is used when the forces for a few members of a large truss are to be determined. Cut the truss in a section where the forces are to be determined (see Figure 11.28). Then consider the section to the left or right (up or down in other cases), draw the FBD, and apply the two-dimensional equilibrium equations for rigid bodies. ***Generally the section considered should not pass or cut more than three members at a time (since only three equilibrium equations are available).***

$$R_x = \Sigma F_x = 0, \quad R_y = \Sigma F_y = 0$$

$$\Sigma M = 0$$

Note that, for some trusses, it is necessary to determine the external forces (reactions) before solving for the internal forces.

Example 11.16

Determine the forces in members CE, CD, and BD of the truss shown.

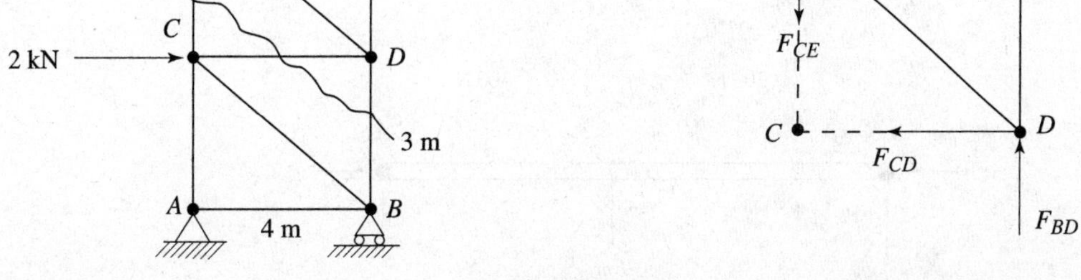

Figure 11.29

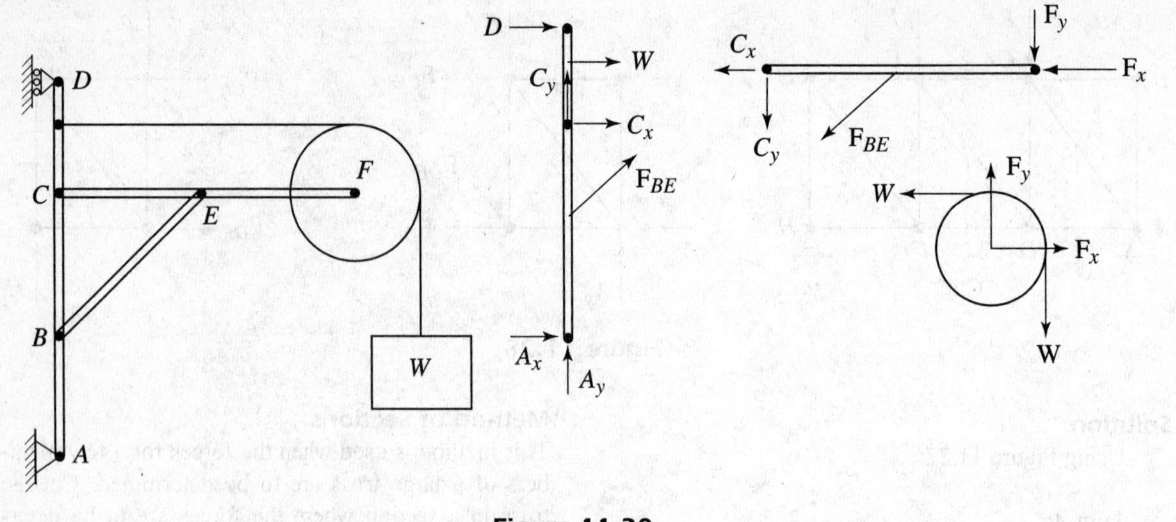

Figure 11.30

Solution:

$\Sigma M_D = 0 \quad \text{CCW} + :$

$F_{CE}(4) - 2(3) - 2(6) = 0$

$F_{CE} = 4.5 \text{ kN T}$

$\Sigma F_x = 0 \Rightarrow F_{CD} = 4 \text{ kN T}$

$\Sigma F_y = 0 \Rightarrow F_{BD} = 4.5 \text{ kN C}$

Frames

Frames are structures containing multiforce members and designed to support applied loads. Frames are usually stationary. The analysis is done by disassembling the frame, shown in Figure 11.30, drawing the FBD for each member, and applying the equilibrium equations (note that some members of a frame can be two-force members).

$$R_x = \Sigma F_x = 0, \quad R_y = \Sigma F_y = 0$$

$$\Sigma M = 0$$

Example 11.17

Determine the components of all forces acting on member *AC* of the frame shown.

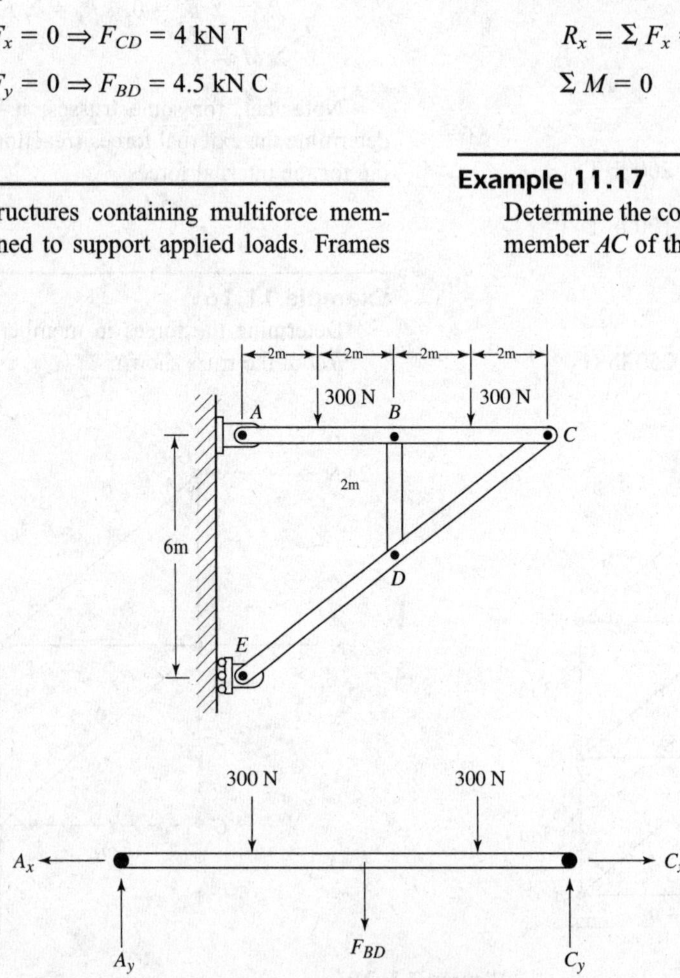

Figure 11.31

Solution:

First determine the reactions without disassembling the frame.

$$\Sigma M_A = 0$$

$$E(6) - 300(2) - 300(6) = 0$$

$$E = 400 \text{ N}$$

$$\Sigma F_x = 0 \Rightarrow A_x = 400 \text{ N} \leftarrow$$

$$\Sigma F_y = 0 \Rightarrow A_y = 600 \text{ N} \uparrow$$

Now use the FBD of member AC, noting that BD is a two-force member.

$$\Sigma M_C = 0$$

$$F_{BD}(4) + 300(2) + 300(6) - 600(8) = 0$$

$$F_{BD} = 600 \text{ N} \downarrow$$

$$\Sigma F_x = 0 \Rightarrow C_x = 400 \text{ N} \rightarrow$$

$$\Sigma F_y = 0 \Rightarrow C_y = 600 \text{ N} \uparrow$$

11.6 Friction

When two surfaces are in contact, the force tangent to the surface that opposes the direction of tendency to motion is called the **friction.** There are two types of friction: dry friction and fluid friction.

To understand the laws of dry friction consider the figure shown below.

The maximum value of friction force (F_{max}) is related to the normal force (N) and the coefficient of static friction (μ_s):

$$F_{max} = \mu_s N \qquad [11.14]$$

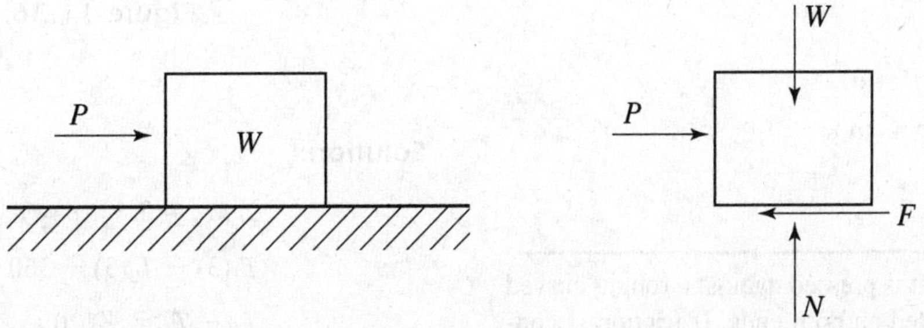

Figure 11.32

Two Types of Friction Problems

There are two distinct types of friction problems:

1. The impending motion exists (the object is about to move). In this case friction has reached its maximum value, and $F = F_{max} = \mu_s N$. Apply the equilibrium equations for the particle or rigid body, and solve for the unknowns.
2. The impending motion is not known (you don't know whether the object is moving or not). In this case assume that the system is in equilibrium, and apply the appropriate equilibrium equations (particle or rigid body) to solve for the friction force. Two outcomes are possible.
   a. If $F < \mu_s N$, then the system is in equilibrium and the friction force calculated is correct.
   b. If $F > \mu_s N$, then the system is in motion and for ***particle problems only*** the correct value of friction force is $F = \mu_k N$, where μ_k is called the coefficient of kinetic friction. In general, μ_k is about 25% smaller than μ_s.

For rigid body problems, a dynamical analysis is used to determine the magnitude of the friction force.

Example 11.18

Determine the value of the friction force.

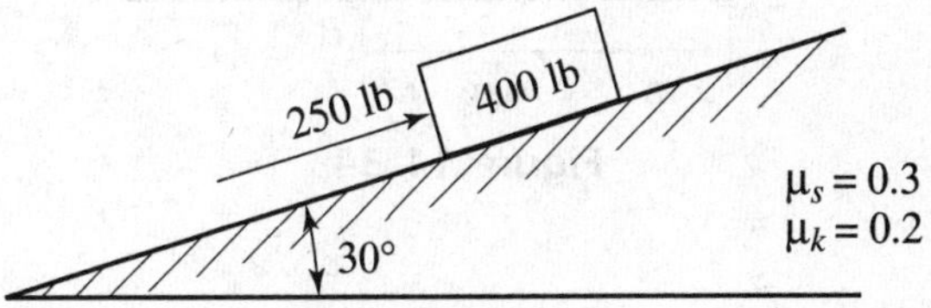

Figure 11.33

Solution:

This is case 2; that is, the impending motion is not known.

$\nwarrow \Sigma F_y = 0$

$N - 400 \cos 30 = 0 \Rightarrow N = 346.4 \text{ lb}$

$\stackrel{+}{\nearrow} \Sigma F_x = 0$

$-F + 250 - 400 \sin 30 = 0 \Rightarrow F = 50 \text{ lb}$

Now check: $\mu_s N = 0.3(364.4) = 103.92$ since $F < \mu_s N$. Then the friction force calculated is correct: $F = 50$ lb.

Example 11.19

If the bar weighs 50 N, determine the minimum value of load P that will initiate the motion (neglect friction at A).

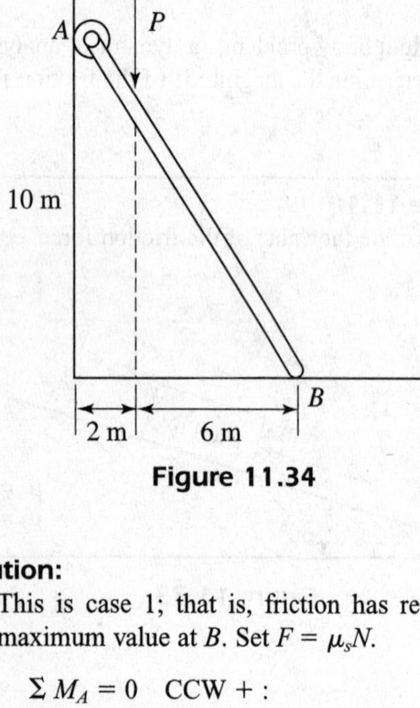

Figure 11.34

Solution:

This is case 1; that is, friction has reached its maximum value at B. Set $F = \mu_s N$.

$\Sigma M_A = 0 \quad \text{CCW} + :$

$N(8) - 0.5N(10) - 50(4) - P(2) = 0$

$3N - 2P = 200$

$\Sigma F_y = 0$

$N - 50 - P = 0$

Solve for P: $P = 50$ N

Belt Friction

Consider a belt that is pressed against a rough, curved surface and is pulled on both ends. If friction is considered, the tensions (T) on both ends are not the same. It can be shown that

$$T_2 = T_1 e^{\mu_s \theta} \qquad [11.15]$$

where θ is the angle of contact between the belt and the drum.

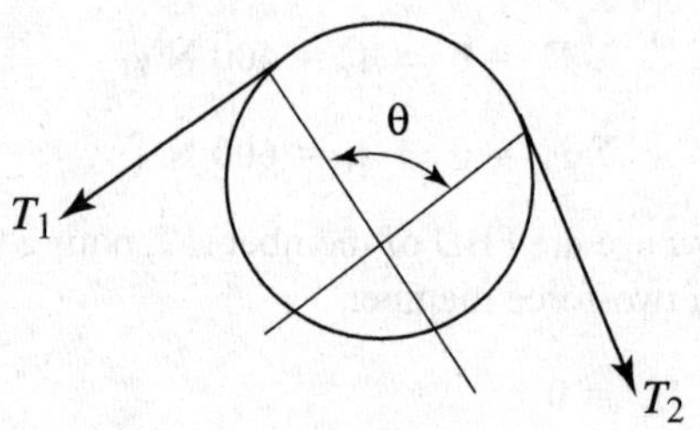

Figure 11.35

Example 11.20

A flat belt transmits a 30 lb-ft torque. Determine the minimum values of tension in both parts of the belt that will prevent slippage. The diameter of the drum is 6 in and $\mu_s = 0.3$.

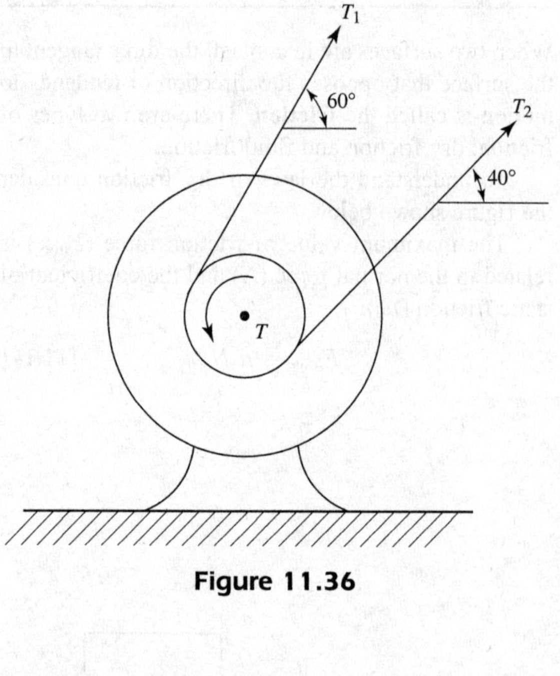

Figure 11.36

Solution:

$\Sigma M_o = 0$

$T_1(3) - T_2(3) + 360 = 0$

$T_1 - T_2 = -120$

The angle of contact between belt and drum is 180°.

$$\theta = 180° = \pi = 3.14 \text{ rad}$$

$$\frac{T_2}{T_1} = e^{0.3(3.14)} = e^{0.942} = 2.565$$

$$T_2 = 2.565T_1$$

$$T_1 = 76.7 \text{ lb}, \quad T_2 = 196.7 \text{ lb}$$

11.7 Center of Gravity

Center of gravity is defined as the point of a body where the weight of the body will pass through. For a homogeneous body the center of gravity is the same as the **centroid.**

In general, to determine the location of centroid of a plane area use the following equations:

$$\overline{X}_c = \frac{\int x_c dA}{A}, \quad \overline{Y}_c = \frac{\int y_c dA}{A} \qquad [11.16]$$

where $\int x_c \, dA$ and $\int y_c \, dA$ are called the first moments of the area with respect to the y-axis and x-axis, respectively.

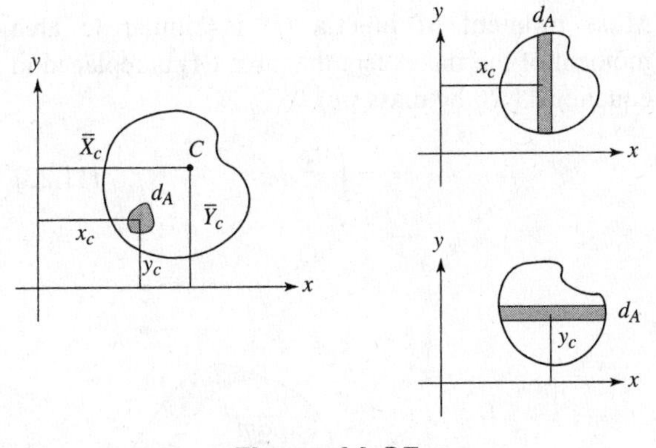

Figure 11.37

If the plane area can be divided into common shapes, as shown in Fig 11.38 (i.e., rectangles, semicircles, triangles), then the discrete form of the equations can be used:

$$\overline{X}_c = \frac{\sum x_i A_i}{A}, \quad \overline{Y}_c = \frac{\sum y_i A_i}{A} \qquad [11.17]$$

Example 11.21

Determine the center of gravity of the shaded plane area shown.

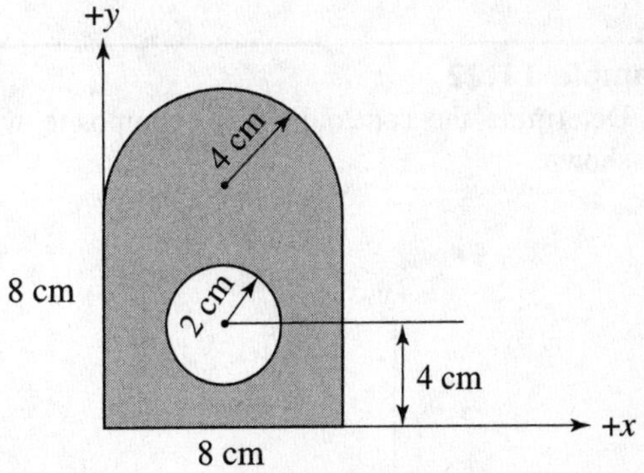

Figure 11.39

Solution:

$$\overline{X}_c = \frac{\sum x_i A_i}{A}$$

$$= \frac{(4)(64) + (4)\left[\frac{1}{2}\pi(4)^2\right] - (4)\left[\pi(2)^2\right]}{64 + \frac{1}{2}\pi(4)^2 - \pi(2)^2} = 4 \text{ cm}$$

$$\overline{Y}_c = \frac{\sum y_i A_i}{A}$$

$$= \frac{(4)(64) + (9.697)\left[\frac{1}{2}\pi(4)^2\right] - (4)\left[\pi(2)^2\right]}{64 + \frac{1}{2}\pi(4)^2 - \pi(2)^2}$$

$$= 5.87 \text{ cm}$$

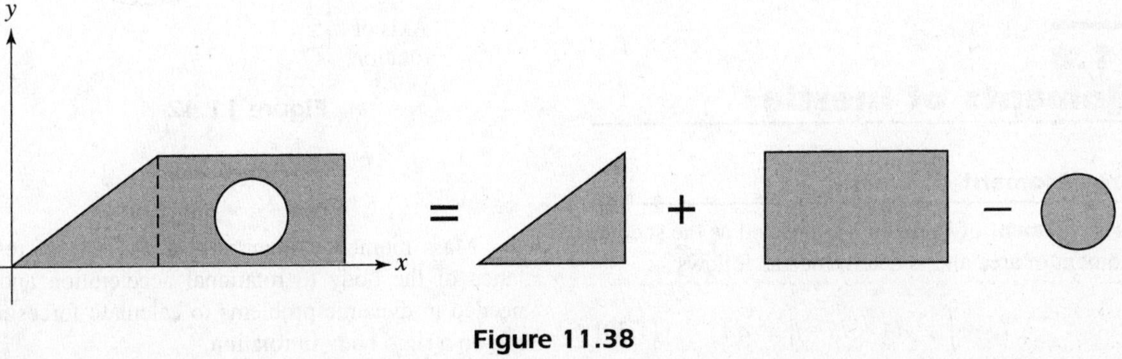

Figure 11.38

To find the centroid of lines (wires) and volumes, use the following similar equations.

For lines:

$$\bar{X}_c = \frac{\sum x_i L_i}{L}, \quad \bar{Y}_c = \frac{\sum y_i L_i}{L} \qquad [11.18]$$

For volumes:

$$\bar{X}_c = \frac{\sum x_i V_i}{V}, \quad \bar{Y}_c = \frac{\sum y_i V_i}{V} \qquad [11.19]$$

Example 11.22

Determine the centroid of the composite wire shown.

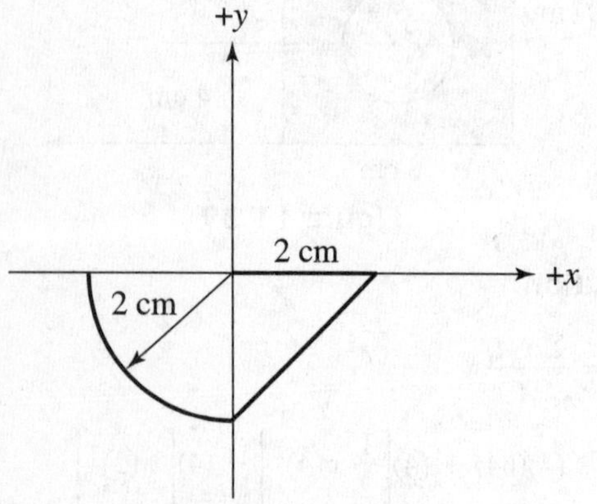

Figure 11.40

Solution:

$$\bar{X}_c = \frac{\sum x_i L_i}{L} = \frac{(1)(2) + (1)(2.83) + (-1.273)(3.14)}{2 + 2.83 + 3.14}$$

$$= 0.1045 \text{ cm}$$

$$\bar{Y}_c = \frac{\sum y_i L_i}{L} = \frac{(0)(2) + (-1)(2.83) + (-1.273)(3.14)}{2 + 2.83 + 3.14}$$

$$= -0.856 \text{ cm}$$

11.8 Moments of Inertia

Area Moment of Inertia

Area moment of inertia (I) is defined as the second moment of area and is determined as follows:

$$I_x = \int y^2\, dA, \quad I_y = \int x^2\, dA \qquad [11.20]$$

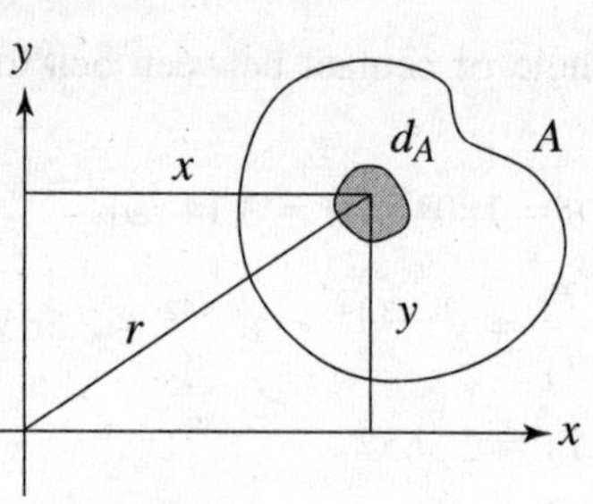

Figure 11.41

Area moment of inertia is a measure of resistance to bending and is needed to calculate stresses due to bending.

Polar Moment of Inertia

Polar moment of inertia (J) is the second moment of area with respect to the z-axis. It represents a resistance to twisting and is needed to calculate shear stresses due to twisting.

$$J = I_z = \int r^2\, dA = \int x^2\, dA + \int y^2\, dA$$
$$= I_x + I_y \qquad [11.21]$$

Mass Moment of Inertia

Mass moment of inertia (I) is similar to area moment of inertia, except that area (A) is replaced in equation 11.20 by mass (m).

$$I = \int r^2\, dm \qquad [11.22]$$

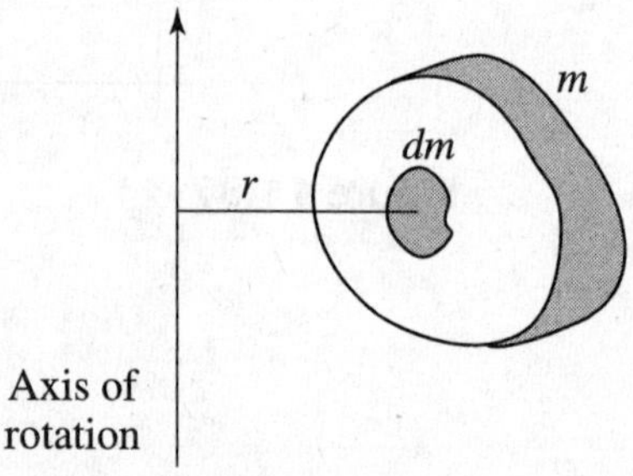

Figure 11.42

Mass moment of inertia is a measure of resistance of the body to rotational acceleration and is needed in dynamic problems to calculate forces acting on a rigid body in rotation.

Table 11.2. Centroids and Area Moments of Inertia of Common Shapes of Areas and Lines

Shape		Area	Centroid	Area Moment of Inertia
Rectangle	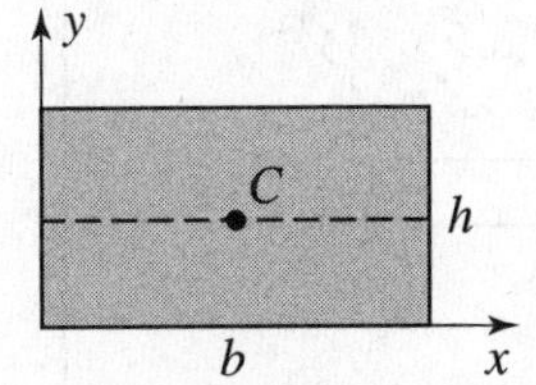	bh	$\bar{x} = \frac{b}{2}$ $\bar{y} = \frac{h}{2}$	$\bar{I}_c = \frac{1}{12}bh^3$ $I_x = \frac{1}{3}bh^3$ $I_y = \frac{1}{3}b^3h$
Triangle	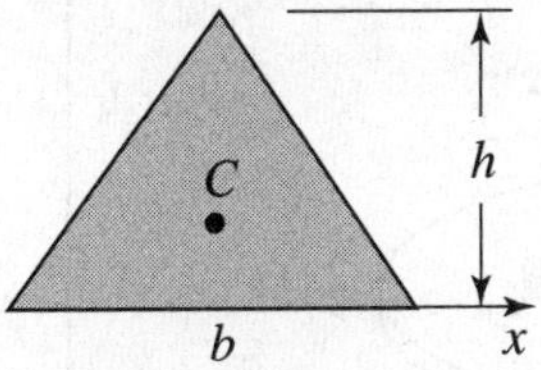	$\frac{1}{2}bh$	$\bar{y} = \frac{h}{3}$	$\bar{I}_c = \frac{1}{36}bh^3$ $I_x = \frac{1}{12}bh^3$
Circle	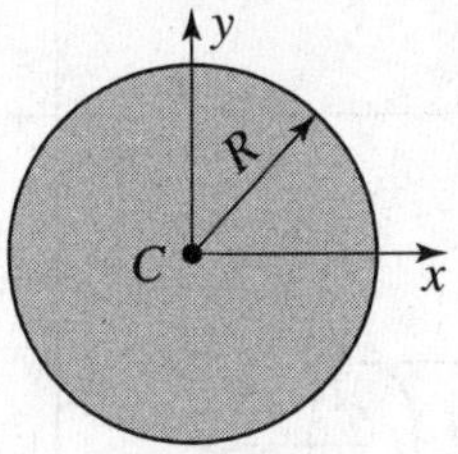	πR^2	$\bar{x} = 0$ $\bar{y} = 0$	$\bar{I}_x = I_y = \frac{\pi R^4}{4}$ $I_z = J = \frac{\pi}{2}R^4$
Semicircle	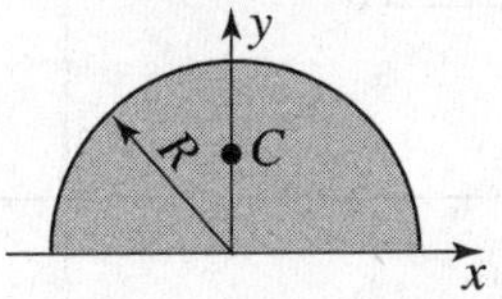	$\frac{\pi R^2}{2}$	$\bar{y} = \frac{4R}{3\pi}$	$\bar{I}_x = I_y = \frac{1}{8}\pi R^4$ $I_z = J = \frac{1}{4}\pi R^4$
Quarter circle	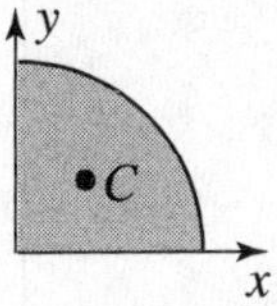	$\frac{\pi R^2}{4}$	$\bar{x} = \frac{4R}{3\pi}$ $\bar{y} = \frac{4R}{3\pi}$	$I_x = I_y = \frac{1}{16}\pi R^4$ $I_z = J = \frac{1}{8}\pi R^4$
Semicircular arc	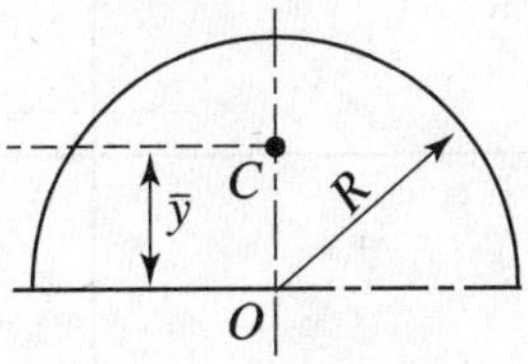		$\bar{x} = 0$ $\bar{y} = \frac{2R}{\pi}$	
Quarter-circular arc	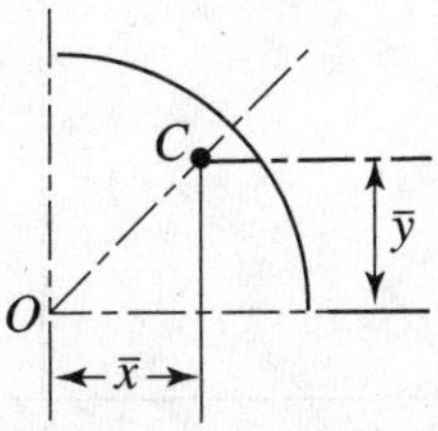		$\bar{x} = \frac{2R}{\pi}$ $\bar{y} = \frac{2R}{\pi}$	

Table 11.3. Mass Moments of Inertia of Common Shapes

Shape		Mass Moment of Inertia
Slender rod	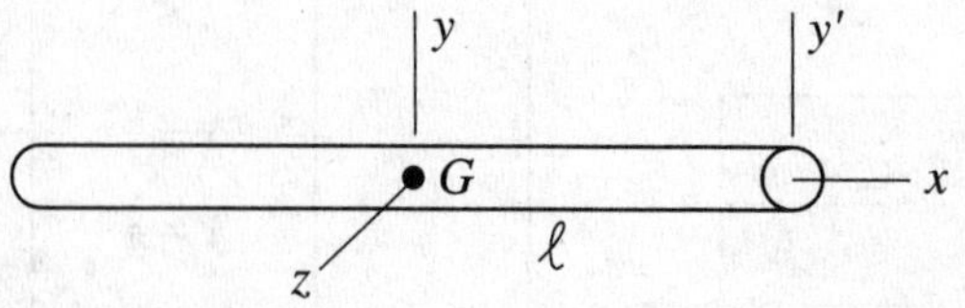	$\bar{I}_y = I_z = \frac{1}{12} m\ell^2$ $I_{y'} = \frac{1}{3} m\ell^2$ $I_x = 0$
Thin disk	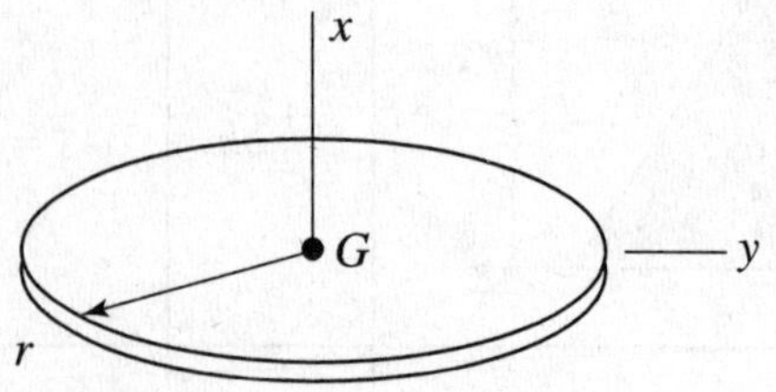	$\bar{I}_x = \frac{1}{2} mr^2$ $\bar{I}_y = \frac{1}{4} mr^2$
Cylinder	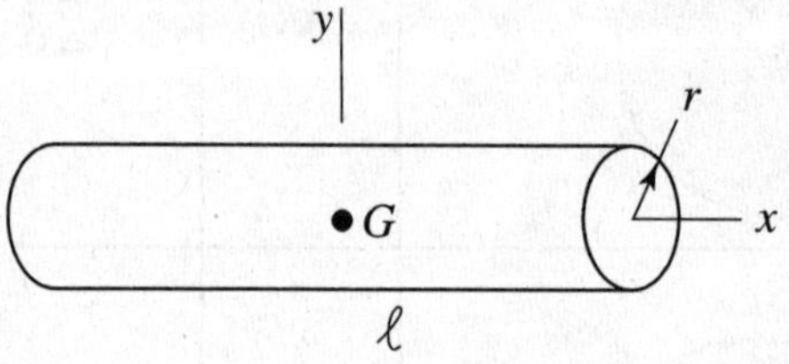	$\bar{I}_x = \frac{1}{2} mr^2$ $\bar{I}_y = \frac{1}{12} m(\ell^2 + 3r^2)$
Rectangular prism	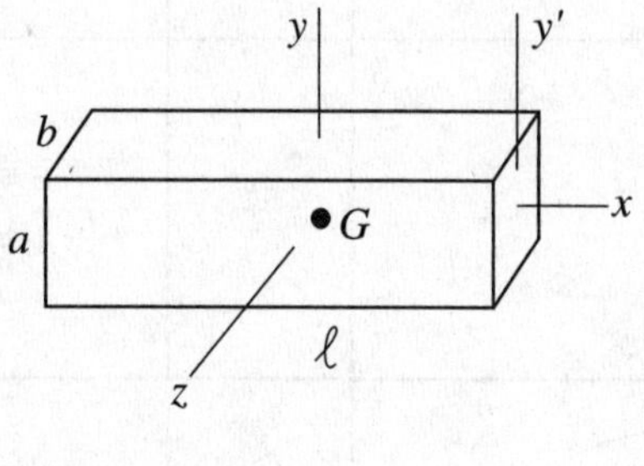	$\bar{I}_x = \frac{1}{12} m(a^2 + b^2)$ $\bar{I}_y = \frac{1}{12} m(\ell^2 + b^2)$ $\bar{I}_z = \frac{1}{12} m(\ell^2 + a^2)$ $\bar{I}_{y'} = \frac{1}{12} m(4\ell^2 + a^2)$
Sphere	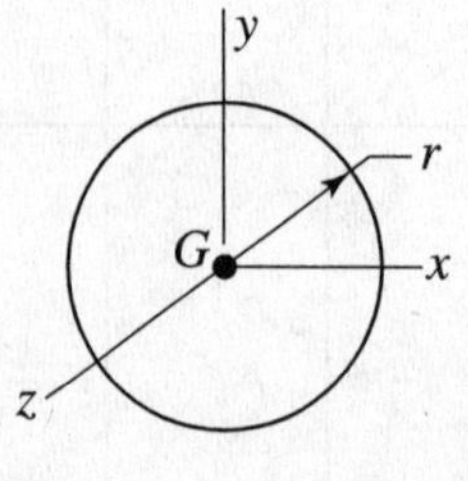	$\bar{I}_x = \bar{I}_y = \bar{I}_z = \frac{2}{5} mr^2$

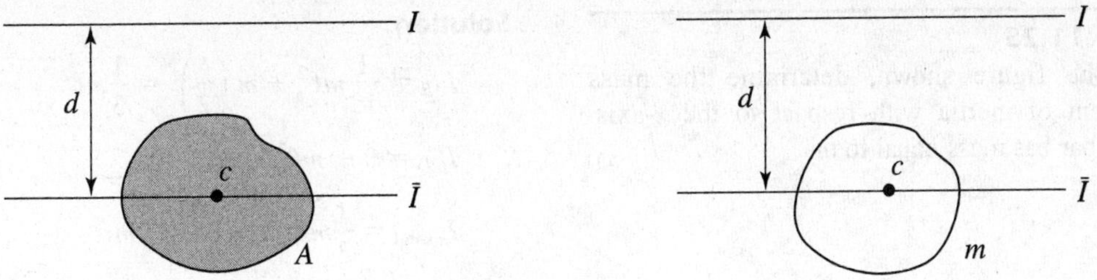

Figure 11.43

Parallel Axis Equation

In many situations the cross-sectional areas are not symmetric. To calculate moment of inertia with respect to an axis that is parallel to the centroidal axis (see Figure 11.43), the following equations can be used:

$$I = \bar{I} + Ad^2, \quad I = \bar{I} + md^2 \qquad [11.23]$$

Example 11.23

For the figure shown, determine the area moment of inertia of the shaded area with respect to the x-axis.

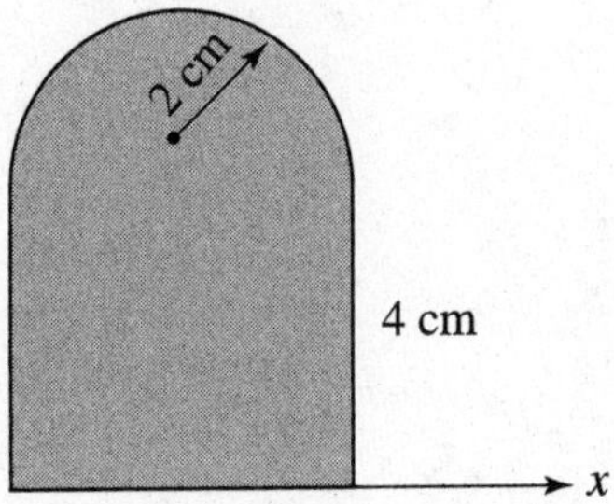

Figure 11.44

Solution:

$$I_{shape} = I_{rect} + I_{semicircle}$$

For the rectangle:

$$I_x = \frac{1}{3}(4)(4)^3 = 85.33 \text{ cm}^4$$

For the semicircle use the parallel axis equation:

$$I_x = \bar{I} + Ad^2$$

$$= 0.007(4)^4 + \frac{\pi}{2}(2)^2\left[4 + \frac{4(2)}{3\pi}\right]^2 = 149.52 \text{ cm}^4$$

$$I_{x\,total} = 85.33 + 149.52 = 234.85 \text{ cm}^4$$

Example 11.24

For the figure shown, determine the area moment of inertia with respect to the horizontal centroidal axis.

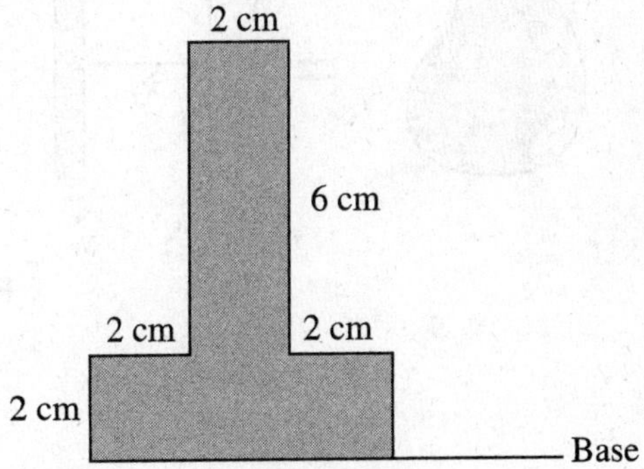

Figure 11.45

Solution:

First locate the centroid of the shape.

$$\bar{Y}_c = \frac{\Sigma y_i A_i}{A} = \frac{(6)(2)(1) + (6)(2)(5)}{(6)(2) + (6)(2)} = \text{3 cm from the base}$$

$$I = I_{flange} + I_{web}$$

$$I_{flange} = \frac{1}{12}(6)(2)^3 + (6)(2)(2)^2 = 52 \text{ cm}^4$$

$$I_{web} = \frac{1}{12}(2)(6)^3 + (6)(2)(2)^2 = 84 \text{ cm}^4$$

$$I = 52 + 84 = 136 \text{ cm}^4$$

Example 11.25

For the figure shown, determine the mass moment of inertia with respect to the x-axis. Each bar has mass equal to m.

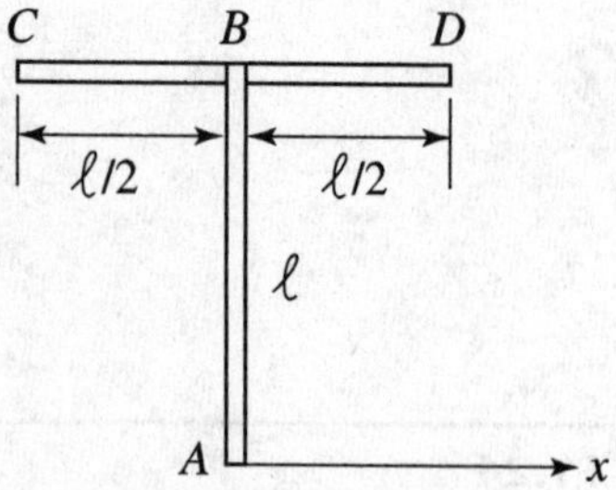

Figure 11.46

Solution:

$$I_{AB} = \frac{1}{12}m\ell^2 + m\left(\frac{\ell}{2}\right)^2 = \frac{1}{3}m\ell^2$$

$$I_{CD} = 0 + m\ell^2 = m\ell^2$$

$$I_{x\text{ total}} = \frac{1}{3}m\ell^2 + m\ell^2 = \frac{4}{3}m\ell^2$$

Radius of Gyration

Radius of gyration (k) represents the distance from the axis at which the area or mass must be concentrated if the moment of inertia is to remain the same. The following equations are used to calculate radius of gyration:

$$k = \sqrt{\frac{I}{A}}, \quad k = \sqrt{\frac{I}{m}} \qquad [11.24]$$

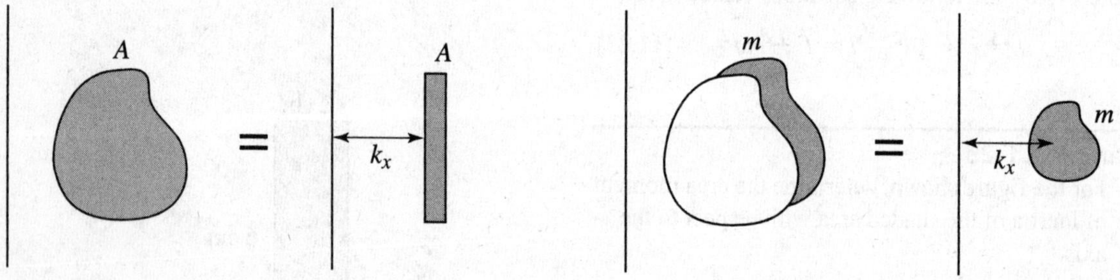

Figure 11.47

PRACTICE PROBLEMS

1. Determine the resultant of the forces.
   (A) 38 N
   (B) 121 N
   (C) 78 N
   (D) 525 N

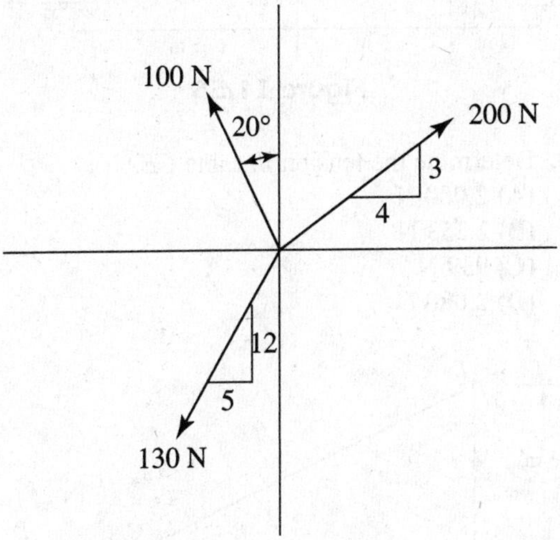

Figure 11.48

2. Determine the resultant of the forces exerted at point B if the tension in each cable is 450 N.
   (A) 735 N
   (B) 472 N
   (C) 375 N
   (D) 250 N

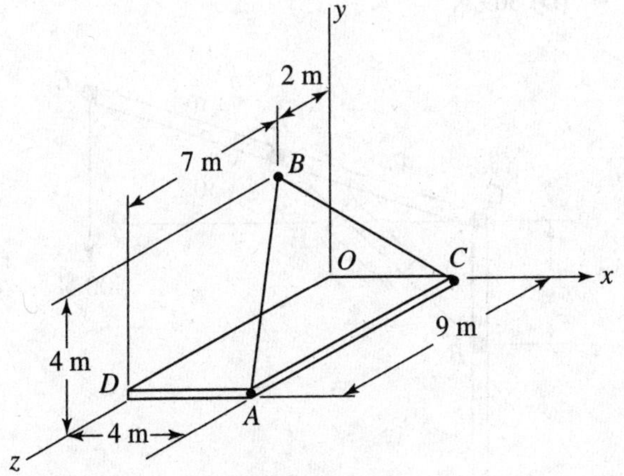

Figure 11.49

3. Determine the moment of force F about point A.
   (A) 30.4 N · m
   (B) 3.8 N · m
   (C) 1.6 N · m
   (D) 20 N · m

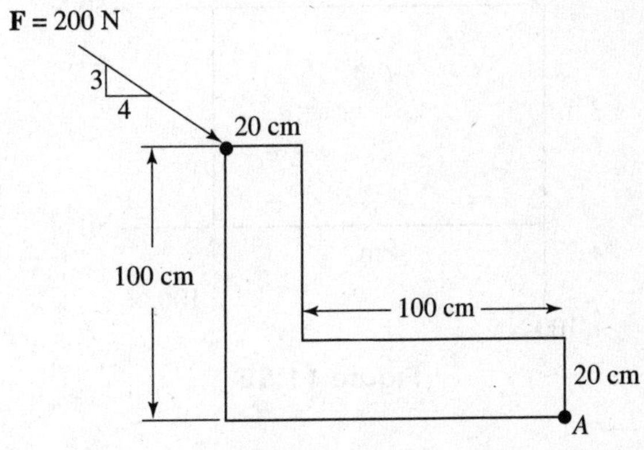

Figure 11.50

4. Determine the moment of force P = 50 N about line OC.
   (A) 3,600 N · m
   (B) 424 N · m
   (C) 1,600 N · m
   (D) 0

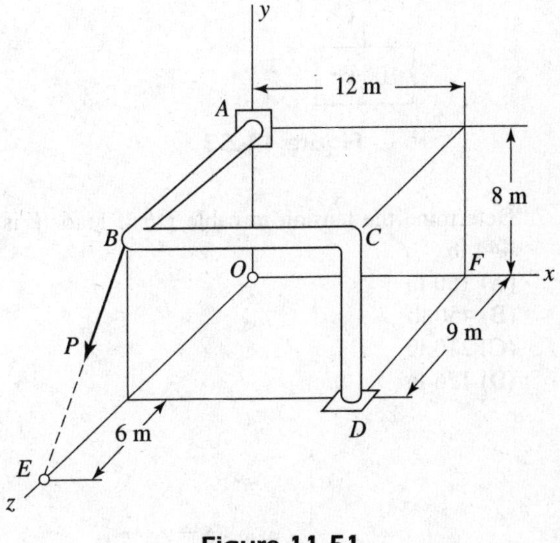

Figure 11.51

5. Determine the resultant of the couples.
   (A) 250 N · m
   (B) 550 N · m
   (C) 1,100 N · m
   (D) 500 N · m

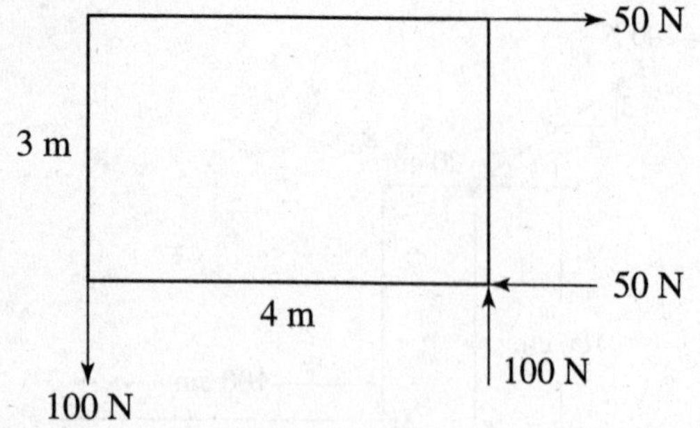

Figure 11.52

6. Determine the tension in cable *AC*.
   (A) 640 N
   (B) 863 N
   (C) 1,200 N
   (D) 550 N

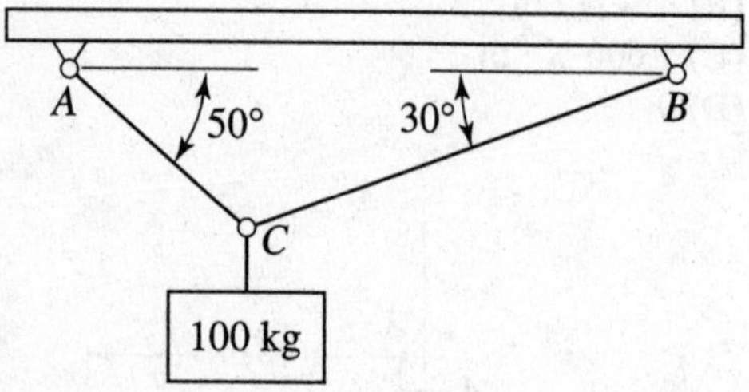

Figure 11.53

7. Determine the tension in cable *DB* if load *W* is 444 lb.
   (A) 150 lb
   (B) 450 lb
   (C) 210 lb
   (D) 156 lb

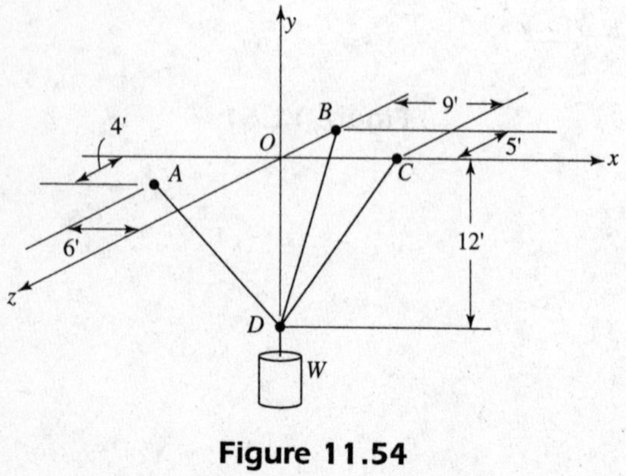

Figure 11.54

8. Determine the reaction at roller support *B*.
   (A) 365 N
   (B) 310 N
   (C) 435 N
   (D) 400 N

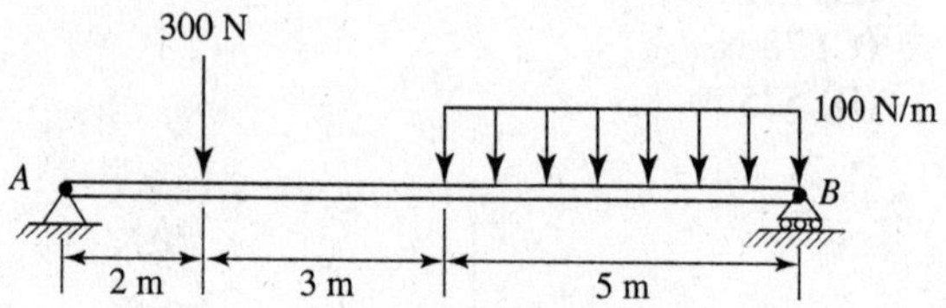

Figure 11.55

9. Determine the tension in cable *CE*.
   (A) 2,000 N
   (B) 2,253 N
   (C) 939 N
   (D) 2,080 N

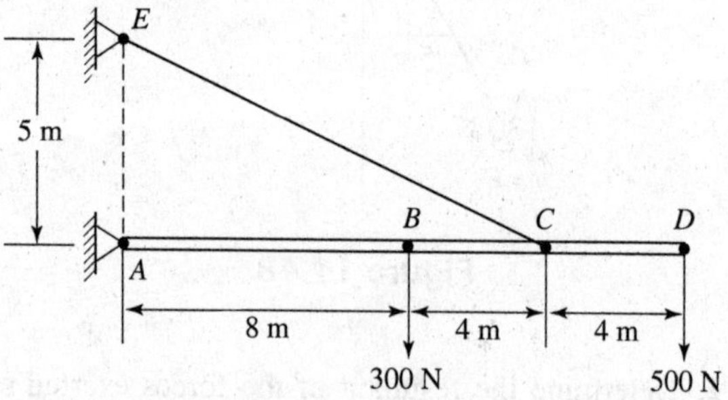

Figure 11.56

10. Determine the force in hydraulic cylinder *BD*.
   (A) 850 N
   (B) 608 N
   (C) 250 N
   (D) 869 N

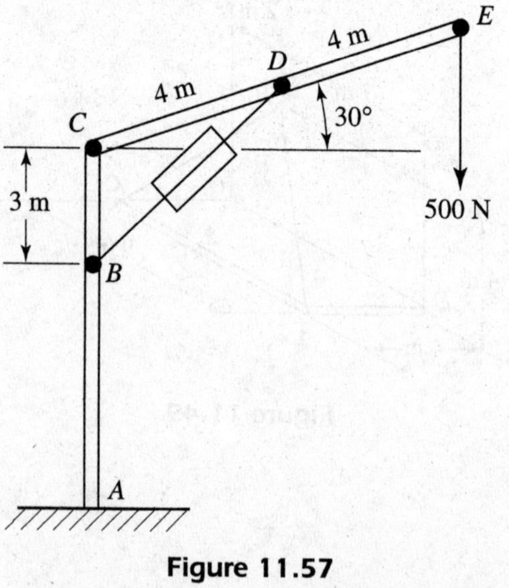

Figure 11.57

11. Determine the tension in cable *BE*.
(A) 2,600 N
(B) 1,310 N
(C) 2,000 N
(D) 917 N

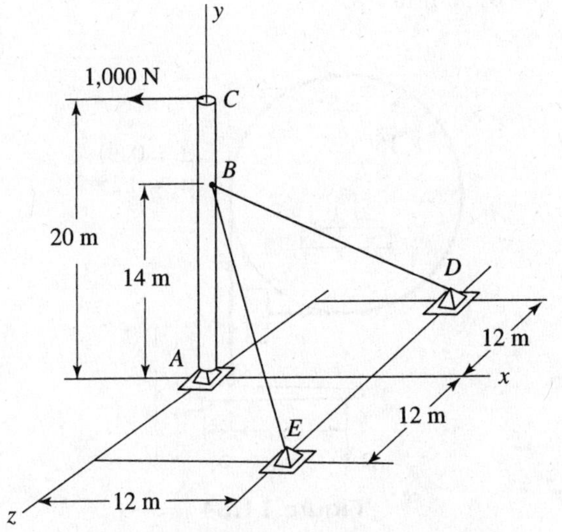

Figure 11.58

12. Determine the force in member *CE* of the truss.
(A) 3 kN
(B) 5 kN
(C) 8 kN
(D) 0

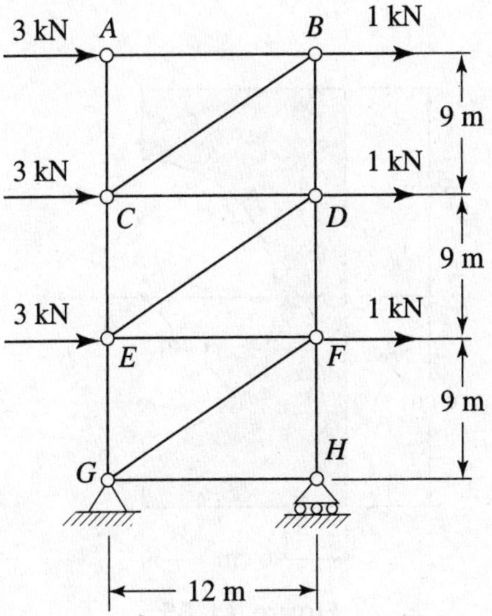

Figure 11.59

13. Determine the force in member *CF* of the truss.
(A) 30 kips
(B) 24 kips
(C) 48 kips
(D) 18 kips

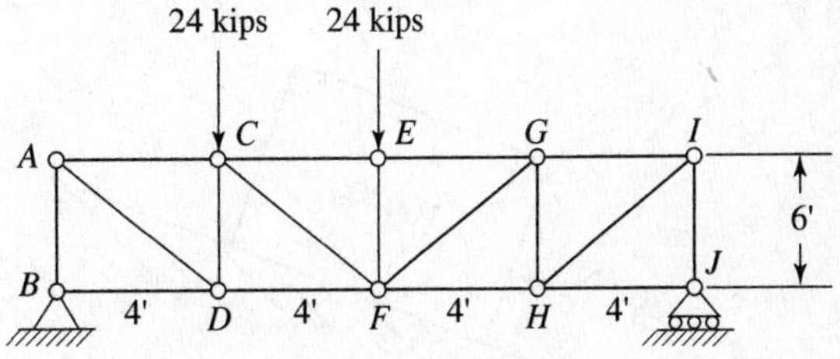

Figure 11.60

14. Determine the resultant reaction at *B* for the frame.
(A) 300 N
(B) 450 N
(C) 200 N
(D) 150 N

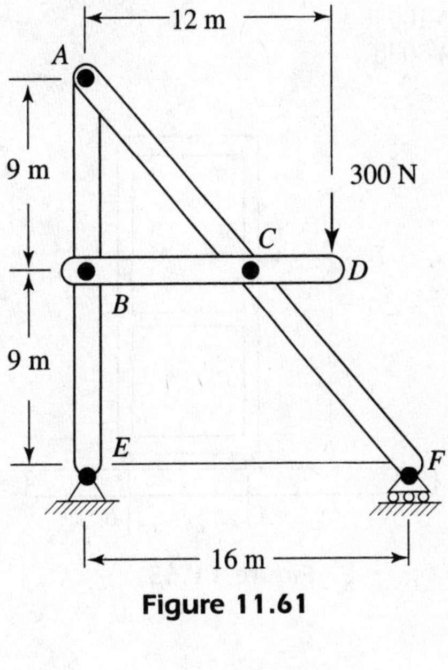

Figure 11.61

15. Determine the friction force if $\mu_s = 0.3$ and $\mu_k = 0.2$.
(A) 170 N
(B) 191 N
(C) 850 N
(D) 294 N

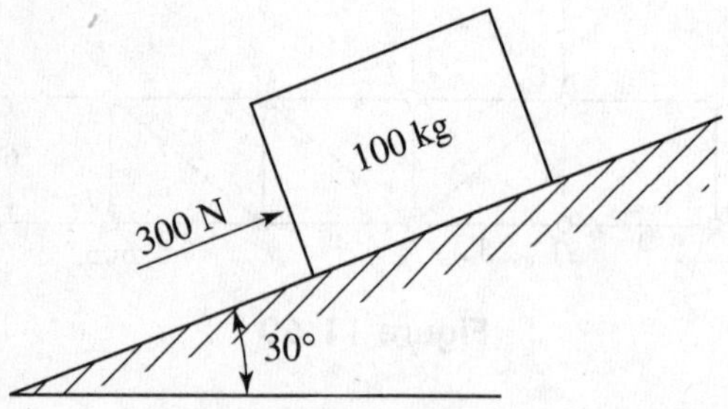

Figure 11.62

16. Determine the force required to move the cabinet. The casters at A and B are locked, the cabinet weighs 100 lb, $h = 30$ in, and $\mu_s = 0.3$.
(A) 30 lb
(B) 60 lb
(C) 100 lb
(D) 50 lb

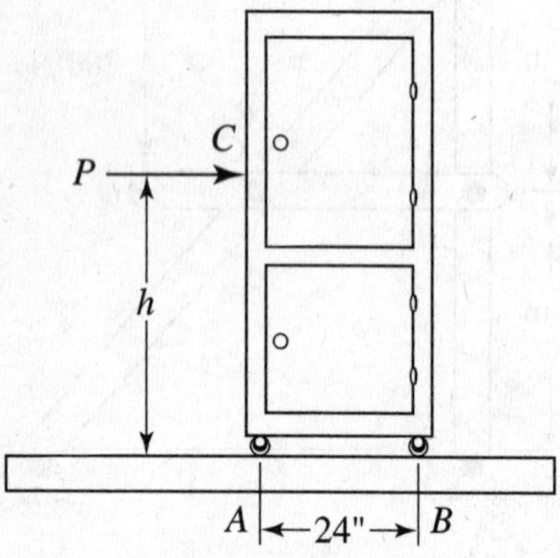

Figure 11.63

17. Determine the torque that must be applied to the flywheel in order to keep it rotating at a constant speed if $P = 8$ lb.
(A) 45 ft-lb
(B) 120 ft-lb
(C) 80 ft-lb
(D) 90 ft-lb

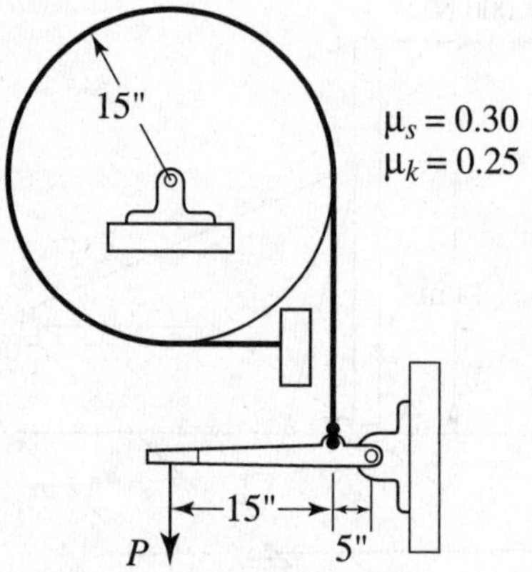

Figure 11.64

18. Determine the x-coordinate of the centroid of the plane area shown.
(A) 2 cm
(B) 6.25 cm
(C) 3.34 cm
(D) 0

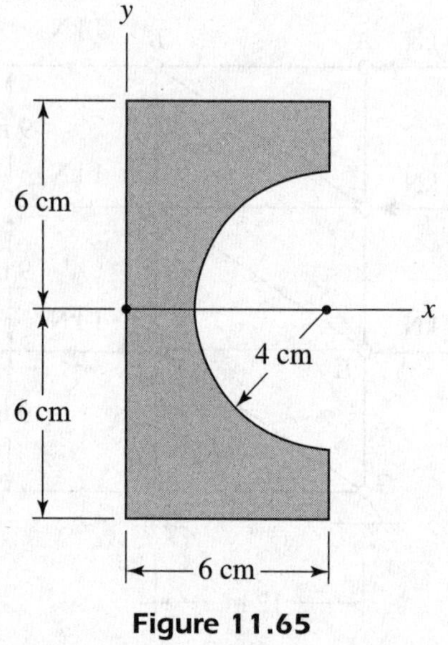

Figure 11.65

19. Determine the area moment of inertia with respect to the x-axis.

(A) 435 cm^4
(B) 525 cm^4
(C) 429 cm^4
(D) 125 cm^4

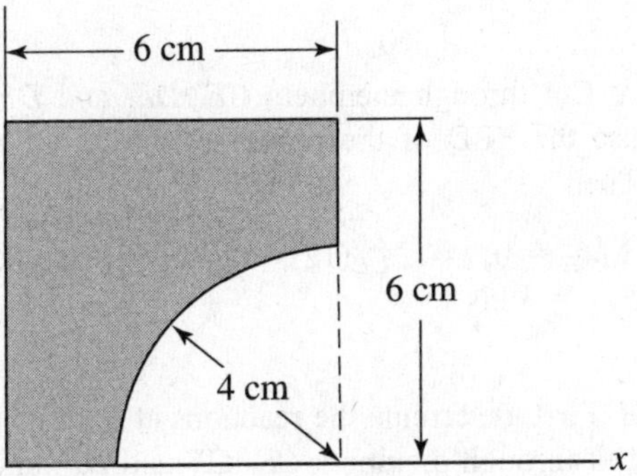

Figure 11.66

20. Determine the centroidal area moment of inertia with respect to the horizontal axis.

(A) 36 cm^4
(B) 257 cm^4
(C) 293 cm^4
(D) 220 cm^4

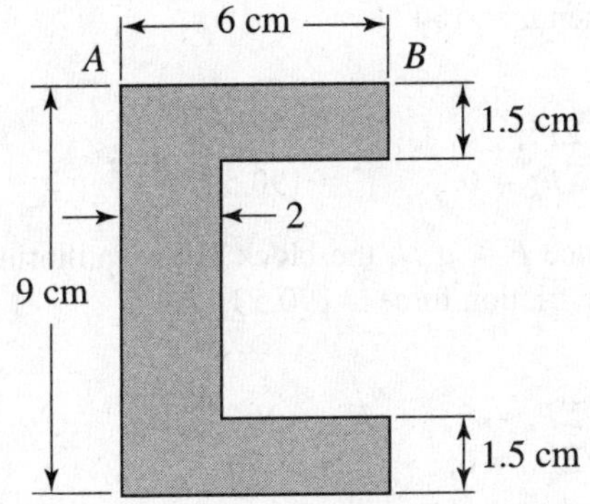

Figure 11.67

21. Determine the mass moment of inertia with respect to the x-axis. The sphere and the slender rod have the same mass, m.

(A) 19.4 ma^2
(B) 24 ma^2
(C) .33 ma^2
(D) 16 ma^2

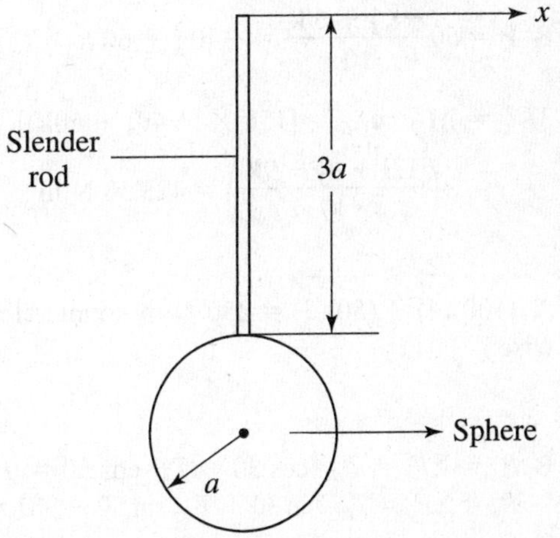

Figure 11.68

Answer Key

1. B	**8.** C	**15.** B
2. A	**9.** B	**16.** A
3. C	**10.** D	**17.** D
4. B	**11.** B	**18.** C
5. A	**12.** A	**19.** C
6. B	**13.** B	**20.** B
7. D	**14.** D	**21.** A

Answers Explained

1. B $R_x = 200\left(\frac{4}{5}\right) - 100 \sin 20 - 130\left(\frac{5}{13}\right)$

$= 75.79$ N

$R_y = 200\left(\frac{3}{5}\right) + 100 \cos 20 - 130\left(\frac{12}{13}\right)$

$= 93.97$ N

$R = \sqrt{(75.79)^2 + (93.97)^2} = 120.7$ N

2. A $\mathbf{T}_{BA} = 450\frac{4\mathbf{i} - 4\mathbf{j} + 7\mathbf{k}}{9}$

$= 200\mathbf{i} - 200\mathbf{j} + 350\mathbf{k}$

$\mathbf{T}_{BC} = 450\frac{4\mathbf{i} - 4\mathbf{j} - 2\mathbf{k}}{6}$

$= 300\mathbf{i} - 300\mathbf{j} - 150\mathbf{k}$

Also, $R_x = 500$ N, $R_y = -500$ N, $R_z = 200$ N.

$R = \sqrt{(500)^2 + (-500)^2 + (200)^2} = 734.8$ N

3. C $M_A = 160(0.1) - 120(0.12) = 1.6$ N·m clockwise

4. B $\mathbf{P} = 50\dfrac{-8\,\mathbf{j} + 6\,\mathbf{k}}{10} = -40\,\mathbf{j} + 60\,\mathbf{k}$

$$M_{OC} = \mathbf{M}_O \cdot \mathbf{u}_{OC} = [15\mathbf{k} \times (-40\mathbf{j} + 60\mathbf{k})] \cdot \left(\frac{12\mathbf{i} + 8\mathbf{j} + 9\mathbf{k}}{17}\right) = 423.53 \text{ N·m}$$

5. A $(100)(4) - (50)(3) = 250$ N·m counterclockwise

6. B $R_x = \Sigma F_x = T_{BC}\cos 30 - T_{AC}\cos 50 = 0$
$R_y = \Sigma F_y = T_{BC}\sin 30 + T_{AC}\sin 50 - 981 = 0$

Solve simultaneously: $T_{AC} = 863$ N.

7. D $\mathbf{T}_{DA} = T_{DA}\left(\dfrac{-6\mathbf{i} + 12\mathbf{j} + 4\mathbf{k}}{14}\right)$

$\mathbf{T}_{DB} = T_{DB}\left(\dfrac{12\mathbf{j} - 5\mathbf{k}}{13}\right)$

$\mathbf{T}_{DC} = T_{DC}\left(\dfrac{9\mathbf{i} + 12\mathbf{j}}{15}\right)$

Then,

$$R_x = 0 \Rightarrow -\frac{3}{7}T_{DA} + \frac{9}{15}T_{DC} = 0$$

$$R_y = 0 \Rightarrow \frac{6}{7}T_{DA} + \frac{12}{13}T_{DB} - 444 = 0$$

$$R_z = 0 \Rightarrow \frac{2}{7}T_{DA} - \frac{5}{13}T_{DB} = 0$$

Solve simultaneously: $T_{DB} = 156$ lb.

8. C $\Sigma M_A = 0,$

$$B(10) - 500(7.5) - 300(2) = 0,$$

$B = 435$ N

9. B $\Sigma M_A = 0,$

$$\left(\frac{5}{13}T_{CE}\right)(12) - (500)(16) - (300)(8) = 0,$$

$T_{CE} = 2{,}253$ N

10. D Use the FBD of member *CDE*. Then:

$$\Sigma M_C = 0, \qquad F_{BD} = 869 \text{ N}$$

11. B $\Sigma M_A = 0, \qquad 2\left(\dfrac{12}{22}T_{BE}\right)(14) - 1{,}000(20) = 0,$

$T_{BE} = 1{,}309.5$ N

12. A Cut through members *CE, DE,* and *DF,* and use the FBD of the upper section of the truss. Then:

$\Sigma M_D = 0, \qquad F_{CE}(12) - 3(9) - 1(9) = 0,$
$F_{CE} = 3$ kN T

13. B First, determine the reactions at *B*. $B = 30$ N. Cut through members *CE, CF,* and *DF*, and use the FBD of the left section of the truss. Then:

$\Sigma M_F = 0, \qquad F_{CE}(6) + 30(8) - 24(4) = 0,$
$F_{CE} = 24$ kips C

14. D First, determine the reactions at *E*. $E_x = 0$ and $E_y = 75$ N. Use the FBD of member *ABE*.

$\Sigma M_A = 0, \qquad B_x = 0 \qquad$ and
$\Sigma F_y = 0, \qquad B_y = 150$ N

Then $B = 150$ N.

15. B $\Sigma F_y = 0, \qquad N = 849.5$ N
$\Sigma F_x = 0, \qquad F = 190.5$ N

Since $F < \mu_s N$, the block is in equilibrium and the friction force is 190.5 N.

16. A $\Sigma F_y = 0, \qquad N_A + N_B = 100$
$\Sigma F_x = 0, \qquad P = 30$ lb

17. D Use the FBD of the lever, and take the moment about the pin:

$$\Sigma M = 0, \qquad T_1 = 32 \text{ lb}$$

Use equation 11.15 with $\mu_k = 0.25$ and $\beta = 270° = 3\pi/2$. Then $T_2 = 103.94$ lb.

Use the FBD of the drum, and take the moment about its center:

$$\Sigma M = 0, \qquad M = 89.925 \text{ ft-lb}$$

18. C $\overline{X}_c = \dfrac{\Sigma x_i A_i}{A}$

$$= \frac{(3)(72) + \left[6 - \frac{4(4)}{3\pi}\right]\left[\frac{1}{2}\pi(4)^2\right]}{72 + \frac{1}{2}\pi(4)^2} = 3.34 \text{ cm}$$

19. C $I_x = \dfrac{6(6)^3}{3} - \dfrac{\pi(4)^2}{16} = 428.86 \text{ cm}^4$

20. B $I = 2I_{\text{flange}} + I_{\text{web}}$

$$I_{\text{flange}} = \frac{1}{12}(6)(1.5)^3 + 9(3.75)^2 = 128.25 \text{ cm}^4$$

$$I_{\text{web}} = \frac{1}{12}(2)(6)^3 = 36 \text{ cm}^4$$

$$I = 2(128.25) + 36 = 292.5 \text{ cm}^4$$

21. A $I_x = I_{\text{rod}} + I_{\text{sphere}}$

$$= \frac{1}{3}m(3a)^2 + \left[\frac{2}{5}ma^2 + m(4a)^2\right]$$

$$= 19.4\, ma^2$$

CHAPTER

12

Thermodynamics

Mohamad Metghalchi, Sc.D.

Robert M. Scott

Introduction

Thermodynamics is the study of the properties of matter—in particular, the relationships among properties and the changes in the values that either occur spontaneously or result through interaction with other objects. The ultimate goal of thermodynamics is to understand the operation of thermal systems, to be able to design these systems, and to recognize opportunities for improving the performance of existing systems.

This presentation is divided into four major sections:

- Definitions of terms: The vocabulary of thermodynamics is developed to provide a framework for the explanation of thermodynamic principles.
- Laws and Principles: The basic laws and principles that describe the relationships among the properties of matter are presented.
- Material Systems: Several types of materials that can form the contents of thermodynamic systems are introduced. For certain special cases, the general expressions for some of the basic laws and principles are simplified, and some new relationships are introduced.
- Applications: The basic principles are applied to systems frequently encountered, and specific methods for analyzing these systems are presented.

12.1 Definitions of Terms

System: A system is specified by a description of the material it contains, and the boundaries that contain it. There are two main classifications of systems.

Open System: Material may enter into or exit from the system. Many sources call this type of system a *control volume.*

Closed System: Material may not enter into or exit from the system. Many sources call this type of system a *control mass.*

Property: A property is an attribute of a system to which a value can be assigned to describe the system. A necessary feature of a property is that the value can be stated at a given time independently of its value at any other time, and independently of the process by which the system arrived at its state.

Intensive properties are independent of the mass of the system; examples are temperature and pressure.

Extensive properties are proportional to the mass of the system; an example is volume.

Specific properties are determined by dividing the value of an extensive property by the mass of the system. A specific property is frequently denoted by the lower-case version of the letter used to represent the extensive property, for example:

$$v = \frac{V}{m} \quad [12.1]$$

where V = volume of system (ft or m^3),
m = mass of system (lbm or kg),
v = specific volume of system (ft^3/lbm or m^3/kg).

State: The state of a system is its condition at an instant of time, determined by the values of a set of independent properties. For a system composed of a single, macroscopically homogeneous substance, the equilibrium state is specified by the values of any two independent properties. The values of all other properties can be determined from these.

Interaction: Changes in the state of a system may either take place spontaneously, without a corresponding change in the environment, or occur through interaction with the environment. All interactions take place through the boundaries of the system. The types of interactions studied here are work interactions, heat interactions, and bulk-flow interactions.

Process: A process is a description of the evolution of a system from one state to another. Some special types of processes are:

Reversible: A process for which there exists another process that can return the system to its original state, leaving no net effect on the system's environment. A true reversible process cannot be achieved in practice. All real processes will experience losses, or transfers of energy that cannot be recovered without changing the state of the environment. The utility of investigating reversible processes is that they provide a limit to the change in state that can occur in any process.

Irreversible: A process for which there does not exist another process that can return the system to its original state, without changing the state of the environment. All real processes are irreversible.

Adiabatic: A process for which all transfers of energy occur through work interactions.

Constant-property: A process during which the value of one property remains constant. When such a process occurs, the analysis of the process is usually simplified.

Isometric: Constant-volume process (energy transfer to a closed rigid container).

Isothermal: Constant-temperature process (condensation or evaporation in a heat exchanger).

Isobaric: Constant-pressure process (weighted piston and cylinder).

Isentropic: Constant-entropy process (ideal turbine).

Isenthalpic: Constant-enthalpy process (flow through a valve).

12.2 Laws and Principles

Few general ideas comprise the science of thermodynamics. Two of these ideas, the first and second laws of thermodynamics, are introduced, along with the concept of the balance equation, in this section.

Mass Balance Equation

Analysis of a thermodynamic system can frequently be accomplished solely through an accounting of all possible changes in the values of additive properties. In general, the time rate of change of the value of an additive property is equal to the algebraic sum of the rate at which an amount of the property crosses the system boundary, and the rate at which an amount of the property is produced or destroyed. For example, in the case of the additive property mass, the balance equation is:

$$\frac{dm}{dt} = \dot{m}_{\text{transferred}} + \dot{m}_{\text{produced or destroyed}} \quad [12.2]$$

where $\dot{m}_{\text{transferred}}$ is the algebraic sum of the mass-flow rates of all material streams into or out of the system. The sign convention for mass-flow rate is positive if the flow of material is into the system, and negative if the flow of material is out of the system. By definition, $\dot{m}_{\text{transferred}} = 0$ for a closed system.

When nuclear reactions can be neglected, mass is neither produced nor destroyed. In terms of equation 12.2, $\dot{m}_{\text{produced or destroyed}} = 0$.

Energy and the Energy Balance Equation

In mechanics, the concept of energy is well defined. There is kinetic energy, related to the motion of a rigid body, and there is potential energy, related to the position of a rigid body in a gravity field.

In thermodynamics, the concept of energy is a little more complicated. Each individual molecule of the substance that makes up a system can possess a finite amount of energy, stored in a number of different modes. For example, each molecule can have kinetic energy due to its translational motion, kinetic energy due to its rotational motion, and potential energy due to vibration of the molecule's atoms with respect to each other. The total energy for a substance is the summation of all types of energy for each molecule that makes up the substance. Because the number of energy modes associated with each molecule can become large, and the number of molecules associated with any real system is extremely large, it is not possible to perform this summation directly.

For a macroscopic system, the easiest types of energy to consider separately are kinetic and potential energy. The energies associated with all other modes of energy storage are grouped together in the property named internal energy and denoted by U. The internal energy of a substance is related to its total energy by the following equation:

$$E = U + \frac{m\overline{V}^2}{2} + mgz \qquad [12.3]$$

where E = total energy of system (Btu or kJ),
U = internal energy of system (Btu or kJ),
m = mass of system (lbm or kg),
$\overline{V}$ = velocity of material in system (ft/sec or m/s),
g = acceleration due to gravity:
= 32.17 ft/sec^2 at sea level,
= 9.81 m/s^2 at sea level,
z = height in gravity field (ft or m);

or, in terms of mass-specific properties (properties per unit mass):

$$e = u + \frac{\overline{V}^2}{2} + gz \qquad [12.4]$$

where e = specific energy of the system (Btu/lbm or kJ/kg),
u = specific internal energy of the system (Btu/lbm or kJ/kg).

The balance equation for energy contains the essence of the principle known as the *first law of thermodynamics* and is given as:

$$\frac{dE}{dt} = \dot{E}_{\text{transferred}} + \dot{E}_{\text{produced or destroyed}} \qquad [12.5]$$

Energy is commonly transferred through work (W), heat (Q), and bulk-flow interactions. All three types of transfer are possible for an open system; bulk flow is not allowed in a closed system.

Work Interaction

Work (W) is energy transfer due to a mechanical interaction between a system and its surroundings. The value of work is considered positive if the system performs work on the surroundings (energy is removed from the system). The types of work commonly encountered are shaft work, boundary work, and flow work, given by the following equations:

$$\dot{E}_{t_{\text{work}}} = -\dot{W}$$

$$\text{Shaft work: } \dot{W}_s = \tau\omega \qquad [12.6]$$

$$\text{Boundary work: } \dot{W}b = p\frac{dV}{dt}$$

$$\text{Flow work: } \dot{W}_f = \dot{m}pv$$

where $\dot{W}$ = rate of energy transfer from a work interaction,
τ = torque applied to shaft,
ω = rotational velocity of shaft (rad/sec),
$\dot{m}$ = mass flow rate entering system,
t = time,
p = pressure in system,
V = volume of system,
v = specific volume of material in system.

A pressure-volume ($p-v$) diagram (Figure 12.1) can be used to graphically compute the boundary work done on or by a closed system during a reversible process, as shown below:

$$W_{b_{rev}} = \int_1^2 p\,dV \qquad [12.7a]$$

or

$$w_{b_{rev}} = \int_1^2 p\,dv \qquad [12.7b]$$

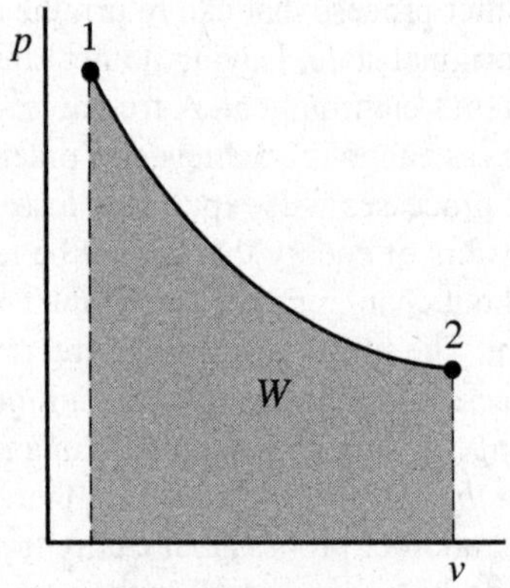

Figure 12.1 Graphical computation of energy transferred in a work interaction

The work done on or by an open system during a reversible process is:

$$w_{rev} = -\int_1^2 v\,dp \qquad [12.8]$$

Heat Interaction

A heat interaction is a transfer of energy that occurs when two systems at different temperatures are placed in contact with each other. In all cases, the transfer of energy is from the high-temperature system to the low-temperature system. We choose to use the sign convention that the energy transfer from a heat interaction is positive if the energy is entering the system.

$$\dot{E}_{t\,\text{Heat}} = \dot{Q} \qquad [12.9]$$

where $\dot{Q}$ = rate of energy transfer from a heat interaction.

Bulk-Flow Interaction

For each material stream that enters the system, two modes of energy transfer occur. The internal energy of the material that enters the system is added to the system, and the material performs flow work on the system. The total energy transferred in a bulk-flow interaction is given by:

$$\dot{E}_{t\,\text{bulk flow}} = \dot{m}\left(u + \frac{\overline{V}^2}{2} + gz\right) + \dot{m}\,pv \qquad [12.10]$$

If enthalpy ($h = u + pv$) is introduced, this equation becomes:

$$\dot{E}_{t\,\text{bulk flow}} = \dot{m}\left(h + \frac{\overline{V}^2}{2} + gz\right) \qquad [12.11]$$

When there are multiple inlet and outlet streams, each of these streams contributes to the transfer of energy. In this case, the total energy transferred because of bulk flow is the sum of the amounts of energy transferred for all fluid streams, or:

$$\dot{E}_{t\,\text{bulk flow}} = \Sigma\,\dot{m}_i\left(h_i + \frac{\overline{V}^2_i}{2} + gz_i\right) - \Sigma\,\dot{m}_e\left(h_e + \frac{\overline{V}^2_e}{2} + gz_e\right) \qquad [12.12]$$

where the subscript i indicates flow into the system, and the subscript e indicates flow out of the system. Again, when nuclear reactions are negligible:

$$\dot{E}_{\text{produced or destroyed}} = 0 \qquad [12.13]$$

Note that, if nuclear reactions cannot be neglected, energy can be produced, but only at the cost of some mass. Conversely, energy can be destroyed, but only if there is a net gain in mass. When nuclear reactions are considered, there must be a conservation of mass and energy together. In other words, the balance equations for mass and energy may only be considered together, and the term for mass produced or destroyed must be related to the term for energy produced or destroyed.

All Interactions Combined (The First Law of Thermodynamics)

The balance equations for all types of interaction may be combined to produce an overall balance equation for energy:

$$\frac{dE}{dt} = \dot{Q} - \dot{W} + \Sigma\,\dot{m}_i\left(h_i + \frac{\overline{V}_i^2}{2} + gz_i\right) - \Sigma\,\dot{m}_e\left(h_e + \frac{\overline{V}_e^2}{2} + gz_e\right) \qquad [12.14]$$

This relationship is commonly known as the **first law of thermodynamics** and is valid when nuclear reactions are negligible.

Example 12.1

A container is filled with water at standard conditions (101 kPa, 25°C) at a rate of 3 kg/min. The velocity of the water as it enters the container through an opening 0.50 m above the average water level is 12 m/s. What is the rate of energy transfer to the container?

Solution:

From equation 12.11:

$$\dot{E}_{t\,\text{bulk flow}} = \dot{m}\left(h + \frac{\overline{V}^2}{2} + gz\right)$$

Then:

$$\dot{E}_{t\,\text{bulk flow}} = \left(3\,\frac{\text{kg}}{\text{min}}\right)\left[419\,\frac{\text{kJ}}{\text{kg}} + \frac{(12\text{ m/s})^2}{2} \times \left(\frac{\text{kJ}}{1{,}000\frac{\text{kg}\cdot\text{m}^2}{\text{s}^2}}\right) + (9.81\text{ m/s}^2)(0.50\text{ m})\left(\frac{\text{kJ}}{1{,}000\frac{\text{kg}\cdot\text{m}^2}{\text{s}^2}}\right)\right]\left(\frac{1\text{ min}}{60\text{ s}}\right)$$

$$= 21\,\frac{\text{kJ}}{\text{s}}$$

$$= 21\text{ kW}$$

Note: In this case, the contributions of kinetic energy transfer (0.072 kJ/kg) and potential energy transfer (0.005 kJ/kg) are negligible compared to the contribution of enthalpy transfer (419 kJ/kg).

Example 12.2

A container that holds 3 kg of water is stirred with a mixer that is powered by the lowering of a 50-kg mass for a distance of 8 ms. The mixing raises the internal energy of the water, a change that is accompanied by an increase in temperature. If the change in temperature is related to the change in internal energy of liquid water according to this equation:

$$\Delta U = mc_p \, \Delta T$$

what is the change in temperature?

Solution:

$$\Delta U = E_{t\,\text{work}} = -W$$

and

$$W = mg(z_2 - z_1)$$
$$= (50 \text{ kg})\left(9.81 \frac{\text{m}}{\text{s}^2}\right)(-8 \text{ m})$$
$$= -3{,}924 \text{ N} \cdot \text{m}$$
$$= -3.92 \text{ kJ}$$
$$\Delta U = 3.92 \text{ kJ}$$
$$\Delta T = \frac{\Delta U}{m_{H_2O}\, c_{p_{H_2O}}}$$
$$= \frac{3.92 \text{ kJ}}{(3 \text{ kg})\left(4.18 \frac{\text{kJ}}{\text{kg} \cdot \text{K}}\right)}$$
$$= 0.31 \text{ K}$$

Cyclic Machines

A cyclic machine is a device, or a collection of devices, that allows a continuous exchange of energy between systems, often changing energy from one form into another. The machine must operate on a thermodynamic cycle, that is, a series of processes in which the ending state of the last process is equivalent to the beginning state of the first process.

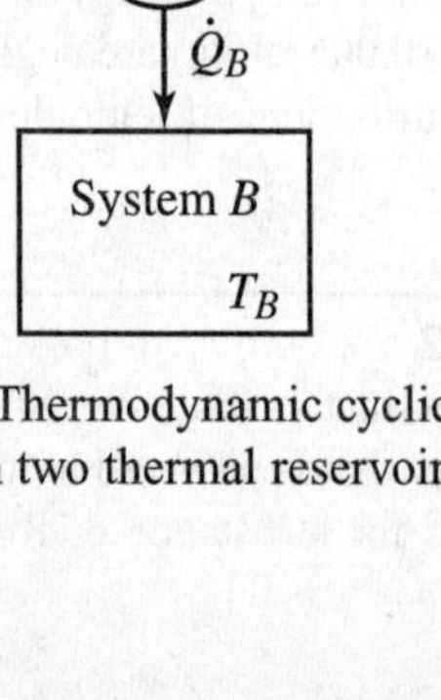

Figure 12.2 Thermodynamic cyclic of machine X, interacting with two thermal reservoirs, system *A* and system *B*

System *A* and system *B* in Figure 12.2 are thermal reservoirs. These are idealized systems that will reject or receive any amount of energy through reversible heat interactions, yet their temperatures will remain the same. A common example of a thermal reservoir is the ocean. Although there are many machines that utilize heat interactions with the ocean (e.g., a water-cooled boat engine or a power-generation plant), the overall temperature of the ocean remains unchanged by interactions with these machines.

Second Law of Thermodynamics

There have been many statements of the **second law of thermodynamics.** All have been descriptions of observations on all types of real thermodynamic systems that have never been violated. These observations are that (1) the transfer of energy occurs only in a preferred direction, namely, from higher temperature to lower temperature in a heat interaction, or from higher pressure to lower pressure in a boundary work interaction, and (2) that no real process is 100% efficient. Three statements of the second law, modified to agree with the language of this discussion, are given below.

Clausius Statement

It is impossible to devise a cyclic machine that produces, as its only effect, the transfer of energy through a heat interaction from a low-temperature body to a high-temperature body.

Kelvin-Planck Statement

It is impossible to devise a cyclic machine that will have no other effect than to extract energy from a reservoir through a heat interaction and to produce an equal amount of energy through a work interaction.

Gyftolpoulous-Barretta Statement

Among all possible states of a system with a given value of energy and with a given set of values of the amounts of constituents and the parameters, there exists one and only one equilibrium state. Moreover, starting from any state of the system, it is possible to reach an equilibrium state with an arbitrarily specified set of values of the amounts of constituents and the parameters. In this definition, the constituents are the substances that make up the system, and the parameters are the volume and any other properties that describe external forces placed on the system.

Availability

Availability (Φ), also called *exergy* or *available energy,* is the theoretical maximum amount of energy that can be extracted from a system in the form of useful work. The availability of the system cannot be specified by itself, but must be specified with reference to an environment large enough that interactions with the system do not measurably change the state of the environment.

The concept of the cyclic machine discussed earlier can serve also to help demonstrate the concept of availability. Assume that a thermodynamic system is connected to the environment through a *reversible* (ideal) cyclic machine, as shown in Figure 12.3.

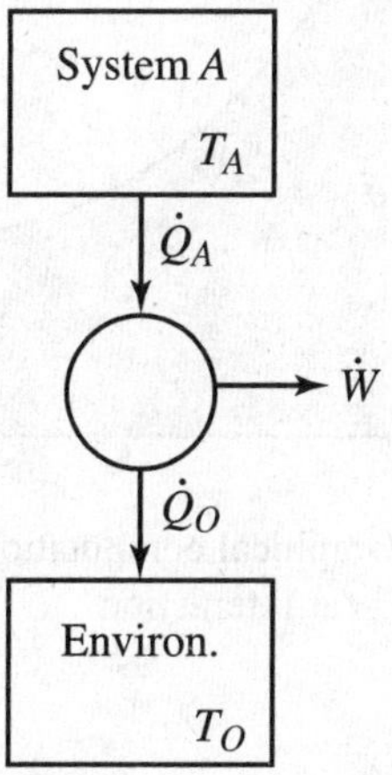

Figure 12.3 Cyclic machine that demonstrates the concept of availability

For the purposes of this description, it is assumed that the temperature of the system (T_A) is greater than the temperature of the environment (T_O), and that the system and the environment interact with the cyclic machine through heat interactions. As this cyclic machine begins to operate, energy is transferred from the thermodynamic system and into the environment. In addition, energy is transferred from the cyclic machine via the work interaction. Because the system has a finite extent, its temperature will begin to drop as energy is removed. The cyclic machine will continue to operate until the temperature of the system equals the temperature of the environment.

The total amount of energy transferred through the work interaction, from the time the cyclic machine begins to operate until it stops, is equal to the system's availability (exergy) in its initial state. Because energy is transferred from the cyclic machine both through the work interaction and the heat interaction into the environment, it is clear that the availability of system A is less than the amount of energy transferred from the system.

The state of the system at which the value of availability is zero is the state at which the cyclic machine stops operating. This state, known as the *dead state* of the system, occurs when the values of certain key properties of the system (e.g., pressure and temperature) are equal to those of the environment.

The balance equation for availability is as follows:

$$\frac{d\Phi}{dt} = \dot{\Phi}_{\text{transferred}} - \dot{\Phi}_{\text{destroyed}} \qquad [12.15]$$

Entropy and the Entropy Balance Equation

Entropy is related to the difference between the amount of system energy and the amount of system availability, or the amount of energy that cannot be used to produce work. This definition can be represented as follows:

$$S = S_{\text{ref}} + \frac{1}{T_o}[(E - E_{\text{ref}}) + p_o(V - V_{\text{ref}}) - (\Phi - \Phi_{\text{ref}})] \qquad [12.16]$$

where T_o is the absolute temperature of the environment, and the subscript ref indicates that the values are taken at an arbitrary reference state of the system.

The balance equation for entropy is:

$$\frac{dS}{dt} = \dot{S}_{\text{transferred}} + \dot{S}_{\text{produced}} \qquad [12.17]$$

Other references may use $\dot{S}_{\text{generated}}$ or $\dot{\sigma}$ instead of $\dot{S}_{\text{produced}}$. This term is related to the irreversibilities of the process as follows:

$$\dot{I} = T_o\dot{S}_p = T_o\dot{S}_g = T_o\dot{\sigma} = \dot{\Phi}_{\text{destroyed}} \qquad [12.18]$$

The balance equation for entropy for all three types of interactions considered here (work, heat, and bulk flow) is:

$$\frac{dS}{dt} = \Sigma\frac{\dot{Q}}{T_b} + \Sigma\,\dot{m}_i\,s_i - \Sigma\,\dot{m}_e\,s_e + \dot{S}_{\text{produced}} \qquad [12.19]$$

where $\Sigma\frac{\dot{Q}}{T_b}$ = total rate of entropy transfer through heat interactions,

$\Sigma\dot{m}_i\,s_i - \Sigma\,\dot{m}_e\,s_e$ = total rate of entropy transfer through bulk-flow interactions.

In equation 12.19, T_b is the temperature of the system boundary at the point where the heat interaction occurs. This temperature may or may not be constant with respect to time and position on the system boundary. There is no transfer of entropy in a work interaction. The entropy-produced term is related to the irreversibilities that occur in any real process.

Clausius Inequality

A historical statement, closely related to the second law of thermodynamics, can be derived from the entropy balance equation for a closed system operating in a cycle. This statement is known as the **Clausius inequality,** and is given as follows:

$$\oint \frac{\delta Q}{T} \leq 0 \qquad [12.20]$$

Example 12.3

What is the rate of entropy production for the cyclic machine diagramed in Figure 12.4?

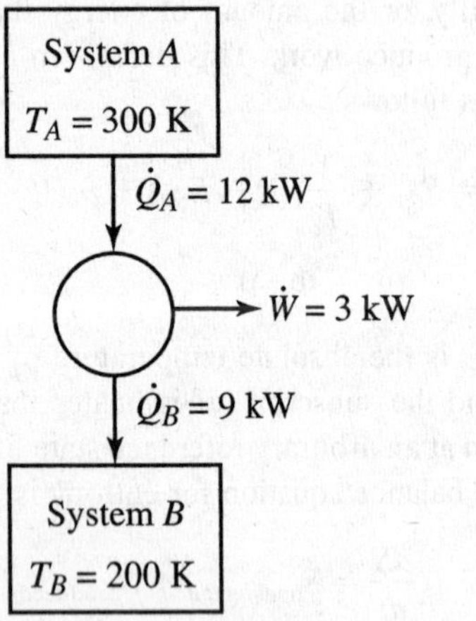

Figure 12.4 Entropy production for a cyclic machine

Solution: From equation 12.19:

$$\frac{dS}{dt} = \Sigma \frac{\dot{Q}}{T_b} + \dot{S}_{\text{produced}}$$

$$0 = \Sigma \frac{\dot{Q}}{T_b} + \dot{S}_{\text{produced}}$$

or

$$\dot{S}_{\text{produced}} = -\Sigma \frac{\dot{Q}}{T_b}$$

$$= -\left(\frac{\dot{Q}_A}{T_A} - \frac{\dot{Q}_B}{T_B}\right)$$

$$= -\left(\frac{12{,}000\ W}{300\ K} - \frac{9{,}000\ W}{200\ K}\right)$$

$$= 5\ \text{W/K}$$

Temperature-Entropy *(T-S)* Diagram

A temperature-entropy (*T-S*) diagram (Figure 12.5) can be used to graphically compute the energy transfer from a reversible heat interaction, as shown below:

$$Q_{\text{rev}} = \int_1^2 T\,dS \qquad [12.21]$$

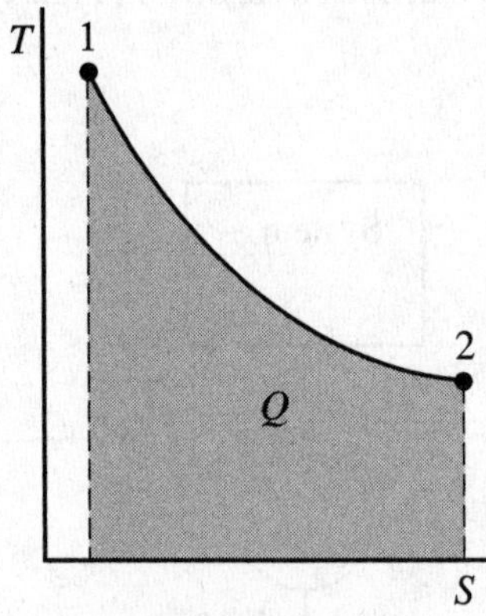

Figure 12.5 Graphical computation of energy transferred in a heat interaction

Availability Balance Equation

The balance equation for availability is:

$$\frac{d\Phi}{dt} = \dot{\Phi}_{\text{transferred}} - \dot{\Phi}_{\text{destroyed}} \qquad [12.22]$$

Availability is never produced, but irreveribilities in the system destroy availability. By the same process used to determine the balance equations for the other additive properties discussed, the balance equation for availability can be derived. This equation is:

$$\frac{d\Phi}{dt} = -\dot{W} + \sum\left(1 - \frac{T_o}{T_b}\right)\dot{Q} + \sum \dot{m}_i \Psi_i - \sum \dot{m}_e \Psi_e + p_o \frac{dV}{dt} - T_o \dot{S}_{\text{produced}} \qquad [12.23]$$

Where Ψ is the *flow availability,* or the amount of availability transferred during a bulk-flow interaction, and is given by:

$$\Psi = (h - h_o) + \frac{\overline{V}^2}{2} + gz - T_o(s - s_o) \qquad [12.24]$$

Flow availability is also the maximum amount of energy that the flowing material can transfer through a work interaction.

Example 12.4

If the heat and work interactions are assumed to be reversible, what is the rate of change of availability for the system shown in Figure 12.6?

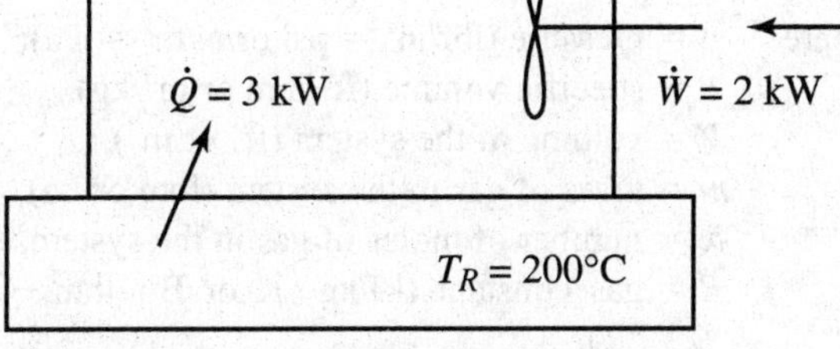

Figure 12.6 A system that undergoes a work interaction and a heat interaction

Solution:

$T_o = 25°C$

$P_o = 101$ kPa

$$\frac{d\Phi}{dt} = -\dot{W} + \left(1 - \frac{T_o}{T}\right)\dot{Q}$$

From equation 12.23:

$$= 2 \text{ kW} + \left[1 - \frac{(25 + 273) \text{ K}}{(200 + 273) \text{ K}}\right](3 \text{ kW})$$

$$= 3.11 \text{ kW}$$

Properties

We now switch our focus from definitions of the basic laws of thermodynamics to descriptions of the substances that make up a thermodynamic system. The first type of substance we will consider is the simple substance. A different type of substance, the ideal gas, is discussed in Section 12.3.

We define a simple substance as a substance that is macroscopically homogeneous and is isotropic. "Homogeneous" means that there is no way to distinguish material in any location of the system from material in any other location. "Isotropic" means that there is no preferred spatial direction in which any interaction will behave differently than if applied from any other spatial direction. This definition can apply to any single substance, such as water, or to a homogeneous mixture of substances, such as air, which is a mixture of oxygen, nitrogen, and other gases.

Enthalpy

Often, when certain types of systems are investigated, a group of properties will arise naturally. One such property is enthalpy, which appears naturally when bulk-flow interactions are considered. By analyzing the energy balance equation for a bulk-flow interaction, we find that the energy transferred is related to the change in value of the following property grouping: $U + pV$. This grouping of properties occurs frequently enough that it has been given its own name, *enthalpy,* and it has become traditional to use this property directly in the analysis of thermodynamic systems.

The expresion for enthalpy is:

$$H = U + pV \qquad [12.25]$$

or, in terms of specific properties:

$$h = u + pv \qquad [12.26]$$

Enthalpy has units of energy (Btu or kJ). Specific enthalpy has units of energy per unit mass (Btu/lbm or kJ/kg).

Gibbs and Hemholtz Free Energy

Just as the idea of enthalpy naturally arises when analyzing bulk flow interactions, two other properties naturally appear when the thermodynamics of chemical reactions are examined.

Gibbs free energy, defined by equation 12.27, appears when chemical reactions at constant pressure and temperature are examined.

$$G = H - TS \qquad [12.27]$$

or, in terms of specific properties:

$$g = h - Ts \qquad [12.28]$$

Hemholtz free energy, defined by equation 12.29, appears when chemical reactions occurring at constant volume and temperature are examined.

$$A = U - TS \qquad [12.29]$$

or, in terms of specific properties:

$$a = u - Ts \qquad [12.30]$$

Both Gibbs free energy and Hemholtz free energy have units of energy (Btu or kJ). In their mass-specific forms, the units are energy per unit mass (Btu/lbm or kJ/kg).

Specific Heat

With current experimental techniques and devices, the thermodynamic properties that are easiest to measure are pressure, volume, and temperature. Given that the equilibrium state of any system comprised of a fixed amount of a simple substance is determined by the values of two independent properties, we know that the internal energy of a system can be expressed as a function of volume and temperature [$(u = u(v, T)$]), and that enthalpy can be expressed as a function of pressure and temperature [$h = h(p, T)$]. These relationships are used to define the thermodynamic property of specific heat.

There are two versions of the property called *specific heat,* the constant-volume and the constant-pressure specific heat, defined as follows:

Constant-volume specific heat: $c_V = \left.\frac{\partial u}{\partial T}\right)_V$ [12.31]

Constant-pressure specific heat: $c_p = \left.\frac{\partial h}{\partial T}\right)_p$ [12.32]

The values of both of these properties vary greatly with temperature for most systems: when small changes in temperature are considered, however, a constant specific heat may be assumed. For solids and incompressible liquids, the difference between the values of c_p and c_V is negligable.

12.3 Material Systems

While the first and second laws of thermodynamics do describe the thermodynamic behavior of all substances, further information is gained by studying how different substances react to thermodynamic interactions.

Ideal Gases

Any equation that states the relationships among the values of the properties of a substance at a given state is called an *equation of state.* It has been observed that relationships among the values of the properties of gases in an equilibrium state, at low pressure, can be expressed in a very simple equation.

Although this equation represents an idealized gas, for most real gases at high temperatures and low pressures the error is negligible. Some gases, such as helium, hydrogen, and nitrogen, behave like an ideal gas for most equilibrium states, while others, such as steam, behave like an ideal gas only at low pressures. A fair indication of the likelihood that a gas will behave like an ideal gas can be obtained by looking at its molecular structure. Monatomic and diatomic gases will almost always behave like an ideal gas; but as the complexity of the molecule increases, the values of the properties of the gas will begin to deviate from those predicted by the ideal gas equation.

The ideal gas equation of state is:

$$pv = RT \quad [12.33a]$$

or

$$pV = mRT \quad [12.33b]$$

or

$$pV = N\overline{R}T \quad [12.33c]$$

where p = pressure (lbf/in^2 = psi or N/m^2 = Pa),
v = specific volume (ft^3/lbm or m^3/kg),
V = volume of the system (ft^3 or m^3),
m = mass of gas in the system (lbm or kg),
N = number of moles of gas in the system,
R = gas constant (kJ/kg · K or Btu/lbm – °R),
$\overline{R}$ = universal gas constant:
= 1,545 ft-lbf/(lbmol-°R),
= 8.314 J/(mol · K),
T = temperature.

While the universal gas constant, $\overline{R}$ is, as its name implies, the same for all gases, the gas constant R is specific to each gas and can be found from the equation

$$R = \frac{\overline{R}}{M} \quad [12.34]$$

where M = molecular weight.
For an ideal gas:

$$R = c_p - c_v \quad [12.35]$$

Example 12.5

If 4 kg of carbon monoxide gas is introduced into a 5.3-m^3 vessel at 25°C, what is the pressure of the gas?

Solution:

From equations 12.33b and 12.34:

$$p = \frac{m\overline{R}T}{MV}$$

$$= \left[\frac{(4\text{ kg})\left(8.314\frac{\text{J}}{\text{mol}\cdot\text{K}}\right)(25+273)\text{ K}}{\left(28\frac{\text{g}}{\text{mol}}\right)(5.3\text{ m}^3)\left(\frac{1\text{ kg}}{1{,}000\text{ g}}\right)}\right]\left(\frac{\text{N}\cdot\text{m}}{\text{J}}\right)\left(\frac{\text{kPa}}{1{,}000\frac{\text{N}}{\text{m}^2}}\right)$$

$$= 66.78\text{ kPa}$$

Example 12.6

What is the gas constant for argon gas?

Solution:

From equation 12.34:

$$R = \frac{\bar{R}}{M}$$

$$= \frac{8.314 \frac{\text{J}}{\text{mol} \cdot \text{K}}}{40 \frac{\text{g}}{\text{mol}}}\left(\frac{1{,}000 \text{ g}}{1 \text{ kg}}\right)$$

$$= 208 \frac{\text{J}}{\text{kg} \cdot \text{K}}$$

$$= 0.208 \frac{\text{kJ}}{\text{kg} \cdot \text{K}}$$

Any two states of an ideal gas can be related as follows:

$$\frac{p_1 v_1}{T_1} = \frac{p_2 v_2}{T_2} \qquad [12.36]$$

The balance equations discussed earlier can be applied to ideal gas systems. When these balance equations are combined with the equation of state, many simplifications and interesting results are found.

For an ideal gas system:

$$\left(\frac{\partial h}{\partial p}\right)_T = 0 \quad \text{and} \quad \left(\frac{\partial u}{\partial v}\right)_T = 0 \qquad [12.37]$$

or

$$h = h(T) \text{ only} \quad \text{and} \quad u = u(T) \text{ only}$$

which leads to

$$c_p = c_p(T) \text{ only} \quad \text{and} \quad c_v = c_v(T) \text{ only.}$$

The case where the specific heat can be considered constant (i.e., when there are relatively small changes in temperature) leads to the following equations:

$$\Delta u = c_v \Delta T \quad \text{and} \quad \Delta h = c_p \Delta T \qquad [12.38]$$

$$\Delta s = c_p \ln\left(\frac{T_2}{T_1}\right) - R \ln\left(\frac{p_2}{p_1}\right) \qquad [12.39]$$

and

$$\Delta s = c_v \ln\left(\frac{T_2}{T_1}\right) + R \ln\left(\frac{v_2}{v_1}\right) \qquad [12.40]$$

Example 12.7

A sample of nitrogen undergoes an isobaric process in which the temperature is raised from 10°C to 45°C. What is the change in entropy per kilogram of nitrogen for this process?

Solution:

From equation 12.39:

$$\Delta s = c_p \ln\left(\frac{T_2}{T_1}\right) - R \ln\left(\frac{p_2}{p_1}\right)$$

Since

$$\ln\left(\frac{p_2}{p_1}\right) = 0$$

Then

$$\Delta s = c_p \ln\left(\frac{T_2}{T_1}\right)$$

$$= \left(1.04 \frac{\text{kJ}}{\text{kg} \cdot \text{K}}\right) \ln\left[\frac{(45 + 273)\text{K}}{(10 + 273)\text{K}}\right]$$

$$= 0.121 \frac{\text{kJ}}{\text{kg K}}$$

Isentropic Process

For any isentropic process of an ideal gas system with constant specific heat:

$$p_1 v_1^{\,k} = p_2 v_2^{\,k} \qquad [12.41]$$

$$T_1 p_1^{(1-k)/k} = T_2 p_2^{(1-k)/k} \qquad [12.42]$$

$$T_1 v_1^{(k-1)} = T_2 v_2^{(k-1)} \qquad [12.43]$$

where $k = \frac{c_p}{c_v}$ = specific heat ratio.

If the isentropic process occurs in a closed system, then:

$$w = \frac{p_2 v_2 - p_1 v_1}{1 - k}$$

$$= \frac{R(T_2 - T_1)}{(1 - k)} \qquad [12.44]$$

$$= \frac{RT_1}{k - 1}\left[1 - \left(\frac{p_2}{p_1}\right)^{(k-1)/k}\right]$$

Example 12.8

If an ideal gas sample ($k = 1.40$) experiences an isentropic process starting from standard conditions (14.69 psia, 77°F) where the temperature drops to 30°F, what is the final pressure?

Solution:

From equation 12.42:

$$T_1 p_1^{(1-k)/k} = T_2 p_2^{(1-k)/k}$$

Then:

$$\frac{T_1}{T_2} = \left(\frac{p_2}{p_1}\right)^{(1-k)/k} \quad \text{or} \quad \left(\frac{T_1}{T_2}\right)^{k/(1-k)} = \frac{p_2}{p_1}$$

$$p_2 = p_1\left(\frac{T_1}{T_2}\right)^{k/(1-k)}$$

$$= (14.69 \text{ psia})\left[\frac{(77 + 460)°\text{R}}{(30 + 460)°\text{R}}\right]^{1.40/(1-1.40)}$$

$$= 10.66 \text{ psia}$$

Example 12.9

If, starting at 200°F, an ideal gas undergoes an isentropic process in which the specific volume quadruples, what is the final temperature? ($k = 1.40$)

Solution:

From equation 12.43:

$$\frac{T_2}{T_1} = \left(\frac{v_1}{v_2}\right)^{k-1}$$

Then: $T_2 = T_1\left(\dfrac{v_1}{v_2}\right)^{k-1}$

$$= [(200 + 460)°\text{R}]\left(\frac{1}{4}\right)^{1.40-1}$$

$$= 379°\text{R}$$

$$= -81°\text{F}$$

Isobaric Process in a Closed System

For an isobaric (constant-pressure) process:

$$w_b = \int_1^2 p\,dv$$

From equation 12.7a:

$$w_b = p\int_1^2 dv \qquad [12.45]$$

$$= p\Delta v$$

and (**Charles's law**):

$$\frac{T_1}{v_1} = \frac{T_2}{v_2} = \text{constant} \qquad [12.46]$$

Isometric Process in a Closed System

For an isometric (constant-volume) process:
From equation 12.7a:

$$w_b = \int_1^2 p\,dv = 0$$

and

$$\frac{T_1}{p_1} = \frac{T_2}{p_2} = \text{constant} \qquad [12.47]$$

Isothermal Process in a Closed System

For an isothermal (constant-temperature) process:

$$w_b = \int_1^2 p\,dv$$

$$= \int_1^2 \frac{RT}{v}\,dv$$

$$= RT\ln\left(\frac{v_2}{v_1}\right)$$

Then:

$$w_b = RT\ln\left(\frac{v_2}{v_1}\right) = RT\ln\left(\frac{p_1}{p_2}\right) \qquad [12.48]$$

and (**Boyle's law**):

$$p_1v_1 = p_2v_2 = \text{constant} \qquad [12.49]$$

Example 12.10

A piston and cylinder system contains 3 kg of air at 15°C. In an isothermal compression in which the final volume is one-third of the initial volume, how much boundary work has been performed?

Solution:

From equation 12.48:

$$w_b = RT\ln\left(\frac{v_2}{v_1}\right)$$

Then:

$$w_b = \left(\frac{8.314\,\frac{\text{J}}{\text{mol}\cdot\text{K}}}{29\,\frac{\text{g}}{\text{mol}}}\right)[(15 + 273)\text{ K}]\ln\left(\frac{v_2}{3v_2}\right)\left(\frac{1{,}000\text{ g}}{\text{kg}}\right)\left(\frac{\text{kJ}}{1{,}000\text{ J}}\right)$$

$$= -90.7\,\frac{\text{kJ}}{\text{kg}} \quad \text{(work performed on the gas)}$$

and

$$W_b = mw_b$$

$$= (3\text{ kg})\left(-90.7\,\frac{\text{kJ}}{\text{kg}}\right)$$

$$= -272\text{ kJ}$$

Polytropic Process in a Closed System

A polytropic process is one for which:

$$p_1 v_1^n = p_2 v_2^n = \text{constant} \quad [12.50]$$

where n is a constant ($n \neq 1$). Note that, when the process is isentropic, $n = k$.

In this case, the work performed during the process is calculated as follows:

$$w = \frac{p_2 v_2 - p_1 v_1}{1 - n} \quad [12.51]$$

Mach Number

The Mach number is a dimensionless parameter used to describe the velocity of an ideal gas. It is defined as the ratio of fluid velocity to the speed of sound, or:

$$M_a = \frac{\overline{V}}{c} \quad [12.52]$$

where M_a = Mach number (dimensionless),
$\overline{V}$ = fluid velocity (ft/sec or m/s),
c = speed of sound (ft/sec or m/s).

For an ideal gas, the speed of sound is defined as:

$$c = \sqrt{kRT} \quad [12.53]$$

where c = speed of sound (ft/sec or m/s),
k = specific heat ratio (c_p/c_v),
R = gas constant (ft-lbf/lbm · °R or kJ/kg · K),
T = absolute temperature of the gas (K or °R).

Ideal Gas Mixtures

When a substance is composed of a mixture of ideal gases, determining the values of its properties and the relationships among its equilibrium states becomes a bit more complicated. To define the mixture, it is necessary to specify the amount of each constituent in the mixture. The common way to do this is to calculate the *mole fraction,* that is, the ratio of the number of moles of each component to the total number of moles in the mixture. The mole fraction is given by:

$$x_i = \frac{N_i}{\sum_i N_i} \quad [12.54]$$

so that

$$\sum_i x_i = 1$$

An equivalent method of defining the composition of the mixture is to determine the *mass fraction,* given by:

$$y_i = \frac{m_i}{\sum_i m^i} \quad [12.55]$$

so that

$$\sum_i y_i = 1$$

It is possible to convert one of these two measures of composition into the other by use of the following formulas:

Mass fraction from mole fraction:

$$y_i = \frac{x_i M_i}{\sum_i x_i M_i} \quad [12.56]$$

Mole fraction from mass fraction:

$$x_i = \frac{y_i / M_i}{\sum_i y_i / M_i} \quad [12.57]$$

Once the composition is defined, it is possible to define the parameters required to apply the ideal gas equation to the mixture, molar mass, and gas constant:

Molar mass of mixture: $M_{\text{mix}} = \sum_i x_i M_i$ [12.58]

Gas constant of mixture: $R_{\text{mix}} = \dfrac{\overline{R}}{M_{\text{mix}}}$ [12.59]

Example 12.11

An ideal gas mixture has the following composition, in terms of mole fractions:

Butane	0.39
Methane	0.42
Propane	0.19

What is the mass fraction of the butane?

Solution:

From equation 12.56:

$$y_i = \frac{x_i M_i}{\Sigma x_i M_i}$$

$$= \frac{(0.39)(58)}{(0.39)(58) + (0.42)(16) + (0.19)(44)}$$

$$= 0.60$$

Analysis of the ideal gas mixture can now be accomplished as if the mixture were a pure ideal gas:

$$pv = R_{\text{mix}}\,T \qquad [12.60a]$$

or

$$pV = \sum_i m_i R_{\text{mix}} T \qquad [12.60b]$$

or

$$pV = \sum_i N_i \overline{R} T \qquad [12.60c]$$

It is sometimes helpful to determine the contribution of each gas to the total pressure or volume of the system. These contributions, called the partial pressure and partial volume of the constituent, are given by:

$$p_i = x_i p = \frac{m_i R_i T}{V} \qquad [12.61]$$

so that

$$\sum_i p_i = p$$

and

$$V_i = x_i V = \frac{m_i R_i T}{p} \qquad [12.62]$$

so that

$$\sum_i V_i = V$$

Equation 12.61 leads to **Dalton's law:**

$$pV = (p_1 + p_2 + p_3 + \ldots + p_n)V \qquad [12.63]$$

Example 12.12

What is the partial pressure of nitrogen in the following mixture (composition given in terms of mass fraction) in a 3-m^3 vessel at 40°C, if the total mass of the mixture is 3 kg?

Argon	0.44
Hydrogen	0.29
Nitrogen	0.27

Solution:

From equation 12.61: $p_i = \dfrac{m_i R_i T}{V}$

Then:

$$m_i = y_i m$$

$$= (0.27)(3\ \text{kg})$$

$$= 0.81\ \text{kg}$$

Also:

$$R_i = \frac{\overline{R}}{M_i}$$

$$= \frac{8.314\ \dfrac{\text{J}}{\text{mol K}}}{28\ \dfrac{\text{g}}{\text{mol}}}\left(\frac{\text{kJ}}{1{,}000\ \text{J}}\right)\left(\frac{1{,}000\ \text{g}}{\text{kg}}\right)$$

$$= 0.297\ \frac{\text{kJ}}{\text{kg K}}$$

$$p_i = \frac{(0.81\ \text{kg})\left(0.297\ \dfrac{\text{kJ}}{\text{kg K}}\right)[(40 + 273)\ \text{K}]}{3\ \text{m}^3}$$

$$= 25.1\ \frac{\text{kJ}}{\text{m}^3}\left(\frac{1{,}000\ \text{N}\cdot\text{m}}{\text{kJ}}\right)\left(\frac{\text{kPa}}{1{,}000\ \dfrac{\text{N}}{\text{m}^2}}\right)$$

$$= 25.1\ \text{kPa}$$

The specific properties for the mixture are obtained from a mass-weighted average of the specific properties for each constituent:

$$u_{\text{mix}} = \sum_i (y_i u_i) \quad \text{and} \quad h_{\text{mix}} = \sum_i (y_i h_i) \qquad [12.64]$$

Simple Compressible Substances

While the ideal gas assumption works for most simple substances at high energy levels, many substances we commonly encounter, such as water, behave in significantly different ways. Water from the tap is a liquid. If, however, we place the water in the freezer, it becomes ice, a solid. If we put the water in a pot and boil it, it becomes steam, a gas. These are the three principal phases in which any substance can exist: solid, liquid, and gas.

An explanation for these phases can be found if we examine the microscopic structure of a substance. At the lowest energy levels of the substance, its molecules arrange themselves into a close-packed, organized structure, called a lattice. Because the energy level is low and the molecules are close together, the intermolecular forces dominate, and the lattice structure is maintained. Because the molecules cannot be easily separated or displaced, the substance appears macroscopically as a solid.

Add energy to the substance through an interaction with its environment, and a change begins to take place. The energy in some molecules will become great enough that the lattice structure will begin to break down. At this stage, the substance still has some structure, but its molecules are easily displaced. The substance now appears macroscopically as a liquid.

Add even more energy to the substance, and eventually all of its molecules will overcome the intermolecular forces. When this happens, the substance will lose all signs of structure, and its molecules will be separated by far greater distances. At this point the molecules can move about randomly, and the substance appears macroscopically as a gas.

Because of this phase-change behavior, we can expect that the equation of state that describes the equilibrium states of most substances will be a great deal more complicated than that of an ideal gas. For the most part we rely on the vast quantity of experimental data that exists to predict the equilibrium states of substances, using either tabulated data, empirical correlations, or graphical thermodynamic surfaces.

The equilibrium state of a simple compressible substance is a function of at most two independent properties. Mathematically, such a relationship can be represented as a surface in three-dimensional space with each axis representing the value of a thermodynamic property. This representation has become a tradition in thermodynamics, with the pressure expressed as a function of the specific volume and the temperature [$p = p(v, T)$]. The projections of such a surface on the p-v and p-T planes are shown in Figure 12.7.

The equilibrium states of most substances can be described with such a diagram. As well as showing the equilibrium states, these diagrams indicate the relationships among phases. The dome-shaped region of the p-v diagram is the vapor dome. States that fall on the left edge of the dome are completely liquid but are on the verge of boiling. For these states, the substance is called a saturated liquid. States that fall on the right edge of the dome are completely gaseous but are on the verge of condensing. For these states, the substance is called a saturated vapor. The two regions are separated by a point at the top of the dome called the critical point. Under the dome, the substance exists in two different homogeneous states; a portion of the substance is a saturated liquid, and the other portion is a saturated vapor. Both portions exist at the same pressure and temperature. There is only one point on the thermodynamic surface at which the substance can exist in all three phases, the triple point.

If lines of constant temperature are drawn on the p-v diagram, an important feature of compressible substances becomes apparent. The constant-temperature lines under the vapor dome are exactly horizontal, indicating that, as long as two phases (liquid and vapor) are present, changes in state that occur at constant pressure will also occur at constant temperature. Any change in the amount of energy will serve to move the overall composition of the substance either closer to the saturated liquid phase or closer to the saturated vapor phase. The same type of behavior is observed as the substance changes between solid and liquid states.

Thermodynamic Tables

Because use of these graphical surfaces for analysis can be cumbersome, the equilibrium-state data for many common substances have been compiled in tabular form. The most common of these tables are the steam tables for water; examples are given at the end of this chapter. Usually there are two tables, one for the saturated liquid and saturated vapor equilibrium states (pages 332–333), and one for the superheated

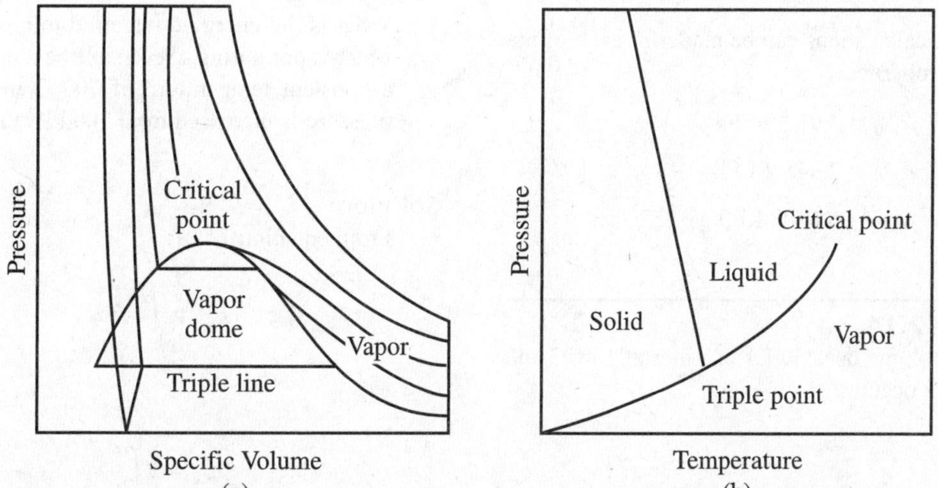

Figure 12.7 The p-v (a) and p-T (b) projections of a thermodynamic surface

vapor (steam) equilibrium states (page 334) of water. These tables give the values of specific volume, specific internal energy, specific enthalpy, and specific entropy as functions of temperature and pressure. The saturated (water) table lists values as functions of either pressure or temperature.

The information available in these tables is limited because the values of only a few states are given. What happens when information is needed about states not listed in the table? For analysis, it is usually sufficient to linearly interpolate the values of the properties for a state that falls between two states given in the tables.

Example 12.13

What is the specific volume of steam at a pressure of 100 kPa and a temperature of 430°C?

Solution:

The superheated steam table (page 334) gives information about properties at a pressure of 100 kPa and a temperature of 400°C or 500°C, as follows:

T (°C)	v (m³/kg)	u (kJ/kg)	h (kJ/kg)	s kJ/(kg · K)
400	3.103	2967.9	3278.2	8.5435
430	v_{430}	u_{430}	h_{430}	s_{430}
500	3.565	3131.6	3488.1	8.8342

By linear interpolation:

$$\frac{v_{430} - 3.103}{3.565 - 3.103} = \frac{430 - 400}{500 - 400}$$

$$v_{430} = 3.242 \text{ m}^3/\text{kg}$$

Similar calculations can be made for each of the other properties:

$$u_{430} = 3{,}017.0 \text{ kJ/kg}$$

$$h_{430} = 3{,}341.2 \text{ kJ/kg}$$

$$s_{430} = 8.6307 \text{ kJ/(kg} \cdot \text{K)}$$

Example 12.14

What volume does 50 kg of water at 130°C and 400 kPa occupy?

Solution:

From equation 12.1:

$$V = mv$$

According to the saturated water table, the saturation pressure of water at 130°C is 270.1 kPa. Since this is less than the state pressure of 400 kPa, the water is in liquid state, and is called a compressed or subcooled liquid. A table for compressed liquid water properties is not supplied; but because the thermodynamic properties of compressed liquid water are primarily functions of temperature, the following approximations can be made:

$$v = v_f(T), \quad u = u_f(T), \quad s = s_f(T)$$

$$h = h_f(T) + v_f(T)[p - p_{sat}(T)]$$

where $v_f(T)$ is the saturated liquid-specific volume at temperature T,
$u_f(T)$ is the saturated liquid-specific internal energy at temperature T,
$s_f(T)$ is the saturated liquid-specific entropy at temperature T,
$h_f(T)$ is the saturated liquid-specific enthalpy at temperature T,
$p_{sat}(T)$ is the saturation pressure of water at temperature T.

From the saturated water table:

$$v_f(130°\text{C}) = 0.001070 \frac{\text{m}^3}{\text{kg}}$$

so

$$V = (50 \text{ kg})\left(0.001070 \frac{\text{m}^3}{\text{kg}}\right) = 0.0535 \text{ m}^3$$

Example 12.15

What is the energy transferred to a container of water vapor during a reversible heat interaction at a constant temperature of 700°C in which the pressure is increased from 100 kPa to 600 kPa?

Solution:

From equation 12.21:

$$Q_{rev} = \int_{s_1}^{s_2} T\,ds$$

Then:

$$Q_{rev} = T\int_{s_1}^{s_2} ds$$

$$= T(s_2 - s_1)$$

Find the values for s_2 and s_1 in the superheated steam table on page 334:

$$Q_{rev} = [(700 + 273)\ \text{K}]\left(8.5107\ \frac{\text{kJ}}{\text{kg}\cdot\text{K}} - 9.3398\ \frac{\text{kJ}}{\text{kg}\cdot\text{K}}\right)$$

$$= -806.7\ \frac{\text{kJ}}{\text{kg}}$$

Example 12.16

What is the flow (open system) availability of a stream of water at 75°C? Consider the dead state to be standard conditions (101 kPa and 25°C), and neglect contributions of potential and kinetic energy.

Solution:

From equation 12.24:

$$\Psi = (h - h_o) - T_o(s - s_o)$$

Find the values for h and s in the saturated steam table (h_f and s_f at $T = 75°\text{C}$):

$$\Psi = \left(313.93\ \frac{\text{kJ}}{\text{kg}} - 104.89\ \frac{\text{kJ}}{\text{kg}}\right) - [(25 + 273)\ \text{K}]\left[\left(1.0155\ \frac{\text{kJ}}{\text{kg}\cdot\text{K}}\right) - \left(0.3674\ \frac{\text{kJ}}{\text{kg}\cdot\text{K}}\right)\right]$$

$$= 15.91\ \frac{\text{kJ}}{\text{kg}}$$

Vapor-Liquid Mixtures

The saturated vapor-liquid (water) table provides data for the region of the thermodynamic surface under the vapor dome. Property data are listed either as functions of temperature or as functions of pressure. Since pressure and temperature are related for a saturated substance, only one value is needed to determine the state of a saturated substance. Usually the value of the other property will be given as a reference.

Each of the dependent properties in the table (specific volume, specific internal energy, specific enthalpy, and specific entropy) is listed for two states, the saturated liquid state with no vapor present, denoted with an f subscript, and the saturated vapor state with no liquid present, denoted with a g subscript. Some values have an fg subscript, which indicates the difference between the values of the property at the saturated liquid and at the saturated vapor state (i.e., $h_{fg} = h_g - h_f$).

As a substance evaporates from a saturated liquid to a saturated vapor, or condenses from a saturated vapor to a saturated liquid, it can be considered as a mixture of two homogeneous substances, a saturated liquid and a saturated vapor. All of the energy added to or removed from the system goes into changing the phase of the fluid. For analysis it is often necessary to determine average values of the properties for the vapor-liquid mixture. Since each of the properties listed in the table is additive in its extensive form, and is reported in its mass specific intensive form, the total value for the substance can be calculated by using a mass-weighted average of the value for each state. This gives rise to a parameter called *quality,* defined as:

$$x = \frac{\text{mass of substance in vapor phase}}{\text{total mass of liquid and vapor combined}}$$

or

$$x = \frac{m_g}{m_f + m_g} \qquad [12.65]$$

The equations that give the mass weighted average of the values of the mass specific properties for a liquid-vapor mixture are as follows:

$$v_{mix} = v_f + x(v_g - v_f)$$
$$= v_f + xv_{fg} \qquad [12.66a]$$

$$u_{mix} = u_f + x(u_g - u_f)$$
$$= u_f + xu_{fg} \qquad [12.66b]$$

$$h_{mix} = h_f + x(h_g - h_f)$$
$$= h_f + xh_{fg} \qquad [12.66c]$$

$$s_{mix} = s_f + x(s_g - s_f)$$
$$= s_f + xs_{fg} \qquad [12.66d]$$

Example 12.17

A vapor-liquid mixture of water at 85°C has a specific volume of 0.75 m^3/kg.

A. What is the quality of the mixture?

B. What is the average specific internal energy of the mixture?

Solutions:

A. From equation 12.66a:

$$x = \frac{v_{mix} - v_f}{v_g - v_f}$$

so that

$$x = \frac{0.75\ \frac{\text{m}^3}{\text{kg}} - 0.001033\ \frac{\text{m}^3}{\text{kg}}}{2.828\ \frac{\text{m}^3}{\text{kg}} - 0.001033\ \frac{\text{m}^3}{\text{kg}}}$$

$$= 0.265$$

B. From equation 12.66b:

$$u_{mix} = u_f + xu_{fg}$$

so that

$$u_{mix} = 355.84\ \frac{kJ}{kg} + (0.265)\left(2132.6\ \frac{kJ}{kg}\right)$$

$$= 921\ \frac{kJ}{kg}$$

Psychrometrics

Often, when an environmental system is analyzed, the substance that makes up the system is found to be air. Normally air is assumed to be a homogeneous mixture of gases, and the values of its thermodynamic properties can be found in tabulated form. However, the values in these tables are for a standard composition of gases, and the composition of the air in an environment can change greatly over time. The component most likely to affect the thermodynamic properties of air is the amount of water vapor the air contains, or its humidity.

To deal with this variation, air is often considered to be a mixture of two gases: dry air, whose thermodynamic properties can be found in standard air tables, and water vapor, whose thermodynamic properties are given in standard steam tables. As with ideal gas mixtures, the pressure of the dry air-water vapor mixture is the sum of the partial pressures of its components, or:

$$p = p_a + p_v \qquad [12.67]$$

where p = total pressure of the mixture,
p_a = partial pressure of the dry air,
p_v = partial pressure of the water vapor.

The composition of an air-water vapor mixture can be expressed in terms of the mass ratio or the mole ratio of the two components, just as with an ideal gas mixture. The mass ratio measure is called the *specific humidity* and is given by:

$$\omega = \frac{m_v}{m_a} = 0.622\frac{p_v}{p - p_v} \qquad [12.68]$$

where: ω = specific humidity or humidity ratio,
m_v = mass of the water vapor,
m_a = mass of the dry air.

The coefficient 0.622 is determined from the ratio of molar masses of water to dry air.

Relative humidity is defined as:

$$\phi = \frac{p_v}{p_g} \qquad [12.69]$$

where ϕ = relative humidity
p_g = saturation pressure of water at the temperature of the air-water vapor mixture.

Dew-Point Temperature

The composition of the air-water vapor mixture is limited to some degree by the equilibrium states of water; that is, there is a maximum amount of water vapor that the mixture can hold. Any water added to the system in excess of this maximum will exist as a liquid. Figure 12.8 illustrates the relationship of the dew-point temperature to the temperature of the air-water mixture.

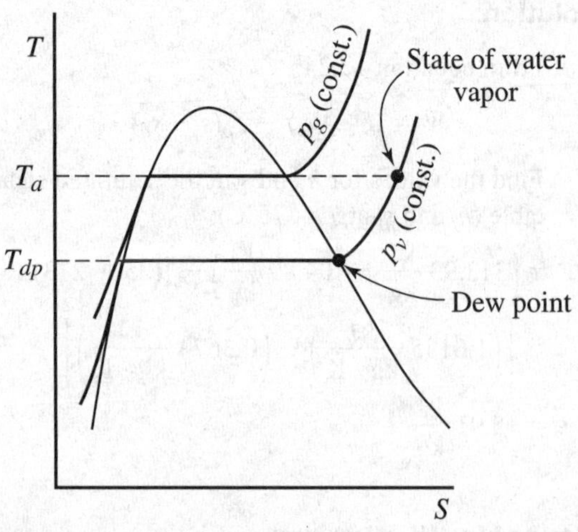

Figure 12.8 *T-s* diagram for water that illustrates the principles of psychrometry

To understand this idea, consider a system that consists of water only at a given temperature. If the pressure of the water is below the saturation pressure for that temperature, the water will exist as a vapor. If the pressure is greater than the saturation pressure, the water will exist as a liquid. For an air-water vapor mixture, the pressure of the water vapor is its partial pressure. As water is added to the system, the partial pressure will increase until it is equal to the saturation pressure of water at the given temperature. At this point, the mixture cannot accept any more water in the vapor phase. Any additional water added to the system will exist in a liquid phase.

The saturation pressure of water is a function of temperature. Therefore, for any given pressure of a water system below the critical pressure, there exists a temperature for which that pressure is the saturation pressure. For an air-water vapor mixture, there exists a temperature for which the partial pressure of the water vapor is equal to the saturation pressure of water. This temperature is called the *dew-point temperature.* If the temperature of the mixture is reduced below its dew point, some of the water vapor will begin to condense into a liquid; this condensation will continue until the partial pressure of water vapor is equal to the saturation pressure of water at the lower temperature. When this happens in our environment, the condensed water collects on solid particles in the air and becomes fog.

Example 12.18

An air-water vapor mixture at a temperature of 80°C has a relative humidity of 27%. What is the dew-point temperature of the mixture?

Solution:

From equation 12.69:

$$p_v = \phi p_g$$

where p_g is the saturation pressure of water at the temperature given, or 46.39 kPa. Then:

$$p_v = 0.27\ (46.39\ \text{kPa}) = 12.53\ \text{kPa}$$

$$T_{dp} = T_{sat}(12.53\ \text{kPa}) \approx 50°\text{C}$$

Wet-Bulb Temperature

A common device used to experimentally determine the amount of water vapor in the air, or the humidity, is a sling psychrometer. This device consists of two glass-tube thermometers, mounted side by side, with a handle attached to the top of the thermometers. The bulb of one thermometer is covered with a fabric wick, which is saturated with water. This is the wet bulb thermometer; the other is the dry-bulb thermometer. The device is operated by swinging it by its handle.

Because there will be some energy transfer due to evaporation of the water in the wick of the wet bulb thermometer, the two thermometers will display different temperatures. This difference is used to determine the humidity of the air. The temperature read from the wet-bulb thermometer is called the *wet-bulb temperature* of the air-water vapor mixture; the temperature read from the dry-bulb thermometer is the dry-bulb temperature.

Psychrometric Chart

A psychrometric chart relates the values of specific volume, specific enthalpy, relative humidity, wet- and dry-bulb temperatures, and humidity ratio for equilibrium states of a mixture at a given pressure. Given the values of any two of these properties, we can determine the values of all others. An example of a psychometric chart is found on page 336.

12.4 Applications

All of the definitions, laws, and concepts given above are combined to analyze and predict the performance of real mechanical devices. Some examples of these devices are discussed below.

Energy-Conversion Devices

There are many energy-conversion devices to which the above laws and relationships can be applied. Each of these systems is a steady-state system, meaning that the rate of change of every property at each location in the device will remain zero. This steady-state assumption greatly simplifies analysis.

The balance equations applied to a steady-state system are as follows:

Mass balance:

$$\frac{dm}{dt} = \dot{m}_{\text{transferred}} = 0 \quad \text{or} \quad \sum \dot{m}_i = \sum \dot{m}_e \quad [12.70]$$

Energy balance:

$$\frac{dE}{dt} = \dot{Q} - \dot{W} + \sum \dot{m}_i\left(h_i + \frac{V_i^2}{2} + gz_i\right) - \sum \dot{m}_e\left(h_e + \frac{\overline{V}_e^2}{2} + gz_e\right) = 0 \quad [12.71]$$

Entropy balance:

$$\frac{dS}{dt} = \sum \frac{\dot{Q}}{T_b} + \sum \dot{m}_i s_i - \sum \dot{m}_e s_e + \dot{S}_{\text{produced}} = 0 \quad [12.72]$$

Nozzles and Diffusers

Nozzles and diffusers, diagrammed in Figure 12.9, are devices used to change the velocity and pressure of a fluid stream; therefore we can expect kinetic energy terms to be significant. Analysis is often simplified by the assumption that effects due to changes in potential energy are negligible.

From mass balance:

$$\dot{m}_i = \dot{m}_e = \dot{m} \quad [12.73]$$

From energy balance:

$$h_e - h_i = \frac{\overline{V}_i^2 - \overline{V}_e^2}{2} \quad [12.74]$$

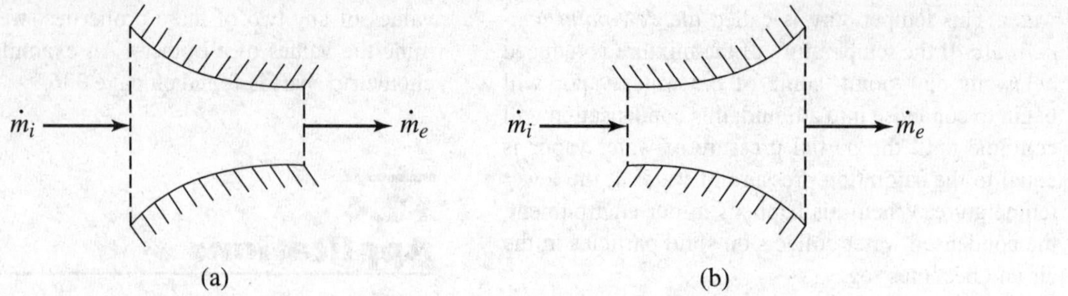

Figure 12.9 A subsonic nozzle (a) and a subsonic diffuser (b)

From entropy balance:

$$\dot{S}_{\text{produced}} = \dot{m}(s_e - s_i) \qquad [12.75]$$

The efficiency of the nozzle or diffuser is given by:

$$\eta = \frac{\text{change in kinetic energy of the actual device}}{\text{change in kinetic energy for an ideal device}}$$

$$= \frac{\overline{V}_e^2 - \overline{V}_i^2}{2(h_i - h_{es})} \qquad [12.76]$$

where η = nozzle or diffuser efficiency,
h_{es} = enthalpy at isentropic exit state.

In a perfectly efficient nozzle, no entropy will be produced, and the value of entropy will be the same at the outlet as at the inlet. In a real nozzle, however, some entropy will be produced, and the value of enthalpy at the exit state will be somewhat higher than that of a perfectly efficient nozzle.

Turbines, Pumps, and Compressors

Turbines, pumps, and compressors, shown in Figure 12.10, are used either to produce mechanical work from some of the internal energy of a substance or to use mechanical work to increase the internal energy of a substance. In a turbine, energy is removed from the substance through a mechanical work interaction; in a pump or compressor, energy is transferrred to the substance through a mechanical work interaction. Whatever device is considered, the conversion of energy is often assumed to take place adiabatically, that is, with no heat interaction, and changes in kinetic and potential energy are often negligible.

From mass balance:

$$\dot{m}_i = \dot{m}_e = \dot{m} \qquad [12.73]$$

From energy balance:

$$\dot{W} = \dot{m}(h_i - h_e) \qquad [12.77]$$

From entropy balance:

$$\dot{S}_{\text{produced}} = \dot{m}(s_e - s_i) \qquad [12.75]$$

The efficiency of turbines, pumps, and compressors can be found by using the following equation:

$$\eta_{\text{turbine}} = \frac{w_{\text{actual}}}{w_{\text{isentropic}}} = \frac{h_i - h_e}{h_i - h_{es}} \qquad [12.78]$$

and

$$\eta_{\text{comp, pump}} = \frac{w_{\text{isentropic}}}{w_{\text{actual}}} = \frac{h_{es} - h_i}{h_e - h_i} \qquad [12.79]$$

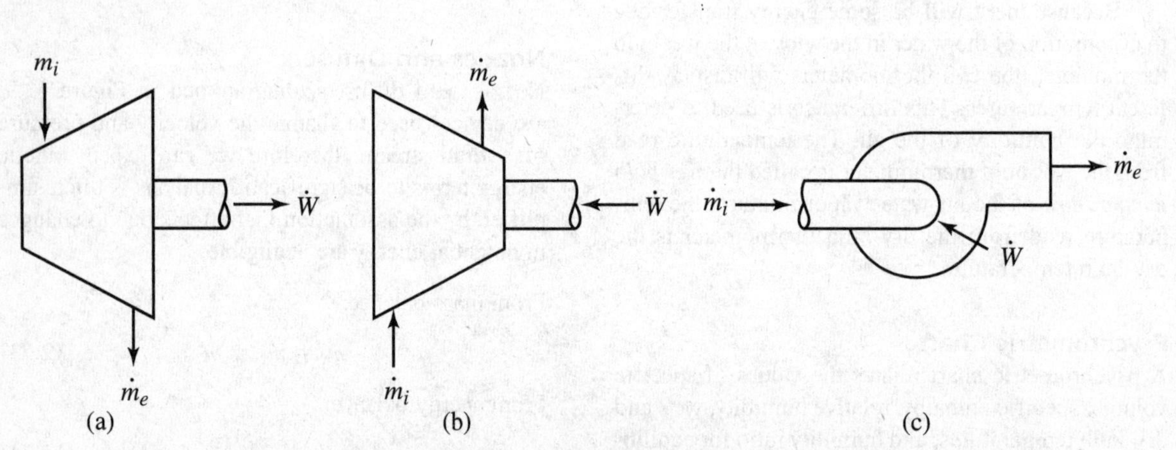

Figure 12.10 Schematic representation of (a) a turbine, (b) a compressor, and (c) a pump.

Example 12.19

A 30-kg/s stream of steam enters a turbine at 800 kPa and 600°C, and exits the turbine at 50 kPa and 300°C

A. What is the rate of energy transferred through turbine work?

B. What is the rate of entropy production?

Solutions:

A. From equation 12.77:

$$\dot{W} = \dot{m}(h_i - h_e)$$

$$= \left(30\frac{\text{kg}}{\text{s}}\right)\left(3{,}699.4\frac{\text{kJ}}{\text{kg}} - 3{,}075.5\frac{\text{kJ}}{\text{kg}}\right)\left(\frac{\text{kW}}{\text{kJ/s}}\right)$$

$$= 19 \text{ kW}$$

B. From equation 12.75:

$$\dot{S}_{\text{produced}} = \dot{m}(s_e - s_i)$$

$$= \left(30\frac{\text{kg}}{\text{s}}\right)\left(8.5373\frac{\text{kJ}}{\text{kg}\cdot\text{K}} - 8.1333\frac{\text{kJ}}{\text{kg}\cdot\text{K}}\right)\left(\frac{\text{kW}}{\text{kJ/s}}\right)$$

$$= 12\frac{\text{kW}}{\text{K}}$$

Example 12.20

How much power is required for an ideal pump ($\eta = 1$) to increase the pressure of a 7-kg/s stream of water at 25°C from 50 kPa to 600 kPa?

Solution:

For a reversible process, equation 12.8 gives:

$$w_{\text{rev}} = -\int_1^2 v\,dp$$

Assume that liquid water is incompressible; then:

$$\dot{W} = -\dot{m}v\int_{p1}^{p2} dp$$

$$= -\dot{m}v(p_e - p_i)$$

$$= -\left(7\frac{\text{kg}}{\text{s}}\right)\left(0.001003\frac{\text{m}^3}{\text{kg}}\right)(600\text{ kPa} - 50\text{ kPa})\left(\frac{1000\text{ N/m}^2}{\text{kPa}}\right)\left(\frac{\text{J}}{\text{N}\cdot\text{m}}\right)\left(\frac{\text{kW}}{1000\text{ J/s}}\right)$$

$$= -3.86 \text{ kW}$$

The pump must supply 3.86 kW of power to the system.

Valves

A valve, represented in Figure 12.11, is a device that can be used to lower the pressure in a fluid system. In most cases the amount of energy transferred through heat interactions is negligible, as are changes in kinetic and potential energy.

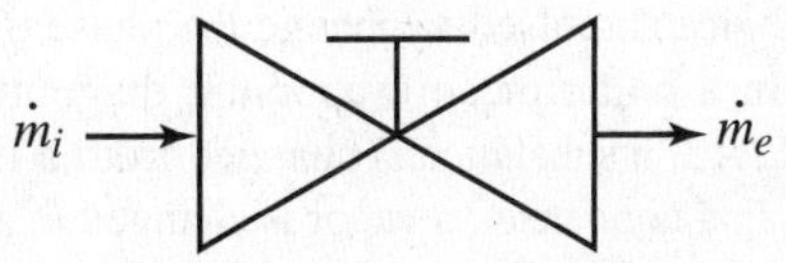

Figure 12.11 Schematic representation of a valve

From mass balance:

$$\dot{m}_i = \dot{m}_e = \dot{m} \quad [12.73]$$

From energy balance:

$$h_i = h_e \quad [12.80]$$

From entropy balance:

$$\dot{S}_{\text{produced}} = \dot{m}(s_e - s_i) \quad [12.75]$$

Example 12.21

Steam flows through a valve. At the inlet of the valve, the steam pressure is 600 kPa, the temperature is 700°C, and the mass flow rate is 4 kg/s. At the outlet of the valve, the steam pressure is 100 kPa. At what rate is entropy produced?

Solution:

From equation 12.75:

$$\dot{S}_{\text{produced}} = \dot{m}(s_e - s_i)$$

Find the values of entropy and enthalpy at the inlet state (p_i = 600 kPa and T_i = 700°C) in the superheated steam table. Then:

$$s_i = 8.51\frac{\text{kJ}}{\text{kg}\cdot\text{K}}$$

$$h_i = 3925.3\frac{\text{kJ}}{\text{kg}}$$

Because flow through a valve is isenthalpic (h = constant), the state of the fluid at the valve outlet can be determined from p_e and $h_e = h_i$. Using the superheated steam table, find the value of entropy at the outlet:

$$s_e = 9.34\frac{\text{kJ}}{\text{kg}\cdot\text{K}}$$

Then:

$$\dot{S}_{\text{produced}} = \left(4\frac{\text{kg}}{\text{s}}\right)\left(9.34\frac{\text{kJ}}{\text{kg}\cdot\text{K}} - 8.51\frac{\text{kJ}}{\text{kg}\cdot\text{K}}\right)$$

$$= 3.32\frac{\text{kJ}}{\text{s K}}$$

Boilers, Condensers, and Evaporators

These devices are used to change the phase of a substance. In a boiler or an evaporator, diagrammed in Figure 12.12, a substance is changed from a liquid to a vapor. In a condenser, a vapor is changed to a liquid. These devices are often used to take advantage of the relatively large amounts of energy transfer required to change the phase of many common fluids. For the most part, boilers, condensers, and evaporators transfer their energy through heat interactions. Changes in potential and kinetic energy are often negligible.

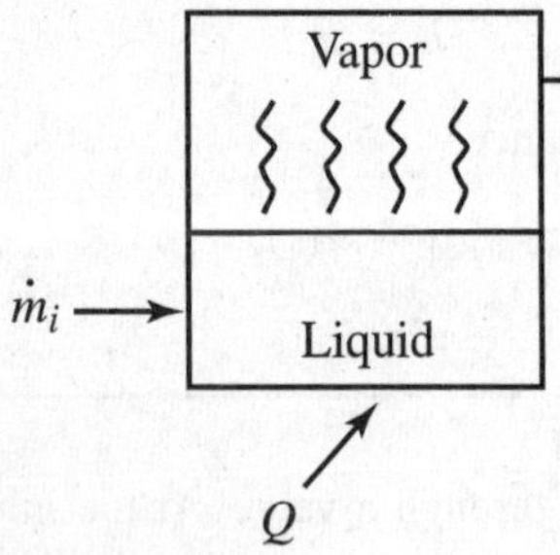

Figure 12.12 Diagram of a boiler or an evaporator

From mass balance:

$$\dot{m}_i = \dot{m}_e = \dot{m} \qquad [12.73]$$

From energy balance:

$$\dot{Q} = \dot{m}(h_e - h_i) \qquad [12.81]$$

From entropy balance:

$$\dot{S}_{\text{produced}} = \dot{m}(s_e - s_i) - \frac{\dot{Q}}{T} \qquad [12.82]$$

where T is the temperature at which the heat interaction occurs.

Example 12.22

A steady-state boiler operates with 5000 kW of energy supplied through heat interaction. If 1.5 kg/s of water at 800 kPa and 25°C enters the boiler, what is the temperature of the steam leaving the boiler?

Solution:

From equation 12.81:

$$h_e = h_i + \frac{\dot{Q}}{\dot{m}}$$

As in Example 12.15, h_i is approximated by $h_f(25°\text{C})$ or $h_i = 104.89$ kJ/kg. Then:

$$h_e = 104.89\frac{\text{kJ}}{\text{kg}} + \frac{5{,}000\ \text{kW}\left(\frac{\text{kJ/s}}{\text{kW}}\right)}{1.5\frac{\text{kg}}{\text{s}}}$$

$$= 3{,}438\frac{\text{kJ}}{\text{kg}}$$

The superheated steam table shows that at 800 kPa, $T_e \approx 480°\text{C}$.

Heat Exchangers

A heat exchanger, diagrammed in Figure 12.13, is a device that allows energy to be exchanged between two substances through a heat interaction. Analysis is simplified by assuming that no other interaction takes place; in particular, that there is no heat interaction between the heat exchanger and its environment.

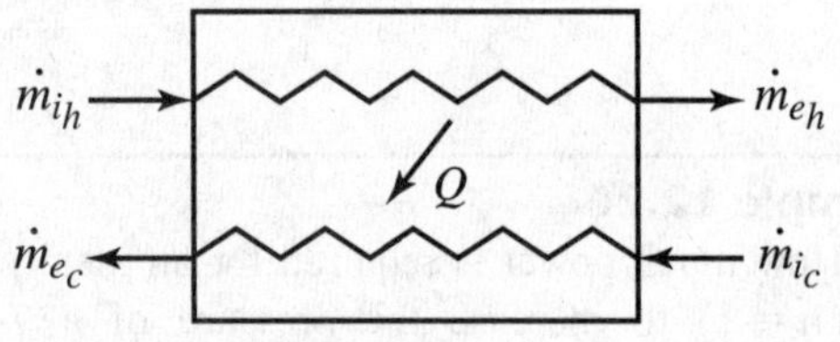

Figure 12.13 Diagram of a heat exchanger

From mass balance:

$$\dot{m}_{ih} = \dot{m}_{eh} = \dot{m}_h \quad \text{and} \quad \dot{m}_{ic} = \dot{m}_{ec} = \dot{m}_c \qquad [12.83]$$

where h = hot stream, and c = cold stream.
From energy balance:

$$\dot{m}_h(h_i - h_e)_h = \dot{m}_c(h_e - h_i)_c \qquad [12.84]$$

In many cases the change in temperature through a heat exchanger is small enough that the constant-pressure specific heat may be considered constant, and the following equation may be used in place of equation 12.84:

$$\dot{m}_h\, c_p(T_i - T_e)_h = \dot{m}_c\, c_p(T_e - T_i)_c \qquad [12.85]$$

From entropy balance:

$$\dot{S}_{\text{produced}} = \dot{m}_c(s_e - s_i)_c - \dot{m}_h(s_i - s_e)_h \qquad [12.86]$$

Example 12.23

In a heat exchanger, 10 kg/s of water enters the hot side at 80°C and 150 kPa, and leaves at 40°C; 12 kg/s of water enters the cold side at 15°C. If there is no pressure drop in the heat exchanger $[(p_e = p_i)_c$ and $(p_e = p_i)_h]$, at what temperature does the cold water leave the heat exchanger?

Solution:

From equation 12.85:

$$\dot{m}_h\, c_p(T_i - T_e)_h = \dot{m}_c\, c_p(T_e - T_i)_c$$

so

$$T_{ec} = \frac{\dot{m}_h\, c_p(T_i - T_e)_h + \dot{m}_c\, c_p T_{ic}}{\dot{m}_c\, c_p}$$

or

$$T_{ec} = T_{ic} + \frac{\dot{m}_h\, c_p}{\dot{m}_c\, c_p}(T_i - T_e)_h$$

$$= 15°\text{C} + \frac{\left(10\,\frac{\text{kg}}{\text{s}}\right)\left(4.18\,\frac{\text{kJ}}{\text{kg K}}\right)}{\left(12\,\frac{\text{kg}}{\text{s}}\right)\left(4.18\,\frac{\text{kJ}}{\text{kg K}}\right)}(80°\text{C} - 40°\text{C})$$

$$= 48°\text{C}$$

Mixers and Separators

Mixers (see Figure 12.14) and separators are devices that combine or separate material streams. For the purposes of this discussion, the mixer or separator will experience no work or heat interactions with its surroundings, and changes in kinetic and potential energy are negligible.

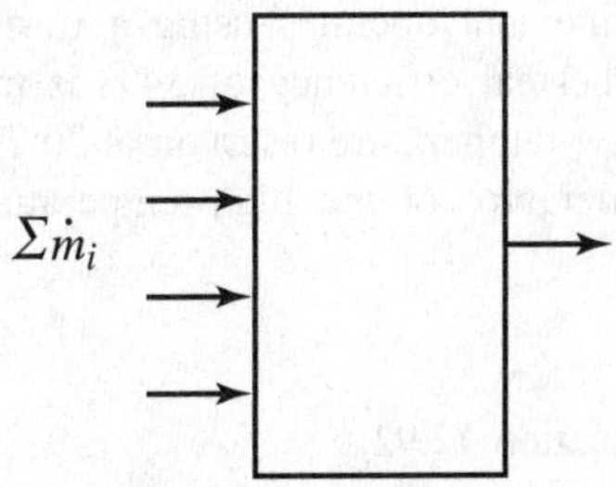

Figure 12.14 Schematic diagram of a mixer

From mass balance:

$$\Sigma\dot{m}_i = \dot{m}_e \qquad [12.87]$$

From energy balance:

$$\Sigma\dot{m}_i\, h_i = \dot{m}_e\, h_e \qquad [12.88]$$

From entropy balance:

$$\dot{m}_e\, s_e - \Sigma\, \dot{m}_i\, s_i = \dot{S}_{\text{produced}} \qquad [12.89]$$

Note that the above equations are valid for a mixer only. For a separator, the summations will be over the outlet terms instead of the inlet terms.

Thermodynamic Cycles

The cyclic machine discussed earlier was a generalization of the many cyclic devices used in industry. All of the devices discussed here operate on a thermodynamic cycle, that is, a series of processes for which the end state of the last process is equivalent to the start state of the first process.

As with energy-conversion devices, it is often desirable to determine the figure of merit for the thermodynamic cycles. The figure of merit for a power-producing thermodynamic cycle is the *thermal efficiency,* while the figure of merit used for refrigeration and heat pump cycles is the *coefficient of performance* (COP).

Carnot Cycle

A Carnot-cycle machine undergoes four processes, which may occur with a cycle of four steady-state components or in a piston and cylinder system. The two types of systems are shown in Figures 12.15 and 12.16.

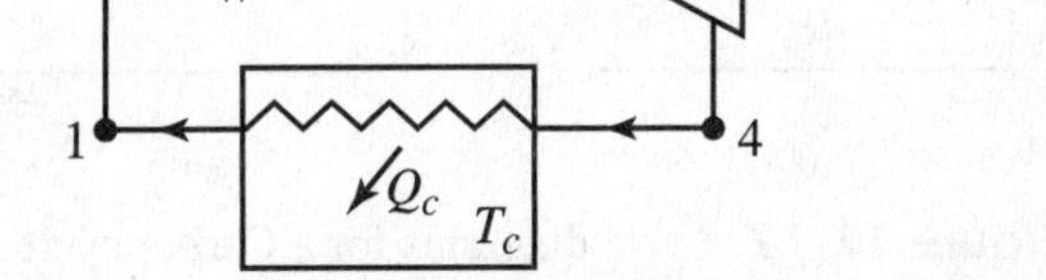

Figure 12.15 Carnot cycle composed of steady-state devices

The processes of an ideal Carnot cycle are as follows:

Process 1-2: Energy is added to the system in a reversible, adiabatic work interaction (isentropic compression).

Process 2-3: Energy is added to the system in a reversible heat interaction with the high-temperature reservoir.

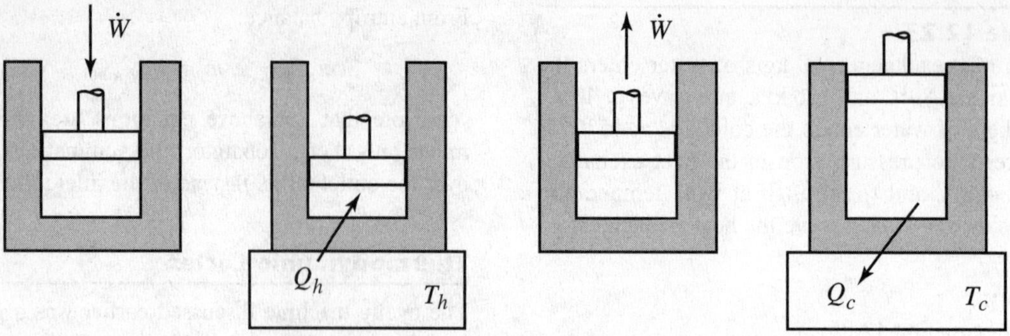

Process 1-2 Process 2-3 Process 3-4 Process 4-1

Figure 12.16 Piston and cylinder Carnot cycle

Process 3-4: Energy is removed from the system in a reversible, adiabatic work interaction (isentropic expansion).

Process 4-1: Energy is removed from the system in a reversible heat interaction with the low-temperature reservoir.

All of the devices considered above are idealized concepts of real devices, which can never be achieved. Irreversibilities in all real devices cause a deviation in performance from that of a Carnot cycle. Figure 12.17 shows plots of a typical Carnot cycle on (a) a *p-v* and (b) a *T-s* diagram.

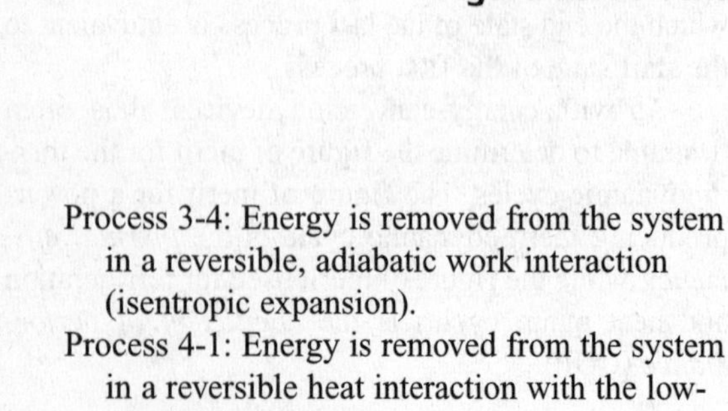

Figure 12.17 Cycle diagrams for a Carnot cycle

When the balance equations are applied to the devices in the Carnot cycle, the thermal efficiency of the cycle is given by:

$$\eta_{\text{Carnot}} = \frac{\dot{W}_{\text{net}}}{\dot{Q}_{\text{in}}} = \frac{\sum \dot{W}}{\dot{Q}_{\text{in}}} = \frac{\sum \dot{Q}}{\dot{Q}_{\text{in}}}$$

$$= \frac{\dot{Q}_{23} + \dot{Q}_{41}}{\dot{Q}_{23}} \qquad [12.90]$$

(Remember that $\dot{Q}_{41}$ is negative because energy is leaving the system.)

Using equation 12.21, we obtain:

$$Q_{\text{rev}} = \int_1^2 T\,dS$$

Equation 12.90 can be rewritten as:

$$\eta_{\text{Carnot}} = \frac{T_H(s_3 - s_2) + T_L(s_1 - s_4)}{T_H(s_3 - s_2)} \qquad [12.91]$$

Since the *T-s* diagram in Figure 12.17 (b) shows that $s_2 = s_1$ and $s_3 = s_4$, equation 12.91 can be simplified to:

$$\eta_{\text{Carnot}} = 1 - \frac{T_L}{T_H} \qquad [12.92]$$

Since the Carnot cycle represents the idealized cyclic machine, no other cycle can operate at the same temperatures with a higher thermal efficiency.

Example 12.24

A machine that operates using a Carnot cycle with a thermal efficiency of 34% is in contact with a low-temperature reservoir at 20°F. What is the temperature of the high-temperature reservoir?

Solution:

From equation 12.92:

$$T_H = \frac{T_L}{1 - \eta_{\text{Carnot}}}$$

Then:

$$T_H = \frac{(20 + 460)°\text{R}}{1 - 0.34}$$

$$= 727°\text{R}$$

$$= 267°\text{F}$$

Example 12.25

For a Carnot cycle, if energy is added at the high-temperature heat interaction at a rate of 4 kW, and energy is removed at the low-temperature heat interaction at a rate of 1.3 kW, what is the efficiency of the cycle?

Solution:

From equation 12.90:

$$\eta_{\text{Carnot}} = \frac{\dot{Q}_{23} + \dot{Q}_{41}}{\dot{Q}_{23}}$$

so

$$\eta_{\text{Carnot}} = \frac{4\text{ kW} + (-1.3\text{ kW})}{4\text{ kW}}$$

$$= 0.67 \text{ or } 67\%$$

Rankine Cycle (Heat Engine)

The most common example of a Rankine cycle is a simple steam power plant. The overall effect is to use energy supplied from the high-temperature reservoir to provide useable energy through a heat interaction.

The processes of an ideal Rankine cycle are as follows:

Process 1-2: The pressure of the working fluid, in liquid phase, is raised with an ideal or isentropic pump (energy added to the system through a work interaction).

Process 2-3: The liquid working fluid is boiled in a heat exchanger connected to the high-temperature reservoir (energy added to the system through a heat interaction).

Process 3-4: The working-fluid vapor is expanded in an ideal or isentropic turbine (energy removed from the system in a work interaction).

Process 4-1: The working-fluid vapor is condensed into a liquid in a heat exchanger connected to the low-temperature reservoir (energy removed from the system in a heat interaction).

The thermal efficiency of a Rankine cycle must be lower than that of a Carnot cycle operating between the same high and low temperatures. By applying the balance equations to each of the devices in the Rankine cycle, the efficiency can be found. The equation for this efficiency is:

$$\eta_{\text{Rankine}} = \frac{(h_3 - h_4) - (h_2 - h_1)}{h_3 - h_2} \qquad [12.93]$$

Vapor-Compression Refrigeration/Heat Pump Cycle

This cycle uses energy provided through a work interaction to transfer energy between two systems at different temperatures. If the purpose of the system is to keep an environment at low temperature, the cycle is called a *refrigeration cycle;* if the purpose is to keep an environment at high temperature, the cycle is called a *heat pump.*

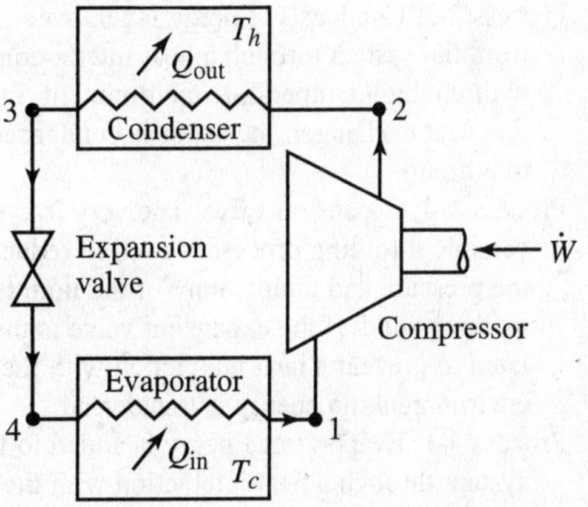

Figure 12.19 Schematic representation of an ideal vapor-compression refrigeration/heat pump system

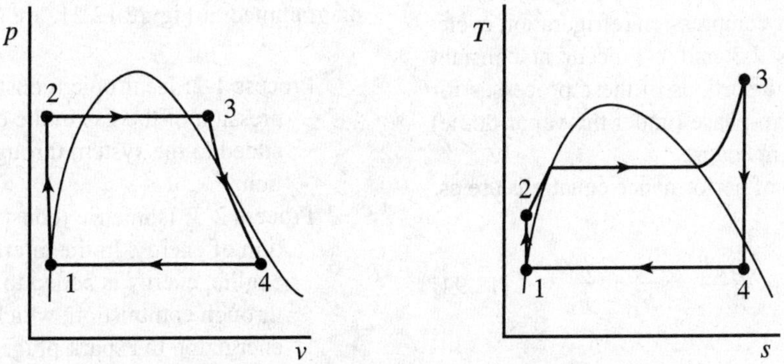

(a) (b)

Figure 12.18 Cycle diagrams for an ideal Rankine cycle

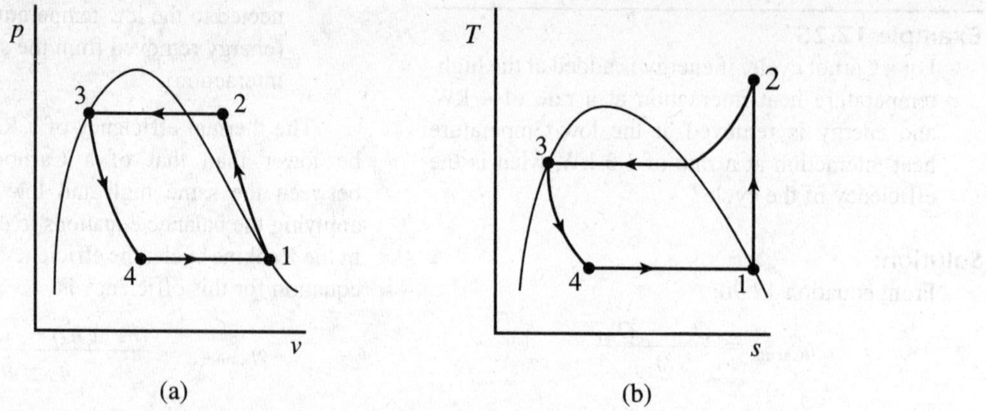

Figure 12.20 Cycle diagrams for a vapor-compression refrigeration cycle

The components of an ideal vapor-compression refrigeration system are as follows:

Process 1-2, Compressor: Energy is added to the working fluid, which is in its vapor phase, through an ideal work interaction.

Process 2-3, Condenser: Energy is removed from the system through a heat interaction with the high temperature environment. In this heat exchanger, the vapor is condensed to a liquid.

Process 3-4, Expansion valve: The very irreversible throttling process is used to reduce the pressure and temperature of the liquid working fluid. If the expansion valve is insulated to prevent a heat interaction with the environment, no energy is transferred.

Process 4-1, Evaporator: Energy is added to the system through a heat interaction with the low-temperature environment. In this heat exchanger, the two-phase working fluid is boiled to a vapor.

Figure 12.20 shows the typical (a) *p-v* and (b) *T-s* diagrams for a vapor compression refrigeration cycle. Note that processes 2-3 and 4-1 occur at constant pressure, and that the portions of these processes for which the fluid is two-phase (under the vapor dome) occur at constant temperature.

The coefficient of performance equations are as follows:

$$COP_{ref} = \frac{\dot{Q}_{4-1}}{\dot{W}_{1-2}} = \frac{h_1 - h_4}{h_2 - h_1} \qquad [12.94]$$

and

$$COP_{hp} = \frac{\dot{Q}_{2-3}}{\dot{W}_{1-2}} = \frac{h_2 - h_3}{h_2 - h_1} \qquad [12.95]$$

The values for entropy in equations 12.94 and 12.95 are determined using a P-h diagram for the refrigerant being used. An example of such a diagram for Refrigerant HFC-134a is provided at the end of this chapter.

Otto Cycle

The Otto cycle is an air-standard cycle that approximates the performance of the typical spark-ignition internal-combustion engine used in an automobile. The main differences between the two are (1) that the compression and the expansion of the piston in the Otto cycle are considered isentropic, unlike the actual process in a spark-ignition engine, and that (2) the working fluid in the Otto cycle is air rather than an air-fuel mixture and products of combustion. Although in an actual spark-ignition engine the values of the working fluid's thermodynamic properties at times vary greatly from those of air, qualitative information can be obtained using a fluid for which large quantities of thermodynamic state data exist.

The processes of an ideal Otto cycle, which is diagrammed in Figure 12.21, are as follows:

Process 1-2: Isentropic (constant-entropy) compression of the gas in the cylinder. Energy is added to the system through a work interaction.

Process 2-3: Isometric (constant-volume) addition of energy. In the internal-combustion engine, energy is added to the system through combustion, which is initiated by energizing the spark plug. For the purposes of the Otto cycle, it is assumed that energy is added to the system through a heat interaction.

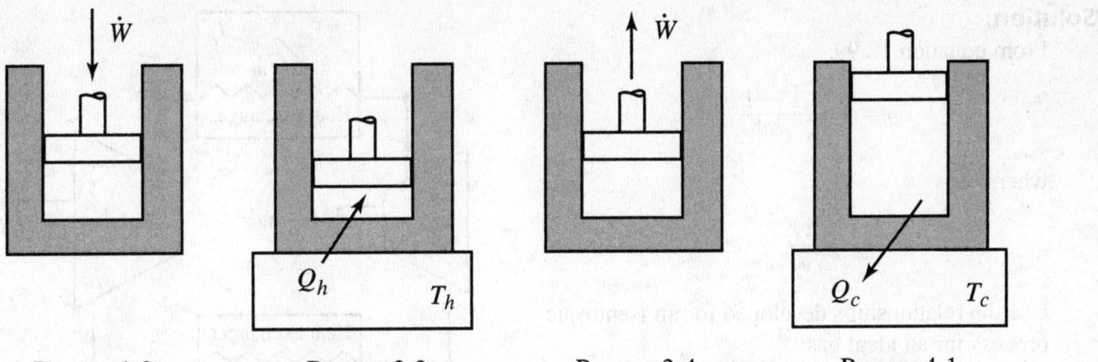

Figure 12.21 Operation of an Otto cycle

Process 3-4: Isentropic expansion of the gas in the cyclinder. Energy is removed from the system through a work interaction.

Process 4-1: Isometric rejection of energy. In the internal-combustion engine, the spent air and combustion products are replaced by fresh air and fuel. For the purposes of the Otto cycle, it is assumed that energy is removed from the system through a heat interaction.

Figure 12.22 shows typical (a) *p-v* and (b) *T-s* diagrams for an Otto cycle. Note that processes 2-3 and 4-1 occur at constant specific volume, while processes 1-2 and 3-4 occur at constant specific entropy.

An important parameter of the Otto cycle is the compression ratio, defined as :

$$r = \frac{v_1}{v_2} \qquad [12.96]$$

Using the ideal gas relationships for an isentropic process, we find that:

$$\frac{T_2}{T_1} = \left(\frac{v_1}{v_2}\right)^{k-1} = r^{k-1} \text{ (constant } k\text{)} \qquad [12.97]$$

$$\frac{T_4}{T_3} = \left(\frac{v_3}{v_4}\right)^{k-1} = \frac{1}{r^{k-1}} \text{ (constant } k\text{)} \qquad [12.98]$$

The thermal efficiency of the Otto cycle is given by:

$$\eta = 1 - \frac{1}{r^{k-1}} \text{ (constant } k\text{)} \qquad [12.99]$$

where k is the specific heat ratio, $k = \frac{c_p}{c_v}$.

Example 12.26

What is the thermal efficiency of an Otto cycle in which air is the working fluid, if the compression process raises the pressure from 100 kPa to 1.8 MPa?

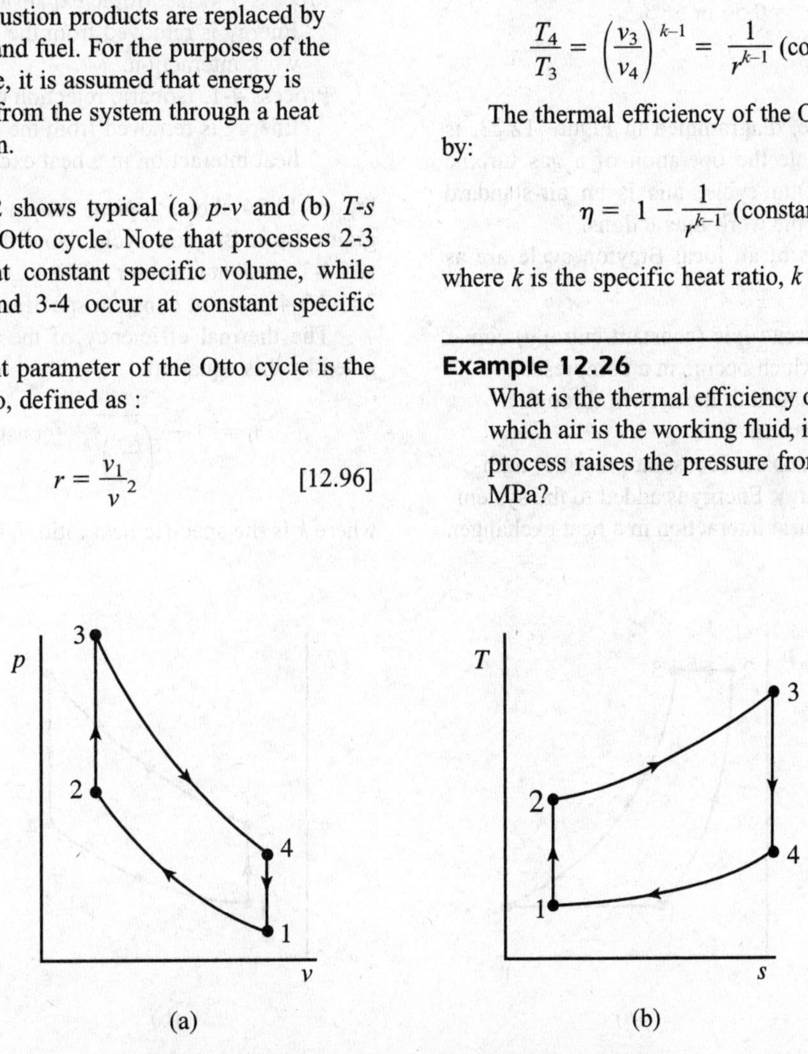

Figure 12.22 Cycle diagrams for an Otto cycle

Solution:

From equation 12.99:

$$\eta = 1 - \frac{1-1}{r^{k-1}}$$

where

$$r = \frac{v_1}{v_2}.$$

Use the relationships developed for an isentropic process for an ideal gas:

$$r^{k-1} = \left(\frac{v_1}{v_2}\right)^{k-1} = \left(\frac{p_2}{p_1}\right)^{\frac{k-1}{k}}$$

$$\eta = 1 - \frac{1}{\left(\frac{p_2}{p_1}\right)^{\frac{k-1}{k}}}$$

$$= 1 - \frac{1}{\left(\frac{1{,}800 \text{ kPa}}{100 \text{ kPa}}\right)^{\frac{1.4-1}{1.4}}}$$

$$= 0.56 \text{ or } 56\%$$

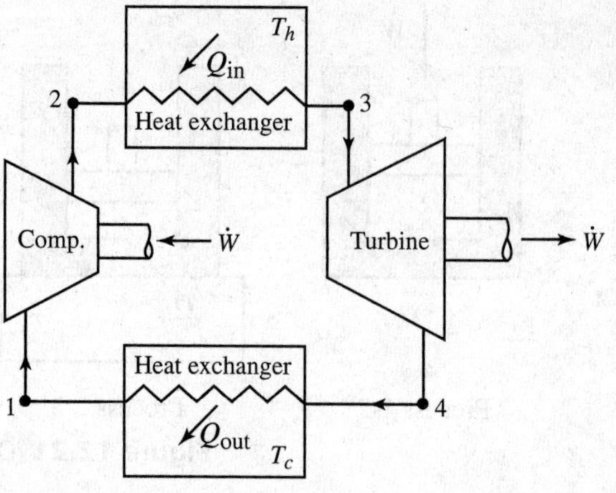

Figure 12.23 Diagram of a system that operates on a Brayton cycle

Brayton Cycle

The Brayton cycle, diagrammed in Figure 12.23, is used to approximate the operation of a gas turbine cycle. Like the Otto cycle, this is an air-standard cycle, with isentropic work interactions.

The processes of an ideal Brayton cycle are as follows:

Process 1-2: Isentropic (constant-entropy) compression, which occurs in a compressor. Energy is added to the system through a work interaction.

Process 2-3: Isobaric (constant-pressure) addition of energy. Energy is added to the system through a heat interaction in a heat exchanger.

Process 3-4: Isentropic expansion in the turbine. Energy is removed from the system through a work interaction.

Process 4-1: Isobaric rejection of energy. Energy is removed from the system through a heat interaction in a heat exchanger.

Figure 12.24 shows typical (a) *p-v* and (b) *T-s* diagrams for a Brayton cycle. Note that processes 2-3 and 4-1 occur at constant pressure, while processes 1-2 and 3-4 occur at constant specific entropy.

The thermal efficiency of the Brayton cycle is given by this equation:

$$\eta = 1 - \frac{1}{\left(\frac{p_2}{p_1}\right)^{\frac{k-1}{k}}} \text{ (constant } k) \quad [12.100]$$

where k is the specific heat ratio, $k = \frac{c_p}{c_v}$.

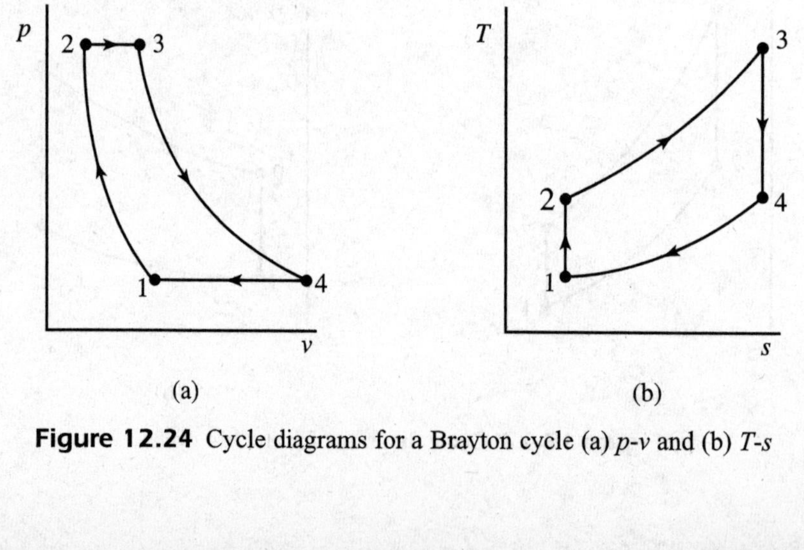

Figure 12.24 Cycle diagrams for a Brayton cycle (a) *p-v* and (b) *T-s*

Specific Heat Data for Gases

Substance	Molecular Weight	c_p Btu/lbm · °R	c_p kJ/kg · K	c_v Btu/lbm · °R	c_v kJ/kg · K	k
Air	29	0.240	1.00	0.171	0.718	1.40
Argon	40	0.125	0.520	0.0756	0.312	1.67
Butane	58	0.415	1.72	0.381	1.57	1.09
Carbon dioxide	44	0.203	0.846	0.158	0.657	1.29
Carbon monoxide	28	0.249	1.04	0.178	0.744	1.40
Ethane	30	0.427	1.77	0.361	1.49	1.18
Helium	4	1.25	5.19	0.753	3.12	1.67
Hydrogen	2	3.43	14.3	2.44	10.2	1.40
Methane	16	0.532	2.25	0.403	1.74	1.30
Neon	20	0.246	1.03	0.148	0.618	1.67
Nitrogen	28	0.248	1.04	0.177	0.743	1.40
Octane vapor	114	0.409	1.71	0.392	1.64	1.04
Oxygen	32	0.219	0.918	0.157	0.658	1.40
Propane	44	0.407	1.68	0.362	1.49	1.12
Steam	18	0.455	1.87	0.335	1.41	1.33

Specific Heat Data for Liquids

Substance	c_p Btu/lbm · °R	c_p kJ/kg · K	Density lbm/ft3	Density kg/m^3
Ammonia	1.146	4.80	38	602
Mercury	0.033	0.139	847	13,560
Water	1.000	4.18	62.4	997

Specific Heat Data for Solids

Substance	c_p Btu/lbm · °R	c_p kJ/kg · K	Density lbm/ft3	Density kg/m3
Aluminum	0.215	0.900	170	2,700
Copper	0.092	0.386	555	8,900
Ice*	0.502	2.11	57.2	917
Iron	0.107	0.450	490	7,840
Lead	0.030	0.128	705	11,310

*Properties for ice taken at 0°C (32°F).

Saturated Water—Temperature Table

Temp.	Saturation Pressure	Specific Volume (m³/kg)		Internal Energy (kJ/kg)			Enthalpy (kJ/kg)			Entropy (kJ/kg · K)		
(°C)	(kPa)	Saturated Liquid	Saturated Vapor	Saturated Liquid	Evap.	Saturated Vapor	Saturated Liquid	Evap.	Saturated Vapor	Saturated Liquid	Evap.	Saturated Vapor
T	P_{sat}	v_f	v_g	u_f	u_{fg}	u_g	h_f	h_{fg}	h_g	s_f	s_{fg}	s_g
0.01	0.6133	0.001000	206.14	0	2375.3	2375.3	0.01	2501.3	2501.4	0	9.1562	9.1562
5	0.8721	0.001000	147.12	20.97	2361.3	2382.3	20.98	2489.6	2510.6	0.0761	8.9496	9.0257
10	0.12276	0.001000	106.38	42.00	2347.2	2389.2	42.01	2477.7	2519.8	0.1510	8.7498	8.9008
15	1.7051	0.001001	77.93	62.99	2333.1	2396.1	62.99	2465.9	2528.9	0.2245	8.5569	8.7814
20	2.339	0.001002	57.79	83.95	2319	2402.9	83.96	2454.1	2538.1	0.2966	8.3706	8.6672
25	3.169	0.001003	43.36	104.88	2304.9	2409.8	104.89	24423	2547.2	0.3674	8.1905	8.558
30	4.246	0.001004	32.89	125.78	2290.8	2416.6	125.79	2430.5	2556.3	0.4369	8.0164	8.4533
35	5.628	0.001006	25.22	146.67	2276.7	2423.4	146.68	2418.6	2565.3	0.5053	7.8478	8.3531
40	7.384	0.001008	19.52	167.56	2262.6	2430.1	167.57	2406.7	2574.3	0.5725	7.6845	8.257
45	9.593	0.001010	15.26	188.44	2248.4	2436.8	188.45	2394.8	2583.2	0.6387	7.5261	8.1648
50	12.349	0.001012	12.03	209.32	2234.2	2443.5	209.33	2382.7	2592.1	0.7038	7.3725	8.0763
55	15.754	0.001015	9.568	230.21	2219.9	2450.1	230.23	2370.7	2600.9	0.7679	7.2234	7.9913
60	19.94	0.001017	7.671	251.11	2205.5	2456.6	251.13	2358.5	2609.6	0.8312	7.0784	7.9096
65	25.03	0.001020	6.197	272.02	2191.1	2463.1	272.06	2346.2	2618.3	0.8935	6.9375	7.831
70	31.19	0.001023	5.042	292.95	2176.6	2569.6	292.98	2333.8	2626.8	0.9549	6.8004	7.7553
75	38.58	0.001026	4.131	313.90	2162.0	2475.9	313.93	2321.4	2635.3	1.0155	6.6669	7.6824
80	47.39	0.001029	3.407	334.86	2147.4	2482.2	334.91	2308.8	2643.7	1.0753	6.5369	7.6122
85	57.83	0.001033	2.828	355.84	2132.6	2488.4	355.90	2296.0	2651.9	1.1343	6.4102	7.5445
90	70.14	0.001036	2.361	376.85	2117.7	2494.5	376.92	2283.2	2660.1	1.1925	6.2866	7.4791
95	84.55	0.001040	1.9820	397.88	2102.7	2500.6	697.96	2270.2	2668.1	1.2500	6.1659	7.4159
100	101.35	0.001044	1.6729	418.94	2087.6	2506.5	419.04	2257.0	2676.1	1.3069	6.0480	7.3549
105	120.82	0.001048	1.4194	440.02	2072.3	2512.4	440.15	2243.7	2683.8	1.3630	5.9328	7.2958
110	143.27	0.001052	1.2102	461.14	2057.0	2518.1	461.3	2230.2	2691.5	1.4185	5.8202	7.2387
115	169.06	0.001056	1.0366	482.30	2041.4	2523.7	482.48	2216.5	2699	1.4734	5.7100	7.1833
120	198.53	0.001060	0.8919	503.50	2025.8	2529.3	503.71	2202.6	2706.3	1.5276	5.6020	7.1296
125	232.1	0.001065	0.7706	524.74	2009.9	2534.6	524.99	2188.5	2713.5	1.5813	5.4962	7.0775
130	270.1	0.001070	0.6685	546.02	1993.9	2539.9	546.31	2174.2	2720.5	1.6344	5.3925	7.0269
135	313.0	0.001075	0.5822	567.35	1977.7	2545.0	567.69	2159.6	2727.3	1.6870	5.2907	6.9777
140	361.3	0.001080	0.5089	588.74	1961.3	2550.0	589.13	2144.7	2733.9	1.7391	5.1908	6.9299
145	415.4	0.001085	0.4463	610.18	1944.7	2554.9	610.63	2129.6	2740.3	1.7907	5.0926	6.8833
150	475.8	0.001091	0.3928	631.68	1927.9	2559.5	632.20	2114.3	2746.5	1.8418	4.9960	6.8379
155	543.1	0.001096	0.3468	653.24	1910.8	2564.1	653.84	2098.6	2752.4	1.8925	4.9010	6.7935
160	617.8	0.001102	0.3071	674.87	1893.5	2568.4	675.55	2082.6	2758.1	1.9427	4.8075	6.7502
165	700.5	0.001108	0.2727	696.56	1876.0	2572.5	697.34	2066.2	2763.5	1.9925	4.7153	6.7078
170	791.7	0.001114	0.2428	718.33	1858.1	2576.5	719.21	2049.5	2768.7	2.0419	4.6244	6.6663
175	892.0	0.001121	0.2168	740.17	1840.0	2580.2	741.17	2032.4	2773.6	2.0909	4.5347	6.6256
	(MPa)											
180	1.0021	0.001127	0.19405	762.09	1821.6	2583.7	763.22	2015.0	2778.2	2.1396	4.4461	6.5857
185	1.1227	0.001134	0.17409	784.10	1802.9	2587.0	785.39	1997.1	2782.4	2.1879	4.3586	6.5465
190	1.2544	0.001141	0.15654	806.19	1783.8	2590.0	807.62	1978.8	2786.4	2.2359	4.2720	6.5079
195	1.3978	0.001149	0.14105	828.37	1764.4	2592.8	829.98	1960.0	2790.0	2.2835	4.1863	6.4698
200	1.5538	0.001157	0.12736	850.65	1744.7	2595.3	852.45	1940.7	2793.2	2.3309	4.1014	6.4323
205	1.7230	0.001164	0.11521	873.04	1724.5	2597.5	875.04	1921.0	2796.0	2.3780	4.0172	6.3952
210	1.9062	0.001173	0.10441	895.53	1703.9	2599.5	897.76	1900.7	2798.5	2.4248	3.9337	6.3585
215	2.1040	0.00118	0.09479	918.14	1682.9	2601.1	920.62	1879.9	2800.5	2.4714	3.8507	6.3221
220	2.318	0.001190	0.08619	940.87	1661.5	2602.4	943.62	1858.5	2802.1	2.5178	3.7683	6.2861
225	2.548	0.001199	0.07849	963.73	1639.6	2603.3	966.78	1836.5	2803.3	2.5639	3.6863	6.2503
230	2.795	0.001209	0.07158	986.74	1617.2	2603.9	990.12	1813.8	2804.0	2.6099	3.6047	6.2146
235	3.06	0.001219	0.06537	1009.89	1594.2	2604.1	1013.62	1790.5	2804.2	2.6558	3.5233	6.1791
240	3.344	0.001229	0.05976	1033.21	1570.8	2604.0	1037.32	1766.5	2803.8	2.7015	3.4422	6.1437
245	3.648	0.001124	0.05471	1056.71	1546.7	2603.4	1061.23	1741.7	2803.0	2.7472	3.3612	6.1083

Saturated Water—Temperature Table (Continued)

Temp.	*Saturation Pressure*	*Specific Volume* (m^3/kg)		*Internal Energy* (kJ/kg)			*Enthalpy* (kJ/kg)			*Entropy* (kJ/kg · K)		
(°C)	**(kPa)**	**Saturated Liquid**	**Saturated Vapor**	**Saturated Liquid**	**Evap.**	**Saturated Vapor**	**Saturated Liquid**	**Evap.**	**Saturated Vapor**	**Saturated Liquid**	**Evap.**	**Saturated Vapor**
T	P_{sat}	v_f	v_g	u_f	u_{fg}	u_g	h_f	h_{fg}	h_g	s_f	s_{fg}	s_g
250	3.973	0.001125	0.05013	1080.39	1522.0	2602.4	1085.36	1716.2	2801.5	2.7927	3.2802	6.0730
255	4.319	0.001263	0.04598	1104.28	1596.7	2600.9	1109.73	1689.8	2799.5	2.8383	3.1992	6.0375
260	4.688	0.001276	0.042211	1128.39	1470.6	2599.0	1134.37	1662.5	2796.9	2.8838	3.1181	6.0019
265	5.081	0.001289	0.03877	1152.74	1443.9	2596.6	1159.28	1634.4	2793.6	2.9294	3.0368	5.9662
270	5.499	0.001302	0.03564	1177.36	1416.3	2593.7	1184.51	1605.2	2789.7	2.9751	2.9551	5.9301
275	5.942	0.001317	0.03279	1202.25	1387.9	2590.2	1210.07	1574.9	2785	3.0208	2.873	5.8938
280	6.412	0.001332	0.03017	1227.46	1358.7	2586.1	1235.99	1543.6	2779.6	3.0668	2.7903	5.8571
285	6.909	0.001348	0.02777	1253.00	1328.4	2581.4	1262.31	1511.0	2773.3	3.113	2.707	5.8199
290	7.436	0.001366	0.02557	1278.92	1297.1	2576.0	1289.07	1477.1	2766.2	3.1594	2.6227	5.7821
295	7.993	0.001384	0.02354	1305.2	1264.7	2569.9	1316.3	1441.8	2758.1	3.2062	2.5375	5.7437
300	8.581	0.001404	0.02167	1332.0	1231.0	2563.0	1344.0	1404.9	2749.0	3.2534	2.4511	5.7045
305	9.202	0.001425	0.019948	1359.3	1195.9	2555.2	1372.4	1366.4	2738.7	3.301	2.3633	5.6643
310	9.856	0.001447	0.018350	1387.1	1159.4	2546.4	1401.3	1326.0	2727.3	3.3493	2.2737	5.623
315	10.547	0.001472	0.016867	1415.5	1121.1	2536.6	1431.0	1283.5	2714.5	3.3982	2.1821	5.5804
320	11.274	0.001499	0.015488	1444.6	1080.9	2525.5	1461.5	1238.6	2700.1	3.448	2.0882	5.5362
330	12.845	0.001561	0.012996	1505.3	993.7	2498.9	1525.3	1140.6	2665.9	3.5507	1.8909	5.4417
340	14.586	0.001638	0.010797	1570.3	894.3	2464.6	1594.2	1027.9	2622.0	3.6594	1.6763	5.3357
350	16.513	0.001740	0.008813	1641.9	776.6	2418.4	1670.6	893.4	2563.9	3.7777	1.4335	5.2112
360	18.651	0.001893	0.006945	1725.2	626.3	2351.5	1760.5	720.3	2481.0	3.9147	1.1379	5.0526
370	21.03	0.002213	0.004925	1844.0	384.5	2228.5	1890.5	441.6	2332.1	4.1106	0.6865	4.7971
374.14	22.09	0.003155	0.003155	2029.6	0	2029.6	2099.3	0	2099.3	4.4298	0	4.4298

Superheated Steam Table

Temp. T (°C)	Specific Volume v (m^3/kg)	Internal Energy u (kJ/kg)	Enthalpy h (kJ/kg)	Entropy s (kJ/kg · K)	Specific Volume v (m^3/kg)	Internal Energy u (kJ/kg)	Enthalpy h (kJ/kg)	Entropy s (kJ/kg · K)
	P = 0.01 MPa (45.81 °C)				P = 0.05 MPa (45.81 °C)			
sat	14.674	2437.9	2584.7	8.1502	3.240	2483.9	2645.9	7.5939
50	14.869	2443.9	2592.6	8.1749				
100	17.196	2515.5	2687.5	8.4479	3.418	2511.6	2682.5	7.6947
150	19.512	2587.9	2783.0	8.6882	3.889	2585.6	2780.1	7.9401
200	21.825	2661.3	2879.5	8.9038	4.356	2659.9	2877.7	8.1580
250	24.136	2736.0	2977.3	9.1002	4.820	2735.0	2976.0	8.3556
300	26.445	2812.1	3076.5	9.2813	5.284	2811.3	3075.5	8.5373
400	31.063	2968.9	3279.6	9.6077	6.209	2968.5	3278.9	8.8642
500	35.679	3132.3	3489.1	9.8978	7.134	3132.0	3488.7	9.1546
600	40.295	3302.5	3705.4	10.1608	8.057	3302.2	3705.1	9.4178
700	44.911	3479.6	3982.7	10.4028	8.981	3479.4	3928.5	9.6599
800	49.526	3663.8	4159.0	10.6281	9.904	3663.6	4158.9	9.8852
900	54.141	3855.0	4396.4	10.8396	10.828	3854.9	4396.3	10.0967
1000	58.757	4053.0	4640.6	11.0393	11.751	4052.9	4640.5	10.2964
1100	63.372	4257.5	4891.2	11.2287	12.674	4257.4	4891.1	10.4859
1200	67.987	4467.9	5147.8	11.4091	13.597	446708	5147.7	10.6662
1300	72.602	4683.7	5409.7	11.5811	14.521	4683.6	5409.6	10.8382
	P = 0.10 MPa (99.63 °C)				P = 0.20 MPa (120.23 °C)			
sat	1.6940	2506.1	2675.5	7.3594	0.8857	2529.5	2706.7	7.1272
100	1.6958	2506.7	2676.2	7.3614				
150	1.9364	2582.8	2776.4	7.6134	0.9596	2576.9	2768.8	7.2795
200	2.172	2658.1	2875.3	7.8343	1.0803	2654.4	2870.5	7.5066
250	2.406	2733.7	2974.3	8.0333	1.1988	2731.2	2971.0	7.7086
300	2.639	2810.4	3074.3	8.2158	1.3162	2808.6	3071.8	7.8926
400	3.103	2967.9	3278.2	8.5435	1.5493	2966.7	3276.6	8.2218
500	3.565	3131.6	3488.1	8.8342	1.7814	3130.8	3487.1	8.5133
600	4.028	3301.9	3704.4	9.0976	2.013	3301.4	3704.0	8.7770
700	4.490	3479.2	3928.2	9.3398	2.244	3478.8	3927.6	9.0194
800	4.952	3663.5	4158.6	9.5652	2..475	3663.1	4158.2	9.2449
900	5.414	3854.8	4396.1	9.7767	2.705	3854.5	4395.8	9.4566
1000	5.875	4052.8	4640.3	9.9764	2.937	4052.5	4640.0	9.6563
1100	6.337	4257.3	4891.0	10.4659	3.168	4257.0	4890.7	9.8458
1200	6.799	4467.7	5147.6	10.3463	3.399	4467.5	5147.5	10.0262
1300	7.260	4683.5	5409.5	10.5183	3.630	4683.2	5409.3	10.1982
	P = 0.40 MPa (143.63 °C)				P = 0.60 MPa (158.85 °C)			
sat	0.4625	2553.6	2738.9	6.8959	0.3157	2567.4	2756.8	6.7600
150	0.4708	2564.5	2752.8	6.9299				
200	0.5342	2646.8	2860.5	7.1706	0.3520	2638.9	2850.1	6.9665
250	0.5951	2726.1	2964.2	7.3789	0.3938	2720.9	2957.2	7.1816
300	0.6548	2804.8	3066.8	7.5662	0.4344	2801.0	3061.6	7.3724
350					0.4742	2881.2	3156.7	7.5464
400	0.7726	2964.4	3273.4	7.8985	0.5137	2962.1	3270.3	7.7079
500	0.8893	3129.2	3484.9	8.1913	0.5920	3127.6	3482.8	8.0021
600	1.0055	3300.2	3702.4	8.4558	0.6697	3299.1	3700.9	8.2674
700	1.1215	3477.9	3926.5	8.6987	0.7472	3477.0	3925.3	8.5107
800	1.2372	3662.4	4157.3	8.9244	0.8245	3661.8	4156.5	8.7367
900	1.3529	3853.9	4395.1	9.1362	0.9017	3853.4	494.4	8.9486
1000	1.4685	4052.0	4639.4	9.3360	0.9788	4051.5	4638.8	9.1485
1100	1.5840	4256.5	4890.2	9.5256	1.0559	4256.1	4889.6	9.3381
1200	1.6996	4467.0	5146.8	9.7060	1.1330	4466.5	5146.3	9.5185
1300	1.8151	4682.8	5408.8	9.8780	1.2102	4682.3	5408.3	9.6906
	P = 0.80 MPa (170.43 °C)				P = 1.00 MPa (179.91 °C)			
sat	0.2404	2576.8	2769.1	6.6628	0.1944	2583.6	2778.1	6.5865
200	0.2608	2630.6	2839.3	6.8158	0.2060	2621.9	2827.9	6.6940
250	0.2931	2715.5	2950.0	7.0384	0.2327	2709.9	2942.6	6.9247
300	0.3241	2797.2	3056.5	7.2328	0.2579	2793.2	3051.2	7.1229
350	0.3544	2878.2	3161.7	7.4089	0.2825	2875.2	3157.7	7.3011
400	0.3843	2959.7	3267.1	7.5716	0.3066	2957.3	3263.9	7.4651
500	0.4433	3126.0	3480.6	7.8673	0.3541	3124.4	3478.5	7.7622
600	0.5018	3297.9	3699.4	8.1333	0.4011	3296.8	3697.9	8.0290
700	0.5601	3476.2	3924.2	8.3770	0.4478	3475.3	3923.1	8.2731
800	0.6181	3661.1	4155.6	8.6033	0.4943	3660.4	4154.7	8.4996
900	0.6761	3852.8	4393.7	8.8153	0.5407	3852.2	4392.9	8.7118
1000	0.7340	4051.0	4638.2	9.0153	0.5871	4050.5	4637.6	8.9119
1100	0.7919	4255.6	4889.1	9.2050	0.6335	4255.1	4888.6	9.1017
1200	0.8497	4466.1	5145.9	9.3855	0.6798	4465.6	5145.4	9.2822
1300	0.9076	4681.8	5407.9	9.5575	0.7261	4681.3	5407.4	9.4543

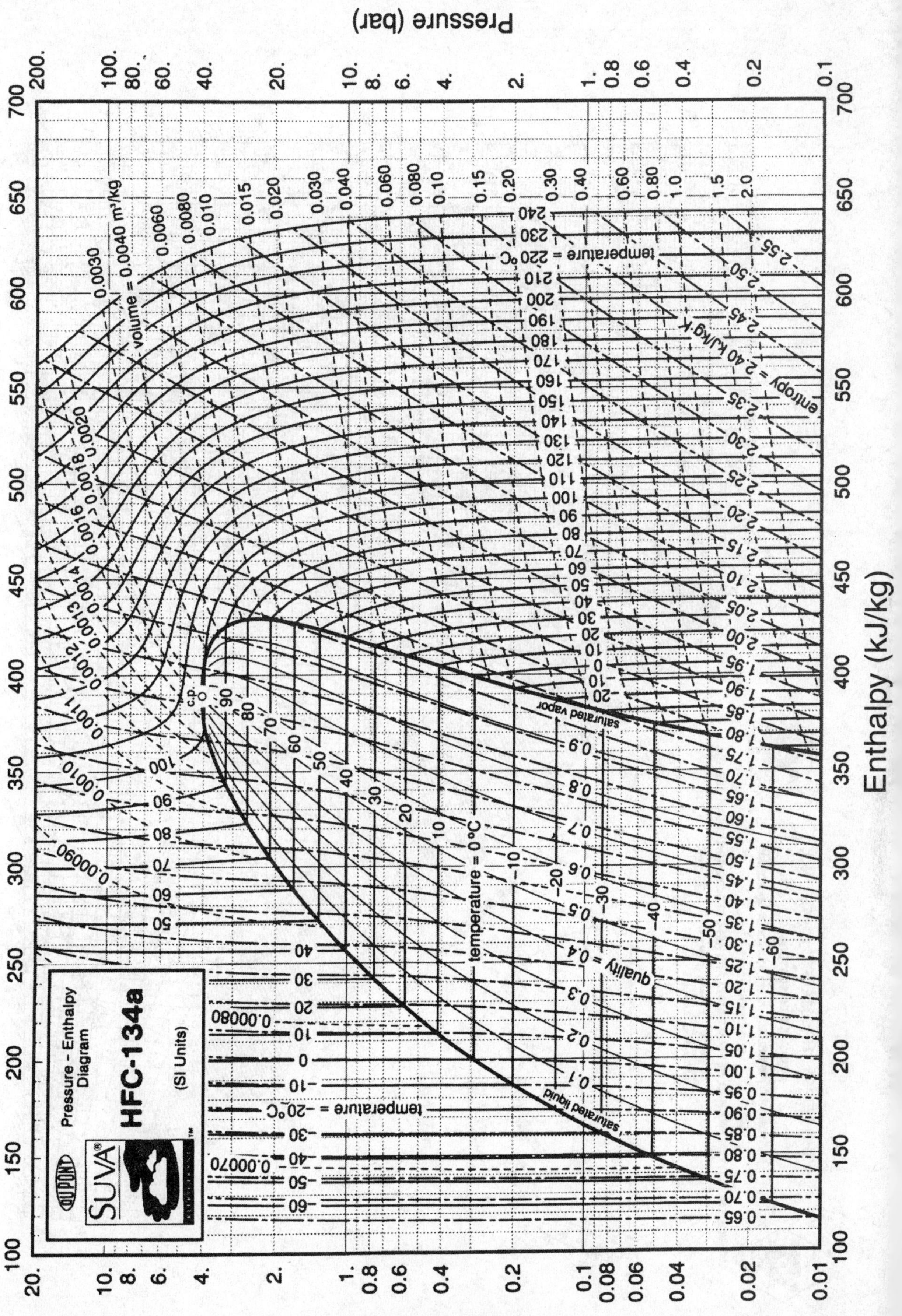

P-h Diagram for Refrigerant HFC-134a in SI units
(reproduced by permission of the DuPont Company)

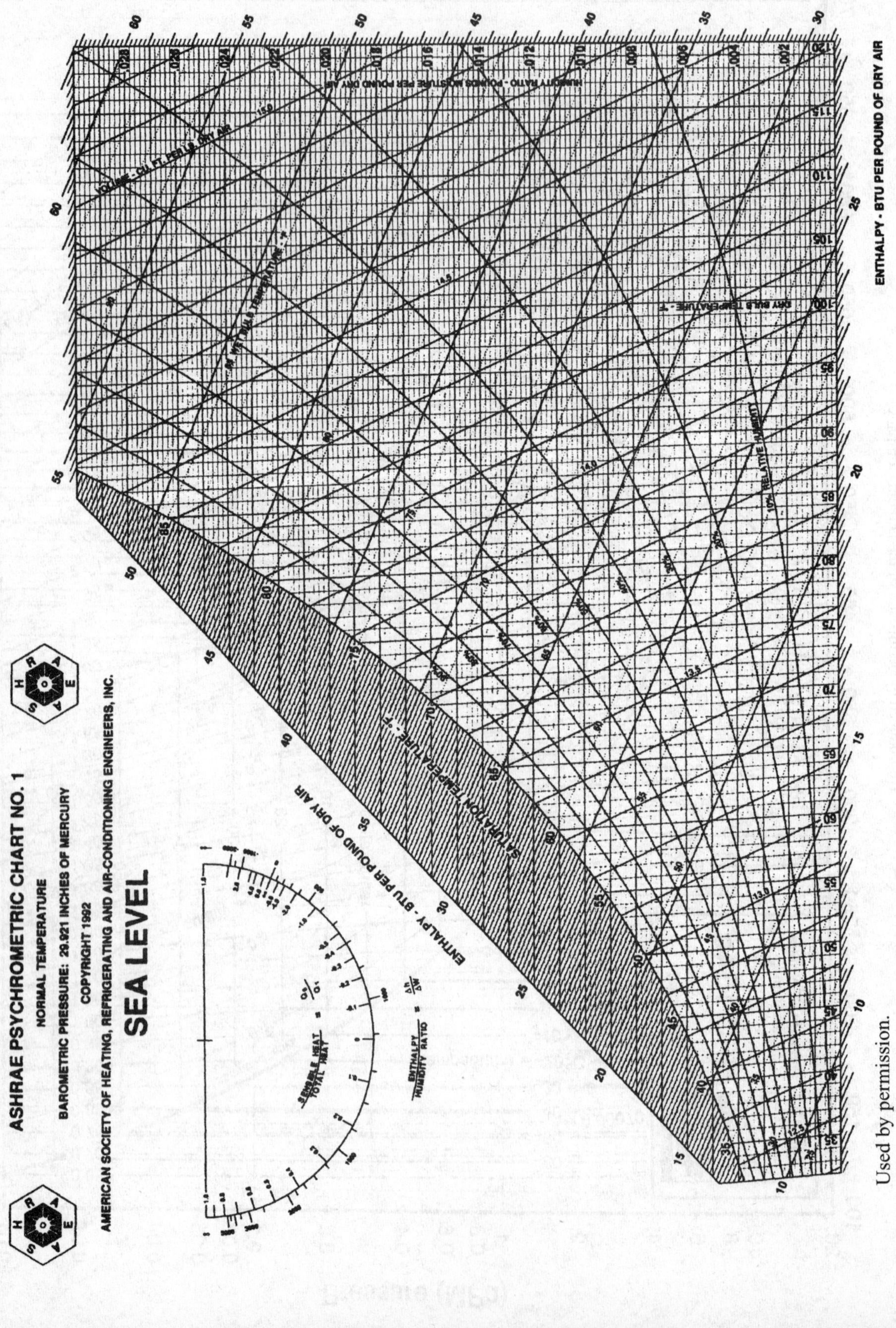

Used by permission.

PRACTICE PROBLEMS

1. The availability of a system:
(A) is the maximum amount of energy that may be removed from the system in an ideal heat interaction
(B) is the maximum amount of energy that may be added to a system in an ideal work interaction.
(C) is the maximum amount of energy that may be removed from a system and its environment in an ideal work interaction.
(D) remains unchanged in an ideal work interaction.

2. What is the change in availability for a system in a closed, rigid container in which 37kJ of energy is transferred to the system through a reversible work interaction, and 42kJ of energy is transferred from the system through a reversible heat interaction with a thermal reservoir at 30°C? Take the dead state of the system to be standard conditions (101 kPa and 25°C).
(A) 5 kJ
(B) 36.3 kJ
(C) 42 kJ
(D) 37.7 kJ

3. What is the mass of oxygen gas in a container with a volume of 25 ft^3, at a pressure of 14.7 psia and a temperature of 75°F?
(A) 2 lbm
(B) 0.0004 lbm
(C) 0.06 lbm
(D) 5 lbm

4. What is the Mach number of air at 25°C flowing with a velocity of 75 m/s?
(A) 0.75
(B) 0.04
(C) 1.27
(D) 0.22

5. What is the mass of water at 400 kPa and 500°C contained in a 6-m^3 vessel?
(A) 6 kg
(B) 6.75 kg
(C) 6000 kg
(D) 60 kg

6. An ideal gas mixture contains the following components:

Oxygen 1 kg
Argon 3 kg
Carbon monoxide2 kg

What is the mass fraction of argon?
(A) 20%
(B) 30%
(C) 40%
(D) 50%

7. What is the molar mass of the following mixture, where the composition is defined in terms of mole fractions?

Argon 0.28
Helium 0.34
Neon 0.38

(A) 4
(B) 22
(C) 20
(D) 40

8. A 6-m^3 vessel contains the following mixture of ideal gases at 20°C:

Nitrogen0.1 kmol
Oxygen 0.3 kmol
Helium 0.05 kmol

What is the total pressure of the vessel?
(A) 100 kPa
(B) 183 kPa
(C) 137 kPa
(D) 12.5 kPa

9. What is the partial pressure of water vapor in an air-water mixture at 15.2 psia if the mole fraction of water vapor in the mixture is 1.6%?
(A) 0.024 psia
(B) 0.24 psia
(C) 2.4 psia
(D) 24 psia

10. What is the specific humidity of an atmospheric air-water mixture at 15.2 psia if the partial pressure of water in the mixture is 0.22 psia?
(A) 0.22
(B) 0.05
(C) 0.022
(D) 0.009

11. What is the velocity of a stream of nitrogen gas at the exit of a diffuser if the inlet velocity is 120 m/s, the inlet temperature is 30°C, and the outlet temperature is 36°C?
(A) 44 m/s
(B) 119.9 m/s
(C) 121.1.m/s
(D) 85. m/s

12. What is the power output of a turbine if 0.5 kg/s of air enters at 750 kPa and 80°C, and exits at 370 kPa and 37°C?
(A) 43 kW
(B) 380 kW
(C) 21 kW
(D) 37 kW

13. An ideal air compressor pressurizes air from standard conditions (14.7 psia, 77°F) to 80 psia What is the air temperature at the exit?
(A) 865°F
(B) 411°F
(C) 125°F
(D) 419°F

14. In a heat exchanger, 8 lbm/s of water enters the cold side at 35°F and exits at 63°F. Hot water enters the other side of the heat exchanger at 90°F and exits at 46°F. What is the flow rate of the hot water?
(A) 5 lbm/sec
(B) 8 lbm/sec
(C) 10 lbm/sec
(D) 15 lbm/sec

15. A Carnot engine operates between 400°C and 30°C. What is the efficiency of the engine?
(A) 92.5%
(B) 60%
(C) 55%
(D) 43%

16. What is the efficiency of an air standard Brayton cycle that operates with a 4:1 pressure ratio?
(A) 48%
(B) 43%
(C) 38%
(D) 33%

17. What type of cycle is represented by the following process?

1-Energy added to the system through an isentropic work interaction.

2-Energy removed from the system through an isobaric heat interaction.

3-Isenthalpic expansion of the working fluid.

4-Energy added to the system through an isobaric heat interaction.

(A) ideal Rankine cycle
(B) ideal Otto cycle
(C) ideal vapor-compression refrigeration cycle
(D) Carnot cycle

18. The average specific volume of water at 80°C is 1 m^3/kg. What is the quality of the water?
(A) 0
(B) 0.3
(C) 0.6
(D) 1

19. The change in entropy of air from 25°C and 1 atm pressure to 200°C and 4 atm pressure is
(A) 0 kJ/kg · K
(B) 0.07 kJ/kg · K
(C) 0.69 kJ/kg · K
(D) 1.69 kJ/kg · K

20. Air expands isentropically in a piston cylinder device from 300°C and 800 kPa to 100 kPa. The work done by the air is
(A) 133 kJ/kg
(B) 181 kJ/kg
(C) 253 kJ/kg
(D) 316 kJ/kg

21. Air expands isentropically in a turbine from 300°C and 800 kPa to 100 kPa. The work output of the turbine is
(A) 133 kJ/kg
(B) 181 kJ/kg
(C) 253 kJ/kg
(D) 316 kJ/kg

22. Steam expands isentropically from 1 MPa and 350°C to atmospheric pressure in a steam turbine. What is the work output of the turbine?
(A) 482 kJ/kg
(B) 502 kJ/kg
(C) 1,500 kJ/kg
(D) 2,739 kJ/kg

23. Refrigerant 134a is isentropically compressed in a compressor from saturated vapor state at 0.1 MPa pressure to 1 MPa pressure. The work required to run the compressor is
(A) 10 kJ/kg
(B) 30 kJ/kg
(C) 50 kJ/kg
(D) 70 kJ/kg

24. What is the coefficient of performance of a Carnot refrigerator operating between 20°F and 75°F?
(A) 0.36
(B) 1.2
(C) 3.5
(D) 8.7

25. What is the coefficient of a Carnot heat pump operating between 1°C and 20°C?
(A) 0.5
(B) 1.05
(C) 7.8
(D) 15.4

26. What is the closed-system availability of steam at 300°C and 0.1 MPa pressure if the environment is at 25°C and 1 atm pressure?
(A) 362 kJ/kg
(B) 514 kJ/kg
(C) 634 kJ/kg
(D) 631 kJ/kg

27. Energy is added to air in a closed system in a reversible and isothermal heat interaction. The pressure of the air decreases from 300 kPa to 100 kPa while the temperature is kept constant at 100°C. The amount of energy transferred in this process is

(A) 31 kJ/kg
(B) 80 kJ/kg
(C) 116 kJ/kg
(D) 410 kJ/kg

Answer Key

1. C	**10.** D	**19.** B
2. B	**11.** B	**20.** D
3. A	**12.** C	**21.** C
4. D	**13.** B	**22.** B
5. B	**14.** A	**23.** C
6. D	**15.** C	**24.** D
7. C	**16.** D	**25.** D
8. B	**17.** C	**26.** C
9. B	**18.** B	**27.** C

Answers Explained

1. C Availability (Φ), also called exergy or available energy, is defined as the theoretical maximum amount of energy that can be extracted from a system and its environment in the form of useful work.

2. B Use equation 12.23; the change in availability is given by the expression

$$\Delta\phi = \left(1 - \frac{T_o}{T_b}\right)Q - W$$

$$= \left[1 - \frac{(25 + 273)\text{K}}{(30 + 273)\text{K}}\right](-42 \text{ kJ}) + 37 \text{ kJ}$$

$$= 36.3 \text{ kJ}$$

3. A From equation 12.33b: $pV = mRT$

or

$$m = \frac{pV}{RT}$$

The only property not given in the problem statement is the gas constant R, which is determined using the property data for oxygen at the end of the chapter and equation 12.35:

$$R = c_p - c_v$$

$$= 0.219\frac{\text{Btu}}{\text{lbm-R}} - 0.157\frac{\text{Btu}}{\text{lbm-R}}$$

$$= 0.062\frac{\text{Btu}}{\text{lbm-R}}$$

Then:

$$m = \frac{pV}{RT}$$

$$= \frac{\left(14.7\frac{\text{lbf}}{\text{in}^2}\right)(25 \text{ ft}^3)}{\left(0.062\frac{\text{Btu}}{\text{lbm-R}}\right)(75 + 460)\text{R}}\left(\frac{144 \text{ in}^2}{\text{ft}^2}\right)$$

$$-\left(\frac{\text{Btu}}{778 \text{ lbf-ft}}\right)$$

$$= 2.05 \text{ lbm}$$

4. D From equation 12.53, the speed of sound in this air stream is determined by

$$c = \sqrt{kRT}$$

Use the property data table at the end of the chapter to determine k and R: $k = 1.40$, and

$$R = c_p - c_v$$

$$= 1.00\frac{\text{kJ}}{\text{kg·K}} - 0.718\frac{\text{kJ}}{\text{kg·K}}$$

$$= 0.282\frac{\text{kJ}}{\text{kg·K}}$$

Then:

$$c = \sqrt{(1.4)\left(0.282\frac{\text{kJ}}{\text{kg·K}}\right)(25 + 273)\text{K}\left[\left(\frac{1{,}000 \text{ N·m}}{\text{kJ}}\right)\left(\frac{\frac{\text{kg·m}}{\text{s}^2}}{\text{N}}\right)\right]}$$

$$= 343 \text{ m/s}$$

From equation 12.52:

$$\text{Ma} = \frac{\overline{V}}{c}$$

$$= \frac{75\frac{\text{m}}{\text{s}}}{343\frac{\text{m}}{\text{s}}}$$

$$= 0.22$$

5. B At these conditions, the water is in the form of superheated steam. To determine the mass of water in the vessel, use the equation

$$m = \rho V$$

or

$$m = \frac{V}{v}$$

From the superheated steam table, $v = 0.8893$ m^3/kg.

Then:

$$m = \frac{6\ \text{m}^3}{0.8893\ \frac{\text{m}^3}{\text{kg}}} = 6.75\ \text{kg}$$

6. D The mass fraction is given by equation 12.55:

$$y_i = \frac{m_i}{\Sigma m_i} = \frac{3\ \text{kg}}{1\ \text{kg} + 3\ \text{kg} + 2\ \text{kg}} = 0.50 = 50\%$$

7. C The gas constant for a mixture of ideal gases is given by equation 12.59:

$$R_{\text{mix}} = \frac{\overline{R}}{M_{\text{mix}}}$$

where, from equation 12.58:

$$M_{\text{mix}} = \Sigma x_i M_i$$

From the property data at the end of the chapter, the molar mass for each constituent is as follows:

Argon:	40 g/mol
Helium:	4 g/mol
Neon:	20 g/mol

Then:

$$M_{\text{mix}} = (0.28)\left(40\ \frac{\text{g}}{\text{mol}}\right) + (0.34)\left(4\ \frac{\text{g}}{\text{mol}}\right) + (0.38)\left(20\ \frac{\text{g}}{\text{mol}}\right) = 20.16\ \text{g/mol}$$

8. B Determine the partial pressure for each constituent from the ideal gas law:

$$p_i = \frac{n_i \overline{R} T}{V}$$

For nitrogen:

$$p_{\text{N}} = \frac{(0.1\ \text{kmol})\left(8.314\ \frac{\text{kJ}}{\text{kmol·K}}\right)(20 + 273)\text{K}}{6\ \text{m}^3} \times \left(\frac{\text{kPa}}{1{,}000\ \frac{\text{N}}{\text{m}^2}}\right)\left(\frac{1{,}000\ \text{N·m}}{\text{kJ}}\right) = 40.6\ \text{kPa}$$

For oxygen:

$$p_{\text{O}} = \frac{(0.3\ \text{kmol})\left(8.314\ \frac{\text{kJ}}{\text{kmol·K}}\right)(20 + 273)\text{K}}{6\ \text{m}^3} \times \left(\frac{\text{kPa}}{1{,}000\ \frac{\text{N}}{\text{m}^2}}\right)\left(\frac{1{,}000\ \text{N·m}}{\text{kJ}}\right) = 121.8\ \text{kPa}$$

For helium:

$$p_{\text{He}} = \frac{(0.05\ \text{kmol})\left(8.314\ \frac{\text{kJ}}{\text{kmol·K}}\right)(20 + 273)\text{K}}{6\ \text{m}^3} \times \left(\frac{\text{kPa}}{1{,}000\ \frac{\text{N}}{\text{m}^2}}\right)\left(\frac{1{,}000\ \text{N·m}}{\text{kJ}}\right) = 20.3\ \text{kPa}$$

The total pressure is the sum of the partial pressures for the three constituents:

$$p = p_{\text{N}} + p_{\text{O}} + p_{\text{He}} = 40.6\ \text{kPa} + 121.8\ \text{kPa} + 20.3\ \text{kPa} = 182.7\ \text{kPa}$$

9. B The partial pressure is given by the equation

$$p_v = x_v p = (0.016)(15.2\ \text{psia}) = 0.243\ \text{psia}$$

10. D The specific humidity for the air-water mixture is given by equation 12.68:

$$\omega = 0.622\frac{p_v}{p - p_v} = 0.622\frac{0.22\ \text{psia}}{14.7\ \text{psia} - 0.22\ \text{psia}} = 0.009$$

11. B From equation 12.74:

$$h_e - h_i = \frac{\overline{V}_i^{\,2} - \overline{V}_e^{\,2}}{2}$$

The change in enthalpy is related to the change in temperature by equation 12.38:

$$h_e - h_i = c_p(T_e - T_i)$$

Find the value of specific heat in the property data tables at the end of the chapter. Then combine and rearrange the equations to determine the outlet velocity:

$$\overline{V}_e = \sqrt{V_i^2 - 2c_p(T_e - T_i)}$$

$$= \sqrt{\left(120\frac{\text{m}}{\text{s}}\right)^2 - 2\left(1.04\frac{\text{kJ}}{\text{kg·K}}\right)(6°\text{ C})}$$

$$= 119.9 \text{ m/s}$$

12. C The power output in a turbine, or the work performed, is given by equation 12.77:

$$\dot{W} = \dot{m}(h_i - h_e)$$

The change in enthalpy is related to the change in temperature by equation 12.38:

$$h_i - h_e = c_p(T_i - T_e)$$

Combine these two equations to find the power output:

$$\dot{W} = \dot{m}c_p(T_i - T_e)$$

$$= \left(0.5\frac{\text{kg}}{\text{s}}\right)\left(1.00\frac{\text{kJ}}{\text{kg·K}}\right)(80°\text{ C} - 37°\text{ C})$$

$$= 21.5\frac{\text{kJ}}{\text{s}} = 21.5 \text{ kW}$$

13. B An ideal compressor operates on an isentropic process. Use equation 12.42 to relate the pressures and temperatures of such a process:

$$T_1 p_1{}^{1-k/k} = T_2 p_2{}^{1-k/k}$$

Rearrange this equation as follows:

$$V = T_1\left(\frac{p_2}{p_1}\right)^{k-1/k}$$

$$= (77 + 460)R\left(\frac{80 \text{ psia}}{14.7 \text{ psia}}\right)^{\frac{1.40-1}{1.40}}$$

$$= 871\ R = 411°\text{ F}$$

14. A From applying an energy balance to the heat exchanger, equation 12.84:

$$\dot{m}_h(h_i - h_e)_h = \dot{m}_c(h_e - h_i)_c$$
$$\dot{m}_h\, c_p(T_i - T_e)_h = \dot{m}_c\, c_p(T_e - T_i)_c$$

Rearrange the second equation:

$$\dot{m}_h = \dot{m}_c\frac{c_p(T_e - T_i)_c}{c_p(T_i - T_e)_h}$$

$$= \left(8\frac{\text{lbm}}{\text{sec}}\right)\frac{\left(1.000\frac{\text{Btu}}{\text{lbm-R}}\right)(63°\text{ F} - 35°\text{ F})}{\left(1.000\frac{\text{Btu}}{\text{lbm-R}}\right)(90°\text{ F} - 46°\text{ F})}$$

$$= 5 \text{ lbm/sec}$$

15. C The efficiency of a Carnot engine is given by equation 12.92:

$$\eta = 1 - \frac{T_L}{T_h}$$

$$= 1 - \frac{(30 + 273)\text{K}}{(400 + 273)\text{K}}$$

$$= 0.55 = 55\%$$

16. D The efficiency of a Brayton cycle is given by equation 12.100:

$$\eta = 1 = \frac{1}{\left(\frac{p_2}{p_1}\right)^{\frac{k-1}{k}}}$$

For air, $k = 1.40$, so the efficiency is:

$$\eta = 1 - \frac{1}{(4)^{\frac{1.4-1}{1.4}}}$$

$$= 0.327 = 33\%$$

17. C The key to this answer is step 3. The only system discussed that includes an isenthalpic expansion of the working fluid is the vapor compression refrigeration cycle.

18. B The average specific volume of a two-phase water mixture is given by equation 12.66a:

$$v_{\text{mix}} = v_f + x(v_g - v_f)$$

The quality is then given by the equation

$$x = \frac{v_{\text{mix}} - v_f}{v_g - v_f}$$

From the saturated water table at the end of the chapter:

$v_f = 0.001029 \text{ m}^3\text{/kg}$ and $v_g = 3.407 \text{ m}^3\text{/kg}$

Then:

$$x = \frac{1.00\frac{\text{m}^3}{\text{kg}} - 0.001029\frac{\text{m}^3}{\text{kg}}}{3.407\frac{\text{m}^3}{\text{kg}} - 0.001029\frac{\text{m}^3}{\text{kg}}}$$

$$= 0.293$$

19. B The change in entropy for a process of an ideal gas is given by equation 12.39:

$$\Delta s = c_p \ln\left(\frac{T_2}{T_1}\right) - R \ln\left(\frac{p_2}{p_1}\right)$$

Determine the specific heat and the gas constant from the property data tables at the end of the chapter:

$$c_p = 1.00\frac{\text{kJ}}{\text{kg·K}}$$

and

$$\begin{aligned} R &= c_p - c_v \\ &= 1.00\frac{\text{kJ}}{\text{kg·K}} - 0.718\frac{\text{kJ}}{\text{kg·K}} \\ &= 0.282 \text{ kJ/kg·K} \end{aligned}$$

The change in entropy is then:

$$\begin{aligned} \Delta s &= c_p \ln\left(\frac{T_2}{T_1}\right) - R \ln\left(\frac{p_2}{p_1}\right) \\ &= \left(1.00\frac{\text{kJ}}{\text{kg·K}}\right)\ln\left(\frac{(200 + 273)\text{K}}{(25 + 273)\text{K}}\right) \\ &\quad - \left(0.282\frac{\text{kJ}}{\text{kg·K}}\right)\ln\left(\frac{4 \text{ atm}}{1 \text{ atm}}\right) \\ &= 0.071 \text{ kJ/kg·K} \end{aligned}$$

20. B Calculate the boundary work performed in an isentropic process in a closed system by using equation 12.44:

$$w = \frac{RT_1}{k-1}\left[1 - \left(\frac{p_2}{p_1}\right)^{\frac{k-1}{k}}\right]$$

where $k = 1.40$, and

$$\begin{aligned} R &= c_p - c_v \\ &= 1.00\frac{\text{kJ}}{\text{kg·K}} - 0.718\frac{\text{kJ}}{\text{kg·K}} \\ &= 0.282\frac{\text{kJ}}{\text{kg·K}} \end{aligned}$$

Then:

$$\begin{aligned} w &= \frac{\left(0.282\frac{\text{kJ}}{\text{kg·K}}\right)(300 + 273)\text{K}}{1.40 - 1} \\ &\quad \times \left[1 - \left(\frac{100 \text{ kPa}}{800 \text{ kPa}}\right)^{\frac{1.40-1}{1.40}}\right] \\ &= 181 \text{ kJ/kg} \end{aligned}$$

21. C Calculate the boundary work performed in an isentropic process in an open system by using the equation

$$w = \left(\frac{k}{k-1}\right)RT_1\left[1 - \left(\frac{p_2}{p_1}\right)^{\frac{k-1}{k}}\right]$$

where $k = 1.40$, and

$$\begin{aligned} R &= c_p - c_v \\ &= 1.00\frac{\text{kJ}}{\text{kg·K}} - 0.718\frac{\text{kJ}}{\text{kg·K}} \\ &= 0.282\frac{\text{kJ}}{\text{kg·K}} \end{aligned}$$

Then:

$$\begin{aligned} w &= \frac{1.40}{1.40 - 1}\left[\left(0.282\frac{\text{kJ}}{\text{kg·K}}\right)(300 + 273)\text{K}\right] \\ &\quad \times \left[1 - \left(\frac{100 \text{ kPa}}{800 \text{ kPa}}\right)^{\frac{1.40-1}{1.40}}\right] \\ &= 253 \text{ kJ/kg} \end{aligned}$$

22. B From equation 12.77:

$$w = h_i - h_e$$

From the superheated steam tables:

$$h_i = 3{,}157.7 \text{ kJ/kg}$$

and

$$s_i = 7.3011 \text{ kJ/kg·K}$$

Since the expansion is isentropic, and the entrance value of entropy is lower than the saturation value of entropy at atmospheric pressure, some condensation will occur. To find the value of enthalpy at the exit state, the quality of the exit steam must be estimated. From equation 12.66d:

$$x = \frac{s_i - s_f}{s_g - s_f}$$

From the saturated water table:

$$s_f = 1.3069 \text{ kJ/kg·K}$$

and

$$s_g = 7.3549 \text{ kJ/kg·K}$$

Then:

$$\begin{aligned} x &= \frac{7.3011\frac{\text{kJ}}{\text{kg·K}} - 1.3069\frac{\text{kJ}}{\text{kg·K}}}{7.3549\frac{\text{kJ}}{\text{kg·K}} - 1.3069\frac{\text{kJ}}{\text{kg·K}}} \\ &= 0.991 \end{aligned}$$

Also, from equation 12.66c:

$$h_e = h_f + x(h_g - h_f)$$

and from the saturated water table:

$h_f = 419.04$ kJ/kg and $h_g = 2676.1$ kJ/kg

Then:

$$h_e = 419.04\frac{\text{kJ}}{\text{kg}} + 0.991\left(2{,}676.1\frac{\text{kJ}}{\text{kg}} - 419.04\frac{\text{kJ}}{\text{kg}}\right)$$
$$= 2{,}655.8 \text{ kJ/kg}$$

and

$$w = h_i - h_e$$
$$= 3{,}157.7\frac{\text{kJ}}{\text{kg}} - 2{,}655.8\frac{\text{kJ}}{\text{kg}}$$
$$= 501.9 \text{ kJ/kg}$$

23. C From equation 12.77:

$$w = h_i - h_e$$

Determine the enthalpy values using the p-h diagram for HFC-134a, provided at the end of the chapter. Locate the entrance state at the intersection of the $p = 0.1$ MPa line and the right side of the vapor dome. Locate the exit state by following the closest constant entropy line until it intersects with the $p = 1.0$ MPa line. The values of entropy are as follows:

$h_i = 380$ kJ/kg and $h_g = 430$ kJ/kg

Then:

$$w = h_i - h_e$$
$$= 380\frac{\text{kJ}}{\text{kg}} - 430\frac{\text{kJ}}{\text{kg}}$$
$$= -50 \text{ kJ/kg}$$

(Note the negative value, indicating that the compressor is adding energy to the system though a work interaction.)

24. D The coefficient of performance for a Carnot refrigeration system is given by the equation

$$\text{COP} = \frac{T_C}{T_H - T_C}$$
$$= \frac{(20 + 460)\text{R}}{(75 + 460)\text{R} - (20 + 460)\text{R}}$$
$$= 8.73$$

25. D The coefficient of performance for a Carnot heat pump system is given by the equation

$$\text{COP} = \frac{T_H}{T_H - T_C}$$
$$= \frac{(20 + 273)\text{R}}{(20 + 273)\text{R} - (1 + 273)\text{R}}$$
$$= 15.42$$

26. C The closed-system availability is given by the equation

$$A = (u - u_0) + p_0(v - v_0) - T_0(s - s_0)$$

From the steam tables at the end of the chapter:

$u = 2{,}810.4$ kJ/kg, $v = 2.639$ m^3/kg, $s = 8.2158$ kJ/kg·K

From the saturated water table at the end of the chapter:

$u_0 = 104.88$ kJ/kg, $v_0 = 0.001003$ m^3/kg, $s_0 = 0.3674$ kJ/kg·K

The dead-state pressure is $p_0 = 101.35$ kPa, and $T_0 = (25 + 273)$K.

Then:

$$A = \left(2{,}810.4\frac{\text{kJ}}{\text{kg}} - 104.88\frac{\text{kJ}}{\text{kg}}\right)$$
$$+ (101.35 \text{ kPa})\left(\frac{1{,}000\frac{\text{N}}{\text{m}^2}}{\text{kPa}}\right)\left(\frac{\text{kJ}}{1{,}000 \text{ N·m}}\right)$$
$$\times \left[2.639\frac{\text{m}^3}{\text{kg}} - 0.001003\frac{\text{m}^3}{\text{kg}}\right]$$
$$- (298 \text{ K})\left[8.2158\frac{\text{kJ}}{\text{kg·K}} - 0.3674\frac{\text{kJ}}{\text{kg·K}}\right]$$
$$= 2{,}705.52\frac{\text{kJ}}{\text{kg}} + 267.36\frac{\text{kJ}}{\text{kg}} - 2{,}338.82\frac{\text{kJ}}{\text{kg}}$$
$$= 634 \text{ kJ/kg}$$

27. C The first law of thermodynamics is often stated as follows:

$$\Delta u = q - w$$

For the given process:

$$\Delta u = c_v \, \Delta T$$
$$= 0$$

which means that

$$q = w = \int p \, dv$$

or, from equation 12.48:

$$q = w = RT\ln\left(\frac{p_1}{p_2}\right)$$

where

$$R = c_p - c_v$$

$$= 1.00\frac{\text{kJ}}{\text{kg·K}} - 0.718\frac{\text{kJ}}{\text{kg·K}}$$

$$= 0.282 \text{ kJ/kg·K}$$

Then:

$$q = w = \left(0.282\frac{\text{kJ}}{\text{kg·K}}\right)[(100 + 273)\text{K}] \times \ln\left(\frac{300 \text{ kPa}}{100 \text{ kPa}}\right)$$

$$= 115.6 \text{ kJ/kg}$$

PRACTICE EXAMINATIONS

General

Taking the practice exams included in this book is an important part of your preparation for the FE/EIT exam. Take the practice exams only after you have thoroughly reviewed the concepts and worked the sample problems presented in this book.

Included are two full-length practice exams. The first practice exam covers the material presented in the Morning Session exam. As on the actual exam, you have four hours to complete the practice test. For examinees not electing to take a discipline-specific afternoon exam, the second practice exam covers the material in the afternoon General Exam option. Again, as on the actual exam, you have four hours to complete the practice test.

Training is the best way to increase your test-taking stamina! For this reason it is strongly recommended that you take these practice exams in two back-to-back, four-hour sessions. Simulate test conditions; use only your calculator and your copy of the "NCEES FE Reference Handbook" while taking the practice exams. Read each question carefully, study the diagrams, and eliminate obviously incorrect answers. Since there is no penalty for wrong answers, make your best guess when you do not know the answer to a question.

Allow enough time in your study program not only to take the practice exams but also to review any problem areas that become evident when you analyze your incorrect answers. Fill in the charts at the end of each exam as you score your results. An analysis of incorrect answers is a useful self-teaching tool and will help you to fine-tune your final study sessions.

ANSWER SHEET: Morning Session

1. Ⓐ Ⓑ Ⓒ Ⓓ
2. Ⓐ Ⓑ Ⓒ Ⓓ
3. Ⓐ Ⓑ Ⓒ Ⓓ
4. Ⓐ Ⓑ Ⓒ Ⓓ
5. Ⓐ Ⓑ Ⓒ Ⓓ
6. Ⓐ Ⓑ Ⓒ Ⓓ
7. Ⓐ Ⓑ Ⓒ Ⓓ
8. Ⓐ Ⓑ Ⓒ Ⓓ
9. Ⓐ Ⓑ Ⓒ Ⓓ
10. Ⓐ Ⓑ Ⓒ Ⓓ
11. Ⓐ Ⓑ Ⓒ Ⓓ
12. Ⓐ Ⓑ Ⓒ Ⓓ
13. Ⓐ Ⓑ Ⓒ Ⓓ
14. Ⓐ Ⓑ Ⓒ Ⓓ
15. Ⓐ Ⓑ Ⓒ Ⓓ
16. Ⓐ Ⓑ Ⓒ Ⓓ
17. Ⓐ Ⓑ Ⓒ Ⓓ
18. Ⓐ Ⓑ Ⓒ Ⓓ
19. Ⓐ Ⓑ Ⓒ Ⓓ
20. Ⓐ Ⓑ Ⓒ Ⓓ
21. Ⓐ Ⓑ Ⓒ Ⓓ
22. Ⓐ Ⓑ Ⓒ Ⓓ
23. Ⓐ Ⓑ Ⓒ Ⓓ
24. Ⓐ Ⓑ Ⓒ Ⓓ
25. Ⓐ Ⓑ Ⓒ Ⓓ
26. Ⓐ Ⓑ Ⓒ Ⓓ
27. Ⓐ Ⓑ Ⓒ Ⓓ
28. Ⓐ Ⓑ Ⓒ Ⓓ
29. Ⓐ Ⓑ Ⓒ Ⓓ
30. Ⓐ Ⓑ Ⓒ Ⓓ
31. Ⓐ Ⓑ Ⓒ Ⓓ
32. Ⓐ Ⓑ Ⓒ Ⓓ
33. Ⓐ Ⓑ Ⓒ Ⓓ
34. Ⓐ Ⓑ Ⓒ Ⓓ
35. Ⓐ Ⓑ Ⓒ Ⓓ
36. Ⓐ Ⓑ Ⓒ Ⓓ
37. Ⓐ Ⓑ Ⓒ Ⓓ
38. Ⓐ Ⓑ Ⓒ Ⓓ
39. Ⓐ Ⓑ Ⓒ Ⓓ
40. Ⓐ Ⓑ Ⓒ Ⓓ
41. Ⓐ Ⓑ Ⓒ Ⓓ
42. Ⓐ Ⓑ Ⓒ Ⓓ
43. Ⓐ Ⓑ Ⓒ Ⓓ
44. Ⓐ Ⓑ Ⓒ Ⓓ
45. Ⓐ Ⓑ Ⓒ Ⓓ
46. Ⓐ Ⓑ Ⓒ Ⓓ
47. Ⓐ Ⓑ Ⓒ Ⓓ
48. Ⓐ Ⓑ Ⓒ Ⓓ
49. Ⓐ Ⓑ Ⓒ Ⓓ
50. Ⓐ Ⓑ Ⓒ Ⓓ
51. Ⓐ Ⓑ Ⓒ Ⓓ
52. Ⓐ Ⓑ Ⓒ Ⓓ
53. Ⓐ Ⓑ Ⓒ Ⓓ
54. Ⓐ Ⓑ Ⓒ Ⓓ
55. Ⓐ Ⓑ Ⓒ Ⓓ
56. Ⓐ Ⓑ Ⓒ Ⓓ
57. Ⓐ Ⓑ Ⓒ Ⓓ
58. Ⓐ Ⓑ Ⓒ Ⓓ
59. Ⓐ Ⓑ Ⓒ Ⓓ
60. Ⓐ Ⓑ Ⓒ Ⓓ
61. Ⓐ Ⓑ Ⓒ Ⓓ
62. Ⓐ Ⓑ Ⓒ Ⓓ
63. Ⓐ Ⓑ Ⓒ Ⓓ
64. Ⓐ Ⓑ Ⓒ Ⓓ
65. Ⓐ Ⓑ Ⓒ Ⓓ
66. Ⓐ Ⓑ Ⓒ Ⓓ
67. Ⓐ Ⓑ Ⓒ Ⓓ
68. Ⓐ Ⓑ Ⓒ Ⓓ
69. Ⓐ Ⓑ Ⓒ Ⓓ
70. Ⓐ Ⓑ Ⓒ Ⓓ
71. Ⓐ Ⓑ Ⓒ Ⓓ
72. Ⓐ Ⓑ Ⓒ Ⓓ
73. Ⓐ Ⓑ Ⓒ Ⓓ
74. Ⓐ Ⓑ Ⓒ Ⓓ
75. Ⓐ Ⓑ Ⓒ Ⓓ
76. Ⓐ Ⓑ Ⓒ Ⓓ
77. Ⓐ Ⓑ Ⓒ Ⓓ
78. Ⓐ Ⓑ Ⓒ Ⓓ
79. Ⓐ Ⓑ Ⓒ Ⓓ
80. Ⓐ Ⓑ Ⓒ Ⓓ
81. Ⓐ Ⓑ Ⓒ Ⓓ
82. Ⓐ Ⓑ Ⓒ Ⓓ
83. Ⓐ Ⓑ Ⓒ Ⓓ
84. Ⓐ Ⓑ Ⓒ Ⓓ
85. Ⓐ Ⓑ Ⓒ Ⓓ
86. Ⓐ Ⓑ Ⓒ Ⓓ
87. Ⓐ Ⓑ Ⓒ Ⓓ
88. Ⓐ Ⓑ Ⓒ Ⓓ
89. Ⓐ Ⓑ Ⓒ Ⓓ
90. Ⓐ Ⓑ Ⓒ Ⓓ
91. Ⓐ Ⓑ Ⓒ Ⓓ
92. Ⓐ Ⓑ Ⓒ Ⓓ
93. Ⓐ Ⓑ Ⓒ Ⓓ
94. Ⓐ Ⓑ Ⓒ Ⓓ
95. Ⓐ Ⓑ Ⓒ Ⓓ
96. Ⓐ Ⓑ Ⓒ Ⓓ
97. Ⓐ Ⓑ Ⓒ Ⓓ
98. Ⓐ Ⓑ Ⓒ Ⓓ
99. Ⓐ Ⓑ Ⓒ Ⓓ
100. Ⓐ Ⓑ Ⓒ Ⓓ
101. Ⓐ Ⓑ Ⓒ Ⓓ
102. Ⓐ Ⓑ Ⓒ Ⓓ
103. Ⓐ Ⓑ Ⓒ Ⓓ
104. Ⓐ Ⓑ Ⓒ Ⓓ
105. Ⓐ Ⓑ Ⓒ Ⓓ
106. Ⓐ Ⓑ Ⓒ Ⓓ
107. Ⓐ Ⓑ Ⓒ Ⓓ
108. Ⓐ Ⓑ Ⓒ Ⓓ
109. Ⓐ Ⓑ Ⓒ Ⓓ
110. Ⓐ Ⓑ Ⓒ Ⓓ
111. Ⓐ Ⓑ Ⓒ Ⓓ
112. Ⓐ Ⓑ Ⓒ Ⓓ
113. Ⓐ Ⓑ Ⓒ Ⓓ
114. Ⓐ Ⓑ Ⓒ Ⓓ
115. Ⓐ Ⓑ Ⓒ Ⓓ
116. Ⓐ Ⓑ Ⓒ Ⓓ
117. Ⓐ Ⓑ Ⓒ Ⓓ
118. Ⓐ Ⓑ Ⓒ Ⓓ
119. Ⓐ Ⓑ Ⓒ Ⓓ
120. Ⓐ Ⓑ Ⓒ Ⓓ

Practice Examination

Morning Session

120 Questions

Directions: For each incomplete statement or question, select the answer that best completes the sentence or answers the question. Then fill in the corresponding space on the answer sheet.

1. The partial derivative $\frac{\partial z}{\partial x}$ of $z = 2x^2y - 2(x + 3y)$ is:
(A) $2x^2 + 3$
(B) $4xy - 2$
(C) $2x^2y$
(D) $4xy + 3$

2. A bag contains 20 balls numbered 1 to 20. If one ball is removed from the bag, what is the probability that the ball is even or is less than 5?
(A) .5
(B) .75
(C) .65
(D) .6

3. The value of the determinant $\begin{vmatrix} -1 & 4 & -2 \\ 6 & 3 & -4 \\ 0 & -2 & 1 \end{vmatrix}$ is:
(A) 5
(B) 0
(C) −1
(D) 6

4. The graph of the general quadratic equation $3x^2 - 10xy + 3y^2 + 8 = 0$ is:
(A) an ellipse
(B) a parabola
(C) a hyperbola
(D) a circle

5. In statistics, the measure of the spread or dispersion of the sample data is usually given by the:
(A) median
(B) standard deviation
(C) mean
(D) mode

6. A geometric interpretation of the first derivative of $y = f(x)$ is:
(A) the area under the curve $y = f(x)$
(B) the volume found by rotating the area under the curve $y = f(x)$ about the x-axis
(C) the slope of the normal to the curve $y = f(x)$
(D) the slope of a tangent to the curve $y = f(x)$

7. The general solution of the differential equation $\frac{dy}{dx} + 3y = 0$ with $y(0) = 1$ is:
(A) $y = e^{-3x}$
(B) $y = e^{3x}$
(C) $y = \ln 3x$
(D) $y = xe^{3x}$

8. The general solution of the differential equation $y'' + 4y' + 4 = 0$ is:
(A) $y = c_1e^{2x}$
(B) $y = e^{-2x}(c_1 + c_2x)$
(C) $y = c_1e^{2x} + c_2xe^{2x}$
(D) $y = c_1e^{-2x} + c_2$

9. A particle travels in a straight line in such a way that its distance s in meters from a given point on the line after time t in seconds is given by the equation $s = 10t^3 - 2t^5$. What is the instantaneous velocity of the particle at $t = 1$ second?
(A) −2 m/s
(B) 15 m/s
(C) 50 m/s
(D) 20 m/s

10. A unit vector perpendicular to the vector $\mathbf{A} = 3\mathbf{i} - 4\mathbf{j}$ is:
(A) $4\mathbf{i} - 3\mathbf{j}$
(B) $\mathbf{i}$
(C) $\frac{3}{5}\mathbf{i} - \frac{4}{5}\mathbf{j}$
(D) $\frac{4}{5}\mathbf{i} + \frac{3}{5}\mathbf{j}$

11. A physical interpretation of the definite integral $\int_a^b f(x)dx$ is:
(A) the instantaneous velocity of an object along the curve $y = f(x)$ from a to b
(B) the acceleration of an object along the curve $y = f(x)$ from a to b
(C) the work done by a variable force $y = f(x)$ in moving an object from a to b
(D) both (A) and (C)

12. The area of Quadrant I that is bounded by $y = x^2$, $x = 3$, and the x-axis is:
(A) 9 square units
(B) 27 square units
(C) 6 square units
(D) 10 square units

13. What is the maximum value of the function f defined by $f(x) = x^3 - 3x$?
(A) -2
(B) 2
(C) 0
(D) 9

14. The slope of the line that passes through points (a,b) and (b,a) is:
(A) 0
(B) 1
(C) -1
(D) undefined

15. The value of $\log_3 50$ is a number between:
(A) 16 and 17
(B) 3 and 4
(C) 0 and 2
(D) 5 and 6

16. What is the inverse of the matrix $\begin{bmatrix} 3 & 1 \\ -5 & -2 \end{bmatrix}$?
(A) $\begin{bmatrix} 2 & 1 \\ -5 & -3 \end{bmatrix}$
(B) $\frac{1}{11}\begin{bmatrix} 2 & -1 \\ 5 & 3 \end{bmatrix}$
(C) $\frac{1}{11}\begin{bmatrix} -2 & 1 \\ 5 & 3 \end{bmatrix}$
(D) undefined

17. The complex number $3 - 3i$ is equivalent to:
(A) $\sqrt{2}e^{(\pi/4)i}$
(B) $3\sqrt{2}e^{(\pi/4)i}$
(C) $3\sqrt{2}e^{(5\pi/4)i}$
(D) $3\sqrt{2}e^{(7\pi/4)i}$

18. The measure of the smallest angle in a triangle with sides that are 4, 5, and 8 meters in length is:
(A) 30.8°
(B) 24.1°
(C) 22.0°
(D) 29.7°

19. What are the coordinates of the center of a sphere whose equation is $x^2 + y^2 + z^2 - 4y + 6z = 0$?
(A) $(0,-2,3)$
(B) $(0, 2,-3)$
(C) $(1,4,9)$
(D) $(1,-2,-3)$

20. What is the sum of the infinite geometric series $\sum_{i=1}^{\infty} (0.3)^i$?
(A) $\frac{3}{10}$
(B) $\frac{1}{2}$
(C) $\frac{2}{5}$
(D) $\frac{3}{7}$

21. The value of the definite integral $\int_2^3 \frac{1}{x-1}dx$ is:
(A) ln 2
(B) ln 3
(C) 1
(D) 0

22. The equation of the tangent to the curve $x^2 + y^2 = 25$ at point $(3,4)$ is:
(A) $4x - 3y = 0$
(B) $3x - 4y = -7$
(C) $4x + 3y = 24$
(D) $3x + 4y = 25$

23. The volume of the solid generated by revolving the area bounded by $y = \sqrt{x}$, $y = 2$, and the y-axis about the y-axis is:
(A) 8π cubic units
(B) $\frac{16\pi}{3}$ cubic units
(C) $\frac{32\pi}{5}$ cubic units
(D) $\frac{8\pi}{3}$ cubic units

24. For $0 < x < \frac{\pi}{2}$, the trigonometric expression $\tan x \csc x \cos x$ is equal to:
(A) 1
(B) 0
(C) $\sin x$
(D) $\cos 2x$

25. If a 100-foot spool of wire has a resistance between its ends of 5 milliohms, what is the resistivity of the wire? The cross-sectional area of the wire is 0.2 sq. in.
(A) $1.666 \times 10^{-6}\ \Omega \cdot m$
(B) $5.242 \times 10^{-6}\ \Omega \cdot m$
(C) $4.233 \times 10^{-7}\ \Omega \cdot m$
(D) $2.115 \times 10^{-8}\ \Omega \cdot m$

26.

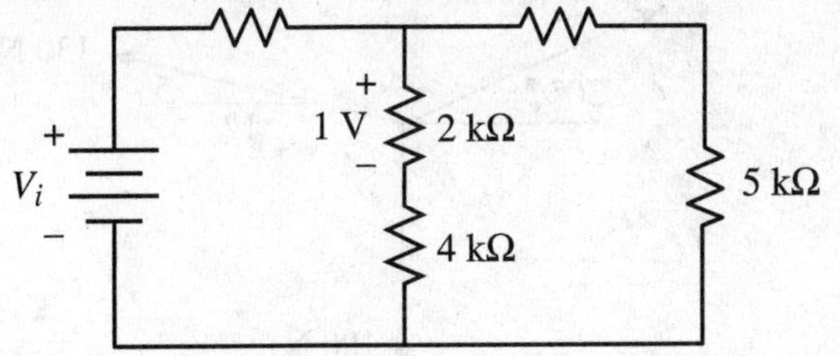

The value of the source voltage, V_i, for the circuit shown above is:

(A) 4 V (C) 5.5 V
(B) 7 V (D) 9.5 V

Questions 27 and 28 are based on the diagram shown below.

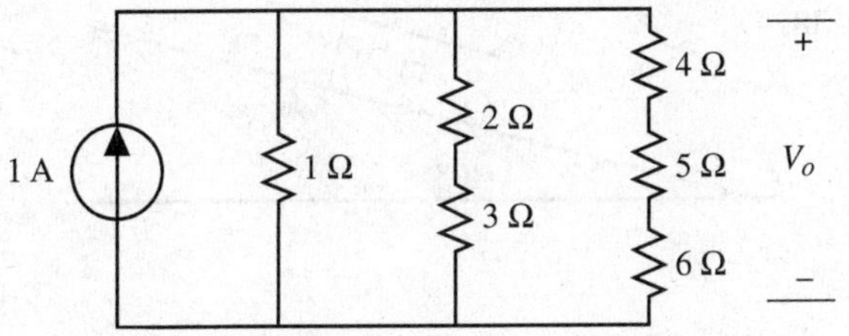

27. What is the value of the output voltage, V_o in this circuit?

(A) 0.789 V (C) 4.321 V
(B) 1.256 V (D) 0.543 V

28. What is the power dissipated by the 2-kiloohm resistor in this circuit?

(A) 1.22 W (C) 0.24 W
(B) 0.31 W (D) 0.05 W

29.

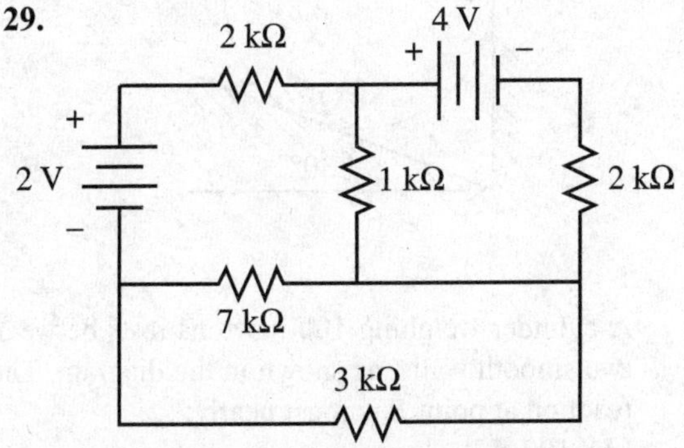

What is the voltage drop across the 1-kiloohm resistor shown in the diagram above?

(A) 0.294 V (C) 3.24 V
(B) 1.43 V (D) 4.56 V

30. The voltage between the terminals of a 0.01microfarad capacitor is 50 volts. What is the charge on the plates of the capacitor?

(A) 50 μC
(B) 5.0 μC
(C) 0.5 μC
(D) 10 μC

31.

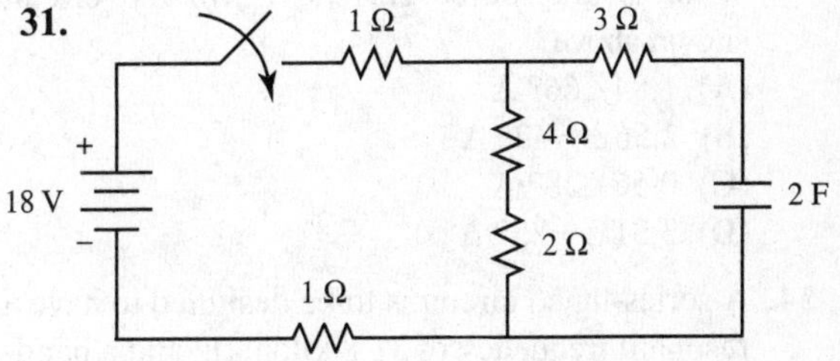

The initial capacitor voltage in the circuit shown above is 0 volt. What voltage will be measured across the capacitor 2 seconds after the switch is closed?

(A) 8.65 V
(B) 1.23 V
(C) 10.64 V
(D) 2.18 V

32.

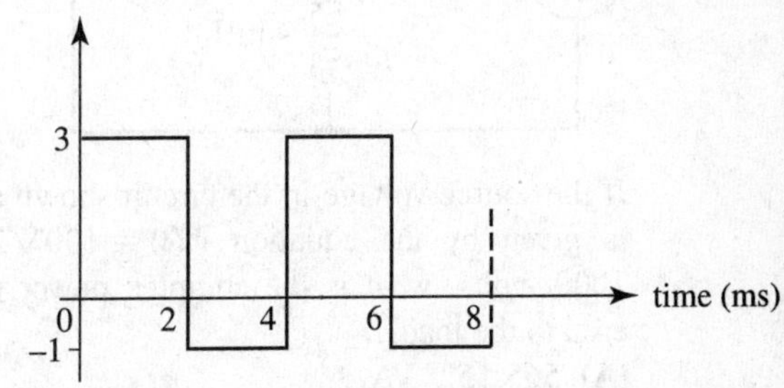

The waveform shown in the above diagram repeats every 4 milliseconds. The average and rms values of the waveform are:

(A) 2.0 V, 2.82 V
(B) 1.0 V, 2.24 V
(C) 0.5 V, 1.0 V
(D) 1.25 V, 2.82 V

33.

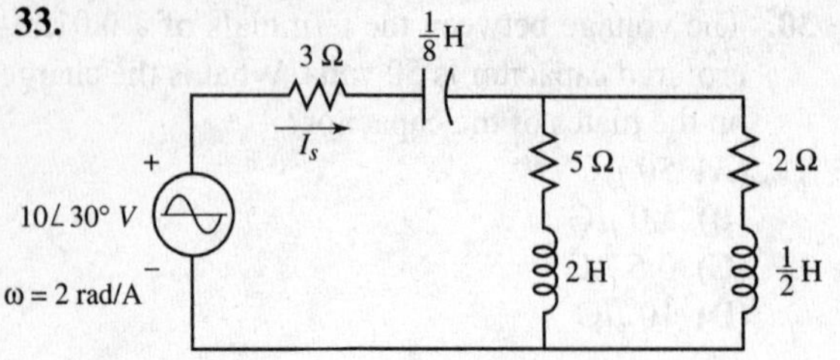

What is the source current, I_s, in the circuit shown above?

(A) 1.84∠66° A
(B) 2.56∠−42° A
(C) 0.56∠28° A
(D) 3.31∠−25° A

34. A series-tuned circuit is to be designed to have a resonant frequency of 31.8 kilohertz and a bandwidth of 2 kilohertz. If the inductor value is 10 millihenrys, the values of the capacitor and the resistor are:

(A) 7.5 μF, 5 Ω
(B) 5.5 μF, 2.5 Ω
(C) 2.5 μF, 125.7 Ω
(D) 4.5 μF, 20 Ω

35.

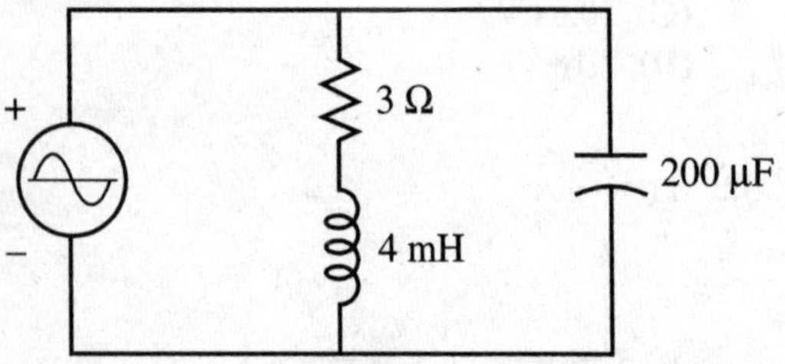

If the source voltage in the circuit shown above is given by the equation $v_s(t) = 100\sqrt{2}\cos 1000t$ volts, what is the complex power delivered to the load?

(A) 565∠52° VA
(B) 12.65∠18.4° VA
(C) 720∠−22.5° VA
(D) 975∠−65° VA

36.

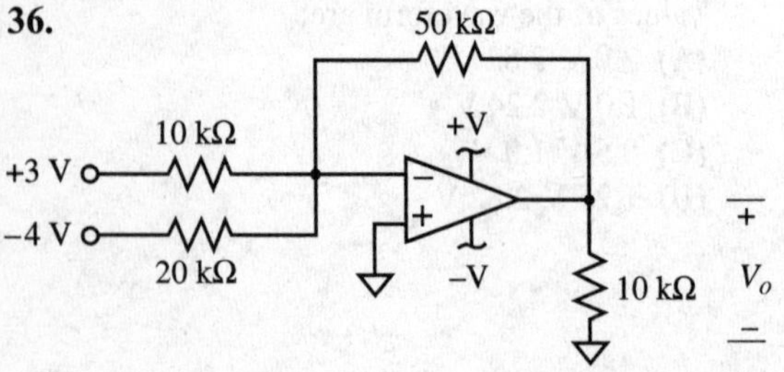

The output voltage, V_o, for the operational amplifier circuit shown above is:

(A) 3.33 V
(B) −2.5 V
(C) 2.5 V
(D) −5.0 V

37.

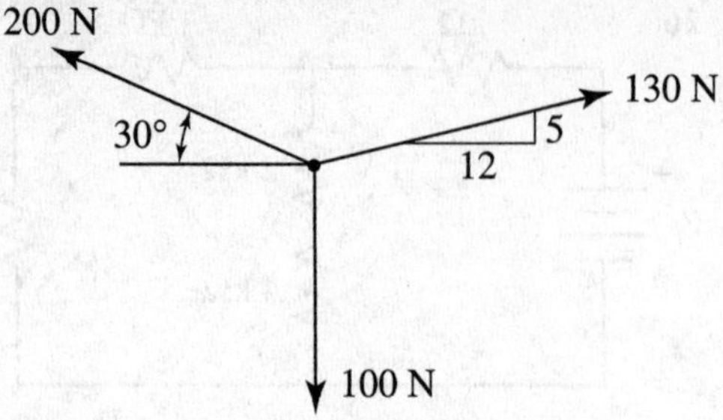

The magnitude of the resultant of the forces shown in the above diagram is most nearly:

(A) 456.6 N
(B) 225.6 N
(C) 73 N
(D) 230 N

38.

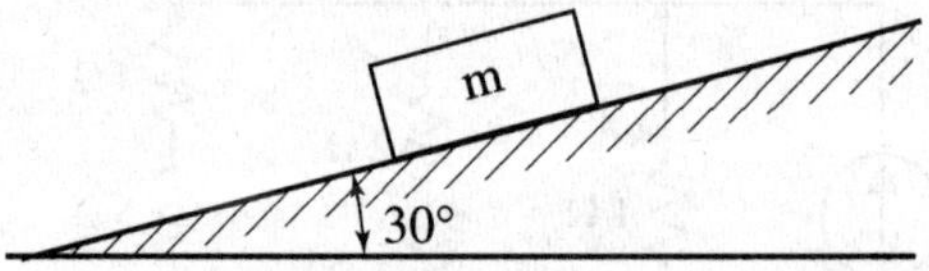

The minimum coefficient of static friction for the block shown in the diagram to be in equilibrium is most nearly:

(A) 0.58
(B) 0.5
(C) 1
(D) 0.87

39.

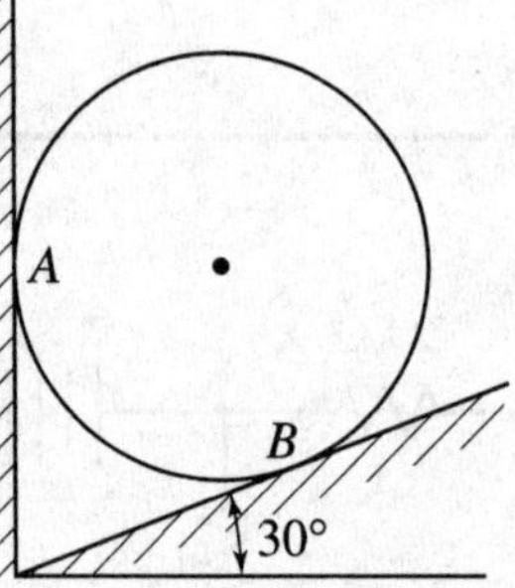

A cylinder weighing 100 newtons rests between two smooth walls, as shown in the diagram. The reaction at point B is most nearly:

(A) 100 N
(B) 115.5 N
(C) 50 N
(D) 86.6 N

40.

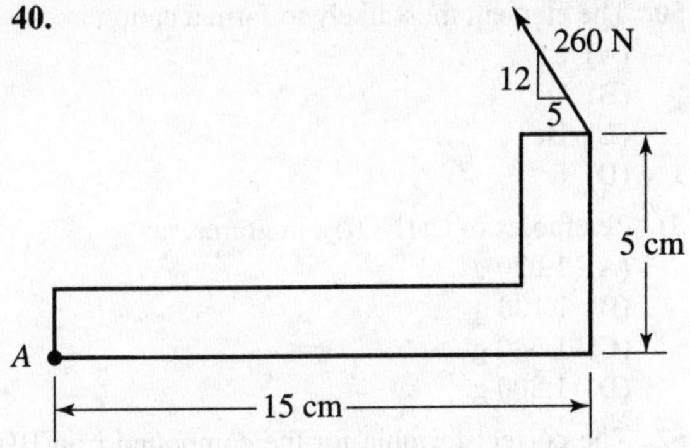

The moment of the 260-newton force about point *A* in the diagram above is most nearly:
(A) 27 N·m
(B) 31 N·m
(C) 18.4 N·m
(D) 41 N·m

41.

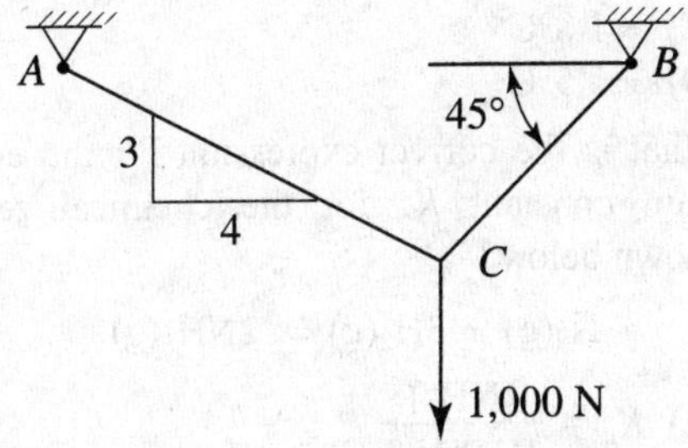

The tension in cable *AC*, shown in the diagram above, is most nearly:
(A) 806.5 N
(B) 714 N
(C) 1414 N
(D) 600 N

42.

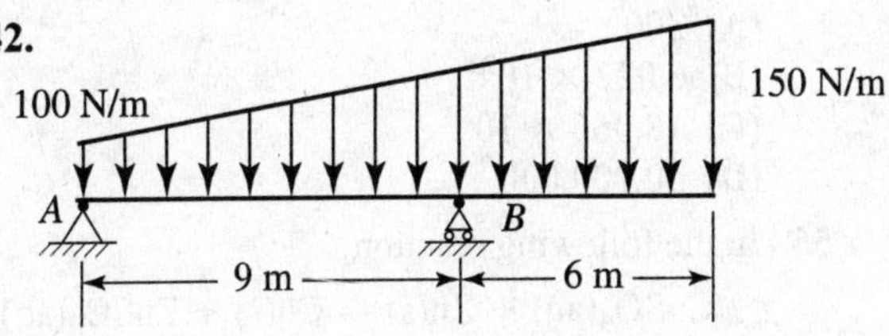

The reaction at point *A* in the diagram is most nearly:
(A) 208 N
(B) 1,625 N
(C) 500 N
(D) 937 N

43.

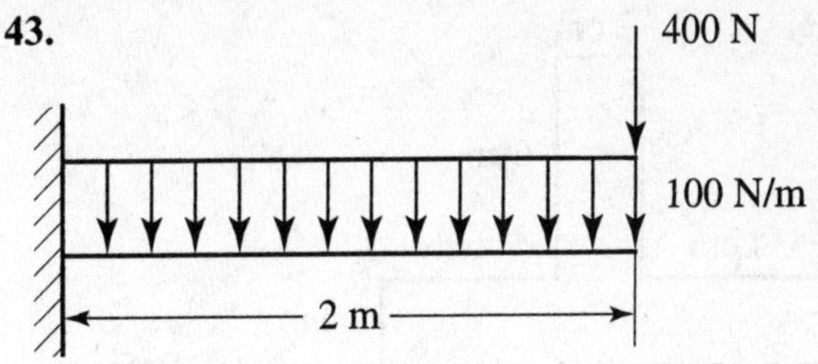

The maximum moment in the beam shown in the diagram is most nearly:
(A) 800 N·m
(B) 1,000 N·m
(C) 200 N·m
(D) 500 N·m

44.

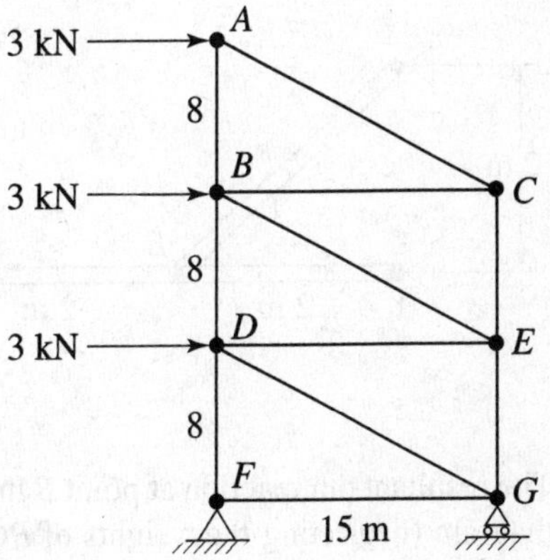

In the above diagram, the force in member *DE* is most nearly:
(A) 9 kN
(B) 24 kN
(C) 6 kN
(D) 9.6 kN

45.

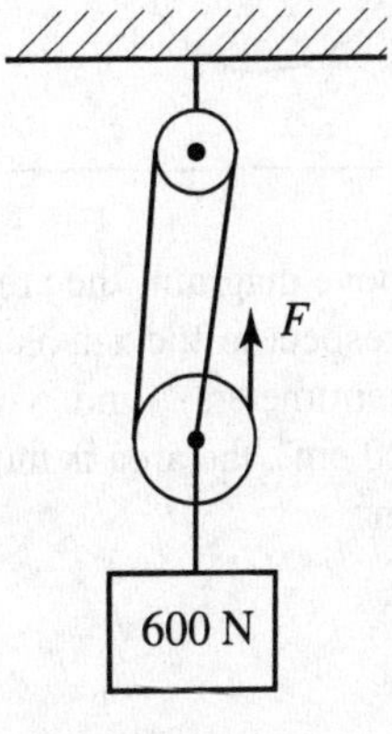

In the above diagram, the force needed for equilibrium is most nearly:
(A) 600 N
(B) 200 N
(C) 300 N
(D) 150 N

46.

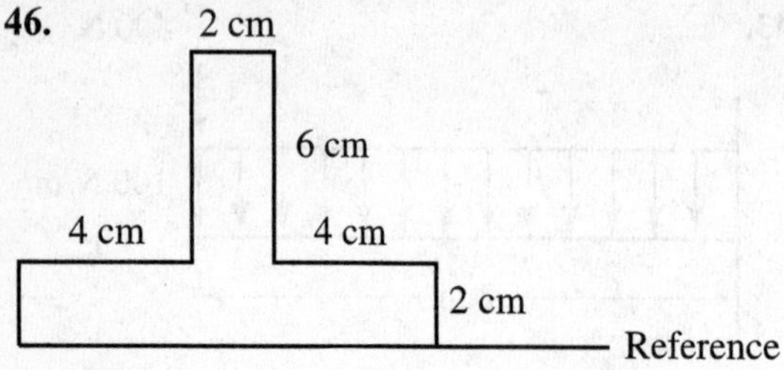

The y-coordinate of the centroid of the plane area shown above is most nearly:
(A) 2 cm
(B) 1.75 cm
(C) 4 cm
(D) 2.5 cm

47.

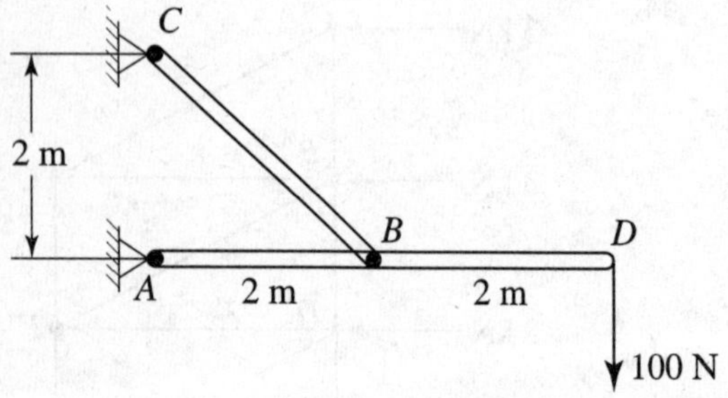

The resultant pin reaction at point B in the above diagram (neglecting the weights of BC and AD) is most nearly:
(A) 283 N
(B) 141.5 N
(C) 100 N
(D) 200 N

48.

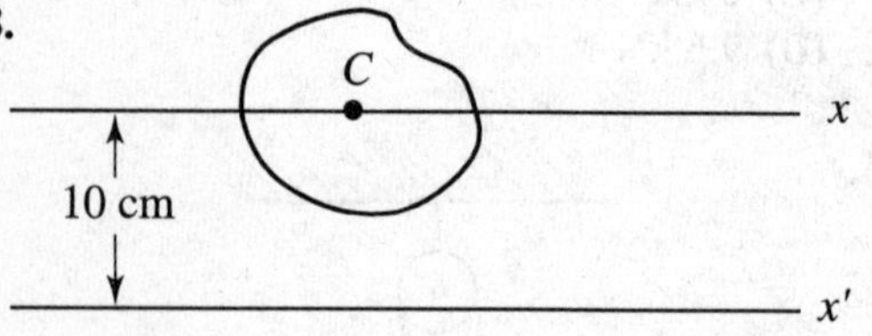

If, in the above diagram, the area moment of inertia with respect to the x-axis (centroidal axis) is 2,000 (centimeters)^4 and with respect to x'-axis is 7,000 cm^4, the area is most nearly:
(A) 100 cm^2
(B) 20 cm^2
(C) 50 cm^2
(D) 90 cm^2

49. What is the valence or oxidation state of sulfur in sodium thiosulfate, $Na_2S_2O_3$?
(A) +1
(B) +2
(C) +3
(D) −2

50. The element most likely to form a cation is:
(A) Li
(B) O
(C) He
(D) F

51. Ten moles of $Ca(NO_3)_2$, in grams, is:
(A) 1,020 g
(B) 1,100 g
(C) 1,640 g
(D) 1,800 g

52. The correct formula for the compound iron(III) hydroxide is:
(A) Fe_3OH
(B) Fe_2O_3
(C) $Fe(OH)_3$
(D) $Fe_3(OH)_3$

53. What is the approximate freezing point of an aqueous solution of 111 grams of $CaCl_2$ dissolved in 1 kilogram of H_2O? [$K_f(H_2O) = 1.86$]
(A) −5.5°C
(B) −3.7°C
(C) −1.8°C
(D) +5.5°C

54. What is the correct expression for the equilibrium constant K_c for the chemical reaction shown below?

$$N_2(g) + 3H_2(g) \Leftrightarrow 2NH_3(g)$$

(A) $K_c = \dfrac{[NH_3]}{[H_2][N_2]}$

(B) $K_c = \dfrac{2[NH_3]}{3[H_2][N_2]}$

(C) $K_c = \dfrac{[NH_3]^2}{[N_2][H_2]^3}$

(D) $K_c = \dfrac{[N_2][H_2]^3}{[NH_3]^2}$

55. The number of oxygen atoms in 100 grams of calcium carbonate, $CaCO_3$, is:
(A) 300
(B) 6.022×10^{23}
(C) 18.066×10^{23}
(D) 30,000,000

56. In the following reaction:

$$CuSO_4(aq) + Zn(s) \rightarrow Cu(s) + ZnSO_4(aq)$$

the oxidizing agent is:
(A) Zn
(B) Cu
(C) $CuSO_4$
(D) $ZnSO_4$

Questions 57 and 58

Ethane gas burns according to this reaction:

$$2C_2H_6 + 7O_2 \rightarrow 4CO_2 + 6H_2O$$

57. How many grams of CO_2 gas are produced from 300 grams of C_2H_6?
(A) 300 g
(B) 440 g
(C) 600 g
(D) 880 g

58. How many liters of CO_2 gas are produced, assuming ideal gas behavior, at STP?
(A) 224 L
(B) 448 L
(C) 660 L
(D) 880 L

---

59. How many liters of a 0.25 M HCl solution are required to neutralize 20 grams of NaOH dissolved in enough water to make 1.0 liter of solution?
(A) 1.0 L
(B) 2.0 L
(C) 4.0 L
(D) 5.0 L

60. Which of the following is an intensive property?
(A) Pressure
(B) Entropy
(C) Internal energy
(D) Enthalpy

61. Which of the following statements is NOT true regarding the state of a system?
(A) It remains unchanged for a steady-state process.
(B) It is determined by the values of any two independent properties in a macroscopically homogeneous substance.
(C) It remains unchanged for a work interaction with a closed system.
(D) It may in some instances change spontaneously until the entropy of the system reaches a maximum value.

62. Which of the following devices is possible?
(A) A cyclic machine that will experience no other interaction than to produce energy through a work interaction, while transferring energy from a high-temperature reservoir to a low-temperature reservoir through heat interactions
(B) A cyclic machine that will experience no other interaction than to transfer to a thermal reservoir an amount of energy equal to the amount of energy it receives from a work interaction
(C) A device that will change the thermodynamic state of a material from one equilibrium state to another without experiencing a change in the amount of energy contained in the material, in the amount of material, or in the external forces placed on the material
(D) A cyclic machine that will experience no other interaction than to accept from a heat interaction with a high-temperature reservoir an amount of energy equal to the amount of energy it receives from a work interaction

63. Energy is added in the amount of 50 kilojoules in a heat interaction to a closed system while 30 kilojoules of work is done by the system. The change in the internal energy of the system is:
(A) 80 kJ
(B) 20 kJ
(C) −20 kJ
(D) −80 kJ

64. If a sample experiencing a change in temperature from 23°C to 46°C also experiences a change in specific enthalpy of 120 kilojoules per kilogram, of what material is the sample most likely to be composed? (Base your answer on the specific heat data provided in Chapter 12.)
(A) Water
(B) Helium
(C) Ammonia
(D) Hydrogen

65. How much energy must be transferred through a heat interaction to raise the temperature of a 4-kilogram sample of methane in a closed system from 15°C to 35°C?
(A) 34.8 kJ
(B) 45 kJ
(C) 139 kJ
(D) 180 kJ

66. For an isentropic process of an ideal gas ($k = 1.40$), with an initial pressure of 50 pounds per square inch absolute, an initial specific volume of 8.2 cubic feet per pound mass, and a final pressure of 120 psia, what is the final value of the specific volume?
(A) 8.2 ft^3/lbm
(B) 3.42 ft^3/lbm
(C) 19.7 ft^3/lbm
(D) 4.39 ft^3/lbm

67. One kilogram of air undergoes an isometric process, starting from 200°C and 600 kilopascals, in which the temperature drops to 110°C. The final pressure is:
(A) 1,091 kPa
(B) 741 kPa
(C) 330 kPa
(D) 486 kPa

68. An ideal gas ($k = 1.4$), with an initial specific volume of 30 cubic meters per kilogram, experiences an isothermal compression from 200 kilopascals to 800 kilopascals. What is the final specific volume of the gas?
(A) 7.5 m^3/kg
(B) 11.14 m^3/kg
(C) 120 m^3/kg
(D) 75 m^3/kg

69. What is the specific internal energy of a liquid water/water vapor mixture with a quality of 58% at 40°C?
(A) 167.56 kJ/kg
(B) 2,262.6 kJ/kg
(C) 2,430.1 kJ/kg
(D) 1,479.8 kJ/kg

70. What is the power output of a turbine operating where 15 kilograms per second of air enters at 750 kilopascals and 280°C, and exits at 370 kilopascals and 37°C?
(A) 2,617 kW
(B) 3,645 kW
(C) 61 kW
(D) 44 kW

71. A rigid body experiences rectilinear motion (x-direction) and has an initial position $X_0 = 7.0$ feet at starting time $t_0 = 0$. The velocity of the body, in feet per second, is known according to the function $V(t) = t^2 - 6t + 9$, where t represents time in seconds. The distance traveled during the first 25.0 seconds of motion is:
(A) 169.9 ft
(B) −36.0 ft
(C) 635.0 ft
(D) 3,558.3 ft

72.

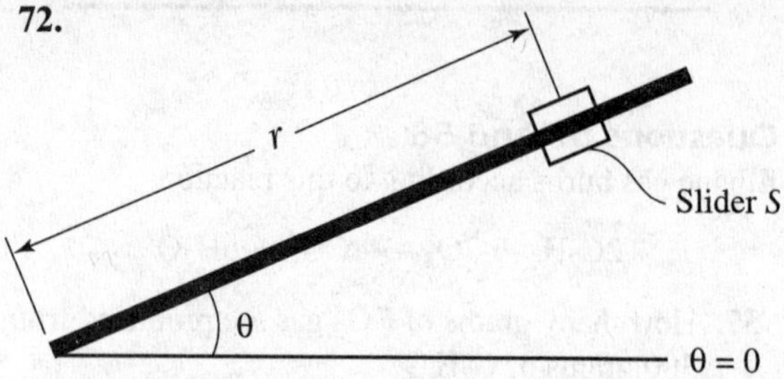

A rod/slider block mechanism rotates in a horizontal plane as shown in the diagram above. The motion is governed by the equations $r(t) = 2.0t^3 - 0.5t^2$ and $\theta(t) = t^2 + 8t$, where the units for r, t, and θ are meters, seconds, and radians, respectively. The mass of the slider block is 2.0 kilograms, and there is negligible friction between the rod and the slider block. The magnitude of the slider block's angular momentum when angular speed $\omega = 20.0$ radians per second is:
(A) 6.85×10^6 kg·m²/s
(B) 1.20×10^3 kg·m²/s
(C) 5.18×10^4 kg·m²/s
(D) 4.06×10^5 kg·m²/s

73.

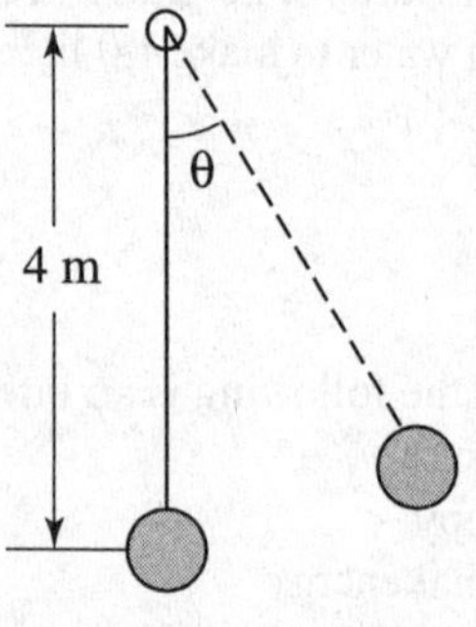

The 15.0-kilogram ball shown in the diagram above is attached to an inextensible cord. The ball swings in a vertical plane, and air resistance is negligible. When $\theta = 30°$, the speed of the ball is known to be 3.0 meters per second. What is the tension in the cord at this instant?
(A) 161.2 N
(B) 3.8 N
(C) 46.7 N
(D) 127.5 N

74. A 6.0-pound-mass rectangular block slides down a 40° incline (from the horizontal), and the kinetic friction coefficient is 0.25. What is the magnitude of the block's total acceleration?
(A) 19.5 ft/sec²
(B) 0.61 ft/sec²
(C) 26.0 ft/sec²
(D) 14.5 ft/sec²

75.

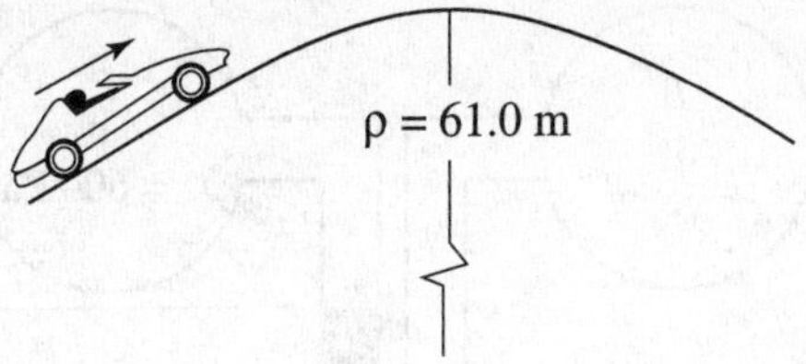

A 1,455-kilogram automobile (including the mass of the driver) is traveling along a hill that has a parabolic shape. The section of the hill near the crest has a radius of curvature of 61.0 meters, as shown in the above diagram. Wind resistance is considered negligible. If the speed of the automobile is 18.3 meters per second at the crest of the hill, the apparent weight of the system at this location should be:

(A) 7,988 N
(B) 22,261 N
(C) 6,285 N
(D) 641 N

76. A 3.0-pound-mass rigid body, **I**, initially moving at 20.0 feet per second along a straight line, collides with a 7.0-pound-mass body, **II**, traveling at 5.0 feet per second in the opposite direction. Body **I** has a postcollision linear momentum of 34.5 pounds mass-feet per second in a direction opposite to its initial motion. The coefficient of restitution for this impact must be:

(A) 0.57
(B) 0.65
(C) 0.80
(D) 0.93

77.

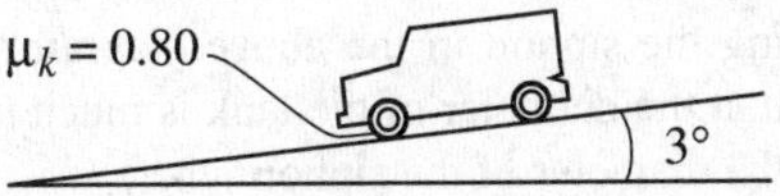

A police officer measures skid marks left by all four wheels of a 1,300-kilogram car to be 20.0 meters along a road surface that has a 3° slope from the horizontal as illustrated in the above diagram. It is known from prevailing conditions that the coefficient of kinetic friction between the tires and the pavement was approximately 0.80 and that the car had a speed of 40.0 kilometers per hour at the end of the skid. The amount of energy dissipated by friction due to the entire skid is:

(A) 203,760 J
(B) 13,350 J
(C) 1,380 J
(D) 101,880 J

78.

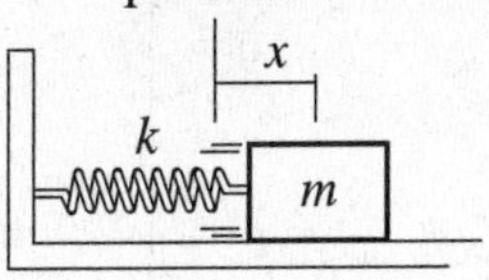

The spring-mass system shown in the above diagram consists of a 1.8-kilogram block and a linear spring with a stiffness of 0.26 kilonewton per meter. The initial displacement of the block is 2.5 centimeters to the right of the equilibrium position, and the block is released from rest. Friction is considered negligible between the block and the horizontal surface. The period of this vibration is necessarily:

(A) 1.81 s
(B) 6.28 s
(C) 0.08 s
(D) 0.52 s

79.

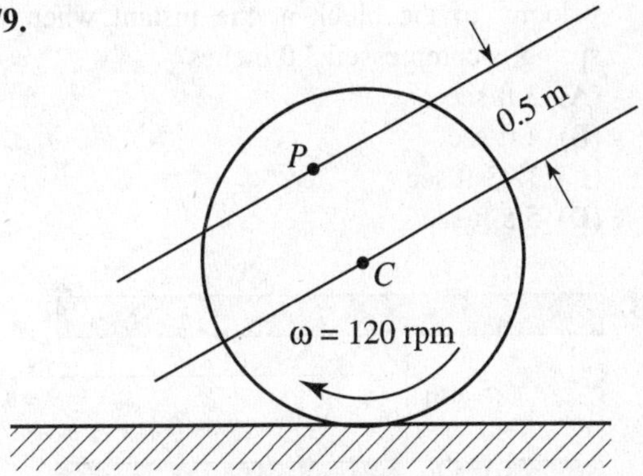

A tractor wheel has a diameter of 1.5 meters and rolls with a constant angular speed of 120 rpm, as illustrated above. The speed of point *P*, measured with respect to the center *C* of the wheel, is:

(A) 9.4 m/s
(B) 60.0 m/s
(C) 6.3 m/s
(D) 18.8 m/s

80.

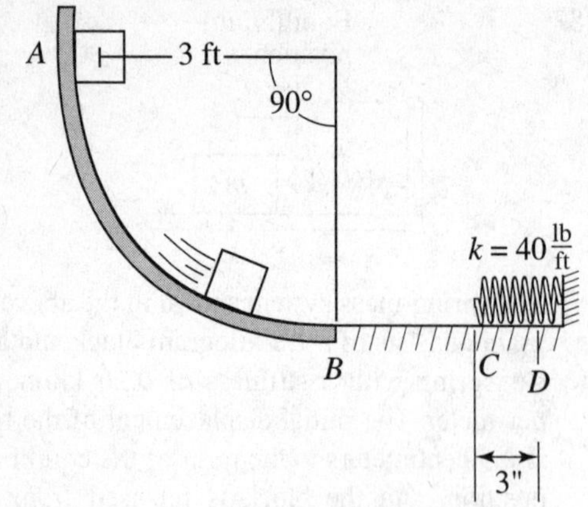

The 5.0-pound block illustrated above is released from rest at *A* and slides along the frictionless circular surface *AB*. It then continues to move across the horizontal surface without friction and proceeds to strike a spring, *C*, having a stiffness of 40 pounds per foot. Assume that the spring is initially undeformed. What will be the velocity of the block at the instant when the spring is compressed 3.0 inches?

(A) 3 ft/sec
(B) 4 ft/sec
(C) 13.3 ft/sec
(D) 5.5 ft/sec

81.

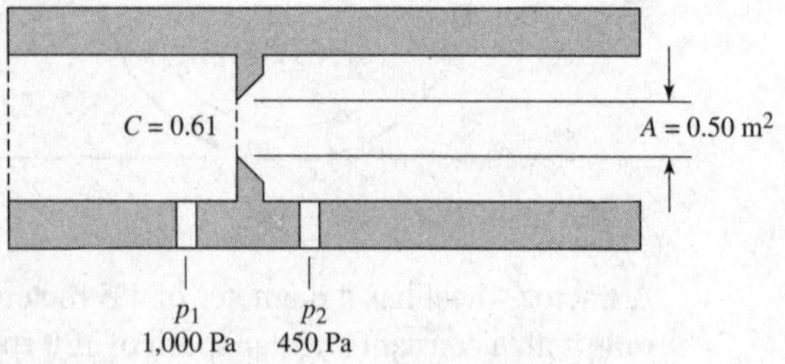

In the above diagram, where *C* is the discharge coefficient, what is the volumetric flow rate through the orifice?

(A) .00542 m^3/s
(B) 0.28 m^3/s
(C) 1.28 m^3/s
(D) 0.65 m^3/s

82.

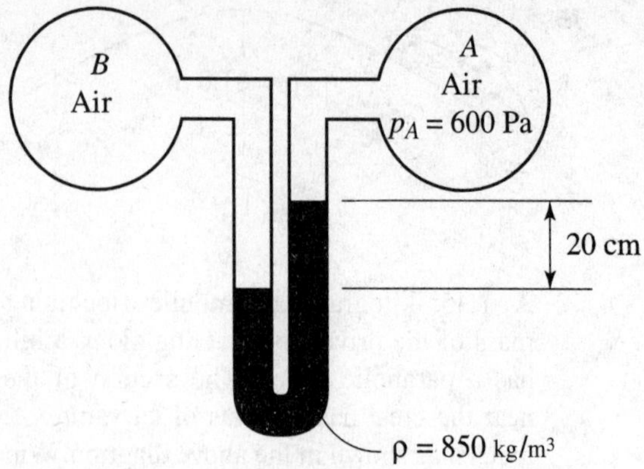

The pressure in vessel *B* shown in the diagram above is most nearly:

(A) 2,268 Pa
(B) 684 Pa
(C) 433 Pa
(D) 767 Pa

83.

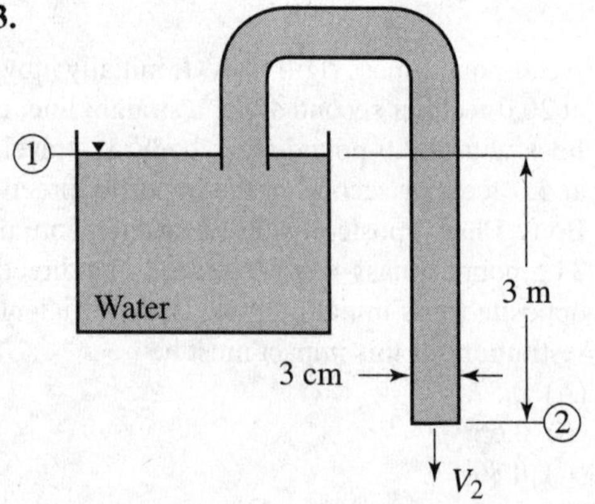

What is the volumetric flow rate of water leaving the siphon in the above diagram? (Assume that the diameter of the tank is much larger than the diameter of the siphon tube.)

(A) 0.32 m^3/s
(B) .00542 m^3/s
(C) 1.28 m^3/s
(D) 0.65 m^3/s

84.

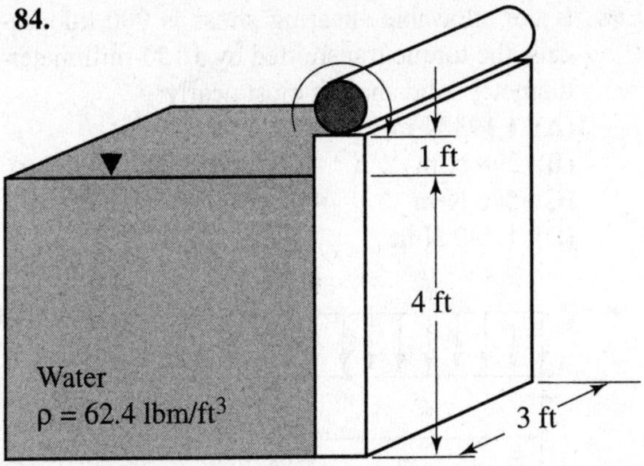

In the above diagram, what is the approximate moment required at the hinge to keep the gate closed?
(A) 3,000 ft-lbf
(B) 4,500 ft-lbf
(C) 5,500 ft-lbf
(D) 4,000 ft-lbf

85.

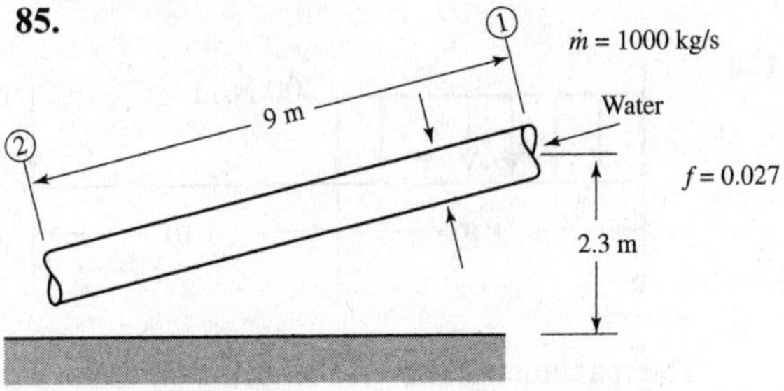

For the pipe shown above, what is the pressure drop $(p_1 - p_2)$?
(A) 2 kPa
(B) −4 kPa
(C) 2.06 kPa
(D) −2 kPa

86. The Reynolds number is:
(A) a measure of the rate of fluid flow
(B) the ratio of inertial forces to viscous forces
(C) the ratio of pressure forces to viscous forces
(D) rarely important in fluid flow analysis

87.

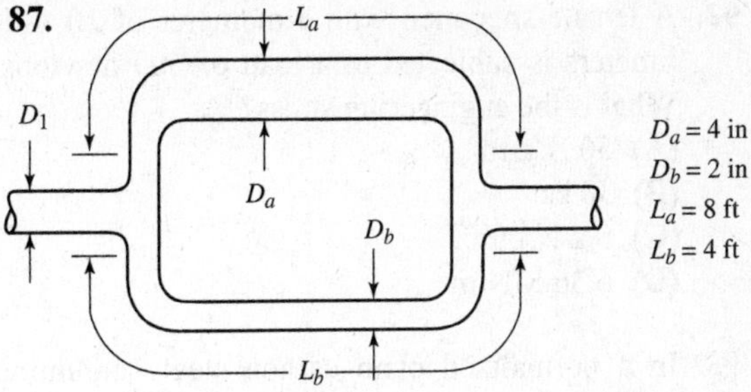

What is the approximate volumetric flow rate through tube a in the above diagram?
(A) 40 ft³/sec
(B) 20 ft³/sec
(C) 50 ft³/sec
(D) 30 ft³/sec

88.

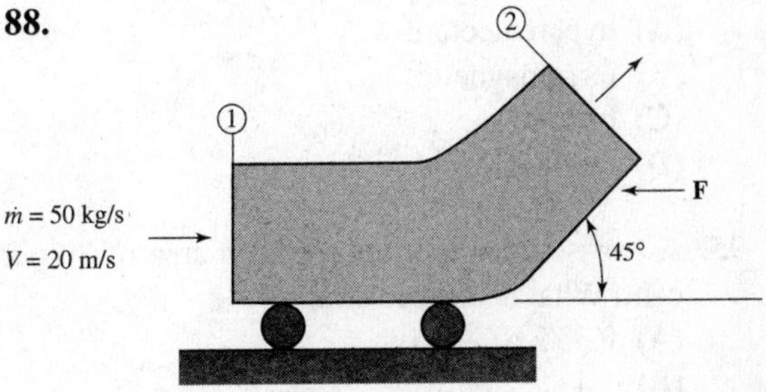

What force, **F**, is required to keep the cart shown above from moving? (Assume in the cross-sectional area that $\text{Area}_1 = \text{Area}_2$)
(A) 1,707 N
(B) 720 N
(C) 707 N
(D) 293 N

89. A copper hook is attached to a plain carbon steel chain below the surface in a saltwater bay. If galvanic corrosion occurs, what will be the anodic reaction?
(A) $Fe \rightleftarrows Fe^{2+} + 2e^-$
(B) $Cu \rightleftarrows Cu^{2+} + 2e^-$
(C) $Cu^{2+} + 2e^- \rightleftarrows Cu$
(D) $NaCl \rightleftarrows Na^+ + Cl^-$

90. A solution is required to be:
(A) a single phase
(B) a liquid composed of two or more components
(C) homogeneous
(D) comprised partly of water

91. Which of the following is the ground-state electronic configuration of a copper atom?
(A) $1s^2 2s^2 2p^6 3s^2 3p^6 4s^1 3d^{10}$
(B) $1s^2 1p^6 2s^2 2p^6 3s^2\ 3p^6 3d^5$
(C) $1s^2 1p^2 2s^2 2p^6 3s^2\ 3p^6 4s^2 4p^6 4d^1$
(D) $1s^2 2s^2 2p^6 3s^2 3p^6 3d^6 4s^2 4p^3$

92. A tensile specimen with a diameter of 10 millimeters is subjected to a load of 500 newtons. What is the engineering stress?
(A) 50 N/mm
(B) 30 ksi
(C) 5.2 N/mm^2
(D) 6.36 MN/m^2

93. In a normalized plain carbon steel containing 0.5 weight percent carbon, approximately what percentage of the alloy is pearlite?
(A) 37%
(B) 63%
(C) 91%
(D) 7.4%

94. At room temperature a plain carbon steel containing 0.2 weight percent carbon is:
(A) hypereutectoid
(B) ferromagnetic
(C) brittle
(D) highly alloyed

95. A bar is rolled to a reduction in area of 30 percent. What is the true strain?
(A) 0.357
(B) 1.43
(C) 0.154
(D) 0.30

96. A material whose electrons cannot be excited across the band gap is considered to be:
(A) a metal
(B) a semiconductor
(C) an insulator
(D) a superconductor

97.

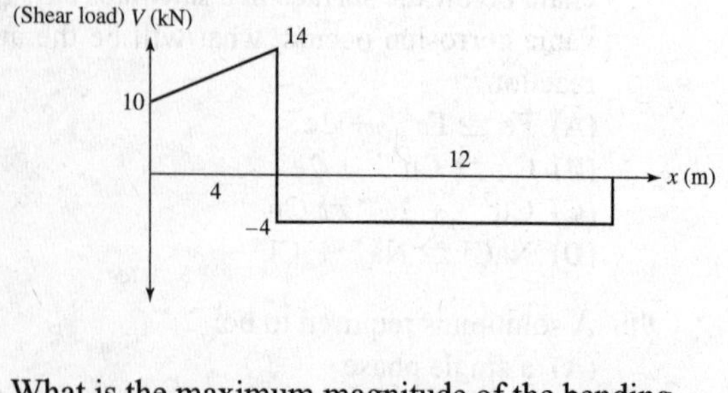

What is the maximum magnitude of the bending moment in the beam shown in the above diagram? The bending moment at each end of the beam is 0, and there are no concentrated couples along the beam.
(A) 96 kN·m
(B) 48 kN·m
(C) 24 kN·m
(D) 40 kN·m

98. If the allowable shearing stress is 900 kilopascals, the torque transmitted by a 150-millimeter-diameter solid shaft is most nearly:
(A) 1,193 N·m
(B) 298 N·m
(C) 596 N·m
(D) 1,590 N·m

99.

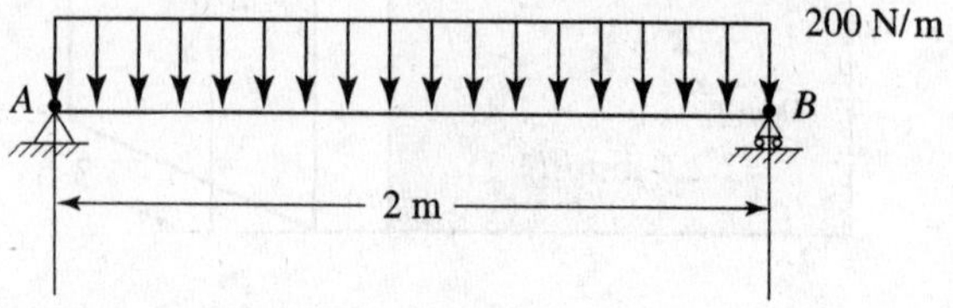

The maximum bending stress for the 4 × 6 centimeter beam shown in the diagram above is most nearly:
(A) 4.17 MPa
(B) 2.08 MPa
(C) 16.7 MPa
(D) 100 MPa

100.

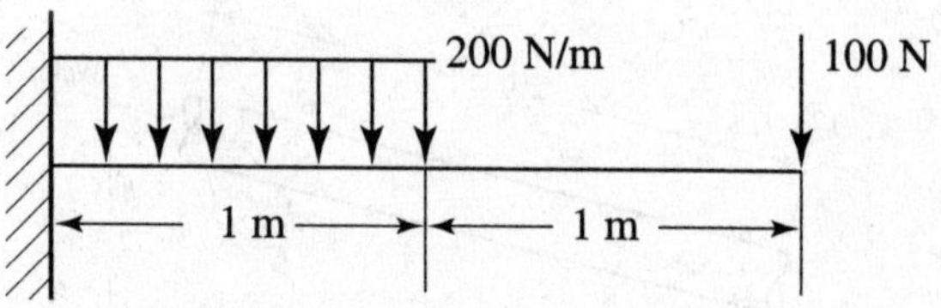

The maximum transverse shearing stress for the 10-centimeter-diameter shaft beam shown in the above diagram is most nearly:
(A) 57.3 kPa
(B) 38.2 kPa
(C) 25.5 kPa
(D) 50.9 kPa

101.

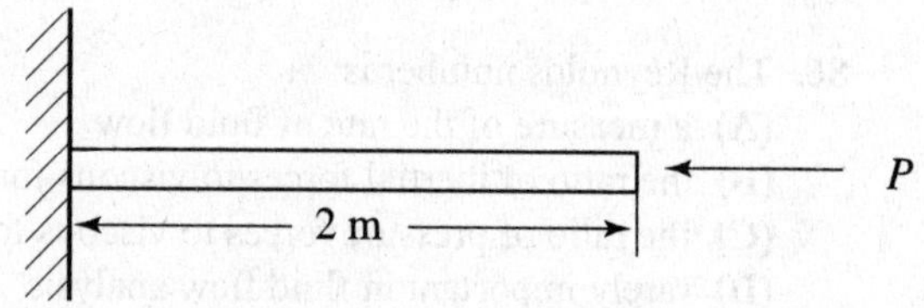

The critical load, P, for the 2-meter long cantilever beam shown in the diagram is most nearly:
(A) 2.468 EI
(B) 1.234 EI
(C) 0.617 EI
(D) 0.5 EI

102.

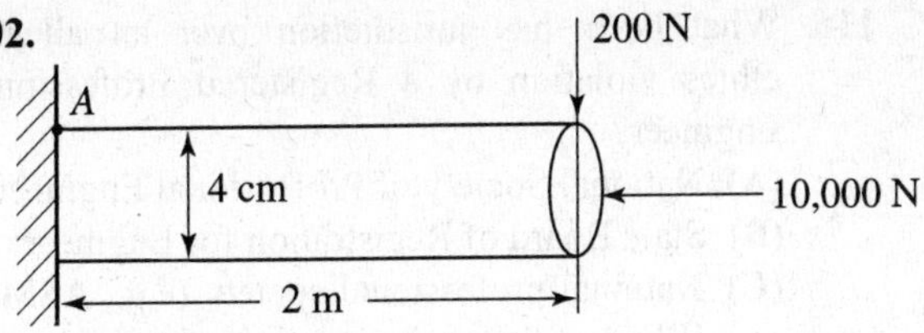

In the above diagram, the normal stress at point *A* is most nearly:

(A) 71.6 MPa
(B) 55.71 MPa
(C) 7.95 MPa
(D) 63.6 MPa

103.

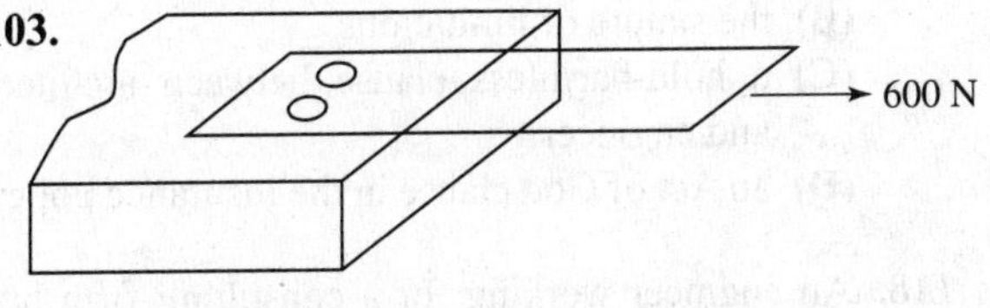

The average shearing stress for each 3-centimeter-diameter bolt shown above is most nearly:

(A) 0.424 MPa
(B) 1.2 MPa
(C) 0.848 MPa
(D) 0.56 MPa

104.

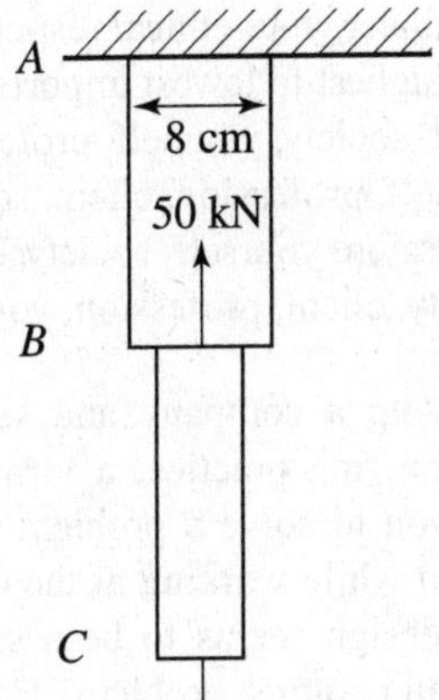

The normal stress in section *AB* of the above diagram is most nearly:

(A) 9.95 MPa
(B) 3.97 MPa
(C) 13.92 MPa
(D) 5.97 MPa

105. What is the base-10 equivalent of the binary whole number 00100111_2?

(A) 12
(B) 24
(C) 39
(D) 56

106. For the base-10 number 47, the binary equivalent is:

(A) 011011_2
(B) 101111_2
(C) 101011_2
(D) 101100_2

107. How many times will the line labeled "START" execute in the following program?

```
        I=4
        J=2
START   J=J+I
        I=J^2
        IF J<100 THEN GO TO START
        ELSE GO TO FINISH
FINISH  PRINT J
```

(A) 3
(B) 4
(C) 5
(D) 6

Questions 108 and 109

The following is a segment of a spreadsheet. Use the data in the cells to answer questions 108 and 109.

	A	B	C	D
1	23	24	25	26
2	7	A2*2	B2*A$1	
3	8	A3*2	B3*B$1	
4	9	A4*2	B4*C$1	
5	10	A5*2	B5*D$1	

108. What will be the top to bottom values in Column B?

(A) 12,14,16,18
(B) 16,18,20,24
(C) 14,16,18,20
(D) 49,64,81,100

109. What will be the top to bottom values in Column C?

(A) 1127,1536,2025,2600
(B) 340,390,460,530
(C) 70,96,126,160
(D) 160,240,320,450

---

110. A flowchart:
(A) is a sequence of instructions to perform operations
(B) is alphabetic code to instruct the computer what to do
(C) defines basic operations and decisions required
(D) is a series of human language statements and common math symbols

111. A European country is experiencing an inflation rate of 25% per month. What is the effective annual rate of interest?
(A) 300%
(B) 25%
(C) 1,355%
(D) 1,455%

112. A company can manufacture parts for a manufacturing cost of $4.00 per unit plus $4,000 for tooling. A semiautomated system has been developed as an alternative. The costs for the proposed method are $40,000 for equipment and $1.00 per unit manufacturing cost per unit. What is the break-even number of units per year?
(A) 12,000
(B) 11,000
(C) 4,000
(D) 15,000

113. An engineer borrows $18,000 at 12% per annum compounded annually. The first payment will be made 3 years from now. The remaining balance at that time will be:
(A) $24,050
(B) $21,554
(C) $25,288
(D) $23,080

114. The annual payment into a fund is $800, and payments will be made for 15 years. Each payment is made at the end of the year. How much will the fund be worth when it matures if interest is 10% per year?
(A) $31,215
(B) $25,418
(C) $35,600
(D) $26,400

115. For an asset costing $25,000, what will be the depreciation charge for the 4th year? (Use the MACRS system.)
(A) $1,680
(B) $1,790
(C) $1,264
(D) $2,150

116. What body has jurisdiction over an alleged ethics violation by a Registered Professional Engineer?
(A) National Society of Professional Engineers
(B) State Board of Registration for Engineers
(C) National professional society (e.g., ASME, IEEE) of the engineer involved
(D) Local district court

117. Snow and ice heavily damaged a building that was designed by Registered Engineers and Architects. The owner was not able to recover damages because of:
(A) the insolvency of the bond holder
(B) the statute of limitations
(C) a hold-harmless clause between architect and engineer
(D) an Act of God clause in the insurance policy

118. An engineer working for a consulting firm has decided to go into private practice. One of her first steps should be to:
(A) submit her letter of resignation
(B) tell colleagues about her plans
(C) send e-mail to the firm regarding her plans
(D) discuss her plans with her supervisor

119. As an engineer, your ethical responsibility, in order from highest to lowest importance, is to:
(A) client, society, yourself, profession
(B) yourself, profession, client, society
(C) profession, yourself, society, client
(D) society, client, profession, yourself

120. After leaving a company and setting up your own engineering practice, a former competitor contacts you to solve a problem similar to one you solved while working at the company. Your previous design seems to be a solution to this former competitor's problem. Can you accept this assignment?
(A) No. Information from the original design would be required.
(B) Yes. Knowledge transfer happens.
(C) No. One should not accept money twice for the same job.
(D) Yes. No stated nondisclosure statement was signed.

Answer Key

Morning Session

1. B
2. D
3. A
4. C
5. B
6. D
7. A
8. B
9. D
10. D
11. C
12. A
13. B
14. C
15. B
16. A
17. D
18. B
19. B
20. D
21. A
22. D
23. C
24. A
25. D
26. A
27. A
28. D
29. B
30. C
31. D
32. B
33. A
34. C
35. B
36. D
37. C
38. A
39. B
40. D
41. B
42. A
43. B
44. C
45. B
46. D
47. A
48. C
49. B
50. A
51. C
52. C
53. A
54. C
55. C
56. C
57. D
58. B
59. B
60. A
61. C
62. A
63. B
64. B
65. C
66. D
67. D
68. A
69. D
70. B
71. D
72. A
73. A
74. D
75. C
76. C
77. A
78. D
79. C
80. C
81. A
82. A
83. B
84. C
85. C
86. B
87. A
88. D
89. A
90. A
91. A
92. D
93. B
94. B
95. A
96. C
97. B
98. C
99. A
100. D
101. C
102. B
103. A
104. D
105. C
106. B
107. A
108. D
109. A
110. C
111. C
112. A
113. C
114. B
115. C
116. B
117. C
118. D
119. D
120. A

Diagnostic Chart

Morning Session Practice Exam

				Reason for Incorrect Answer			
Subject Area	*Total Number of Questions*	*Number Correct*	*Number Incorrect*	*Lack of Knowledge*	*Misread Problem*	*Careless or Mathematical Error*	*Wrong Guess*
Mathematics (1–24)	24						
Electric Circuits (25–36)	12						
Statics (37–48)	12						
Chemistry (49–60)	12						
Thermodynamics (61–70)	10						
Dynamics (71–80)	10						
Fluid Mechanics (81–88)	8						
Materials Science (89–96)	8						
Mechanics of Materials (97–104)	8						
Computers (105–110)	6						
Ethics (111–115)	5						
Economics (116–120)	5						
Total	120						

Answers Explained

1. **B** Treat y as a constant to obtain $\frac{\partial z}{\partial z} = 4xy - 2$.

2. **D** $P(A \text{ or } B) = P(A) + P(B) - P(A \text{ and } B)$

$$= \frac{10}{20} + \frac{4}{20} - \frac{2}{20} = \frac{12}{20} \text{ or } .6.$$

3. **A** Expand about the third row to obtain

$$2\begin{vmatrix} -1 & -2 \\ 6 & -4 \end{vmatrix} + 1\begin{vmatrix} -1 & 4 \\ 6 & 3 \end{vmatrix} = 2(16) + 1(-27) = 5$$

4. **C** The discriminant

$$B^2 - 4AC = (-10)^2 - 4(3)(3) = 64 > 0$$

Hence, the graph is a hyperbola.

5. **B** This defines the standard deviation. The median is the value of the middle term. The mean is the average of the terms. The mode is the most frequently occurring value. These are basic definitions that should be memorized.

6. **D** The first derivative is equal to the slope of the tangent to the curve, $y = f(x)$. The area under the curve is equal to the integral of the function $f(x)$. The other responses do not mean anything.

7. **A** The equation is linear in y with integrating factor $e^{\int 3dx} = e^{3x}$. Hence, the general solution is $ye^{3x} = c$, or $y = ce^{-3x}$. For $y(0) = 1$, $c = 1$. Therefore, $y = e^{-3x}$.

8. **B** The solution of the auxiliary equation $m^2 + 4m + 4 = 0$ is the repeated root $m = -2$. Hence, the general solution is $y = c_1e^{-2x} + c_2xe^{-2x}$ or $y = e^{-2x}(c_1 + c_2x)$.

9. **D** $v = \frac{ds}{dt} = 30t^2 - 10t^4$. Therefore, at $t = 1$ s, $v = 20$ m/s.

10. **D** $\mathbf{B} = 4\mathbf{i} + 3\mathbf{j}$ is perpendicular to $\mathbf{A} = 3\mathbf{i} - 4\mathbf{j}$, since $\mathbf{A} \cdot \mathbf{B} = 0$. Since $|\mathbf{B}| = 5$, a unit vector perpendicular to $\mathbf{A}$ is $\frac{4}{5}\mathbf{i} + \frac{3}{5}\mathbf{j}$.

11. **C** The work done by a variable force in moving an object is equal to the definite integral $\int_a^b f(x)dx$. The instantaneous velocity is equal to the first derivative of $f(x)$, and instantaneous acceleration is equal to the second derivative of $f(x)$.

12. **A** Area $= \int_0^3 x^2\,dx = \frac{x^3}{3}\Big|_0^3 = 9$ square units.

13. **B** $f'(x) = 3x^2 - 3$ and $f''(x) = 9x$. Solving $f'(x) = 0$ yields $x = \pm 1$, with $f(1) = -2$, and $f(-1) = 2$. Since $f''(-1) = -9 < 0$, the maximum value of f is 2.

14. **C** Slope $m = \frac{a - b}{b - a} = -1$.

15. **B** Since $3^3 = 27$ and $3^4 = 81$, the value of $\log_3 50$ must be a number between 3 and 4.

16. **A** $|A| = \begin{vmatrix} 3 & 1 \\ -5 & -2 \end{vmatrix} = -1$. $A^T = \begin{bmatrix} 3 & -5 \\ 1 & -2 \end{bmatrix}$ implies $\text{adj}(A) = \begin{bmatrix} -2 & -1 \\ 5 & 3 \end{bmatrix}$. Hence:

$$A^{-1} = \frac{\text{adj}(A)}{|A|} = \begin{bmatrix} 2 & 1 \\ -5 & -3 \end{bmatrix}$$

17. **D** $r = \sqrt{3^2 + (-3)^2} = 3\sqrt{2}$.
Also, $\theta = \tan^{-1}(-1) = -\pi/4$, which is equivalent to $7\pi/4$. Hence, $3 - 3i = 3\sqrt{2}e^{(7\pi/4)i}$.

18. **B** The smallest angle is opposite the smallest side. Thus, by the law of cosines, $4^2 = 5^2 + 8^2 - 2(5)(8)\cos\theta$, which implies that $\theta = 24.1°$.

19. B Complete the squares, and rewrite the equation as $(x-0)^2+(y-2)^2+(z+3)^2=13$. Hence, the center of the sphere is at $(0,2,-3)$.

20. D $a_1 = 0.3$ and $r = 0.3$. Hence,

$$S = \frac{0.3}{1-0.3} = \frac{3}{7}$$

21. A $\int_2^3 \frac{1}{x-1}dx = \ln|x-1|\Big|_2^3 = \ln 2 - \ln 1$

$= \ln 2.$

22. D Differentiate implicitly to obtain $2x + 2y\frac{dy}{dx} = 0$, which implies $\frac{dy}{dx} = -\frac{x}{y}$. Now, at (3,4), slope $m = -3/4$. Hence, the equation of the tangent is $(y-4) = -\frac{3}{4}(x-3)$ or $3x + 4y = 25$.

23. C Volume $= \pi\int_0^2 (y^2)^2\ dy = \pi\left(\frac{y^5}{5}\right)\Big|_0^2 = \frac{32\pi}{2}$ cubic units.

24. A Rewrite the expression as $\frac{\sin x}{\cos x}\cdot\frac{1}{\sin x}\cdot\frac{\cos x}{1}$, which, if $\sin x \neq \cos x \neq 0$, is equal to 1.

25. D Rearrange eq. 4.4:

$$\rho = \frac{RA}{l}$$

$$= \frac{(5\times10^{-3}\ \Omega)(0.2\ \text{in}^2)(2.54\ \text{cm/in})(1\ \text{m}/100\ \text{cm})}{100\ \text{ft}\times 12\ \text{in/ft}}$$

$$= 2.115\times10^{-8}\ \Omega\cdot\text{m}$$

26. A Solve for the current through the center branch:

$$I_2 = \frac{1\ \text{V}}{2\ \text{k}\Omega} = 0.5\ \text{mA}$$

The voltage across the 2-kΩ and 4-kΩ resistors is:

$$V_2 = (0.5\ \text{mA})(2\ \text{k}\Omega + 4\ \text{k}\Omega) = 3\ \text{V}$$

The voltage across the 1-kΩ and 5-kΩ resistors is also 3 V. Therefore the current through this combination is:

$$I_3 = \frac{3\ \text{V}}{1\ \text{k}\Omega + 5\ \text{k}\Omega} = 0.5\ \text{mA}$$

The total current is

$$I_1 = I_2 + I_3 = 0.5\ \text{mA} + 0.5\ \text{mA} = 1.0\ \text{mA}$$

The voltage across R_1 (the first 1-kΩ resistor) is

$$V_1 = (1.0\ \text{mA})(1\ \text{k}\Omega) = 1\ \text{V}$$

Apply Kirchhoff's voltage law around the input loop:

$$V_i = V_1 + V_2 = 1\ \text{V} + 3\ \text{V} = 4\ \text{V}$$

27. A Determine the total equivalent resistance "seen" by the current source. First, find the equivalent resistance of each branch.

Branch 1: 1 Ω
Branch 2: 2 Ω + 3 Ω = 5 Ω
Branch 3: 4 Ω + 5 Ω + 6 Ω = 15 Ω
Apply eq. 4.17(b):

$$R_T = \frac{1}{\frac{1}{1\ \Omega}+\frac{1}{5\ \Omega}+\frac{1}{15\ \Omega}} = 0.789\ \Omega$$

Voltage $V_o = (1\ \text{A})(0.789\ \Omega) = 0.789\ \text{V}$

28. D From Problem 27, the voltage across each branch is known to be 0.789 V. Therefore the current through the center branch is:

$$I = \frac{0.789\ \text{V}}{2\ \Omega + 3\ \Omega} = 0.1578\ \text{A}$$

Apply eq. 4.9:

$$P = I^2\times R = (0.1578\ \text{A})^2(2\ \Omega) = 0.05\ \text{W}$$

29. B Select the loop currents so that only one (I_A for this problem) flows through the 1-kΩ resistor. Therefore, only loop current I_A will have to be calculated before applying Ohm's law to solve for the voltage.

Loop A path includes the 2-V source, resistors 2 kΩ, 1 kΩ, and 7 kΩ.

Loop B path includes the 2-V and 4-V sources, resistors 2 kΩ, 2 kΩ, and 3 kΩ.

Loop C path includes resistors 7 kΩ and 3 kΩ.

Assume all loop currents are chosen in a clockwise direction.

Loop A: 10 kΩ + 2 kΩ − 7 kΩ = 2 V
Loop B: 2 kΩ + 7 kΩ + 3 kΩ = −4 V + 2 V
Loop C: −7 kΩ + 3 kΩ + 10 kΩ = 0

Solve for I_A (note the answer will be in mA):

$$I_A = \frac{\begin{vmatrix} 2 & 2 & -7 \\ -2 & 7 & 3 \\ 0 & 3 & 10 \end{vmatrix}}{\begin{vmatrix} 10 & 2 & -7 \\ 2 & 7 & 3 \\ -7 & 3 & 10 \end{vmatrix}} = \frac{204}{143} = 1.43\ \text{mA}$$

$$V = (1.43\ \text{mA})(1\ \text{k}\Omega) = 1.43\ \text{V}$$

30. C Apply eq. 4.26:

$$Q = C \times V = (0.01 \times 10^{-6}\ \text{F}) \times 50\ \text{V}$$
$$= 0.5\ \mu\text{C}$$

31. D To determine the maximum voltage the capacitor can charge to and the time constant, first obtain the Thévenin equivalent circuit. The Thévenin equivalent resistance is found by replacing the voltage source with 0 Ω; then the 1-Ω and 2-Ω resistors are in series, and this series combination is in parallel with the series combination of 4 Ω and 2 Ω.

Let R_a = 1 Ω + 2 Ω = 3 Ω

and R_b = 4 Ω + 2 Ω = 6 Ω. Then:

$$R_{\text{Th}} = \frac{3\ \Omega \times 6\ \Omega}{3\ \Omega + 6\ \Omega} + 3\ \Omega = 5\ \Omega$$

The Thévenin equivalent voltage is found by removing the capacitor and measuring the voltage across R_b (the voltage across the resistor combination of 4 Ω and 2 Ω). This Thévenin voltage may be calculated by using the voltage division law:

$$V_{\text{Th}} = \frac{R_b}{R_a + R_b} \times 18\ \text{V}$$
$$= \frac{6\ \Omega}{3\ \Omega + 6\ \Omega} \times 18\ \text{V} = 12\ \text{V}$$

The time constant is τ = 5 Ω × 2 F = 10 s. Apply eq. 4.33:

$$v_c(t) = 12\ \text{V} \times (1 - e^{-2/10}) = 2.18\ \text{V}$$

32. B For the average value of this waveform, apply eq. 4.36(b):

$$I_{avg} = \frac{(3\ \text{V} \times 2\ \text{ms}) + (-1\ \text{V} \times 2\ \text{ms})}{4\ \text{ms}}$$
$$= 1.0\ \text{V}$$

For the rms value of this waveform, apply eq. 4.37 or use

$$I_{rms} = \sqrt{\frac{(9\ \text{V}^2 \times 2\ \text{ms}) + (1\ \text{V}^2 \times 2\ \text{ms})}{4\ \text{ms}}}$$
$$= 2.24\ \text{V}$$

33. A Solve for the impedance of each branch:

$$Z_1 = 3\ \Omega - j\frac{1}{(2\ \text{rad/s} \times \frac{1}{8}\ \text{H})}$$
$$= (3 - j4)\ \Omega$$
$$Z_2 = 5\ \Omega + j(2\ \text{rad/s} \times 2\ \text{H}) = (5 + j4)\ \Omega$$
$$Z_3 = 2\ \Omega + j(2\ \text{rad/s} \times \frac{1}{2}\ \text{H}) = (2 + j1)\ \Omega$$

Find the total impedance:

$$Z_T = Z_1 + \frac{Z_2 \times Z_3}{Z_2 + Z_3}$$
$$= (3 - j4)\ \Omega + \frac{(5 + j4)\ \Omega \times (2 + j1)\ \Omega}{(5 + j4)\ \Omega + (2 + j1)\ \Omega}$$
$$= (4.45 - j3.18)\ \Omega$$

Apply Ohm's law:

$$I_s = \frac{10\angle 30°\text{V}}{(4.45 - j3.18)\ \Omega} = 1.84\angle 66°\ \text{A}$$

34. C Rearrange eq. 4.48 to solve for C:

$$C = \frac{1}{(2\pi \times 31.8 \times 10^3\ \text{Hz})^2 \times (10 \times 10^{-3}\ \text{H})}$$
$$= 2.5 \times 10^{-9}\ \text{F} = 2.5\ \mu\text{F}$$

Rearrange eq. 4.52(b) to solve for R:

$$R = 2\pi \times BW \times L$$
$$= 2\pi \times (2 \times 10^3\ \text{Hz}) \times (10 \times 10^{-3}\ \text{H})$$
$$= 125.7\ \Omega$$

35. B Determine the impedance of each branch.

Let $Z_a = R + j\omega L = (3 + j(1{,}000)(4\ \text{mH}))$
$= (3 + j4)\ \Omega$

and $Z_b = 0 - j\dfrac{1}{(1{,}000\ \text{rad/s})(200\ \mu\text{F})}$
$= -j5\ \Omega$

Then:

$$Z_T = \frac{Z_a Z_b}{Z_a + Z_b} = \frac{(3 + j4)\ \Omega \times (-j5)\ \Omega}{(3 + j4)\ \Omega + (-j5)\ \Omega}$$

$$= (7.5 - j2.5)\ \Omega$$

The input voltage phasor is $10.0\angle 0°$ V. Apply Ohm's law; then:

$$I = \frac{10.0\angle 0°\ \text{V}}{(7.5 - j2.5)\ \Omega} = 1.265\angle 18.4°\ \text{A}$$

Complex power = $10.0\angle 0°$ V × $1.265\angle 18.4°$ A = $12.65\ \angle 18.4°$ VA

36. D Apply eq. 4.64:

$$V_o = -\left(\left(\frac{50\ \text{k}\Omega}{10\ \text{k}\Omega} \times 3\ \text{V}\right) + \left(\frac{50\ \text{k}\Omega}{20\ \text{k}\Omega} \times (-4\ \text{V})\right)\right)$$

$$= -5.0\ \text{V}$$

37. C $R_x = \Sigma F_x = 130\left(\frac{12}{13}\right) - 200(\cos 30)$

$$= -53.2\ \text{N}$$

$$R_y = \Sigma F_y = 130\left(\frac{5}{13}\right) + 200(\sin 30) - 100$$

$$= 50\ \text{N}$$

$$R = \sqrt{R^2_x + R^2_y} = 73\ \text{N}$$

38. A $\mu_s = \tan\theta = \tan(30) = 0.577 = 0.58$

39. B $\Sigma F_y = 0 \qquad B\cos(30) = 100$

$$B = 115.5\ \text{N}$$

40. D $M_A = 260\left(\frac{12}{13}\right)(0.15) + 260\left(\frac{5}{13}\right)(0.05)$

$$= 41\ \text{N·m}$$

41. B $\Sigma F_x = 0 \quad \frac{4}{5}T_{AC} = T_{BC}\cos 45$

$$\Sigma F_y = 0 \quad \frac{3}{5}T_{AC} + T_{BC}\sin 45 - 1{,}000 = 0$$

Solve for T_{AC}: $T_{AC} = 714$ N

42. A $\Sigma M_B = 0 \quad A(9) - 1{,}500(1.5) + 375(1) = 0$

$$A = 208.33\ \text{N}$$

43. B Maximum moment occurs at the support.

$$M_{max} = 400(2) + 200(1) = 1{,}000\ \text{N·m}$$

44. C Cut the truss through members *BD*, *DE*, and *EG*, and use the FBD of the upper section of the truss:

$$\Sigma F_x = 0 \qquad F_{DE} = 6\ \text{kN}$$

45. B $\Sigma F_y = 0 \qquad 3F = 600$

$$F = 200\ \text{N}$$

46. D $\overline{Y} = \frac{\Sigma \overline{y} A}{A} = \frac{1(20) + 5(12)}{20 + 12} = 2.5\ \text{cm}$

47. A $\Sigma M_A = 0 \qquad (F_{BC}\cos 45)(2) - 100(4) = 0$

$$F_{BC} = 283\ \text{N}$$

48. C $I_{x'} = I_x + A\,d^2$

$$A = \frac{I_{x'} - I_x}{d^2} = \frac{7{,}000 - 2{,}000}{10^2} = 50\ \text{cm}^2$$

49. B See Example 1.4. Sulfur may have more than one valence or oxidation state. Set up a simple algebraic equation, letting *x* equal the unknown valence of sulfur. Sodium has a valence of +1, and oxygen has a valence of −2. The net charge on $Na_2S_2O_3$ is 0, since it's uncharged. Sum up the individual atomic charges and set them equal to 0. Thus:

$$2(+1) + 2(x) + 3(-2) = 0$$

$$x = +2$$

50. A Look for a metal, since metals generally form positively charged ions, called cations. The only metal listed is lithium, Li.

51. C The molar mass of $Ca(NO_3)_2$ is 164 g/mol. Thus, 10 moles is 1,640 gs.

52. C Iron(III) hydroxide is an ionic compound. Hence, use the criss-cross method of formula writing. Iron(III) is Fe^{3+}. Hydroxide is OH^-. Criss-crossing gives $Fe(OH)_3$.

53. A This is a freezing-point-depression problem, so use eq. 1.11. The solute is $CaCl_2$, and the solvent is water. $CaCl_2$ is a strong electrolyte, so $i = 3$.

The K_f of water is given as 1.86. The molality *m* of the solution is:

$$m = \frac{111\ \text{g}/111\ \text{g/mol}}{1.0\ \text{kg}} = 1.0\ \text{molal}$$

Substitute these numbers into eq. 1.11, and solve for ΔT. Thus, $\Delta T = 5.5°C$. Hence, the freezing point T_f of the solution is $-5.5°C$.

54. C The correct expression for the equilibrium constant K_c is given by eq. 1.28. Of the choices given, only $K_c = \frac{[NH_3]^2}{[N_2][H_2]^3}$ is in this form.

55. C First convert 100 g to moles of $CaCO_3$; the answer is 1 mol of $CaCO_3$. There are 3 moles of oxygen in 1 mole of $CaCO_3$; this gives 3 mol of O. Then multiply by Avogadro's number to convert to the number of atoms.

$$\text{molar mass} = 40 + 12 + 3(16) = 100\text{g/mol } CaCO_3$$

$$1 \text{ mol } CaCO_3 \Leftrightarrow 3 \text{ mol O}$$

$$3 \text{ mol O}\left(\frac{6.022 \times 10^{23} \text{ atoms O}}{1 \text{ mol O}}\right) = 18.066 \times 10^{23} \text{ atoms of oxygen}$$

56. C The oxidizing agent is the reactant species that removes electrons from another reactant. Since copper is in the +2 oxidation state in $CuSO_4$ and goes to the zero or uncharged state on the product side, it must gain 2 electrons by removing them from zinc. Thus, $CuSO_4$ is the oxidizing agent.

57. D The reaction is already balanced; assume O_2 is in excess. Use the factor-label method:

$$300 \text{ g } \cancel{C_2H_6}\ \frac{(1.0 \cancel{\text{ mol } C_2H_6})}{(30.0 \cancel{\text{ g } C_2H_6})}\ \frac{(4.0 \cancel{\text{ mol } CO_2})}{(2.0 \cancel{\text{ mol } C_2H_6})}\ \frac{(44.0 \text{ g } CO_2)}{(1.0 \cancel{\text{ mol } CO_2})} = 880 \text{ g}$$

58. B Since CO_2 can be regarded as an ideal gas, convert 880 g to liters using the ideal gas law:

$$PV = nRT$$

where $n = \text{m/MM} = \frac{880 \text{ g}}{44.0 \text{ g/mol}} = 20.0 \text{ mol.}$

STP means that $T = 273$ K and $P = 1.0$ atm. Also $R = 0.0821$ L·atm/K·mol. Substitute the numbers, and solve for V: $V = 448$ L.

59. B Use $(M_A)(V_A) = (M_B)(V_B)$, since moles of acid must equal moles of base.

$$M_A = 0.25 \text{ M}, V_A = \text{unknown}$$

$$M_B = \frac{20 \text{ g NaOH/40 g/mol}}{1.0 \text{ L}} = 0.500 \text{ M}$$

$$V_B = 1.0 \text{ L}$$

Substitute the numbers and solve for V_A: $V_A = 2.0$ L.

60. A The values of entropy (S), internal energy (U), and enthalpy (H) are each proportional to the mass of the system. For purposes of analysis, the mass specific forms of these properties are often used. The mass-specific form is defined as the value of the property divided by the mass of the system; thus:

$$s = \frac{S}{m}, \quad u = \frac{U}{m}, \quad h = \frac{H}{m}$$

The value of pressure, however, does not depend on the mass of the system, and therefore pressure is an intensive property.

61. C A steady-state system is defined as a system in which the state remains constant with time; therefore the state of a system remains unchanged for a steady-state process, and statement (A) is true.

It can be shown that the state of a system that is comprised of a macroscopically homogeneous substance is determined by the values of any two independent properties, so statement (B) is true.

Because during a work interaction, energy is exchanged between the system and its surroundings, the state of the system must change; therefore statement (C) is false.

One statement of the second law of thermodynamics is that there exists one stable equilibrium state for which the value of entropy is a maximum for a given value of energy. If the value of entropy is lower than this maximum value, it is possible that it will increase spontaneously, so statement (D) is true.

62. A If an energy balance and an entropy balance is applied to the system described in statement (A), it is possible to configure the system in such a way that the values of energy and entropy do not change with time. Device (A) is possible.

By applying an entropy balance to the system described in statement (B), it can be shown that the value of entropy must be continuously decreasing; therefore, device (B) is not possible.

By applying an energy balance to statement (D), it can be shown that the value of energy must be continuously increasing; therefore, device (D) is not possible.

An equilibrium state is determined by the amount of energy contained in the material, the amount of material, and the external forces placed on the material; therefore, there cannot be two equilibrium states under these conditions. Device (C) is not possible.

63. B When the energy balance equation, eq. 12.14, is applied to this system, it can be simplified as follows:

$$\Delta E = Q - W$$

where Q = the amount of energy transferred to a system during a heat interaction,
W = the amount of energy transferred from a system during a work interaction.

Substitute the given values:

$$\Delta E = 50 \text{ kJ} - 30 \text{ kJ} = 20 \text{ kJ}$$

64. B The relationship between a change in specific enthalpy and the temperature of a system is given by eq. 12.38:

$$\Delta h = c_p(\Delta T)$$

Then:

$$c_p = \frac{\Delta h}{\Delta T} = \frac{120 \dfrac{\text{kJ}}{\text{kg}}}{46°\text{C} - 23°\text{C}} = 5.22 \frac{\text{kJ}}{\text{kg}\cdot°\text{C}} \text{ or } 5.22 \frac{\text{kJ}}{\text{kg}\cdot\text{K}}$$

Therefore, based on the property data tables at the end of Chapter 12, the substance is most likely helium, which has a constant-pressure specific heat of 5.19 kJ/kg·K.

65. C The change in internal energy for a closed system is equal to:

$$\Delta U = m\,\Delta u$$

The change in specific internal energy is related to the change in temperature by eq. 12.38:

$$\Delta u = c_v\,\Delta T$$

so that

$$\Delta U = m\,c_v\,\Delta T = (4 \text{ kg})\left(1.74 \frac{\text{kJ}}{\text{kg}\cdot\text{K}}\right)(35°\text{C} - 15°\text{C}) = 139.2 \text{ kJ}$$

66. D For an isentropic process in a system composed of an ideal gas, from eq. 12.41:

$$p_1 v_1^{\,k} = p_2 v_2^{\,k}$$

$$v_2 = v_1\left(\frac{p_1}{p_2}\right)^{1/k} = \left(8.2 \frac{\text{ft}^3}{\text{lbm}}\right)\left(\frac{50 \text{ psia}}{120 \text{ psia}}\right)^{\frac{1}{1.40}} = 4.39 \text{ ft}^3/\text{lbm}$$

67. D From eq. 12.47, for an isometric process of a system composed of an ideal gas:

$$\frac{T_1}{p_1} = \frac{T_2}{p_2}$$

$$p_2 = p_1\frac{T_2}{T_1} = (600 \text{ kPa})\frac{(110 + 273)\text{K}}{(200 + 273)\text{K}} = 486 \text{ kPa}$$

68. A One relationship that describes an isothermal process of an ideal gas is Boyle's law, eq. 12.49:

$$p_1 v_1 = p_2 v_2$$

$$v_2 = v_1\frac{p_1}{p_2} = \left(30 \frac{\text{m}^3}{\text{kg}}\right)\frac{(200 \text{ kPa})}{(800 \text{ kPa})} = 7.5 \text{ m}^3/\text{kg}$$

69. D For a two-phase mixture of water, the average value of the specific internal energy is given by eq. 12.66b:

$$u_{\text{mix}} = u_f + x(u_g - u_f)$$

From the saturated water table at the end of Chapter 12, at 40°C:

$u_f = 167.56$ kJ/kg, $u_g = 2{,}430.1$ kJ/kg

so that:

$$u_{\text{mix}} = 167.56 \frac{\text{kJ}}{\text{kg}} + 0.58 \times \left(2{,}430.1 \frac{\text{kJ}}{\text{kg}} - 167.56 \frac{\text{kJ}}{\text{kg}}\right) = 1{,}479.8 \text{ kJ/kg}$$

70. B For a turbine, from eq. 12.77:

$$\dot{w} = \dot{m}(h_i - h_e)$$

where, from eq. 12.33:

$$h_i - h_e = c_p(T_i - T_e)$$

Find the value of the constant-pressure specific heat of air in the property data table at the end of Chapter 12:

$$c_p = 1.00 \text{ kJ/kg·K}$$

Substitute known values:

$$\dot{w} = \dot{m}\, c_p(T_i - T_e)$$

$$= \left(15\frac{\text{kg}}{\text{s}}\right)\left(1.00\frac{\text{kJ}}{\text{kg·K}}\right)(280°\text{C} - 37°\text{C})$$

$$= 3{,}645\frac{\text{kJ}}{\text{s}} = 3{,}645 \text{ kW}$$

71. D Distance traveled is determined by calculating the absolute value of the area of the velocity graph from $0 \le t \le 25.0$ s. It is necessary to determine the time(s) when $V = 0$.

$$V(t) = t^2 - 6t + 9$$

Factoring, $V = 0$ at $t = 3.0$ s.

Distance traveled =

$$\left|\int_0^3 (t^2 - 6t + 9)\, dt\right| + \left|\int_3^{25} (t^2 - 6t + 9)\right|$$

$$= \left(\frac{t^3}{3} - 3t^2 + 9t\right)$$

$$= |9 - 0| + |(3{,}558.33 - 9)|$$

$$= 3{,}558.3 \text{ ft.}$$

72. A Given: $r(t) = 2.0t^3 - 0.5t^2$ and $\theta(t) = t^2 + 8t$.

Then:

$$\omega = \dot{\theta} = \frac{d\theta}{dt} = 2t + 8 = 20.0 \text{ rad/s}$$

$$t = \frac{20 - 8}{2} = 6.0 \text{ s.}$$

Angular momentum is

$$H = mr^2\dot{\theta} = (2.0 \text{ kg})[2(6)^3 - 0.5(6)^2]^2(20.0 \text{ rad/s})$$
$$= 6.85 \times 10^6 \text{ kg·m}^2\text{/s.}$$

73. A For cord tension when $\theta = 30°$, use the tangential and normal coordinates system.

FBD of ball involves only tension and weight forces (neglecting air friction).

$$\Sigma F_n = \frac{mV^2}{R} = \frac{(15 \text{ kg})(3.0 \text{ m/s})^2}{4.0 \text{ m}} = 33.75 \text{ N}$$

From the FBD of the ball:

$$\Sigma F_n = T - \text{W} \cos 30°$$

$$= T - (15 \text{ kg})(9.81 \text{ m/s}^2)(0.866) = 33.75$$

Then:

$$T = 33.75 + 127.4 = 161.2 \text{ N}$$

74. D Draw the FBD of the block, using inclined and normal coordinates. External forces are normal reaction N_R, weight, and kinetic friction F_{FK}.

Block's acceleration is along inclined direction. Solve:

$$a_{\text{I}} = \frac{\Sigma F_{\text{I}}}{m} = \frac{\text{W} \sin 40° - F_{FK}}{6.0 \text{ lbm}}$$

$$= \frac{6.0 \sin 40° - 0.25\, N_R}{6.0 \text{ lbm}}$$

From equilibrium in normal direction,

$$N_R = \text{W} \cos 40° = (6.0)(0.766) = 4.6 \text{ lbf}$$

$$a_{\text{I}} = \frac{3.86 - 0.25(4.6 \text{ lb})}{6.0 \text{ lbm}}$$

$$= \frac{(2.71 \text{ lb})(32.2)}{6.0 \text{ lbm}} = 14.5 \text{ ft/sec}^2$$

75. C Apparent weight is reaction N_R. Draw the FBD of the car, and identify weight and normal and friction forces.

Normal direction is toward center of curvature.

$$\Sigma F_n = \frac{mV^2}{R} = \frac{(1{,}455 \text{ kg})(18.3 \text{ m/s})^2}{61.0 \text{ m}}$$

$$= 7{,}988.0 \text{ N}$$

$$= W_c - N_R = 7{,}988.0 \text{ N}$$

$$N_R = (1{,}455 \text{ kg})(9.81 \text{ m/s}^2) - 7{,}988$$

$$= 6{,}285 \text{ N}$$

76. C Employ the conservation of linear momentum principle for impact.

Let $V_{\text{I}} = 20.0$ ft/sec and $V_{\text{II}} = -5.0$ ft/sec.

Since $m_{\text{I}} = 3.0$ lbm, postcollision velocity is:

$$V_{\text{I}}' = \frac{mV_{\text{I}}'}{m} = \frac{-34.5 \text{ lb-ft/sec}}{3.0 \text{ lb}} = -11.5 \text{ ft/sec}$$

For coefficient of restitution e:

$$e(V_{\text{I}} - V_{\text{II}}) = V_{\text{II}}' - V_{\text{I}}'$$

Also:

$$m_I V_I + m_{II} V_{II}$$
$$= m_I V_I' + m_{II} V_{II}' \rightarrow V_{II}'$$
$$= \frac{(3.0)(20.0) + (7.0)(-5.0) - (-34.5)}{7.0}$$
$$= \frac{59.5}{7.0} = 8.5 \text{ ft/sec}$$

Substitute known values and solve for e:

$$e = \frac{8.5 - (-11.5)}{20.0 - (-5.0)} = 0.80$$

77. A The equation for work of a force is $W_{1\to2} = \int F\cdot dr$. For a constant-friction force, $W_{1\to2} = (F_F)(20.0 \text{ m})$ since the friction force and displacement are in the same direction. $F_F = 0.8N_R$, where N_R is the normal reaction between the tires and pavement, given by $N_R = W \cos 3°$ (from equilibrium in the direction perpendicular to incline). Then

$$N_R = (1{,}300)(9.81)\cos 3° = 12{,}735.5 \text{ N}$$

Energy dissipated is friction work, so:

$$W_{1\to2} = (0.8 \times 12{,}735.5\text{N})(20.0 \text{ m})$$
$$= 203{,}768.4 \text{ N·m}$$
$$W_{1\to2} \approx 203{,}760 \text{ J}$$

78. D Period of vibration τ is independent of the initial displacement.

$$\tau = \frac{1}{f_n} \quad \text{and} \quad f_n = \frac{\omega_n}{2\pi} = \frac{1}{2\pi}\sqrt{\frac{k}{m}}$$

Then:

$$\tau = 2\pi\sqrt{\frac{m}{k}}$$

where $k = 0.260$ kN/m $= 260.0$ N/m. Substitute known values:

$$\tau = 2\pi\sqrt{\frac{1.8 \text{ kg}}{260.0 \text{ N/m}}} = 2\pi\sqrt{0.00688\text{s}^2}$$
$$= 6.28(0.083\text{s}) = 0.523 \text{ s}$$

79. C The speed of point P relative to the center C of the wheel is simply the tangential speed.

$$V_{p/c} = r\omega = (0.5\text{m})(120 \text{ rpm})$$
$$= (0.5 \text{ m})(120)\left(\frac{2\pi}{60} \text{ rad/s}\right)$$
$$= 6.28 \text{ m/s} \approx 6.3 \text{ m/s}$$

80. C First determine the speed of the block at point B, utilizing the conservation of energy principle for a frictionless process from A to B:

$$KE_A + PE_A = KE_B + PE_B$$

Let $PE_B = 0$(datum), and $PE_A = mgh_A = (5.0$ lbm)(32.2 ft/sec^2) (3.0 ft) = 15.0 ft-lbf. Since $V_A = 0$, then $KE_A = 0$, and the conservation of energy equation becomes

$$0 + 15.0 \text{ ft-lbf} = \frac{1}{2}mV_B^2 + 0$$

Solve:

$$V_B = \sqrt{\frac{2(15.0 \text{ ft-lbf})}{m}}$$
$$= \sqrt{\frac{(30.0 \text{ ft-lb})(32.2)}{5.0 \text{ lbm}}} = 13.9 \text{ ft/sec}$$

Since there is no work on the block between point B and spring C, $V_C = V_B = 13.9$ ft/sec. Use the work and kinetic energy principle from C to the 3.0-in compressed position (point D): $KE_C + W_{\text{net } C\to D} = KE_D$. The work from C to D is spring work only, so

$$W_{\text{net } C\to D} = \frac{1}{2}k(X_C^2 - X_D^2)$$

Substitute known values:

$$15.0 \text{ ft-lbf} + \frac{1}{2}(40.0 \text{ lbf/ft})[0 - (0.25 \text{ ft})^2]$$
$$= \frac{1}{2}(5.0 \text{ lbm})V_D^2$$

Solve:

$$V_D = \sqrt{\frac{2(15.0 - 1.25)\text{ft-lbf}(32.2)}{5.0 \text{ lbm}}} = 13.3 \text{ ft/sec}$$

81. A The flow rate of fluid through an orifice flow meter is given by the equation

$$Q = CA\sqrt{2g\left[\left(\frac{p_1}{\gamma} + z_1\right) - \left(\frac{p_2}{\gamma} + z_2\right)\right]}$$

Because z_1 is equal to z_2, this equation can be simplified to:

$$Q = CA\sqrt{2g\left(\frac{p_1 - p_2}{\gamma}\right)}$$

Substitute known values:

$$Q = (0.61)(0.50\ \text{m}^2) \times \sqrt{2\left(9.81\ \frac{\text{m}}{\text{s}^2}\right)\left(\frac{1{,}000\ \text{Pa} - 450\ \text{Pa}}{9{,}810\ \frac{\text{N}}{\text{m}^3}}\right)\left(\frac{\frac{\text{N}}{\text{m}^2}}{\text{Pa}}\right)}$$

$$= 0.32\ \text{m}^3/\text{s}$$

82. A Because the density of air has a much smaller value than that of the manometer fluid, pressure differences within the air sections are negligible compared to pressure differences within the manometer fluid. Therefore, p_A is very nearly the pressure at the top of the manometer fluid exposed to vessel *A*, and p_B is very nearly the pressure at the surface of the manometer fluid exposed to vessel *B*. The two pressures can be related as follows:

$$p_B - p_A = \rho_m g h_m$$

This equation is rearranged as:

$$p_B = p_A + \rho_m g h_m$$
$$= 600\ \text{Pa} + \left(850 \frac{\text{kg}}{\text{m}^3}\right)\left(9.81 \frac{\text{m}}{\text{s}^2}\right)(0.20\ \text{m}) \times \left(\frac{\text{N}}{\frac{\text{kg}\cdot\text{m}}{\text{s}^2}}\right)\left(\frac{\text{Pa}}{\frac{\text{N}}{\text{m}^2}}\right)$$
$$= 2{,}268\ \text{Pa}$$

83. This problem is solved using the Bernoulli equation:

$$\frac{p_1}{\gamma} + \frac{\overline{V}_1^{\,2}}{2g} + z_1 = \frac{p_2}{\gamma} + \frac{\overline{V}_2^{\,2}}{2g} + z_2$$

In this case, because the diameter of the tank is assumed to be much larger than the diameter of the siphon tube, the average velocity at section 1 is nearly 0. Also, the pressures of the fluid at section 1 and section 2 are equal to the atmospheric pressure. Using these facts, simplify the Bernoulli equation and solve for $\overline{V}_2$:

$$\frac{\overline{V}_2^{\,2} - \overbrace{\overline{V}_1^{\,2}}^{=0}}{2g} = \frac{\overbrace{p_1 - p_2}^{=0}}{\gamma} + (z_1 - z_2)$$
$$\overline{V}_2 = \sqrt{2g(z_1 - z_2)}$$
$$= \sqrt{2\left(9.81\ \frac{\text{m}}{\text{s}^2}\right)(3\text{m})}$$
$$= 7.67\ \text{m/s}$$

The volumetric flow rate is determined from the average velocity using $Q = \overline{V}A$, where the area *A* is given by the equation

$$A = \frac{\pi D^2}{4}$$

and where *D* is the diameter of the siphon tube.

$$Q = \overline{V}\left(\frac{\pi D^2}{4}\right)$$
$$= \left(7.67 \frac{\text{m}}{\text{s}}\right)\left[\frac{\pi(0.03\ \text{m})^2}{4}\right]\left(\frac{3{,}600\ \text{s}}{\text{h}}\right)$$
$$= .00542\ \frac{\text{m}^3}{\text{s}}$$

84. C The total force acting on the gate, applied by the water pressure, can be modeled as a point force located at the center of pressure. Using the magnitude of this point force and its distance from the axis of the hinge, the required moment is determined. (Refer to the figure below.)

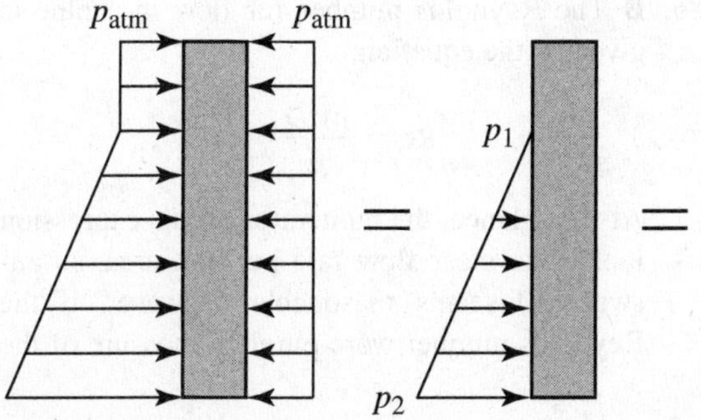

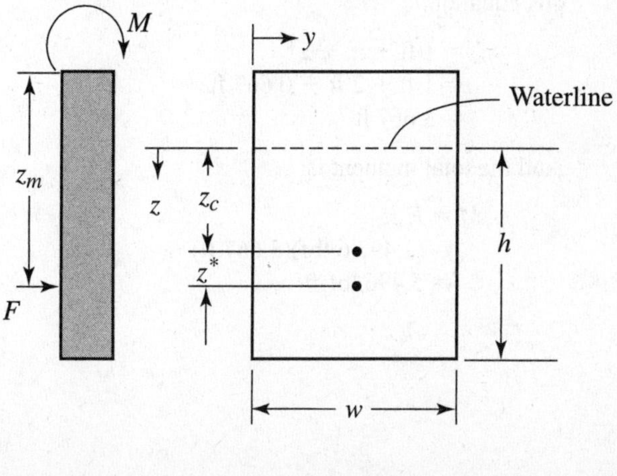

To determine the magnitude of the point force, use these equations:

$$F = \frac{p_1 + p_2}{2} A_v$$

$$p_1 = \overbrace{\rho g z_1}^{=0} = 0 \frac{\text{lbf}}{\text{ft}^2}$$

$$p_2 = \rho g z_2 = \left(62.4 \frac{\text{lbm}}{\text{ft}^3}\right)\left(32.2 \frac{\text{ft}}{\text{sec}^2}\right)(4 \text{ ft})\left(\frac{\text{lbf}}{32.2 \frac{\text{lbm-ft}}{\text{sec}^2}}\right) = 249.6 \frac{\text{lbf}}{\text{ft}^2}$$

$$A_v = (3 \text{ ft})(4 \text{ ft}) = 12 \text{ ft}^2$$

$$F = \frac{0 \frac{\text{lbf}}{\text{ft}^2} + 249.6 \frac{\text{lbf}}{\text{ft}^2}}{2}(12 \text{ ft}^2) = 1{,}497.6 \text{ lbf}$$

To determine the center of pressure, use these equations:

$$z^* = \frac{\rho g I_{y_c} \overbrace{\sin(90°)}^{=1}}{F}$$

$$I_{y_c} = \frac{wh^3}{12} = \frac{(3 \text{ ft})(4 \text{ ft})^3}{12} = 16 \text{ ft}^4$$

$$z^* = \frac{\left(62.4 \frac{\text{lbm}}{\text{ft}^3}\right)\left(32.2 \frac{\text{ft}}{\text{sec}^2}\right)(16 \text{ ft}^4)}{1497.6 \text{ lbf}}\left(\frac{\text{lbf}}{32.2 \frac{\text{lbm-ft}}{\text{sec}^2}}\right) = 0.667 \text{ ft}$$

To determine the length of the moment arm, use this equation:

$$z_m = 1 \text{ ft} + z_c + z^* = 1 \text{ ft} + 2 \text{ ft} + 0.667 \text{ ft} = 3.667 \text{ ft}$$

And the total moment is:

$$M = F z_m = (1{,}497.6 \text{ lbf})(3.667 \text{ ft}) = 5{,}496 \text{ lbf-ft}$$

85. C Solve this problem using the Bernoulli equation, modified to include the frictional head loss:

$$\frac{p_1}{\gamma} + \frac{\overline{V}_1^2}{2g} + z_1 = \frac{p_2}{\gamma} + \frac{\overline{V}_2^2}{2g} + z_2 + h_f$$

In this case, the average velocity at the outlet is equal to the average velocity at the inlet, so the pressure loss is given by the equation

$$p_1 - p_2 = \gamma(z_2 - z_1 + h_f)$$

The frictional head loss is expressed as

$$h_f = f\left(\frac{L}{D}\right)\left(\frac{\overline{V}^2}{2g}\right)$$

Also:

$$\overline{V} = \frac{\dot{m}}{\rho A}$$

where

$$A = \frac{\pi(0.20 \text{ m})^2}{4} = 0.157 \text{ m}^2$$

Then:

$$\overline{V} = \frac{\left(1000 \frac{\text{kg}}{\text{s}}\right)}{\left(1{,}000 \frac{\text{kg}}{\text{m}^3}\right)(0.157 \text{ m}^2)} = 6.37 \text{ m/s}$$

and

$$h_f = (0.027)\left(\frac{9 \text{ m}}{0.20 \text{ m}}\right)\left(\frac{\left(6.37 \frac{\text{m}}{\text{s}}\right)^2}{2\left(9.81 \frac{\text{m}}{\text{s}^2}\right)}\right) = 2.51 \text{ m}$$

Finally:

$$p_1 - p_2 = \left(9{,}810 \frac{\text{N}}{\text{m}^3}\right)(-2.3 \text{ m} + 2.51 \text{ m})\left(\frac{\text{Pa}}{\frac{\text{N}}{\text{m}^2}}\right) = 2{,}060 \text{ Pa}$$

86. B The Reynolds number for flow in a pipe is given by the equation:

$$\text{Re} = \frac{\rho \overline{V} D}{\mu}$$

At first glance, the numerator of this expression looks like mass flow rate per unit area, so answer (A) seems reasonable. However, if the Reynolds number were purely a measure of the rate of fluid flow, there would be no need of viscosity in the relationship, so it can be inferred that the meaning may be somewhat broader. Examine the other choices for a better fit.

The pressure of the fluid does not appear in the relationship for the Reynolds number, nor is it easy to derive a pressure-force term from the parameters used. Answer (C) seems unlikely.

An inertial force term would be proportional to

$$F_i \approx \rho \overline{V}^2$$

And a viscous force would be proportional to

$$F_v \approx \mu \frac{V}{L}$$

where L is a characteristic length for the flow. The ratio of these two forces is as follows:

$$\frac{F_i}{F_v} \approx \frac{\rho \overline{V}^2}{\mu \frac{V}{L}} = \frac{\rho \overline{V} L}{\mu} = \mathrm{Re}_L$$

Therefore, the answer is (B).

Choice (D) is incorrect because the Reynolds number is always an important parameter when analyzing a fluid-flow situation. It gives an indication of whether the flow is likely to be laminar or turbulent.

87. A Since the head loss through each pipe must be equal:

$$f_a \frac{L_a}{D_a} \frac{\overline{V}_a^{\,2}}{2g} = f_b \frac{L_b}{D_b} \frac{\overline{V}_b^{\,2}}{2g}$$

With $f_a = f_b$:

$$\begin{aligned}\frac{V_a}{V_b} &= \sqrt{\frac{D_a}{D_b} \frac{L_b}{L_a}} \\ &= \sqrt{\frac{4 \text{ in}}{2 \text{ in}} \frac{4 \text{ ft}}{8 \text{ ft}}} \\ &= 1 \\ &(\overline{V}_a = \overline{V}_b)\end{aligned}$$

Use this result in the continuity equation:

$$\begin{aligned}\overline{V}A &= \overline{V}_a A_a + \overline{V}_b A_b \\ &= V_a(A_a + A_b) \\ &= V_a\left(\frac{\pi D_a^2}{4} + \frac{\pi D_b^2}{4}\right) \\ &= \frac{\pi V_a}{4}(D_a^2 + D_b^2)\end{aligned}$$

Then:

$$\begin{aligned}\overline{V}_a &= (\overline{V}A)\frac{4}{\pi(D_a^2 + D_a^2)} \\ &= \left(260 \frac{\text{ft}^3}{\text{min}}\right)\left[\frac{4}{\pi[(4 \text{ in})^2 + (2 \text{ in})^2]}\right] \\ &\quad \left(\frac{144 \text{ in}^2}{\text{ft}^2}\right)\left(\frac{\text{min}}{60 \text{ sec}}\right) \\ &= 39.7 \text{ ft}^3/\text{sec}\end{aligned}$$

88. D Use the impulse-momentum principle to solve this problem:

$$\vec{F} = \dot{m}\vec{V}_2 - \dot{m}\vec{V}_1$$

In this case, only the horizontal, or x-direction, component is important. The x-direction equation for the impulse momentum principle is as follows:

$$|\vec{F}_x| = \dot{m}|\vec{V}_2| \cos \alpha - \dot{m}|\vec{V}_1|$$

Also, since $A_1 = A_2$, $|\vec{V}_1| = |\vec{V}_2| = 20$ m/s, so

$$\begin{aligned}|\vec{F}_x| &= \dot{m}|\vec{V}_1|(\cos \alpha - 1) \\ &= \left(50 \frac{\text{kg}}{\text{s}}\right)\left(20 \frac{\text{m}}{\text{s}}\right)(\cos 45 - 1)\left(\frac{\text{N}}{\frac{\text{kg}\cdot\text{m}}{\text{s}^2}}\right) \\ &= -293 \text{ N}\end{aligned}$$

89. A Use the standard Emf Series in Table 8.4 as an approximation of the behavior of dissimilar metals in salt water. Iron is anodic with respect to copper. Therefore, the anodic oxidation half-cell reaction for iron will occur.

90. A Although the solute and solvent may be in different phases (as, e.g., when the solute is table salt, a solid, and the solvent is water, a liquid), the solution has only a single phase (in this example, liquid).

91. A In choices (B) and (C), the 1p level does not exist. In choice (D), the 3d level is a higher energy level than the 4s level.

92. D Engineering stress, σ, is defined as load per area. Here, the load is 500 N and the area is

$$\pi r^2 = 7.85 \text{ mm}^2 = 7.85 \times 10^{-6} \text{ m}^2$$

Then the stress is

$$\sigma = \frac{500 \text{ N}}{7.85 \times 10^{-6}} = 6.36 \times 10^6 \frac{\text{N}}{\text{m}^2} = 6.36 \text{ MN/m}^2$$

93. B For a plain carbon steel containing 0.5 wt. %C, the lever law for amount of pearlite should be drawn in the austenite plus ferrite region, just above the eutectoid temperature. The amount of austenite at this temperature is the amount of pearlite when the austenite is cooled to room temperature:

$$f_\gamma = \frac{0.5 - 0.02}{0.8 - 0.02} \cong \frac{5}{8} \cong 63\%$$

94. B Refer to the phase diagram for steel-carbon.

95. A Reduction in area can be espressed as a fraction:

$$RA = \frac{A_0 - A}{A_0}$$

True strain ϵ, is $\ln\frac{1}{1_0} = \ln\frac{A_0}{A}$. Therefore,

$$\epsilon = \ln\frac{1}{1 - RA} = \ln\frac{1}{0.7} = 0.357$$

96. C Metal is a conductor; free electrons can easily move through it. A semiconductor allows some electrons to move through it. A superconductor has no electrical resistance.

97. B The net moment is equal to the area under the shear diagram. Therefore, area = 48 kN·m, the net moment is 48 kN·m. The area of the trapezoid is equal to the area of the rectangle = 48 kN·m.

98. C For a solid shaft, $\tau = \frac{16\,T}{\pi\,d^3}$. Then

$$T = \frac{\tau\pi d^3}{16} = 596.4 \text{ N·m}$$

99. A Here, M_{max} = 100 N·m. Then:

$$\sigma_{max} = \frac{M_{max}C}{I} = \frac{100(0.03)}{\frac{1}{12}(0.04)(0.06)^3}$$
$$= 4.166 \text{ MPa}$$

100. D Here, V_{max} = 300 N. For a circular cross section,

$$\tau = \frac{4\,V}{3A} = \frac{4(300)}{3\frac{\pi}{4}(0.1)^2} = 50.9 \text{ kPa}$$

101. C The critical load is given by the equation

$$P_{cr} = \frac{\pi^2 EI}{L_e^{\,2}} = \frac{\pi^2 EI}{4^2} = 0.617 \text{ EI}$$

Note that $L_e = 2L = 2(2) = 4$ m.

102. B The normal stress at point A is given by the equation

$$\sigma_A = \frac{Mc}{I} - \frac{P}{A}$$
$$= \frac{(400)(0.02)}{\frac{\pi}{64}(0.04)^4} - \frac{10{,}000}{\frac{\pi}{4}(0.04)^2} = 55.7 \text{ MPa}$$

103. A For each 3-cm-diameter bolt:

$$\tau = \frac{V}{A_s} = \frac{300}{\frac{\pi}{4}(0.03)^2} = 0.424 \text{ MPa}$$

104. D The normal stress in section AB is given by the equation

$$\sigma_{AB} = \frac{P_{AB}}{A_{AB}} = \frac{30{,}000}{\frac{\pi}{4}(0.08)^2} = 5.968 \text{ MPa}$$

105. C $2^0 = 1$
$2^1 = 2$
$2^2 = 4$ $1 + 2 + 4 + 32 = 39$
$2^3 = 8$ or
$2^4 = 16$ 00100111_2
$2^5 = 32$

106. B Use values given for Problem 105. Then:

$$32 + 8 + 4 + 2 + 1 = 47$$

or

101111_2

107. A First time: J = 2 + 4
I = 6
I = 6^2 or 36
Second time: J = 6 + 36 = 42
I = 42
I = 42^2 or 1764
Third time: J > 100

108. D

	A	B	C	D
1	23	24	25	26
2	7	**49**	**49*23=1127**	
3	8	**64**	**64*24=1536**	
4	9	**81**	**81*25=2025**	
5	10	**100**	**100*26=2600**	

109. A Refer to the solution for problem 108 and look at Column C.

110. C A flowchart consists of graphic symbols to show how information would flow through a program running on a computer. Choices (A), (B), and (D) indicate that written instructions are involved. Instructions are expressed as symbols, making choice (C) the correct answer.

111. C Effective annual rate of interest

$$= (1 + \text{rate per month})^n - 1$$
$$= (1 + 0.25)^{12} - 1$$
$$= 14.55 - 1 = 13.55$$
$$= 1{,}355\%$$

112. A Use the following equation:

$$4.00x + 4{,}000 = 1.00x + 40{,}000$$
$$3x = 36{,}000$$
$$x = 12{,}000$$

113. C

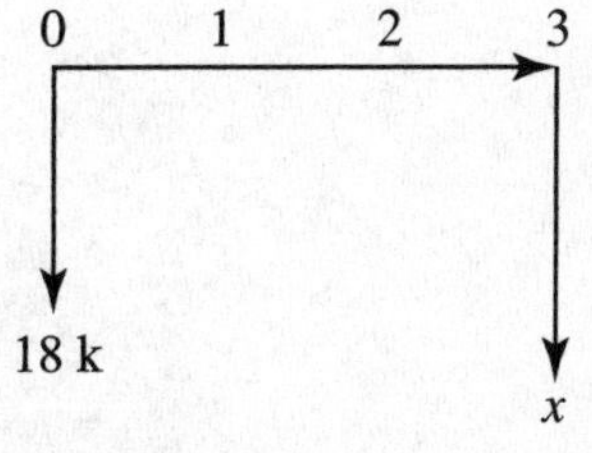

$$x = 18{,}000(F/P, 12, 3)$$
$$= 18{,}000(1.4049) = \$25{,}288$$

114. B

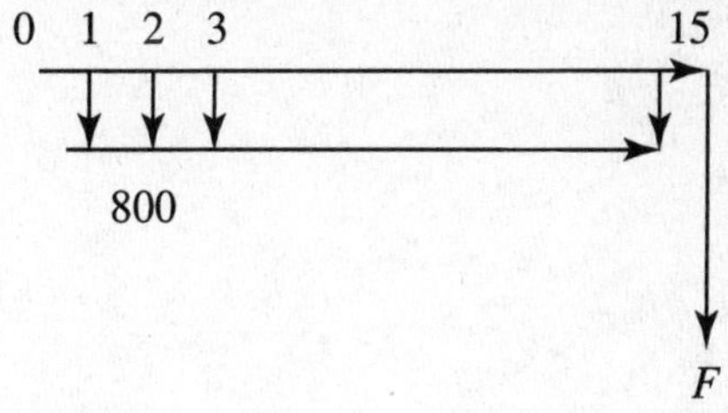

$$F = 800(F/A, 10, 15)$$
$$= 800(31.7725)$$
$$= \$25{,}418$$

115. C

Year	Opening Balance	Depreciation Write-off %	Depreciation	Balance at End of Year
1	25,000	0.20	5,000	20,000
2	20,000	0.32	6,400	13,600
3	13,600	0.192	2,611	10,989
4	10,989	0.115	**1,264**	9,725

116. B Choices (A) and (C) are professional societies representing PEs and specific engineering disciplines including PEs. They do not have power to settle disputes of any nature. Ethics violations are civil suits and could be settled in court; however, the Board of Registration in each state is empowered to handle ethics violations. Choice (B) is the best response.

117. C Insolvency of the bond holder would not release a party. There is no mention of a time constraint; therefore, (A) and (B) are incorrect. Ice recurs based on temperature, not an Act of God, and should be a design consideration. Therefore, (C) is the correct answer.

118. D Choices (B) and (C) are unethical at this point in time. Formal resignation is required but again not now. A discussion with her supervisor is the first step in the process. Choice (D) is the correct response.

119. D The hierarchy of ethical responsibility is stated in the Code of Ethics. Choice (D) is the correct response.

120. A Knowledge transfer does not include replicating a previous design. A contact paid for the original design and ownership resides with the purchaser. The absence of a nondisclosure statement does not make the assignment legitimate. Choices (B), (C), and (D) are not acceptable. Choice (A) is the correct response.

ANSWER SHEET: Afternoon Session

1. Ⓐ Ⓑ Ⓒ Ⓓ	13. Ⓐ Ⓑ Ⓒ Ⓓ	25. Ⓐ Ⓑ Ⓒ Ⓓ	37. Ⓐ Ⓑ Ⓒ Ⓓ	49. Ⓐ Ⓑ Ⓒ Ⓓ
2. Ⓐ Ⓑ Ⓒ Ⓓ	14. Ⓐ Ⓑ Ⓒ Ⓓ	26. Ⓐ Ⓑ Ⓒ Ⓓ	38. Ⓐ Ⓑ Ⓒ Ⓓ	50. Ⓐ Ⓑ Ⓒ Ⓓ
3. Ⓐ Ⓑ Ⓒ Ⓓ	15. Ⓐ Ⓑ Ⓒ Ⓓ	27. Ⓐ Ⓑ Ⓒ Ⓓ	39. Ⓐ Ⓑ Ⓒ Ⓓ	51. Ⓐ Ⓑ Ⓒ Ⓓ
4. Ⓐ Ⓑ Ⓒ Ⓓ	16. Ⓐ Ⓑ Ⓒ Ⓓ	28. Ⓐ Ⓑ Ⓒ Ⓓ	40. Ⓐ Ⓑ Ⓒ Ⓓ	52. Ⓐ Ⓑ Ⓒ Ⓓ
5. Ⓐ Ⓑ Ⓒ Ⓓ	17. Ⓐ Ⓑ Ⓒ Ⓓ	29. Ⓐ Ⓑ Ⓒ Ⓓ	41. Ⓐ Ⓑ Ⓒ Ⓓ	53. Ⓐ Ⓑ Ⓒ Ⓓ
6. Ⓐ Ⓑ Ⓒ Ⓓ	18. Ⓐ Ⓑ Ⓒ Ⓓ	30. Ⓐ Ⓑ Ⓒ Ⓓ	42. Ⓐ Ⓑ Ⓒ Ⓓ	54. Ⓐ Ⓑ Ⓒ Ⓓ
7. Ⓐ Ⓑ Ⓒ Ⓓ	19. Ⓐ Ⓑ Ⓒ Ⓓ	31. Ⓐ Ⓑ Ⓒ Ⓓ	43. Ⓐ Ⓑ Ⓒ Ⓓ	55. Ⓐ Ⓑ Ⓒ Ⓓ
8. Ⓐ Ⓑ Ⓒ Ⓓ	20. Ⓐ Ⓑ Ⓒ Ⓓ	32. Ⓐ Ⓑ Ⓒ Ⓓ	44. Ⓐ Ⓑ Ⓒ Ⓓ	56. Ⓐ Ⓑ Ⓒ Ⓓ
9. Ⓐ Ⓑ Ⓒ Ⓓ	21. Ⓐ Ⓑ Ⓒ Ⓓ	33. Ⓐ Ⓑ Ⓒ Ⓓ	45. Ⓐ Ⓑ Ⓒ Ⓓ	57. Ⓐ Ⓑ Ⓒ Ⓓ
10. Ⓐ Ⓑ Ⓒ Ⓓ	22. Ⓐ Ⓑ Ⓒ Ⓓ	34. Ⓐ Ⓑ Ⓒ Ⓓ	46. Ⓐ Ⓑ Ⓒ Ⓓ	58. Ⓐ Ⓑ Ⓒ Ⓓ
11. Ⓐ Ⓑ Ⓒ Ⓓ	23. Ⓐ Ⓑ Ⓒ Ⓓ	35. Ⓐ Ⓑ Ⓒ Ⓓ	47. Ⓐ Ⓑ Ⓒ Ⓓ	59. Ⓐ Ⓑ Ⓒ Ⓓ
12. Ⓐ Ⓑ Ⓒ Ⓓ	24. Ⓐ Ⓑ Ⓒ Ⓓ	36. Ⓐ Ⓑ Ⓒ Ⓓ	48. Ⓐ Ⓑ Ⓒ Ⓓ	60. Ⓐ Ⓑ Ⓒ Ⓓ

Practice Examination

Afternoon Session

60 Questions

Directions: For each incomplete statement or question, select the answer that best completes the sentence or answers the question. Then fill in the corresponding space on the answer sheet.

Questions 1–3

A weight attached to a spring moves up and down, so that the equation of motion is $\frac{d^2x}{dt^2} + 64x = 0$, where x is the displacement in feet of the weight from its equilibrium position at any time t. Suppose that at $t = 0$ second the displacement is 3 inches $[x(0) = \frac{1}{4}]$ and the velocity is 1 foot per second $[x'(0) = 1]$.

1. The displacement x of the weight at any time t is given by:
(A) $x = -\sin 8t$
(B) $x = \frac{1}{4} \cos 8t + \frac{1}{8} \sin 8t$
(C) $x = 2 \cos 8t$
(D) $x = \cos 8t - \sin 8t$

2. What is the amplitude of motion?
(A) $\frac{1}{4}$ ft
(B) $\frac{1}{3}$ ft
(C) $\frac{\sqrt{3}}{2}$ ft
(D) $\frac{\sqrt{5}}{8}$ ft

3. The period of motion is:
(A) $\frac{\pi}{8}$ sec
(B) $\frac{\pi}{3}$ sec
(C) $\frac{\pi}{2}$ sec
(D) $\frac{\pi}{4}$ sec

Questions 4–6

A function f is defined by a determinant as follows:

$$f(x) = \begin{vmatrix} 2x^2 & x \\ 8 & 2 \end{vmatrix}$$

4. The x-intercept(s) of the graph of this function is (are):
(A) 1
(B) −3
(C) 0 and 2
(D) 2 and −2

5. What is the minimum value of this function?
(A) −4
(B) −2
(C) 1
(D) 0

6. The area bounded by this curve and the x-axis is:
(A) 1 square unit
(B) 3 square units
(C) $\frac{16}{3}$ square units
(D) $\frac{32}{3}$ square units

Questions 7–9

Vectors **A** and **B** are defined as follows:

$$\mathbf{A} = 2\mathbf{i} - 2\mathbf{j} - \mathbf{k}, \mathbf{B} = \mathbf{i} - \mathbf{k}$$

7. The dot product of vectors **A** and **B** is:
(A) 12
(B) 3
(C) −6
(D) 0

8. What is the magnitude of the cross product of vectors **A** and **B**?
(A) 7
(B) 12
(C) 1
(D) 3

9. The angle between vectors **A** and **B** is:
(A) 45°
(B) 38°
(C) 105°
(D) 97°

Questions 10–12

An area in Quadrant I is bounded by $y = x^3$, $x = 2$, and the x-axis.

10. What is the area of this region?
(A) 6 square units
(B) 8 square units
(C) 4 square units
(D) 2 square units

11. The volume generated by revolving this area about the y-axis is:
(A) 8π cubic units
(B) 14π cubic units
(C) $\frac{64\pi}{5}$ cubic units
(D) $\frac{8\pi}{3}$ cubic units

12. The first moment of this area with respect to the x-axis is:
(A) 6
(B) $\frac{64}{7}$
(C) $\frac{46}{5}$
(D) $\frac{13}{2}$

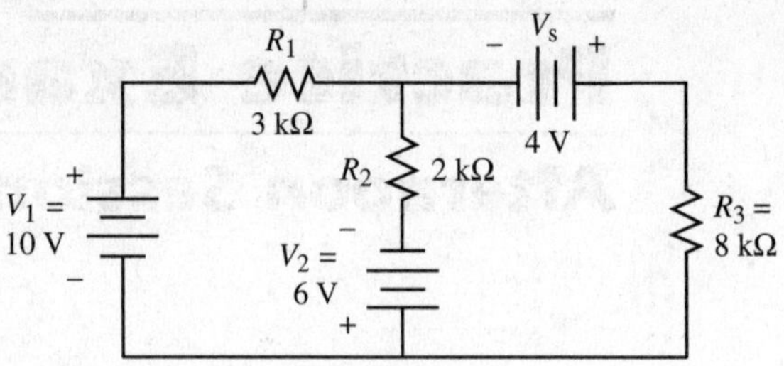

13. What is the power dissipated by R_3 in the circuit shown in the diagram?
(A) 3.42 mW
(B) 2.18 mW
(C) 1.83 mW
(D) 5.76 mW

Questions 14 and 15 relate to the figure shown below.

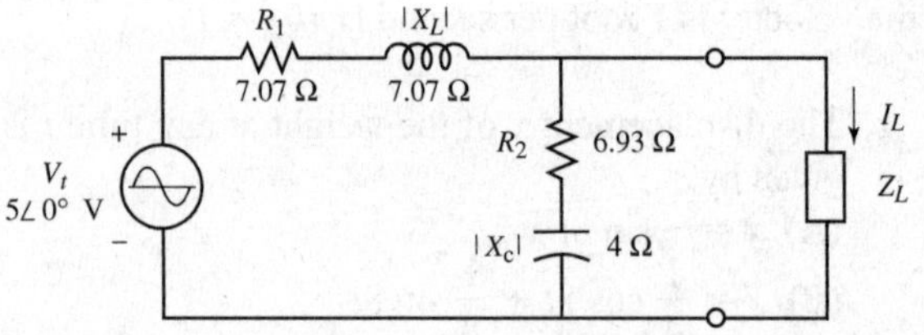

14. Determine the Thévenin equivalent circuit, V_{Th} and Z_{Th}, for the load impedance, Z_L, in the circuit.
(A) 5.51 $\angle 32.2°$ V; 3.67 $\angle -17.4°$ Ω
(B) 2.79 $\angle -42.4°$ V; 5.58 $\angle 2.63°$ Ω
(C) 1.9 $\angle$ 63.4° V; 4.12 $\angle -31.5°$ Ω
(D) 3.47 $\angle -17.8°$ V; 7.83 $\angle 8.9°$ Ω

15. What is the load current, I_L, if the load impedance is $(5 - j7)$ Ω?
(A) 0.223 $\angle -9.87°$ A
(B) $(1.24 + j0.84)$ A
(C) 0.517 $\angle -21.3°$ A
(D) $(3.13 + j1.87)$ A

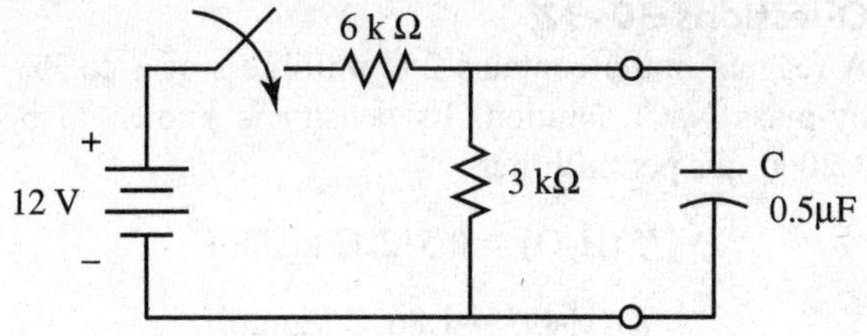

16. For the circuit shown in the diagram, how long will the capacitor take to charge to 2 volts after the switch is closed? The initial voltage across the capacitor is 0 volt.
(A) 2.33 ms
(B) 1.86 ms
(C) 0.318 ms
(D) 0.693 ms

Questions 17 and 18 relate to the figure shown below.

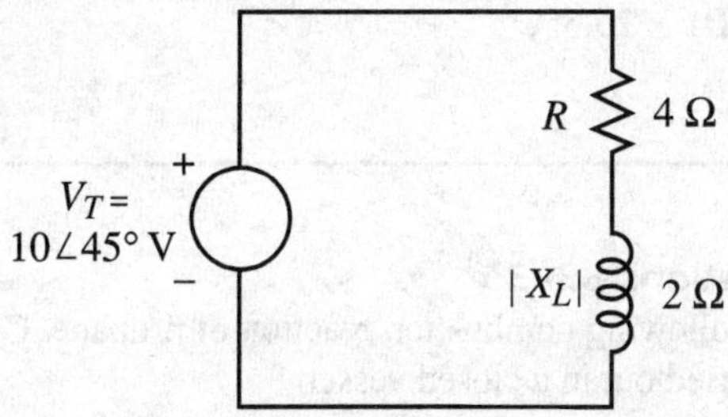

17. The total volt amperes (VA) for the circuit are:
(A) $(15.3 + j12)$ VA
(B) $18.6 \angle -16.4°$ VA
(C) $22.4 \angle -26.6°$ VA
(D) $(19 - j4.3)$ VA

18. If the frequency of the source is 400 hertz, what capacitor value must be connected in series with *R* and *L* so that the circuit has unity power factor?
(A) 87.3 μF
(B) 26.6 μF
(C) 142 μF
(D) 199 μF

Questions 19–21 relate to the figure shown below.

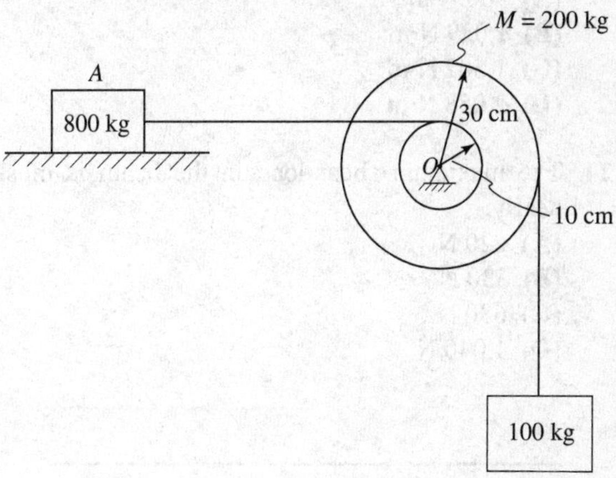

19. The minimum coefficient of static friction between block *A* and the surface is most nearly:
(A) 0.3
(B) 0.375
(C) 1
(D) 0.5

20. The resultant bearing reaction at *O* is most nearly:
(A) 2,943 N
(B) 424 N
(C) 141 N
(D) 4,162 N

21. The tension in the cable connected to block *A* is most nearly:
(A) 2,943 N
(B) 300 N
(C) 100 N
(D) 981 N

Questions 22–24 relate to the figure shown below.

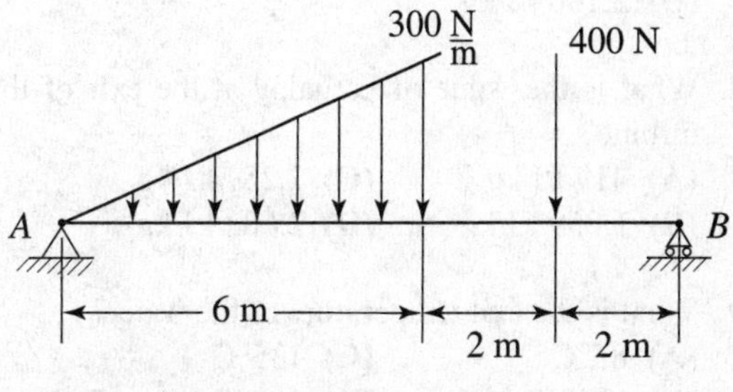

22. The reaction at point *B* is most nearly:
(A) 350 N
(B) 680 N
(C) 1,040 N
(D) 450 N

23. The maximum moment in the beam is most nearly:
(A) 900 N·m
(B) 1,029 N·m
(C) 1,507 N·m
(D) 2,058 N·m

24. The maximum shear load in the beam is most nearly:
(A) 620 N
(B) 330 N
(C) 680 N
(D) 1,040 N

Questions 25–29

Steam enters an adiabatic turbine at 1 megapascal and 300°C and expands to atmospheric pressure. The turbine efficiency is 80%.

25. What would the temperature of the water exiting the turbine be if the turbine were ideal?
(A) 60°C
(B) 80°C
(C) 100°C
(D) 120°C

26. What would be the approximate work output of an ideal turbine with the same inlet and exit conditions of water?
(A) 375 kJ/kg
(B) 461 kJ/kg
(C) 789 kJ/kg
(D) 2,632 kJ/kg

27. What is the approximate actual work of this turbine?
(A) 369 kJ/kg
(B) 461 kJ/kg
(C) 576 kJ/kg
(D) 2,100 kJ/kg

28. What is the value of enthalpy at the exit of this turbine?
(A) 419 kJ/kg
(B) 1,859 kJ/kg
(C) 2,257 kJ/kg
(D) 2,682 kJ/kg

29. What is the exit temperature of the water?
(A) 85°C
(B) 103°C
(C) 135°C
(D) 183°C

Questions 30–32

A reagent bottle contains 250 milliliters of a 26.3%-by-mass NaCl solution. Its density is known to be 1.20 grams per milliliter.

$$K_b(H_2O) = 0.512°C·kg/mol$$

$$K_f(H_2O) = 1.86°C·kg/mol$$

30. What is the molal concentration of the solution?
(A) 0.539 m
(B) 3.75 m
(C) 6.10 m
(D) 26.3 m

31. What is the boiling point of this solution?
(A) 106.2°C
(B) 102.6°C
(C) 101.9°C
(D) 98.5°C

32. What is the freezing point of this solution?
(A) −6.25°C
(B) −10.0°C
(C) −20.0°C
(D) −25.5°C

Questions 33–35

The following combustion reaction of propane, C_3H_8, is carried out in a closed vessel:

$$C_3H_8(g) + 5O_2(g) \rightarrow 4H_2O(l) + 3CO_2(g)$$

33. How many grams of CO_2 will be produced from 88.0 grams of propane and 360 grams of oxygen?
(A) 88.0 g
(B) 132 g
(C) 176 g
(D) 264 g

34. The limiting reagent is:
(A) propane
(B) oxygen
(C) water
(D) carbon dioixde

35. How many grams of oxygen will remain at the end of the reaction?
(A) 20.0 g
(B) 40.0 g
(C) 60.0 g
(D) 80.0 g

Questions 36–38

A mother is pulling her child, seated on a sled, at a constant speed of 2.5 feet per second up a snow-covered incline that is 10° from the horizontal. The mass of the child plus the sled is 50.0 pounds mass, and the kinetic friction coefficient between the sled and snow surfaces is 0.1. The mother pulls with a force that is constantly directed at 20° from the inclined surface.

36. The magnitude of the mother's pulling force is necessarily:
(A) 8.9 lbf **(C)** 17.8 lbf
(B) 6.6 lbf **(D)** 14.0 lbf

37. The friction force acting on the sled is nearly:
(A) 13.1 lbf **(C)** 5.3 lbf
(B) 4.5 lbf **(D)** 6.6 lbf

38. The work done by the pulling force for a 120.0-foot displacement of the sled along the incline is approximately
(A) 1,580 ft-lbf **(C)** 660 ft-lbf
(B) 0 **(D)** 1,680 ft-lbf

Questions 39–41

A flying-trapeze acrobat jumps off a platform while holding onto an inextensible rope having a length of 25.0 feet. As indicated in the diagram below, the mass of the acrobat is 130.0 pounds mass, and he swings from the rope at point *A* with an initial tangential velocity of 3.0 feet per second. The effects of rope friction at the hinge point and of wind resistance are considered negligible.

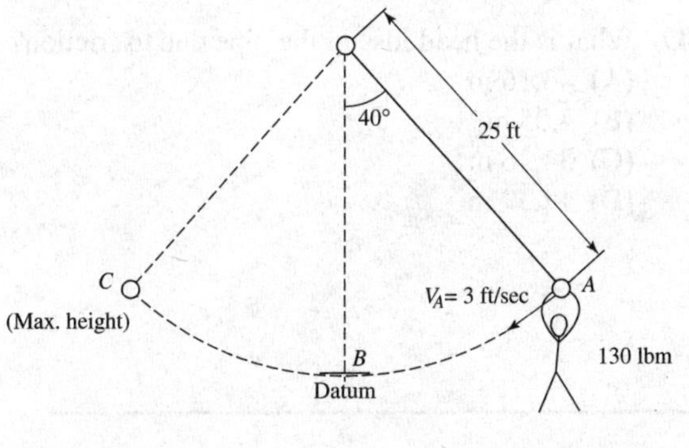

39. The speed of the acrobat at elevation datum point *B* should be:
(A) 25.8 ft/sec
(B) 61.3 ft/sec
(C) 8.7 ft/sec
(D) 19.6 ft/sec

40. What is the angular velocity of the rope when the acrobat's normal acceleration is 1.0 foot per second squared?
(A) 0.2 rad/sec
(B) 6.7 rad/sec
(C) 2.5 rad/sec
(D) 0.88 rad/sec

41. When the acrobat has swung to the maximum height at point *C*, the elevation of the free end of the rope above the datum is:
(A) 0.8 ft
(B) 0.15 ft
(C) 6.0 ft
(D) 1.6 ft

Questions 42–45 relate to the figure shown below.

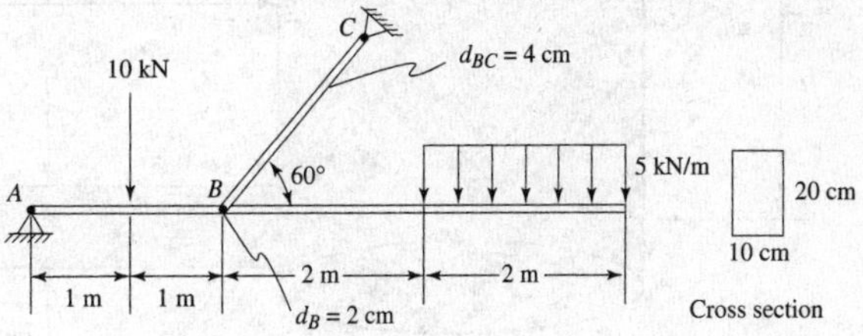

42. The average normal stress in bar *BC* is most nearly:
(A) 10 MPa
(B) 28.8 MPa
(C) 27.56 MPa
(D) 120 MPa

43. The maximum bending stress in the beam is most nearly:
(A) 180 MPa
(B) 30 MPa
(C) 90 MPa
(D) 15 MPa

44. The average shear stress in the pin at B (double shear) is most nearly:
(A) 55.6 MPa
(B) 55.13 MPa
(C) 87.8 MPa
(D) 25 MPa

45. The maximum transverse shear stress in the beam is most nearly:
(A) 3.75 MPa
(B) 4.5 MPa
(C) 1.5 MPa
(D) 3 MPa

Questions 46–49

Water flows from the tank shown in the diagram through a cast-iron pipe that is 75 meters long and has a 10-centimeter inside diameter. The jet of water leaving the pipe is expected to turn a turbine. The turbine operates most efficiently when the horizontal force (F_x) on the blade is at least 100 newtons. (The density of water is 1,000 kg/m^3, and its viscosity is 8×10^{-4} N·s/m^2. The roughness for cast-iron pipe is 0.25 mm.)

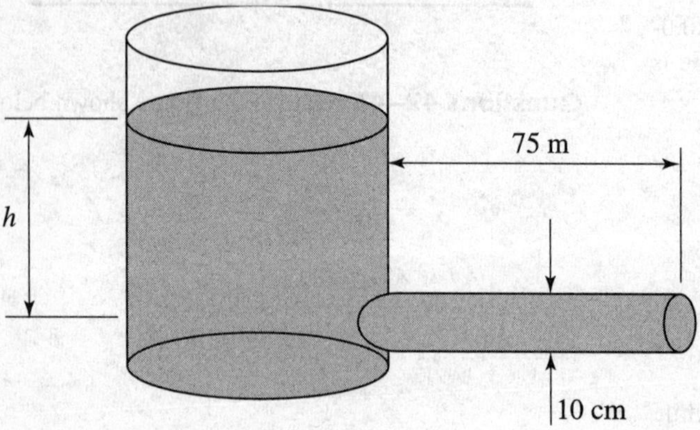

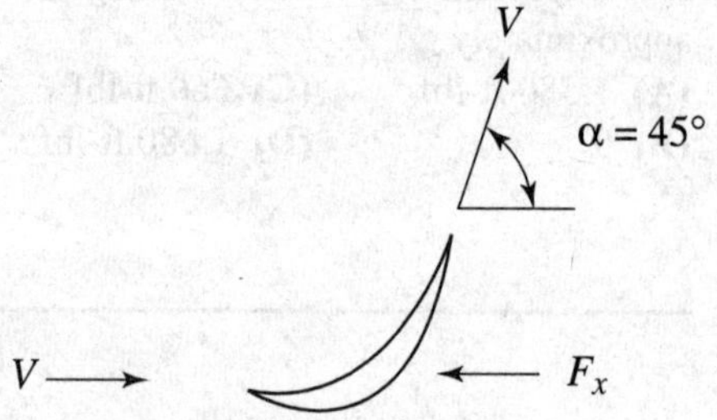

46. What should the velocity of the water leaving the pipe be in order to produce a horizontal force of 100 newtons?
(A) 6.59 m/s
(B) 8.00 m/s
(C) 8.50 m/s
(D) 5.44 m/s

47. What is the Reynolds number of the water at this velocity?
(A) 1.00×10^{-6}
(B) 6.80×10^{-5}
(C) 5.30×10^{-5}
(D) 1.06×10^{-5}

48. What is the friction factor for this water velocity and this pipe?
(A) 0.25
(B) 0.026
(C) 0.05
(D) 0.018

49. What is the head loss in the pipe due to friction?
(A) 43.16 m
(B) 4.05 m
(C) 34.36 m
(D) 12.37 m

50. The crystal structure of iron at room temperature is:
(A) FCC
(B) BCC
(C) HCP
(D) BCT

51. When carbon is dissolved in iron to a concentration of 0.5 weight percent carbon and the alloy is heated to 900°C, what phase is present?
(A) ferrite
(B) austenite
(C) pearlite
(D) martensite

52. What is (are) present in the alloy described in Problem 51 after it cools slowly to 720°C from 900°C?
(A) ferrite
(B) ferrite and pearlite
(C) austenite
(D) martensite

53. The diffusion coefficient of carbon in iron at 720°C is:
(A) 4.4×10^{-13} cm^2/s
(B) 2.4×10^{-7} cm^2/s
(C) 2.7×10^{-9} cm^2/s
(D) 8.5×10^{-11} cm^2/s

54. What is the most common number of bits per byte?
(A) 2
(B) 4
(C) 8
(D) 16

55. What is 17 in straight binary code?
(A) 10000
(B) 10001
(C) 1111
(D) 1001

56. How many times will the second line of the following program be executed?

```
              D = 38
LOOPSTART     D = D-1
              F = INTEGER PART OF (D/2)
              IF F > 12, THEN GO TO
                LOOPSTART, OTHERWISE
                GO TO END
END           PRINT "DONE"
```

(A) 14
(B) 13
(C) 9
(D) 17

57. An unlicensed engineer interviews for a position as Director of Plant Operations at a university. On his resume, he states that he is a member of the National Society of Professional Engineers (NSPE) and includes his membership number. He is, in fact, an associate member of NSPE. Does his claim that he is a member violate the Engineers' code of ethics?
(A) Yes. It implies that he is a licensed engineer.
(B) No. He was implying membership, not licensure.
(C) Yes. A member number could be construed as a PE registration number.
(D) No. He was indicating professional society involvement.

58. A forensic engineer accepts a retainer from an attorney for a plaintiff and receives selected documentation from the attorney. Subsequently the engineer bills for work that includes a review of the case documentation. Still later, because of a disagreement with the attorney, she ceases to perform the work without delivering a report to the attorney or receiving any additional payment for her services. Thereafter, the engineer returns the full retainer fee to the attorney and all of the file documentation provided earlier. Several months later, the engineer is approached by the defense attorneys in the same case and accepts an assignment to function as an expert for the defense in the same legal dispute. Was it ethical for the engineer to accept the assignment?
(A) No. She drew no conclusions during the first review of the material.
(B) Yes. She returned all moneys paid to her.
(C) No. She did not have the consent of all concerned parties.
(D) Yes. Several months passed before she was approached by the defense attorneys.

59. Superior Air Flights is considering the purchase of a helicopter to connect service between its base airport and a new field being built about 25 miles away. The choppers are assumed to be needed for only 6 years until a rapid transit service is completed. Estimates for the two craft under consideration are as follows:

	Whirl 2B	ROT8
First cost	\$95,000	\$120,000
Annual maintenance	\$3,000	\$9,000
Salvage value	\$12,000	\$25,000
Life in years	3	6

What is the annual cost advantage of selecting ROT8?
(A) $0
(B) $700
(C) $2,100
(D) $4,216

60. It costs Superior Air Flights $1,200 to run a particular flight, empty or full. Additionally, each passenger generates costs of $40. Regular tickets sell for $90. A plane holds 65 people, but each flight carries only about 35 passengers. The Marketing Manager proposes to sell special tickets for $50 to people not normally flying this route. He thinks he can sell 15 additional seats for each flight without cutting into the regular business. If he is correct, how much will the total profit on this flight be?
(A) $200
(B) $500
(C) $700
(D) $1,000

Answer Key

Afternoon Session

1. B
2. D
3. D
4. C
5. A
6. C
7. B
8. D
9. A
10. C
11. C
12. B
13. C
14. B
15. A
16. D
17. C
18. D
19. B
20. D
21. A
22. B
23. D
24. C
25. C
26. B
27. A
28. D
29. B
30. C
31. A
32. C
33. D
34. A
35. B
36. D
37. B
38. A
39. D
40. A
41. C
42. C
43. A
44. B
45. A
46. A
47. C
48. B
49. A
50. B
51. B
52. B
53. B
54. C
55. B
56. B
57. A
58. C
59. D
60. C

Diagnostic Chart

Afternoon Session Practice Exam

				Reason for Incorrect Answer			
Subject Area	*Total Number of Questions*	*Number Correct*	*Number Incorrect*	*Lack of Knowledge*	*Misread Problem*	*Careless or Mathematical Error*	*Wrong Guess*
Mathematics (1–12)	12						
Electric Circuits (13–18)	6						
Statics (19–24)	6						
Thermodynamics (25–29)	5						
Chemistry (30–35)	6						
Dynamics (36–41)	6						
Mechanics of Materials (42–45)	4						
Fluid Mechanics (46–49)	4						
Materials Science (50–53)	4						
Computers (54–56)	3						
Ethics (57–58)	2						
Economics (59–60)	2						
Total	60						

Answers Explained

1. B The solutions of the auxiliary equation $m^2 + 64 = 0$ are $\pm 8i$. Hence:

$$x = c_1 \cos 8t + c_2 \sin 8t \text{ and}$$
$$x' = -8c_1 \sin 8t + 8c_2 \cos 8t$$

The initial condition $x(0) = \frac{1}{4}$ implies $c_1 = \frac{1}{4}$, and the initial condition $x'(0) = 1$ implies $c_2 = \frac{1}{8}$. Thus, the displacement of the weight at any time t is given by

$$x = \frac{1}{4} \cos 8t + \frac{1}{8} \sin 8t$$

2. D The amplitude of motion is $\sqrt{c_1{}^2 + c_2{}^2}$

$$= \sqrt{\left(\frac{1}{4}\right)^2 + \left(\frac{1}{8}\right)^2} = \frac{\sqrt{5}}{8} \text{ ft.}$$

3. D The period of motion is $\frac{2\pi}{\omega} = \frac{2\pi}{8} = \frac{\pi}{4}$ secs.

4. C The function f may be rewritten as $f(x) = 4x^2 - 8x$. The x-intercepts of the graph of f are the real solutions of the quadratic equation $4x^2 - 8x = 0$. Hence, the x-intercepts are 0 and 2.

5. A For $f(x) = 4x^2 - 8x$:

$$f'(x) = 8x - 8 \quad \text{and} \quad f''(x) = 8$$

Solving yields $f'(x) = 0$, which implies $x = 1$. Since $f''(1) = 8 > 0$, there is a minimum at $x = 1$, and this minimum value is $f(1) = -4$.

6. C Area $= \int_0^2 [0 - (4x^2 - 8x)]\, dx$

$$= -\frac{4x^3}{3} + 4x^2 \Big|_0^2 = \frac{16}{3} \text{ square units.}$$

7. B $\mathbf{A} \cdot \mathbf{B} = (2)(1) + (-2)(0) + (-1)(-1) = 3.$

8. D $\mathbf{A} \times \mathbf{B} = \begin{vmatrix} \mathbf{i} & \mathbf{j} & \mathbf{k} \\ 2 & -2 & -1 \\ 1 & 0 & -1 \end{vmatrix} = \mathbf{i}\begin{vmatrix} -2 & -1 \\ 1 & 1 \end{vmatrix}$

$$+\mathbf{j}\begin{vmatrix} 2 & -1 \\ 1 & -1 \end{vmatrix} + \mathbf{k}\begin{vmatrix} 2 & -2 \\ 1 & 0 \end{vmatrix} = 2\mathbf{i} - \mathbf{j} + 2\mathbf{k}.$$

Hence, $|\mathbf{A} \times \mathbf{B}| = \sqrt{2^2 + (-1)^2 + 2^2} = 3.$

9. A Angle $\theta = \cos^{-1}\left(\frac{\mathbf{A} \cdot \mathbf{B}}{|\mathbf{A}||\mathbf{B}|}\right) = \cos^{-1} \frac{1}{\sqrt{2}} = 45°.$

10. C Area $= \int_0^2 x^3\, dx = \frac{x^4}{4}\Big|_0^2 = 4$ square units.

11. C Take the volume of the outer cylinder, and subtract from it the volume of the hollowed-out region:

$$\text{Volume} = \pi(2)^2(8) - \pi\int_0^8 (\sqrt[3]{y})^2\, dy$$
$$= 32\pi - \frac{3\pi}{5} y^{5/3}\Big|_0^8 = \frac{64\pi}{5} \text{ cubic units.}$$

12. B $M_x = \int_0^8 y(2 - \sqrt[3]{y})\, dy$

$$= \int_0^8 (2y - y^{4/3})dy = y^2 - \frac{3}{7}y^{7/3}\Big|_0^8 = \frac{64}{7}.$$

13. C Apply Kirchhoff's voltage law to both loops:

Loop A includes V_1, V_2, R_1, and R_2.
Loop B includes V_2, V_3, R_2, and R_3.

Choose a clockwise direction for loop currents. Then:

Loop A: $5I_A - 2I_B = 10\text{ V} + 6\text{ V}$
Loop B: $-2I_A + 10I_B = -6\text{ V} + 4\text{ V}$

Solve for I_B:

$$I_B = \frac{\begin{vmatrix} 5 & 16 \\ -2 & -2 \end{vmatrix}}{\begin{vmatrix} 5 & -2 \\ -2 & 10 \end{vmatrix}} = \frac{-10 + 32}{50 - 4} = 0.478 \text{ mA}$$

Apply eq. 4.9:

$$P = I_B^2 \times R_3 = (0.478 \text{ mA})^2 \times 8 \text{ k}\Omega = 1.83 \text{ mW}$$

14. B The Thévenin equivalent voltage is determined by using the voltage division law:

$$V_{Th} = \frac{Z_2}{Z_1 + Z_2} \times V_T$$

$$= \frac{(6.93 - j4)\ \Omega}{(7.07 + j7.07)\ \Omega + (6.93 - j4)\ \Omega} \times 5\angle 0°\ \text{V} = 2.79\angle -42.4°\ \text{V}$$

The Thévenin equivalent impedance is determined as follows:

$$Z_{Th} = \frac{Z_1 \times Z_2}{Z_1 + Z_2}$$

$$= \frac{(7.07 + j7.07)\ \Omega \times (6.93 - j4)\ \Omega}{(7.07 + j7.07)\ \Omega + (6.93 - j4)\ \Omega}$$

$$= (5.57 + j0.256)\ \Omega = 5.58\angle 2.63°\ \Omega$$

15. A Use the Thévenin equivalent values to obtain the load current:

$$I_L = \frac{V_{Th}}{Z_{Th} + Z_L}$$

$$= \frac{2.79\angle 42.4°\ \text{V}}{(5.57 + j0.256)\ \Omega + (5 - j7)\ \Omega}$$

$$= 0.223\angle -9.87°\ \text{A}$$

16. D The maximum or final voltage the capacitor could charge to is

$$V_f = \frac{3\ \text{k}\Omega}{6\ \text{k}\Omega + 3\ \text{k}\Omega} \times 12\ \text{V} = 4\ \text{V}$$

The resistance "seen" by the capacitor is

$$R = \frac{3\ \text{k}\Omega \times 6\ \text{k}\Omega}{3\ \text{k}\Omega + 6\ \text{k}\Omega} = 2\ \text{k}\Omega$$

The time constant for this circuit is $\tau = 2\ \text{k}\Omega \times 0.5\ \mu\text{F} = 1.0\ \text{ms}$.

Apply eq. 4.33:

$$2\ \text{V} = 4\ \text{V}(1 - e^{-t/\tau})$$

Substitute for τ and solve for t:

$$t = 0.693\ \text{ms}.$$

17. C Solve for the load current:

$$I_L = \frac{10\angle 45°\ \text{V}}{(4 + j2)\ \Omega} = 2.24\angle 18.4°\ \text{A}$$

The phase angle from voltage to current is 26.6° (45° − 18.4°).

Apply eqs. 4.45 and 4.46:

$$P = 10\ \text{V} \times 2.24\ \text{V} \times \cos(26.6°) = 20\ \text{W}$$
$$Q = 10\ \text{V} \times 2.24\ \text{A} \times \sin(26.6°) = 10\ \text{VAR}$$

For an inductive circuit the power factor is lagging, so applying eq. 4.47:

$$S = (20 - j10)\ \text{VA} = 22.4\angle -26.6°\ \text{VA}$$

18. D $X_L = X_C = \frac{1}{\omega C} = 2\ \Omega$

Solve for C:

$$C = \frac{1}{(2\ \Omega)(2\pi)(400\ \text{Hz})} = 199\ \mu\text{F}$$

19. B Use the FBD of the pulley, and take the moment about its center:

$$T(10) = 981(30) \qquad T = 2{,}943\ \text{N}$$

Use the FBD of the block.

Then:

$$\Sigma F_x = 0 \qquad F = T = 2{,}943\ \text{N}$$

$$\Sigma F_y = 0 \qquad N = 800(9.81) = 7{,}848\ \text{N}$$

$$\mu_s = \frac{F}{N} = \frac{2{,}943}{7{,}848} = 0.375$$

20. D $O = \sqrt{(2{,}943)^2 + (2{,}943)^2} = 4{,}162\ \text{N}$

21. A Refer to the solution to Problem 19: $T = 2{,}943$ N.

22. B $\Sigma M_A = 0 \qquad B(10) - 400(8) - 900(4) = 0$
$B = 680$ N

23. D Draw the shear and bending-moment diagrams. The maximum moment will occur about 4.98 m to the left of point A, where shear is equal to 0.

The equation for the shear in the section where the distributed load is acting is

$$V = -25x^2 + 620x$$

and the equation for the bending moment in the same section is

$$M = \frac{-25}{3}x^3 + 620$$

Then:

$$M_{max} = 2{,}058\ \text{N·m}$$

24. C The maximum shear load can be determined from the shear diagram drawn for Problem 23. But by inspection the maximum shear load is equal to the reaction at B, which is 680 N. Then:

$$V_{max} = 680 \text{ N}$$

25. C From the superheated steam tables at the end of Chapter 12, the value of entropy at the entrance state of the turbine is 7.1229 kJ/kg·K. Since normal atmospheric pressure is 101.35 kPa, the table for superheated steam at 100 kPa will provide values very close to those expected at atmospheric pressure. Since the value of entropy for saturated vapor at this pressure is greater than the value at the turbine inlet, some condensation will occur. Therefore, the temperature of the exiting stream of water will be equal to the saturation temperature of water at atmospheric pressure, or 100°C.

26. B Turbine work is determined using eq. 12.77:

$$\dot{W} = \dot{m}(h_i - h_e) \quad \text{or} \quad w = (h_i - h_e)$$

The value of enthalpy in the inlet is taken from the superheated steam table:

$$h_i = 3051.2 \text{ kJ/kg}$$

To find the value of enthalpy in the outlet stream of an ideal turbine, the quality of the exit stream for the ideal turbine must be determined. Use eq. 12.66d:

$$s_{mix} = s_f + x(s_g - s_f) \quad \text{or} \quad x = \frac{(s_{mix} - s_f)}{(s_g - s_f)}$$

Find the values of s_f and s_g using the saturated water table:

$$s_f = 1.3069 \text{ kJ/kg·K}, \qquad s_g = 7.3549 \text{ kJ/kg·K}$$

In this case, the value of s_{mix} is equal to the value of entropy in the inlet stream of the turbine:

$$s_{mix} = 7.1229 \text{ kJ/kg·K}$$

Substitute known values:

$$x = \frac{s_{mix} - s_f}{s_g - s_f} = \frac{\left(7.1229 \frac{\text{kJ}}{\text{kg·K}} - 1.3069 \frac{\text{kJ}}{\text{kg·K}}\right)}{\left(7.3549 \frac{\text{kJ}}{\text{kg·K}} - 1.3069 \frac{\text{kJ}}{\text{kg·K}}\right)} = 0.962$$

Using this value for quality, determine the value of enthalpy for the exit stream of the ideal turbine by applying eq. 12.66c, where $h_e = h_{mix}$:

$$h_e = h_f + x(h_g - h_f)$$

Find the values of h_f and h_g using the saturated water table:

$$h_f = 419.04 \text{ kJ/kg}, \qquad h_g = 2{,}676.1 \text{ kJ/kg}$$

Then:

$$h_e = 419.04 \frac{\text{kJ}}{\text{kg}} + 0.962\left(2{,}676.1 \frac{\text{kJ}}{\text{kg}} - 419.04 \frac{\text{kJ}}{\text{kg}}\right) = 2590.3 \text{ kJ/kg}$$

The work produced in an ideal turbine under these conditions is:

$$\dot{w} = (h_I - h_e) = \left(3{,}051.2 \frac{\text{kJ}}{\text{kg}} - 2{,}590.3 \frac{\text{kJ}}{\text{kg}}\right) = 460.9 \text{ kJ/kg}$$

27. A Turbine efficiency as given is defined as the amount of work a turbine produces, divided by the amount of work produced in an ideal turbine operating at the same conditions:

$$\eta_{turb} = \frac{w_{real}}{w_{ideal}}$$

Then:

$$w_{real} = (\eta_{turb})(w_{ideal}) = (0.80)\left(461 \frac{\text{kJ}}{\text{kg}}\right) = 368.8 \text{ kJ/kg}$$

28. D Determine the value of enthalpy for the exit state of the real turbine as follows:

$$w = (h_i - h_e)$$
$$h_e = h_i - w = 3{,}051.2 \frac{\text{kJ}}{\text{kg}} - 368.8 \frac{\text{kJ}}{\text{kg}} = 2{,}682.4 \text{ kJ/kg}$$

29. B Use the 100 kPa (0.10 MPa) section of the saturated steam table and the value of enthalpy determined for Problem 28 to find the outlet temperature of the turbine.

	Temperature (°C)	*Enthalpy*
Saturated steam table at 100 kPa	100	2,676.2
Exit state of real turbine	t_e	2,682.4
Saturated steam table at 100 kPa	150	2,776.4

Use linear interpolation to generate a more accurate estimate of t_e:

$$\frac{t_e - 100}{150 - 100} = \frac{2{,}682.4 - 2{,}676.2}{2{,}776.4 - 2{,}676.2}$$

$$t_e = (150 - 100)\left(\frac{2{,}682.4 - 2{,}676.2}{2{,}776.4 - 2{,}676.2}\right) + 100$$

$$= 103.1°\text{C}$$

30. C Use the factor-label method. Remember to distinguish among solute, solvent, and solution.

$$\frac{(26.3\ \text{g NaCl})}{(100\ \text{g sol'n})}\frac{(100\ \text{g sol'n})}{(73.7\ \text{g H}_2\text{O})}\frac{(1.0\ \text{mol NaCl})}{(58.5\ \text{g NaCl})}\frac{(1{,}000\ \text{g H}_2\text{O})}{(1.0\ \text{kg H}_2\text{O})} = 6.10\ \text{m}$$

31. A Use eq. 1.10, and substitute the molality calculated for Problem 30. The van't Hoff factor $i = 2$ for NaCl (a strong electrolyte), and $K_b(H_2O)$ is given in the introductory data for Problems 30–32.

32. C Use eq. 1.11, and substitute the known molality and i values. $K_f(H_2O)$ is given in the introductory data for Problems 30–32.

33. D Since amounts of *both* reactants are given, the limiting reagent must be determined. First:

$88.0\ \text{g}\ C_3H_8 = 2.0\ \text{mol}\ C_3H_8$ and

$360\ \text{g}\ O_2 = 11.25\ \text{mol}\ O_2$

The ratio of propane to oxygen is 1 mol to 5 mol in the balanced reaction. Since 2 mol C_3H_8 are actually present, 10 mol O_2 are required to completely react with the propane. However, 11.25 mol O_2 are actually present and available for reaction. Hence, O_2 is present in excess while C_3H_8 is in short supply and hence is the limiting reagent.

Use the factor-label method, and start with the limiting reagent, since it determines the maximum product yield:

$$2.0\ \text{mol}\ C_3H_8 \frac{(3\ \text{mol}\ CO_2)}{(1.0\ \text{mol}\ C_3H_8)}\frac{(44.0\ \text{g}\ CO_2)}{(1.0\ \text{mol}\ CO_2)} = 264\ \text{g}\ CO_2$$

34. A The limiting reagent was evaluated in Problem 33 as C_3H_8 (propane).

35. B Find the amount of O_2 that will remain after the reaction as follows:

11.25 mol (initially present)
− 10.0 mol (used up)
= 1.25 mol (left over)

Convert moles into grams: 1.25 mol O_2 is 40.0 g O_2.

36. D Use the inclined and normal coordinate system. Consider child plus sled as a combined free body. Draw the FBD of the child/sled system, and identify external forces: normal reaction N_R, weight W, pulling force F_p, and kinetic friction F_{FK}.

Solve F_p using Newton's second law (let the positive inclined direction be along the 10° upward slope).

$\Sigma F_I = ma_I$ Since the speed along the incline is constant, $a_I = 0$ and $\Sigma F_I = 0$.

Also, $F_p \cos 20° - F_{FK} - W_I = 0$

$0.94F_p - 0.1N_R - W \sin 10° = 0$

Then:

$$0.94F_p - 0.1N_R - (50.0\ \text{lbf})(0.174) = 0 \quad \text{(eq. I)}$$

$$\Sigma F_n = 0$$

$$F_p \sin 20° + N_R - (50.0\ \text{lbf}) \cos 10° = 0$$

Then:

$$0.342F_p + N_R - 49.24\ \text{lbf} = 0 \quad \text{(eq. II)}$$

Solve eqs. I and II simulataneously for N_R:

$$N_R = \frac{0.94F_p - 8.68}{0.1} = 9.4F_p - 86.8$$

Substitute into II:

$$0.342F_p + (9.4F_p - 86.8) - 49.24 = 0$$

$$F_p = \frac{136.04}{9.74} = 13.96 \text{ lbf} \approx 14.0 \text{ lbf}$$

37. B The kinetic friction force acting on the sled is $0.1N_R$. Use the value of F_p obtained for Problem 36: $N_R = 9.4(14.0 \text{ lb}) - 86.8 = 44.8$ lbf.

$$F_{FK} = 0.1(44.8) = 4.48 \text{ lbf}$$

38. A Work done by pulling force F_p for a 120.0-ft displacement:

$$W_{1\to2} = (F_{pl})(\Delta l) = (14.0 \text{ lb})\cos 20°(120.0 \text{ ft}) = 1{,}578.7 \text{ ft-lbf} \approx 1{,}580 \text{ ft-lbf}$$

39. D Employ the conservation of energy equation between points A and B. Since the elevation datum is at B, potential energy at B is 0. The equation is:

$$KE_A + PE_A = KE_B + PE_B$$

Solve KE_B, and then obtain velocity V_B.

$$\frac{1}{2}(130.0 \text{ lbm})(3.0 \text{ ft/sec})^2 + mgh_A = \frac{1}{2}mV_B^2 + 0$$

$$h_A = 25.0 \text{ ft} - (25.0 \text{ ft})\cos 40° = 5.85 \text{ ft}$$

Substitute and solve:

$$585.0 \text{ lbm ft}^2/\text{sec}^2 + (130.0 \text{ lbm})(32.2 \text{ ft/sec}^2) \times (5.85 \text{ ft}) = 65.0 \text{ lbm } V_B^2$$

$$V_B^2 = 9.0 \text{ ft}^2/\text{sec}^2 + 376.7 \text{ ft}^2/\text{sec}^2$$

$$V_B = \sqrt{385.7} = 19.6 \text{ ft/sec}$$

40. A Angular velocity is ω. Use the tangential and normal coordinate system. Tangential speed $V = R\omega$.

$$\text{Normal acceleration} = a_N = \frac{V^2}{R} = 1.0 \text{ ft/sec}^2 \text{ (given).}$$

Then:

$$V = \sqrt{(R)(a_N)} = \sqrt{(25.0 \text{ ft})(1.0 \text{ ft/sec}^2)} = 5.0 \text{ ft/sec}$$

and

$$\omega = \frac{V}{R} = \frac{5.0 \text{ ft/sec}}{25.0 \text{ ft}} = 0.20 \text{ rad/sec}$$

41. C At maximum height, point C, let $V_C = 0$ and $KE_C = 0$. Use the conservation of energy equation from point B to C:

$$KE_B + PE_B = KE_C + PE_C$$

Since elevation h_C is desired, solve PE_C and use $PE_C = mgh_C$.

$$\frac{1}{2}(130.0 \text{ lbm})(19.6 \text{ ft/sec})^2 + 0 = 0 + (130.0 \text{ lbm})(32.2 \text{ ft/sec}^2)h_C$$

$$\frac{24{,}970.4 \text{ lbm-ft}^2/\text{sec}^2}{4{,}186.0 \text{ lbm-ft/sec}^2} = h_C$$

$$h_C = 5.96 \text{ ft} \approx 6.0 \text{ ft}$$

42. C $\Sigma M_A = 0$

$$F_{BC} \sin 60(2) - 10(1) - 10(5) = 0$$

$$F_{BC} = 34.64 \text{ kN}$$

Then:

$$\sigma_{AB} = \frac{F_{BC}}{A_{BC}} = \frac{34{,}640}{\frac{\pi}{4}(0.04)^2} = 27.56 \text{ MPa}$$

43. A The maximum moment occurs at the right end of the beam and is equal to

$$M_{max} = 120 \text{ kN·m}$$

Therefore:

$$\sigma_{max} = \frac{M_{max}C}{I} = \frac{120{,}000(0.1)}{\frac{1}{12}(0.1)(0.2)^3} = 180 \text{ MPa}$$

44. B $\tau = \dfrac{V}{A_s} = \dfrac{\frac{34{,}640}{2}}{\frac{\pi}{4}(0.02)^2} = 55.13 \text{ MPa}$

45. A $V_{max} = 50{,}000$ kN

Then:

$$\tau = \frac{3}{2}\frac{V}{A} = \frac{3(50{,}000)}{2(0.1)(0.2)} = 3.75 \text{ MPa}$$

46. A The force on a fixed blade is given by the equation

$$|\mathbf{F}_x| = \dot{m}(|\mathbf{V}_1| - |\mathbf{V}_2|\cdot\cos\alpha)$$

Because friction along the face of the blade can be neglected, $|\mathbf{V}_1| = |\mathbf{V}_2|$, and

$$|\mathbf{F}_x| = \dot{m}|\mathbf{V}_1|(1 - \cos\alpha)$$
$$\dot{m} = \rho Q$$
$$= \rho|\mathbf{V}_1|A$$
$$= \rho|\mathbf{V}_1|\left(\frac{\pi D^2}{4}\right)$$

and

$$|\mathbf{F}_x| = \rho\left(\frac{\pi D^2}{4}\right)|\mathbf{V}_1|^2(1 - \cos\alpha)$$

Then:

$$|\mathbf{V}_1| = \sqrt{\left[\frac{1}{\rho}\left(\frac{4}{\pi D^2}\right)\left(\frac{1}{1 - \cos\alpha}\right)\right]|\mathbf{F}_x|}$$

$$= \sqrt{\left[\frac{1}{\left(1{,}000\frac{\text{kg}}{\text{m}^3}\right)}\left(\frac{4}{\pi(0.10\text{ m})^2}\right)\left(\frac{1}{1 - \cos 45°}\right)\right](100\text{ N})\left(\frac{\frac{\text{kg·m}}{\text{s}^2}}{\text{N}}\right)}$$

$$= 6.59\text{ m/s}$$

47. C Find the Reynolds number as follows:

$$\text{Re} = \frac{\rho\bar{V}D}{\mu}$$

$$= \frac{\left(1{,}000\frac{\text{kg}}{\text{m}^3}\right)\left(6.59\frac{\text{m}}{\text{s}}\right)(0.10\text{ m})}{8 \times 10^{-4}\frac{\text{N·s}}{\text{m}^2}}\left(\frac{\text{N}}{\frac{\text{kg·m}}{\text{s}^2}}\right)$$

$$= 0.000053 \text{ or } 5.30 \times 10^{-5}$$

48. B The friction factor is determined using the Moody diagram at the end of Chapter 7. The parameters required are the Reynolds number and the relative roughness. The Reynolds number was determined for Problem 47. The relative roughness is found as follows:

$$\frac{e}{D} = \frac{0.25\text{ mm}}{10\text{ cm}}$$
$$= \frac{0.00025\text{ m}}{0.10\text{ m}}$$
$$= 0.0025$$

From the Moody diagram, the friction factor is found to be 0.026.

49. A The head loss in the pipe due to friction is found as follows:

$$h_f = f\left(\frac{L}{D}\right)\left(\frac{\bar{V}^2}{2g}\right)$$

$$= 0.026\left(\frac{75\text{ m}}{0.10\text{ m}}\right)\left(\frac{\left(6.59\frac{\text{m}}{\text{s}}\right)^2}{2\left(9.81\frac{\text{m}}{\text{s}^2}\right)}\right)$$

$$= 43.16\text{ m}$$

50. B Refer to the iron-carbon phase diagram.

51. B Refer to the iron-carbon phase diagram.

52. B Refer to the iron-carbon phase diagram.

53. B At 720°C, iron is body centered cubic. According to Table 8.3, D_0 is 3.9×10^{-7} m²/s and Q is 80 kJ/mol. Therefore:

$$D = D_0 e^{-\frac{Q}{RT}} = 3.9 \times 10^{-7}\, e^{-\frac{80{,}000}{(8.31)(993)}}\text{ m}^2/\text{s}$$
$$= 2.4 \times 10^{-11}\text{ m}^2/\text{s} = 2.4 \times 10^{-7}\text{ cm}^2/\text{s}$$

54. C The most common number of bits per byte is 8.

55. B

2^0	1	
2^1		
2^2		or 10001
2^3		
2^4	16	
	17	

56. B

1st, 2nd	F=18
3rd, 4th	F=17
5th, 6th	F=16
7th, 8th	F=15
9th, 10th	F=14
11th, 12th	F=13
13th	F=12

57. A Choices (B) and (D) are the least reasonable responses. A registered engiineer would state membership and a number, making (C) a possible selection. However, (A) is the best choice because the implication is that the applicant is registered, which is unethical.

58. C Not writing written conclusions, returning moneys paid, and passing time do not make it ethical to accept the other assignment. If all parties had agreed and thus they are informed, the engineer could have accepted the assignment. Choices (A), (B), and (D) are not acceptable.

59. D

$$\begin{aligned} AC(2B) &= 95K + 3K - 12K(A/F, 10, 3) \\ &= 95K + 3K - 12K(0.3021) \\ &= \$37{,}566 \end{aligned}$$

and

$$\begin{aligned} AC(ROT) &= 120K + 9K - 25K(A/F, 10, 6) \\ &= 120K + 9K - 25K(0.1296) \\ &= \$33{,}350 \end{aligned}$$

Then:

$$\begin{aligned} \text{Difference in annual cost} &= \$37{,}566 - \$33{,}350 \\ &= \$4{,}216 \end{aligned}$$

60. C Use this equation:

$$\begin{aligned} \text{Profit} &= \text{revenues} - \text{costs} \\ &= [(35 \cdot \$90) + (15 \cdot \$50)] - [(35+15) \cdot \$40] - \$1{,}200 \\ &= [(\$3{,}150) + (\$750)] - [(50)(\$40)] - \$1{,}200 \\ &= \$700 \end{aligned}$$

INDEX